Tomart's Price Guide to Worldwide

STAR WARS ® Collectibles

SECOND EDITION

by Stephen J. Sansweet & T.N. Tumbusch

Edited by Stephen J. Sansweet

Section Updates by Josh Ling and T.N. Tumbusch

Authorized by Lucasfilm Ltd.

Tomart Studio Color Photography
by Tom Schwartz and Kelly McLees

Sansweet Collection Color Photography
by Steve Essig

Additional Black & White Photography
by Tom Schwartz, Tom Tumbusch, and Steve Essig

TOMART PUBLICATIONS
Division of Tomart Corporation
Dayton, Ohio

To Adam, Sammy and Daniel: the "next generation" awaiting the next Trilogy...
...and to Daren Murrer, who finds the stuff everyone else threw away.

Edition Note

This revised edition of the only Lucasfilm-authorized *Star Wars* memorabilia price guide has been updated and expanded in several key areas, notably Toys, since that is the main interest of the majority of collectors. The Toy list has been updated to include all items issued since the first edition was published, prices have been revised and the section is printed in full color. Several other sections have undergone major changes, including Books, Trading Cards, Model Kits, several sections of the Food Containers/Premiums listings, Coins and Stamps. Additional items and fixes are scattered throughout the book. This revised edition, like the first, concentrates in most collecting areas on the classic *Star Wars* merchandise issued from 1976 through 1986.

Acknowledgements

This book couldn't have been compiled without the help of scores of individuals. On a personal level, my utmost appreciation goes to Bob Canning for his behind-the-scenes help, understanding and support. Deep thanks to those who helped me gather, organize—and appreciate—my collection, and who in some way ultimately helped in the compilation of this guide: Eimei Takeda, Tom Nelson, Josh Ling, Wade Lageose, Lance Worth, Jeff Kilian, Darlene Parsons, Bill Plumb, Dov Kelemer, Jim Baumgart, Jim Stevenson, Ann Young, Judy Hovey, Mike Stannard, Chuck Redin, Rick Sherman, Scott Weiss, Mike Fulmer, Don Bies, Gary Kurtz, Les David, Elaine Wein, Steve Denny, Tom Neiheisel, Robert "Boba" Fisher, Harry Freidenberg & sons Fritz and Mike, Jim Latta, Albert McFadden, Eric Larson, Scott Tice, Matt Borchers, Kevin Mayne...and about a hundred more.

Thanks also go to a man who has become the king of the *Star Wars* collectibles photographers, Steve Essig, who never fails to do excellent work no matter how strange the conditions. Thanks go to a contingent from Down Under that supplied shots of Australian merchandise: The irrepressible Shane Morrissey, Darren Grant Reid, Michael Wilson, Cath & Steve Scholz and Jan MacNally.

Special thanks for their help and suggestions for this revised edition go to Josh Ling, Cameron Ellison, Duncan Jenkins, Laura Kyro, Lance Worth, Kevin LaNeave, Gus Lopez and Shawn Kerkhoff.

At Lucasfilm, thanks to a crew that's always a pleasure to work with: Howard Roffman, Lucy Autrey Wilson, Sue Rostoni, Kathleen Scanlon, Julia Russo, Kathleen Holliday, Stacy Mollema, Rachel Milstein, André Lake Mayer, Yvonne Nolasco and Marc Wendt.

Steve Sansweet

Information and/or items for photography were provided by John Alcantar, Chris Arbizzani, Linda Baker, Ron Bogacki, Frank Buckzo, Vivian Coe, Vinnie D'Alleva, Brian Doyle, T.O. Epps, Jr., Jeff Freeman, Richard Hawran, Mark Huckabone, Jeff Kilian, Erik Ko, Israel "Lev" Levarek, Andrew McGinley, Steve Miller, Daren and Kathy Murrer, Don Post, David S. Reeves, Basil Shiveley, Bill Sikora, Brian W. Hager Strand, Alonso Vilches, Dave Welch, Jerry and Joan Wesolowski, Mark Yungblut, and Bruce Zalkin.

Several contributors to previous Tomart publications have indirectly assisted this book, including Carol Markowski, Daniel Rous, and E.J. Benstock.

Tomart studio color photography is the work of Tom Schwartz, assisted by Terry Cavanaugh and the Tomart staff. Page imaging and color separations were done by Prism Color Group; printing by Central Printing and Carpenter Lithographing.

Many images were originally processed for the first edition by Nathan Zwilling and Elisabeth Cline. Thanks also go to Charles Sexton, who performed galactic feats of organization for the original project.

Lastly, special thanks to the Tomart Staff: Publisher and father Thomas E., whose foresight and expertise have made this book much better than it would otherwise have been; Mark Cela for archiving and providing additional stuff for photography; Rebecca Trissel and Robert Welbaum for data compilation; Kerrie Cela for cheerfully talking to all those people on the phone; Kelly McLees for digital photography; Nathan Hanneman and Marijke Smith for image processing.

T.N. Tumbusch

First printing, 1997

®, ™ & © 1997 Lucasfilm Ltd. All Rights Reserved. Used Under Authorization.
Photographs used previously in *Space Adventure Collectibles* and *Action Figure Digest* © Tomart Publications

Published by Tomart Publications, Dayton, Ohio.

Library of Congress Catalog Card Number: 93-60870

ISBN: 0-914293-37-0   Manufactured in the United States of America

1 2 3 4 5 6 7 8 9 0   8 7 6 5 4 3 2 1 9 0

Howard Chaykin's art for the first *Star Wars* poster.

IN THE BEGINNING...

Most important, of course, was the film.

And what a film it was! The opening crawl climbed and faded off the screen like the chapter headings from fondly-remembered 10-cent Saturday matinee serials at the Bijou. And then that miles-long ship seemed to pass directly over our heads with a roar from the back of the theater that made us crane our heads upward to see if the illusion were somehow real. Back on the screen there was a tough young woman with two blackberry Danish for hair, giving something to an trash can-like robot and his exasperated, upright golden friend. What more could we...whoops! Where are all those guys coming from, the ones in the hard white costumes with guns blazing? And that big dude, all in black, who sounds like he's had asthma all his life. All this in just the first five minutes!

The merchandise just trickled out at first from surprised manufacturers who had never heard of a movie spawning successful licensed products, much less one with weird sounding character names like Luke Skywalker, Princess Leia Organa of Alderaan or Obi-Wan Kenobi (Ben to his friends). There had been a few pre-film items such as the comic-art poster. A thousand of the Howard Chaykin-designed sheets were produced as a promotional item and sold at fan conventions at cost ($1 each) by Lucasfilm employees. But they couldn't give them away. Today they're going for $400 or more. Then a paperback novelization of the screenplay, released six months before the film, did very well—it sold out, in fact—but the publisher decided to hold off on any reprints until the film came out, so that it could print a movie tie-in edition. The Marvel comic book, a six-part serialization, also did well—and got at least a certain segment of the hoped-for audience clued in. There were a couple of advance theatrical posters—one pretty neat because it was printed on silvery "mylar" stock—and a couple of cast and crew promotional items, and that was it.

Then came May 25, 1977, and things were never the same again in our corner of the galaxy. The movie-going public went absolutely bonkers, and the lines and crowds and enthusiasm for this new film, *Star Wars*, literally became front-page news across the country as well as network-TV news fodder. What had George Lucas wrought? Single-handedly, he seemed to have rescued the movies from the angst-driven trough they had been in for much of the 1970s. And he won a new, if grudging respect for the fantasy and science fiction genres that, for most folks, meant the mostly amateurish space-monster films of the 1950s. Here was a powerful story of good and evil, soon to be spun out in additional chapters, in which an entire new universe had been created—from planets and spaceships down to eating utensils in the kitchen of a moisture farmer on a twin-sun planet named Tatooine.

A SOUVENIR FROM A GALAXY FAR, FAR AWAY

Moviegoers, caught up in this new universe, wanted to take a piece of it home. At first there were T-shirts and iron-on transfers, some jewelry and badges that spelled the arch-villain's name wrong (Darth Vadar?). Those $1 posters which fantasy and comics conventioneers had spurned for a buck started commanding $10, and there were other, commercially produced posters to buy. Some sheets and pillow cases, the first of many sets of stickers and gum cards (yes, they used to wrap them in wax paper and give you a hard slab of bubble gum), sheet music, a couple of books...

But where were the toys? If ever there had been a "toyetic" movie, in the words of one toy industry visionary, this was it. And four months before *Star Wars* opened, Kenner Products decided to give it a shot. Kenner, which had successfully licensed such TV shows as *The Six Million Dollar Man*, wasn't convinced that the new Lucas film would be a big hit, but that didn't matter. Space toys had been sort of moribund since the early 1950s, yet this one film had enough action, adventure and neat ships and gadgets to make a natural toy line.

Bernie Loomis, then Kenner president, had read a brief article in the *Hollywood Reporter* about an upcoming space movie from Twentieth Century Fox called *Star Wars*. He was intrigued by the movie's name and asked Fox for a script and some photos. He liked the characters and thought the vehicles would be fun to make into toys.

Still, he assumed that the film would come and go quickly, and that when the toys came out a year later they would have to stand on their own. Kenner's contract called only for one "all-family action board game" in 1977 and perhaps three different playsets with figures the following year. But the design department was working overtime to come up with ideas and prototypes to present to Fox and Lucas, who had the right of final approval.

Giving Birth to Action Figures

As recounted in co-author Steve Sansweet's book *Star Wars: From Concept to Screen to Collectible* (Chronicle Books: 1992), the key decision in the launch of the *Star Wars* line—one that not only insured its success but affected the entire toy industry—was made in Loomis' office early one March morning in 1977. Loomis called head designer David Okada a little after 7 a.m. and asked him to come upstairs to help figure out "what we're going to do with these *Star Wars* figures."

Kenner had been successful with 12-inch tall *Six Million Dollar Man* dolls, as Hasbro had been with *G.I. Joe*. But if the only Han Solo figure was going to be 12 inches, the Millennium Falcon would have to be five-feet in diameter and cost several hundred dollars. No way!

"We were hashing it around, trying to decide what to do, when Bernie held up his right hand, the thumb and forefinger apart, and asked, 'How about that big, Dave?'" Okada recounts. The designer took a six-inch steel ruler from his shirt pocket, measured the open space at 3¾ inches, and both men decided that would be as good a height as any for Luke Skywalker with the other figures scaled to size.

Display and certificate package for the Kenner Early Bird Kit.

Kenner thought kids would pick and choose among their favorite characters. As it turned out, with a price point around $2 a figure, they wanted them all—a line that would grow to 115 different figures, plus all kinds of packaging and other variations—by 1985. The size of the figures also led to affordable vehicles and playsets.

The initial plan was to turn out three vehicles and six "mini-action figures," but the lead time in the toy industry is usually 18 months (a year if pushed). Then *Star Wars* opened and six figures and three craft became more than 30 products in development overnight. Kenner managed to get out some boxed puzzles, paint-by-number sets and even a board game by late fall, but it just couldn't produce action figures or vehicles in time for Christmas. So the toy makers sold a promise. For about $10 you could buy a tightly-sealed certificate package containing a thin cardboard "stage" for the first 12 action figures, a few assorted pieces of paper and a certificate redeemable by mail for the first four action figures. About 600,000 were shipped, although many weren't sold. But those who mailed in their coupons got the first set of four *Star Wars* figures early in 1978—the first of some 250 million small action figures that would be sold worldwide over the next eight years.

There were many figure variations. The first Luke had a hard plastic lightsaber embedded in his arm which telescoped twice, but it was complicated and expensive, so later original Lukes had lightsabers which telescoped once. Other versions of Luke had snap-on weapons.

Han Solo was re-sculpted since his original pinhead was out of proportion to his muscular body—yet both versions continued to show up even on *Jedi* cards. The tiny Jawa went from wearing a vinyl cape to a somewhat richer looking cloth cape. Today, the "cheap-looking" vinyl-caped Jawa sells for thousands. Takara Corp., the Japanese sub-licensee, also made some changes. It added a higher-gloss gold finish to C-3PO and new heads for the droid and for Darth Vader.

Mistakes were made. Kenner's Cantina Adventure Set, a Sears exclusive for Christmas 1978, included four new action figures. One was Snaggletooth, a 3¾-inch figure dressed in royal blue with beige gloves and tall silver boots. The only photo Kenner had showed the creature cut off at the waist, so designers had to guess. Actually, Snaggletooth was short, had hairy hands and large, ugly paws for feet. The Snaggletooth released later on a card was only 3 inches tall and wore a red uniform and no boots or gloves.

The most notable of all changes took place before production. The figure of bounty hunter Boba Fett was to be used as a mail-in promotional offer. It was widely advertised as having a spring-loaded, missile-firing backpack. But shortly before the figure was to ship, there was a widely publicized product recall of vehicles whose small spring-loaded missiles had injured young children.

Kenner quickly remade the toys and covered up packaging and signs advertising the missile-firing feature. Rumors persist that some missile-firing figures were mailed. The truth is that a bunch of production-test figures, called "first shots," did make it back to Kenner for inspection, but these were unpainted, bluish-gray plastic without any copyright or manufacturer lines. Some copies of these first shots have been made and are being passed off as originals. A second, painted missile-firing Fett with a "J-hook" slot in the backpack also exists.

Beyond the 3¾ Inch Universe

In the initial rush to get *something* out the door, there were other glitches. An early puzzle had so much black sky and small stars that it was almost impossible to assemble.

A lot of concepts didn't make it past the prototype stage. One was a three-dimensional game with an eight-inch diameter plastic Death Star in the center. The Death Star had a "sweet spot." At the board's corners were four X-wing fighters on flexible support rods. The Death Star "exploded" when the right spot was hit. There was an incredibly detailed, foot-tall remote-control R2-D2 with opening compartments; a pull-string talking Yoda; a 12-inch Lando Calrissian doll; C-3PO walkie-talkies; Jedi and Boba Fett role-play outfits—child-size plastic accessories to turn kids into a hero or the bounty hunter; and many, many more.

Some unproduced concepts were photographed for Kenner's retailer catalog. Catalogs for Kenner's foreign affiliates went to press earlier and had photos of early prototypes of *Star Wars* toys, some not looking much like the finished product. The 1980 French Meccano catalog has a photo of the unproduced large Lando Calrissian doll; but it's really a Parker Stevenson *Hardy Boys* doll with its face painted brown. The Lando doll and additional Micro Collection miniature playsets weren't produced because the initial items in their respective lines didn't sell all that well.

Kenner didn't slap *Star Wars* labels on everything in sight. But Luke Skywalker's headset radio was a *Six Million Dollar Man* design, molded in black plastic instead of blue. The large and expensive X-wing Aces Target Game was a variation of an earlier Aerial Aces target game. Kenner also used existing molds for a battery-operated toothbrush and Super Sonic Power vans done in *Star Wars* versions. Kenner Canada produced separate boxed Luke, Leia and Darth Vader plastic belts with guns and other accessories—none of which looked like anything from the movie. Kenner U.S. asked permission to sell them too, but when Lucasfilm saw the rather unimpressive toys, production was immediately halted. They are probably the rarest Kenner-labeled items actually produced.

Up to a dozen handmade prototypes of some of the toys were made. A few have found their way to the collectors' market and

Utility belts manufactured by Kenner Canada are among the rarest Kenner items produced.

command high prices. The same with packaging. When George Lucas changed the name of the final film in the trilogy six months before release, Kenner destroyed more than $30,000 worth of *Revenge of the Jedi* packaging. The pieces that have survived and found their way to collectors are highly prized.

By 1985 the *Star Wars* line was fading despite the best efforts of Kenner and its many foreign affiliates. There were no more films in the series—at least for the foreseeable future. Attempts to do lines based on the short-lived *Droids* and *Ewoks* television cartoon series were more popular in some European countries than the U.S.

From Costumes to Mugs to Wallpaper

While *Star Wars* collecting is toy-driven, there have been thousands of other products worldwide. More than a thousand licensees have sold more than $4 billion worth of products tied to the classic *Star Wars* Trilogy and the *Special Edition*, *Droids*, *Ewoks*, *Star Tours* and all their offshoots. In the last few years, as collecting older *Star Wars* items has become a super-hot hobby, scores of new manufacturers have started producing new items ranging from a ever-expanding body of novels and comic books to pewter replicas of the saga's most famous spacecraft. There's also a killer arcade-size electronic pinball game.

As George Lucas continues filming the next trilogy, there will be new as well as familiar names cropping up on new products. Among the early major licensees for the first trilogy was the Bibb Co. with a line of *Star Wars* sheets, pillow cases, blankets, bedspreads, sleeping bags, curtains, beach pads, beach towels, bathroom towels and washcloths. Bibb had *eight* different designs: Galaxy, Space Fantasy, Lord Vader and Jedi Knight; and special designs for Sears, J.C. Penney, Montgomery Ward and Ratcliffe Bros. in England. New sheets are from Westpoint-Stevens.

Don Post Studios, a small California mask maker, saw its business soar as it produced authentic-looking over-the-head masks of six different characters, and then added more for the next two films. While the home Super 8-millimeter film business was giving way to home video, Ken Films did its best business ever by selling a few minutes of *Star Wars* excerpts.

By 1979 there were *Star Wars* Halloween costumes and masks, overalls and jackets, digital and analog wristwatches, T-shirts, socks, shoes and sneakers and sandals, plastic tableware, greeting cards, gift wrap, a syndicated newspaper comic strip, flying rockets, plastic model kits, wallpaper, buttons and patches, lunch boxes, belts and buckles, jewelry, school supplies, ceramic mugs and banks and cookie jars, posters, gum trading cards, records and tapes, books and comics, pajamas and robes, sheets and towels—and, of course, lots of toys.

The U.S. merchandising success was repeated worldwide. In the United Kingdom alone there were 36 manufacturers with 136 different products. England's Helix International made one of the few three-dimensional representations of the Death Star: a round metal pencil sharpener for 35 pence. In Spain Ediciones Manantial made an R2-D2 rotating calendar and a C-3PO mobile. Italy's Edizioni Panini produced a stamp album story book.

You could eat *Star Wars* in Europe and Asia—and eventually the U.S. In England there were ice lollies, lemon chew bars and molded marshmallows in the shapes of C-3PO, R2-D2 and Darth Vader. Italy had licorice twists. There were ice cream bars in Australia and Malaysia. In Japan, those with a hankering could buy chocolate or caramel candy, rice snacks and dry bread sticks—all with small *Star Wars* premiums like Cracker Jack prizes. For *Jedi*, England's Bridge Farm Dairies offered *Star Wars* lowfat yogurt in eight varieties: Jabba the Hutt peach melba, anyone?

Promotional tie-ins are also highly collectible. *Star Wars* trading cards were stuffed in with 65 million loaves of Wonder Bread. General Mills ran promotions with plastic tumblers, kites, cards, stickers, and miniature cardboard vehicles. (The

The U.K. Death Star playset (also sold in other countries) is one of the few international items with no U.S. equivalent.

cereal boxes themselves are quite collectible, as are the hundreds of different in-store point-of-purchase displays that manufacturers used to attract buyers.) There were collectors' cards on six-pack trays of Hershey candy bars; and hats, placemats and even a sweepstakes to win an in-home appearance by Darth Vader from the maker of Dixie cups. R2-D2 and C-3PO promoted childhood immunization campaigns in the U.S. and Australia and a savings campaign for the German Post Office and a bank in Australia.

The biggest tie-in was with the Coca-Cola Co. In the U.S. there were dozens of different plastic cups and glasses to collect from fast-food outlets and convenience stores. Coke also offered a flying disc, collectors' cards and a stamp album. In Asia, many of the offers were tied to collecting bottle caps with photos of characters or vehicles inside. In Japan there were 50 different caps and an R2-D2 radio with a Coca-Cola logo as a premium. Pepsi took over in 1997.

Although the foreign toy market was dominated by Kenner replicas, there were some notable exceptions. In England, France, Australia and Canada, a brightly-colored chipboard Death Star playset—which is highly prized by collectors—was sold. In Japan, Takara's separate line of toys included a sonic-controlled R2-D2 which "spits" plastic discs and another with a viewer in its stomach showing seven different scenes from *Star Wars*. Takara also produced four different seven-inch tall action figures; transformable X-wing fighters; wooden model kits; working die-cast figures and vehicles; inflatable toys; and one of George Lucas' favorite toys, a two-inch tall wind-up walking R2-D2 that was also sold on a card by Kenner Canada.

Besides the licensed products, there are other, non-mass produced items that *Star Wars* fans seek for their collections. These include various size posters and lobby cards made for movie theaters, along with press books and press kits. In the U.S. alone, the original trilogy produced an amazing 29 different one-sheets, the standard 27" x 41" posters theaters hang in outdoor and lobby frames. Distinctive foreign posters from Israel to Hong Kong to Poland and advertising sheets for products worldwide swell the number of different posters to well over 1,500.

There are also limited-edition promotional items, including Lucite stars from charity screenings of *Star Wars* and *The Empire Strikes Back*, brass paperweights with the films' names, and even a "passport" used to admit VIPs to the set of *The Empire Strikes Back* in England. Some collectors seek original art from the posters or books, and there are even some props and costumes that have made it into the collecting world. Lucasfilm has occasionally given away such things as a piece of the Death Star in a fan club sweepstakes. And sometimes it has donated items for charity auctions. These have included an original script autographed by Lucas ($3,500), a C-3PO hand ($5,000) and a mounted Darth Vader helmet, mask and shoulder plate from Empire ($20,000). But unlike nearly every other filmmaker, Lucas has kept most of the props and costumes in the company's archives. So most allegedly authentic props and costumes offered by dealers and even usually reputable auction houses have turned out to be bogus. Buyer beware!

Timothy Zahn's *Heir to the Empire* trilogy has sparked renewed interest in the *Star Wars* universe.

ON TO STARDOM AGAIN

Things were fairly quiet on the *Star Wars* front between 1985 and 1992. Still, there were events such as the 10th Anniversary celebration of *Star Wars*, a 1987 fan convention, which got lots of media coverage. There are now *Star Tours* rides—and merchandise—at four Disney theme parks on three continents. Collectors' silver and gold coins released in 1988 have zoomed through the stratosphere. Coin dealers say there were only 14 complete sets of all 24 coins minted, and they are now quoted at $20,000 to $25,000 for the full set. There have also been hand-painted cels from the *Ewoks* and *Droids* TV cartoon series.

But things didn't get *really* crazy again until early 1997 when, as a 20th Anniversary treat, Lucasfilm and 20th Century Fox released the *Star Wars Trilogy Special Edition*. Filled with new scenes and surprises, and in cleaned-up prints with digital sound, the trilogy sent the world headlong into *Star Wars* mania again. Fans new and old mobbed box offices for a chance to see the Trilogy the way it was meant to be seen: on a big screen, with great sound and as a shared expeience with a large audience. And of course, *Star Wars* collecting became red-hot again.

Star Wars collecting has gone through several phases. At first, diehard collectors were a source of amusement for some. "You collect *that*? But isn't that stuff still in the stores?" some would ask. "Trekkers" would smirk. Toy show promoters even six or seven years ago had to be cajoled into letting any *Star Wars* merchandise out on dealers' tables. "It's just that there seems to be so much of it around; are people really buying those things?" the promoters asked. Yes, they were. They still are. Only more so.

At first, the 12-inch dolls took off in price, a cross-over for *Star Wars* and doll collectors. A few of the rarer ones were bid up to $400 or so in mint boxes. Then the vehicles became popular. And the posters. And finally the action figures, which have been red-hot since about 1991.

What has driven the current round of *Star Wars* mania? For one thing, an entire generation of youngsters has grown up with the Trilogy and the toys as early and wonderful childhood memories. Now that many of them are entering the work force, they have the money to try to recreate those warm feelings. An even newer generation of kids, born after 1977, has watched the films over and over on video. But the renaissance really kicked in with the publication of Timothy Zahn's trilogy of new *Star Wars* novels, the first of which—surprisingly and unexpectedly—zoomed to first place on the all-important New York Times bestseller list. Other books started coming out, and after years of being in deep freeze, the *Star Wars* license suddenly became hot again.

With George Lucas now in production on three *Star Wars* prequels—the first for release around May 1999, and then in 2001 and 2003—companies around the world are gearing up to make everything from limited edition prop replicas to kids' shoes. Collectibles from the *original* Trilogy are likely to be in even more demand than they are today.

THE ONLY RULE YOU NEED TO KNOW

If anything is absolutely true about *any* collectible, it's that there are no sure things. In a cover story on collectibles in Forbes magazine in the fall of 1993, more than 20 different fields were rated from ice-cold to overheated. One category stood on its own: Movie and rock 'n' roll memorabilia. That was rated "insane," meaning that prices were already high but that the demand was so great they would probably go much higher. While the writer specifically referred to original props, costumes and the like, its easy to extrapolate to toys, posters and the other items covered in this guide.

Still, if you're buying *Star Wars* memorabilia mainly to make a fortune, we have one word of advice: *don't*. No one, not the biggest collectors or the most savvy manufacturers, can guess what will tickle a buyer's fancy tomorrow, much less five or ten years from now. You've seen that ceramic salt and pepper shaker go up in value 15-fold, and some rare action figures have soared 50,000%. (Yes, that's fifty-thousand percent!) But it's also possible that a $75 Darth Vader telephone will still be worth about the same price a decade later and that certain Ewok children's books will go for less than cover price. Collectors should be in it for the fun, the challenge, the thrill of the search, and the chance to meet like-minded friendly folks all over the world.

SCOUTING THE GALAXY

Okay. So you've bought the book. Now where in the world do you find some of the goodies that have you salivating? Well, everywhere. But it takes work.

Since *Star Wars* collectibles are of relatively recent vintage, there's a very good chance that a lot of them—some even untouched—were stored away by kids or parents and are finally being brought out at garage or estate sales. Most towns also have flea markets or swap meets, some weekly, where toys and books from the trilogy have become popular sellers. And there are an abundance of toy, comic, card, science fiction and related shows all across the country every weekend in your town or in one not too far away. Even dealers at *Star Trek* conventions usually carry some *Star Wars* items. Lately, *Star Wars* items have even shown up at major auctions.

There are also many publications—some of them born in just the past few years—that run stories and have ads relating to old and new collectibles. You can write (or in some cases where a phone number is listed, call with a credit card) to subscribe. Among the best are:

- *The Star Wars Insider*, the Official *Star Wars* Fan Club's quarterly magazine, with a full mail-order section of old and new goodies (some exclusive)
  P.O. Box 111000
  Aurora, CO 80042
  1-800-TRUE FAN

- Topp's *Star Wars Galaxy Magazine*, another Lucasfilm-licensed quarterly publication with a heavy emphasis on merchandise and collectibles.
  Subscription Department
  Star Wars Galaxy Magazine
  P.O. Box 555
  Mt. Morris, IL 61054
  815/734-5822

- Tomart's *Action Figure Digest*, Tomart Publications' entry, with full-color coverage of old and new figures. *AFD* publishes updates of *Star Wars*-related action figures, playsets, and associated items, domestic and international, in every issue. It's also the official price update publication for this book.
  3300 Encrete Lane
  Dayton, OH 45439
  937/294-2250

Tomart's *Action Figure Digest* Magazine features regular updates of *Star Wars* action figures and related merchandise.

- *Action Figure News and Toy Review*, which includes regular stories and price guides.
  556 Monroe Turnpike
  Monroe CT 06468
  203/452-7286

- *Starlog*, the longest-running science-fiction media magazine, with occasional collectibles articles and ads, and a collectible in itself when it runs trilogy stories.
  475 Park Avenue South
  New York, NY 10016

- *Toy Shop*, a twice-a-month tabloid which is mostly advertising, and usually has a ton of trilogy stuff, including rarities. These folks also publish *Today's Collector*. On the whole, expect to pay more if you buy from ads in these publications.
  700 E. State Street
  Iola, WI 54990
  1-800-258-0929

- *The Star Wars Collector*, an excellent bi-monthly fan newsletter by and for advance Trilogy collectors. Highly recommended.
  Martin Thurn
  20982 Homecrest Court
  Ashburn, VA 20147-4015

- *Movie Collector's World*, a twice-a-month tabloid with lots of ads for posters, press kits and related material.
  P.O. Box 309
  Fraser MI 48026
  313/774-4311

ABOUT THIS BOOK

Tomart's Price Guide to Worldwide Star Wars Collectibles is the only memorabilia price guide ever authorized by Lucasfilm Ltd., and was produced with the company's full cooperation. It has been compiled after thorough searches of the famous LFL "Toy Bay"—a repository of most of the worldwide merchandise; photo scrapbooks of thousands of items; and massive lists compiled from reports that licensees were required to produce. As a backstop, it also has made extensive use of the collections of both the authors and other collectors.

The manufacturers list in the back of this book is the most complete and extensive ever compiled; even Lucasfilm didn't have such a resource in one place. The list, like this book, covers every manufacturer anywhere in the world that was officially licensed first by Twentieth Century Fox and then by Lucasfilm to produce merchandise related to the *Star Wars* universe. It starts before *Star Wars* was released and includes all manufacturers who had signed contracts through the middle of 1997 to make licensed merchandise. For the enthusiast, it can be a cross-reference and a way to identify manufacturer, country of origin and, in some cases, approximate year of manufacture.

While every collector who does an inventory arranges things in a slightly different way, we have attempted to organize this book into well-defined categories. We also have instituted a totally new numbering system so that this book alone can be your *Star Wars* collecting bible. Each item is assigned its own alphanumeric code, and the black and white photos are cross-referenced with this code. The first two letters of the code refer to the overall category; the four numbers give it a unique identification number. There are frequent breaks in the numbers to leave room for updates and fill-ins in future editions of this guide. We hereby give permission—and in fact encourage—buyers and dealers to make use of these codes to buy, sell and trade *Star Wars* collectibles. Now both parties to a distant transaction will be able to know exactly which watch, for example, is being offered. Be aware, however, that all rights to any *other* use of these codes is reserved, and must be cleared with the publisher. This includes, but is not limited to, checklists, reporting values in newsletters, independent updates, or advisory services.

We know many of you collect just small action figures, or just posters, or just books. On the other hand, some of you try to be "completists" (one of everything, thank you). We have planned this book to serve all types of collectors.

This book sticks strictly to licensed items or authentic memorabilia related to the making of the trilogy. Fan-made items and fanzines may be tacky or great, but they usually aren't widely available, anyone can make them at any time, and they aren't done with the permission or quality control of Lucasfilm. Thus fan items aren't included here. While there has been some commercial bootlegging of *Star Wars* items over the years (especially things like paint-it-yourself ceramics, stickers and posters), Lucasfilm has been extraordinarily vigilant, so there's less than the rush of phony *E.T.* merchandise that flooded the market shortly after the film came out. Also, in appropriate sections of the listings we've tried to point out the existence of counterfeit items made to look like licensed products.

We've also made the decision not to individually list items that are so rare (prototypes, props, original art, etc.) that each individual transaction sets a new, negotiated price. But again, we mention some of these throughout the book.

We have made every attempt to be complete and accurate. However, because of the groundbreaking nature of a project like this and the fact that there have been some limitations on time and space, there will be some omissions and possibly some errors in this first edition. We urge you to write to Tomart with any corrections, additions and suggestions so that the next edition of this guide can be even better. Send your letter to:

Star Wars Price Guide Update
P.O. Box 292102
Dayton, OH 45429

THE VALUES IN THIS PRICE GUIDE

Many readers will find this book valuable enough just for the first-time listing of so many *Star Wars* products. (Granted, some very passionate collectors may get sick seeing how much more is out there.) But the reason a lot of dealers and collectors buy a guide like this is for its prices, so we want to explain what our figures mean and how we arrived at some of our decisions.

Because we list a lot of non-U.S. merchandise, and we expect that this book will sell worldwide, we at first contemplated trying to list prices of foreign-made items at the native-currency rate they are selling at in the countries where they were made. Talk about a wrong-headed idea! While there are *Star Wars* collectors all over the world, the vast majority are based in the U.S. Collectors in countries like the United Kingdom, France, Germany and Japan are mainly interested in items made in the U.S., while American "completists" are the ones searching for foreign goods. Then there's the problem of constantly fluctuating currency rates on top of constantly fluctuating

Four Conditions of an Action Figure: 1) Loose, no weapons or accessories, worth less than the values quoted in this guide. 2) Loose with all pieces originally sold in package. 3) Mint in package (frequently quoted as MOC or MIB — Mint on Card or Mint in Box) usually refers to condition of figure or other item...in a hobby where the package can be more valuable than its contents, this is often misleading. 4) Mint in Mint Package, used to describe and value perfect specimens.

collectibles prices. So this book's prices are based on buying everything listed in the U.S.

Of course, there are still major problems in putting prices into type. On some really hot items, prices can change monthly or even weekly. The mini-action figures are a good example of this. On the other hand, a full warehouse find of 100,000 Yak Face figures on *Power of the Force* cards would quickly bring the price of that rarity down. (That's just a "for example," folks. Nobody has made such a find.)

The prices listed here are a guide to what items might sell for in the open market to collectors. When a dealer—who has to pay for rent, utilities, travel, shipping and other expenses—buys an item from a collection, the seller can expect to get an agreed-upon fraction of our listed prices. As we have stated in past Tomart Photo Price Guides, the real value of any particular item is what a ready buyer is willing to pay. No more. No less. Prices go up, but they also go down. Prices are different on the East and West coasts at major conventions than they are at a garage sale in Dubuque. Or look through the pages of any publication with lots of dealers' ads. You'll see the same item pages apart from one dealer for $100 and another for $250. Who'll get *your* order? And prices are usually negotiable, especially if you buy a number of items. Also, more dealers are conducting monthly auctions; that may mean you'll have to pay a bit more, but you'll also get a chance to buy an item that probably would have been sold before you even saw the ad.

Price Ranges

The prices in this book reflect, to the best of the authors' and publisher's ability, the current market value at time of publication as determined through research at toy shows throughout the country, the scanning of thousands of ads, and the advice of some of the world's top *Star Wars* collectors and dealers. In some instances we list a range of prices, in others (primarily toys) we use more specific categories.

Let there be no mistake about the price spreads set down on the following pages. In all cases, the highest prices listed are for mint items in mint packaging, what you'll see in some ads as MIMB (mint in mint box), MIMP (package), MISB (sealed box), Gem Mint, C-10/C-10 (item and package in Condition 10—or tops), etc.

"Mint" should mean the same thing to everyone, but we've found that it doesn't. Our definition: Like-new condition. No scratches, no marks, never played with, never repaired, nothing (like decals) added, free of any defects. Same goes for the pack-

aging. Basically, the shape you'd find an item in if you hopped in your time machine, set it back 15 years or so, walked into a really clean and well-tended shop and bought store stock off the shelf (or—since we're dreaming—as the clerk is unpacking the master carton.)

Our low-end price range describes items in "good" condition. This means first and foremost that the item is complete with absolutely no parts or pages missing. Creases, dirt, marks, chips, tears, bends, scratches, minor rust or corrosion damage, repairs without original materials, and similar shortcomings are factors that relegate items to the complete, but "good" classification. When a range of prices is provided, the lower amount shown assumes an unboxed item, except when the box is an integral part of a complete item (for example, board games).

Anything other than mint should go for a discount from mint prices. While there may be a reason to buy an item advertised to be in "poor" condition—repair parts for example—most collectors would pass it by. Many would also pass on "good." Many items are found in "very good," "fine," "very fine," or "near-mint" condition. For those who prefer the numerical scale, that would probably be in the C-5 or C-6 to C-9 range. The best way to tell is to look. Most reputable mail-order dealers will give you at least a week's return privilege if you're not satisfied with condition.

All prices shown in this book are in U.S. dollars. Prices appear in one of two formats. For most items, this is a low-high range between the "good" and "mint" price as defined above. Items found in less than "good" condition should be considered at less than the lowest price shown.

Action Figure Price Categories

In the case of action figures and related accessories, the exact condition of the item as well as its packaging has a greater influence on the perceived value of an item. For these sections, the general price ranges used elsewhere have been divided into three categories: Complete No Package (CNP), Mint In Package (MIP), and Mint in Mint Package (MMP).

Complete No Package (CNP) refers to loose items with all weapons, decals, and other items found in the original bubble pack or box. Items without all the original items are therefore worth less than the value listed for "loose" but complete items.

Mint In Package (MIP) means an unopened figure on a card or in a box that is at least in fine condition with no tears, prominent creases, battered corners, or price-sticker damage. The item *inside* the box is mint, but collectors value the box as much, if not more, than the contents. Vehicles, playsets, accessories, and other toys may have been opened, decals applied, and assembled—but still complete and undamaged—in a fine or better original box.

The phrase "Mint In Package" can be misleading. This is frequently interpreted by dealers to mean the item *inside* the package is mint, but the package itself could be re-glued, bent, faded, marred, or covered with adhesive tags that are difficult to remove without damage.

Mint in Mint Package (MMP) means the item is in perfect condition, just like it rolled from the manufacturer's assembly line. See our definition of "mint" above for more details.

The values in this guide are based on the experience of the authors and the national panel of dealers and collectors credited here and in the acknowledgements. That doesn't mean that they have the items for sale at those prices; neither of the authors sell *Star Wars* collectibles—they are collectors. Also, neither Lucasfilm nor any of its employees supplied any prices for this guide; the prices don't reflect any belief by Lucasfilm that any particular item should or shouldn't sell for around its listed price.

WHERE TO BUY AND SELL

Many readers select this book because they want to get connected to the *Star Wars* network or have items they wish to sell. Apart from the ideas previously presented, special mention of the dealers and collectors who have been particularly helpful to Tomart Publications in publishing this book is due.

Those listed are by no means the total number of dealers or collectors from whom items were purchased. These are, however, the ones who were most cooperative, handled orders without delay or foul-up, and sent items in a condition consistent with the way they were advertised. Unfortunately, there were others who sent shabby material, did not attend to orders promptly, or shorted the order.

This list also contains the names of dealers and collectors who spent the time to review an early version of the manuscript for this book, make suggestions, and provide value estimates. The people listed here came through for us. It seems likely they would do the same for anyone wishing to buy or sell. Along with each name and address are included any special areas of interest.

Amok Time Inc.
18 Wolcott Road
Levittown, NY 11756
Phone: 516/520-0975
E-mail: amoktime@aol.com
    One-stop *Star Wars* shop.

Chris Arbizzani (Collector/Dealer)
1102 Market St. Apt. B
DeKalb, IL 60115
Phone: 815/754-5368
E-mail: chris@netsector.com
Web: www.netsector.com/chris
    Collectible toys and action figures. Please enclose a self-addressed stamped envelope (SASE) with mail inquiries.

The Emporium
13 Lower Goat Lane
Nowich, Norfolk
England NR2 1EL
    U.K. and other international *Star Wars* toys.

The Final Frontier
7411 Monterey St.
Gilroy, CA 95020
Phone: 408/847-1050
    Star Wars, Science Fiction, Super Heroes and other action figures.

Frank Buczko
Essener Str. 45a, Postfach 100427
D-44704 Bochum
Germany
Phone: Germany 234-13327
Fax: Germany 234-683795
    German and other international toys.

Collectible Toys
P.O. Box 329
Sun City, CA 92586
Attn: Ann or Judy
Phone: 909/672-9502
E-mail: colltoy@pe.net
    Buying, selling, and trading movie and TV toys and related items, with an emphasis on *Star Wars*.

The Falcon's Hanger
115-A West 9th St.
Auburn, IN 46706
Attn: Jeff Freeman
    Star Wars and action figure collectibles.

Figures Co.
P.O. Box 19482
Johnston, RI 02919
Phone: 401/946-5720   Fax: 401/946-8492
E-mail: FigInc@aol.com
Web: www.ewtech.com/figures
    Has large catalog of *Star Wars*, Super Heroes, Space, Wrestling and other collectible figures. Send $2.00 for a copy. Wholesale to dealers available.

Growell Company
330 Clement St.
San Francisco, CA 94118
Phone: 415/221-6788
Web: www.citysearch.com/sfo/growell
    Star Wars and other action figures.

Heroes
Attn: Mark Huckabone
23640 W. Highway 120
Grayslake, IL 60030
Phone: 847/546-8677
    Star Wars, Mego figures, 3¾" *G.I. Joe*, Super Heroes, and other scarce action figures, vehicles, and playsets.

Meltdown Comics & Collectibles
7529 Sunset Blvd.
Los Angeles, CA 90046
Phone: 213/851-7223
    Owner Gaston Dominguez seeks and sells cool stuff from around the world.

John's Collectible Toys and Gifts
57 Bay View Dr.
Shrewsbury, MA 01545
Phone: 508/852-0005
E-mail: JDicicco@aol.com
Web: www.ewtech.com/Johns
    Star Wars and other character merchandise

Kathy & Daren Murrer
The Earth
Cincinatti, Ohio
Phone: 513/561-TOYS (8697)
E-mail: theearth@theearth.net
Web: www.theearth.net
    Specializing Kenner *Star Wars* toys and collector supplies. Buying, selling, and trading.

Outer Limits
433 Piaget Ave.
Clifton, NJ 07013
Phone: 973/340-9393
E-mail: outerl@aol.com
    Star Wars and other toys, domestic and international

Star Force Collectibles
Attn: Lance Worth
367 N. Magnolia #103
EL Cajon, CA 92020
Phone: 619/588-7697
    Star Wars and nothing but *Star Wars*.

Star Wars Trader
Attn: Brian Semling
W730 Hwy 35
Fountain City, WI 54629
Phone: 608/687-7572
    Star Wars specialist. Buying, selling, and trading old and new *Star Wars* toys.

Super Collector
16547 Brockhurst St.
Fountain Valley, CA 92708
Attn: John Alcantar
    Star Wars, comics.

Tom and T.N.Tumbusch
P.O. Box 292102
Dayton, OH 45429
    Buying unusual *Star Wars* items and items not shown in this book.

Toy Tokyo
P.O. Box 337
New York, N.Y. 10021-0009
Fax: 212/517-5450
    Star Wars, Super Heroes, and other collectible items, harder to find items from around the world.

Toys 'N' Stuf
P.O. Box 2037
San Bernardino, CA 92406
Phone: 909/880-8558
    Older and unusual figures, Mego, Super Heroes, *Star Wars*, Major MATT MASON, store displays, all kinds of TV, movie, and character related toys from around the world.

Trilogy Collectibles (Private Collector)
Attn: Brian W. Hagerstrand
1140 Aldoro Dr.
Waukesha, WI 53188
Phone: 414/650-1662
    Buying and trading *Star Wars* collectibles.

Jerry & Joan Wesolowski
22 Allison
Toledo, OH 43605
Phone: 419/691-1810
    Science Fiction, Space, Movie, TV, Military, character toys, figures, and model kits.

AN0020

AN0020

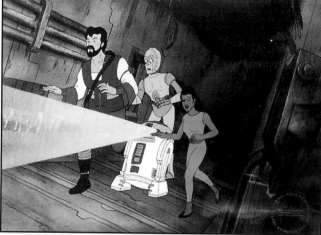

AN0021

AN0041

AP0020

AP0023

AP0025

AP0029

AP0010

AN0020	*Droids* cels w/out backgrounds	150 - 200
AN0021	*Droids* cels w/backgrounds	175 - 250
AN0030	*The Great Heep* cels w/out backgrounds	150 - 200
AN0031	*The Great Heep* cels w/backgrounds	175 - 250
AN0040	*Ewoks* cels w/out backgrounds	150 - 200
AN0041	*Ewoks* cels w/backgrounds	175 - 250
Royal Animated Art Seri-Cels		
AN1010	Best Friends (DR1)	70 - 90
AN1012	Battle Cruiser (DR2)	70 - 90
AN1014	Stranded (DR3)	70 - 90
AN1016	Boba Fett: Bounty Hunter (DR4)	70 - 90
AN1020	The Big Hug (EW1)	70 - 90
AN1022	Celebration (EW2)	70 - 90

ANIMATION ART

An animation celluloid (cel) is one frame of a cartoon. It requires up to 24 of these drawings to photograph one second of animated film, and thousands for an entire cartoon. Because each picture is slightly different, every cel is a unique item. *Star Wars* cels are from the *Droids* and *Ewoks* television shows and a related animated special, *The Great Heep*. There was also a *Star Wars* Holiday Special produced in 1978. The show was mostly live-action, but included an animated sequence which introduced Boba Fett for the first time.

The value of any particular cel must be evaluated on a case-by-case basis, taking into account the character(s) depicted, the completeness of character(s) shown (partial, full-figure, etc.), the pose, and the presence (if at all) of the original background. Also, there are some larger-size "panorama" cels that are at least twice the length of a regular cel. Backgrounds should be examined carefully, as some modern cels are framed with color photocopies of the original background. Cel collectors with artistic talent have also been known to paint their own backgrounds. Because of the fragile nature of cels, it is not uncommon to find them in damaged condition.

In addition to production cels, licensee Royal Animated Art has produced high-quality reproductions of key scenes, known as seri-cels (or serigraphs on celluloid) and limited-edition hand-painted cels.

APPAREL

All sorts of wearables were available in stores during the first run of the trilogy, and more have been released in recent years. Specialty items available through the Fan Club or promotional items issued in conjunction with the *Star Wars* 10 Anniversary Convention and the release of the *Star Wars Trilogy Special Edition* are even more collectible. Apparel items also are listed under other categories, mainly **CAST AND CREW**, **FOOTWARE**, and **STAR TOURS**. There isn't much collector interest in most apparel items, so the values for the most part haven't risen much above initial purchase price. Much of it, in the right size, is still great to wear—especially for that "retro" look—and there are certain completists who want a good selection in their collection.

HATS/CAPS/VISORS

In addition to novelty "baseball" caps, a replica of the cap worn by Imperial officers and a Yoda cap with "ears" were manufactured. Make sure to check for a copyright tag inside the cap, however, as fan-produced and non-licensed items are common.

AP0010   Fan Club, navy w/embroidered *Star Wars* logo
and stars on bill (Factors)   25 - 35

AP2070

AP2060

AP1362

AP1363

AP1400

AP1370

AP2490

AP2072

AP0011	Fan Club, yellow	15 - 20
AP0012	Fan Club, black w/embroidered logo patch	10 - 15
AP0020	*SW* Rebel Forces cap (made for *ESB*) (Thinking Cap Co.)	5 - 25
AP0021	Imperial cap w/metal rank insignia (Thinking Cap)	15 - 25
AP0023	*ESB* logo cap (Thinking Cap)	8 - 12
AP0025	Yoda cap w/ears (Thinking Cap)	15 - 25
AP0027	Black mesh w/sticker of battle scene and Kenner-type *SW* logo (General Mills premium)	20 - 30
AP0028	Black mesh w/sticker of Kenner *ESB* logo (General Mills premium)	12 - 15
AP0029	Navy mesh w/printed sketch of main characters and *ESB* logo (Dixie Cups premium)	15 - 20
AP0040	Darth blue mesh and bill	5 - 10

ROTJ printed caps (Sales Corp. of America)

AP0050	*ROTJ* logo	5 - 12
AP0051	Jabba the Hutt	5 - 12
AP0052	Luke and Vader w/raised lightsabers	5 - 12
AP0053	Luke and Vader fighting	5 - 12
AP0054	Vader and Royal Guards	5 - 12
AP0055	Admiral Ackbar	5 - 12
AP0056	Gamorrean Guard	5 - 12

ROTJ cuffed knit caps (Grossman Cap/Sales Corp.) AP0060-66

AP0060	*ROTJ* logo	6 - 14
AP0061	C-3PO	6 - 14
AP0062	R2-D2	6 - 14
AP0063	Wicket	6 - 14
AP0064	Paploo	6 - 14
AP0065	Gamorrean Guard	6 - 14
AP0066	Chewbacca	6 - 14
AP0070	X-wing embroidered logo (LucasArts Games)	10 - 15

Australia

AP1361	*ESB* black/silver cap (B&W Character Merchandising)	8 - 12
AP1362	*ESB* black and silver visor (B&W)	8 - 12
AP1370	*Jedi* black corduroy cap	5 - 7
AP1371	*ROTJ* black mesh	5 - 7

Canada

| AP1400 | C-3PO's cereal premium hat (mail-in) | 20 - 40 |

See also—CAST AND CREW; PARTY ITEMS

JACKETS AND PONCHOS

| AP2001 | Skywalker Fatigue Jacket (*ESB*, Fan Club) | 85 - 125 |
| AP2002 | Han Solo Vest (*ROTJ*, Fan Club) | 55 - 100 |

Bright Red Group

AP2010	*SW* windbreaker, quilted. Blue w/white trim	10 - 25
AP2012	*SW* windbreaker, quilted. *SW* logo patch, blue w/white trim	10 - 25
AP2013	*SW* windbreaker, quilted. "May the Force be with You" patch, white w/black trim.	10 - 25

AP2730   AP2720   AP2731   AP2721

AP2014	*SW* windbreaker, quilted. Black w/white trim.	10 - 25
AP2015	*SW* windbreaker, quilted. Red w/white trim.	10 - 25
AP2016	*SW* windbreaker, quilted. "Darth Vader Lives" patch, red w/white trim	10 - 25
AP2030	*SW* unlined jacket w/logo patch, blue and white	10 - 25
AP2031	*SW* unlined jacket w/"Darth Vader Lives" patch, black w/white trim	10 - 25

Adam Joseph Industries

AP2060	C-3PO and R2-D2 blue rain jacket	10 - 12
AP2061	C-3PO and R2-D2 blue rain poncho	10 - 12
AP2070	Darth and Royal Guards gold rain jacket	10 - 12
AP2071	Darth and Royal Guards silver or yellow rain poncho	10 - 12
AP2072	Darth and Royal Guards yellow rain jacket	10 - 12

Australia

| AP2490 | *ESB* plastic rain cape (B&W Character Merch.) | 6 - 10 |

Italy

| AP2540 | *SW* wool jacket (Baltro Italiana) | 25 - 45 |

OUTERWEAR

Earmuffs

| AP2600 | *ROTJ* earmuffs (Rayman/Ridless Products Group) | 5 - 10 |

Gloves/Mittens (Grossman/Sales Corp.)

| AP2710 | C-3PO gloves, black | 5 - 10 |
| AP2711 | C-3PO mittens, navy | 5 - 10 |

AP2016

AP2012   AP2013   AP2030   AP2031

AP2710 AP2750 AP2751 AP2711 AP2760 AP2740 AP2770

AP29067 AP29063

AP2902 AP2904 AP2906 AP29061 AP3100 AP3101 AP3700 AP3701

AP3000 AP3010 AP3040 AP3050 AP3020 AP3030 AP3550 AP3706

AP2720	Chewbacca gloves, brown		5 - 10
AP2721	Chewbacca mittens, blue		5 - 10
AP2730	Darth gloves, black		5 - 9
AP2731	Darth mittens, red		5 - 9
AP2740	Paploo mittens, blue		5 - 9
AP2750	R2-D2 gloves, tan		5 - 9
AP2751	R2-D2 mittens black		5 - 9
AP2760	Wicket mittens red		5 - 9
AP2765	*ROTJ* girls mittens, Ewoks		5 - 9
AP2766	*ROTJ* boys mittens and gloves: R2-D2, C-3PO, Chewbacca, or Darth Vader, each		5 - 9

Japan

AP2870	X-wing gloves (Tomokuni)		10 - 15

Leg Warmers (Grossman/Sales Corp.)

AP2901	C-3PO orange and white		4 - 10
AP2902	Ewok blue and white		4 - 10
AP2903	Ewok pink and white		4 - 10
AP2904	*Jedi* black and red		4 - 10
AP2905	*Jedi* black, red, white		4 - 10
AP2906	R2-D2 blue and red		4 - 10
AP2907	*ROTJ* logo		4 - 10

Japan

AP2960	*SW* high socks (Reknown)		10 - 15

Scarves (Grossman/Sales Corp.)

AP3000	C-3PO black and yellow		4 - 10
AP3002	Chewbacca brown and beige		4 - 10
AP3004	Darth black and beige		4 - 10
AP3006	Ewok white and brown		4 - 10
AP3008	*Jedi* red and black		4 - 10
AP3010	R2-D2 blue and red		4 - 10
AP3012	*ROTJ* girls knit scarf, Ewoks		4 - 10

PANTS/SKIRTS

Jeans

AP3100	*SW* royal blue w/overall pattern (Liberty Trouser Co.)	10 - 15
AP3101	*SW* navy w/overall pattern (Liberty Trouser)	10 - 15
AP3102	*SW* brown w/overall pattern (Liberty Trouser)	10 - 15
AP3103	*SW* corduroy jeans (Bibb)	7 - 10
AP3104	*SW* chambray jeans (Bibb)	7 - 10
AP3105	*ROTJ* Boys denim jeans, Darth Vader, Robots (Gans Enterprises/Sales Corp.)	7 - 10
AP3106	*ROTJ* Boys denim jeans, Darth Vader, Paploo, *Jedi* logo (Gans Enterprises)	7 - 10

Canada

AP3320	*SW* pants (Harley Inc.)	10 - 15

Overalls

AP3550	*SW* overalls (Liberty Trouser)	10 - 15
AP3551	*SW* sunsuit (short pants overalls, Liberty Trouser)	10 - 15
AP3552	*SW* toddler suits (Bibb)	10 - 15

Shorts

AP3700	*SW* brown overall pattern (Liberty Trouser)	10 - 12
AP3701	*SW* blue overall pattern (Liberty Trouser)	10 - 12
AP3702	*SW* navy overall pattern (Liberty Trouser)	10 - 12
AP3705	Boys fleece gym shorts, *Jedi* logo (Sales Corp.)	5 - 10
AP3706	Boys gym shorts, *Jedi* logo (Sales Corp.)	5 - 10
AP3707	Boys athletic shorts, *Jedi* logo (Mr. Seb Sportswear)	5 - 10
AP3708	Boys athletic shorts, *Jedi* logo (Mr. Seb Sportswear)	5 - 10
AP3710	Boys gym shorts (Bibb)	5 - 10

Canada

AP3810	*SW* shorts (Harley Inc.)	5 - 10

Japan

AP3840	*SW* short pants (Reknown)	5 - 10

Skirts		AP4000		AP4001	
AP3900	*SW* overall pattern (Liberty Trouser)				8 - 12
AP3905	Girls top and skirt, Ewoks (Little Laura of California/Sales Corp.)				8 - 12
Italy					
AP3950	*SW* cord and denim pants and skirts (Baltro Italiana)				5 - 15

Warm-up Suits (Sales Corp.)

AP4000	Toddlers warm-up, Wicket and Paploo	8 - 15
AP4001	Toddlers warm-up, Wicket and R2-D2	8 - 15
AP4002	Toddlers warm-up, Wicket and Woklings	8 - 15
AP4003	Toddlers warm-up, Wicket and Paploo	8 - 15
AP4004	Toddlers warm-up, Baby Ewoks	8 - 15
AP4010	Toddlers fleece hooded, Wicket and Paploo	8 - 15
AP4011	Toddlers fleece hooded, Wicket and R2-D2	8 - 15
AP4015	Girls Wicket and R2-D2, long or short sleeves	8 - 15
AP4016	Girls Wicket and Paploo, long or short sleeves	8 - 15
AP4017	Girls Wicket, long or short sleeves	8 - 15
AP4021	Girls Rebo Band, long sleeves	8 - 15
AP4025	Boys Luke and Darth (duel), long sleeves w/pants	8 - 15
AP4026	Boys Luke and Darth (duel), w/hood & shorts	8 - 15
AP4027	Boys *Jedi* logo, long sleeves w/pants	8 - 15
AP4028	Boys *Jedi* logo, w/hood & shorts	8 - 15
AP4029	Boys Paploo, long sleeves w/pants	8 - 15
AP4030	Boys Paploo, w/hood & shorts	8 - 15
AP4031	Boys Ackbar and vehicles, long sleeves w/pants	8 - 15
AP4032	Boys Ackbar and vehicles, w/hood & shorts	8 - 15
AP4033	Boys Darth and guards, long sleeves w/pants	8 - 15
AP4034	Boys Darth and guards, w/hood & shorts	8 - 15
AP4035	Boys Darth w/cape, long sleeves w/pants	8 - 15
AP4036	Boys Darth w/cape, w/hood & shorts	8 - 15
AP4041	Boys combinations, *Jedi* logo	8 - 15
AP4042	Boys combinations, Darth and Luke	8 - 15
AP4043	Boys combinations, Jabba the Hutt	8 - 15
AP4044	Boys combinations, Darth and logo	8 - 15
AP4045	Boys combinations, Darth and Royal Guards	8 - 15
Canada		
AP4350	*SW* jogging suits (Harley Inc.), ea.	8 - 15

SHIRTS

Sweatshirts

AP4510	Admiral Ackbar, white and blue w/blue pants	20 - 30
AP4511	Admiral Ackbar, gray sleeveless hooded	15 - 20
AP4530	C-3PO parts identification, white (Uniprints)	15 - 20
AP4531	C-3PO, Wicket and R2-D2, blue and gray w/pants	20 - 30
AP4551	Darth and Luke, gray w/blue sleeves and gray pants	20 - 30
AP4552	Darth and Luke, gray w/gray pants	20 - 30
AP4553	Darth, gray and black w/red trim and gray pants	20 - 30
AP4554	Darth, white and red w/red pants	20 - 30
AP4555	Darth, gray w/black sleeves and gray pants	20 - 30
AP4556	Darth, sleeveless gray hooded	15 - 20
AP4557	Darth and guards, sleeveless gray and blue	15 - 20
AP4580	Ewoks planting a tree, gray w/skirt (Sales Corp.)	20 - 30
AP4581	Ewoks planting a tree, pink w/pants (Sales Corp.)	20 - 30
AP4582	Ewoks, light pink w/skirt (Sales Corp.)	20 - 30
AP4583	Ewoks, light turquoise w/pants (Sales Corp.)	20 - 30
AP4590	Jabba, gray w/gray pants	20 - 30
AP4610	*ROTJ*, black, red and white crew w/long pants	20 - 30
AP4612	*ROTJ*, black and red short sleeve w/shorts	15 - 20
AP4640	R2-D2 parts identification, white (Uniprints)	15 - 20
AP4650	*ROTJ*, black sleeveless	15 - 20
AP4670	Wicket & Paploo, gray & red hooded w/gray pants	15 - 25

AP4553 AP4555 AP4556 AP4557

AP4650

AP4581 AP4583 AP4590 AP4610

AP4670 AP4672 AP5221 AP5222 AP5450

AP5540 AP5541 AP5542 AP5543 AP5870

AP5771 AP5772 AP5773

AP4671	Wicket & Paploo, white & blue hooded w/blue pants	15 - 25
AP4672	Wicket & R2-D2, white & gray hooded w/pants	15 - 25
AP4673	Wicket & R2-D2, white & red hooded w/red pants	15 - 25
AP4674	Wicket and R2-D2/rainbow, w/pants (Sales Corp.)	15 - 25
AP4675	Wicket and R2-D2/rainbow, w/skirt (Sales Corp.)	15 - 25

Australia

AP5200	May The Force.../Vader, top and pants (Kortex)	20 - 30
AP5210	*ESB* (Perfect Fit Clothing Co.)	15 - 20
AP5211	*ESB* hooded (Perfect Fit Clothing Co.)	15 - 20
AP5221	*ROTJ* R2-D2 and C-3PO (Kortex)	15 - 20
AP5222	*ROTJ* AT-AT (Kortex)	15 - 20

Canada (Harley Inc.)

| AP5300 | *SW* sweatshirts, ea. | 15 - 20 |

Denmark (Thyrring Agency)

| AP5355 | *ROTJ* | 15 - 20 |

England (Distribution Network)

| AP5400 | *SW* | 15 - 20 |

France (MSD International)

| AP5450 | Darth Vader *ESB*, yellow | 15 - 20 |

Germany (Mondragon)

AP5500	Baby Ewoks, cream	
AP5510	C-3PO, Wicket and R2-D2, cream	15 - 20
AP5520	Cantina Band, cream	15 - 20
AP5530	Darth and Luke Duel, cream	15 - 20
AP5540	*Die Rückkehr der Jedi-Ritter*, Vader head/duel	15 - 20
AP5541	*Die Rückkehr der Jedi-Ritter*, Ewok, R2-D2, C-3PO w/star background, light yellow	15 - 20
AP5542	*Die Rückkehr der Jedi-Ritter*, Woklings	15 - 20
AP5543	*Die Rückkehr der Jedi-Ritter*, Sy Snootles and Rebo Band, light yellow	15 - 20

Japan (Reknown)

| AP5650 | *SW* sweatshirts | 15 - 20 |

Mexico (Amate Textile)

AP5770	*El Regreso del Jedi*, Scout Walker	15 - 20
AP5771	*El Regreso del Jedi*, Darth Vader/Luke	15 - 20
AP5772	*El Regreso del Jedi*, Darth Vader	15 - 20
AP5773	*El Regreso del Jedi*, Duel	15 - 20

AP6001 AP6003 AP6007 AP6009 AP6015 AP6017

AP6027 AP6029 AP6031 AP6033 AP6039 AP6041

AP6037

AP6211 AP6213 AP6225 AP6233 AP6241 AP6243 AP6244

T-shirts

What is a T-shirt worth? Not much if it has been washed to death, is stained or ripped. But a mint condition, unworn shirt can have nice graphics and be appealing to wear or put into a collection as a symbol of how *Star Wars* quickly became part of the popular culture. Special **CAST AND CREW** shirts, of course, have a higher value and will be found under that heading. Many of the earliest T-shirts were made from Factors Inc. iron-on decals available only to T-shirt specialty shops. In fact, some collectors search for the original unused iron-on decals still attached to their backing sheets, or decals that have been applied to a piece of cloth or felt. Here is a large, but by no means exhaustive, selection of licensed T-shirts.

Factors
AP6001	C-3PO	10 - 15
AP6003	C-3PO and R2-D2	10 - 15
AP6005	C-3PO and R2-D2 on sand	10 - 15
AP6007	Chewbacca	10 - 15
AP6009	Darth Vader	10 - 15
AP6011	Darth Vader Lives	10 - 15
AP6013	Darth Vader helmet and X-wing	10 - 15
AP6015	Dogfight	10 - 15
AP6017	Han Solo	10 - 15
AP6019	Han Solo and Chewbacca	10 - 15
AP6021	Hildebrant Bros. art	10 - 15
AP6023	Jawas	10 - 15
AP6025	Leia	10 - 15
AP6027	Luke	10 - 15
AP6029	May The Force be with You	10 - 15
AP6031	Obi Wan and Darth Vader	10 - 15
AP6033	R2-D2	10 - 15
AP6035	*Star Wars* logo	10 - 15
AP6037	*Star Wars* logo, version 2	10 - 15
AP6039	*Star Wars:* May the Force be with You	10 - 15
AP6041	Stormtrooper on Dewback	10 - 15

Factors Glitter Shirts AP6051-67
AP6051	C-3PO	10 - 15
AP6053	Chewbacca	10 - 15
AP6055	Darth Vader	10 - 15
AP6057	Jawa	10 - 15
AP6059	Leia	10 - 15
AP6061	Luke	10 - 15
AP6063	R2-D2	10 - 15
AP6065	*Star Wars*	10 - 15
AP6067	Stormtrooper	10 - 15

Uniprints AP6080-6244
AP6080	*SW* and TIE-fighter, rust	10 - 15
AP6081	*SW*, white w/red sleeves	10 - 15
AP6082	*SW* X-wing, cream	10 - 15
AP6100	*ESB*, light blue	10 - 15
AP6101	*ESB*, white w/blue sleeves	10 - 15
AP6103	*ESB* Tauntaun, denim blue w/navy trim	10 - 15
AP6105	*ESB* Probe Droid white w/blue sleeves	10 - 15
AP6107	*ESB* X-wing, rust	10 - 15
AP6109	*ESB* Yoda, cream	10 - 15
AP6211	*ROTJ* C-3PO and R2-D2, cream	10 - 15
AP6213	*ROTJ* Stormtrooper and AT-ST	10 - 15
AP6221	Cast, cream	10 - 15
AP6223	Chewbacca, cream	10 - 15
AP6225	Darth Vader, gray	10 - 15
AP6227	Han Solo, denim blue w/navy trim	10 - 15
AP6229	Luke, denim blue w/navy trim	10 - 15
AP6231	Millennium Falcon, light blue	10 - 15
AP6233	Wicket	10 - 15
AP6241	*Ewoks*	10 - 15
AP6243	*Ewoks* Wicket	10 - 15
AP6244	*Ewoks* Wicket on vine	10 - 15
AP6250	Ewoks "Color Me" T-shirts (Patty Marsh Productions)	10 - 15
AP6255	*SW* 10th Anniversary Convention T-shirts (Creation Conventions Inc.)	15 - 20
AP6260	*SW* (Ralph Marlin)	10 - 15
AP6270	*SW* w/reproduction of Hollywood Boulevard artwork (Melanie Taylor Kent Ltd.)	10 - 15
AP6280	Topps *Star Wars* Galaxy I art (various) (American Marketing Enterprises), ea.	10 - 15
AP6285	*SW* trilogy for Musicland, Suncoast Video, and Sci-Fi Channel, various designs (Barrett Sportswear), ea.	18 - 25

Australia
AP6510	May The Force be with You/Darth Vader (Kortex)	20 - 30
AP6520	R2-D2, C-3PO and *ESB* logo (Perfect Fit)	20 - 30
AP6530	*ROTJ* Baby Ewoks on light blue sleeveless	20 - 30
AP6531	*ROTJ* Baby Ewoks on white tank top (Kortex)	20 - 30
AP6532	*ROTJ* Han Solo and Millennium Falcon (Kortex)	20 - 30
AP6533	*ROTJ* Luke Skywalker and stormtrooper (Kortex)	20 - 30
AP6534	*ROTJ* R2-D2 and C-3PO on tan (Kortex)	20 - 30
AP6535	*ROTJ* Baby Ewoks on white tank top (Kortex)	20 - 30
AP6536	*ROTJ* Speeder Bike on white w/red sleeves	20 - 30
AP6537	*ROTJ* white on blue (Kortex)	20 - 30
AP6538	*ROTJ* Wicket on light blue tank top (Kortex)	20 - 30
AP6539	*ROTJ* Wicket on white sleeveless (Kortex)	20 - 30

AP6510   AP6520   AP6532   AP6533   AP6534   AP6536

AP6537   AP7020   AP7110   AP7120   AP7121   AP7130

AP7040   AP7023

AP7331   AP7333   AP7334   AP7336

AP7340   AP7651   AP7652   AP7654   AP7655

AP7510   AP7653   AP7658   AP7660   AP7901

AP6560	Wicket and baby Ewoks on white sleeveless	20 - 30
AP6561	Wicket and R2-D2 on light blue sleeveless	20 - 30
AP6570	SW 6 designs (Maryborough Knitting Mills), ea	20 - 30
Canada		
AP6790	SW T-shirts (Harley Inc.)	20 - 30
AP6791	SW tank tops (Harley Inc.)	20 - 30
AP6792	SW polo shirts (Harley Inc.)	20 - 30
Denmark		
AP6800	ROTJ T-shirts (Thyrring Agency)	20 - 30
Germany (Mondragon)		
AP6910	Die Rückkehr der Jedi-Ritter, Vader head & duel	20 - 30
AP6911	Die Rückkehr der Jedi-Ritter; Ewok; R2-D2; C-3PO	
	w/star background, light blue	20 - 30
AP6912	Die Rückkehr der Jedi-Ritter, Woklings	20 - 30
France (MSD International)		
AP7001	SW logo, cream w/red and silver letters	20 - 30
AP7002	SW gray letters w/red outline, white	20 - 30
AP7020	L'Empire Contre-Attaque, R2-D2 & C-3PO, white	20 - 30
AP7023	L'Empire Contre-Attaque, Yoda, white	20 - 30
AP7040	Le Retour du Jedi, cream w/red letters	20 - 30
AP7041	Le Retour du Jedï, red letters on white	20 - 30
Japan		
AP7105	SW silk screened T-shirts, various designs	
	(Tsurumoto Room Co.), ea.	20 - 30

AP7110	Hildebrandt Bros. art (Reknown)	20 - 30
AP7120	R2-D2 and C-3PO (Reknown)	20 - 30
AP7121	R2-D2 and C-3PO (Reknown)	20 - 30
AP7130	SW logo (Reknown)	20 - 30
AP7140	ESB logo (Yagi Shoten Co.)	20 - 30
AP7141	Darth Vader (Yagi Shoten Co.)	20 - 30
AP7142	Millennium Falcon (Yagi Shoten Co.)	20 - 30
AP7150	ROTJ T-shirts (Seio Insatsu Co.), ea.	20 - 30
Mexico (Amate Textile), El Regreso del Jedi		
AP7331	Biker Scouts	20 - 30
AP7332	Darth and Luke	20 - 30
AP7333	Luke and Darth duel	20 - 30
AP7334	Luke, Han Solo, Leia	20 - 30
AP7335	Vader head/dogfight	20 - 30
AP7336	AP7335 on black	20 - 30
AP7340	Baby Ewoks	20 - 30
New Zealand (Bing Harris Sargood)		
AP7450	ROTJ	20 - 30
Singapore (Playthings)		
AP7510	Chewbacca, Luke, Leia, and Han Solo	20 - 30
Sweden (Wright and Co.)		
AP7651	ROTJ, black logo and speeder bike	20 - 30
AP7652	ROTJ, black logo on white	20 - 30
AP7653	ROTJ, Darth Vader and red circle on white	20 - 30

AP8010   AP8020   AP8021   AP8117   AP8119

AP8101   AP8121   AP8315   AP8318   AP8327   AP8366

AP8475   AP8477   AP8495   AP8497   AP8498   AP8499   AP8512

AP7654	*ROTJ* red logo and Yoda	15 - 25
AP7655	*ROTJ* red logo, black Storm Trooper and grid	15 - 25
AP7658	*ROTJ* logo, "*Revenge*" poster art	15 - 25
AP7660	Ewoks	10 - 20

Other Shirts

AP7900	X-wing polo shirt (for LucasArts Games)	20 - 25
AP7901	*SW* "chambray" shirts	20 - 30

SLEEPWEAR

Bathrobes/Shavecoats

AP8010	Darth Vader (Wilker Bros.)	10 - 25
AP8020	May the Force be with You (Wilker Bros.)	10 - 25
AP8021	Darth Vader dressing gown	10 - 25

Australia (Mr. Australia Garments)

AP8050	Darth Vader and stormtroopers	10 - 25
AP8051	R2-D2 (large/gray)	10 - 25
AP8052	R2-D2 (small/red)	10 - 25
AP8053	C-3PO head	10 - 25
AP8054	C-3PO full figure	10 - 25
AP8055	Luke on Tauntaun	10 - 25
AP8056	Yoda	10 - 25
AP8057	Han and Chewbacca	10 - 25

Nightgowns (Wilker Bros.)

AP8101	Darth and Death Star	10 - 20
AP8103	Luke and Leia	10 - 20
AP8105	R2-D2 and C-3PO	10 - 20
AP8107	Star field, R2-D2 and C-3PO	10 - 20
AP8115	Darth and Luke	10 - 20
AP8117	Darth	10 - 20
AP8119	Yoda	10 - 20
AP8121	Yoda and Luke	10 - 20
AP8130	Princess Kneesaa, white w/pink sleeves & trim	10 - 20

England

AP8202	*ESB* dressing gown (Penshield Ltd.)	30 - 60

Pajamas (Wilker Bros.)

AP8301	Admiral Ackbar, blue short sleeves and pants	10 - 30
AP8302	Admiral Ackbar, blue sleeves and pants	10 - 30
AP8305	Baby Ewoks, blue sleeves & pants	10 - 30
AP8306	Baby Ewoks, yellow sleeves & pants	10 - 30

AP8310	Biker Scouts	10 - 30
AP8316	Boba Fett	10 - 30
AP8317	Boba Fett and Darth Vader, long sleeve	10 - 30
AP8318	Boba Fett, Chewbacca, C-3PO, and R2-D2	10 - 30
AP8325	C-3PO and Ewoks	10 - 30
AP8326	C-3PO and Luke	10 - 30
AP8327	C-3PO and R2-D2, long sleeves	10 - 30
AP8328	C-3PO and R2-D2, white w/royal blue trim & pants	10 - 30
AP8329	C-3PO, R2-D2 and Royal Guards	10 - 30
AP8330	C-3PO, R2-D2, and Chewbacca	10 - 30
AP8335	Cantina Band, white w/navy trim, blue sleeves	10 - 30
AP8336	Cantina Band, white w/royal blue trim and pants	10 - 30
AP8340	Chewbacca and Millennium Falcon	10 - 30
AP8341	Chewbacca	10 - 30
AP8342	Chewbacca, R2-D2 & C-3PO, blue sleeves & pants	10 - 30
AP8343	Chewbacca, droids, yellow sleeves & pants	10 - 30
AP8350	Darth and C-3PO, short sleeves	10 - 30
AP8351	Darth and Death Star	10 - 30
AP8352	Darth and Royal Guards, blue sleeves and pants	10 - 30
AP8353	Darth and Royal Guards, yellow sleeves and pants	10 - 30
AP8354	Darth and Royal Guards, red sleeves and pants	10 - 30
AP8360	Darth and Luke	10 - 30
AP8361	Darth, short sleeves	10 - 30
AP8362	Darth, white w/navy trim, blue short sleeves & pants	10 - 30
AP8363	Darth, white w/navy trim, blue sleeves and pants	10 - 30
AP8364	Darth, white w/navy trim, yellow sleeves and pants	10 - 30
AP8365	Darth, white w/navy trim, yellow sleeves and pants	10 - 30
AP8366	Darth helmet montage, short sleeves	10 - 30
AP8367	Darth Vader Lives	10 - 30
AP8368	Darth and Boba Fett	10 - 30
AP8380	Droopy McCool	10 - 30
AP8390	*ESB* long sleeves	10 - 30
AP8418	Ewoks in village, yellow sleeves and pants	10 - 30
AP8419	Ewoks in village, red trim and pants	10 - 30
AP8440	Gamorrean Guards	10 - 30
AP8445	Han Solo and Chewbacca	10 - 30
AP8446	Han Solo and Darth Vader	10 - 30
AP8460	Jabba and Boba Fett, blue sleeves and pants	10 - 30
AP8461	Jabba and Boba Fett yellow sleeves and pants	10 - 30
AP8462	Jabba, Bib Fortuna and Gamorrean Guards	10 - 30
AP8463	Jabba the Hutt blue sleeves and pants	10 - 30
AP8464	Jabba the Hutt, yellow sleeves and pants	10 - 30
AP8470	Latara	10 - 30

| AP8520 | AP8522 | AP8523 | AP8524 | AP8525 | AP8526 | AP8527 | AP8530 |

| AP8531 | AP8533 | AP8534 | AP8535 | AP8536 | AP8540 |

| AP8545 | AP8546 | AP8547 | AP8810 | AP8538 |

| AP8820 | AP8821 | AP8830 | AP8831 | AP9101 |

AP8475	Luke and Darth, short sleeves	10 - 30
AP8476	Luke and Leia	10 - 30
AP8477	Luke on Tauntaun, long sleeves	10 - 30
AP8478	Luke on Tauntaun, short sleeves	10 - 30
AP8490	Max Rebo, white w/navy trim, blue sleeves & pants	10 - 30
AP8492	Paploo on Speeder Bike yellow sleeves and pants	10 - 30
AP8493	Paploo on Speeder Bike, blue short sleeves & pants	10 - 30
AP8495	Princess Kneesaa, blue sleeves and pants	10 - 30
AP8497	Princess Kneesaa, yellow sleeves and pants	10 - 30
AP8498	Kneesaa on swing	10 - 30
AP8499	Kneesaa skipping rope	10 - 30
AP8500	R2-D2 and C-3PO, blue short sleeves and pants	10 - 30
AP8501	R2-D2 and C-3PO yellow sleeves and pants	10 - 30
AP8502	R2-D2 and C-3PO (alt. version), yellow sleeves/pants	10 - 30
AP8503	R2-D2 and C-3PO blue sleeves and pants	10 - 30
AP8504	R2-D2 and C-3PO	10 - 30
AP8505	R2-D2, C-3PO and Darth	10 - 30
AP8506	R2-D2, C-3PO and X-wing	10 - 30
AP8510	Star field, R2-D2 and C-3PO	10 - 30
AP8511	*Star Wars* logo and "May the Force be with You"	10 - 30
AP8512	Stormtrooper and R2-D2, long sleeves	10 - 30
AP8515	Stormtrooper	10 - 30
AP8516	Wicket and R2-D2	10 - 30
AP8520	Wicket the Ewok, yellow sleeves and pants	10 - 30
AP8521	Wicket the Ewok, blue sleeves and pants	10 - 30
AP8522	Wicket w/butterfly net	10 - 30
AP8523	Wicket and Kneesaa on vine	10 - 30
AP8524	Wicket w/balloons	10 - 30
AP8525	Wicket w/walking stick	10 - 30
AP8526	Wicket in basket	10 - 30
AP8527	Wicket and Kneesaa in bush	10 - 30
AP8530	Wicket and Kneesaa on skateboard	10 - 30

AP8531	Wicket and Kneesaa playing drum and tambourine	10 - 30
AP8533	Wicket on vine	10 - 30
AP8534	Wicket and Kneesaa on teeter-totter	10 - 30
AP8535	Wicket and Kneesaa tug-of-war	10 - 30
AP8536	Wicket and Kneesaa w/flowers	10 - 30
AP8538	Wicket zip-up	10 - 30
AP8540	Wiley the Ewok	10 - 30
AP8545	Yoda and Luke, short sleeves	10 - 30
AP8546	Yoda, long sleeves	10 - 30
AP8547	Yoda II, long sleeves	10 - 30
AP8548	Yoda, short sleeves	10 - 30
Canada (Harley Inc.)		
AP8700	*SW* pajamas	10 - 30
England		
AP8810	*SW* (Marks and Spencer)	10 - 30
AP8820	*ESB* Montage (Penshiel)	10 - 30
AP8821	*ESB* Darth and Luke (Penshiel)	10 - 30
AP8830	*ROTJ* Montage (Penshiel)	10 - 30
AP8831	*ROTJ* Luke, Jabba, Darth (Penshiel)	10 - 30
Japan (Reknown)		
AP8900	*SW* pajamas	10 - 30
New Zealand (Bing Harris Sargood)		
AP9040	*ROTJ*	10 - 30

SOCKS/HOSIERY

These white socks, with various colored stripes and decals of characters from the trilogy, are better worn than collected; but in mint condition they are valued at $5 - $15 a pair.

Charleston Hosiery Mills

AP9101	*SW* Chewbacca	5 - 15
AP9102	*SW* Darth Vader	5 - 15

18

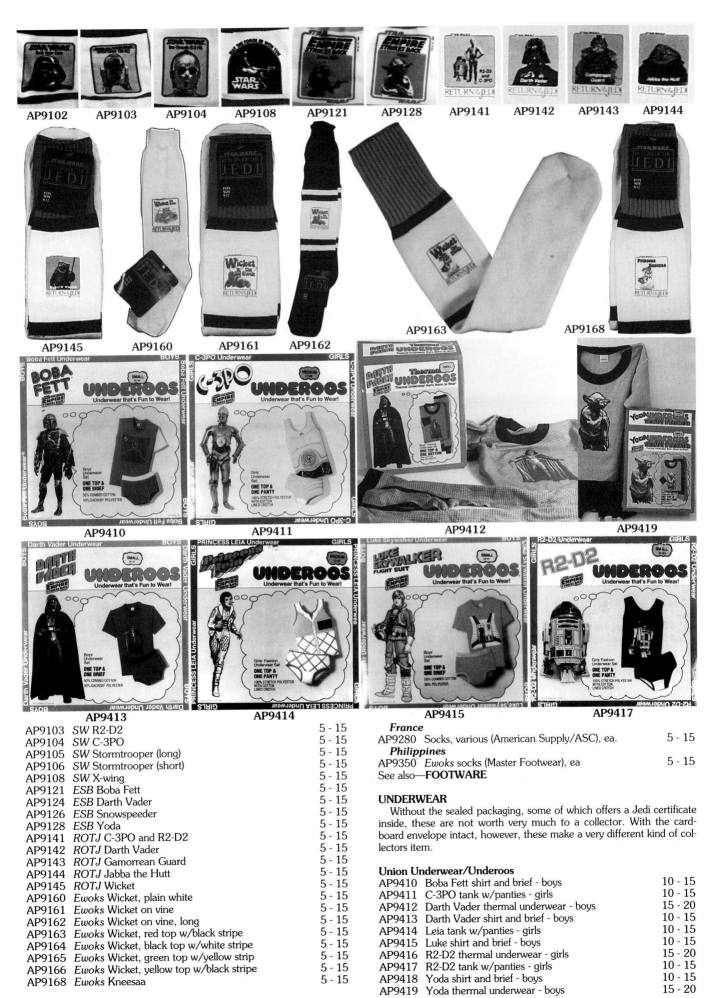

AP9102 · AP9103 · AP9104 · AP9108 · AP9121 · AP9128 · AP9141 · AP9142 · AP9143 · AP9144

AP9145 · AP9160 · AP9161 · AP9162 · AP9163 · AP9168

AP9410 · AP9411 · AP9412 · AP9419

AP9413 · AP9414 · AP9415 · AP9417

AP9103	*SW* R2-D2	5 - 15
AP9104	*SW* C-3PO	5 - 15
AP9105	*SW* Stormtrooper (long)	5 - 15
AP9106	*SW* Stormtrooper (short)	5 - 15
AP9108	*SW* X-wing	5 - 15
AP9121	*ESB* Boba Fett	5 - 15
AP9124	*ESB* Darth Vader	5 - 15
AP9126	*ESB* Snowspeeder	5 - 15
AP9128	*ESB* Yoda	5 - 15
AP9141	*ROTJ* C-3PO and R2-D2	5 - 15
AP9142	*ROTJ* Darth Vader	5 - 15
AP9143	*ROTJ* Gamorrean Guard	5 - 15
AP9144	*ROTJ* Jabba the Hutt	5 - 15
AP9145	*ROTJ* Wicket	5 - 15
AP9160	*Ewoks* Wicket, plain white	5 - 15
AP9161	*Ewoks* Wicket on vine	5 - 15
AP9162	*Ewoks* Wicket on vine, long	5 - 15
AP9163	*Ewoks* Wicket, red top w/black stripe	5 - 15
AP9164	*Ewoks* Wicket, black top w/white stripe	5 - 15
AP9165	*Ewoks* Wicket, green top w/yellow strip	5 - 15
AP9166	*Ewoks* Wicket, yellow top w/black stripe	5 - 15
AP9168	*Ewoks* Kneesaa	5 - 15

France

AP9280	Socks, various (American Supply/ASC), ea.	5 - 15

Philippines

AP9350	*Ewoks* socks (Master Footwear), ea	5 - 15

See also—**FOOTWARE**

UNDERWEAR

Without the sealed packaging, some of which offers a Jedi certificate inside, these are not worth very much to a collector. With the cardboard envelope intact, however, these make a very different kind of collectors item.

Union Underwear/Underoos

AP9410	Boba Fett shirt and brief - boys	10 - 15
AP9411	C-3PO tank w/panties - girls	10 - 15
AP9412	Darth Vader thermal underwear - boys	15 - 20
AP9413	Darth Vader shirt and brief - boys	10 - 15
AP9414	Leia tank w/panties - girls	10 - 15
AP9415	Luke shirt and brief - boys	10 - 15
AP9416	R2-D2 thermal underwear - girls	15 - 20
AP9417	R2-D2 tank w/panties - girls	10 - 15
AP9418	Yoda shirt and brief - boys	10 - 15
AP9419	Yoda thermal underwear - boys	15 - 20

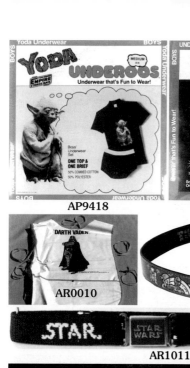

AP9418   AP9423   AP9710   AP9716   AP9715

AP9711

AR1024

AR1025

AR0010   AR1010

AR1011

AR1026

AR1013

AR1330

AR1014

AR1341

AR1016

AP9420	Chewbacca - boys	10 - 15
AP9421	Han - boys	10 - 15
AP9422	Han thermal - boys	15 - 20
AP9423	Wicket - boys	10 - 15
AP9424	Wicket thermal - boys	15 - 20
AP9440	*SW* boxer shorts (Ralph Marlin and Co.)	10 - 15
	Australia **(Kortex)**	
AP9710	Baby Ewoks, white top	10 - 15
AP9711	Baby Ewoks, white panties	10 - 15
AP9715	*Ewoks* Wicket, light blue top	10 - 15
AP9716	*Ewoks* Wicket, light blue panties	10 - 15

For other Apparel, see also—**CAST AND CREW; STAR TOURS**

APPAREL ACCESSORIES

APRONS

AR0010	Plastic art smock	10 - 15

BELTS/BUCKLES

Elastic Fabric or vinyl belts (Lee Co.)

AR1010	Brown or blue vinyl w/silk-screened art of Darth Vader, Luke, Leia and droids and *SW* logo in silver, ea	15 - 20
AR1011	*SW* fabric, navy w/white stitched *SW* logo, w/*SW* blue and silver sticker on buckle	10 - 15
AR1012	*SW* fabric, tan w/navy stitched *SW* logo, w/*SW* blue and silver sticker on buckle	10 - 15
AR1013	*SW* fabric, light blue w/red stitched *SW* logo, w/*SW* silver on red enamel buckle	10 - 15
AR1014	*SW* fabric, olive drab w/yellow stitched *SW* logo, w/*SW* silver on olive enamel buckle	10 - 15
AR1015	*ROTJ* fabric, red w/brass & red enamel logo buckle	10 - 15
AR1016	*ROTJ* fabric, red, white & blue w/*Star Wars* and *Return of the Jedi* printed, brass & red enamel logo buckle	10 - 15
AR1017	AR1016, brass and white enamel logo buckle	10 - 15
AR1018	*ROTJ* fabric, red, black & gray w/*Star Wars* and *Return of the Jedi* printed, brass & red enamel logo buckle	10 - 15

AR1019	*ROTJ* fabric, tan, brown, red, & yellow w/*Star Wars* & *Return of the Jedi* printed, brass & red enamel logo buckle	6 - 8
AR1020	*ROTJ* fabric, brown and yellow w/*Star Wars* and *Return of the Jedi* printed, brass and white enamel Darth Vader bust buckle	8 - 10
AR1021	*ROTJ* fabric, blue and red w/*Star Wars* and Return of the Jedi printed, round brass buckle w/enameled sketch of Jabba the Hutt	6 - 8
AR1022	*ROTJ* fabric, navy, light blue and red w/*Star Wars* and *Return of the Jedi* printed, round brass buckle w/enameled sketch of Wicket on blue background	6 - 8
AR1023	*ROTJ* fabric, tan and navy, w/*Star Wars* and *Return of the Jedi* printed, round brass buckle w/enameled sketch of Wicket on yellow	6 - 8
AR1024	*Droids* fabric, navy, light blue and red with droids in landspeeder, dimensional pewter buckle w/cartoon R2-D2, C-3PO and speeder	10 - 12
AR1025	*Droids* fabric, navy, yellow and red with droids in landspeeder, dimensional brass buckle w/cartoon R2-D2, C-3PO and speeder	10 - 12
AR1026	*Ewoks* fabric, mainly pink and green with dancing Ewoks, pink Wicket sticker on buckle	6 - 8

Leather Belts
The Leather Shop

AR1330	*SW* tan w/Obi-Wan and Vader pattern in black	20 - 25
AR1331	*SW* tan w/repeated pattern of Han and Chewbacca blasting stormtrooper, droids & Luke, Leia & Darth	20 - 25
AR1332	*SW* black w/oval brass Darth Vader bust buckle	15 - 20

Lee Co.

AR1341	*SW* black or brown leather belt, w/C-3PO and R2-D2 on blue enameled brass buckle, boxed	15 - 20
AR1342	AR1341 on hanger tag	
AR1343	*SW* black or brown leather belt, w/Darth Vader on black enameled brass buckle, boxed	15 - 20
AR1344	AR1343 on hanger tag	
AR1345	*SW* brown plain belt, w/*SW* logo on red or blue enameled brass buckle, boxed	15 - 20

AR1343

AR1345

AR1346

AR1383

AR1401

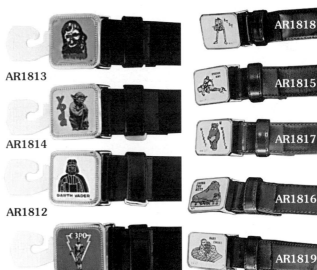

AR1813
AR1814
AR1812
AR1811
AR1818
AR1815
AR1817
AR1816
AR1819

AR1851

AR1852

AR2010   AR2011

AR2012   AR2013   AR2014

AR1405

AR1810

AR1346	AR1345 on hanger tag	10 - 15
AR1361	*ESB* tan, brown or black plain belt, w/*ESB* logo on red or blue enameled brass buckle	15 - 20
AR1363	*ESB* black or brown plain belt, w/Darth Vader dimensional bust on oval brass buckle	15 - 20
AR1365	*ESB* black or brown plain belt, w/Darth Vader dimensional bust on black-enameled brass buckle	15 - 20
AR1367	*ESB* black or brown plain belt, w/dimensional Yoda on round brass buckle	15 - 20
AR1381	*ROTJ* bonded leather belt in brown or blue w/silk-screened circular portraits of Luke, Darth Vader, Lando, TIE fighter, X-wing and logo	10 - 15
AR1383	*ROTJ* bonded leather belt in brown or blue w/silk-screened *SW* and *ROTJ* logos, Jabba, Darth, Wicket, the droids, baby Ewoks, skiff and shuttle	10 - 15
AR1385	*ROTJ* embossed light brown belt w/*ROTJ* logo on brass and red-enameled rectangular buckle	15 - 25
AR1387	*ROTJ* embossed light brown belt w/dimensional Jabba the Hutt on rectangular brass buckle	15 - 25
AR1401	*Droids* brown or blue bonded leather with silk-screened logo and droids in landspeeder	8 - 12
AR1405	*Droids* light brown or black belts embossed with rockets, planets and stars, and w/brass or pewter dimensional buckles w/cartoon C-3PO and R2-D2	15 - 25

France (American Supply)
AR1700	Belts, assorted, ea.	10 - 12

Mexico (El Buen Equipaje/Tudor brand)
AR1810	*ESB* black or brown vinyl, silk-screened w/*ESB* logo, TIE fighter, R2-D2, Yoda, Luke, Leia Chewbacca, droids, Darth Vader	5 - 8
AR1811	*ESB* black or brown vinyl w/enameled C-3PO buckle	8 - 10

AR1812	*ESB* black or brown vinyl w/enameled Vader buckle	8 - 10
AR1813	*ESB* black or brown vinyl w/enameled "Chewie" buckle	8 - 10
AR1814	*ESB* black or brown vinyl w/enameled Yoda buckle	8 - 10
AR1815	*ROTJ* black or brown vinyl w/enameled speeder buckle	5 - 7
AR1816	*ROTJ* black or brown vinyl w/enameled Jabba buckle	5 - 7
AR1817	*ROTJ* black or brown vinyl w/enameled Wicket buckle	5 - 7
AR1818	*ROTJ* black or brown vinyl w/enameled AT-ST buckle	5 - 7
AR1819	*ROTJ* black or brown vinyl w/enameled baby Ewoks buckle	5 - 7

Japan (Nishimura Seni Kogyo)
AR1850	*SW* vinyl in three colors w/brass buckle	10 - 15
AR1851	*SW* vinyl w/movie photos in four colors	10 - 15
AR1852	*SW* leather belt	15 - 25

Spain (Textile Artesa SA)
AR1880	*SW* assorted belts, ea.	5 - 7

BUCKLES (Leathershop Inc.)

This early licensee made five varieties of sculpted, heavy brass buckles to sell alone in 1977. Another company, Basic Tool and Supply Co.—apparently without a direct license—made almost exact duplicates of the same buckles, yet somehow a bit more refined. Also, the Basic Tool buckles have a polished finish while the Leathershop buckles have a flat finish. Not listed here are buckles made by Lee which are frequently found at flea markets and toy shows; they have all been removed from Lee belts and are valued at around $5 to $10. There were also scores of non-licensed buckles produced.

AR2010	*SW* logo on rectangular buckle	20 - 30
AR2011	C-3PO and R2-D2 on rectangular buckle	20 - 30
AR2012	R2-D2 on oval buckle	20 - 30
AR2013	Darth Vader bust on oval buckle	20 - 30
AR2014	Dogfight on rectangular buckle w/rounded sides	25 - 35

AR4011   AR4013

AR4021   AR4031

HANDKERCHIEFS

Japan

AR4011	*ESB* C-3PO and R2-D2 (Iwamota Co.)	8 - 12
AR4013	*ESB* Luke (Iwamota)	8 - 12
AR4021	*ESB* Darth Vader (Marubeni Co.)	8 - 12
AR4031	*ROTJ* R2-D2 and Wicket (Marubeni)	8 - 12

AR6010

AR6012

NECKTIES (Ralph Marlin & Co.)

AR6010	*SW* character tie	15 - 25
AR6012	TIE fighter tie	15 - 25

AR7010   AR7011   AR7510

SUSPENDERS (Lee Co.)

Knitted cloth suspenders came in a wide variety of striped color patterns. Each came with one of three different plastic badges attached to one side only. In mint condition, they include a blue, black and white header card with a drawing of Darth Vader's helmet.

AR7010	Darth Vader helmet, die-cut and dimensional	15 - 20
AR7011	Yoda face on round white badge	15 - 20
AR7012	C-3PO and R2-D2, die-cut but flat	15 - 20

Spain (Textile Artesa SA)

AR7080	*SW*, various suspenders, ea.	3 - 6

UMBRELLAS (Adam Joseph Industries)

AR7510	Clear plastic w/C-3PO and R2-D2	8 - 10

AR8010   AR8020   AR8030

AR8011   AR8021   AR8031

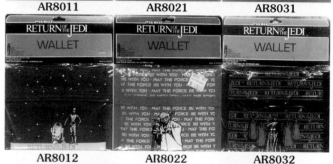

AR8012   AR8022   AR8032

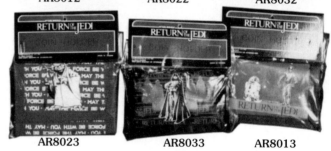

AR8023   AR8033   AR8013

AR7513	Clear plastic w/Darth Vader & Emperor's Guards	8 - 10

Australia (B&W Character Merchandise)

AR7830	*ESB*, various storm sticks (umbrellas)	5 - 8

WALLETS

Billfolds/Purses/Coin Holders (Adam Joseph Industries)

Adam Joseph sold five different *ROTJ* varieties of pocket-sized money holders, each in three different designs. The Droids pattern had a properly colored R2-D2 and C-3PO with a red and yellow *ROTJ* logo on a royal blue background. The Yoda design had a green Yoda on a red background with a repeat pattern of "May the Force be with you." The Darth Vader and Emperor's Royal Guards design was red on black, with the *ROTJ* logo in a repeat pattern in the background.

Small, squeeze-open vinyl change containers were produced in the U.K. They were sold in eight different designs, each produced in many different colors. While they are usually encountered loose, they are occasionally found sealed on a *ROTJ* card with sketches of Darth Vader and R2-D2 and the heading "Smile Money Bag." High prices assume they are mint on the card.

AR8010	Droids vinyl wallet	10 - 12
AR8011	Droids vinyl billfold	10 - 12
AR8012	Droids nylon purse	8 - 10
AR8013	Droids nylon coin holder	8 - 10
AR8014	Droids nylon pocket pal	6 - 8
AR8020	Yoda vinyl wallet	10 - 12

AR8040 **AR8803** **AR8806**

AR8801 **AR8804** **AR8805** **AR8806**

AR8803 **AR8802** **AR8800** **AR8807**

AR8021	Yoda vinyl billfold	10 - 12
AR8022	Yoda nylon purse	6 - 8
AR8023	Yoda nylon coin holder	6 - 8
AR8024	Yoda nylon pocket pal	6 - 8
AR8030	Darth Vader vinyl wallet	10 - 12
AR8031	Darth Vader vinyl billfold	10 - 12
AR8032	Darth Vader nylon purse	6 - 8
AR8033	Darth Vader nylon coin holder	6 - 8
AR8034	Darth Vader nylon pocket pal	6 - 8
AR8040	Wicket the Ewok vinyl wallet	10 - 15

Mexico (Personajes Registrados)

AR8655	*ROTJ* plastic wallets: Wicket, R2-D2 & Vader designs	3 - 5

Spain (Industrias CYS S.A.)

AR8770	*SW* and *Droids* school wallets in various designs, ea	3 - 5

United Kingdom (Touchline Promotions Ltd./Hi-Toys Ltd.)

AR8800	Darth Vader change purse	5 - 30
AR8801	C-3PO change purse	5 - 30
AR8802	R2-D2 change purse	5 - 30
AR8803	Stormtrooper change purse	5 - 30
AR8804	Ewok change purse	5 - 30
AR8805	Chewbacca change purse	5 - 30
AR8806	Admiral Ackbar change purse	5 - 30
AR8807	Jabba the Hutt change purse	5 - 30

BA0005

BA0006

BANKBOOKS AND PREMIUMS

Passbook savings account bankbooks were issued by the N.S.W. Building Society Ltd. in Sydney, Australia. The first bankbook had a color photo of R2-D2 and C-3PO in the forest of the Endor moon. A version of the same photo inside had spaces to mark off 10 deposits of at least $2 each; depositors got a poster, and for each deposit got one

BA0007/BA0008 **BA0015** **BA0016**

BA0017 **BA0018** **BA0019**

of 10 *ROTJ* character stickers to place on the poster. There was also a chance to win Kenner toys. A second passbook, with Wicket on the cover, was offered, as well as second poster and a "gift pack" (school kit) for opening a savings account or adding to the first one. This offer also featured a drawing for free passes to *Caravan of Courage*.

Australia

BA0005	Promotional folder for *SW* savings account	1 - 2
BA0006	Passbook w/R2-D2 and C-3PO on cover	15 - 25
BA0007	*ROTJ* poster	10 - 15
BA0008	Stickers for *ROTJ* poster, 10 different, ea.	.50 - 1
BA0015	Promotional folder for opening or adding to *SW* savings account	1 - 2
BA0016	Passbook w/Wicket on cover	10 - 20
BA0017	*Ewok Adventure* poster	10 - 15
BA0018	Stickers for Ewok poster, 10 different, ea.	.50 - 1
BA0019	Gift Pack—School kit	3 - 5

BA1012 **BA1011** **BA1010**

BANKS

The first banks were made in 1978 by Roman Ceramics in the shape of R2-D2, C-3PO and a bust of Darth Vader. Towle/Sigma Giftware also made ceramic banks for *ROTJ* in 1983. A number of vinyl banks were made by Adam Joseph Industries, also for *ROTJ*. The rarest of those is the Gamorrean Guard bank. Although pictured on the box with the other banks, it was never distributed in the U.S. It was sold later, however, in Canada, Australia and perhaps a few other countries, and is difficult to find mint in its original box.

Roman Ceramics Corp.

BA1010	R2-D2 ceramic bank	30 - 50
BA1011	C-3PO ceramic bank	40 - 80
BA1012	Darth Vader ceramic bank	50 - 90

BA1040

BA1045

BA1050

BA1051

BA1052

BA1055

BA1060 BA1061 BA1062 BA1064 BA1063
BA1065

WICKET THE EWOK BANK
BA1064

PRINCESS KNEESAA BANK
BA1065

BA8085

BA8087

BA8790

BA8791

BA8792

BA8950

Metal Box Ltd.

BA1040	Darth lithographed tin box w/combination dials	15 - 25
BA1041	Yoda lithographed tin box w/combination dials	15 - 25
BA1045	*ESB* lithographed tin octagonal	15 - 25

Towle/Sigma/Leonard Silver

BA1050	Chewbacca figural bank	25 - 45
BA1051	Yoda figural bank	25 - 45
BA1052	Jabba the Hutt figural bank	25 - 45
BA1055	Darth Vader anodized silver plated full-figure metal	75 - 125

Adam Joseph Industries

BA1060	Gamorrean Guard	75 - 125
BA1061	Emperor's Royal Guard	30 - 50
BA1062	Darth Vader	20 - 45
BA1063	R2-D2	15 - 22
BA1064	Wicket	8 - 15
BA1065	Kneesaa	8 - 15

Thinkway (talking electronic)

BA1101	C-3PO & R2-D2	20 - 30
BA1102	Darth Vader	20 - 25

Australia

BA8080	Darth Vader ceramic (Roy Lee Cin)	25 - 40

Commonwealth Savings Bank of Sydney

BA8085	Darth Vader plastic	10 - 15
BA8086	R2-D2 - white	10 - 15
BA8087	R2-D2 - light blue	10 - 15
BA8088	R2-D2 - dark blue	10 - 15

Mexico **(Vinolos Romay)**

BA8790	Darth Vader plastic	5 - 10
BA8791	R2-D2 plastic	5 - 10
BA8792	Yoda plastic	5 - 10

Spain

BA8950	Droids Money Box	10 - 20

United Kingdom

BA9100	*ROTJ* plastic coin sorter bank (J.&L. Randall Ltd.)	35 - 50

BED AND BATH

SHEETS, PILLOWS, PILLOWCASES, BLANKETS, BEDSPREADS, SLEEPING BAGS, AND DRAPES

Bibb Co., based in New York City, produced and sold more than a dozen different patterns of bedroom items during the trilogy, many exclusive to the large national department store chains. Foreign affiliates sold similar items, and other manufacturers outside the U.S. designed different patterns. There hasn't been much collector interest in sheets and the like, although there has been some indication of a pickup in interest since 1993 or so as some collectors look for the items that they actually slept on as kids. Others praise the funky textile graphics. Still, these items haven't risen much in price and aren't likely to in the near future. Always look for these unused in their original packages. What follows is an extensive, but by no means exhaustive, list of different products. Most came in various sizes, but that doesn't affect price as much as condition and packaging.

BA9100

BE1023

BE1024

BE1025

BE1026

BE1028

BE1030

BE1031

BE1035

BE1320

BE1523

BE1527

Beachpad

BE0010	*SW* "Galaxy" design seabee beach pad	15 - 20

Bedspreads/Comforters/Quilts

BE1011	*SW* "Jedi Knights" design	20 - 30
BE1012	*SW* "Galaxy" design	15 - 25
BE1013	*SW* "Lord Vader" design	15 - 25
BE1014	*SW* "Space Fantasy" design	15 - 25
BE1015	*SW* Aztec Gold coloration	20 - 30
BE1021	*ESB* "Darth's Den" design	20 - 30
BE1022	*ESB* "Lord Vader" design	15 - 25
BE1023	*ESB* "Lord Vader's Chamber" design	15 - 25
BE1024	*ESB* "Spectre" design w/Vader and Yoda	15 - 25
BE1025	*ESB* "Boba Fett" design	20 - 30
BE1026	*ESB* "Yoda" design	20 - 30
BE1027	*ESB* "Ice Planet" design	20 - 30
BE1028	*ESB* J.C. Penney firing Boba Fett design	20 - 30
BE1030	*ROTJ* montage w/Jabba, Ewoks, Skiff, etc.	20 - 30
BE1031	*ROTJ* montage w/Duel, AT-ST, Ewoks, etc.	20 - 30
BE1035	*ROTJ* "Star Wars Saga" design	20 - 30
BE1036	*ROTJ* design w/logos of all three films	20 - 30

Australia **(Noveau Intl./Pillow Pals)**

BE1320	*ROTJ* Bibb designs, ea.	15 - 20

England **(Hayjax Manufacturing)**

BE1380	*ROTJ* Bibb designs, ea.	15 - 20

Spain **(Artemur, SA)**

BE1460	*SW* quilted bedspreads, ea.	15 - 20

Blankets

BE1511	*SW* "Jedi Knights" design	15 - 25
BE1512	*SW* "Galaxy" design	15 - 25
BE1513	*SW* "Lord Vader" design	15 - 25
BE1514	*SW* "Space Fantasy" design	15 - 25
BE1515	*SW* Aztec Gold design	15 - 25

BE2515

BE2523

BE1521	*ESB* "Darth's Den" design	15 - 25
BE1522	*ESB* "Lord Vader" design	15 - 25
BE1523	*ESB* "Lord Vader's Chamber" design	15 - 25
BE1524	*ESB* "Spectre" design	15 - 25
BE1525	*ESB* "Boba Fett" design	15 - 25
BE1526	*ESB* "Yoda" design	15 - 25
BE1527	*ESB* "Ice Planet" design	15 - 25
BE1528	*ESB* J.C. Penney firing Boba Fett design	15 - 25
BE1530	*ROTJ* montage w/Jabba, Ewoks, Skiff, etc.	15 - 25
BE1531	*ROTJ* montage w/duel, AT-ST, Ewoks, etc.	15 - 25
BE1535	*ROTJ* "Star Wars Saga" design	15 - 25
BE1536	*ROTJ* design w/logos of all three films	15 - 25

Australia

BE1610	Bibb designs, ea.	15 - 20

Curtains/Drapes

BE2511	*SW* "Jedi Knights" design	10 - 20
BE2512	*SW* "Galaxy" design	10 - 20
BE2513	*SW* "Lord Vader" design	10 - 20
BE2514	*SW* "Space Fantasy" design	10 - 20
BE2515	*SW* Aztec gold design	10 - 20

BE2524   BE2526   BE2530   BE2810

BE3580   BE4000   BE4001   BE4002   BE4531

BE4532   BE4533   BE4535   BE4830   BE5036

BE2521	*ESB* "Darth's Den" design	10 - 20
BE2522	*ESB* "Lord Vader" design	10 - 20
BE2523	*ESB* "Lord Vader's Chamber" design	10 - 20
BE2524	*ESB* "Spectre" design	10 - 20
BE2525	*ESB* "Boba Fett" design	10 - 20
BE2526	*ESB* "Yoda" design	10 - 20
BE2527	*ESB* "Ice Planet" design	10 - 20
BE2528	*ESB* J.C. Penney firing Boba Fett design	10 - 20
BE2530	*ROTJ* montage w/Jabba, Ewoks, Skiff, etc.	10 - 20
BE2531	*ROTJ* montage w/Duel, AT-ST, Ewoks, etc.	10 - 20
BE2535	*ROTJ* "Star Wars" Saga" design	10 - 20
BE2536	*ROTJ* design w/logos of all three films	10 - 20

Australia

BE2810	*SW* cotton drapes, various designs, ea.	5 - 15

England

BE2975	*ROTJ* curtains, ea.	5 - 15

Duvet Covers
England

BE3580	*SW* Marks & Spencer Ltd. design	15 - 20
BE3581	*ROTJ* Bibb designs by Hayjax Mfg., ea.	15 - 20

New Zealand (Bing Harris Sargood)

BE3685	*ROTJ* Bibb designs, ea.	15 - 20

Switzerland (Schneidinger Freres)

BE3790	*ROTJ* designs, ea.	15 - 20

Pillows (Adam Joseph Industries)

BE4000	Darth Vader full figure sculptural pillow	15 - 25
BE4001	R2-D2 sculptural pillow	15 - 25
BE4002	Jabba the Hutt sculptural pillow	15 - 25

Pillowcases

One of the most interesting items for the bedroom was Bibb's set of three reversible pillowcases for *ESB*. They came packaged in colorful square boxes illustrated with characters from the film. All the sheets had matching pillowcases either sold separately for *SW* or *ESB* or packaged as sheet and pillowcase sets for *ESB* and *ROTJ*. There were two separate pillowcase designs also sold for *ESB*.

BE5511   BE5512

BE4510	*SW* sheet designs, ea.	5 - 12
BE4520	*ESB* sheet designs, ea.	5 - 12
BE4531	*ESB* boxed reversible Darth Vader/Boba Fett	20 - 30
BE4532	*ESB* boxed reversible C-3PO /R2-D2	20 - 30
BE4533	*ESB* boxed reversible Yoda/Chewbacca	20 - 30
BE4534	*ESB* "Star Wars" Bog Planet" design	8 - 12
BE4535	*ESB* "Star Wars" Cloud City" design	8 - 12

Australia (Noveau)

BE4826	*ESB* Yoda	5 - 12
BE4830	*ROTJ* montage w/Jabba, Ewoks, Skiff, etc.	5 - 12
BE4831	*ROTJ* montage w/Duel, AT-ST, Ewoks, etc.	5 - 12

England

BE4850	*SW* Bibb designs by Marks & Spencer Ltd., ea.	8 - 10
BE4870	*ROTJ* Bibb designs by Hayjax Mfg., ea.	8 - 10

New Zealand (Bing Harris Sargood)

BE4930	*ROTJ* designs, ea.	5 - 12

Switzerland (Schneidinger Freres)

BE4970	*ROTJ* designs, ea.	5 - 12

Pillow Shams

BE5036	*ROTJ* design w/all three film logos	10 - 20
BE5037	*ROTJ* red background w/Luke and Darth fight	10 - 20

Sheets/Sheet sets

BE5511	*SW* "Jedi Knights" design	15 - 30
BE5512	*SW* "Galaxy" design	15 - 30
BE5513	*SW* "Lord Vader" design	15 - 30

BE5514   BE5524   BE5528   BE5536

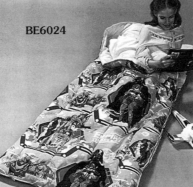

BE6023   BE6024   BE6026

BE6030

BE7003

BE7103

BE5514	*SW* "Space Fantasy" design	15 - 30
BE5515	*SW* Aztec Gold design	15 - 30
BE5521	*ESB* "Darth's Den" design	15 - 30
BE5522	*ESB* "Lord Vader" design	15 - 30
BE5523	*ESB* "Lord Vader's Chamber" design	15 - 30
BE5524	*ESB* "Spectre" design	15 - 30
BE5525	*ESB* "Boba Fett" design	15 - 30
BE5526	*ESB* "Yoda" design	15 - 30
BE5527	*ESB* "Ice Planet" design	15 - 30
BE5528	*ESB* J.C. Penney firing Boba Fett design	15 - 30
BE5530	*ROTJ* montage w/Jabba, Ewoks, Skiff, etc.	15 - 30
BE5531	*ROTJ* montage w/Duel, AT-ST, Ewoks, etc.	15 - 30
BE5535	*ROTJ* "Star Wars Saga" design	15 - 30
BE5536	*ROTJ* design w/all three film logos	15 - 30
Australia (Nouveau)		
BE5630	*ROTJ* multicolor design	5 - 10
England		
BE5710	*SW* designs from Marks & Spencer, ea.	5 - 15
BE5730	*ROTJ* designs from Hayjax Mfg., ea.	5 - 15
New Zealand (Bing Harris Sargood)		
BE5830	*ROTJ* designs, ea.	5 - 10
Spain (Artemur, SA)		
BE5910	*SW* designs, ea.	5 - 15
Sleeping (Slumber) Bags		
BE6012	*SW* "Galaxy" design	35 - 40
BE6020	*ESB* "Star Wars Empire" design	35 - 40
BE6024	*ESB* "Spectre" design	35 - 40
BE6023	*ESB* "Lord Vader's Chamber" design	35 - 40
BE6026	*ESB* "Yoda" design	35 - 45
BE6028	*ESB* J.C. Penney firing Boba Fett design	25 - 40
BE6030	*ROTJ* montage w/Jabba, Ewoks, Skiff, etc.	25 - 40

BE6035	*ROTJ* "Star Wars Saga" design	25 - 40
BE6036	*ROTJ* design w/all three film logos	25 - 40
BE6037	*ROTJ* "Star Wars Adventure" design	30 - 50
England (Hayjax Mfg.)		
BE6710	*SW* trilogy sleeping bags, ea.	25 - 40
Spain (Artemur, SA)		
BE6910	*SW* sleeping bags, ea.	25 - 40

TOWELS

Towels, like T-shirts, are easy to knock off, and there were a number of cheap bootleg beach towels using characters and scenes from the trilogy. But many of the towels and washcloths from the sole U.S. manufacturer Bibb Co., some under its Barth and Dreyfuss brand, have unique supergraphics and are nice to look at or display. Collectors need to find them in unused condition, because once washed, they lose much of their brightness and charm. Collectors value towels even less than sheets, so prices have stayed low. The exceptions are some of the sturdier oversized bath sheets or beach towels from *ESB* and *ROTJ* that are nicer than some framed lithographs.

Bath Sheets/Beach Towels

BE7000	*SW*: C-3PO, R2-D2 w/red logo, blue & orange planets	10 - 18
BE7001	*SW*: Darth Vader, TIE fighters, logo in red	10 - 18
BE7002	*SW*: Horizontal art w/Vader head, Jawas, stormtroopers and Death Star	15 - 20
BE7003	*SW*: Horizontal art w/Vader head, Chewbacca, Leia, Luke and the droids	10 - 18
BE7103	*ESB*: Horizontal art w/Boba Fett, Vader, Yoda, the droids, snowspeeders, Cloud City	10 - 18
BE7104	*ESB*: Boba Fett/Vader over Luke, Leia, & R2-D2	10 - 18
BE7105	*ESB*: Vader & Boba Fett over Han, droids, Leia, Luke, Chewie	10 - 18

BE7001   BE7104   BE7106   BE7107

BE7109   BE7210   BE7212   BE7213   BE7502

BE7514   BE7515   BE7535   BE7536   BE7750   BE7755

BE7106	*ESB*: Vader, red background w/planets	20 - 35
BE7107	*ESB*: Yoda in front of tree on yellow background	20 - 35
BE7108	*ESB*: Chewbacca, blue background w/planets	20 - 35
BE7109	*ESB*: C-3PO & R2-D2, black background w/planets	20 - 35
BE7210	*ROTJ*: Scenes of Ewoks, heroes and Jabba's palace	10 - 18
BE7211	*ROTJ*: Circles w/*Jedi* characters	15 - 25
BE7212	*ROTJ*: Rebo band, Wicket/R2-D2 and Jabba	15 - 25
BE7213	*ROTJ*: Velvet finish Luke and Vader duel	35 - 50
BE7214	*ROTJ*: "Wicket the Ewok"	10 - 18

Bath Towels

BE7500	*SW*: Vader over Chewie, Han, Luke, Leia, droids	8 - 12
BE7501	*SW*: R2-D2 in mirror image on each half of towel	8 - 12
BE7502	*SW*: Leia and Luke, Vader head, R2-D2 and C-3PO	8 - 12
BE7514	*ESB*: Vader and Boba Fett on one half w/Yoda, droids and Cloud City on other half	8 - 12
BE7515	*ESB*: Vader and Boba Fett on one half w/Yoda, droids and Millenium Falcon on other half	8 - 12
BE7535	*ROTJ*: Bath towel w/Ewok wash mitt	10 - 15
BE7536	*ROTJ*: Bath towel/hand towel/washcloth set	10 - 15

Australia (**Nouveau from Bibb designs**)

BE7750	*ESB*: Darth Vader and rebellion heroes on on white	8 - 12
BE7751	Chewbacca, Gamorrean Guard, Royal Guard, Han Solo, Vader, Leia, Boba Fett, Ewok	8 - 15
BE7752	Darth and Luke duel *ROTJ* Logo	15 - 25
BE7753	Ewoks, cast, Jabba	8 - 15

BE7756   BE7760   BE8001

BE7755	*ROTJ*: 8 round scenes and space ships on white	8 - 15
BE7756	*ROTJ*: Darth Vader and rebellion heroes on red	8 - 15
BE7760	*ROTJ*: Cast on white	8 - 15
BE7761	*ROTJ*: Cast on blue	8 - 15

New Zealand (**Bing, Harris Sargood**)

BE7865	*ROTJ*: R2-D2, Wicket, Chewbacca, C-3PO, Vader	8 - 15
BE7866	*ROTJ*: Ewoks	8 - 15
BE7867	*ROTJ*: Jedi Knights	8 - 15
BE7868	*ROTJ*: Chewbacca, R2-D2 and C-3PO	8 - 15
BE7869	*ROTJ*: Darth and Guards	8 - 15

BE8015	**BE8511**

Spain (Humet Textile SA)		
BE7980	*Droids* designs	10 - 20

Hand Towels

BE8000	*SW:* Darth Vader w/raised lightsaber and dogfight	8 - 12
BE8001	*SW:* R2-D2 in blue and turquoise	8 - 12
BE8002	*SW:* C-3PO, R2-D2, Leia, Luke w/blaster	8 - 12
BE8003	*SW:* C-3PO and R2-D2	8 - 12
BE8015	*ESB:* Vader and Boba Fett, snowspeeders	8 - 12
Australia		
BE8310	*ROTJ:* Cast, red on white	8 - 12

Washcloths

BE8510	*SW:* X-wing fighter	5 - 10
BE8511	*SW:* R2-D2 in blue and turquoise	5 - 10
BE8512	*SW:* Vader head, blue outlined logo	5 - 10
BE8513	*SW:* C-3PO and R2-D2	5 - 10
BE8615	*ESB:* Yoda	5 - 10
BE8616	*ESB:* Vader and Boba Fett	5 - 10
BE8617	*ESB:* Ice planet	5 - 10
Australia		
BE8910	*ROTJ:* Cast, red on white	5 - 10

BOOKS

First, there was the word. From the original novelization of *Star Wars*, which initially appeared as a paperback about nine months before the film arrived, the trilogy has spawned hundreds of books in scores of languages. In addition to the books directly related to the initial trilogy, noted science-fiction novelists have expanded the *Star Wars* universe. In fact, many believe that it was the publication in hardcover of the first of Timothy Zahn's trilogy, *Heir to the Empire*, that launched the revival of interest in *Star Wars*. That book also launched an ambitious new publishing program by Lucasfilm.

There also have been numerous coloring, activity, information, young-reader and even "horror" books. The major American imprints include Ballantine and its Del Rey affiliate; Bantam and its Bantam Doubleday Dell imprint; Random House; Chronicle Books; Dark Horse; FPG; Berkley Books; Topps Co.; Prima Publishing; Ziff-Davis; Fun Works; Golden Books; Scholastic; Little, Brown and Co.; and West End Games. Some hardcover editions of novels are available only by mail order through the Science Fiction Book Club; the Club also publishes its own, slightly smaller versions of many of the hardcovers. Comic, stamp, sticker and role-playing game books are listed elsewhere. What follows is as complete a selection as possible of books that were licensed by Lucasfilm and published or distributed in the U.S. (That leaves out a huge number of books that make mention of the *Star Wars* trilogy, but aren't official *Star Wars* products.) There are also scattered examples of foreign translations. The pricing of foreign books remains mixed. Sometimes there's little interest. Other times, because of a particularly good or unusual cover–or the novelty interest in the "foreignness" of the language—the price may be 50% or even 100% greater than the U.S. version.

ACTIVITY
Random House, BO0001-BO0004

BO0001	*SW: Artoo Detoo's Activity Book*	5 - 8
BO0002	*SW: Luke Skywalker's Activity Book*	5 - 8
BO0003	*SW: Chewbacca's Activity Book* no printed price	5 - 8
BO0004	*SW: Darth Vader's Activity Book*	5 - 8
BO0005	*SW: The Star Wars Iron-On Transfer Book* (Ballantine)	15 - 25
BO0006	*SW: Punch-Out and Make-It Book*	10 - 20
BO0020	*ESB: The ESB Mix or Match Storybook*	10 - 15
BO0022	*ESB: Yoda's Activity Book*	5 - 10

BE8617	**BE8910**

BO0023	*ESB: Punch-Out and Make-It Book*	10 - 20
BO0040	*ROTJ: How to Draw Star Wars Heroes, Creatures, Spaceships, and other Fantastic Things*	5 - 12
BO0041	*ROTJ: Star Wars Word Puzzles*	2 - 5
BO0042	*ROTJ: Punch-Out and Make It Book*	10 - 20
BO0043	*ROTJ: Picture Puzzle Book* (Happy House)	1 - 5
BO0044	*ROTJ: Dot-to-Dot Fun* (Happy House)	1 - 5
BO0045	*ROTJ: Things to Do and Make* (H.H.)	1 - 5
BO0046	*ROTJ: Word Puzzle Book* (H.H.)	1 - 5
BO0047	*ROTJ: Monster Activity Book* (H.H.)	1 - 5
BO0048	*ROTJ: Mazes* (Happy House)	1 - 5
BO0049	*ROTJ: The Star Wars Book of Masks*	18 - 20
BO0055	*Ewoks: Winter Dot-to-Dot* (Happy House)	15 - 20
Golden Books, 1997		
BO0200	*SW: A New Hope* (with tattoos)	4 - 5
BO0201	*SW: The Empire Strikes Back* (tattoos)	4 - 5
BO0202	*SW: Return of the Jedi* (tattoos)	4 - 5
BO0203	*SW: Pilots and Spacecraft* (glow in dark)	4 - 5
BO0204	*SW: The Rebel Alliance vs. The Imperial Forces* (puzzles, mazes)	2 - 3
BO0205	*SW: The Training of a Jedi Knight* (puzzles, mazes)	2 - 3
BO0206	*SW: Tell-A-Story Sticker Book*	3 - 4
Canada		
BO0400	*ROTJ: Word Puzzle Book*, slightly smaller than US version BO0046 (Happy House)	1 - 5
England		
BO0406	*SW: Punch-Out and Make-It Book* (Collins)	8 - 12
Japan		
BO0431	*SW: Iron-On Transfer Book*	15-28
BO0449	*ROTJ: Activity Book*	10-18
BO0450	*ROTJ: Punch-Out Mask Book*	20-30
Spain		
BO0481	*SW: Punch-Out and Make it Book* (Editorial Norma)	18-26

ART/SKETCH
Ballantine, BO0500-BO0510

BO0500	*The Art of Star Wars*, hardcover	45 - 75
BO0502	*The Art of Star Wars*, trade paperback	20 - 25
BO0502a	*The Art of Star Wars*, trade paperback (revised 1994 cover)	18 - 20
BO0502b	*The Art of Star Wars*, trade paperback (1997 Special Edition section)	19 - 20
BO0503	*The Star Wars Sketchbook*, softcover only	10 - 15
BO0504	*The Art of The Empire Strikes Back*, hardcover	45 - 75
BO0505	*The Art of The Empire Strikes Back*, trade paper	20 - 25
BO0505a	*The Art of The Empire Strikes Back*, trade paper (1994 cover)	18 - 20
BO0505b	*The Art of The Empire Strikes Back*, trade paper (1997 Special Edition section)	19 - 20
BO0506	*The Empire Strikes Back Sketchbook*, trade paperback only	10 - 12
BO0507	*The Empire Strikes Back Notebook*, trade paperback only (script plus storyboards)	8 - 12
BO0508	*The Art of Return of the Jedi*, hardcover	45 - 75
BO0509	*The Art of Return of the Jedi*, trade paperback	20 - 25
BO0509a	*The Art of Return of the Jedi*, trade paperback (revised 1994 cover)	18 - 20
BO0509b	*The Art of Return of the Jedi*, trade paperback (1997 Special Edition section)	19 - 20
BO0510	*Return of the Jedi Sketchbook*, trade paperback only	8 - 12
BO0520	*The Art of Star Wars Galaxy*, trade paperback (Topps)	18 - 25
BO0520a	*The Art of Star Wars Galaxy*, trade paperback (Topps/ QVC exclusive - includes special 9-up card sheet)	18 - 25

29

	The Art of Star Wars Galaxy, limited edition, bound and boxed maroon box (Underwood-Miller Inc.)	150 - 175
	The Art of Star Wars Galaxy, limited edition, bound and boxed purple box (Underwood-Miller Inc.)	150 - 175
BO0523	*The Art of Star Wars Galaxy II*, trade paperback,	18 - 25
BO0524	*The Art of Star Wars Galaxy II*, foil cover, trade paperback,	18 - 25
BO0530	*The Illustrated Star Wars Universe*, hardcover (Ballantine)	35 - 40
BO0540	*SW: The Art of Dave Dorman*, hardcover (numbered, signed [FPG])	75 - 80
BO0541	*SW: The Art of Dave Dorman*, trade paper (FPG)	22 - 25
BO0545	*SW: The Art of Drew Struzan*, hardcover (numbered, signed [FPG] 1997)	75 - 80
BO0546	*SW: The Art of Drew Struzan*, trade paper (FPG 1997)	22 - 25

Japan
BO0650	*ROTJ Sketchbook*	15-20
BO0660	ROTJ: N. "Olai" [Orai] Original Sketch Collection	20-25

ART PORTFOLIOS/BOXES

Ralph McQuarrie's pre-production and other artwork for the *Star Wars* saga was published by Ballantine upon the release of each film. Just like fine art, each piece was printed on a separate sheet and placed, unbound, in a cardboard portfolio. Each has been reprinted several times.

BO0700	*SW portfolio*	20 - 45
BO0702	*ESB portfolio*	15 - 25
BO0704	*ROTJ portfolio*	15 - 25
BO0710	Post Card Art Portfolio (Classico)	10 - 20
BO0800	*The Art of Ralph McQuarrie* Art Box (Chronicle)	15 - 25

BLANK BOOKS/DIARIES
BO0900	*My Jedi Journal*, with Yoda cover (Ballantine)	10 - 20

Antioch
BO0901	*Truce at Bakura* journal w/matching bookmark	8 - 10
BO0902	*The Crystal Star* journal w/matching bookmark	8 - 10
BO0903	*The Courtship of Princess Leia* journal w/matching bookmark	8 - 10
BO0904	Jedi battle scene journal w/bookmark	8 - 10
BO0905	Hildebrandt art journal w/bookmark	8 - 10
BO0906	20th Anniversary journal, montage on front only. Includes Rystáll bookmark and two wallet cards. Numbered limited ed.	12 - 14
BO0930	SW Book of Days	13 - 15

BLUEPRINTS/TECHNICAL
Ballantine
BO1000	SW blueprints in plastic folder	10 - 20
BO1005	The SW Intergalactic Passport	2 - 8

Starlog Technical Journals
BO1010	Vol. 1: *Tatooine*	5 - 10
BO1011	Vol. 1: *Tatooine* with foil cover	12 - 15
BO1012	Vol. 1: *Tatooine* with *Special Edition* insert	8 - 10
BO1013	Vol. 2: *Imperial Forces*	5 - 10
BO1014	Vol. 2: *Imperial Forces* with *Special Edition* insert	8 - 10
BO1015	Vol. 3: *Rebel Forces*	5 - 10
BO1016	Vol. 3: *Rebel Forces* with Special Edition insert	8 - 10
BO1020	*SW Technical Journal* compiles Starlog volumes, hardcover (Ballantine)	25 - 35
BO1030	SW Blueprint portfolio (Zanart)	15 - 18

Germany
BO1101	*Technisches Handbuch: Des Planeten Tatooine*	30 - 35

Japan
BO1150	SW Book of Blueprints (Bandai)	5 - 15

BOOKMARKS

A series of 16 bookmarks was produced by Random House in 1983. They were made in both a plain-surface and high-gloss finish

BO1201	#1 Luke	2 - 5
BO1202	#2 Darth Vader	2 - 5
BO1203	#3 Princess Leia	2 - 5
BO1204	#4 R2-D2	2 - 5
BO1205	#5 C-3PO	2 - 5
BO1206	#6 Lando, Skiff disguise	2 - 5
BO1207	#7 Chewbacca	2 - 5
BO1208	#8 Yoda	2 - 5

BO0660   BO1760

BO1209	#9 Obi-Wan	2 - 5
BO1210	#10 Han Solo	2 - 5
BO1211	#11 Boba Fett	2 - 5
BO1212	#12 Wicket the Ewok	2 - 5
BO1213	#13 Emperor's Royal Guard	2 - 5
BO1214	#14 Imperial Stormtrooper	2 - 5
BO1215	#15 Jabba the Hutt	2 - 5
BO1216	#16 Admiral Ackbar	2 - 5

Anitoch Publishing
with tassel
BO1220	SW art from The Lost City of the Jedi	2 - 3
BO1221	SW art from Zorba the Hutt's Revenge	2 - 3
BO1222	SW art from The Glove of Darth Vader	2 - 3
BO1223	SW art from Truce at Bakura	2 - 3
BO1224	SW art from The Courtship of Princess Leia	2 - 3
BO1225	SW art from The Crystal Star	2 - 3
BO1226a	Han Solo	2 - 3
BO1226b	Darth Vader	2 - 3
BO1226c	Princess Leia	2 - 3
BO1226d	Luke Skywalker	2 - 3
BO1226e	Ben Kenobi	2 - 3
BO1226f	Lando Calrissian	2 - 3
BO1226g	C-3PO	2 - 3
BO1226h	Chewbacca	2 - 3
BO1226i	Rystáll	2 - 3
BO1226j	Special Edition montage	2 - 3

shapemarks (die-cut, no tassel)
BO1228a	Chewbacca	2 - 3
BO1228b	Stormtrooper	2 - 3
BO1228c	Boba Fett	2 - 3
BO1228d	Yoda	2 - 3
BO1228e	C-3PO	2 - 3
BO1228f	R2-D2	2 - 3
BO1228g	Tusken Raider	2 - 3
BO1228h	Darth Vader	2 - 3
BO1228i	Jawa	2 - 3

Fantasma
BO1230	Darth Vader 3D honeycomb pattern	2 - 3
BO1231	Luke and Vader 3D noneycomb pattern	2 - 3

A.H. Prismatic
BO1232	B-wing, Falcon, TIE fighter hologram	2 - 3
BO1233	Falcon, Vader, Star Destroyer hologram	2 - 3
BO1234	X-wing, TIE Interceptor, AT-AT hologram	2 - 3

Bantam cardboard booklist/bookmarks
BO1240	Die-cut Vader/Shadows of the Empire	1 - 2
BO1241	Rectangular "The Adventure Continues" Jedi holding lightsaber	1 - 2

BOOKPLATES

Random House made boxed sets of 50 gummed bookplates for ROTJ. They came in four different patterns

BO1500	ROTJ: Yoda bookplates	3 - 10
BO1501	ROTJ: R2-D2 and C-3PO bookplates	3 - 10
BO1502	ROTJ: Darth Vader bookplates	3 - 10
BO1503	ROTJ: Wicket the Ewok bookplates	3 - 10

Antioch

BO1510	Dark Empire (boxed)	5 - 8
BO1511	R2-D2 & C-3PO (boxed)	5 - 8
BO1512	R2-D2 & C-3PO (hanger pack)	5 - 8
BO1513	Hildebrandt art (hanger pack)	5 - 8

Netherlands

BO1650	ROTJ scenes on school book labels (Introduct Holland)	2 - 4

COLORING BOOKS

Kenner Products made a series of coloring books for the trilogy and beyond, distinguishable by the cover illustration or photo. The coloring books for *Star Wars* were produced only by Kenner Canada, and thus the back-cover logo reads *La Guerre des Étoiles* for French-speaking Canadians. For the *Star Wars Special Edition*, the coloring books were produced by Golden Books.

BO1720	ESB: Leia, Chewbacca, C-3PO	2 - 5
BO1721	ESB: Lando, Leia, Han, Chewbacca	2 - 5
BO1722	ESB: Luke	2 - 5
BO1724	ESB: R2-D2	2 - 5
BO1725	ESB: Yoda	3 - 5
BO1726	ESB: Darth Vader and stormtroopers	3 - 5
BO1740	ROTJ: The Max Rebo Band	2 - 5
BO1741	ROTJ: Luke	2 - 5
BO1742	ROTJ: Lando in battle	2 - 5
BO1750	ROTJ: Wicket's World	1 - 5
BO1751	ROTJ: Wicket the Ewok	1 - 5
BO1752	EWOKS: Ewoks coloring book	1 - 5
BO1760	Dental Health Adventure Book (Oral-B premium)	5-10

Golden Books, 1997

BO1800	*SW: Galactic Adventures*	1 - 2
BO1801	*SW: Heroes and Villains*	1 - 2
BO1802	*SW: An Ewok Adventure*	2 - 3
BO1803	*SW: Posters to Color*	3 - 4
BO1804	*SW: Mark & See Magic*	4 - 5

Canada (Kenner Canada)

BO1900	SW: Chewbacca	10 - 25
BO1901	SW: R2-D2	10 - 25
BO1902	SW: C-3PO and Luke	10 - 25
BO1903	SW: Chewbacca and Luke	10 - 25

England/United Kingdom (Dragon Books/Collins)

BO1950	*DROIDS: The Droid Colouring Book of the Future*	2 - 4
BO1960	*EWOKS: The Ewok Fun Colouring Book*	1 - 3

France (Editions Hemma)

BO2000	*Les Ewoks*, Wicket cover	1 - 4
BO2001	*Les Ewoks*, Kneesaa w/flute	1 - 4
BO2002	*Les Ewoks*, Kneesaa eating fruit	1 - 4
BO2003	*Les Ewoks*, Chief Chirpa	1 - 4

Philippines (Presswell Enterprises)

BO2100	Ewoks	1 - 3

COMIC PAPERBACKS (Marvel)

This section includes only those Marvel Comics adaptations which have been re-printed in paperback format. See the **COMICS: COMIC BOOKS** section for items in comic book format.

BO2200	*The Marvel Comics Illustrated Version of Star Wars*, black & white (Del Rey, 1977)	5 - 12

Marvel Illustrated Books

BO2201	SW: Four New Adventures in Full Color, paperback	15 - 25
BO2202	SW 2: *World of Fire*, paperback, black & white	15 - 25
BO2210	ESB: The Marvel Comics Version, paperback, color	5 - 12
BO2220	ROTJ: The Official Comics Version, paperback, color	4 - 10

EDUCATIONAL

Random House, as part of its in-school "Attack on Reading" program published a set of workbooks and study guides in 1979 and 1980 using the *Star Wars* film as a way to teach reading comprehension and word skills. The softcover manuals are colorful, contain interesting quizzes and make an unusual collectible. Pendulum Press at about the same time produced a remedial reading kit for slow learners. The kit, which came in a cardboard "suitcase," consisted of a filmstrip, a separate audio track, five follow-along specially-prepared black and white digest-sized comic books that were written to encourage reading, and a special full-color poster by the comic artist. There were also spirit-master tests for the teacher to run off on the old duplicating machine (before photocopiers were common in schools). Finding one of these kits, with every item present and in unused condition, isn't like finding the holy grail—but close.

For *Jedi*, the Happy House imprint of Random House moved out of the classroom and into the stores with a series of six workbooks to improve verbal and mathematical skills for children in kindergarten through third grade. The original price of the books was deliberately kept to only 99 cents to be affordable to a wider public. Random House also published a number of "about" books using *Star Wars* characters to explain certain subject areas.

BO2500	*SW Attack on Reading: Teacher's Guide*	10 - 25
BO2501	*SW Attack on Reading: Comprehension 1*	10- 20
BO2502	*SW Attack on Reading: Comprehension 2*	10 - 20
BO2503	*SW Attack on Reading: Word Study*	10 - 20
BO2504	*SW Attack on Reading: Study Skills*	10 - 20
BO2508	*Star Wars* TV and Movie Tie-ins (Creative Education)	15 - 20

Pendulum Press

BO2510	SW remedial reading multimedia kit	150 - 200

Random House

BO2515	*C-3PO's Book about Robots*, softcover	5 - 10
BO2516	*The Star Wars Book about Flight*, softcover	5- 10
BO2517	*The Star Wars Question and Answer Book about Space*, hardcover	10 - 15
BO2518	Softcover of BO2517 (Scholastic Book Services)	5 - 10
BO2519	*ROTJ: The Star Wars Question & Answer Book about Computers*, softcover	5 - 15

Happy House

BO2520	*ROTJ: Multiplication workbook*	2 - 5
BO2521	*ROTJ: Addition and Subtraction workbook*	2 - 5
BO2522	*ROTJ: Reading and Writing*	2 - 5
BO2523	*ROTJ: Spelling*	2 - 5
BO2524	*ROTJ: Early Numbers*	2 - 5
BO2525	*ROTJ: ABC Readiness*	2 - 5

England

BO2730	SW: Easy Reading edition (Longman Publishers)	5 - 12
BO2732	SW: Easy Reading edition (Sphere)	5 - 12

Japan

BO2750	*Star Wars* screenplay	10 - 20
BO2751	*The Empire Strikes Back* screenplay	10 - 20
BO2752	*Return of the Jedi* screenplay	10 - 20

GUIDES (Ballantine/Del Rey)

BO2800	*A Guide to the Star Wars Universe*, paperback (Velasco)	5 - 10
BO2801	*A Guide to the Star Wars Universe*, 2nd ed., paperback (Slavicsek)	10 - 15
BO2802	*The Essential Guide to Characters*	15 - 18
BO2802a	*The Essential Guide to Characters*, special condensed edition	1 - 2
BO2803	*The Essential Guide to Vehicles and Vessels*	15 - 18
BO2803a	*The Essential Guide to Vehicles and Vessels*, special condensed edition	1 - 2
BO2804	*The Essential Guide to Weapons and Technology* (1997)	15 - 18
BO2805	*The Essential Guide to Planets and Moons*	undetermined
BO2806	*The Essential Guide to Droids* (1998)	15 - 18
BO2810	*The World of Star Wars* (Paradise Press)	5 - 10
BO2820	*Star Wars Encyclopedia* (1998)	undetermined
BO2830	*Tomart's Price Guide to Worldwide SW Collectibles* (Tomart, 1994)	24 - 28
BO2840	*The Complete Star Wars Trilogy Scrapbook* (Scholastic)	6 - 8

Japan

BO2950	*All About the Star Wars*	30 - 40

"MAKING OF" BOOKS

BO3000	*SW Compendium* (Paradise Press)	8 - 18
BO3001	*The Star Wars Album* (Ballantine, 1977)	10 - 20
BO3002	*SW: The Making of the Movie* (Step-Up Books/ Random House)	7 - 15
BO3020	*Once Upon a Galaxy: A Journal of The Making of ESB* (softcover with photos, Del Rey/Ballantine)	5 - 10
BO3030	*The Making of ROTJ* (softcover with photos, Del Rey/Ballantine)	5 - 10
BO3035	*The Secrets of Shadows of the Empire*, trade paperback (Ballantine)	15 - 18

Australia

BO3300	*The Star Wars Album* (Marvel Comics Intl.)	8 - 16

Belgium

BO3325	*The Making of ROTJ* (Orbit)	10 - 20

France

BO3350	*The Star Wars Album* (Hachette)	12 - 24

Germany

BO3370	*The Star Wars Album*	12 - 24
BO3375	*The Making of ROTJ*	10 - 20

Japan

BO3410	*The Star Wars Album*	12 - 24
BO3420	*The Making of ROTJ*	10 - 20

Netherlands

BO3450	*The Star Wars Album*	8 - 16

NON-FICTION

BO3500	*Industrial Light & Magic: The Art of Special Effects*, hardcover (Del Rey)	50 - 75
BO3505	*Industrial Light & Magic: Into the Digital Realm*, hardcover (Del Rey)	50 - 75

Chronicle Books

BO3510	*Star Wars: From Concept to Screen to Collectible*, hardcover	20 - 30
BO3511	*Star Wars: From Concept to Screen to Collectible*, trade paperback	15 - 20
BO3520	*From Star Wars to Indiana Jones: The Best of the Lucasfilm Archives*, hardcover	40 - 50
BO3521	*From Star Wars to Indiana Jones: The Best of the Lucasfilm Archives*, trade paperback	20 - 25
BO3522	*SW: The Toys* postcard book	10 - 12
BO3523	*SW: Behind the Scenes* postcard book	10 - 12
BO3524	*SW: Aliens and Creatures* postcard book	10 - 12
BO3530	*Star Wars Chronicles*	130 - 150
BO3540	*SW: The Myth of Magic*, hardcover (1997 Bantam)	45 - 50
BO3541	*SW: The Myth of Magic*, trade paperback (1997 Bantam)	22 - 25
BO3550	*George Lucas: The Creative Impulse*, hardcover (1992 Abrams)	35 - 40
BO3555	*George Lucas: The Creative Impulse* 2nd ed., hardcover (1997 Abrams)	35 - 40
BO3560	*I'd Just as Soon Kiss a Wookie: The Quotable SW* (Ballantine)	5 - 7
BO3561	*I'd Just as Soon Kiss a Wookie: The Quotable SW*, special condensed edition (Ballantine)	1 - 2

Germany

BO3810	*Von Star Wars bis Indiana Jones: Das Beste aus den Lucasfilm Archiven*	40 - 50

Japan

BO3900	*The Modeling of Star Wars* (Hobby Japan)	30 - 45
BO3901	*Industrial Light & Magic*	30 - 60
BO3902	*Star Wars: From Concept to Screen to Collectible*	30 - 40
BO3905	*The George Lucas Exhibition*, trade paperback catalog of 1993-94 Japanese exhibition of Lucasfilm props (Hata Stichting/Foundation)	50 - 75
BO3906	*George Lucas Museum*, hardcover version of catalog with added Lucas interview in Japanese (Bungeishunju Ltd.)	60 - 100
BO3910	*Star Wars Chronicles* w/slipcover and inserts	250 - 300
BO3912	*Cinefex ILM/Star Wars* (hardcover)	40 - 45
BO3913	*Cinefex ILM/Star Wars* (softcover)	30 - 35

United Kingdom

BO3950	*The Star Wars Archives*	40 - 50

NOVELS

The first edition of *Star Wars* as a novel by George Lucas was the December, 1976 paperback edition from Ballantine with a noir cover by Ralph McQuarrie of a very dark Darth Vader peering down on an early concept of Luke, the droids and Chewbacca. There have been dozens of paperback reprintings, with several cover variations. Del Rey also printed a gold-jacketed hardcover in October, 1977, and the Science Fiction Book Club printed a blue-jacketed version after that. Most of the hardcover editions of the movie and early Han Solo and Lando Calrissian novels that are found today are the book club editions. Publishers editions have the month of first printing on the copyright page; the book club editions just have the year. While none of the books are especially valuable, the publishers' editions would be worth at least 50% more than those of the book club.

BO4010	*Star Wars* novelization by George Lucas (First edition paperback, Del Rey, Dec 1976)	10 - 20
BO4011	2nd - 6th printing, "Now a Spectacular Motion Picture"	4 - 6
BO4012a	7th & 8th printing, "Best Movie of the Year"	4 - 6
BO4012b	9th - 19th printing, "Best Movie of the Year," photos removed	4 - 6
BO4012c	20th - 26th printing, "Over 5 Million in Print"	4 - 6
BO4012d	27th - 46th printing, "Over 5 Million in Print" SW logo in green	4 - 6
BO4012e	47th - 51st printing. A New Hope added to title "Classic" cover	4 - 6
BO4012f	52nd + printing, Special Edition Cover	4 - 6
BO4013	*Star Wars* novel, hardcover Ballantine Books edition, Oct. 1977 (gold dust jacket, black cloth w/ SW in gold on book)	45 - 75
BO4014	*Star Wars* novel, hardcover Science Fiction Book Club edition (blue dust jacket, gray cardboard cover)	7 - 20
BO4015	*Star Wars* novel, hardcover video art cover edition, 1995	16 - 18
BO4020	*Splinter of the Mind's Eye*, hardcover (Ballantine/Book Club, 1978)	5 - 15
BO4021	paperback w/red logo (Del Rey, 1978)	2 - 6
BO4022	paperback w/white logo (Del Rey, 1978)	2 - 6
BO4023	paperback w/"Classic" cover (1994)	4 - 6
BO4030	*Han Solo at Stars' End*, hardcover (Ballantine/Book Club, 1979)	5 - 15
BO4031	paperback (Del Rey, 1979)	2 - 6
BO4031a	paperback "New York Times Best Seller" (1997)	4 - 6
BO4032	*Han Solo's Revenge*, hardcover (Ballantine/Book Club, 1979)	5 - 15
BO4033	paperback w/yellow logo (Del Rey, 1979)	2 - 6
BO4033a	paperback w/brown logo (Del Rey, 1979)	2 - 6
BO4033b	paperback w/white logo (Del Rey, 1979)	2 - 6
BO4034	*Han Solo and the Lost Legacy*, hardcover (Ballantine/Book Club, 1980)	5 - 15
BO4035	paperback (Del Rey, 1980)	2 - 6
BO4036	Han Solo paperback boxed set	20 - 25
BO4040	*The Empire Strikes Back* novel, hardcover (Ballantine/Book Club, 1980)	5 - 18
BO4040a	*The Empire Strikes Back* novel, hardcover video art cover edition (1995)	16 - 18
BO4041	*The Empire Strikes Back* novel, paperback w/blue cover (Del Rey, 1983)	2 - 6
BO4041a	*The Empire Strikes Back* novel, paperback w/red cover (Del Rey, 1983)	2 - 6
BO4041b	*The Empire Strikes Back* novel, paperback "Classic" cover	4 - 6
BO4041c	*The Empire Strikes Back* novel, paperback Special Edition cover	4 - 6
BO4042	*ESB: The Illustrated Edition*, paperback only (Del Rey)	5 - 10
BO4050	*Return of the Jedi* novel, hardcover (Ballantine/Book Club, 1983)	5 - 15
BO4050a	*Return of the Jedi* novel, hardcover video art cover edition (1995)	16 - 18
BO4051	*Return of the Jedi* novel, paperback (Del Rey, 1983)	2 - 6
BO4051a	*Return of the Jedi* novel, paperback "Classic" cover	4 - 6
BO4051b	*Return of the Jedi* novel, paperback Special Edition cover	4 - 6
BO4052	*ROTJ: The Illustrated Edition*, paperback only (Del Rey)	5 - 10
BO4060	*Lando Calrissian and the Mindharp of Sharu*, hardcover (Del Rey/Book Club)	20 - 30
BO4061	paperback (Del Rey, 1983)	2 - 5
BO4062	*Lando Calrissian and the Flamewind of Oseon*, hardcover (Del Rey/Book Club)	20 - 30
BO4063	paperback (Del Rey)	2 - 5
BO4064	*Lando Calrissian and the Starcave of ThonBoka*, hardcover (Del Rey/Book Club)	20 - 30
BO4065	paperback (Del Rey)	2 - 5
BO4070	*The Star Wars Trilogy*, 10th Anniversary Omnibus Edition, trade paper (Del Rey)	6 - 10
BO4070a	*The Star Wars Trilogy*, Omnibus Edition, trade paper (Del Rey)	6 - 10
BO4071	*The Star Wars Trilogy*, paperback boxed set	20 - 25
BO4072	*The Star Wars Trilogy*, paperback compilation	4 - 6
BO4073	*The Star Wars Trilogy*, trade paperback	8 - 10
BO4080	*The Han Solo Adventures*, paperback compilation	4 - 8
BO4081	*The Han Solo Adventures*, trade paperback	8 - 10
BO4085	*The Lando Calrissian Adventures*, paperback compilation	4 - 8
BO4086	*The Lando Calrissian Adventures*, trade paperback	8 - 10

Bantam

BO4100	*SW: Heir to the Empire*, hardcover	15 - 25
BO4101	*SW: Heir to the Empire*, hardcover (Book Club)	15 - 25
BO4102	paperback	4 - 8
BO4103	signed & numbered limited edition w/slipcover	125 - 150
BO4105	*SW: Dark Force Rising*, hardcover	15 - 22

BO0001

BO0003

BO0004

BO0005

BO0020

BO0040

BO0043

BO0044

BO0045

BO0046

BO0047

BO0048

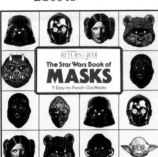
BO0049

BO0200

BO0201

BO0202

BO0203

BO0204

BO0205

BO0206

BO0431

BO0449

BO0460

BO0481

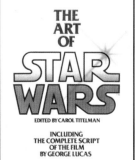
BO0502

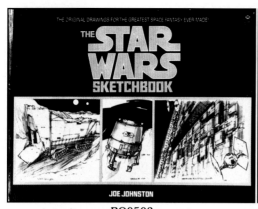

BO0503

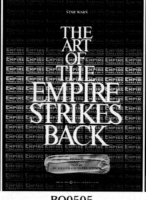

BO0505

BO0509

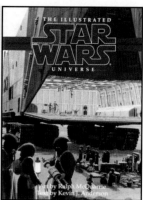

BO0530

BO0510

BO0650

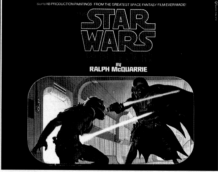

BO0700

BO0702

BO0704

BO0710

BO0900

BO1000

BO1005

BO1010

BO1011

BO1013

BO1101

BO1150

BO1722

BO1726

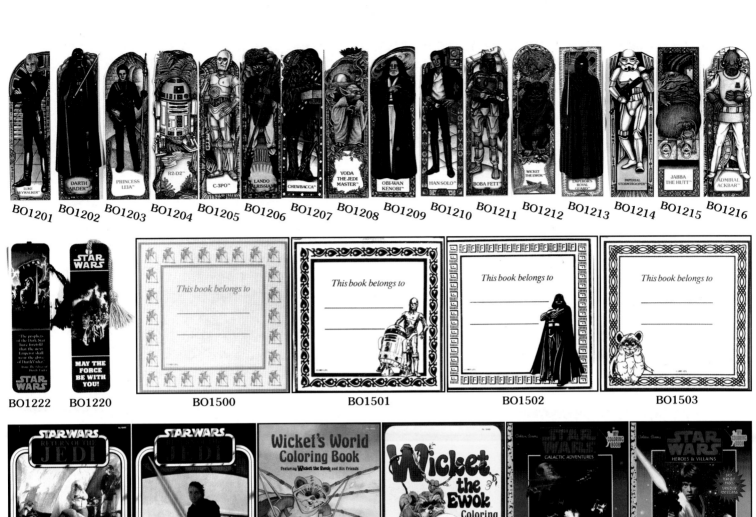

BO1201   BO1202   BO1203   BO1204   BO1205   BO1206   BO1207   BO1208   BO1209   BO1210   BO1211   BO1212   BO1213   BO1214   BO1215   BO1216

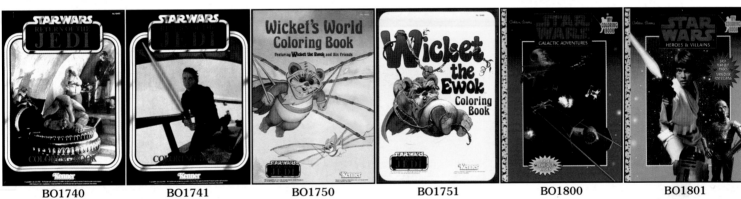

BO1222   BO1220   BO1500   BO1501   BO1502   BO1503

BO1740   BO1741   BO1750   BO1751   BO1800   BO1801

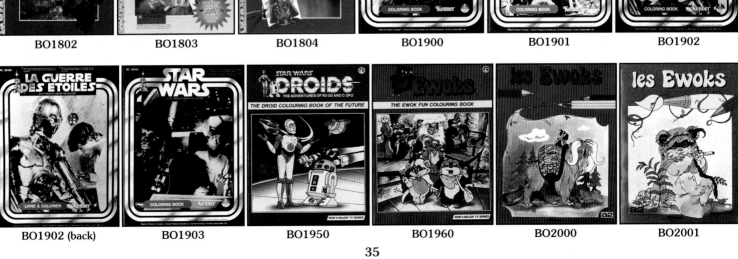

BO1802   BO1803   BO1804   BO1900   BO1901   BO1902

BO1902 (back)   BO1903   BO1950   BO1960   BO2000   BO2001

BO2002

BO2003

BO2200

BO2210

BO2502

BO2517

BO2510

BO2519

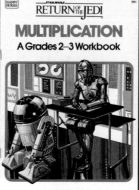
BO2520

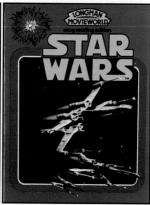
BO2730

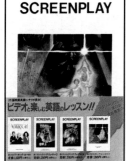
BO2750

BO2751

BO2752

BO2800

BO2801

BO2803

BO2830

BO2840

BO2950

BO3000

BO3001

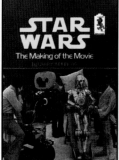
BO3002

BO3020

BO3300

BO3325

BO3350

BO3370

BO3375

BO3410

BO3420

BO3450

BO3510

BO3530

BO3810

BO3900

BO3901

BO3902

BO3905

BO3906

BO3910

Inserts from BO3910

BO3950

BO4011

BO4012

BO4012f

BO4041c

BO4051b

BO4014

BO4020

BO4030

BO4031

BO4032

BO4034

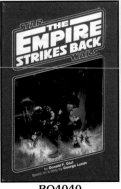
BO4040

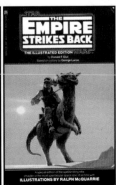
BO4042

BO4050

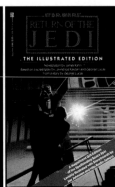
BO4052

BO4060   BO4063   BO4065   BO4070   BO4101   BO4106

BO4111   BO4120   BO4125   BO4130   BO4132   BO4135

BO4140   BO4165   BO4166   BO4167   BO4200   BO5501

BO5503   BO5505   BO5515   BO5530   BO5535   BO5540

BO5541   BO5550   BO5552   BO5580   BO5582   BO5585   BO5601

BO5602

BO5615

BO5616

BO5617

BO5621

BO5625

BO5630

BO5638

BO5701

BO5705

BO5707

BO5709

BO5711

BO5720

BO5721

BO5722

BO5731

BO5735

BO5748

BO5750

BO5790

BO5792

BO5794

BO5797

BO5805

BO5810

BO5850

BO5852

BO5855

BO5860

BO5872

BO5874

BO5877

BO5901

BO5903

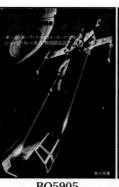
BO5905

BO5910

BO5923

BO5931

BO5933

BO5935

BO5950

BO6030

BO6060

BO6061

BO6065

BO6066

BO6067

BO6073

BO6083

BO6085

BO6104

BO6110

BO6140

BO6141

BO6161

BO6170

BO6171

BO6180

BO6180

BO6230

BO6250

BO6251

BO6253

BO6260

BO6270	BO6300	BO6400

BO4106	SW: Dark Force Rising, hardcover (Book Club)	15 - 22
BO4107	paperback	4 - 8
BO4108	signed & numbered limited edition w/slipcover	125 - 150
BO4110	SW: The Last Command, hardcover	18 - 22
BO4111	SW: The Last Command, hardcover (Book Club)	18 - 22
BO4112	paperback	4 - 7
BO4113	signed & numbered limited edition w/slipcover	125 - 150
BO4115	Thrawn Trilogy paperback boxed set	15 - 20
BO4120	The Truce at Bakura, hardcover (Bantam/Book Club)	18 - 22
BO4121	The Truce at Bakura, hardcover (Book Club)	10 - 12
BO4122	The Truce at Bakura, paperback	4 - 6
BO4123	The Truce at Bakura, paperback "New York Times Bestseller"	4 - 6
BO4125	The Courtship of Princess Leia, hardcover (Bantam/Book Club)	18 - 22
BO4126	The Courtship of Princess Leia, hardcover (Book Club)	10 - 12
BO4127	The Courtship of Princess Leia, paperback	4 - 6
BO4130	Jedi Search, paperback	4 - 6
BO4132	Dark Apprentice, paperback	4 - 6
BO4134	Champions of the Force, paperback	4 - 6
BO4135	Jedi Academy Trilogy paperback boxed set	15 - 20
BO4135	Jedi Academy Trilogy hardcover book club compilation	10 - 12
BO4140	The Crystal Star, hardcover (Bantam/Book Club)	20 - 25
BO4141	The Crystal Star, hardcover (Book Club)	10 - 12
BO4142	The Crystal Star, paperback	4 - 6
BO4145	Ambush at Corellia, paperback	4 - 6
BO4146	Assault on Selonia, paperback	4 - 6
BO4147	Showdown at Centerpoint, paperback	4 - 6
BO4148	Corellian Trilogy paperback boxed set	15 - 20
BO4149	Corellian Trilogy hardcover bookclub compilation	15 - 20
BO4155	Children of the Jedi, hardcover	20 - 25
BO4156	Children of the Jedi, hardcover (Book Club)	10 - 12
BO4157	Children of the Jedi, paperback	4 - 6
BO4160	Darksaber, hardcover	20 - 25
BO4161	Darksaber, hardcover (Book Club)	10 - 12
BO4162	Darksaber, paperback	4 - 6
BO4165	Tales from Jabba's Palace, paperback	4 - 6
BO4166	Tales from the Mos Eisley Cantina, paperback	4 - 6
BO4167	Tales of the Bounty Hunters, paperback	4 - 6
BO4170	X-wing book 1: Rogue Squadron, paperback	4 - 6
BO4171	X-wing book 2: Wedge's Gamble, paperback	4 - 6
BO4172	X-wing book 3: The Krytos Trap, paperback	4 - 6
BO4173	X-wing book 4: The Bacta War, paperback	4 - 6
BO4190	Before the Storm, paperback	4 - 6
BO4191	Shield of Lies, paperback	4 - 6
BO4192	Tyrant's Test, paperback	4 - 6
BO4193	Black Fleet Crisis Trilogy hardcover Book Club compilation	15 - 20
BO4195	Shadows of the Empire, hardcover	20 - 25
BO4196	Shadows of the Empire, hardcover (Book Club)	10 - 12
BO4197	Shadows of the Empire, paperback	20 - 25
BO4200	The New Rebellion, hardcover	20 - 25
BO4201	The New Rebellion, hardcover (Book Club, 1997)	10 - 12
BO4202	The New Rebellion, paperback (1997)	4 - 6
BO4205	Planet of Twilight, hardcover	20 - 25
BO4206	Planet of Twilight, hardcover (Book Club 1997)	10 - 12
BO4207	Planet of Twilight, paperback (1998)	4 - 6
BO4210	Paradise Snare, paperback (1997)	5 - 7
BO4211	Hutt Gambit, paperback (1997)	5 - 7
BO4212	Rebel Dawn, paperback (1998)	5 - 7
BO4215	Specter of the Past, hardcover (1997)	20 - 25

BO4217	Specter of the Past, paperback (1998)	5 - 7
BO4220	Vision of the Future, hardcover (1998)	20 - 25
BO4222	Vision of the Future, paperback (1999)	5 - 7
BO4225	I, Jedi, hardcover (1998)	20 - 25
BO4227	I, Jedi, paperback (1999)	5 - 7
BO4230	Star Wars Chronology, hardcover (1998)	28 - 30
BO4231	Star Wars Chronology, trade paperback (1998)	16 - 18

Brazil (Editora Record)

BO5501	SW: Guerra nads Estrelas, trade paper	5 - 15
BO5503	ESB: O Império Contra-Ataca, trade paper	5 - 15
BO5505	ROTJ: O Retorno de Jedi, trade paper	5 - 15
BO5515	A Última Ordem	5 - 15

Denmark

BO5550	Imperiets Arving	5 - 15
BO5551	Dark Force Rising	5 - 15
BO5552	Den Sidste Kommando	5 - 15

Finland

BO5580	SW: Tähtien Sota	20 - 30
BO5582	Mustan Lordin Paluu	20 - 30
BO5585	ESB: Imperium Vastaisku	20 - 30
BO5590	ROTJ: Jedin Paluu	20 - 30

France

BO5601	SW: La Guerre des Étoiles, trade paper (Presses de la Cité)	10 - 30
BO5602	paperback	5 - 20
BO5615	ESB: L'Empire Contre-Attaque, trade paper	10 - 30
BO5616	paperback	5 - 15
BO5617	hardcover	20 - 25
BO5621	ROTJ: Le Retour du Jedi, paperback	5 - 10
BO5625	La Guerre Des Étoiles (trilogy), trade paperback	15 - 20
BO5630	L'Héritier de l'Empire	20 - 25
BO5631	La Bataille des Jedi	20 - 25
BO5632	The Last Command	20 - 25
BO5638	Le Mariage de la Princesse Leia	20 - 25

Germany (Wilhelm Goldmann)

BO5701	SW: Krieg der Sterne, softcover	10 - 25
BO5705	Die neuen Abenteuer des Luke Skywalker	5 - 15
BO5707	Han Solos Rache, paperback	5 - 12
BO5709	Han Solo auf Stars' End, paperback	5 - 12
BO5711	Han Solo und das Verlorene Vermächtnis, paperback	5 - 12
BO5720	ESB: Das Imperium Schlägt Zurück, paperback	5 - 15
BO5721	alternate cover	15 - 25
BO5722	alternate cover, wide	15 - 25
BO5731	ROTJ: Die Rückkehr der Jedi-Ritter, paperback	5 - 10
BO5735	Die Star Wars Saga, all three novels, paperback	10 - 12
BO5748	Entführung nach Dathomir	5 - 10
BO5750	Der Kristallstern	5 - 10

Hungary (Kozmosz Könyvek)

BO5790	SW: Csillagok Háborúja, trade paper	10 - 15
BO5792	ESB: A Birodalom Visszavág, trade paper	10 - 15
BO5794	ROTJ: A Jedi Visszatér, trade paper	10 - 15
BO5797	Lando Calrissian és Sharu varázskulcsa	10 - 15
BO5805	Különbéke	10 - 15
BO5810	Szökevények	10 - 15

Italy (Arnoldo Mondadori Editore)

BO5850	SW: Guerre Stellari, hardcover	20 - 35
BO5852	SW: Guerre Stellari, paperback w/slipcase	20 - 45
BO5855	Han Solo Guerriero Stellare	15 - 25
BO5860	ESB: L'Imperio Colpisce Ancora, hardcover	18 - 30
BO5872	L'ultima Missione	10 - 15
BO5874	La Tregua di Bakura	10 - 15
BO5877	Un Amore per la Principessa	10 - 15

Japan

BO5901	Star Wars, hardcover	20 - 35
BO5903	Star Wars, paperback (Hildebrandt art)	10 - 22
BO5905	Star Wars, paperback (dogfight)	8 - 20
BO5910	Splinter of the Mind's Eye, hardcover	20 - 30
BO5923	The Empire Strikes Back	20 - 30
BO5931	Return of the Jedi, hardcover	20 - 30
BO5933	Return of the Jedi, paperback	10 - 22
BO5935	Return of the Jedi, paperback (alternate cover)	10 - 25
BO5950	Dark Apprentice (2 vol.)	20 - 35

Korea

BO6030	Heir to the Empire	20 - 30

Netherlands

BO6060	SW: Strijd Tussen de Sterren, trade paperback	15 - 25
BO6061	paperback w/photo	5 - 15
BO6065	Gevangenen van de Oerwoudplaneet	20 - 30
BO6066	De Wraak van Han Solo	15 - 25

BO6500

BO6505

BO6507

BO6510

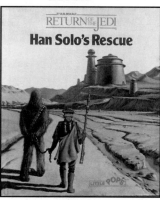
BO6520

BO6521

BO6530

BO6570

BO6067	*Han Solo in Star's End*	15 - 25
BO6071	*ESB: Wraakuit het Heelal*, paperback	5 - 10
BO6073	photo cover	10 - 15
BO6081	*ROTJ: De terugkeer van de Jedi*, paperback	5 - 10
BO6083	photo cover	5 - 10
BO6085	illustrated trade paperback	5 - 15

Norway (Fredhøis Forlag)

BO6100	*SW: Stjerne Krigen*, paperback	15 - 25
BO6104	*Evighetens Øye*	10 - 15
BO6110	*ESB: Imperiet Slår Tilbake*, paperback	5 - 15
BO6120	*ROTJ: Jedi Ridderen Vender Tilbake*, paperback	20 - 25

Poland

BO6140	*Dziedzic Imperium*	15 - 25
BO6141	*Ciemna Strona Mocy*	15 - 25

Portugal (Europa-América)

BO6161	*SW: A Guerra das Estrelas*, paperback	20 - 30
BO6170	*ESB: O Império Contra-Ataca*, trade paperback	20 - 30
BO6171	paperback	8 - 15
BO6180	*ROTJ: O Regresso de Jedi*, trade paperback	10 - 20
BO6181	paperback	8 - 15

Singapore

BO6230	*Return of the Jedi*	10 - 20

Spain

BO6250	*SW: La Guerra de las Galaxias*, trade paperback (Libreria Editorial Argos)	10 - 20
BO6251	paperback	
BO6253	*El Ojo de la Mente*	
BO6260	*ESB: El Imperio Contraataca*, trade paperback	10 - 20
BO6270	*ROTJ: El Retorno del Jedi*, trade paperback (Editorial Planeta)	10 - 20
BO6281	*Estrella de cristal*	10 - 20

Trilogia de la Academia Jedi BO6291-93

BO6291	*La búsqueda del Jedi*	10 - 20
BO6292	*El discipulo de la Fuerza Oscura*	10 - 20
BO6293	*Campeones de la Fuerza*	10 - 20
BO6295	*Herederos de la Fuerza*	10 - 20

Sweden

BO6300	*SW: Stjärnornas Krig*, paperback (Tidena Forlag)	5 - 15

United Kingdom

BO6340	*SW: Softcover first edition (Sphere)*	5 - 15
BO6345	*ESB: Softcover first ed w/color insert (Sphere)*	5 - 15
BO6350	*ROTJ: Hardcover (Macdonald Film Tie-In)*	10 - 20
BO6351	*ROTJ: Softcover, first & special junior ed. (Futura)*	5 - 10
BO6370	*Tales from Jabba's Palace*, paperback	4 - 6

BO6375	*Ambush at Corellia*	4 - 6
BO6376	*Assault at Selonia*	4 - 6
BO6377	*Showdown at Centerpoint*	4 - 6

Yugoslavia

BO6400	*SW: Zvezdani Ratovi*, trade paperback (Minotaur)	15 - 25

POP-UP AND MECHANICAL

Random House

BO6500	*SW* Pop-Up Book	10 - 20
BO6505	*ESB* Pop-Up Book	10 - 20
BO6507	*ESB* Panorama Book	15 - 25
BO6510	*ROTJ* Pop-Up Book	10 - 15
BO6520	*ROTJ: Han Solo's Rescue*, hardcover	8 - 10
BO6520a	*ROTJ: Han Solo's Rescue*, softcover	10 - 15
BO6521	*ROTJ: The Ewoks Save the Day*, hardcover	8 - 10
BO6521a	*ROTJ: The Ewoks Save the Day*, softcover	10 - 15
BO6522	*SW* Lift the Flap book	10 - 12

Dark Horse

BO6530	*Battle of the Bounty Hunters* Pop-Up book	18 - 20

Fun Works

BO6540	*Heroes in Hiding* Pop-Up book	8 - 10
BO6541	*A New Hope* shimmer book	8 - 10
BO6550	*SW: A New Hope* flip book	3 - 4
BO6551	*SW: The Empire Strikes Back* flip book	3 - 4
BO6552	*SW: Return of the Jedi* flip book	3 - 4

Little, Brown

BO6560	Mos Eisley Cantina Pop-Up book	18 - 20
BO6561	Jabba's Palace Pop-Up book	18 - 20
BO6565	The Rebel Alliance action flap book	15 - 17
BO6566	The Galactic Empire action flap book	15 - 17
BO6570	Death Star Pop-Up book	15 - 17
BO6571	Millennium Falcon Pop-Up book	15 - 17

Publications International

BO6580	*Star Wars* Play a Sound book	14 - 16

England

BO6620	SW Pop-Up Book (Collins)	10 - 15

France

BO6650	*SW: La Guerre des Etoilles* (Flammarion)	15 - 20

Italy

BO6680	*SW: Guerre Stellari* (Sperling & Kupfer Editori)	15 - 20

Japan

BO6701	*SW: Star Wars* (Bandai)	15 - 20

Spain

BO6730	*SW: La Guerra de las Galaxias* (Editorial Norma)	15 - 20

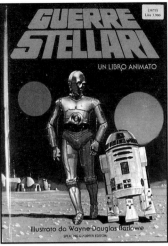

| BO6650 | BO6680 | BO6701 | BO6730 |

| BO6760 | BO6761 | BO6762 | BO6763 |

| BO6765 | BO6766 | BO6767 | BO6768 |

DROIDS pop-up books
BO6760	*Trigon*	1 - 4
BO6761	*Capturados*	1 - 4
BO6762	*Las Aventuras de Mungo Babab*	1 - 4
BO6763	*La Desaparicion de C3-PO*	1 - 4

EWOKS pop-up books:
BO6765	*Amenaza sobre la Aldea*	1 - 4
BO6766	*Fuego en el Bosque*	1 - 4
BO6767	Latara	1 - 4
BO6768	Asha	1 - 4

QUIZ/GAMES
BO6800	*The Jedi Master's Quizbook*, paperback black cover (Del Rey)	4 - 8
BO6800a	*The Jedi Master's Quizbook*, paperback blue cover (Del Rey)	4 - 8
BO6801	*Diplomatic Corps Entrance Exam*, trade paperback (Ballantine 1997)	10 - 12
BO6809	*SW Nintendo Hint Book* (LucasArts mail-away exclusive)	10 - 12

Prima
BO6810	*Super SW Official Game Secrets*, trade paper	10 - 13
BO6810a	*Super ESB Official Game Secrets*, trade paper	10 - 13

| BO6800 | BO6930 |

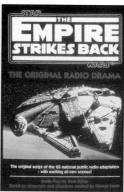

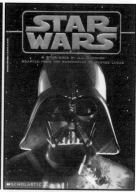

BO6970   BO6975   BO6976   BO7001   BO7001a

BO7003   BO7003a   BO7004   BO7004a   BO7006

BO6810b	*Super ROTJ Official Game Secrets*, trade paper	10 - 13
BO6811	*X-Wing: The Official Strategy Guide*, trade paper	15 - 20
BO6812	*X-Wing Collector's CD-Rom: The Official Strategy Guide*, trade paperback	15 - 20
BO6813	*TIE Fighter: The Official Strategy Guide*, trade paperback	15 - 20
BO6814	*TIE Fighter: Authorized Strategy Guide*, trade paperback (Brady Publishing)	12 - 14
BO6815	*TIE Fighter Collector's CD-Rom: The Official Strategy Guide*, trade paperback	15 - 20
BO6816	*Defender of the Empire: Official Secrets and Solutions*, trade paperback	12 - 15
BO6817	*Dark Forces: Official Player's Guide*, trade paper	18 - 20
BO6818	*Rebel Assault: The Official Insiders Guide*, trade paperback	15 - 20
BO6819	*Rebel Assault II: Official Player's Guide*, trade paper	15 - 20
BO6820	*Shadows of the Empire: Official Player's Guide*, trade paperback	12 - 14
BO6821	*X-wing vs. TIE Fighter Strategy Guide*, trade paperback (1997)	15 - 20
BO6822	*Jedi Knight Strategy Guide*, trade paperback (1997)	15 - 20

SCRIPTS/SCREENPLAYS

Premiere Magazine produced screenplays for all three films. The original versions of The Empire Strikes Back and Return of the Jedi were sold briefly, but recalled and destroyed because of a misprint.

Ballantine

BO6900	*SW: NPR Radio Dramatization*	10 - 12
BO6901	*ESB: NPR Radio Dramatization*	10 - 12
BO6902	*ROTJ: NPR Radio Dramatization*	10 - 12

OSP/Premiere

BO6930	*Star Wars*	8 - 15
BO6931	*The Empire Strikes Back* (recalled version)	50 - 75
BO6932	*The Empire Strikes Back*	8 - 15
BO6933	*Return of the Jedi*; red cover (recalled version)	50 - 75
BO6934	*Return of the Jedi*	8 - 15
BO6935	*SW Trilogy scripts boxed set*	55 - 60
BO6940	*SW: The Annotated Scripts*, trade paperback (Ballantine 1997)	10 - 13

United Kingdom

BO6970	*Star Wars: The Scripts*	25 - 35
BO6975	*Star Wars: The Original Radio Drama*	10 - 15
BO6976	*ESB: The Original Radio Drama*	10 - 15

See also - **BOOKS: Art/Sketch; BOOKS: Educational**

STORY/YOUNG READER

BO7000	*SW Storybook*, hardcover (Random House)	10 - 15
BO7001	softcover (Scholastic Book Service)	5 - 10
BO7001a	softcover (Scholastic 1997)	5 - 6
BO7002	*ESB Storybook*, hardcover (Random House)	10 - 12
BO7003	softcover (Scholastic Book Service)	5 - 10
BO7003a	softcover (Scholastic 1997)	5 - 6
BO7004	*ROTJ Storybook*, hardcover (Random House)	8 - 10
BO7005	softcover (Scholastic)	5 - 10
BO7005a	softcover (Scholastic 1997)	5 - 6
BO7006	*SW Treasury*—all three softcovers in a slipcase (Scholastic)	10 - 15
BO7007	*SW Movie Storybook Trilogy*—all three in one trade paperback	8 - 12
BO7010	*SW: Step-Up Movie Adventure* (Random House)	5 - 12
BO7010a	BO7010, 1995 edition	4 - 5
BO7011	*ESB: Step-Up Movie Adventure* (Random House)	5 - 12
BO7011a	BO7011, 1995 edition	4 - 5
BO7012	*ROTJ: Step-Up Movie Adventure* (Random House)	5 - 12
BO7012a	BO7012, 1995 edition	4 - 5
BO7020	*SW: The Maverick Moon*, softcover, day sky (Random House)	1 - 4
BO7020a	*SW: The Maverick Moon*, softcover, night sky (Random House)	1 - 4
BO7021	*SW: The Mystery of the Rebellious Robot* (Random House)	1 - 4
BO7025	*SW: The Wookiee Storybook*, hardcover (Random House)	5 - 12

ROTJ: Ewok mini-storybooks, softcover (Random House)

BO7060	*The Baby Ewoks' Picnic Surprise*	1 - 3
BO7061	*Three Cheers for Kneesaa!*	1 - 3
BO7062	*The Ewoks' Hang-Gliding Adventure*	1 - 3
BO7063	*Wicket Finds a Way*	1 - 3
BO7064	*ROTJ: The Ewoks Join the Fight*, softcover (Random House)	2 - 5
BO7064a	*ROTJ: The Ewoks Join the Fight*, library bound (Random House)	2 - 5
BO7065	*ROTJ: The Adventures of Teebo*, written/illustrated by Joe Johnston, hardcover (Random House)	20 - 25
BO7066	*ROTJ: How the Ewoks Saved the Trees*, hardcover (Random House)	5 - 12
BO7066a	*ROTJ: How the Ewoks Saved the Trees*, softcover (Random House)	5 - 12
BO7067	*The Ewoks and the Lost Children*, based on *The Ewok Adventure* movie, hardcover (Random House)	4 - 10

| BO7010 | BO7010a | BO7011a | BO7012 | BO7012a |

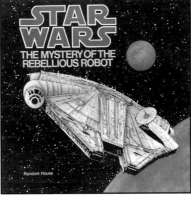

| | | BO7060 | BO7061 | BO7062 |

| BO7020 | BO7021 | BO7063 | BO7064 | BO7066 |

| BO7067 | BO7081 | BO7083 | BO7084 | BO7121 |

| BO7123 | BO7125 | BO7127 | BO7129 | BO7131 |

Droids Books (Random House)
BO7080	*The Pirates of Tarnoonga*, hardcover	18 - 20
BO7081	*The Lost Prince*, hardcover	18 - 20
BO7082	*Escape from the Monster Ship*, softcover	15 - 18
BO7083	*Shiny as a Droid*	4 - 10
BO7084	*Droids: The Adventures of R2-D2 and C-3PO*	2 - 8

Ewoks Books (Random House)
BO7090	*Fuzzy as an Ewok*	4 - 10
BO7091	*Wicket and the Dandelion Warriors*, hardcover	2 - 8

BO7092	*The Shadow Stone*, softcover	3 - 8
BO7093	*The Ring, the Witch and the Crystal*, softcover	2 - 6
BO7094	*The Red Ghost*, softcover	2 - 5
BO7095	*Wicket goes Fishing* (hard and softcover)	5 - 10
BO7096	*The Ewok Who Was Afraid* (softcover)	5 - 10

SW: Young adult series, softcover BO7121-35 (Bantam Skylark)
BO7121	*The Glove of Darth Vader*	3 - 4
BO7122	*The Glove of Darth Vader*, new gold foil logo cover	3 - 4
BO7123	*The Lost City of the Jedi*	3 - 4

| BO7182 | BO8701 | BO8705 | BO8740 | BO8761 |

| BO8762 | BO8800 | BO8811 | BO8821 | BO8822 | BO8823 |

BO7124	*The Lost City of the Jedi*, new gold foil logo cover	3 - 4
BO7125	*Zorba the Hutt's Revenge*	3 - 4
BO7126	*Zorba the Hutt's Revenge*, new gold foil logo cover	3 - 4
BO7127	*Mission from Mount Yoda*	3 - 4
BO7128	*Mission from Mount Yoda*, new gold foil logo cover	3 - 4
BO7129	*Queen of the Empire*	3 - 4
BO7130	*Queen of the Empire*, new gold foil logo cover	3 - 4
BO7131	*Prophets of the Dark Side*	3 - 4
BO7132	*Prophets of the Dark Side*, new gold foil logo cover	3 - 4
BO7135	Boxed set of books 1 - 3	12 - 15
BO7138	Hardcover compilation of books 1 - 3 (Barnes and Noble Books)	8 - 10
BO7139	Hardcover compilation of books 4 - 6 (Barnes and Noble Books)	8 - 10
BO7150	*Luke's Fate*, paperback (Random House, "brand new" on cover)	4 - 5
BO7151	*Luke's Fate*, paperback (Random House)	4 - 5
BO7155	*Shadows of the Empire* Junior Novelization (Bantam)	4 - 6

Galaxy of Fear series (Bantam)

BO7161	*Eaten Alive*	4 - 6
BO7162	*City of the Dead*	4 - 6
BO7163	*Planet Plague*	4 - 6
BO7164	*The Nightmare Machine*	4 - 6
BO7165	*The Ghost of the Jedi* (1997)	4 - 6
BO7166	*Army of Terror* (1997)	4 - 6

Junior Jedi Knights series (Berkely)

BO7171	*The Golden Globe*	4 - 6
BO7172	*Lyric's World*	4 - 6
BO7173	*Promises*	4 - 6
BO7174	*Anakin's Quest*	4 - 6
BO7175	*Vader's Fortress* (1997)	4 - 6
BO7176	*Kenobi's Blade* (1997)	4 - 6

Young Jedi Knights series (Berkely)

BO7181	*Heirs of the Force*	4 - 5
BO7182	*Shadow Academy*	4 - 5
BO7183	*The Lost Ones*	4 - 5
BO7184	*Lightsabers*	4 - 5
BO7185	*Darkest Knight*	4 - 5
BO7186	*Jedi Under Siege*	4 - 5
BO7187	Boxed paperback set of first three books	14 - 16
BO7188	Compilation of first six books, hardcover (Book Club)	10 - 12
BO7191	*Shards of Alderaan*	4 - 5
BO7192	*Diversity Alliance*	4 - 5
BO7193	*Delusions of Grandeur* (1997)	4 - 5
BO7194	*Jedi Bounty* (1997)	4 - 5
BO7195	*The Emperor's Plague* (1997)	4 - 5

Little Chronicles (Chronicle)

BO7250	*SW: A New Hope*, mini hardcover	8 - 10

BO7251	*The Empire Strikes Back*, mini hardcover	8 - 10
BO7252	*Return of the Jedi*, mini hardcover	8 - 10

Toy Spine Books (Fun Works 1997)

BO7260	*R2-D2's Mission: A Little Heroes Journey*, w/minature toy R2-D2 bound into spine	6 - 8
BO7261	*Darth Vader's Mission: The Search for the Secret Plans*, w/minature toy Darth Vader bound into spine	6 - 8

Super Shape Books (Golden Books 1998)

BO7280	*Luke Skywalker, Jedi Knight*	2 - 4
BO7281	*Princess Leia*	2 - 4
BO7282	*R2-D2 & C-3PO Droid Duo*	2 - 4

Pull Out Poster Books BO7290-92 (Scholastic)

BO7290	*SW: A New Hope*	4 - 6
BO7291	*The Empire Strikes Back*	4 - 6
BO7292	*Return of the Jedi*	4 - 6
BO7300	*Monsters and Aliens from George Lucas*, hardcover (Abrams)	15 - 20

Brazil

BO8701	*Guerra nas Estrelas*	5 - 15
BO8705	*Destaque e Brinque*	5 - 15

England (Collins Publishing)

BO8740	*SW Storybook*, hardcover	5 - 15
BO8741	paperback	4 - 8
BO8761	*ROTJ Storybook*, paperback	4 - 8
BO8762	*ROTJ Storybook*, St. Michael hardback version	3 - 6
BO8780	*DROIDS: The White Witch* softcover	3 - 6
BO8781	*DROIDS: Escape intoTerror* softcover	3 - 6
BO8782	*DROIDS: The Trigon Unleashed* softcover	3 - 6
BO8783	*DROIDS: A Race to the Finish* softcover	3 - 6
BO8784	*EWOKS: The Haunted Village* softcover	3 - 6
BO8785	*EWOKS: To Save Deej* softcover	3 - 6
BO8786	*EWOKS: Sun Star against Shadow Stone* softcover	3 - 6
BO8787	*EWOKS: Wicket's Wagon*	3 - 6

France

BO8800	*SW: Histoire Illustrée de La Guerre des Étoiles*	10 - 20
BO8811	*La Victoire des Ewoks*	4 - 8
BO8821	*Les Ewoks: La Pierre Mystérieuse*	4 - 8
BO8822	*Les Ewoks: Wicket et le Lutin Volant*	4 - 8
BO8823	*Les Ewoks: Wicket et la Poudre Magique*	4 - 8
BO8841	*The Glove of Darth Vader*	5 - 10
BO8842	*The Lost City of the Jedi*	5 - 10
BO8843	*La vengeance de Zorba le Hutt*	5 - 10
BO8844	*Mission from Mount Yoda*	5 - 10
BO8845	*Queen of the Empire*	5 - 10
BO8846	*Le Prophète Suprême du Côte Obscur*	5 - 10

Germany

BO8850	*ROTJ: Die Rückkehr der Jedi-Ritter*	10 - 15
BO8855	*Ewoks: Karawane Der Tapferen*	10 - 15

| BO8843 | BO8846 | BO8850 | BO8855 | BO8858 | BO8861 | BO8880 |

| BO8883 | BO8900 | BO8905 | BO8907 | BO8909 |

| BO8921 | BO8923 | BO8950 |

BS0010	"I saw *SW* at Mann's Chinese Theater (or The Avco Cinema)" (orange on blue star field)	1 - 3
BS0020	*SW* 10th Anniversary Convention gold foil (Creation Conventions)	1 - 3
BS0030	*SW* laser reflective (Fantasma)	2 - 3

BUTTONS AND BADGES

Like bumper stickers, there were tons of bootleg Stars Wars buttons and badges—but there were also plenty of licensed ones from Factors Inc. for the first films through Adam Joseph Industries for *ROTJ*. One of the most interesting early sets was made by Factors and available only to early members of the *Star Wars* Fan Club. This 14-button set is distinguished for having one picturing a very young, frazzled-looking George Lucas.

BU0001	Fan Club Button	5 - 10
BU0002	Fan Club Luke	5 - 10
BU0003	Fan Club Han Solo	5 - 10
BU0004	Fan Club Princess Leia	5 - 10
BU0005	Fan Club Chewbacca	5 - 10
BU0006	Fan Club Artoo	5 - 10
BU0007	Fan Club Threepio	5 - 10
BU0008	Fan Club Ben Kenobi	5 - 10

Hungary
BO8858	Young Adult series, each	8 - 15

Israel
BO8861	*The Glove of Darth Vader*	8 - 15
BO8862	*The Lost City of the Jedi*	8 - 15
BO8863	*Zorba the Hutt's Revenge*	8 - 15
BO8864	*Mission from Mount Yoda*	8 - 15
BO8865	*Queen of the Empire*	8 - 15
BO8866	*Prophets of the Dark Side*	8 - 15

Italy
BO8880	*SW: Il fotolibro di Guerre Stellari*	20 - 30
BO8883	*ESB: fotolibro L'Impero Colpisce Ancora*	20 - 30

Japan
BO8900	*SW Storybook*	25 - 50
BO8903	*ESB Storybook*	25 - 50
BO8905	*ROTJ Storybook*	20 - 40
BO8907	*ROTJ Movie Adventure*	20 - 40
BO8909	*The Ewoks and the Lost Children*	5 - 10
BO8921	*The Glove of Darth Vader*	5 - 10
BO8923	*The Lost City of the Jedi*	5 - 10

Spain
BO8950	*SW: La Guerra de las Galaxias*	20 - 30

SOUVENIR
BO9000	Stalog Salutes *Star Wars*, 10th Anniversary souvenir program	4 - 12

Japan
BO9810	Program booklet for US-Japan Robot Exhibition	5 - 15

BUMPER STICKERS

There are dozens of *Star Wars* bumper stickers, especially since the films coincided with the end of bumper-sticker mania. But few of the stickers are licensed or authorized; most were done in local print shops. They may be fun to collect, but not worth more than $1 or so apiece.

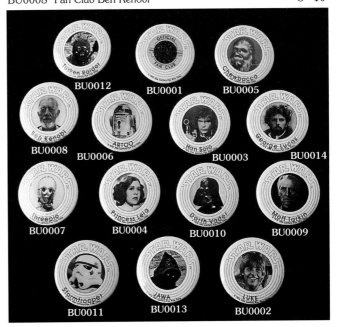

| BU0020 | BU1008 | BU1025 | BU1025 | BU3004 | BU3005 | BU3011 |

| BU1000 | BU1001 | BU1002 | BU1003 | BU1004 | BU1005 |

| BU1006 | BU1007 | BU1008 | BU1018 | BU1019 | BU1020 |

| BU2000 | BU2001 | BU2002 | BU2003 | BU2004 | BU2005 |

BU0009	Fan Club Moff Tarkin	5 - 10
BU0010	Fan Club Darth Vader	5 - 10
BU0011	Fan Club Stormtrooper	5 - 10
BU0012	Fan Club Tusken Raider	5 - 10
BU0013	Fan Club Jawa	5 - 10
BU0014	Fan Club George Lucas	5 - 10
BU0020	Fan Club Rebel Recruiter	5 - 15

SW 3" pin back badges (Factors Inc.)

BU1000	May the Force be With You	2 - 8
BU1001	R2-D2	2 - 8
BU1002	C-3PO	2 - 8
BU1003	Luke Skywalker	2 - 8
BU1004	Chewbacca	2 - 8
BU1005	Ben (Obi-Wan) Kenobi	2 - 8
BU1006	Solo & Chewbacca	2 - 8
BU1007	Princess Leia Organa	2 - 8
BU1008	R2-D2 and C-3PO/SW logo	4 - 10
BU1018	Darth Vader (photo button)	2 - 8
BU1019	Darth Vader w/lightsaber	2 - 8
BU1020	Darth Vadar (misspelled) Lives (sketch of mask)	2 - 8
BU1021	Darth Vadar mirror-backed button as key chain	4 - 10
BU1022	Darth Vadar mirror-backed button as necklace	4 - 10
BU1023	SW/May the Force...w/Kenner logo	10 - 25
BU1024	Pendulum Press has SW	5 - 10
BU1025	SW/Natl. Public Radio buttons, each	5 - 10
BU1100	Yoda Goes Public/NPR	10 - 15

ESB 3" pin back badges (Factors Inc.)

BU2000	Darth Vader	2 - 6
BU2001	Yoda	2 - 6
BU2002	C-3PO and R2-D2	2 - 6
BU2003	Boba Fett	2 - 6
BU2004	Chewbacca	2 - 6
BU2005	Luke X-wing pilot	2 - 6

ROTJ 2¼" pin back badges (Adam Joseph Industries)

BU3000	Revenge logo	4 - 10
BU3001	Return logo	1 - 5
BU3002	Max Rebo	1 - 5
BU3003	Gamorrean guard	1 - 5
BU3004	Revenge 1-sheet art	1 - 5
BU3005	R2-D2 and C-3PO	1 - 5
BU3006	Darth Vader	1 - 5
BU3007	Jabba	1 - 5
BU3008	Heroes in forest	1 - 5
BU3009	Chewbacca	1 - 5
BU3010	Baby Ewok	1 - 5
BU3011	Royal guard	1 - 5
BU3012	Yoda	1 - 5

Ewoks cartoon 2¼" pin back badges (Adam Joseph) BU4003-16

BU4003	Wicket the Ewok logo	1 - 2
BU4004	Shoveling snow	1 - 2
BU4005	Basket on head	1 - 2
BU4006	Lessons in forest	1 - 2
BU4007	Sitting and thinking	1 - 2
BU4008	Flying	1 - 2
BU4009	Wicket and R2-D2	1 - 3
BU4010	Kneesaa and Baga	1 - 2
BU4011	Feeding Baga	1 - 2
BU4012	Baby grouping	1 - 2
BU4013	Wicket tells a story	1 - 2
BU4014	Swinging on a vine	1 - 2
BU4015	Ice Capades and Ewoks (3½" pin back)	3 - 5
BU4016	Ice Capades and Ewoks (2¼" eyes light up)	4 - 8
BU4100	Ask me for your ROTJ glasses (Burger King)	5 - 10
BU4110	I sat through the Trilogy Sept. 2-3 1984, LA Con	5 - 10
BU4111	The SW Trilogy, March 28, 1985	5 - 10

10th Anniversary buttons, BU4500-BU4510

BU4500	SW: The First Ten Years	4 - 8

BU3000　　BU3001　　BU3002　　BU3003　　BU3004　　BU3005

BU3006　　BU3007　　BU3008　　BU3009　　BU3010　　BU3011

BU3012　　BU4013　　BU4015　　BU4700　　BU4760　　BU6050

BU1023　　BU4003　　BU4004　　BU4005　　BU4006　　BU4007

BU4008　　BU4009　　BU4010　　BU4011　　BU4012　　BU4014

BU4500　　　　　　　BU4750

BU4501	Leia and Luke	4 - 8
BU4502	C-3PO and R2-D2	4 - 8
BU4503	Darth Vader	4 - 8
BU4510	Pewter First 10 Years pin	10 - 20

BU4700	Trilogy Video Re-release button	3 - 5
BU4750	Special Edition button	2 - 5
BU4760	*Droids* Animated Classics	3 - 5
	England/United Kingdom	
BU6050	*ESB* 1st anniv.; Darth Vader "Happy Empire Day"	5 - 10
Touchline		
BU6051	Stormtrooper, white on black	3 - 5
BU6052	R2-D2, white on lt. blue	3 - 5
BU6053	Darth Vader, white on black	3 - 5
BU6054	Jabba the Hutt, orange	3 - 5
BU6055	C-3PO, gold on blue	3 - 5
BU6065	Ewok, brown and yellow	3 - 5
BU6066	Chewbacca, brown on red	3 - 5
BU6067	Admiral Ackbar, brown on white	3 - 5
Present Needs Ltd.		
BU6081	Baby Ewoks	2 - 4
BU6082	Vader and Royal guard	2 - 4
BU6083	May the Force be With You	2 - 4

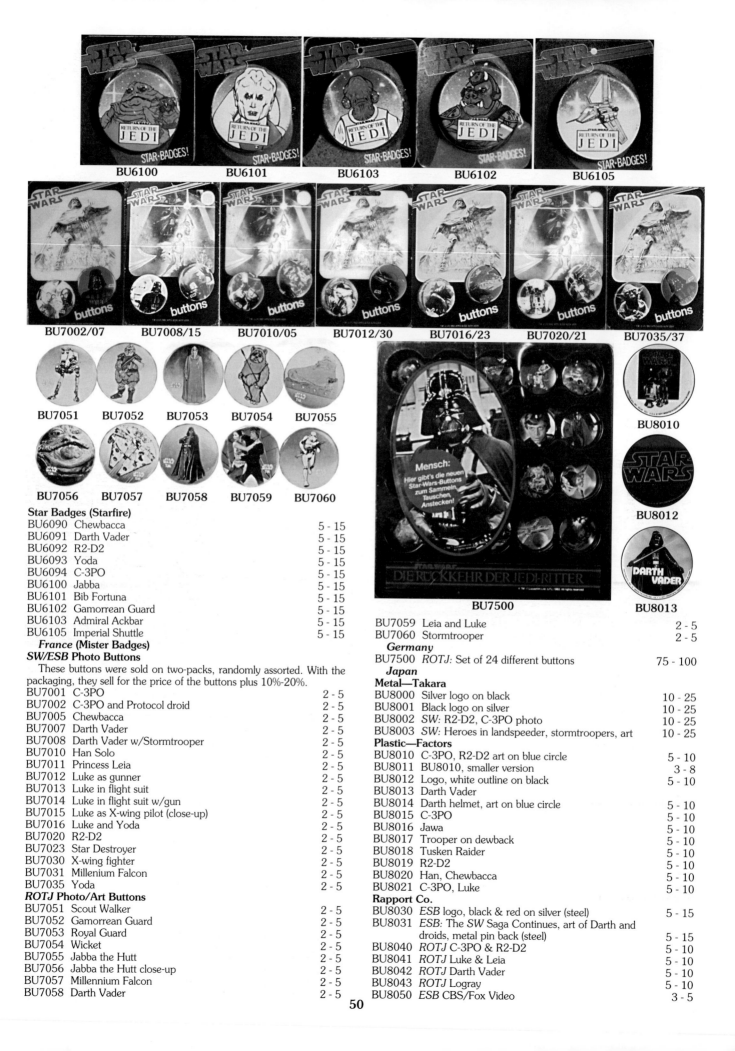

Row 1: BU6100　BU6101　BU6103　BU6102　BU6105

Row 2: BU7002/07　BU7008/15　BU7010/05　BU7012/30　BU7016/23　BU7020/21　BU7035/37

BU7051　BU7052　BU7053　BU7054　BU7055

BU7056　BU7057　BU7058　BU7059　BU7060

BU8010

BU8012

BU8013

BU7500

Star Badges (Starfire)

BU6090	Chewbacca	5 - 15
BU6091	Darth Vader	5 - 15
BU6092	R2-D2	5 - 15
BU6093	Yoda	5 - 15
BU6094	C-3PO	5 - 15
BU6100	Jabba	5 - 15
BU6101	Bib Fortuna	5 - 15
BU6102	Gamorrean Guard	5 - 15
BU6103	Admiral Ackbar	5 - 15
BU6105	Imperial Shuttle	5 - 15

France (Mister Badges)

SW/ESB Photo Buttons

These buttons were sold on two-packs, randomly assorted. With the packaging, they sell for the price of the buttons plus 10%-20%.

BU7001	C-3PO	2 - 5
BU7002	C-3PO and Protocol droid	2 - 5
BU7005	Chewbacca	2 - 5
BU7007	Darth Vader	2 - 5
BU7008	Darth Vader w/Stormtrooper	2 - 5
BU7010	Han Solo	2 - 5
BU7011	Princess Leia	2 - 5
BU7012	Luke as gunner	2 - 5
BU7013	Luke in flight suit	2 - 5
BU7014	Luke in flight suit w/gun	2 - 5
BU7015	Luke as X-wing pilot (close-up)	2 - 5
BU7016	Luke and Yoda	2 - 5
BU7020	R2-D2	2 - 5
BU7023	Star Destroyer	2 - 5
BU7030	X-wing fighter	2 - 5
BU7031	Millenium Falcon	2 - 5
BU7035	Yoda	2 - 5

ROTJ Photo/Art Buttons

BU7051	Scout Walker	2 - 5
BU7052	Gamorrean Guard	2 - 5
BU7053	Royal Guard	2 - 5
BU7054	Wicket	2 - 5
BU7055	Jabba the Hutt	2 - 5
BU7056	Jabba the Hutt close-up	2 - 5
BU7057	Millennium Falcon	2 - 5
BU7058	Darth Vader	2 - 5

BU7059	Leia and Luke	2 - 5
BU7060	Stormtrooper	2 - 5

Germany

BU7500	*ROTJ*: Set of 24 different buttons	75 - 100

Japan

Metal—Takara

BU8000	Silver logo on black	10 - 25
BU8001	Black logo on silver	10 - 25
BU8002	*SW*: R2-D2, C-3PO photo	10 - 25
BU8003	*SW*: Heroes in landspeeder, stormtroopers, art	10 - 25

Plastic—Factors

BU8010	C-3PO, R2-D2 art on blue circle	5 - 10
BU8011	BU8010, smaller version	3 - 8
BU8012	Logo, white outline on black	5 - 10
BU8013	Darth Vader	
BU8014	Darth helmet, art on blue circle	5 - 10
BU8015	C-3PO	5 - 10
BU8016	Jawa	5 - 10
BU8017	Trooper on dewback	5 - 10
BU8018	Tusken Raider	5 - 10
BU8019	R2-D2	5 - 10
BU8020	Han, Chewbacca	5 - 10
BU8021	C-3PO, Luke	5 - 10

Rapport Co.

BU8030	*ESB* logo, black & red on silver (steel)	5 - 15
BU8031	*ESB*: The *SW* Saga Continues, art of Darth and droids, metal pin back (steel)	5 - 15
BU8040	*ROTJ* C-3PO & R2-D2	5 - 10
BU8041	*ROTJ* Luke & Leia	5 - 10
BU8042	*ROTJ* Darth Vader	5 - 10
BU8043	*ROTJ* Logray	5 - 10
BU8050	*ESB* CBS/Fox Video	3 - 5

| BU8030 | BU8031 | BU9020 | BU9088 |

BU9070

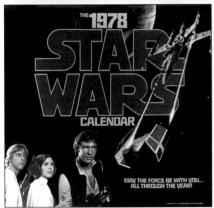

| CA0100 | CA0107 | CA0120 |

BU8061 Caravan of Courage logo	2 - 5	
BU8062 Caravan of Courage photo	2 - 5	
BU8063 Endor, girl and creature	3 - 5	
BU8064 Endor, girl alone	3 - 5	

Netherlands (ESB—Apple and Egg Productions)

BU9001 C-3PO	2 - 5
BU9002 C-3PO and Protocol droid	2 - 5
BU9005 Chewbacca	2 - 5
BU9006 Darth Vader	2 - 5
BU9007 Darth Vader w/Stormtrooper	2 - 5
BU9008 Han Solo	2 - 5
BU9009 Princess Leia	2 - 5
BU9010 Luke as gunner	2 - 5
BU9011 Luke in flight suit	2 - 5
BU9012 Luke in flight suit w/gun	2 - 5
BU9013 Luke as X-wing pilot (close-up)	2 - 5
BU9014 Luke and Yoda	2 - 5
BU9015 R2-D2	2 - 5
BU9016 Star Destroyer	2 - 5
BU9017 X-wing fighter	2 - 5
BU9018 Millenium Falcon	2 - 5
BU9019 Yoda	2 - 5
BU9020 Retailer Tray	45 - 65

New Zealand (ROTJ—Bing Harris Sargood)

BU9050 Darth Vader	2 - 5
BU9051 Darth and Luke duel	2 - 5
BU9052 R2-D2 and C-3PO	2 - 5
BU9053 Wicket	2 - 5

BU9054 Death Star	2 - 5
BU9055 C-3PO, Chewbacca, Leia	2 - 5

Spain (Chocolates la Cibeles Mieres/Siero)

BU9070 Cardboard adhesive badges inside lids of chocolate spread cocoa, ea.	2 - 5

Sweden (Ide and Resultat AB)

BU9088 *SW* light-up badges, ea.	8 - 15
BU9090 *ROTJ* light-up badges, ea.	5 - 10

CALENDARS

Star Wars calendars were produced each year between 1978 and 1981, then sporadically after that. The first two years, the calendars came in printed cardboard sleeves.

Random House/Ballantine, CA0100-075

CA0100 1978 *SW*	10 - 20
CA0101 1979 *SW*	10 - 20
CA0102 1980 *SW* (poster art)	20 - 30
CA0103 1981 *ESB*	10 - 15
CA0106 1984 *ROTJ*	10 - 15
CA0107 1984 *ROTJ* Ewok stickers	5 - 10
CA0120 1990 Trilogy (Cedco Publishing)	10 - 15
CA0121 1991 Trilogy (Cedco Publishing)	10 - 15
CA0123 1991 Lucasfilm 20th anniv. (Abrams)	8 - 12
CA0128 1995 Trilogy (Antioch)	5 - 10
CA0129 1995 Trilogy 3D (Andrews and McMeel	5 - 10
CA0130 1995 Trilogy (Landmark)	5 - 10
CA0131 1996 *SW* (Hallmark)	5 - 10

CA0140

CA8050

CA9000

CA9510

CC0001

CC0002

CC0004

CC0005

CC0006

CC0007

CC0008

CC0009

CA0132	1996 Wide Image Calendar (Cedco)	10 - 15
CA0133	1996 Wide Image Datebook (Cedco)	5 - 10
CA0134	1997 20th anniversary (Shooting Star Press)	5 - 10
CA0135	1997 20th anniversary (Golden Turtle Press)	5 - 10
CA0136	1997 *ESB* (Hallmark)	5 - 10
CA0137	1997 Art of SW Calendar (Cedco)	10 - 15
CA0138	1997 Art of SW Datebook (Cedco)	5 - 10
CA0140	1997 20th anniv. Collector's Edition	5 - 10

England

CA8050	*ESB* 1981 (Thomas Forman)	10 - 15

Japan

CA8500	1988 promo/Trilogy (Namco Ltd.)	10 - 15

Spain

CA9000	*SW*: Calendario Robot (R2-D2) (Ediciones Manantial)	25 - 35
CA9001	*ROTJ* 1983 customer calendar (Kodak, S.A.)	5 - 10

Sweden

CA9510	*SW* Advent calendar (Ide and Resultat)	10 - 20

CAST AND CREW

This is one of the most fascinating, yet frustrating, areas of collecting for it involves items that were usually made only in the hundreds, if that. On the other hand, it's unlikely that many were discarded, so cast and crew items show up more often than a collector might think. Some of these items—or versions of them—were later turned into commercial products. This is a partial list drawn mainly from co-author Sansweet's collection. Unlike merchandise, no one at Lucasfilm ever thought to catalog cast, crew and promotional items.

CHRISTMAS & OTHER CARDS

It helps to have been on someone's Christmas-card list to get these, although with several hundred or more sent out each year, they occasionally show up at dealers' tables. Some have original art by Ralph

McQuarrie that was painted especially for the cards. Lucasfilm Christmas cards had a *Star Wars* theme from 1977 through 1986.

CC0001	1976: Hollywood Blimp, commercial card w/*SW* Corp. logo imprinted	25 - 35
CC0002	1977: John Alvin's Concert poster art of C-3PO and R2-D2	25 - 40
CC0003	1978: C-3PO and R2-D2 Christmas shopping by McQuarrie	25 - 40
CC0004	1979: Moving announcement, art by McQuarrie (*SW* character parade down Lankershim Blvd.)	25 - 40
CC0005	1979: Christmas w/R2-D2/antlers, C-3PO/Santa	25 - 40
CC0006	CC0005, Christmas party invitation version	25 - 40
CC0007	1980: Droids in Santa's workshop (McQuarrie)	25 - 40
CC0008	1981: Yoda as Santa, white & blue versions (McQ)	25 - 40
CC0009	1982: Yoda on sleigh w/Yoda license plate (McQ)	25 - 40
CC0010	1983: Ewok Santa (McQ)	25 - 40
CC0011	1984: Ewoks watching Santa ride past moon	15 - 25
CC0012	1985: Ewoks and Droids party at decorated house	15 - 25
CC0013	1986: Ewoks build a snowman, montage (David Craig)	15 - 25
CC0021	1994: Jawas making toys (McQ)	15 - 25
CC0022	1995: Cantina Band in snow globe (McQ)	15 - 25

CLOTHING

Caps

CC1020	Gray w/embroidered Blue Harvest patch	65 - 100

Sweaters

CC1030	Gray wool, w/knitted *ESB* logo in blue and silver; one sleeve has knitted film strip	125 - 250

CC0010

CC0011

CC0021

CC0022

CC0012

CC0013

CC1020

CC3000

CC3001

CC3002

CC3005

CC3006

CC3007

CC5000

CC5005

CC6000

CC6001

CC8500

T-shirts

CC1040	Triangular early *SW* icon on yellow shirt	15 - 25
CC1041	Royal blue w/silver mesh *SW* logo	20 - 30
CC1042	"*SW*: Marin Unit" (Vader in hot tub w/ducky). Back reads: "The Empire Lays Back"	25 - 40
CC1043	*ESB*: Vader in flames art w/Black Falcon copyright	25 - 40
CC1044	*ESB*: Fallen "wind-up" AT-AT w/"Industrial Light & Magic"	25 - 40
CC1045	*ESB*: Dancing probot in light bulb labeled ILM '79-'80	25 - 40
CC1046	*ESB*: "*SW* II Night Crew" w/sleepy Vader holding candle and teddy bear	25 - 40
CC1047	*ESB*: Tusken Raider w/earphones holding mike labeled *ESB*: "Sound People...or worse"	25 - 40
CC1048	*ROTJ*: "Blue Harvest"	50 - 75

COMMEMORATIVE

Lucite stars came in either a blue velvet pull-string bag or in a see-through thin plastic box. They were made to give out at charity screenings and some went to cast and crew. Some have a clear sticker from the distributor "Two's Company."

CC3000	Lucite star: *Star Wars*	150 - 300
CC3001	Lucite star: May the Force be with you	150 - 300
CC3002	Lucite star: The Empire Strikes Back	150 - 300
CC3003	Square cardboard coasters printed w/early *ESB* logo in gray and blue	10 - 20

CC3004	Round *ESB* coasters, metallic art of R2-D2	10 - 20
CC3005	Pen & pencil set, matte black & gold, engraved w/gold *SW* logo in tan velvet case	75 - 125
CC3006	*ESB* square pewter paperweight	50 - 75
CC3007	*Revenge of the Jedi* brass rectangular paperweight w/maroon velvet pull-string bag	150 - 300
CC3008	Engraved invitation, tickets for crew screening of *ESB*	25 - 40
CC3009	Engraved invitation, tickets for crew screening of *ROTJ*	25 - 40

PATCHES

CC5000	*SW*: early style lettering, solid white on blue w/white border	25 - 55
CC5005	*SW*: white outline lettering on rounded blue rectangle; separate long blue strip: Norwegian Unit	25 - 50
CC5010	*ESB*: Crew version of Vader in flames patch, thin white border, different from fan club version	20 - 50
CC5020	*ROTJ* Crew version of Yoda *Revenge* patch, slightly sharper than fan club version	35 - 55

PASSPORT

This blue, cloth-covered, hard cardboard booklet is stamped "Intergalactic Passport" in silver on the front cover. It is die-cut in two places, one for a stamped number and one for the name of the VIP who would be using the passport to gain access to the *ESB* sound

53

CE0000   CE0001   CE0002   CE0003

CE0004   CE0005   CE0006   CE0007

CE0010   CE0021   CE0022   CE0023

CE2225   CE1050   CE1051   CE1052   CE1052

stages in England. There are two versions, one with the numerical stamp on the cover and several full-page stamps inside, and one which says "Special Guest."

| CC6000 | Passport, stamped "special guest" | 75 - 100 |
| CC6001 | Passport, unstamped | 50 - 75 |

STATIONERY

CC7000	Paper & envelope for The *Star Wars* Corp. w/early lettering & McQ. art	20 - 30
CC7005	*SW "The Empire Strikes Back,"* Chapter II Co.	20 - 30
CC7010	Blue Harvest (cover name for *ROTJ*)	20 - 30

STICKERS

CC8500	Triangle, early Luke w/lightsaber before orange planet: *The Star Wars*, large	10 - 20
CC8501	small version of CC8500	5 - 10
CC8502	As CC8500, but: *Star Wars*	3 - 6
CC8510	*ESB:* Stylized Darth Vader helmet in flames	2 - 5
CC8520	*ROTJ:* Yoda in circle on blue rectangle: *Revenge of the Jedi*	10 - 15

CERAMICS

BANKS, CERAMIC—See BANKS

COLLECTOR PLATES

The Hamilton Collection produced a series of eight collector plates in the late 1980s, then added a larger ninth plate to commemorate the 10th anniversary of *Star Wars* in 1987. In 1993, Hamilton introduced a new series of three plates, one for each of the *Star Wars* films. A series of eight coffee mugs using the art of the first eight plates were also made.

CE0000	Han Solo	65 - 125
CE0001	Princess Leia	45 - 65
CE0002	Luke and Darth Vader	45 - 65
CE0003	Falcon cockpit	55 - 95
CE0004	Luke and Yoda	45 - 65
CE0005	Wicket and R2-D2	45 - 65
CE0006	Imperial Walkers	45 - 65
CE0007	Space Battle	75 - 150
CE0010	10th Anniversary plate	60 - 125

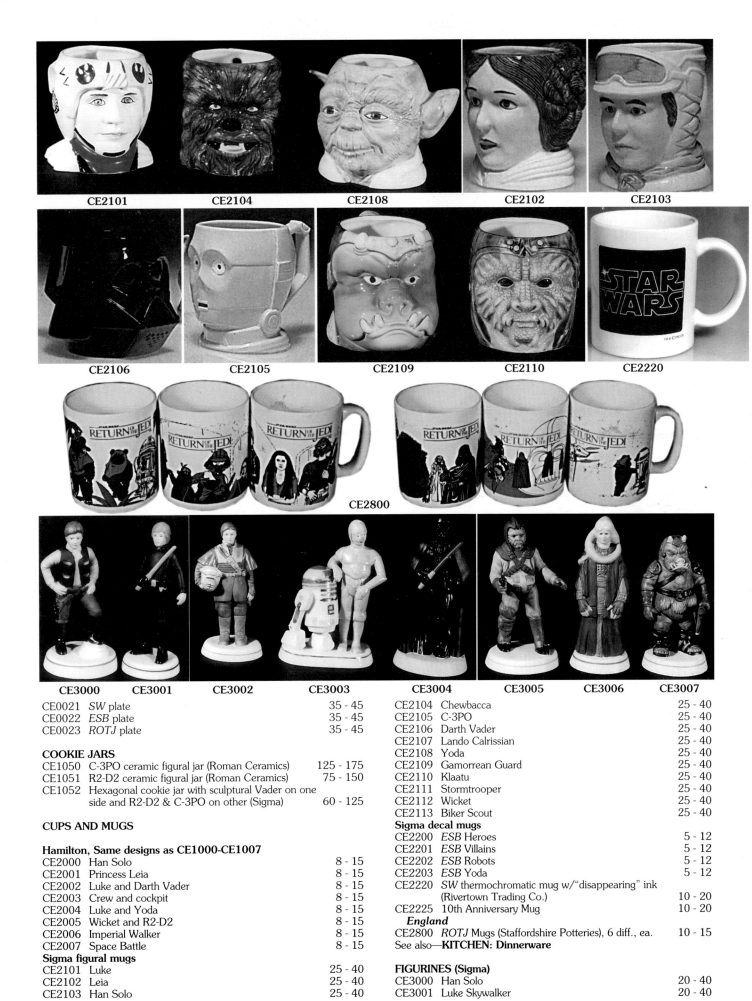

CE2101	CE2104	CE2108	CE2102	CE2103

CE2106	CE2105	CE2109	CE2110	CE2220

CE2800

CE3000	CE3001	CE3002	CE3003	CE3004	CE3005	CE3006	CE3007

CE0021	*SW* plate	35 - 45
CE0022	*ESB* plate	35 - 45
CE0023	*ROTJ* plate	35 - 45

COOKIE JARS

CE1050	C-3PO ceramic figural jar (Roman Ceramics)	125 - 175
CE1051	R2-D2 ceramic figural jar (Roman Ceramics)	75 - 150
CE1052	Hexagonal cookie jar with sculptural Vader on one side and R2-D2 & C-3PO on other (Sigma)	60 - 125

CUPS AND MUGS

Hamilton, Same designs as CE1000-CE1007

CE2000	Han Solo	8 - 15
CE2001	Princess Leia	8 - 15
CE2002	Luke and Darth Vader	8 - 15
CE2003	Crew and cockpit	8 - 15
CE2004	Luke and Yoda	8 - 15
CE2005	Wicket and R2-D2	8 - 15
CE2006	Imperial Walker	8 - 15
CE2007	Space Battle	8 - 15

Sigma figural mugs

CE2101	Luke	25 - 40
CE2102	Leia	25 - 40
CE2103	Han Solo	25 - 40

CE2104	Chewbacca	25 - 40
CE2105	C-3PO	25 - 40
CE2106	Darth Vader	25 - 40
CE2107	Lando Calrissian	25 - 40
CE2108	Yoda	25 - 40
CE2109	Gamorrean Guard	25 - 40
CE2110	Klaatu	25 - 40
CE2111	Stormtrooper	25 - 40
CE2112	Wicket	25 - 40
CE2113	Biker Scout	25 - 40

Sigma decal mugs

CE2200	*ESB* Heroes	5 - 12
CE2201	*ESB* Villains	5 - 12
CE2202	*ESB* Robots	5 - 12
CE2203	*ESB* Yoda	5 - 12
CE2220	*SW* thermochromatic mug w/"disappearing" ink (Rivertown Trading Co.)	10 - 20
CE2225	10th Anniversary Mug	10 - 20

England

CE2800	*ROTJ* Mugs (Staffordshire Potteries), 6 diff., ea.	10 - 15

See also—**KITCHEN: Dinnerware**

FIGURINES (Sigma)

CE3000	Han Solo	20 - 40
CE3001	Luke Skywalker	20 - 40

CE3008	**CE3009**	**CE3010**	**CE3011**

CE3002	Princess Leia	20 - 40
CE3003	C-3PO/R2-D2	25 - 45
CE3004	Darth Vader	20 - 40
CE3005	Klaatu	20 - 40
CE3006	Bib Fortuna	20 - 40
CE3007	Gamorrean Guard	20 - 40
CE3008	Wicket W. Warrick	20 - 40
CE3009	Lando Calrissian	20 - 40
CE3010	Boba Fett	20 - 40
CE3011	Galactic Emperor	25 - 45
CE3012	Jabba the Hutt	40 - 60

HOUSEHOLD ITEMS

CE4000	Yoda salt and pepper shakers	35 - 45
CE4001	R2-D2 & R5-D4 salt and pepper shakers	65 - 150
CE4003	R2-D2 string dispenser/scissors	50 - 60
CE4004	Yoda vase	35 - 50
CE4005	C-3PO pencil tray	25 - 45
CE4006	C-3PO tape dispenser	40 - 60
CE4007	Yoda tumbler/pencil cup	25 - 40
CE4008	C-3PO picture frame	30 - 45
CE4009	R2-D2 picture frame	25 - 40
CE4010	Darth Vader picture frame	30 - 50
CE4011	Snow speeder toothbrush holder	25 - 50
CE4012	Landspeeder soap dish	25 - 45
CE4013	Yoda backpack box	20 - 40
CE4030	Ewoks w/drum	20 - 35
CE4032	Darth Vader mirror	35 - 55
CE4033	Chewbacca/Vader bookends	50 - 75
CE4036	Luke on Tauntaun teapot	75 - 150
CE4037	Stormtrooper cup/box	20 - 40
CE4041	Yoda candlestick holder	25 - 50
CE4042	Yoda tumbler/pencil box	25 - 45

MUSIC BOXES (Sigma)

CE5000	Turret w/C-3PO	55 - 115
CE5002	Sy Snootles and Rebo Band	50 - 100
CE5003	Wicket and Kneesaa	45 - 80

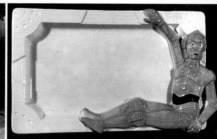

CE4000	**CE4001**	**CE4003**	**CE4004**	**CE4005**

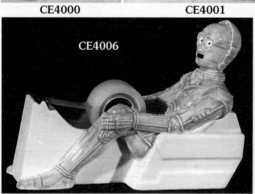

CE4006

	CE4008	**CE4009**	**CE4032**

CE4011	**CE4012**	**CE4013**	**CE5003**	**CE4010**

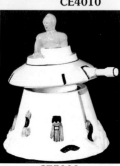

CE4033	**CE4036**	**CE4037**	**CE4042**	**CE5000**

CE6000 **CE6001** **CE6003**

Folder for Rarities Mint coins   Rarities Mint advertisement

TANKARDS

Large, dimensional "toby" mugs were produced in 1977-1978 by California Originals (Mind Circus) and were sculpted by Jim Rumpf.

CE6000	Darth Vader	60 - 125
CE6001	Obi-Wan Kenobi	60 - 125
CE6002	Chewbacca	60 - 125

COINS

Perhaps the rarest and most expensive commercially available *Star Wars* item is a full set of numbered collectors' coins from Rarities Mint, issued in 1987 and 1988 to commemorate the film's 10th anniversary. The company produced six different sculpted designs, each of which was available in one ounce and five ounce silver, and one-quarter ounce and one ounce gold.

The five-ounce silver coins came in blue, padded velveteen snap-open jewelry boxes (except for coin #1; it's case was maroon). All the other coins came in colorful cardboard folders with the *SW* 10th anniversary logo and a pull-out insert with the coin that gave its name, registration number and the total number of that mintage—or at least the total number that Rarities had hoped to mint. For despite the fact that the one-ounce gold coins say "1 of 10,000," these were just cards left over from the end of the run of the smaller silver coins (about 15,000 copies of the first coin were sold). In fact, dealers with access to Rarities records say that serial numbers of the gold coins began at 50—and there were only 14 of the once-ounce gold coins sold. Thus there can be only 14 complete sets of all 24 coins. In addition one coin was produced in a one-tenth ounce size for the Japanese market alone and sold there as the "charm" on a necklace. The coins weren't cheap to begin with, with the one-ounce gold going for around $1,000 each.

In 1992, Catch A Star collectibles produced a one-ounce silver 15th anniversary *Star Wars* coin that was first available on a QVC shopping network *Star Wars* special.

The most common coins are the 62 silver-toned aluminum coins produced by Kenner Products for its action-figure line under the "Power of the Force" logo. These coins were produced in 1984, and each was available by mail in exchange for a proof-of-purchase seal, although you couldn't choose the coin you wanted. Persistent collectors pestered Kenner, and the toy company got Lucasfilm's permission to

sell the entire 62-coin set for $29. but only to those who called and wrote inquiring if they could buy the whole set; such an offer was never made known to the general public. Later 23 of the coins were included on matching "Power of the Force" action figure packages in the U.S. and more on POTF cards distributed in Canada, Australia and Europe. Coins that were available only by mail have higher values, as do coins packaged with some of the rarer figures. The Droids and Ewoks figures were also packaged with similar coins, but these were copper or gold toned. There are many coin variations—misstruck coins, coins with errors that had to be revised, coins struck in the wrong color, prototype coins (both regular size and a smaller size), etc. In addition there is a 63rd coin—Jedi Knight, with hands holding a lightsaber erect—that Kenner had planned to use as a mail-in promotion that never took place.

Three brass-colored coins came with Just Toys BendEms in 1994.

SILVER AND GOLD COINS

One ounce silver (Rarities Mint)

CI0011	Tenth Anniversary (Leia and Luke)	75 - 95
CI0012	C-3PO and R2-D2	100 - 110
CI0013	Han Solo and Chewbacca	100 - 110
CI0014	Imperial Stormtroopers	115 - 125
CI0015	Mos Eisley Cantina Band	115 - 125
CI0016	Darth Vader & Ben (Obi-Wan) Kenobi	125 - 135

Five ounce silver (Rarities Mint)

CI0021	Tenth Anniversary (Leia and Luke)	125 - 250
CI0022	C-3PO and R2-D2	150 - 250
CI0023	Han Solo and Chewbacca	150 - 250
CI0024	Imperial Stormtroopers	150 - 250
CI0025	Mos Eisley Cantina Band	150 - 250
CI0026	Darth Vader & Ben (Obi-Wan) Kenobi	150 - 250

One-quarter ounce gold (Rarities Mint)

CI0031	Tenth Anniversary (Leia and Luke)	450 - 750

CI0011   **CI0012**   **CI0013**

CI0014   **CI0015**   **CI0016**   **CI2070**

CI2001	CI2002	CI2003
CI2004	CI2005	CI2006
CI2007	CI2008	CI2009
CI2010	CI2011	CI2012
CI2013	CI2014	CI2015
CI2016	CI2017	CI2018
CI2019	CI2020	CI2021
CI2022	CI2023	CI2024
CI2025	CI2026	CI2027
CI2028	CI2029	CI2030

CI0032	C-3PO and R2-D2	500 - 750
CI0033	Han Solo and Chewbacca	500 - 750
CI0034	Imperial Stormtroopers	500 - 750
CI0035	Mos Eisley Cantina Band	500 - 750
CI0036	Darth Vader & Ben (Obi-Wan) Kenobi	500 - 750

One ounce gold (Rarities Mint) CI0041-46

CI0041	Tenth Anniversary (Leia and Luke)	2,000 - 2,500
CI0042	C-3PO and R2-D2	2,300 - 2,800
CI0043	Han Solo and Chewbacca	2,300 - 2,800
CI0044	Imperial Stormtroopers	2,250 - 2,750
CI0045	Mos Eisley Cantina Band	2,250 - 2,750
CI0046	Darth Vader & Ben (Obi-Wan) Kenobi	2,300 - 2,800
CI0048	Ad for above coin sets	4 - 8
CI0050	15th Anniversary one ounce silver (Luke, Leia and droids, limited to 5,000, Catch A Star)	35 - 45

Japan

CI0500	One-tenth ounce gold in necklace, Tenth Anniversary (Luke and Leia) design only	500 - 750

ACTION FIGURE COINS (Kenner Products)

Power of the Force (aluminum)

CI2001	Amanaman	5 - 10
CI2002	Anakin Skywalker	30 - 40

CI2003	AT-AT	50 - 60
CI2004	AT-ST Driver	10 - 15
CI2005	A-wing Pilot	5 - 10
CI2006	Barada	5 - 10
CI2007	Bib Fortuna	75 - 90
CI2008	Biker Scout	10 - 15
CI2009	Boba Fett	50 - 60
CI2010	B-wing Pilot	5 - 10
CI2011	Chewbacca	10 - 15
CI2012	Chief Chirpa	30 - 40
CI2013	Creatures: Hammerhead, Snaggletooth and Greedo, text reads "at local cantinas"	50 - 60
CI2013a	Creatures, text reads "at local cafes"	250 - 300
CI2014	C-3PO	10 - 15
CI2015	Darth Vader	10 - 15
CI2016	Droids	50 - 60
CI2017	Emperor	10 - 15
CI2018	Emperor's Royal Guard	35 - 45
CI2019	EV-9D9, torture droid	5 - 10
CI2020	FX-7, medical droid	75 - 90
CI2021	Gamorrean Guard	20 - 30
CI2022	Greedo	75 - 90
CI2023	Han Solo, carbon freeze	10 - 15
CI2024	Han Solo, rebel (Endor)	15 - 20

CI2031	CI2032	CI2033	CI2034	CI2035	CI2036
CI2037	CI2038	CI2039	CI2040	CI2041	CI2042
CI2043	CI2044	CI2045	CI2046	CI2047	CI2048
CI2049	CI2050	CI2051	CI2051a	CI2052	CI2053
CI2054	CI2055	CI2056	CI2057	CI2058	CI2059

CI2024a	"Hans" Solo	250 - 300	CI2046	Princess Leia	75 - 90
CI2025	Han Solo, rebel fighter (Falcon Ramp)	75 - 90	CI2047	Princess Leia in Endor outfit	10 - 15
CI2026	Han Solo, rebel hero (Hoth)	50 - 60	CI2048	Princess Leia, head, w/R2-D2	75 - 90
CI2027	Hoth Stormtrooper	75 - 90	CI2049	Romba	5 - 10
CI2028	Imperial Commander	50 - 60	CI2050	R2-D2	5 - 10
CI2029	Imperial Dignitary	5 - 10	CI2051	Sail Skiff w/*Star Wars* logo	75 - 90
CI2030	Imperial Gunner	5 - 10	CI2051a	Sail Skiff w/o *Star Wars* logo	200 - 250
CI2031	Jawas	10 - 15	CI2051b	Sail Barge	250 - 300
CI2032	Lando Calrissian w/Millennium Falcon	5 - 10	CI2052	Star Destroyer Commander	50 - 60
CI2033	Lando Calrissian w/Cloud City	50 - 60	CI2053	Stormtrooper	10 - 15
CI2034	Luke Skywalker in Stormtrooper armor, with or without eyes	10 - 15	CI2054	Teebo	10 - 15
CI2035	Luke Skywalker on tauntaun	50 - 60	CI2055	TIE fighter Pilot	35 - 45
CI2036	Luke Skywalker w/landspeeder	35 - 45	CI2056	Too-One Bee	75 - 90
CI2037	Luke Skywalker on scout bike	5 - 10	CI2057	Tusken Raider	75 - 90
CI2038	Luke Skywalker, Jedi	10 - 15	CI2058	Warok	5 - 10
CI2039	Luke Skywalker, Jedi knight/head	10 - 15	CI2059	Wicket	10 - 15
CI2040	Luke Skywalker, Jedi knight/Dagobah	75 - 90	CI2060	Yak Face	30 - 40
CI2041	Logray	30 - 40	CI2061	Yoda	15 - 20
CI2042	Lumat	5 - 10	CI2062	Zuckuss	75 - 90
CI2043	Millenium Falcon (Millennium misspelled)	50 - 60	CI2063	Jedi Knight	300 - 500
CI2043a	Millenium Falcon, back describes generic rebel	250 - 300	CI2064	Smaller Luke X-wing Coin	20 - 30
CI2044	Obi-Wan Kenobi	10 - 15	CI2068	62-coin set	2,000 - 2,500
CI2045	Paploo	5 - 10	CI2070	62-coin double set, framed (10 produced)	3,500 - 6,000

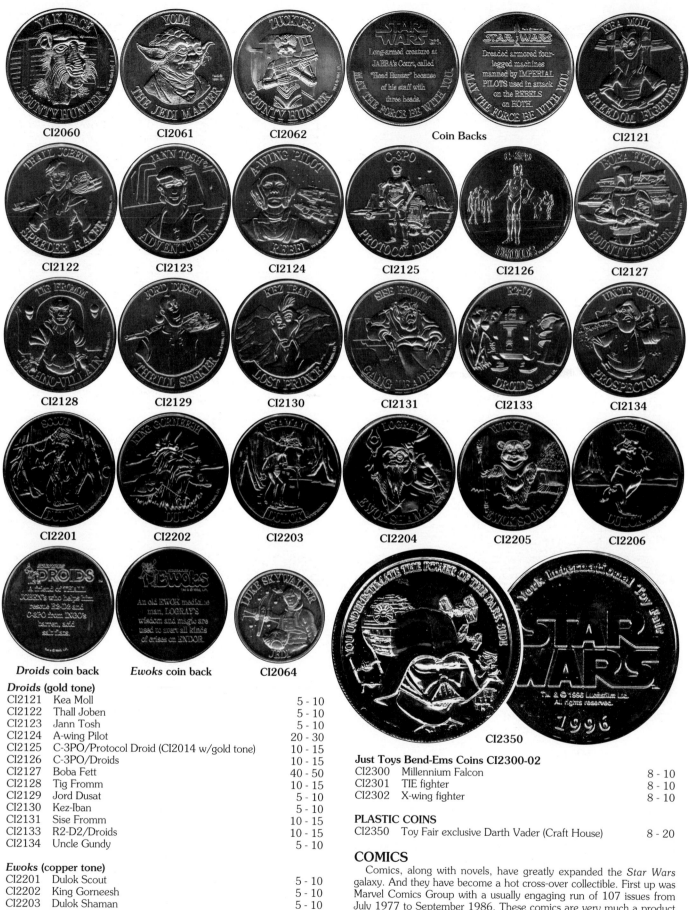

CI2060 CI2061 CI2062 Coin Backs CI2121

CI2122 CI2123 CI2124 CI2125 CI2126 CI2127

CI2128 CI2129 CI2130 CI2131 CI2133 CI2134

CI2201 CI2202 CI2203 CI2204 CI2205 CI2206

Droids coin back *Ewoks* coin back CI2064

CI2350

Droids (gold tone)

CI2121	Kea Moll	5 - 10
CI2122	Thall Joben	5 - 10
CI2123	Jann Tosh	5 - 10
CI2124	A-wing Pilot	20 - 30
CI2125	C-3PO/Protocol Droid (CI2014 w/gold tone)	10 - 15
CI2126	C-3PO/Droids	10 - 15
CI2127	Boba Fett	40 - 50
CI2128	Tig Fromm	10 - 15
CI2129	Jord Dusat	5 - 10
CI2130	Kez-Iban	5 - 10
CI2131	Sise Fromm	10 - 15
CI2133	R2-D2/Droids	10 - 15
CI2134	Uncle Gundy	5 - 10

Ewoks (copper tone)

CI2201	Dulok Scout	5 - 10
CI2202	King Gorneesh	5 - 10
CI2203	Dulok Shaman	5 - 10
CI2204	Lograw	10 - 15
CI2205	Wicket W. Warrick	10 - 15
CI2206	Urgah Lady Gorneesh	5 - 10

Just Toys Bend-Ems Coins CI2300-02

CI2300	Millennium Falcon	8 - 10
CI2301	TIE fighter	8 - 10
CI2302	X-wing fighter	8 - 10

PLASTIC COINS

CI2350	Toy Fair exclusive Darth Vader (Craft House)	8 - 20

COMICS

Comics, along with novels, have greatly expanded the *Star Wars* galaxy. And they have become a hot cross-over collectible. First up was Marvel Comics Group with a usually engaging run of 107 issues from July 1977 to September 1986. These comics are very much a product of their time, and most of the latter story lines judged by today's standards seem fairly "cartoony." For the most part, they aren't considered part of the *Star Wars* canon.

The revival of the *Star Wars* line by Dark Horse Comics in late 1991 brought a new surge of excitement. From the first issue of *Dark*

CO0000 Left: Original Right: Reprint CO0011 CO0139 CO0150

CO0175 CO0207 CO0211 CO0212 CO0213 CO0260

CO0301 CO0310 CO0352

Empire, it was clear that—for the most part—this would be a darker, more adult visit to that far away galaxy, both in story and in art. In a bold leap, the editors, writers and artists have also expanded the galaxy back in time some 5,000 years before the events depicted in *Star Wars: A New Hope*. And there has been a liberal cross-over of characters and events between the comics and novels, adding deeper dimension to both.

There are also the oddities: three issues of a 3-D comic from Blackthorne; weekly—sometimes monthly—comics from Marvel U.K. with different covers and occassionally exclusive comics; and more than a dozen non-U.S. versions of both the Marvel and Dark Horse series, a few of which are noted below.

After years of stagnation, the Marvel comics have taken off in price (as have many of the early or special Dark Horse issues), but not every issue and not to the level that some other guides would have you believe. There is usually no price difference between newsstand and direct-sales (comic specialty shop) versions of either the Marvel or Dark Horse issues. The single most valuable comic is a price-test version of the first Marvel. It has 35 cents (instead of 30 cents) in the price box at the upper left, and a UPC code (bar stripes) in a box at the lower left. Supposedly only 1,500 to 2,000 copies were distributed.

COMIC BOOKS

Star Wars (Marvel)
CO0000 #1 (available as 30¢ [w/ UPC code {price in a square or price in a diamond} and w/o UPC code] and as 35¢ [w/o UPC code]) 15 - 20
CO0001 #1 35¢ w/ UPC code 250 - 350

CO0002-6 #2 - 6 (available as 30¢ [w/ UPC code {price in a square or price in a diamond} and w/o UPC code] and as 35¢ [w/ and w/o UPC code], ea. 3 - 7
CO0007-9 #7 - 9 (NS & DS), ea. 2 - 6
CO0010 Reprints of #1-6 (available as 30¢ [w/ and w/o UPC code] and as 35¢ [w/ and w/o UPC code]), ea. 2 - 3
CO0011 Bagged set (#1-#3 reprints) 8 - 12
CO0012 Bagged set (#4-#6 reprints) 8 - 12
CO0013 Bagged set (#1-#6 reprints) 10 - 15
CO0014 Bagged set (#7-#9) 8 - 12
CO0015 Bagged set (#10-#12) 20 - 25
CO0016 Bagged set (#13-#15) 20 - 25
CO0017 Bagged set (#16-#18) 20 - 25
CO0110-67,69 #10 - 67,69 (NS & DS), ea. 2 - 6
CO0168 #68 (origin of Boba Fett - NS & DS) 15-20
CO0170-79 #70 - 79 (NS & DS), ea. 3-5
CO0180-89 #80 - 89 (NS & DS), ea. 4-6
CO0190-99 #90 - 99 (NS & DS), ea. 5-7
CO0200-206 #100 - 106 (NS & DS), ea. 8-10
CO0207 #107 (NS & DS) 50-75
CO0211 Star Wars Annual #1 (NS & DS - '79) 2 - 5
CO0212 Star Wars Annual #2 (NS & DS -'82) 2 - 5
CO0213 Star Wars Annual #3 (NS & DS -'83) 2 - 5
CO0221-3 Star Wars treasury sized #1, #2, #3 (combines 1 and 2) Whitman or Marvel, ea. 3 - 5
CO0231-2 Marvel Movie Showcase #1, #2 (reprints SW first 6 issues - NS & DS), ea. 2 - 3
CO0250 The Empire Strikes Back treasury sized #2 (Parker's Run or Marvel) 2 - 5
CO0260 Marvel Comics Super Special #16 (ESB) 2 - 5
CO0301-4 Return of the Jedi Limited Series, #1-#4 (NS & DS), ea. 2 - 5
CO0310 Return of the Jedi (Magazine sized Official Comics Ed.) 8 - 10
CO0350 Marvel Age #4 (SW cover) 2 - 5
CO0352 Marvel Age #10 (SW cover) 2 - 5
CO0354 Marvel Age #19 (Star Comics/Ewoks cover) 2 - 5
CO0360 Marvel Comics Super Special #27 (ROTJ) 2 - 5
Droids (Marvel)
CO0401-8 Droids comics, #1-#8 (NS & DS), ea. 4 - 6
Ewoks (Marvel)
CO0451-64 Ewoks comics, #1-#14 (NS & DS), ea. 4 - 6
CO0471-3, 5 Marvel Star Comics #1-#3, #5 (Ewoks, digest size), ea. 2 - 4
Pizzazz (Marvel)
CO0481-96 Issues #1-#16 (included Marvel comic series), ea. 4 - 6

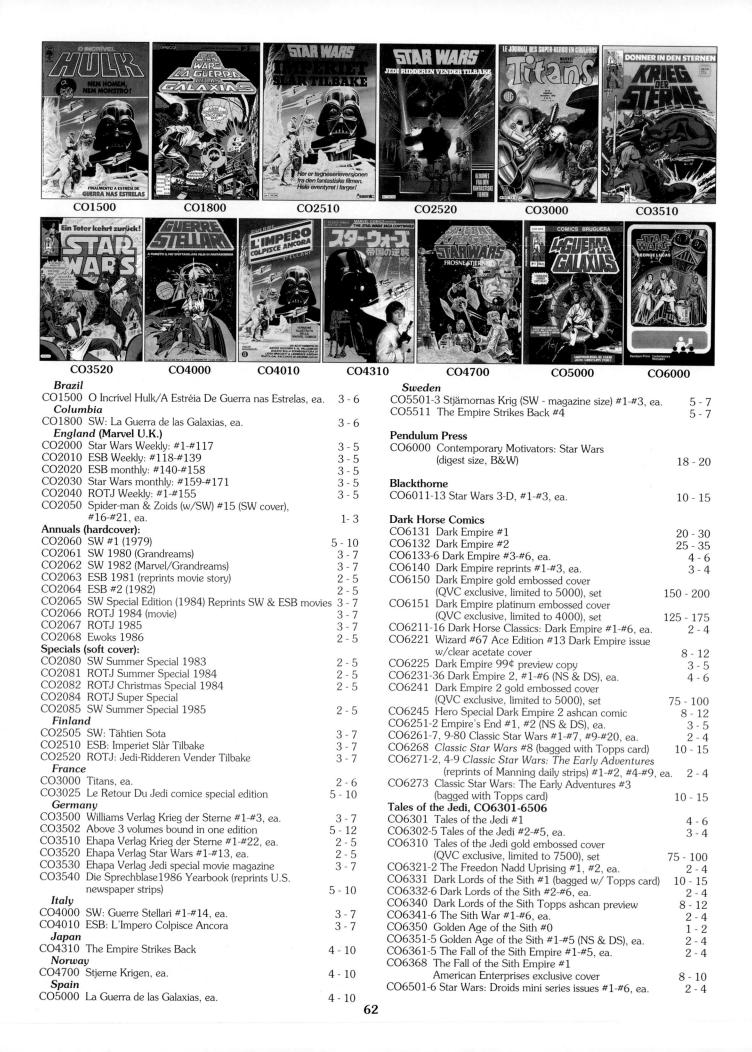

CO1500	CO1800
CO2510	CO2520
CO3000	CO3510
CO3520	CO4000
CO4010	CO4310
CO4700	CO5000
CO6000	

Brazil
CO1500 O Incrível Hulk/A Estréia De Guerra nas Estrelas, ea.   3 - 6
Columbia
CO1800 SW: La Guerra de las Galaxias, ea.   3 - 6
England (Marvel U.K.)
CO2000 Star Wars Weekly: #1-#117   3 - 5
CO2010 ESB Weekly: #118-#139   3 - 5
CO2020 ESB monthly: #140-#158   3 - 5
CO2030 Star Wars monthly: #159-#171   3 - 5
CO2040 ROTJ Weekly: #1-#155   3 - 5
CO2050 Spider-man & Zoids (w/SW) #15 (SW cover),
       #16-#21, ea.   1- 3
Annuals (hardcover):
CO2060 SW #1 (1979)   5 - 10
CO2061 SW 1980 (Grandreams)   3 - 7
CO2062 SW 1982 (Marvel/Grandreams)   3 - 7
CO2063 ESB 1981 (reprints movie story)   2 - 5
CO2064 ESB #2 (1982)   2 - 5
CO2065 SW Special Edition (1984) Reprints SW & ESB movies 3 - 7
CO2066 ROTJ 1984 (movie)   3 - 7
CO2067 ROTJ 1985   3 - 7
CO2068 Ewoks 1986   2 - 5
Specials (soft cover):
CO2080 SW Summer Special 1983   2 - 5
CO2081 ROTJ Summer Special 1984   2 - 5
CO2082 ROTJ Christmas Special 1984   2 - 5
CO2084 ROTJ Super Special
CO2085 SW Summer Special 1985   2 - 5
Finland
CO2505 SW: Tähtien Sota   3 - 7
CO2510 ESB: Imperiet Slår Tilbake   3 - 7
CO2520 ROTJ: Jedi-Ridderen Vender Tilbake   3 - 7
France
CO3000 Titans, ea.   2 - 6
CO3025 Le Retour Du Jedi comice special edition   5 - 10
Germany
CO3500 Williams Verlag Krieg der Sterne #1-#3, ea.   3 - 7
CO3502 Above 3 volumes bound in one edition   5 - 12
CO3510 Ehapa Verlag Krieg der Sterne #1-#22, ea.   2 - 5
CO3520 Ehapa Verlag Star Wars #1-#13, ea.   2 - 5
CO3530 Ehapa Verlag Jedi special movie magazine   3 - 7
CO3540 Die Sprechblase1986 Yearbook (reprints U.S.
       newspaper strips)   5 - 10
Italy
CO4000 SW: Guerre Stellari #1-#14, ea.   3 - 7
CO4010 ESB: L'Impero Colpisce Ancora   3 - 7
Japan
CO4310 The Empire Strikes Back   4 - 10
Norway
CO4700 Stjerne Krigen, ea.   4 - 10
Spain
CO5000 La Guerra de las Galaxias, ea.   4 - 10

Sweden
CO5501-3 Stjärnornas Krig (SW - magazine size) #1-#3, ea.   5 - 7
CO5511 The Empire Strikes Back #4   5 - 7

Pendulum Press
CO6000 Contemporary Motivators: Star Wars
      (digest size, B&W)   18 - 20

Blackthorne
CO6011-13 Star Wars 3-D, #1-#3, ea.   10 - 15

Dark Horse Comics
CO6131 Dark Empire #1   20 - 30
CO6132 Dark Empire #2   25 - 35
CO6133-6 Dark Empire #3-#6, ea.   4 - 6
CO6140 Dark Empire reprints #1-#3, ea.   3 - 4
CO6150 Dark Empire gold embossed cover
      (QVC exclusive, limited to 5000), set   150 - 200
CO6151 Dark Empire platinum embossed cover
      (QVC exclusive, limited to 4000), set   125 - 175
CO6211-16 Dark Horse Classics: Dark Empire #1-#6, ea.   2 - 4
CO6221 Wizard #67 Ace Edition #13 Dark Empire issue
      w/clear acetate cover   8 - 12
CO6225 Dark Empire 99¢ preview copy   3 - 5
CO6231-36 Dark Empire 2, #1-#6 (NS & DS), ea.   4 - 6
CO6241 Dark Empire 2 gold embossed cover
      (QVC exclusive, limited to 5000), set   75 - 100
CO6245 Hero Special Dark Empire 2 ashcan comic   8 - 12
CO6251-2 Empire's End #1, #2 (NS & DS), ea.   3 - 5
CO6261-7, 9-80 Classic Star Wars #1-#7, #9-#20, ea.   2 - 4
CO6268 *Classic Star Wars* #8 (bagged with Topps card)   10 - 15
CO6271-2, 4-9 *Classic Star Wars: The Early Adventures*
      (reprints of Manning daily strips) #1-#2, #4-#9, ea.   2 - 4
CO6273 Classic Star Wars: The Early Adventures #3
      (bagged with Topps card)   10 - 15
Tales of the Jedi, CO6301-6506
CO6301 Tales of the Jedi #1   4 - 6
CO6302-5 Tales of the Jedi #2-#5, ea.   3 - 4
CO6310 Tales of the Jedi gold embossed cover
      (QVC exclusive, limited to 7500), set   75 - 100
CO6321-2 The Freedon Nadd Uprising #1, #2, ea.   2 - 4
CO6331 Dark Lords of the Sith #1 (bagged w/ Topps card)   10 - 15
CO6332-6 Dark Lords of the Sith #2-#6, ea.   2 - 4
CO6340 Dark Lords of the Sith Topps ashcan preview   8 - 12
CO6341-6 The Sith War #1-#6, ea.   2 - 4
CO6350 Golden Age of the Sith #0   1 - 2
CO6351-5 Golden Age of the Sith #1-#5 (NS & DS)   2 - 4
CO6361-5 The Fall of the Sith Empire #1-#5, ea.   2 - 4
CO6368 The Fall of the Sith Empire #1
      American Enterprises exclusive cover   8 - 10
CO6501-6 Star Wars: Droids mini series issues #1-#6, ea.   2 - 4

CO6011	CO6131	CO6161	CR8000

CO6510	*Droids* Special one-shot issue (reprint of Dark Horse Comics 17-19)	2 - 4
CO6511-8	Droids #1-#8, ea.	2 - 4
CO6521	The Mixed Up Droid (mini w/Time-Warner cassette)	1 - 3
CO6525	Droids: The Protocol Offensive (1997)	4 - 6
CO6531	*Classic Star Wars: The Vandelhelm Mission* (reprint of Marvel *Star Wars* #98)	2 - 4
CO6541-2	*Classic Star Wars: A New Hope* (reprint of Marvel *Star Wars* 1-6) #1, #2, ea.	4 - 6
CO6551-2	*Classic Star Wars: The Empire Strikes Back* (reprint of Marvel *Star Wars* 39-44) #1, #2, ea.	4 - 6
CO6561	*Classic Star Wars: Return of the Jedi* (reprint of Marvel *ROTJ* 1, 2 - w/Topps card) #1	10 - 15
CO6562	*Classic Star Wars: Return of the Jedi* (reprint of Marvel *ROTJ* 3, 4) #2	4 - 6
CO6571	Jabba the Hutt: The Garr Suppoon Hit	2 - 4
CO6572	Jabba the Hutt: The Hunger of Princess Nampi	2 - 4
CO6573	Jabba the Hutt: The Dynasty Trap	2 - 4
CO6574	Jabba the Hutt: Betrayal (NS & DS)	2 - 4
CO6581-4	River of Chaos #1-#4, ea.	2 - 4

X-wing Rogue Squadron CO6601-6670

CO6601-4	The Rebel Opposition #1-#4 (NS & DS), ea.	2 - 4
CO6611-4	The Phantom Affair #1-#4, ea.	2 - 4
CO6621-4	Battle Ground Tatooine #1-#4, ea.	2 - 4
CO6631-4	The Warrior Princess #1-#4, ea.	2 - 4
CO6641-4	Requiem for a Rogue #1-#4, ea.	2 - 4
CO6651	(Apple Jacks cereal mail-in premium)	8 - 10
CO6660	X-wing Rogue Squadron #½ white logo (Wizard mail-in premium)	8 - 10
CO6665	X-wing Rogue Squadron #½ platinum logo (Wizard subscription premium)	10 - 12
CO6670	X-wing Rogue Squadron *Empire Strikes Back* 1st Day Presentation (Limited to 150,000)	8 - 10
CO6701-6	Heir to the Empire #1-#6 (NS & DS), ea.	2 - 4
CO6711-6	Dark Force Rising #1-#6, ea.	2 - 4
CO6721-6	The Last Command #1-#6 (1997), ea.	2 - 4
CO6731-4	Splinter of the Mind's Eye #1-#4 (NS & DS), ea.	2 - 4
CO6741	Boba Fett: Bounty on Bar-Kooda (NS & DS)	15 - 20
CO6743	Boba Fett #2: When the Fat Lady Swings (NS & DS)	2 - 4
CO6744	Boba Fett #3: Murder Most Foul (NS & DS)	2 - 4
CO6751-6	Shadows of the Empire #1-#6 (NS & DS), ea.	3 - 5
CO6761	Kenner Shadows of the Empire (Boba Fett/IG-88)	2 - 4
CO6762	Kenner Shadows of the Empire comic (Vader/Xizor)	2 - 4
CO6765	Shadows of the Empire mini-comic w/AMT models kits, Luke/Xizor/Fett cover	3 - 5

Shadows of the Empire mini-comics (w/Galoob sets) CO6771-73

CO6771	Dash Rendar cover	3 - 5
CO6772	Xizor/Emperor cover	3 - 5
CO6773	Vader cover	3 - 5
CO6781-5	*Shadows of the Empire: Evolution* #1-#5 (1998), ea.	3 - 5
CO6791-2	*Classic Star Wars: Devil Worlds* (reprints of UK *Star Wars* weekly) #1, #2 (NS & DS), ea.	2 - 4

SW Galaxy magazine comic reprints, CO6801-03

CO6801	Tales from Mos Eisley	3 - 5
CO6802	Boba Fett: Twin Engines of Destruction	2 - 4
CO6803	Shadow Stalker	2 - 4
CO6811-4	Star Wars: A New Hope (SE:Special Edition) #1-#4 (NS & DS), ea.	2 - 4
CO6821-3	Classic Star Wars: Han Solo at Star's End #1-#3 (NS & DS), ea.	2 - 4
CO6830	Star Wars #0 (American Entertainment exclusive, Pizzazz comic reprint)	8 - 10
CO6841-6	Crimson Empire #1-#6 (1998), ea.	3 - 5
CO6907-9,	17-19 Dark Horse Comics #7-#9, #17-#19, ea.	4 - 6
CO6925-30	Dark Horse Insider #15-#20, ea.	4 - 6
CO6941	San Diego Comicon #4 (SW cover 1995)	15 - 20
CO6951	Decade of Dark Horse #2	10 - 15

Comic 3-packs, CO6961-3

CO6961	Shadows #1, #2, River of Chaos #4	8 - 10
CO6962	Droids #1, Heir to the Empire #1, Sith War #1	8 - 10
CO6963	Dark Lords of the Sith #1, #2, Classic SW #18	8 - 10
CO6964	*Indiana Jones/SW* 4-pack (Early Adventures #1, #3, and 2 *Indiana Jones* comics)	8 - 10

England **(Dark Horse U.K.)**

CO8800	Star Wars #1-#10, ea.	2 - 4

COMIC STRIPS

CO9000	SW syndicated comic strip (Los Angeles Times Syndicate) Dailies, ea.	1 - 2
CO9010	SW Sunday color strips, ea.	2 - 10

COMPILATIONS

CO9050	Star Wars: 3 volume slipcased hardcover, reprinting all strips by Al Williamson, B&W, signed and numbered, pub. by Russ Cochran	135 - 160
CO9155	Dark Empire softcover	18 - 20
CO9156	Dark Empire leather-bound hardcover (limited to 1000, signed)	125 - 150
CO9158	Dark Empire 2 softcover, 1st printing (embossed)	18 - 20
CO9159	CO9158, further printings (no embossing)	18 - 20
CO9161	Dark Empire 2 leather-bound hardcover (limited to 1000, signed)	125 - 150
CO9165	*Classic Star Wars* Volume 1 (reprints *CSW* #1-#7)	15 - 17
CO9166	*Classic Star Wars* Volume 2: The Rebel Storm (reprints *CSW* #8-#14)	16 - 18
CO9167	*Classic Star Wars* Volume 3: Escape to Hoth (reprints *CSW* #15-#20)	16 - 18
CO9168	*Classic Star Wars* Volume 4: The Early Adventures (reprints *CSW: The Early Adventures* #1-#9)	16 - 18
CO9201	*Tales of the Jedi: The Collection*	15 - 17
CO9202	*TOTJ Volume 2: Dark Lords of the Sith*	18 - 20
CO9203	*TOTJ Volume 3: The Sith War*	18 - 20
CO9204	*TOTJ Volume 4: The Golden Age of the Sith*	18 - 20
CO9205	*TOTJ Volume 5: Fall of the Sith Empire (1998)*	18 - 20
CO9301	*Droids: The Kalarba Adventures*, 1st printing (embossed cover)	18 - 20
CO9302	CO9301, further printings (no embossing)	18 - 20
CO9303	*Droids: The Kalarba Adventures* leather-bound hardcover w/dustjacket (limited to 1000, signed)	100 - 125
CO9305	*Droids: Rebellion*	15 - 17
CO9310	*Star Wars: The Comic-Book Adaptation* ('95 video release cover)	10 - 12
CO9311	*The Empire Strikes Back: The Comic Adaptation* ('95 video release cover)	10 - 12
CO9312	*Return of the Jedi: The Comic Adaptation* ('95 video release cover)	10 - 12
CO9315	Slipcase set of CO9310-12 w/ different covers	28 - 32
CO9320	*Star Wars: The Comic Book Adaptation*, new art, new cover by Hildebrandt brothers	9 - 11
CO9321	CO9320 w/Special Edition ingot cover exclusive to Act III theaters	10 - 15
CO9325	*The Empire Strikes Back: The Comic-Book Adaptation*, new cover by Hildebrandt brothers	9 - 11
CO9330	*Return of the Jedi: The Comic-Book Adaptation*, new cover by Hildebrandt brothers	9 - 11
CO9341	Heir to the Empire, 1st printing (embossed cover)	20 - 22
CO9342	CO9341, further printings (no embossing)	20 - 22
CO9343	Heir to the Empire leather-bound hardcover (limited to 1000, signed)	100 - 125
CO9351	Dark Force Rising (1998)	20 - 22
CO9355	The Last Command (1998)	20 - 22
CO9360	Splinter of the Mind's Eye	15 - 17
CO9365	Shadows of the Empire	18 - 20
CO9366	Shadows of the Empire leather-bound hardcover (limited to 1000, signed)	100 - 125
CO9371	Han Solo at Star's End (1997)	20 - 22
CO9375	X-wing Rogue Squadron: The Phantom Affair (1997)	18 - 20
CO9380	Crimson Empire (1998)	20 - 22

COMPUTER-RELATED
See also—**GAMES: Video**

UTILITY PROGRAMS (Sound Source Unlimited)

CR8000	*SW* Visual Clips (for Mac only)	45 - 60
CR8001	*SW* Visual Clips add-on (mail offer)	20 - 30
CR8010	*SW* Audio Clips (for Mac or PC)	35 - 45
CR8011	*SW* Audio Clips add-on (mail offer)	15 - 25

CS0000   CS0007   CS0006   CS0002

CS0022   CS0042   CS0045

CS0046   CS0047   CS0048

COSTUMES/MASKS

Star Wars was filled with bizarre creatures wearing strange clothing. What better than costumes and masks to bring the fantasy home? The trilogy—especially such popular and recognizable characters as Darth Vader and Yoda—has become a perennial Halloween dress-up favorite. Ben Cooper manufactured Halloween costumes in the U.S. These typically consisted of a molded thin plastic mask and a one- or two-piece vinyl apparel set. For the first year, costumes were sold in a black box; later costumes were sold in a blue box. *Empire* costumes were originally sold in the blue *Star Wars* box with a label applied to the end flap, then later in black *ESB* boxes. Four of the costumes were produced with a *Revenge of the Jedi* imprint, making them even more desirable.

Don Post, an old-line Hollywood mask company, got a very positive jolt out of the trilogy. Some of the more popular Don Post masks are still being sold, with new items being added to the collection. Rubie's Costumes has recently begun making low-cost costumes and masks.

CS1100   CS1150

CS1170

CS1300

CS0001   CS0010

COSTUMES (Film designation indicates box or costume logo)

CS0000	*SW*: Lord Darth Vader, #740, black box	15 - 30
CS0001	*SW*: Luke Skywalker, #741, black box	15 - 30
CS0002	*SW*: Golden Robot (C-3PO), #742, black box	15 - 30
CS0003	*SW*: Luke X-wing Pilot	10 - 25
CS0004	*SW*: R2-D2, #744, black box	15 - 30
CS0005	*SW*: Princess Leia, #745, black box	20 - 35
CS0006	*SW*: Chewbacca, #746, black box	15 - 30
CS0007	*SW*: Stormtrooper, #747, black box	15 - 30
CS0008	*SW*: Boba Fett, #748, black box	20 - 35
CS0010	*SW*: Lord Darth Vader, #740, blue box	15 - 30
CS0011	*SW*: Luke Skywalker, #741, blue box	15 - 30
CS0012	*SW*: Golden Robot (C-3PO), #742, blue box	15 - 30
CS0014	*SW*: R2-D2, #744, blue box	15 - 30
CS0015	*SW*: Princess Leia, #745, blue box	20 - 35
CS0016	*SW*: Chewbacca, #746, blue box	15 - 30
CS0017	*SW*: Stormtrooper, #747, blue box	15 - 30
CS0018	*SW*: Boba Fett, #748, blue box	20 - 35
CS0020	*ESB*: Lord Darth Vader, #740	10 - 20
CS0021	*ESB*: Luke Skywalker, #741	8 - 18
CS0022	*ESB*: Golden Robot (C-3PO), #742	8 - 18
CS0023	*ESB*: Luke X-wing Pilot	8 - 18
CS0024	*ESB*: R2-D2, #744	8 - 18
CS0025	*ESB*: Princess Leia, #745	20 - 35
CS0026	*ESB*: Chewbacca, #746	20 - 35
CS0027	*ESB*: Stormtrooper, #747	15 - 30
CS0028	*ESB*: Boba Fett, #748	15 - 30
CS0029	*ESB*: Yoda, #749	15 - 30
CS0035	*Revenge*: Wicket, #735	30 - 55
CS0036	*Revenge*: Adm. Ackbar, #736	30 - 55
CS0037	*Revenge*: Gamorrean Guard, #737	30 - 55
CS0038	*Revenge*: Klaatu, #738	30 - 55
CS0042	*ROTJ*: Wicket the Ewok (tiny tot), #202	15 - 30
CS0045	*ROTJ*: Wicket, #735	15 - 30
CS0046	*ROTJ*: Adm. Ackbar, #736	15 - 30
CS0047	*ROTJ*: Gamorrean Guard, #737	15 - 30
CS0048	*ROTJ*: Klaatu, #738	15 - 30
CS0050	*ROTJ*: Lord Darth Vader, #740	15 - 30
CS0051	*ROTJ*: Luke Skywalker, #741	15 - 30
CS0052	*ROTJ*: Golden Robot (C-3PO), #742	15 - 30
CS0053	*ROTJ*: Luke X-wing Pilot	15 - 30
CS0054	*ROTJ*: R2-D2, #744	15 - 30
CS0055	*ROTJ*: Princess Leia, #745	15 - 30
CS0056	*ROTJ*: Chewbacca, #746	15 - 30
CS0057	*ROTJ*: Stormtrooper, #747, blue box	15 - 30
CS0058	*ROTJ*: Boba Fett, #748	15 - 30
CS0059	*ROTJ*: Yoda, #749	15 - 30
Australia		
CS1100	C-3PO (Croner Trading)	15 - 20
CS1110	Darth Vader (Croner Trading)	15 - 20
CS1150	Stormtrooper (Croner Trading)	15 - 20
CS1160	Darth Vader (Fonsash Party Ltd.)	15 - 20
CS1170	Luke Skywalker (Fonsash Party Ltd.)	15 - 20

CS2003   CS2006   CS2011   CS2020

CS2025

CS2035   CS2030   CS2040   CS2045

Belgium (J.P. Belgium)		
CS1250	Darth Vader	15 - 25
CS1251	Stormtrooper	15 - 25
CS1252	Chewbacca	15 - 25
CS1253	C-3PO	15 - 25
Canada (Norben Products)		
CS1270	Darth Vader, child	15 - 20
CS1271	Darth Vader, adult	15 - 20
England (Acamas Toys)		
CS1300	C-3PO	25 - 35
CS1305	Chewbacca	25 - 35
CS1310	Darth Vader	25 - 35
CS1315	Ewok	25 - 35
CS1320	Gamorrean Guard	25 - 35
CS1321	Leia	25 - 35
CS1322	Klaatu	25 - 35
CS1325	Luke Skywalker	35 - 45
CS1330	Stormtrooper	25 - 35
CS1335	Yoda	25 - 35
France		
CS1400	C-3PO (Le Panache Blanc)	25 - 35
CS1410	*SW* full Leia dress (Society Anselme)	65 - 125

MASKS

Masks by Don Post Studios are among the most highly-sought *Star Wars* items. Early versions of the Don Post masks came only in a plastic bag. Later versions were packed in a blue box. All should have tags attached. Pay close attention to which version of a mask is offered for sale, as values can be dramatically different.

The original Darth Vader helmet (1977) was made of heavy plastic, had very dark eye lenses, and is the rarest variation found. Because the mask was cast in a metal mold using a centrifugal process, it was not possible to stamp any lettering on the mask. A sticker on the inside of the helmet carried the Twentieth Century Fox copyright. Both the eyeholes and the faceplate grille were separate pieces which were glued in. A lighter, injection-molded version of the helmet, made the following year, had the Twentieth Century copyright molded on the inside. The lenses were heat-set, and easier to see through. (The difference in eyehole tint was due to the stock which was available at the time.) In 1983 the mask was once again revised: the end points on the respirator were removed and replaced with a flat, silver-painted dot. A fourth version, released in 1993-94, changed the copyright to LFL. A fifth revision of the mask used molded plastic nose and respirator tips. Most elaborate of all, however, is the deluxe edition of the helmet released in 1995. Molded from one of the original masks used in filming *The Empire Strikes Back*, it is the closest thing to the film prop ever licensed.

Stormtrooper helmets were injection-molded in heavy PVC plastic with dark lenses in 1977. The Twentieth Century Fox copyright was molded on the back of the helmet. They were revised in '78 with lighter PVC plastic, and had clearer lenses. The lenses were glued in on both versions. The third version of the Stormtrooper mask, first produced in 1988, was a slightly different shape, because the new plastic used reacted to the mold differently. The eyes were no longer separate pieces of smoky-colored plastic, and were painted black with many holes drilled for vision. The 1989-90 version replaced the foam band around the front of the helmet with a molded-in piece. All variations of the Stormtrooper mask have a tendency to yellow with age, as a result of the plastic used. A 1994-95 version of the mask shows the LFL copyright, and once again has clear plastic eye lenses.

All versions of the C-3PO mask were done in latex. The first version had gold pigment in the plastic itself, which has caused some collectors to mistake it for vinyl. These tended to get a "tarnished" look as a result of this process. The 1978 version was molded in black latex which was painted gold. The 1994 release of C-3PO is similar to the '78 version, but with the modified LFL copyright.

Chewbacca masks were first produced with a fierce, open-mouthed face. Don Post Studios was dissatisfied with the look of the mask when cast, and resculpted it with a closed mouth for 1978. About 500 of the vicious Chewie masks were sold before the revision was produced.

Yoda was first issued in conjunction with *The Empire Strikes Back*. The mask was re-sculpted each time a mold wore out. Three different molds were used in succession: the second in 1983, the third in 1987. The three masks are very similar, as no changes were intended.

The Darth Vader helmet, Stormtrooper helmet, and C-3PO masks have been produced continuously from 1977 until the time of this book's publication. Re-issues of many original masks, with LFL copyrights and "Made in China" molded in, have been around since 1994. These include a Tusken Raider with larger eyes and shorter breathing apparatus, Klaatu, Gamorrean Guard, and the Emperor. New masks include Boba Fett and the Imperial Guard.

Japan's Ogawa-Gomu Co. produced rubber pull-over masks in plastic bags w/header cards.

Special thanks to Don Post of Don Post Studios and to Bill Sikora for their assistance in compiling this section.

Don Post Studios

CS2001	Darth Vader helmet, original w/sticker, 1977	100 - 300
CS2002	Darth, molded 20th Fox copyright, 1978	75 - 125
CS2003	Darth, 3rd version w/o end points, 1983	40 - 50
CS2004	Darth, 4th version w/LFL copyright, 1993	40 - 50
CS2005	Darth, plastic nose & respirator tips, 1994	40 - 50
CS2006	Darth Vader Deluxe helmet, (fiberglass) 1995	400 - 1,200

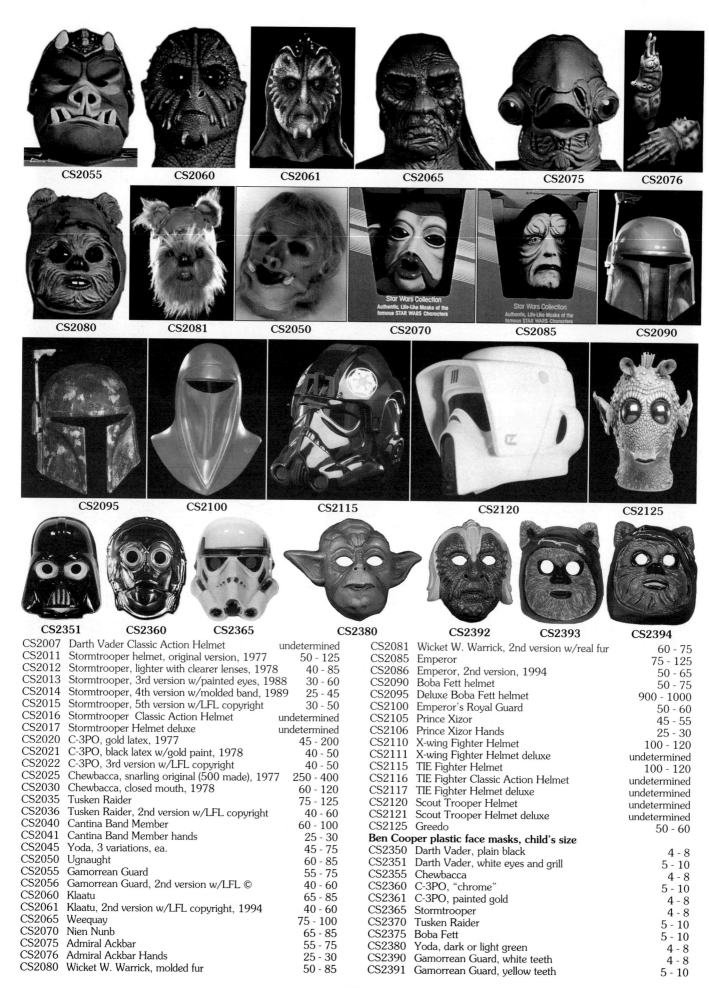

CS2055 CS2060 CS2061 CS2065 CS2075 CS2076

CS2080 CS2081 CS2050 CS2070 CS2085 CS2090

CS2095 CS2100 CS2115 CS2120 CS2125

CS2351 CS2360 CS2365 CS2380 CS2392 CS2393 CS2394

CS2007	Darth Vader Classic Action Helmet	undetermined
CS2011	Stormtrooper helmet, original version, 1977	50 - 125
CS2012	Stormtrooper, lighter with clearer lenses, 1978	40 - 85
CS2013	Stormtrooper, 3rd version w/painted eyes, 1988	30 - 60
CS2014	Stormtrooper, 4th version w/molded band, 1989	25 - 45
CS2015	Stormtrooper, 5th version w/LFL copyright	30 - 50
CS2016	Stormtrooper Classic Action Helmet	undetermined
CS2017	Stormtrooper Helmet deluxe	undetermined
CS2020	C-3PO, gold latex, 1977	45 - 200
CS2021	C-3PO, black latex w/gold paint, 1978	40 - 50
CS2022	C-3PO, 3rd version w/LFL copyright	40 - 50
CS2025	Chewbacca, snarling original (500 made), 1977	250 - 400
CS2030	Chewbacca, closed mouth, 1978	60 - 120
CS2035	Tusken Raider	75 - 125
CS2036	Tusken Raider, 2nd version w/LFL copyright	40 - 60
CS2040	Cantina Band Member	60 - 100
CS2041	Cantina Band Member hands	25 - 30
CS2045	Yoda, 3 variations, ea.	45 - 75
CS2050	Ugnaught	60 - 85
CS2055	Gamorrean Guard	55 - 75
CS2056	Gamorrean Guard, 2nd version w/LFL ©	40 - 60
CS2060	Klaatu	65 - 85
CS2061	Klaatu, 2nd version w/LFL copyright, 1994	40 - 60
CS2065	Weequay	75 - 100
CS2070	Nien Nunb	65 - 85
CS2075	Admiral Ackbar	55 - 75
CS2076	Admiral Ackbar Hands	25 - 30
CS2080	Wicket W. Warrick, molded fur	50 - 85

CS2081	Wicket W. Warrick, 2nd version w/real fur	60 - 75
CS2085	Emperor	75 - 125
CS2086	Emperor, 2nd version, 1994	50 - 65
CS2090	Boba Fett helmet	50 - 75
CS2095	Deluxe Boba Fett helmet	900 - 1000
CS2100	Emperor's Royal Guard	50 - 60
CS2105	Prince Xizor	45 - 55
CS2106	Prince Xizor Hands	25 - 30
CS2110	X-wing Fighter Helmet	100 - 120
CS2111	X-wing Fighter Helmet deluxe	undetermined
CS2115	TIE Fighter Helmet	100 - 120
CS2116	TIE Fighter Classic Action Helmet	undetermined
CS2117	TIE Fighter Helmet deluxe	undetermined
CS2120	Scout Trooper Helmet	undetermined
CS2121	Scout Trooper Helmet deluxe	undetermined
CS2125	Greedo	50 - 60

Ben Cooper plastic face masks, child's size

CS2350	Darth Vader, plain black	4 - 8
CS2351	Darth Vader, white eyes and grill	5 - 10
CS2355	Chewbacca	4 - 8
CS2360	C-3PO, "chrome"	5 - 10
CS2361	C-3PO, painted gold	4 - 8
CS2365	Stormtrooper	4 - 8
CS2370	Tusken Raider	5 - 10
CS2375	Boba Fett	5 - 10
CS2380	Yoda, dark or light green	4 - 8
CS2390	Gamorrean Guard, white teeth	4 - 8
CS2391	Gamorrean Guard, yellow teeth	5 - 10

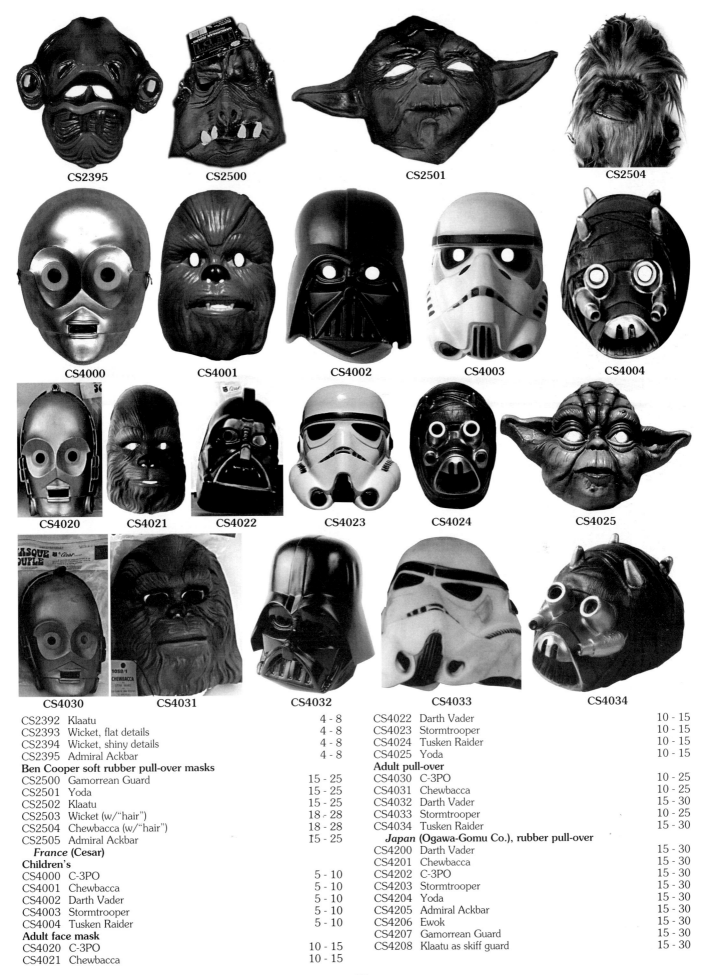

CS2395   CS2500   CS2501   CS2504

CS4000   CS4001   CS4002   CS4003   CS4004

CS4020   CS4021   CS4022   CS4023   CS4024   CS4025

CS4030   CS4031   CS4032   CS4033   CS4034

CS2392	Klaatu	4 - 8
CS2393	Wicket, flat details	4 - 8
CS2394	Wicket, shiny details	4 - 8
CS2395	Admiral Ackbar	4 - 8
Ben Cooper soft rubber pull-over masks		
CS2500	Gamorrean Guard	15 - 25
CS2501	Yoda	15 - 25
CS2502	Klaatu	15 - 25
CS2503	Wicket (w/"hair")	18 - 28
CS2504	Chewbacca (w/"hair")	18 - 28
CS2505	Admiral Ackbar	15 - 25
France (Cesar)		
Children's		
CS4000	C-3PO	5 - 10
CS4001	Chewbacca	5 - 10
CS4002	Darth Vader	5 - 10
CS4003	Stormtrooper	5 - 10
CS4004	Tusken Raider	5 - 10
Adult face mask		
CS4020	C-3PO	10 - 15
CS4021	Chewbacca	10 - 15

CS4022	Darth Vader	10 - 15
CS4023	Stormtrooper	10 - 15
CS4024	Tusken Raider	10 - 15
CS4025	Yoda	10 - 15
Adult pull-over		
CS4030	C-3PO	10 - 25
CS4031	Chewbacca	10 - 25
CS4032	Darth Vader	15 - 30
CS4033	Stormtrooper	10 - 25
CS4034	Tusken Raider	15 - 30
Japan (Ogawa-Gomu Co.), rubber pull-over		
CS4200	Darth Vader	15 - 30
CS4201	Chewbacca	15 - 30
CS4202	C-3PO	15 - 30
CS4203	Stormtrooper	15 - 30
CS4204	Yoda	15 - 30
CS4205	Admiral Ackbar	15 - 30
CS4206	Ewok	15 - 30
CS4207	Gamorrean Guard	15 - 30
CS4208	Klaatu as skiff guard	15 - 30

CS4200

CS4201

CS4202

CS4204

CS4205

CS4206

CS4207

CS4208

CS4400

CS4401

CS4402

CS4425

CS4426

CS4427

CS4428

CS4404

CS4403

CS4405

CS4429

CS4430

CS4431

CS4502

CS4504

CS4505

CS4432

CS4433

CS4434

Mexico

Papeles Troquelados, paper

CS4400	Darth Vader	5 - 10
CS4401	Stormtrooper	5 - 10
CS4402	C-3PO	5 - 10
CS4403	Chewbacca	5 - 10
CS4404	Yoda	5 - 10
CS4405	Boba Fett	5 - 10

Creaciones Juanin, plastic

CS4425	C-3PO	7 - 12
CS4426	Chewbacca	7 - 12
CS4427	Darth Vader	7 - 12
CS4428	Stormtrooper	7 - 12
CS4429	Yoda	7 - 12
CS4430	TIE Fighter Pilot	7 - 12
CS4431	Admiral Ackbar	7 - 12
CS4432	Gamorrean Guard	7 - 12
CS4433	Wicket	7 - 12
CS4434	Biker Scout	7 - 12

CS6300　　　　　　　　　　　CS6550

CS9000	*ESB* five-pattern set	10 - 25
CS9005	*ROTJ* shirt	8 - 15
CS9010	*ROTJ* night wear	8 - 15
CS9015	*ROTJ* Ewok costumes	10 - 15

CRAFTS

COLORING/PAINTING

Poster sets for coloring and painting were among the earliest *Star Wars* merchandise from Kenner. One set featured a three-dimensional cardstock Darth Vader mask which was attached to the finished poster. Paint-by-number boxed sets for *ESB* and *ROTJ* used glow-in-the-dark paint for accents. Vinyl figurine paint sets were produced by Kenner's Craft Master affiliate. New craft sets are from RoseArt.

Coloring Sets

| CT0001 | *SW* Dip Dots paint set | 15 - 25 |
| CT0010 | *ESB* Color & Clean Machine | 15 - 35 |

Figurine Paint Sets

CT0100	*ESB* Leia	15 - 25
CT0101	*ESB* Luke on Tauntaun	15 - 25
CT0102	*ESB* Yoda	15 - 25
CT0103	*ESB* Han Solo	15 - 25
CT0104	*ESB* Boba Fett	15 - 25
CT0120	*ROTJ* Admiral Ackbar	15 - 25
CT0121	*ROTJ* Wicket	15 - 25
CT0122	*ROTJ* C-3PO & R2-D2	15 - 25

New Zealand (Bing Harris Sargood Ltd.)

CS4500	Yoda	10 - 15
CS4501	Chewbacca	10 - 15
CS4502	Wicket	10 - 15
CS4504	Gamorrean Guard	10 - 15
CS4505	Admiral Ackbar	10 - 15
CS4506	Jabba the Hutt	10 - 15

Switzerland (Urweider)

CS4780	Darth Vader	10 - 15
CS4781	Stormtrooper	10 - 15
CS4782	Chewbacca	10 - 15
CS4783	C-3PO	10 - 15

See also—**BOOKS: Activity; FOOD**

PLAY SUITS (Ben Cooper)

CS5000	C-3PO	15 - 35
CS5001	Darth Vader	15 - 35
CS5002	Stormtrooper	15 - 35
CS5010	Chewbacca 3 piece disguise kit	10 - 20

Australia (Croner)

| CS6300 | Darth Vader | 10 - 20 |
| CS6305 | Stormtrooper | 8 - 15 |

England (Cheryl Playthings Ltd.)

| CS6550 | C-3PO | 20 - 45 |

Spain (Josman)

| CS6800 | *Droids:* C-3PO | 8 - 15 |

PONCHOS (Ben Cooper)

CS7000	C-3PO	5 - 15
CS7005	Darth Vader	5 - 15
CS7010	Yoda	5 - 15

Australia (General Mills Fun Group)

| CS8500 | *ESB* assorted ponchos | 5 - 10 |

PATTERNS (McCall's)

A McCall's pattern set included paper design patterns to make costumes of Chewbacca, Princess Leia, Yoda, a Jawa and Darth Vader. Other sets could be used to make an *ROTJ* shirt, *ROTJ* night wear (both with iron-on transfers) or Ewok costumes.

Paint by Number

CT0210	*ESB* Battle on Hoth paint set	9 - 18
CT0211	*ESB* Chase through the Asteroids	9 - 18
CT0220	*ESB* Darth Vader	9 - 18
CT0221	*ESB* Luke Skywalker	9 - 18
CT0222	*ESB* Princess Leia	9 - 18
CT0223	*ESB* Yoda	9 - 18
CT0224	*ESB* Boba Fett	9 - 18
CT0230	*ROTJ* Lando & Boushh	9 - 18
CT0231	*ROTJ* Jabba the Hutt	9 - 18
CT0232	*ROTJ* Rebo Band	9 - 18
CT0233	*ROTJ* C-3PO & R2-D2	9 - 18
CT0240	*Ewoks:* Wicket and Baga	9 - 18
CT0241	*Ewoks:* Ewok Gliders	9 - 18
CT0242	*Ewoks:* Ewok Village	9 - 18

Poster Sets

CT0410	*SW* Playnts 5-poster set	15 - 25
CT0411	*SW* Poster Art: Galactic dogfight/The forces of good and evil	15 - 25
CT0412	*SW* Poster Art: Darth Vader lives/May the Force...	15 - 25
CT0413	*SW* Poster Art: Heroes and villains/Cantina & aliens	15 - 25
CT0414	*SW* 3-D Darth Vader Poster Art	15 - 35
CT0415	*ESB* Poster Art: On Dagobah w/Yoda/Battle on Hoth	10 - 20

CS6800　　　CS7000　　　CS7005　　　CS9000　　　CT0010

CT0100　　　CT0101　　　CT0102　　　CT0210　　　CT0211

CT0220   CT0221   CT0222   CT0223   CT0231   CT0232

CT0240   CT0241   CT0242

IRON-ON APPLIQUES

Besides the iron-on transfer book listed under the **BOOKS** heading (Ballantine's least successful *Star Wars* publishing project), there were dozens of *SW* and *ESB* transfer sheets. These were sold both poly-bagged directly to the consumer and also to stores that used a heat process to put the transfers on T-shirts. Since they're stuck on the sheets in reverse, they must be held up to the light to see the correct image. All of the transfers listed below sell in the range of $5 to $10—often less in quantity. The U.S. transfers were all made by Factors Inc.

By the time *ROTJ* was released, the market had changed, and stores sold T-shirts with designs already silk-screened or imprinted.

Star Wars Iron-On Designs

CT1001	Hildebrandt poster, #2099	5 - 10
CT1002	Battle, Vader head, #2100	5 - 10
CT1003	R2-D2, C-3PO in corridor, #2101	5 - 10
CT1004	C-3PO, Luke, #2102	5 - 10
CT1005	Chewbacca, Han Solo, #2103	5 - 10
CT1006	May the Force..., #2104	5 - 10
CT1007	Darth Vadar lives, #2105	5 - 10
CT1008	Logo, #2106	5 - 10
CT1009	Droids before star field, #2130	5 - 10
CT1010	Vader full figure, #2131	5 - 10
CT1011	"Chewie," #2132	5 - 10
CT1012	Jawas, #2133	5 - 10
CT1013	Princess Leia, #2221	5 - 10
CT1014	Luke firing blaster, #2222	5 - 10

"Foto-Dazzlers" (glitter effect)

CT1030	Logo, #1019	5 - 10
CT1031	R2-D2, #1138	5 - 10

CT0410   CT0411   CT0413   CT0414

CT1001   CT1002   CT1003   CT1004   CT1005   CT1006   CT1009

CT1008   CT1030   CT1010   CT1011   CT1012   CT1013   CT1014   CT1031

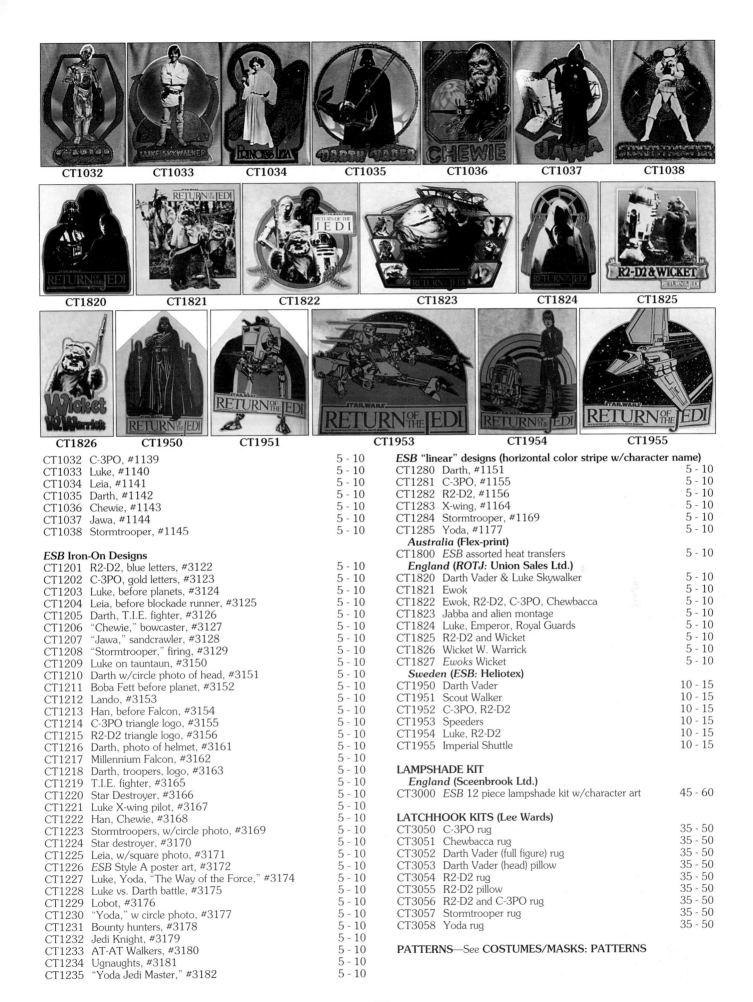

CT1032	CT1033	CT1034
CT1035	CT1036	CT1037
CT1038		

CT1820	CT1821	CT1822
CT1823	CT1824	CT1825

CT1826	CT1950	CT1951
CT1953	CT1954	CT1955

CT1032	C-3PO, #1139	5 - 10
CT1033	Luke, #1140	5 - 10
CT1034	Leia, #1141	5 - 10
CT1035	Darth, #1142	5 - 10
CT1036	Chewie, #1143	5 - 10
CT1037	Jawa, #1144	5 - 10
CT1038	Stormtrooper, #1145	5 - 10

ESB Iron-On Designs

CT1201	R2-D2, blue letters, #3122	5 - 10
CT1202	C-3PO, gold letters, #3123	5 - 10
CT1203	Luke, before planets, #3124	5 - 10
CT1204	Leia, before blockade runner, #3125	5 - 10
CT1205	Darth, T.I.E. fighter, #3126	5 - 10
CT1206	"Chewie," bowcaster, #3127	5 - 10
CT1207	"Jawa," sandcrawler, #3128	5 - 10
CT1208	"Stormtrooper," firing, #3129	5 - 10
CT1209	Luke on tauntaun, #3150	5 - 10
CT1210	Darth w/circle photo of head, #3151	5 - 10
CT1211	Boba Fett before planet, #3152	5 - 10
CT1212	Lando, #3153	5 - 10
CT1213	Han, before Falcon, #3154	5 - 10
CT1214	C-3PO triangle logo, #3155	5 - 10
CT1215	R2-D2 triangle logo, #3156	5 - 10
CT1216	Darth, photo of helmet, #3161	5 - 10
CT1217	Millennium Falcon, #3162	5 - 10
CT1218	Darth, troopers, logo, #3163	5 - 10
CT1219	T.I.E. fighter, #3165	5 - 10
CT1220	Star Destroyer, #3166	5 - 10
CT1221	Luke X-wing pilot, #3167	5 - 10
CT1222	Han, Chewie, #3168	5 - 10
CT1223	Stormtroopers, w/circle photo, #3169	5 - 10
CT1224	Star destroyer, #3170	5 - 10
CT1225	Leia, w/square photo, #3171	5 - 10
CT1226	*ESB* Style A poster art, #3172	5 - 10
CT1227	Luke, Yoda, "The Way of the Force," #3174	5 - 10
CT1228	Luke vs. Darth battle, #3175	5 - 10
CT1229	Lobot, #3176	5 - 10
CT1230	"Yoda," w circle photo, #3177	5 - 10
CT1231	Bounty hunters, #3178	5 - 10
CT1232	Jedi Knight, #3179	5 - 10
CT1233	AT-AT Walkers, #3180	5 - 10
CT1234	Ugnaughts, #3181	5 - 10
CT1235	"Yoda Jedi Master," #3182	5 - 10

ESB "linear" designs (horizontal color stripe w/character name)

CT1280	Darth, #1151	5 - 10
CT1281	C-3PO, #1155	5 - 10
CT1282	R2-D2, #1156	5 - 10
CT1283	X-wing, #1164	5 - 10
CT1284	Stormtrooper, #1169	5 - 10
CT1285	Yoda, #1177	5 - 10

Australia (Flex-print)

CT1800	*ESB* assorted heat transfers	5 - 10

England (*ROTJ:* Union Sales Ltd.)

CT1820	Darth Vader & Luke Skywalker	5 - 10
CT1821	Ewok	5 - 10
CT1822	Ewok, R2-D2, C-3PO, Chewbacca	5 - 10
CT1823	Jabba and alien montage	5 - 10
CT1824	Luke, Emperor, Royal Guards	5 - 10
CT1825	R2-D2 and Wicket	5 - 10
CT1826	Wicket W. Warrick	5 - 10
CT1827	*Ewoks* Wicket	5 - 10

Sweden (*ESB:* Heliotex)

CT1950	Darth Vader	10 - 15
CT1951	Scout Walker	10 - 15
CT1952	C-3PO, R2-D2	10 - 15
CT1953	Speeders	10 - 15
CT1954	Luke, R2-D2	10 - 15
CT1955	Imperial Shuttle	10 - 15

LAMPSHADE KIT

England (Sceenbrook Ltd.)

CT3000	*ESB* 12 piece lampshade kit w/character art	45 - 60

LATCHHOOK KITS (Lee Wards)

CT3050	C-3PO rug	35 - 50
CT3051	Chewbacca rug	35 - 50
CT3052	Darth Vader (full figure) rug	35 - 50
CT3053	Darth Vader (head) pillow	35 - 50
CT3054	R2-D2 rug	35 - 50
CT3055	R2-D2 pillow	35 - 50
CT3056	R2-D2 and C-3PO rug	35 - 50
CT3057	Stormtrooper rug	35 - 50
CT3058	Yoda rug	35 - 50

PATTERNS—See COSTUMES/MASKS: PATTERNS

CT3000 CT3050 CT3051 CT3053 CT3054

CT3055 CT3056 CT3057 CT3058

CT4000 CT4020 CT4021

CT4025 CT4026 CT4035 CT4041 CT4042 CT4043

CT4050 CT4051 CT5010 CT5011 CT5012

RUB-DOWN TRANSFERS (American Publishing Corp./Presto Magix)

Boxed sets

CT4000	*Star Wars (ESB)* Activity Set	10 - 20
CT4020	*ROTJ* Battle on Endor	10 - 15
CT4021	*ROTJ* Jabba the Hutt Throne Room	10 - 15
CT4025	Wicket the Ewok: Ewoks at Home	5 - 10
CT4026	Wicket the Ewok: Ewok Village	5 - 10

Poly-bagged small sets

CT4030	*ESB* Asteroid Storm	2 - 5
CT4031	*ESB* Beneath Cloud City	2 - 5
CT4032	*ESB* Cloud City Battle	2 - 5
CT4033	*ESB* Dagobah Bog Planet	2 - 5
CT4034	*ESB* Deck of Star Destroyer	2 - 5

CT4035	*ESB* Ice Planet Hoth	2 - 5
CT4036	*ESB* Rebel Base	2 - 5
CT4040	*ROTJ* Ewok Village	2 - 5
CT4041	*ROTJ* Jabba the Hutt Throne Room	2 - 5
CT4042	*ROTJ* Sarlacc Pit	2 - 5
CT4043	*ROTJ* Death Star	2 - 5

Poly-bagged large sets

CT4050	*ROTJ*/Wicket the Ewok: Ewoks at Play	3 - 6
CT4051	*ROTJ*/Wicket the Ewok: Ewok Hut scene	3 - 6

England

Letraset Poly-bagged large sets

CT5010	*SW* Battle at Mos Eisley	3 - 6
CT5011	*SW* Escape from Death Star	3 - 6

CT5021 CT5022 CT5023 CT5024 CT5025 CT5026 CT5027 CT5028 CT5029 CT5030

CT5035 CT5040 CT5062 CT5065 CT5075 CT5215 CT5217

CT5250 CT5326 CT5401-3, CT5410 CT5520 CT5521 CT6550

CT5501-14 CT5505

CT5012	*SW* Rebel Air Attack	3 - 6
Letraset Poly-bagged small sets		
CT5021	*SW* Part 1: Kidnap of Princess Leia	2 - 5
CT5022	*SW* Part 2: Sale on Tattooine (sic)	2 - 5
CT5023	*SW* Part 3: Action at Mos Eisley	2 - 5
CT5024	*SW* Part 4: Escape from Stormtroopers	2 - 5
CT5025	*SW* Part 5: Flight to Alderaan	2 - 5
CT5026	*SW* Part 6: Inside the Death Star	2 - 5
CT5027	*SW* Part 7: Prison Break Out	2 - 5
CT5028	*SW* Part 8: Death Star Escape	2 - 5
CT5029	*SW* Part 9: Rebel Air Base	2 - 5
CT5030	*SW* Part 10: Last Battle	2 - 5
CT5035	Display box for CT5021-30, empty	5 - 10
Thomas Salter Ltd. (duplicate of U.S. Presto Magix)		
Boxed sets		
CT5040	*ROTJ* Battle on Endor	10 - 12
CT5041	*ROTJ* Hutt Throne Room	10 - 12
CT5042	*ROTJ* Ewoks at home	5 - 10
CT5043	*ROTJ* Ewok Village	5 - 10
Poly-bagged large sets		
CT5060	*ROTJ* Sarlacc Pit	3 - 6
CT5062	*ROTJ* Ewok Village	3 - 6
CT5065	Display box for large sets, empty	5 - 10
Poly-bagged small sets		
CT5070	*ROTJ* Jabba the Hutt	2 - 5
CT5072	*ROTJ* The Ewoks	2 - 5
CT5075	Display box for small sets, empty	5 - 10
Premiums		
CT5100	*SW* Letraset packs w/purchase (Wimpy International Ltd.), ea.	2 - 5
CT5110	*ESB* 4 different sets (Kraft Foods Ltd.), ea.	3 - 6
France (Kenner Joux et Jouets)		
CT5210	*ROTJ* Action Transfers, assorted, (Jesco) ea.	2 - 5
CT5215	*Les Ewoks* transrama: poster size	4 - 8
CT5217	*Les Ewoks* transrama: Au Village, "giant" size	3 - 6
CT5218	*Les Ewoks* transrama: Le Sous Bois, "giant" size	3 - 6
CT5220	*Les Ewoks* transrama: La Maison, pocket size	2 - 5
CT5221	*Les Ewoks* transrama: Le Gouter, pocket size	2 - 5
CT5222	*Les Ewoks* transrama: Le Bain, pocket size	2 - 5
CT5223	*Les Ewoks* transrama: Les Jeux, pocket size	2 - 5
Germany (BSB)		
CT5250	German versions of English Letraset sets, ea.	
Mexico (Editorial Magro)		
CT5325	*ESB*: C-3PO and R2-D2	1 - 3

CT5326	*ESB*: Battle in Cloud City	1 - 3
Spain		
Smash Transfers		
CT5401	*Il Trono di Jabba*	3 - 6
CT5402	*La Fossa Di Sarlacc*	3 - 6
CT5403	*Il Villaggio degli Ewoks*	3 - 6
CT5410	Display box for CT5401-3	3 - 6
See also—**STATIONERY**		

RUBBER STAMPS (Adam Joseph Industries) Carded *ROTJ*

CT5501	Chewbacca	2 - 5
CT5502	Yoda	2 - 5
CT5503	Millennium Falcon	2 - 5
CT5504	TIE fighter,	2 - 5
CT5505	Biker Scout	2 - 5
CT5506	X-wing fighter pilot logo	2 - 5
CT5507	Darth Vader	2 - 5
CT5508	Admiral Ackbar	2 - 5
CT5509	Wicket	2 - 5
CT5510	Gamorrean Guard	2 - 5
CT5511	C-3PO	2 - 5
CT5512	Imperial Guard	2 - 5
CT5513	Stormtrooper	2 - 5
CT5514	Obi-Wan	2 - 5
CT5516	Display box for CT5501-14	5 - 15
CT5520	Wicket 3-in-1 stamp set	2 - 4
CT5521	Kneesaa 3-in-1 stamp set	2 - 4
See also—**STAR TOURS**		

SEWING KIT (Craft Master)

CT6550	*ROTJ* Wicket and Friends Sew 'N Show Cards	10 - 15

SUN CATCHERS ("STAINED GLASS")
***ESB*: Lee Wards**

CT9001	C-3PO	8 - 15
CT9002	Darth Vader (head)	8 - 15

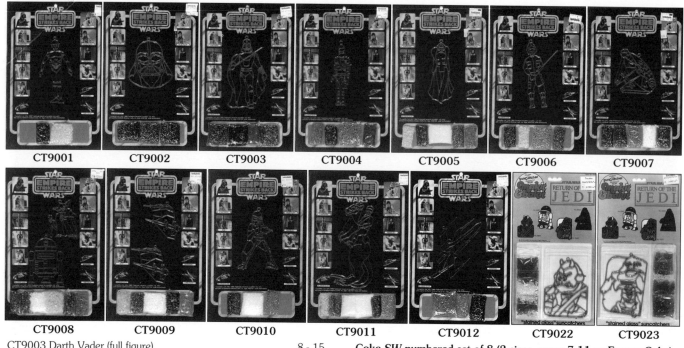

CT9001	CT9002	CT9003	CT9004	CT9005	CT9006	CT9007

CT9008	CT9009	CT9010	CT9011	CT9012	CT9022	CT9023

"stained glass" suncatchers   "stained glass" suncatchers

CT9003	Darth Vader (full figure)	8 - 15
CT9004	IG-88	8 - 15
CT9005	Leia	8 - 15
CT9006	Luke lightsaber	8 - 15
CT9007	Millennium Falcon	8 - 15
CT9008	R2-D2 and Yoda	8 - 15
CT9009	Snowspeeder	8 - 15
CT9010	Stormtrooper	8 - 15
CT9011	Luke on Tauntaun	8 - 15
CT9012	X-wing	8 - 15

ROTJ: Fundimensions

CT9020	R2-D2	4 - 10
CT9021	Darth Vader	4 - 10
CT9022	Gamorrean Guard	4 - 10
CT9023	Jabba and Salacious Crumb	4 - 10

CUPS/GLASSES—COLLECTOR'S

COLLECTOR'S CUPS

Until the 1997 Pepsi deal, Coca-Cola Co. cornered the market on collectors cups and glasses worldwide, often distributing the same items under different chain names including such well-known ones as Burger King, Kentucky Fried Chicken, and 7-11 Stores; regional chains like Koolee; and foreign chains such as Hungry Jack in Australia. The exceptions include a plastic cup promotion from Pepperidge Farm for *Star Wars* cookies (one free cup with purchase, four more available as a mail-in offer) and mustard-jar glasses in France and Germany (see Food category). Our definition of cups here is drinking containers that are opaque; glasses (whether glass or hard plastic) you can see through.

Coke first *SW* numbered set of 20 (sometimes marked Koolee)

CU0001	Stormtroopers	5 - 15
CU0002	Chewbacca & Han Solo	5 - 15
CU0003	Trapped in trash compactor	5 - 15
CU0004	Duel of the lightsabers	5 - 15
CU0005	Darth, X-wing & T.I.E. ftr.	5 - 15
CU0006	Dogfight	5 - 15
CU0007	Stopped on Mos Eisley	5 - 15
CU0008	Luke Skywalker	5 - 15
CU0009	Luke trains w/lightsaber	5 - 15
CU0010	Darth and Moff Tarkin	5 - 15
CU0011	Chewie escorted by Luke, Han	5 - 15
CU0012	R2-D2 & C-3PO	5 - 15
CU0013	Princess Leia	5 - 15
CU0014	Tusken Raiders	5 - 15
CU0015	Jawas carry off R2-D2	5 - 15
CU0016	Tusken Raider attacks	5 - 15
CU0017	Darth chokes underling	5 - 15
CU0018	Luke, Leia swing to safety	5 - 15
CU0019	Leia, Luke, Han triumphant	5 - 15
CU0020	Kenobi shuts tractor beam	5 - 15

Coke *SW* numbered set of 8 (2 sizes, some 7-11 or Frozen Coke)

CU0031	Han & Chewbacca	3 - 10
CU0032	Final Chase (X-wing., T.I.E. ftr.)	3 - 10
CU0033	Tusken Raiders, Jawas	3 - 10
CU0034	Darth Vader	3 - 10
CU0035	R2-D2, C-3PO	3 - 10
CU0036	Ben (Obi-Wan) Kenobi	3 - 10
CU0037	Luke & Leia	3 - 10
CU0038	The Lightsabers (Ben, Darth duel)	3 - 10

Coke third *SW* set (1979), unnumbered set of 8

CU0040	Boba Fett	3 - 10
CU0041	The final chase	3 - 10
CU0042	Ben Kenobi	3 - 10
CU0043	Darth & Moff Tarkin	3 - 10
CU0044	Luke & Leia	3 - 10
CU0045	R2-D2 and C-3PO	3 - 10
CU0046	Han Solo	3 - 10
CU0047	Chewbacca	3 - 10

Coke *ESB* 1982 theater promotion (free w/purchase)

CU0050	20-oz cup w/*SW* art on one side, *ESB* on the other	2 - 5
CU0051	32-oz. cup	3 - 6
CU0052	Pitcher, 50 oz.	5 - 10

Coke *ROTJ* 1983 theater promotion

CU0060	20-oz cup w/ Darth-Luke duel, Jabba's throne room, other art	2 - 5

CU0001	CU0002	CU0003	CU0004	CU0005	CU0007	CU0006

CU0010	CU0009	CU0019	CU0018	CU0017	CU0008

CU0020	CU0016	CU0013	CU0015	CU0012	CU0014	CU0011

| CU0031 | CU0032 | CU0033 | CU0034 |

| CU0035 | CU0036 | CU0037 | CU0038 |

| CU0047 | CU0044 | CU0042 | CU0045 |

| CU0074 | CU0076 | CU0079 | CU0072 | CU0073 |

| CU0081 | CU0077 | CU0080 | CU0074 | CU0075 |

| CU5004 | CU5001 | CU5003 | CU5002 |

| CU5013 | CU5011 | CU5014 | CU5012 |

| CU5021 | CU5023 | CU5024 | CU5022 |

CU0061 Pitcher, 50 oz.   5 - 10

Coke *ROTJ* 1983 set of 12 unnumbered (7-11 U.S. and Canada/ Kentucky Fried Chicken in Puerto Rico)

CU0070 Front: Han, Leia, Chewie at bunker; Back: Droids in grass 3 - 6
CU0071 F: Bikers; B: Han & Biker Scout   3 - 6
CU0072 F: Ackbar; B: Nein Nunb, Lando   3 - 6
CU0073 F: Throne room elevator; B: Guards leave shuttle   3 - 6
CU0074 F: Barge & skiff; B: Yak Face, C-3PO, Ree-Yees   3 - 6
CU0075 F: Bib Fortuna, Jabba, guard; B: Max Rebo band   3 - 6
CU0076 F: Han, Luke, Chewie, Lando/skiff; B: Kenobi & Luke   3 - 6
CU0077 F: Luke, Darth duel; B: Darth, Emperor, shuttles   3 - 6
CU0078 F: Moff Jerjerrod/control room; B: Dignitaries   3 - 6
CU0079 F: Klaatu, Jawas, Ishi; B: Lando/skiff   3 - 6
CU0080 F: Wicket; B: Wicket, Ewok, AT-ST   3 - 6
CU0081 F: Ackbar, Lando, droids, Luke; B: Han in carbonite   3 - 6

Coke/Kenner ROTJ 1985 theater promotion: "Win SW Toys"

CU0090 32-ox. waxed paper cup w/game piece attached   2 - 5
CU0091 Cup w/out game piece   1 - 2

Pepperidge Farm *Star Wars* Cookies cups

CU0100 C-3PO, R2-D2 & Wicket—in-store, free w/purchase   5 - 10
CU0101 The Rebels—mail-in offer   5 - 10
CU0102 The Vehicles—mail-in   5 - 10
CU0103 The Villains—mail-in   5 - 10
CU0104 The Creatures—mail-in   5 - 10

Australia (Coca-Cola Export Corp.)

CU4521 *ESB* McDonald's (red) Darth, Boba Fett,
         Stormtroopers   5 - 10
CU4522 *ESB* McDonald's (blue) Han, Yoda, Luke, Chewie, Leia   5 - 10
CU4523 *ESB* McDonald's cup (yellow) AT-AT, droids,
         Star Destroyer   5 - 10
CU4526 *ROTJ* souvenir plastic cup, Endor scene   3 - 6

Philippines

CU4850 *ROTJ* logo (Jollibee Food Corp./Coke)   3 - 6
See also—**KITCHEN**

COLLECTOR'S GLASSES

Burger King, in conjunction with Coca-Cola, sold four different glasses for each of the films in the trilogy. Only one was sold each week, to keep customers coming back to complete a set. For *ROTJ*, because of a new regulation in the state of Massachusetts, the "glasses" were a hard see-through plastic in that state only.

***Star Wars* glasses**

CU5001 Luke   10 - 15
CU5002 R2-D2 and C-3PO   10 - 15
CU5003 Chewbacca   10 - 15
CU5004 Darth Vader   12 - 18

***The Empire Strikes Back* glasses**

CU5011 Luke   4 - 8
CU5012 R2-D2 and C-3PO   4 - 8
CU5013 Lando Calrissian   4 - 8
CU5014 Darth Vader   4 - 8

***Return of the Jedi* glasses**

CU5021 Jabba the Hutt   3 - 6
CU5022 Tatooine desert   3 - 6
CU5023 Ewok village   3 - 6
CU5024 Emperor's throne room   3 - 6

***Return of the Jedi* plastic tumblers (Massachusetts only)**

CU5031 Jabba the Hutt   4 - 8
CU5032 Tatooine desert   4 - 8

CU9000

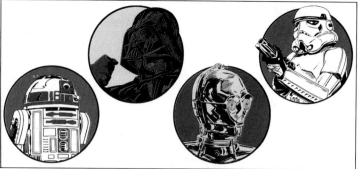

Box for CU9000

CU5022   CU5032

Book Cover from FA0001

FA0002

FA0012

FA0014

Photo card from FA0020

FA0022

FA0032

CU5033	Ewok village	4 - 8
CU5034	Emperor's throne room	4 - 8
Australia (Coca-Cola Export Corp. Hungry Jack)		
CU8500	Jabba	10 - 12
CU8501	Tatooine desert	10 - 12
CU8502	Ewok village	10 - 12
CU8503	Emperor's throne room	10 - 12
Thailand		
CU9000	Trilogy boxed 4-pack	35 - 50

FAN CLUB

The official *Star Wars* Fan Club was originally an in-house division of Lucasfilm. Members received a quarterly newsletter, originally published by Factors, which became known as *Bantha Tracks* when Lucasfilm took over publication with issue #5. Every year, when membership was renewed, there was a small renewal kit usually consisting of a membership card, some photos, a decal, a cloth patch and often some other special goodie. Early versions of the pre-*ROTJ* kits contained a Revenge logo cloth patch and the fan club sold separately a Yoda Revenge patch. Among the other special items were *SW* and *ESB* pencils and photo albums, and a lenticular photo, one with a plastic ridged lens attached that makes the photo look like a moving scene (the Darth-Luke lightsaber battle) when it is twisted.

The in-house club folded in 1987, but it was soon replaced by a licensed Lucasfilm Fan Club, which turned the newsletter into a (usually) quarterly magazine. The name was changed back to the Official *Star Wars* Fan Club in the spring of 1994, and the quarterly magazine was dubbed the *Star Wars* Insider. All along, the club has offered some exclusive merchandise (see **APPAREL, BUTTONS AND BADGES, PATCHES, POSTERS**, etc.) as well as occasional finds of older items.

The hardest issues of the club newsletter are the first four, which were published by Factors. The highlights of these were assembled into a compilation issue published by Lucasfilm. *Bantha Tracks* #34 included a vinyl record from Sprocket Systems, the Lucasfilm post-production department. The final issue, #35, was in the form of a large fold-out poster celebrating 10 years of *Star Wars* mania.

The UK fan club kit included a patch, lenticular photo, phrase stickers, and four of a possible twelve character stickers (see SR9210).

The Japanese *Star Wars* Fan Club published a separate quarterly color magazine (in Japanese, of course). Although it started relatively late in the cycle (1983) the club offered some nifty exclusive items during its four year existence. It also produced a beautifully-printed membership kit, with a pop-up photo inside the cover.

FA0001	Original *SW* Fan Club kit	20 - 40
FA0002	Ad slick for *SW* Fan Club	3 - 6
FA0012	Bantha member T-shirt	15 - 30
FA0014	Key chain	5 - 10
FA0020	*ESB* renewal kit	10 - 25
FA0022	Ad slick showing *ESB* kit	2 - 5
FA0030	*ROTJ* advance kit w/*Revenge* logo patch	25 - 40
FA0031	*ROTJ* advance kit w/*Return* logo patch	10 - 20
FA0032	*ROTJ* 1984 renewal kit	10 - 20
FA0041-4	*Star Wars* Fan Club Newsletter (Factors) #1-#4, ea.	10 - 18
FA0045	Newsletter compilation, highlights of #1-#4	4 - 10
FA0055-83	Bantha Tracks, #5-#33, ea.	3 - 10
FA0084	Bantha Tracks #34 (Sprocket Systems sound sheet)	5 - 15
FA0085	Bantha Tracks #35 (last issue)	4 - 12
FA0091-99	Lucasfilm Fan Club Magazine, #1-#9, ea.	2 - 6
FA0100-12	Lucasfilm Fan Club Magazine, #10-#22, ea.	2 - 4
FA0113	*Star Wars* Insider, #23+	2 - 4

FA0041   FA0045   FA0084   FA0085   FA0091

FA8201   FA8203   FA8224

England/UK

FA7930	Official *Star Wars* Lucasfilm Fan Club kit	10 - 20

Japan

FA8201-14	Japanese *SW* Fan Club Magazine, Vol. #1-#14, ea.	4 - 10
FA8220	JSWFC logo blue bath towel	15 - 30
FA8222	JSWFC logo white T-shirt	10 - 20
FA8224	JSWFC logo blue binder for magazines	10 - 20
FA8226	1984 Calendar	10 - 12
FA8228	JSWFC membership kit	25 - 45
FA8230	*SW* logo green nylon luggage/carry bags (5 sizes)	20 - 95
FA8232	JSWFC logo membership card	3 - 6
FA8234	JSWFC 1985 calendar	4 - 10
FA8236	JSWFC logo nylon wallet	5 - 15
FA8238	JSWFC logo audio cassette carrying case	5 - 15

FILM/VIDEO/SLIDES

FILM CLIPS

Star Wars was released at the dawn of the home video age, when home movies were dying. Even Super 8 was too much of a hassle once the easier and eventually cheaper home videos took hold. *Star Wars* gave the Super 8 format one last hurrah, and was the final big seller—and all-time bestseller—for Ken Films and many of its foreign affiliates and licensees. Since few people have projectors these days, they are collected more for their packaging and nostalgic value.

SW Super 8 films (Ken Films)

FM0010	Black and white	15 - 20
FM0020	Color/silent	20 - 30
FM0030	Color/sound, 4 min.	25 - 40
FM0040	Color/sound, 8 min.	30 - 45
FM0045	Color/sound, 17 min.	60 - 95

ESB Super 8 films

FM0050	Color/sound, 4 min.	15 - 20
FM0051	Color/sound, 8 min.	25 - 45
FM0052	Color/sound, 17 min.	60 - 95
FM0053	Color/sound, 17 min., Part 2	60 - 95

Spanish language

FM0068	*Star Wars* w/sticker: "Sonido en Español"	45 - 60
FM0070	*SW: La Guerra de las Galaxias* Color/sound, 8 min.	30 - 45
FM0072	*SW: La Guerra de las Galaxias* Color/sound, 17 min.	45 - 60
FM0075	*ESB: El Imperio Contraataca* Color/sound, 17 min.	45 - 60

France

FM0460	*SW: La Guerre des Etoiles* Color/sound, 8 min.	30 - 45

Germany (Marketing Film)

FM0550	*SW: Krieg der Sterne* Color/sound, 8 min.	30 - 45
FM0551	*SW: Krieg der Sterne* Color/sound, 17 min.	45 - 60
FM0555	*ESB: Das Imperium schlägt zurück* Color/sound, 4 min. (UFA)	25 - 40

Italy (IE International)

SW: Guerre Stellari Color/sound

FM0701	SOS nella galassia	45 - 75
FM0702	Trappola mortale	45 - 75
FM0703	Duello col Laser	45 - 75
FM0704	La cattura dell' Astronave	45 - 75
FM0705	Messaggio dallo Spazio	45 - 75
FM0706	La liberazione di Leia	45 - 75
FM0707	Battaglia spaziale	45 - 75

Japan (Fuji Film)

FM0850	*SW* Color/sound, 8 min.	45 - 60
FM0851	*SW* Color/Sound, 17 min.	75 - 125

FM0010   FM0020   FM0040   FM0068   FM0072   FM0460

FM0075   FM0550   FM0551   FM0555   FM0850   FM0851

FM0701　FM0702　FM0703　FM0704　FM0705　FM0706　FM0707

FM1001　　　FM2620　　　　FM2670　　　　FM2820

FM1003　　　　　FM3001　　　　　　FM3010

FILMSTRIPS/PROJECTORS

Kenner's *Star Wars* movie viewer was crank-operated and designed for special cartridges containing Super 8 film. One cartridge was packed with the viewer and others were available for separate purchase. Kenner also made "Give a Show" projectors with strips of rudimentary "slides" to tell a story. Viewers and projectors were also sold in other countries.

Movie Viewers (Kenner Products)

FM1001	*SW* Movie Viewer w/"May the Force..." cassette	25 - 60
FM1002	Destroy Death Star cassette	10 - 20
FM1003	Danger at the Cantina	10 - 20
FM1004	Battle in Hyperspace	10 - 20
FM1005	Assault on Death Star	10 - 20

France (Meccano)

FM2620	*SW: La Guerre des Etoiles* Cinevue w/cassette	25 - 50

Germany

FM2670	*SW: Kreig der Sterne* Cinevue w/cassette	30 - 65

Japan (Nakajima)

FM2820	*SW* Movie Viewer w/one of three cassettes (package is numbered 1, 2 or 3)	35 - 60

SLIDE PROJECTORS

FM3000	*SW* Give-a-Show Projector (Kenner Products)	25 - 45
FM3001	*ESB* Give-a-Show Projector w/Scooby Doo	30 - 50
FM3005	*ESB* Give-a-Show Projector (Kenner)	20 - 40
FM3010	*Ewoks* Give-a-Show Projector (Kenner)	15 - 30

Australia (Toltoys)

FM3700	*SW* Give-A-Show Projector	45 - 55

England (Chad Valley)

FM3750	*SW* Slide Projector Set (box w/pop-up battle scene)	45 - 75

Italy (Harbert)

FM3800	*SW* Projettore festacolor (slide projector)	25 - 45

SLIDES

Slides of trilogy scenes, or reference shots of props or characters, can occasionally be found. Some are stamped with official Lucasfilm markings, meaning that they were originally issued to the press or a merchandiser. Such marked slides generally sell for $5 to $10 each.

TRAILERS

Twentieth Century Fox Film, through National Screen Service, made more than a dozen different trailers to promote the upcoming films of the trilogy and their re-release. They can be purchased mostly from film dealers in the 35 mm format, although some were released in the wider 70 mm format. The ideal way to find them is on small plastic cores, perhaps even with the National Screen Service outer paper tag still attached. Trilogy trailers generally run from $25 to $50, although the 70 mm *Revenge* trailer could top $200.

VIDEO

The *Star Wars* trilogy helped launch the home video age. Many who were born after the first film played in theaters have come to love the trilogy by playing the tapes—and now video disks—over and over again. The first and rarest *Star Wars* cassette came from 20th Century-Fox Video (before it became CBS-Fox Video, only to revert to Fox Video in the early 1990s). The 1982 cassette comes in a plastic case with a pasted-on label, with "Video Rental Library" in large letters on front, back and spine. You couldn't buy this tape for love or money—although you might be able to find one of the rare unplayed ones today, still shrink-wrapped, for $100 to $200. The rarest disks are the now obsolete RCA CED Videodisks. Foreign versions of the videos, in different scanning formats, dubbed or sub-titled, are abundant. Since most of the videos remain in production, there are few "rare" ones, and cassette collecting hasn't become a nostalgic pastime yet—but give it time.

Video Cassettes (Fox or CBS-Fox Video)

FM5001	*SW* Video Rental Library 1982 plastic-case	100 - 200
FM5002	*SW* First sale version, "drawer" case (1982)	35 - 45
FM5005	*SW* (CBS-Fox Video)	15 - 30
FM5010	The Making of *Star Wars*/SP FX: *The Empire Strikes Back* Original 1983 "drawer" box	25 - 35
FM5011	FM5010, regular boxed version	10 - 25
FM5020	*ESB* (CBS-Fox Video)	10 - 25
FM5025	SP FX: *The Empire Strikes Back*	10 - 25
FM5030	*ROTJ*	10 - 25
FM5035	Classic Creatures: *Return of the Jedi*	10 - 20
FM5036	From *SW* to *Jedi:* The Making of a Saga, 3 package designs, ea.	10 - 20
FM5040	*SW* Trilogy, box and slipcase w/new packaging for all three cassettes (1990)	35 - 45

FM3750 FM3800   FM5005 FM5020 FM5050

FM5055 FM5066 FM5072 FM5081 FM6030 FM6330 FM6333 FM6340

FM5045	*SW* Trilogy Special Collectors edition: Letterboxed versions of the 3 films; "From *SW* to Jedi," book, certificate, hologram on gift box	85 - 100
FM5050	*SW* Trilogy boxed set, 1996	40 - 60
FM5051	*SW*, 1996	10 - 15
FM5052	*ESB*, 1996	10 - 15
FM5053	*ROTJ*, 1996	10 - 15
FM5055	The Making of *Star Wars*, Corn Pops premium	15 - 25
FM5056	*SWSE* boxed set	25 - 30
FM5057	*SWSE* boxed set (letterbox)	35 - 40

MGM/UA Home Video Cassettes

FM5060	The Ewok Adventure	10 - 20
FM5061	*Ewoks: The Battle for Endor*	10 - 20

The *SW* Trilogy Animated Collection (J2 Communications)

FM5070	*Droids: The White Witch/Escape into Terror*	8 - 15
FM5071	*Droids: The Lost Prince/The New King*	8 - 15
FM5072	*Droids: The Pirates and the Prince*	4 - 10
FM5080	*Ewoks: Cries of the Trees/The Tree of Light*	8 - 15
FM5081	*Ewoks: The Haunted Village/Blue Harvest*	8 - 15

FM5082	*Ewoks: The Tree of Light*	4 - 10
France		
FM6030	*Les Ewoks: Épisode N° 1*	8 - 16
Japan		
FM6325	*SW* "Best Library"	20 - 40
FM6326	*ESB* "Best Library"	20 - 40
FM6327	*ROTJ* "Best Library"	20 - 40
FM6330	*Classic Creatures* (VAP Inc.)	25 - 45
FM6333	From *SW* to *Jedi*: The Making of a Saga (VAP)	25 - 45
FM6340	*Droids*: Volume 1 (CBS/Fox)	10 - 20
FM6350	*Ewoks*: Volume 1 (CBS/Fox)	10 - 20

Video Disks (RCA CED system)

FM6500	*SW*	25 - 50
FM6501	*ESB*	25 - 50
FM6502	The Making of *SW*; SP FX: *ESB*	35 - 70
FM6505	*ROTJ* (2 disk set)	75 - 100

CBS-Fox Video laser disks

FM7010	*SW* standard play	25 - 65
FM7011	*SW* extended play	25 - 45
FM7012	*SW* wide screen, extended play	25 - 70
FM7020	*ESB* standard play	25 - 65
FM7021	*ESB* extended play	25 - 45
FM7022	*ESB* wide screen, extended play	25 - 70
FM7030	The Making of *SW*; SP FX: *ESB*	45 - 100
FM7041	*ROTJ* extended play	25 - 45
FM7042	*ROTJ* wide screen, extended play	25 - 70
FM7050	Trilogy Collectors' Edition: wide screen, THX sound, standard play, added materials, booklet and book	185 - 250

MGM-UA Home Video laser disks

FM8000	The Ewok Adventure	15 - 25
FM8011	*Ewoks: The Battle for Endor*	15 - 25
Japan		
FM9010	*SW*, extended play	45 - 65
FM9011	*SW*, standard play	65 - 95

FM6325 FM6326 FM6327

FM7011 FM7021 FM7041 FM9011

FO0050

FO0053

FO0065

FO0060

FO0060

FO0060

FO0060

FO0070

FO0075

FO0080

FO1025

FO1026

Stickers for FO1027

FO1028   FO1027

FO1225

FO1230

FO1950, 51, 52

FM9020	*ESB*, extended play	45 - 65
FM9021	*ESB*, standard play	65 - 95
FM9025	The Making of *SW*; SP FX: *ESB*	45 - 65
FM9030	*ROTJ*, extended play	45 - 65
FM9031	*ROTJ*, standard play	65 - 95
FM9035	*Classic Creatures*	45 - 65
FM9037	From *SW* to *Jedi*: The Making of a Saga	45 - 65
FM9040	Trilogy Collectors' Edition	300 - 450

FOOD CONTAINERS/PREMIUMS
See also—**POSTERS; STORE DISPLAYS; TOYS: Action Figures**

After overcoming some initial reluctance, Lucasfilm licensed *Star Wars* trilogy themes and characters to the food and beverage industry worldwide. Mostly, the representations were confined to the packaging or involved a mail-in or in-pack premium offer. But occasionally, the products themselves took on *SW* shapes—ranging from marshmallow candies in England to cookies and vitamins in the U.S. While some collectors still have, intact, full boxes of cookies from 1983 or even Japanese rice snacks from 1978, the prices listed below are for empty containers, packaging or premiums in as fresh and clean condition as possible. For some items, such as cereal boxes, there are even a few examples available of box "flats"—the printed cardboard sheets before they are folded and glued. We would consider such rarities "gem mint," valued at a 50% to 100% premium over the listed prices.

Among the earliest and rarest items is a Coca-Cola/Burger Chef set of seven different *SW* Fun Meal trays. These cardstock trays had punch-out figures, vehicles and games and, for a collector, must be in the unpunched state. There was also a matching table card promoting the offer as well as extensive in-store displays and signs.

In 1997, PepsiCo products featured *Star Wars* characters on their products worldwide for about six months, crossing over into a wide variety of Pepsi and Frito-Lay products, including beverages, snack foods, premiums from fast food restaurants, and an exclusive action figure tie-in with Kenner. Finding them all is a real challenge, since a vast number of new items were created in a very short period of time.

BEVERAGES
FO0049	*ROTJ* Hi-C cans w/droids and T-shirt & cap offer	15 - 30
FO0050	Hi-C label only	3 - 5
FO0051	Hi-C premium *ROTJ* T-shirt	10 - 20
FO0052	Hi-C premium *ROTJ* cap	10 - 20
FO0053	Hi-C *ROTJ* double sticker sheet mail-in offer	3 - 5
FO0060	Pepsi products 24-packs, each	5 - 10
FO0065	Pepsi products 12-packs, each	3 - 5
FO0070	Pepsi products 2-liter bottles, each	2 - 5
FO0075	Pepsi products 20 oz bottles, each	2 - 5
FO0080	Darth Vader glow-in-the-dark cup	3 - 5

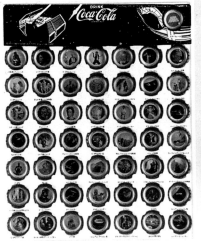

FO1852

FO1851

FO1310/FO1365

FO1370

FO2010

FO2015

FO2025

FO2030

FO2041

FO2042

FO2043

FO2045

FO2046

Australia (Sunburst Regency Foods Pty Ltd.)

FO1025	Break boxed fruit drinks w/Ewok illustrations on back	2 - 4
FO1026	Plastic grocery bags w/Break ad & poster offer	2 - 5
FO1027	Break *Ewok Adventure* build-a-poster and stickers	15 - 35
FO1028	Display ad for poster offer	4 - 8

Hong Kong (Coca Cola Export) Sprite *ESB* premiums

FO1225	Book marks, ea.	3 - 5
FO1230	Rulers, ea.	4 - 10
FO1235	Book covers, ea.	4 - 10
FO1240	Badges w/Luke, C-3PO & R2-D2, Leia, Han, Vader, ea.	3 - 8

Japan

FO1310	*SW* Inside of crowns, or tops of bottle-caps: 50 different color photos on underside (Coke, Fanta, Sprite), ea.	5 - 10
FO1365	Display tray for FO0310 w/Death Star, TIE ftr.	75 - 125
FO1370	R2-D2/Coca Cola premium radio	750 - 1,500

Singapore (Coca-Cola Export) Sprite *ESB*

FO1825	T-shirts w/C-3PO, Darth Vader, *ESB* logo, Leia	5 - 15
FO1830	Poster	5 - 10
FO1835	Pen and pencil cases	5 - 10

Spain (Concessiones de Bebidas Caronicas)

FO1850	Konga cola w/*ROTJ* action figure giveaway label	3 - 5
FO1851	Display ad for Konga cola giveaway	4 - 6
FO1852	Konga cola ceiling dangler	10 - 15

Sweden (Spendrups Bryggeri AB)

FO1950-52	Jedi Läsk carbonated drinks w/labels of Yoda, Luke & Leia, Paploo & neck band w/Yoda, ea.	10 - 15

See also—**CUPS/GLASSES—COLLECTOR'S**

CANDY

FO2010	*SW* Nestlé chocolate bar wrappers and Nestlé's Quik w/on pack promotion for *SW* pendant, ea.	10 - 20
FO2015	*ESB* dimensional candy containers (Topps), full box	30 - 45
FO2016	Individual containers, ea.	1 - 3
FO2025	*ESB*-Yoda series candy containers, full box	30 - 45
FO2026	Individual containers, ea.	1 - 3
FO2030	*ROTJ* dimensional candy containers (Topps), full box	30 - 50
FO2031	Individual containers, ea.	1 - 3

ESB photo cards on 6-pack cartons of Hershey products (uncut)

FO2041	Milk Chocolate: C-3PO & R2-D2	10 - 25
FO2042	Milk Chocolate w/almond: Chewie	10 - 25
FO2043	Kit Kat: Luke on tauntaun	10 - 25
FO2044	Whatchamacallit: Darth Vader	10 - 25
FO2045	Reese's Peanut Butter Cups: Boba Fett	10 - 25
FO2046	Reese's Crunchy Peanut Butter Cups: Darth Vader	10 - 25

PEZ dispensers, carded (2 card variations)

FO2201	Stormtrooper	3 - 6
FO2202	Darth Vader	2 - 3
FO2203	C-3PO	2 - 3
FO2204	Yoda	2 - 3
FO2205	Chewbacca	2 - 3

PEZ dispensers, bagged

FO2211	Stormtrooper	3 - 6
FO2212	Darth Vader	2 - 3
FO2213	C-3PO	2 - 3
FO2214	Yoda	2 - 3

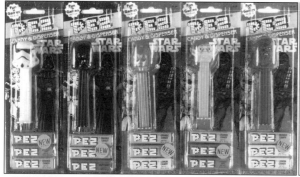

FO2201   FO2202   FO2203   FO2204   FO2205

FO2211-15

FO2216

FO3010

FO3110, 11

FO3011

FO3130

FO3131   FO3132

FO3133

FO3134

Jelly Shapes from FO3131-34

FO3150

FO3300

Mini-toys from FO3302 & FO3303

FO2215 Chewbacca	2 - 3	
FO2216 PEZ Display Box	10 - 20	
Australia (Red Tulip Chocolates)		
FO3010 *ESB* jelly candies: C-3PO, R2-D2 or Darth, ea.	5 - 10	
FO3011 *ESB* suckers (Red Tulip), ea.	5 - 10	
Costa Rica (Salvesa)		
FO3050 *SW* lollipops, ea.	3 - 5	
England		
FO3100 *SW* Mallow Shapes: box w/C-3PO, R2-D2,		
Darth Vader (Tavener Rutledge Ltd.), box	5 - 15	
FO3110 *ESB* Chewbar (Trebor Sharps Ltd.), carton	15- 35	
FO3111 Individual Chewbars, ea.	1 - 2	
FO3115 *ESB* Smarties chocolate candy (Rowntree-Mackintosh)	3 - 5	
FO3120 *ROTJ* sugar and chocolate candy (Maynards)	3 - 5	
FO3130 *SW* chocolate shapes (Kinnerton Confectionery)	2 - 4	

Jelly Shapes (Kinnerton Confectionery Ltd., 1996-97)		
FO3131 R2-D2 (metal cannister)	5 - 7	
FO3132 R2-D2 (paperboard box)	2 - 4	
FO3133 R2-D2 tin w/plastic topper	3 - 7	
FO3134 Darth Vader tin w/plastic topper	3 - 7	
Finland (Halva)		
FO3150 *SW* licorice: Darth Vader on pack front, other		
characters on back	3 - 5	
France (Nestlé Co.)		
FO3200 *SW* Nestlé Crunch bar wrappers	3 - 5	
Greece (Vasilios Dagiacos)		
FO3270 *ROTJ* chocolate wafers	3 - 5	
FO3271 *ROTJ* collector cards in wafers packs, ea.	1 - 2	
Italy (LIF-SUD SpA)		
FO3290 *SW* licorice twists	3 - 5	

| FO3460 | FO3465 | FO3470 | FO3475 |

| FO3100 | FO3615 | FO3631-34 | FO3641 |

FO3650

FO3680   FO3700

Japan

FO3300	*SW* choco-bowl w/stamp or mini-toy (Meija Seika Co.)	15 - 25
FO3302	*SW* rice snacks w/mini-toy in cup package (Morinaga and Co.)	15 - 25
FO3303	*SW* caramels w/mini-toy premium (Morinaga and Co.)	15 - 25

Singapore (Playthings)

FO3400	*ESB* lollipops, ea.	3 - 5

Spain

FO3450	SW candy or gum w/Droids images (General de Confiteria), ea.	2 - 4

Chupa Chups (1997)

FO3460	Fantasy Ball Gum Lollipops w/stickers, ea.	1 - 2
FO3465	Pen Pops, ea.	2 - 4
FO3470	Port-a-Chups, ea.	2 - 4
FO3475	Chupa Chups display boxes, ea.	10 - 20

CEREAL

Star Wars ads and premium offers appeared on General Mills cereals, mainly in 1978 (while General Mills owned Kenner Products). Kellogg's produced C-3POs cereal in 1984, but it didn't last much more than a year. However Kellogg's used its *Star Wars* license on other cereal boxes in Canada, Australia and New Zealand. Prices are for complete boxes.

General Mills

FO3610	*SW* Cheerios boxes w/various promotions/toy rebates	35 - 50
FO3612	*SW*/Cheerios kite mail-in	35 - 50
FO3615	*SW*/Hildebrandt mini-poster	5 - 15
FO3616	*SW*/Droids mini poster	5 - 15

FO3617	*SW* Star Destroyer mini poster	5 - 15
FO3618	*SW* X-wing. & characters mini-poster	5 - 15
FO3620	*SW*/Cheerios 16-oz tumbler w/photos (mail-in)	15 - 25
FO3630	*SW* Lucky Charms box showing mobiles	35 - 50
FO3631	X-wing fighter mobile (Lucky Charms)	10 - 25
FO3632	TIE fighter mobile (Lucky Charms)	10 - 25
FO3633	Millennium Falcon mobile (Lucky Charms)	10 - 25
FO3634	Landspeeder mobile (Lucky Charms)	10 - 25

Boxes promoting *SW* Stick-ons FO3641-46

FO3641	Trix	25 - 50
FO3642	Lucky Charms	25 - 50
FO3643	Cocoa Puffs	25 - 50
FO3644	Count Chocula	35 - 50
FO3645	Franken Berry	35 - 50
FO3646	Boo Berry	35 - 50
FO3650	*SW* Stick-ons, 3¼x4 inches, 16 different, ea.	3 - 6

Boxes promoting *SW* paper "cards" FO3671-76

FO3671	Crazy Cow, strawberry	35 - 50
FO3672	Crazy Cow, chocolate	35 - 50
FO3673	Cocoa Puffs	25 - 50
FO3674	Count Chocula	25 - 50
FO3675	Franken Berry	25 - 50
FO3676	Boo Berry	25 - 50
FO3680	*SW* white bordered paper "cards," 18 different, ea.	2 - 4
FO3700	*SW* white bordered paper cards, complete set in *SW* logo vinyl card case, mail-in offer	35 - 90

Kellogg's C-3PO's (complete boxes)

FO3701	Darth Vader mask	20 - 40

FO3701   FO3702   FO3703   FO3704   FO3705   FO3706

FO3720   FO3726   FO3727   FO4520   FO4521

FO4530   FO4531   FO3745   FO3746   FO3747

FO4603   FO4603   FO4603   FO4603   FO4603   FO4603   FO4603   FO4603

FO3702	Yoda mask	20 - 40
FO3703	Chewbacca mask	20 - 40
FO3704	Luke mask	20 - 40
FO3705	Stormtrooper mask	20 - 40
FO3706	C-3PO mask	20 - 40
FO3720	C-3POs box w/plastic rocket & stickers in box	15 - 30

Plastic "Rebel Rocket" w/sticker sets FO3725-27

FO3725	R2-D2/Luke	15 - 30
FO3726	C-3PO/Darth	15 - 30
FO3727	Chewie/Stormtrooper	15 - 30
FO3730	C-3POs box w/*SW* Stick'R trading cards promotion	15 - 30
FO3731	*SW/ROTJ* Stick'R trading cards, 10 numbered blue bordered cards covered by white bordered sticker, ea.	2 - 4
FO3745	Kellogg's Froot Loops w/Han Solo mail-in offer	5 - 20
FO3746	Kellogg's Corn Pops w/Video Tape offer	5 - 10
FO3747	Kellogg's Apple Jacks w/comic offer	5 - 10

Australia

FO4500	*SW* Weeties cereal box (Nabisco Ltd.)	20 - 45
FO4501	*SW* mini-posters in Weeties boxes	5 - 10
FO4520	Kellogg's Corn Flakes and RiceBubbles w/*ROTJ* sweepstakes promotion	20 - 45
FO4521	Action picture name decoder discs w/silver rub-off to reveal character name for sweepstakes, 16 diff., ea.	4 - 6
FO4530	Kellogg's *Ewok Adventure* promotion boxes: Froot Loops, Honey Smacks, or Coco Pops, ea.	5 - 12
FO4531	Kellogg's *Ewok Adventure* punch-out game and trading cards, 16 different designs, ea.	3 - 5

Canada

FO4601	General Mills Golden Grahams w/*ROTJ* poster offer	25 - 35
FO4603	Kellogg's Cereal boxes, 1997, 8 different, ea.	10 - 30

General Mills boxes w/*SW/ESB/ROTJ* booklet and poster offer:

FO4605	Cheerios	45 - 60
FO4606	Honey Nut Cheerios	45 - 60
FO4607	Trix	45 - 60
FO4608	Lucky Charms	45 - 60
FO4609	Cocoa Puffs	45 - 60
FO4610	Count Chocula	45 - 60
FO4611	Franken Berry	25 - 35

General Mills 8-page color premium booklets FO4621-28

FO4621	*SW*	5 - 10
FO4622	*ESB*	5 - 10

FO4605

FO4621-28

FO4635

FO4636

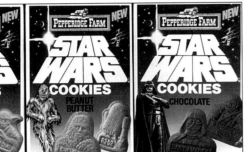

FO5001   FO5002   FO5003

FO5750

FO4623	The Rebel Alliance	5 - 10
FO4624	The Imperial force	5 - 10
FO4625	Jabba the Hutt	5 - 10
FO4626	Green Moon of Endor	5 - 10
FO4627	Rescue of Han Solo	5 - 10
FO4628	Battle w/the Empire	5 - 10
FO4635	Kellogg's C-3POs box w/offer for 20 trading cards	30 - 50
FO4636	C-3POs 20 in-box trading cards, (like U.S. set but cards replace stickers), ea.	4 - 8

See also—APPAREL: Hats, Caps, and Visors; POSTERS
England

FO4700	*SW* Shreddies box w/in-pack offer (Nabisco Ltd.)	35 - 45
FO4701	Letraset transfer sheet in boxes of Shreddies	2 - 4

Spain

FO4950	Cheerios box w/in-pack offer	25 - 35
FO4951	*SW* booklet inside Cheerios	5 - 7

COOKIES/CAKES (Pepperidge Farm)
Cookie boxes (2 versions: Mail-in cup offer, photos of cookies)

FO5001	Vanilla - Rebel Alliance I	10 - 25
FO5002	Peanut Butter - Rebel Alliance II	10 - 25
FO5003	Chocolate - The Imperial Forces	10 - 25

See also—CUPS/GLASSES—COLLECTOR'S
Australia

FO5700	*SW* biscuits (Arnott's Biscuits Pty. Ltd.)	5 - 15

England

FO5750	*ROTJ* biscuits: (Burton's Gold Medal Biscuits)	5 - 15

France (Ceraliment Lu Brun)

FO5800	*ESB* Petit Brun Biscuits	4 - 12
FO5801	*ESB* premium on Petit Brun packages: 12 different plastic vacuum-molded squares of *ESB* characters, ea.	2 - 4

Italy

FO5850	Sweet biscuits (General Biscuits Italia)	3 - 8

FUN MEAL AND FAST FOOD-RELATED ITEMS

In addition to the classic Burger Chef Funmeal trays, a number of kids' meal promotions were run worldwide in conjunction with the 20th Anniversary and *Special Edition* release. One of the more prolific premiums available from this time is a set of four sipper cups which were available in Hawaii, Australia, Canada, Great Britain, and elsewhere. These were Taco Bell or KFC premiums depending on the country. Apart from Hawaii, they were not available at retail in the U.S., but many sets have been imported by collectors.

Australian Pizza Hut restaurants offered four PVC figures with cardboard backgrounds in 1995. These figures were made from Kenner *Action Masters* molds. Most notable is the Chewbacca figure, which was never produced for *Action Masters*. Quick restaurants in Australia produced a kids' meal box in 1996, and used Galoob *Micro Machines* as premiums.

SW Coke/Burger Chef Funmeal tray promotion FO6010-17

FO6010	Flight (game w/spinner)	15 - 40
FO6011	Darth Vader card game	15 - 40
FO6012	Landspeeder	15 - 40
FO6013	R2-D2 droid puppet	15 - 40
FO6014	TIE fighter	15 - 40
FO6015	C-3PO droid puppet	15 - 40
FO6016	X-wing fighter	15 - 40

Cookies from FO5001   Cookies from FO5002   Cookies from FO5003

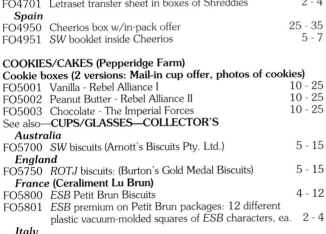

FO6010 FO6011 FO6012 FO6013 FO6014 FO6015 FO6016

FO6017 FO6031 FO6033 FO6034 FO6051 FO6052 FO6053 FO6054

FO6061 FO6062 FO6063 FO6064 FO6070

FO6073 FO6080 FO6081 FO6082 FO6101

FO6102 FO6103 FO6104 FO6105

FO6017	*SW* Fun Meal table tent	10 - 20
FO6030	*SW/ESB* Coke/Burger King set of 36 photo	
	trading cards, 3 perforated cards per panel	25 - 45
FO6031	*ESB* Coke/Burger King Darth Vader Frisbee promo	20 - 45
FO6032	*ESB* Coke/Burger King unused rub-off ticket	3 - 6
FO6033	*ESB* Coke/Burger King set of 48 photo stickers	35 - 45
FO6034	*ESB* Coke/Burger King 4-page album for stickers	15 - 25
Sipper Cups (Various PepsiCo Restraunts, Hawaii & Worldwide)		
FO6051	Stormtrooper	5 - 15
FO6052	Darth Vader	5 - 15
FO6053	R2-D2	5 - 15
FO6054	C-3PO	5 - 15
Pizza Hut (1997)		
FO6061	Darth Vader pizza box	2 - 5
FO6062	Stormtrooper pizza box	2 - 5
FO6063	R2-D2 pizza box	2 - 5
FO6064	C-3PO pizza box	2 - 5
FO6070	Take-out Cup	2 - 5

FO6073	Placemat	1 - 2
FO6080	*SW* Premium Poster	2 - 5
FO6081	*ESB* Premium Poster	2 - 10
FO6082	*ROTJ* Premium Poster	2 - 5
Taco Bell (1997)		
FO6101	Puzzle Cube	1 - 3
FO6102	Millennium Falcon Gyro	1 - 3
FO6103	R2-D2 Playset	1 - 3
FO6104	Magic Cube (Darth Vader/Yoda)	1 - 3
FO6105	Floating Cloud City	1 - 3
FO6106	Balancing Boba Fett	1 - 3
FO6107	Exploding Death Star Spinner	3 - 7
FO6108	Yoda (Under 3 Premium)	3 - 7
FO6110	*SW* fun meal box	1 - 4
FO6111	*ESB* fun meal box	1 - 4
FO6112	*ROTJ* fun meal box	1 - 4
FO6115	Large cup (Darth Vader)	1 - 3
FO6116	Medium cup (C-3PO)	1 - 3

FO6106

FO6107

FO6108

Insert from FO6101-08

FO6110

FO6111

FO6112

FO6115   FO6116   FO6117

FO6121

FO6122

FO6123

FO6201   FO6202   FO6203   FO6204

FO6211

FO6117	Small cup (R2-D2)	1 - 2
FO6121	Large bag (C-3PO)	1 - 2
FO6122	Small bag (R2-D2)	1 - 2
FO6123	Food wrapper (C-3PO)	1 - 2

Australia

Pizza Hut PVC figures with backgrounds FO6201-04

FO6201	Chewbacca	2 - 5
FO6202	Darth Vader	2 - 5
FO6203	C-3PO	2 - 5
FO6204	R2-D2	2 - 5
FO6211	Kids' Meal box	3 - 7

England

KFC Kids' Meal Premiums

FO6251	AT-ST Walker	2 - 4
FO6252	AT-AT w/AT-AT driver	2 - 4

FO6251

FO6252

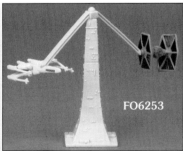

FO6253

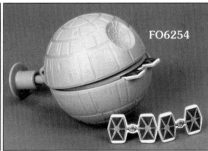

FO6254

FO6255

FO6256

FO6260

FO6301	FO6302	FO6303	FO6304	FO6305
FO6501	FO6507 FO6501	FO6502	FO6503	FO6504 FO6511
FO6512	FO6515	FO6525 FO6526	FO6530	FO6531
FO6610 FO6600 FO6600	FO6660	FO6871 FO6872	FO6891	FO6892 FO6901

FO6253	X-wing/TIE Fighter spinner	2 - 4
FO6254	Shooting Death Star	2 - 4
FO6255	Sandcrawler w/R2-D2	2 - 4
FO6256	Darth Vader Spinner	2 - 4
FO6260	Kids' meal box	1 - 3

France
Pizza Hut Kids' Meal Premiums (also available in UK)

FO6301	Death Star 3-D puzzle	2 - 4
FO6302	Han Solo in Carbonite puzzle	2 - 4
FO6303	Repair C-3PO magnetic puzzle	2 - 4
FO6304	MIllennium Falcon Asteroid Field game	2 - 4
FO6305	Placemat	1 - 2

ICE CREAM/ICE TREAT

Boxes and individual wrappers for licensed Australian iced treats are beautifully printed and make for unusual collectibles. A quantity of the unused wrappers—in various colors and designs that almost look like stone litho—has made it to the collectors market.

Australia
Iced treats in boxes w/cut-outs on the back, FO6501-12 (Streets)

FO6501	*SW* Luke, Chewie, Tusken Raider	15 - 45
FO6502	*SW* Darth X-wing., R2-D2	15 - 45
FO6503	*SW* Leia, C-3PO, Star Destroyer	15 - 45
FO6504	*SW* Stormtrooper, Landspeeder, Jawas	15 - 45
FO6507	*SW* unused wrappers for iced treats	10 - 30
FO6511	*ESB* Luke, Tauntaun, Star Destroyer	15 - 45
FO6512	*ESB* Yoda, Boba Fett, AT-ATs	15 - 45
FO6515	*ESB* unused wrappers for iced treats	10 - 30
FO6525	*ROTJ* iced confection w/Jedi Jelly (Pauls/Peters/ Australian United Foods), boxes, ea.	10 - 25
FO6526	Unused wrappers for Iced Treat w/Jedi Jelly	10 - 25
FO6528	*ROTJ* popsicles (Peters), box	10 - 25
FO6529	Unused wrappers for *ROTJ* popsicles, ea.	10 - 25

| FO6530 | *SW* Popsicles (Pauls, 1983), box | 10 - 25 |
| FO6531 | Unused wrappers for *SW* Popsicles | 10 - 25 |

Chile
| FO6580 | *ESB* Ice Cream w/collectible stamps (Savory) | 10 - 20 |

England (Lyons Maid)
FO6600	*SW* Ice Lolly w/characters on back of wrapper, ea.	5 - 10
FO6610	*ESB* ice lolly w/characters on back of wrapper, ea.	5 - 15
FO6611	*ESB* Ice Lolly w/sticker under a coat of wax, ea.	5 - 15

France (Mota Ice Cream)
| FO6650 | *ESB* ice cream treats, wrappers | 5 - 10 |
| FO6660 | *ESB* poster and 30 stickers (premium offer) | 25 - 55 |

Netherlands (Campina Ijsfabbrieken B.V.)
| FO6850 | *ROTJ* Ice Confection, Darth Vader, X-wing, snowspeeder on wrapper | 3 - 8 |
| FO6851 | *ROTJ* premium stickers: Darth & Royal Guard, Stormtrooper, Luke & Yoda, Darth, C-3PO & R2-D2, or Star Destroyer, ea. | 2 - 3 |

New Zealand (Tip Top Ice Cream)
FO6870	*SW/ESB* R2-D2 Space Ice wrapper	2 - 5
FO6871	R2-D2 Race in Space Galaxy Game (paper premium)	10 - 25
FO6872	*SW* stickers w/each R2 Space Ice, 15 different, ea.	2 - 4

ESB cut-out paper masks, premium, FO6891-94
FO6891	C-3PO	5 - 20
FO6892	Darth Vader	5 - 20
FO6893	Stormtrooper	5 - 20
FO6894	Chewbacca	5 - 20
FO6895	*ESB* frozen confections, R2-D2 & Darth Vader wrapper	3 - 5
FO6900	*ROTJ* frozen confections w/Jedi Jelly, wrapper	3 - 5
FO6901	*ROTJ*—4 "Jedi Jelly" in-pack stickers, ea.	2 - 4

Singapore/Malaysia (Walls)
| FO6920 | *ESB* Ice Cream wrapper | 3 - 7 |
| FO6925 | *ESB* Ice Lolly wrapper | 3 - 7 |

Sweden (Hemglass)
| FO6950 | Star Mint Ice Cream | 3 - 5 |

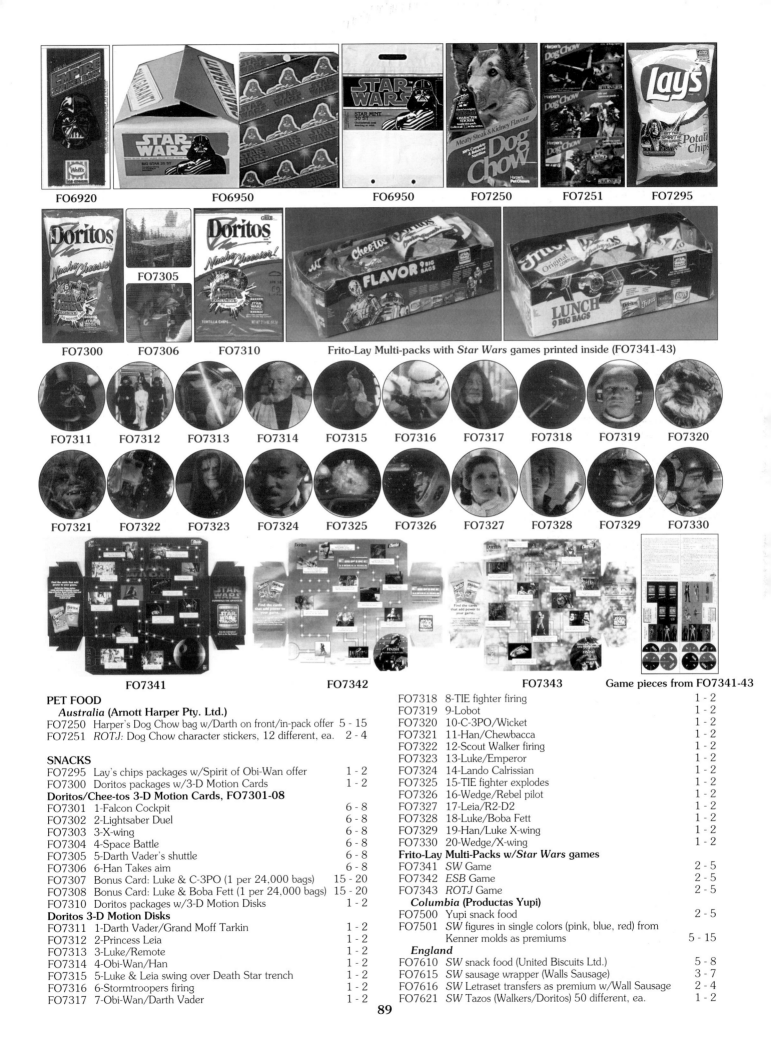

FO6920 FO6950 FO6950 FO7250 FO7251 FO7295

FO7300 FO7306 FO7310

FO7305

Frito-Lay Multi-packs with *Star Wars* games printed inside (FO7341-43)

FO7311 FO7312 FO7313 FO7314 FO7315 FO7316 FO7317 FO7318 FO7319 FO7320

FO7321 FO7322 FO7323 FO7324 FO7325 FO7326 FO7327 FO7328 FO7329 FO7330

FO7341 FO7342 FO7343 Game pieces from FO7341-43

PET FOOD

Australia (Arnott Harper Pty. Ltd.)

FO7250	Harper's Dog Chow bag w/Darth on front/in-pack offer	5 - 15
FO7251	*ROTJ:* Dog Chow character stickers, 12 different, ea.	2 - 4

SNACKS

FO7295	Lay's chips packages w/Spirit of Obi-Wan offer	1 - 2
FO7300	Doritos packages w/3-D Motion Cards	1 - 2

Doritos/Chee-tos 3-D Motion Cards, FO7301-08

FO7301	1-Falcon Cockpit	6 - 8
FO7302	2-Lightsaber Duel	6 - 8
FO7303	3-X-wing	6 - 8
FO7304	4-Space Battle	6 - 8
FO7305	5-Darth Vader's shuttle	6 - 8
FO7306	6-Han Takes aim	6 - 8
FO7307	Bonus Card: Luke & C-3PO (1 per 24,000 bags)	15 - 20
FO7308	Bonus Card: Luke & Boba Fett (1 per 24,000 bags)	15 - 20
FO7310	Doritos packages w/3-D Motion Disks	1 - 2

Doritos 3-D Motion Disks

FO7311	1-Darth Vader/Grand Moff Tarkin	1 - 2
FO7312	2-Princess Leia	1 - 2
FO7313	3-Luke/Remote	1 - 2
FO7314	4-Obi-Wan/Han	1 - 2
FO7315	5-Luke & Leia swing over Death Star trench	1 - 2
FO7316	6-Stormtroopers firing	1 - 2
FO7317	7-Obi-Wan/Darth Vader	1 - 2
FO7318	8-TIE fighter firing	1 - 2
FO7319	9-Lobot	1 - 2
FO7320	10-C-3PO/Wicket	1 - 2
FO7321	11-Han/Chewbacca	1 - 2
FO7322	12-Scout Walker firing	1 - 2
FO7323	13-Luke/Emperor	1 - 2
FO7324	14-Lando Calrissian	1 - 2
FO7325	15-TIE fighter *explodes*	1 - 2
FO7326	16-Wedge/Rebel pilot	1 - 2
FO7327	17-Leia/R2-D2	1 - 2
FO7328	18-Luke/Boba Fett	1 - 2
FO7329	19-Han/Luke X-wing	1 - 2
FO7330	20-Wedge/X-wing	1 - 2

Frito-Lay Multi-Packs w/*Star Wars* games

FO7341	*SW* Game	2 - 5
FO7342	*ESB* Game	2 - 5
FO7343	*ROTJ* Game	2 - 5

Columbia (Productas Yupi)

FO7500	Yupi snack food	2 - 5
FO7501	*SW* figures in single colors (pink, blue, red) from Kenner molds as premiums	5 - 15

England

FO7610	*SW* snack food (United Biscuits Ltd.)	5 - 8
FO7615	*SW* sausage wrapper (Walls Sausage)	3 - 7
FO7616	*SW* Letraset transfers as premium w/Wall Sausage	2 - 4
FO7621	*SW* Tazos (Walkers/Doritos) 50 different, ea.	1 - 2

FO7621

FO7622

FO8420

FO8420

FO7700

FO7802

FO7901

FO9530

FO7622	Tazo Force Pack album (Walkers/Doritos)	5 - 10
France (Gringoire Brossard)		
FO7650	Snack cakes	2 - 4
Japan (Morinaga)		
FO7700	Slim Stick (breadstick) w/mini-toy	10 - 25
Netherlands (Preservenbedrijj B.V.)		
FO7800	ESB UFO's Potato Chips bag	3 - 5
FO7801	UFO's ESB poster (free at point of purchase)	10 - 20
FO7802	UFO's ESB six round stickers to put on poster: Chewbacca, Yoda, Darth Vader, Luke, Leia, C-3PO, ea.	2 - 4
New Zealand (General Foods Corp.)		
FO7900	ESB Twinkies snack cakes	2 - 5
FO7901	ESB round stickers w/Twinkies: Yoda, Luke, Chewbacca, Leia, Darth Vader, C-3PO, ea.	2 - 4
Portugal (Panrico S.A.)		
FO8100	SW snack cakes	2 - 4
FO8101	SW polyethylene figurines w/snack cakes	5 - 15
Puerto Rico (Frito Lay of Puerto Rico)		
FO8200	ESB Frito Lay chips	2 - 3
FO8201	ESB poster and plastic stickers in pack to add on	5 - 15
Spain		
FO8400	SW cakes w/paper sheets w/characters (Nupa S.A.)	2 - 5
FO8420	Snacks w/in-pack Droids/Ewoks stickers (Crecspan S.A.)	1 - 2

YOGURT

England (Bridge Farm Dairies Ltd.)		
FO8500	SW Yogurt (ROTJ); 8 different plastic containers: Yoda, Ewoks, Luke, Darth, Ackbar, Chewie, Leia, or Jabba, ea.	4 - 10
Spain		
FO8850	Four posters and stickers (Yoplait Yogurt mail-in)	15 - 25

OTHER GROCERY STORE ITEMS

FO9000	SW bread promotion; Wonder Bread wrapper	20 - 45
FO9001	SW bread cards (Bakers Promotions), set of 16	15 - 30
FO9002	Individual cards, ea.	1 - 2
FO9020	SW vitamin tablets (Natural Balance) bottle	5 - 10

FO8500

Canada

FO9430	(Metric Media, Inc.) York peanut butter promotion: 6 circular ESB photo trading cards, ea.	3 - 6
England		
FO9500	SW school set w/Heinz Baked Beans w/Sausage labels (H.J. Heinz and Co.)	2 - 4

FO8850

FO9001

FO9650

FO9430   FO9630   FO9800

FT0010   FT0015

FT2530   FT2525

FT2710

FT3010   FT3011

FT3013   FT3014

FT3021   FT3025

FO9530	Dairylea cheese triangles, package w/Ewoks & Droids video offer (Kraft Foods Ltd.)	3 - 10
France		
FO9630	*ROTJ* mustard glass container (Amora), 4 diff., ea.	10 - 20
FO9635	La Vach qui Rit cheese, 18 stickers (Fromagerie Bel), set	25 - 35
Germany		
FO9650	*ESB* & *ROTJ* mustard containers, 6 per set (Hengstenberg Mustard), ea.	10 - 15
FO9660	*ROTJ* bubble gum w/*SW* pictures on wrappers (Fleer GmbH)	1 - 2
Spain		
FO9800	*ROTJ* pastry, 3 wrapper designs (Panrico S.A.), ea.	2- 4
FO9805	24 *ROTJ* stickers and 4 posters w/pastries, set	25 - 40
FO9850	Ready-mixed custards w/Ewoks on package (CPC Espana SA)	5 - 10

FOOTWEAR

Connecticut-based Clarks of England manufactured a large line of *Star Wars* shoes. They ranged from sandals to dress shoes, and many had *SW* characters embossed on the soles. The shoes came in colorful boxes, and toward the end of the line, the *ESB* logo replaced the *SW* logo. For a collector, the shoes themselves are worth little without the boxes and the special *SW* plastic bag packed inside most boxes to carry the shoes home. For *ROTJ*, Stride Rite had the license and made a line of mostly casual shoes, some of which also had characters on the soles. The shoe box served as a spacecraft hangar and each pair of shoes came with a thin cardboard punch-out sheet with stand-up figures of Lando, Darth Vader, C-3PO, R2-D2 and Luke. There is also a Stride Rite plastic bag. The value of unworn boots, sandals, shoes and sneakers in their original box with all related material ranges from about $20 to $125.

BOOTS (Stride Rite)

FT0010	Ewoks, black vinyl	See preceeding
FT0015	Darth Vader, black vinyl	paragraph for
Japan (Nippon Gohu Co.)		Footwear prices
FT1010	*SW* boots	
Spain (Calzados Nimer S.A.)		
FT1210	*SW* children's footwear	

SANDALS (Clarks)

FT2510 Cosmic Rambler: tan, blue, or red leather
FT2520 Landspeeder: blue, white, or tan leather
FT2525 Solar Racer: blue, white or tan leather
FT2530 Star Rider: amber, blue, silver, gold, or pink
  Australia (Fairlane Investments)
FT2710 *ESB* Darth, R2-D2, or C-3PO PVC thongs

SHOES (Clarks)

FT3010 C-3PO: navy suede/leather, brown suede/leather, burgundy leather, black and gold fabric
FT3011 Chewbacca: sand suede, blue denim brown leather
FT3013 Darth Vader: brown, navy leather
FT3014 Darth Vader Lives: tobacco, blue leather
FT3015 Princess Leia I: black, blue, white, tan leather
FT3020 Princess Leia II: blue, tobacco leather
FT3021 Princess Leia III: blue, tan leather
FT3025 R2-D2: navy, brown, black

FT3027

FT3031

FT3026

FT8005

FT6440 FT6450

FT8010

FT8011

FT8012

FT8014

FT8022

FT8013

FT8020

FT8232

FT8234

FT8235

FT8240

FT8250

FT5010   FT5012   FT5014   FT6010

FT6011   FT6012   FT6015   FT6016

FT6430   FT6431   FT6432   FT6433   FT6434

FT3026   Luke Skywalker: burgundy/blue/tan
FT3027   Stormtrooper: blue suede, green, or black suede
         w/white fabric
FT3031   Tusken Raider: chocolate & tobacco suede,
         brown leather
   Philippines (Master Footwear)
FT3510   *Ewoks* character shoes

SHOELACES (Stride Rite)

Shoelaces on cards were produced by Stride Rite for *ROTJ*, even though the first one has the *Star Wars* logo on the card. All others have the *ROTJ* logo on the card.

FT5010	*SW* logo blue outline on gray (*SW* logo on card)	1 - 3
FT5011	Red *SW* logo on gray, Vader head	1 - 3
FT5012	Red *ROTJ* logo on blue/white	1 - 3
FT5013	*SW* yellow logo outlined in red on blue w/spacecraft	1 - 3
FT5014	Blue *SW* logo outlined in red on blue w/droids	1 - 3
FT5015	Blue *Ewoks* & *ROTJ* logos on yellow w/Ewoks	1 - 3

SLIPPERS (Stride Rite)

FT6010	C-3PO and R2-D2 navy corduroy	5 - 12
FT6011	C-3PO and R2-D2 blue and white slipper socks	5 - 12
FT6012	Darth Vader red and white slipper socks	5 - 12
FT6015	Darth white and black slippers	5 - 12
FT6016	*Ewoks* blue and light blue slippers	3 - 10
FT6017	*Ewoks* pink and white slippers	3 - 10
FT6018	Wicket red and white slipper socks	3 - 10
	England	
FT6430	Ewok (British Shoe)	5 - 12
FT6431	Leia (British Shoe)	5 - 12

FT6432 Robots (British Shoe)

FT8251

FT6432	Robots (British Shoe)	5 - 12
FT6433	*Star Wars* (British Shoe)	5 - 12
FT6434	Darth Vader (British Shoe)	5 - 12
FT6435	Ewoks swing on rope (British Shoe)	3 - 10
FT6440	*SW* slippers, blue and red (Cleveley's)	5 - 12
FT6450	*SW* slippers (Marks & Spencer)	5 - 15
FT6455	*SW* slippers II (Marks & Spencer)	5 - 15
	Philippines (Master Footwear)	
FT6860	*Ewoks* characters, various designs	3 - 10

SNEAKERS
Clarks

FT8005	*SW*, blue	See Footwear paragraph
FT8010	C-3PO, red canvas	on page 87 for prices
FT8011	Darth Vader, royal blue canvas/silver trim, or	
	black canvas/silver trim	
FT8012	Darth Vader jogger: black suede/black nylon/yellow	
FT8013	TIE fighter jogger: royal blue suede/yellow nylon,	
	brown suede/beige nylon, gray suede/silver nylon	
FT8014	Luke, orange/blue canvas, yellow/black canvas	
FT8017	Princess Leia: white w/blue, green or yellow trim	
FT8020	R2-D2	
FT8022	The Force jogger, gold suede/red nylon, blue	
	suede/silver nylon, brown suede/beige nylon	

Stride Rite

FT8232	Darth Vader: navy suede
FT8233	Darth Vader: royal blue suede
FT8234	Ewoks, blue
FT8235	R2-D2 & C-3PO, gray suede w/blue
FT8236	R2-D2 & C-3PO, tan suede w/blue
FT8237	X-wing, blue
FT8240	Millennium Falcon
FT8250	Stride Rite shoe bag

FV1110

FV0121

FV1115

FV2010

FV2520   FV2523

FV3125   FV3130

FV3020

FV4010

FV4020

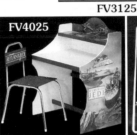
FV4025

FV4240

FV4710

FV5010

FV5011

FV5012

FV5060

FV5061

FT8251   Stride Rite shoe box
   Brazil (Sao Paulo Alpagatas SA)
FT8750   *SW* sneakers, various designs
   Japan (Nippon Gohu Co.)
FT9100   *SW* sneakers, various designs

FURNITURE

In the U.S, American Toy & Furniture sold a fairly extensive line of knock-down children's furniture, the kind that is shipped flat and must be assembled at home. The original line in 1983 had *ROTJ* designs, while the furniture the following year was mostly Ewoks-related. By far the most collectible item is the already assembled R2-D2 rolling toy chest. Some of the items were hard to find except through chain-store catalogs, but the boxes they were shipped in didn't have the usual colorful photographic tip-on sheets pasted to the front. The highest value on these items are assigned to furniture in unopened boxes with the color photos of the assembled contents.

BEDS
   Ireland (Kidnap Furniture Ltd.)
FV0120	Headboard: Darth Vader, Luke and stormtrooper	40 - 50
FV0121	Bed end: R2-D2, C-3PO & Ewoks	40 - 50

BOOKCASES/SHOWCASES (American Toy & Furniture)
FV1110	*ROTJ* bookcase/showcase	45 - 75
FV1115	Ewoks bookcase/toy chest	45 - 60

CHAIRS (AT&F)
FV2010	Wicket the Ewok rocker	45 - 60

   Australia (Brava Soft Furnishings)
FV2520	*ESB* beanbag chair	20 - 45
FV2522	*ROTJ* logo beanbag chair	20 - 45
FV2523	*ROTJ* beanbag chair, quilted w/vinyl back	20 - 45
FV2524	*ROTJ* Ewoks beanbag chair	20 - 35

CLOTHES RACKS
FV3020	Darth Vader, Luke & Darth dueling (AT&F)	35 - 55
FV3125	Max Rebo Band (Adam Joseph Industries)	20 - 45
FV3130	C-3PO (Adam Joseph Industries)	20 - 45

DESKS (AT&F)
FV4010	Wicket the Ewok activity desk w/bench	45 - 60
FV4020	*Ewoks* twin peg desk w/benches	45 - 60
FV4025	*ROTJ* desk and chair set	45 - 75

   Ireland (Kidnap Furn.)
FV4240	Darth Vader desk	45 - 70

EASELS (AT&F)
FV4710	*Ewoks*	45 - 60

LAMPS/NIGHT LIGHTS (Adam Joseph Industries)
FV5010	R2-D2	3 - 6
FV5011	C-3PO	3 - 6

93

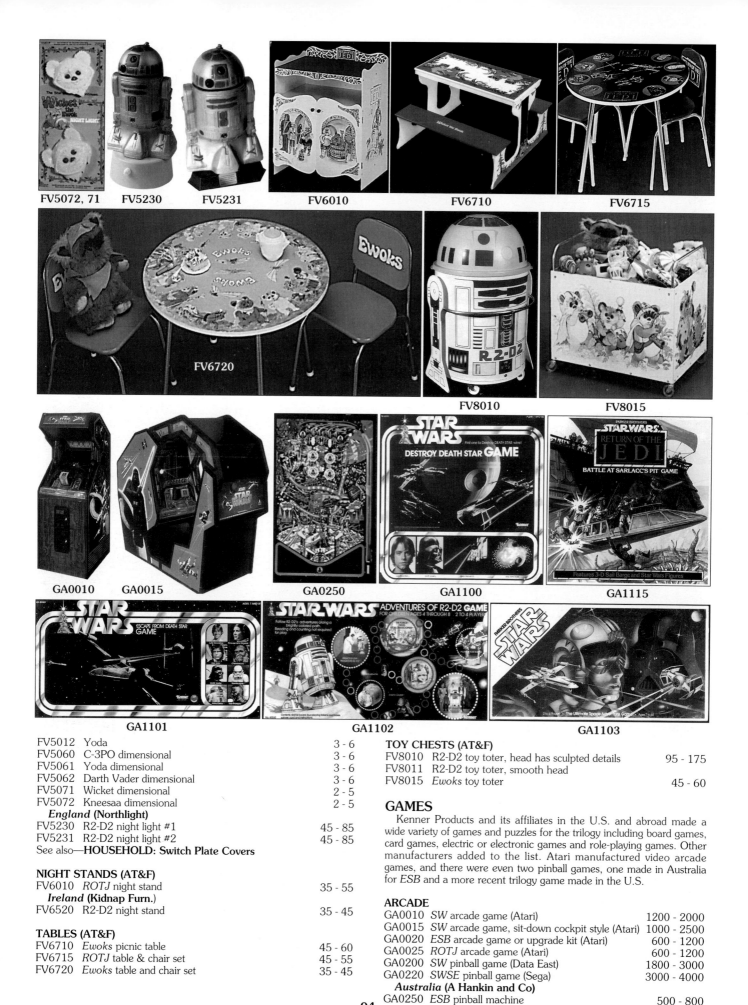

FV5072, 71   FV5230   FV5231   FV6010   FV6710   FV6715

FV6720

FV8010   FV8015

GA0010   GA0015   GA0250   GA1100   GA1115

GA1101   GA1102   GA1103

FV5012	Yoda	3 - 6
FV5060	C-3PO dimensional	3 - 6
FV5061	Yoda dimensional	3 - 6
FV5062	Darth Vader dimensional	3 - 6
FV5071	Wicket dimensional	2 - 5
FV5072	Kneesaa dimensional	2 - 5

England (Northlight)

| FV5230 | R2-D2 night light #1 | 45 - 85 |
| FV5231 | R2-D2 night light #2 | 45 - 85 |

See also—HOUSEHOLD: Switch Plate Covers

NIGHT STANDS (AT&F)

| FV6010 | *ROTJ* night stand | 35 - 55 |

Ireland (Kidnap Furn.)

| FV6520 | R2-D2 night stand | 35 - 45 |

TABLES (AT&F)

FV6710	*Ewoks* picnic table	45 - 60
FV6715	*ROTJ* table & chair set	45 - 55
FV6720	*Ewoks* table and chair set	35 - 45

TOY CHESTS (AT&F)

FV8010	R2-D2 toy toter, head has sculpted details	95 - 175
FV8011	R2-D2 toy toter, smooth head	
FV8015	*Ewoks* toy toter	45 - 60

GAMES

Kenner Products and its affiliates in the U.S. and abroad made a wide variety of games and puzzles for the trilogy including board games, card games, electric or electronic games and role-playing games. Other manufacturers added to the list. Atari manufactured video arcade games, and there were even two pinball games, one made in Australia for *ESB* and a more recent trilogy game made in the U.S.

ARCADE

GA0010	*SW* arcade game (Atari)	1200 - 2000
GA0015	*SW* arcade game, sit-down cockpit style (Atari)	1000 - 2500
GA0020	*ESB* arcade game or upgrade kit (Atari)	600 - 1200
GA0025	*ROTJ* arcade game (Atari)	600 - 1200
GA0200	*SW* pinball game (Data East)	1800 - 3000
GA0220	*SWSE* pinball game (Sega)	3000 - 4000

Australia (A Hankin and Co)

| GA0250 | *ESB* pinball machine | 500 - 800 |

GA1110   GA1112   GA1120   GA1121

GA1470   GA1472   GA1488   GA1490

GA1495   GA1600   GA1606   GA2105

GA1650   GA2805   GA3051   GA3052   GA3053   GA3260   GA3300

GA1605

GA3900   GA3900

GA2470   GA2472   GA2475

BOARD

GA1100	Destroy Death Star (Kenner/Parker Bros.)	15 - 40
GA1101	Escape From Death Star (Kenner/Parker Bros.)	10 - 35
GA1102	Adventures of R2-D2 (Kenner/Parker Bros.)	10 - 25
GA1103	*Star Wars* (Kenner/Parker Bros.)	10 - 30
GA1110	Yoda the Jedi Master (Kenner/Parker Bros.)	10 - 25
GA1112	Hoth Ice Planet Adventure.(Kenner/Parker Bros.)	10 - 30
GA1115	Battle at Sarlacc's Pit (Kenner/Parker Bros.)	10 - 30
GA1120	Wicket the Ewok (Kenner/Parker Bros.)	5 - 15
GA1121	The Ewoks Save the Trees.(Kenner/Parker Bros.)	5 - 10
GA1470	Assault on Hoth (West End Games)	20 - 30
GA1472	Battle for Endor (West End Games)	20 - 30
GA1475	Escape from the Death Star (West End Games)	20 - 30
GA1488	Death Star Assault (Parker Bros.)	15 - 25
GA1490	*Star Wars* Video Board Game (Parker Bros.)	20 - 30
GA1495	*Star Wars* Monopoly (Limited Edition)	35 - 60
GA1496	*Star Wars* Monopoly (Unlimited Edition)	25 - 30

France		
GA1600	*les Ewoks Sauvons la forêt* (Editions Volumétrix)	15 - 30
GA1605	*les Ewoks: Dominos* (Editions Volumétrix)	15 - 30
GA1606	*les Ewoks: Formes et Couleurs*	15 - 30
Germany **(Parker)**		
GA1650	Krieg der Sterne	15 - 35
Italy **(General Mills Fun Group)**		
GA1870	Guerre Stellari	15 - 35
Japan		
GA2100	Escape from Death Star (Takara)	15 - 35
GA2105	*Star Wars* Game (Takara)	20 - 35
GA2470	Endor (Tsukuda Hobby Co.)	20 - 35
GA2472	Hoth Planet (Tsukuda Hobby Co.)	20 - 35
GA2475	Death Star (Tsukuda Hobby Co.)	20 - 35
Philippines **(Presswell Enterprises)**		
GA2700	Ewok board games	5 - 10
Spain		
GA2800	La Guerra de las Galaxias (General Mills Fun Group)	15 - 35
GA2805	*SW* Classic table games (Didactecnica SA)	5 - 12
GA2810	*SW* Classic dominos (Didactecnica SA)	5 - 12

GA3101-03   GA3105

GA4010   GA4012   GA4015

GA4126   GA4127   GA4140   GA4141   GA4240

GA4450   GA5014   GA5015   GA5016

CARD GAMES (Parker Bros.)

GA3050	*ROTJ* Play-for-Power	5 - 12
GA3051	*Ewoks* Say "Cheese"	2 - 6
GA3052	*Ewoks* Paw Pals	2 - 6
GA3053	*Ewoks* Favorite Five	2 - 6

Customizable Card Game (Decipher/Parker Bros.) GA3101-05

GA3101	Rare cards, each	1.50 - 50
GA3102	Uncommon cards, each	3¢ - 5¢
GA3103	Common cards, each	1¢ - 2¢
GA3105	Boxed starter set (Parker Bros.)	10 - 15
GA3110	Empire starter set (Parker Bros.)	12 - 20

France

GA3260	World of Ewoks	10 - 20

***Germany* (F. X. Schmid)**

GA3300	Quartett Spiel Krieg der sterne	10 - 20

***Spain* (Heraclio Fournier SA)**

GA3700	*Droids* cards	5 - 15

CHESS SETS (Danbury Mint)

GA3900	*SW* pewter set	700 - 850

ELECTRONIC/ELECTRIC

Kenner

GA4010	Electronic Laser Battle	65 - 125
GA4012	Electronic Battle Command	45 - 90
GA4015	X-Wing Aces target game	300 - 750

Micro Games of America

GA4125	*SW* hand held game (boxed or rack card)	15 - 25
GA4126	*ESB* hand-held game (box or card)	15 - 25
GA4127	*ROTJ* hand-held game (box or card)	15 - 25

GA4140	*SW* Game Wizard	10 - 15
GA4141	*SW* Intimidator	10 - 15

***England* (Palitoy)**

GA4240	Destroy Death Star (electric version)	65 - 150

***France* (Meccano)**

GA4300	La Bataille Spatiale

***Japan* (Tsukuda Hobby Co.)**

GA4450	*SW* LCD hand-held game	35 - 65

PUZZLES

Kenner jigsaw puzzles were among the earliest *Star Wars* items. First series puzzles were available in early blue or purple boxes before all the puzzles were switched to black-bordered boxes. No American puzzles were produced for *ESB*, but they came back in abundance for *ROTJ*, produced by Kenner's Craft Master affiliate. Puzzles were also popular outside the U.S., and many manufacturers issued series of six, eight or twelve boxed mini-puzzles. The Japanese issued a wide variety of puzzles, and the Spanish produced *Star Wars* "rompecabezas," literally head-breakers: block puzzles where each piece is a cube and there's a different puzzle part on all six sides to make up six different puzzles.

Kenner boxed puzzles for *SW* Series #1

GA5010	Luke, 500 pcs., purple box	5 - 15
GA5011	Luke, 500 pcs., black box	5 - 10
GA5012	Space Battle, 500 pcs., purple box	5 - 15
GA5013	Space Battle, 500 pcs., black box	5 - 10
GA5014	R2-D2 C-3PO, 140 pcs., blue box	5 - 15
GA5015	R2-D2/C-3PO, 140 pcs., black box	5 - 10
GA5016	Han/Chewbacca, 140 pcs., blue box	5 - 15

FM5002 Early Video Package

Candy and snack header cards (Mexico)

FO6650 Ice Cream
Wrappers from France

FO6051-54 Taco Bell/KFC Sipper Cups

BE6012 Sleeping Bag

BE1012 Bedspread

FO1370 Coca-Cola radio

FO3300-03 & FO7700 Candy and snacks from Japan

FO6512 Streets Ice Treats

FT3010-31 & FT8005-22 Clark's Shoes

Offer for FO3620

TO9315 Cobot R2-D2

SZ7012 Burger King

Poster for PO5235-37

PO1971 Yogurt from the UK

Translite for CU5001-04 Burger King Glasses

PO5013 Burger Chef Fun Meal Translites

PO4015 New Zealand Frozen Treat

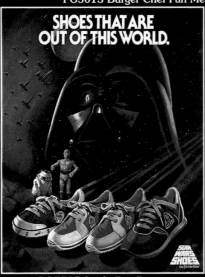

PO5705 Stride Rite Poster

SZ7017 Burger King Contest Translite

PO5206 Burger King Glasses Translite

SZ7140 CBS Fox Counter Display

Poster for PO5230

Chocolate Easter Egg and Candies from England.

Doritos from the U.S. and Fruit Lolly Pops from England.

Mexican Snack Foods Promotional Poster and Display

Lay's Potato Chip Bag with Special Figure Offer; Cookie Displays from Mexico; and Doritos Snack Food Bag from England.

1997 Cookie Boxes from Mexico Offered Trading Cards and a Figure in one of every 50 Boxes.

Pepsi (Mexico); Snack Bags from Great Britain; and Pizza Hut Sign from Mexico.

MA5011 Chewbacca maquette

MA5013 Jabba the Hutt maquette

MA5005 Boba Fett maquette

MA5015 Han Solo
in Carbonite replica

JE6751
JE6753
JE6755
JE6757
JE6759
JE6761
JE6763
JE6765
JE6767
JE6769
JE6773
JE6775
JE6771
JE6777
JE6779
JE6781
JE6783
JE4351
JE6785
JE6791
JE6793
JE6787
JE6789
JE4353
JE6795
JE6800
JE6811
JE6813
JE6815
JE6817
JE6819

Hollywood Pins

MA5001 Yoda maquette

MA5003 Admiral Ackbar maquette

TO8600 & TO8501 Plush Chewbaccas

PT5500 1st Kenner
Star Wars catalog

FO3612
Cheerios
Premium Kite

TO9925 Bagatelle Game
(Italy)

TO8601 Plush Jawa
(Canada)

STAR WARS
PRODUCTS FOR DELIVERY
BEGINNING JANUARY AND FEBRUARY, 1978

Kenner

PO0014 *SW* 'A' Sheet

PO0030 *SW* 'C' Sheet

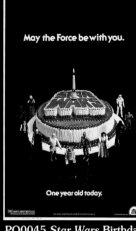
PO0044 *SW* 'D' Sheet

PO0045 *Star Wars* Birthday

PO0120 *Empire* 'A' Sheet

PO0130 *ESB* 'B' Sheet

PO0150 *ESB* '82 Rerelease

PO0210 *Revenge* Advance

PO5040 SW Concert (1978)

PO0220 *Jedi* 'A' Sheet

PO0230 *Jedi* 'B' Sheet

PO0245 *Jedi* '85 Rerelease

PO5295 NPR *SW* Blank

PO5297 NPR *Empire* Blank

PO5020 *SW* Chaykin (1976)

PO2869 Yamakatsu (Japan)

PO4523 *Star Wars* (Poland)

PO4525 *Jedi* (Poland)

PO0017 *Star Wars* Horizontal 'A' Sheet

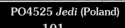

    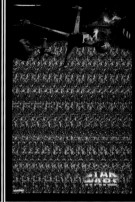

PO5896a *SW* Video Key   PO5896b *ESB* Video Key   PO5896c *ROTJ* Video Key   PO5885 Nintendo poster   PO5982e Magic Eye

PO3107 Sezon Museum   PO3108 Sezon Museum   PO5605 Melanie Taylor Kent   PO5880 Michael Whelan Yoda Litho

   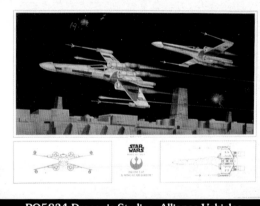

PO2160 German SDI   PO5842 *ESB* 15th Ann.   PO5912 *ROTJ* 10th Ann.   PO5834 Draconis Studios: Alliance Vehicles

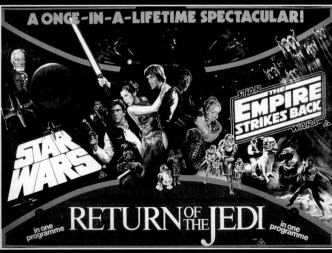 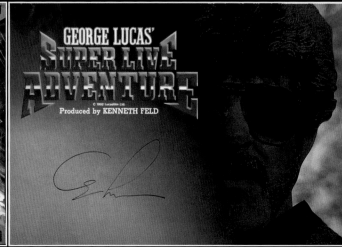

PO1964 British Trilogy Poster   PO2999 George Lucas Super Live Adventure

OFFICIAL **STAR WARS** WATCHES

ANTI-MAGNETIC
PRECISION SWISS MOVEMENTS
ELECTRONICALLY TIMED

WT5214   WT5210   WT5212   WT5228

WT5118   WT5114   WT5620

BRADLEY TIME
A DIVISION OF ELGIN NATIONAL IND. INC.

Display for WT5111

WT5710

WT5625   WT5610   WT5615   ST9733   WT5710

OFFICIAL **STAR WARS** Microelectronic Digital Watch

TEXAS INSTRUMENTS

OFFICIAL **STAR WARS**

TEXAS INSTRUMENTS

WT5001 Original Texas Instruments Watch

WT9250

WT5124   WT0010   WT5715   WT5720 Sci-Fi Channel Watch

103

SZ8282 Burger King *Jedi* Glasses Counter Display

PE0105 FAO Schwarz Pewter

TO7500 Cinemacast

WT9500 Duracell Watch (Mexico)

BA1101 Droids Talking Bank

BA1102 Vader Talking Bank

One-of-a-kind Humm-V, Grand Prize from
Taco Bell "Feel the Force" contest.

GA5019	GA5021	GA5022	GA5023	GA5024
GA5030	GA5033	GA5160	GA5161	GA5162
GA5182	GA5184	GA5185	GA5186	GA5187 GA5300 GA5301
GA5321	GA5322	GA5323	GA5325	

GA5017	Han/Chewbacca, 140 pcs., black box	5 - 10	
Series #2			
GA5018	Luke and Leia leap, 500 pcs.	5 - 12	
GA5019	Vader & Kenobi duel, 500 pcs.	5 - 12	
GA5020	In trash compactor, 140 pcs	5 - 8	
GA5021	Luke meets R2-D2, 140 pcs.	5 - 8	
Series #3			
GA5022	X-wing fighters prepare, 500 pcs.	5 -12	
GA5023	Victory Celebration, 500 pcs.	5 - 12	
GA5024	Attack of Sand People, 140 pcs.	5 - 8	
GA5025	Troopers stop landpeeder, 140 pcs.	5 - 8	
Series #4			
GA5030	Cantina Band, 500 pcs.	5 - 12	
GA5033	Selling of Droids, 500 pcs.	5 - 12	
GA5035	The Bantha, 140 pcs.	5 - 8	
GA5037	Jawas Capture R2-D2, 140 pcs.	5 - 8	
Larger puzzles			
GA5100	*Star Wars* Adventure (Hildebrandt movie poster art), 1000 pcs.	8 - 15	
GA5110	Aboard the Millennium Falcon, 1000 pcs.	8 - 15	
GA5120	Corridor of Lights, 1500 pcs.	10 - 20	
GA5130	Millennium Falcon in Hyper-Space, 1500 pcs.	10 - 20	
Craft Master *ROTJ* boxed puzzles			
GA5150	Battle on Endor, 170 pcs.	5 - 10	
GA5151	Ewok Leaders, 170 pcs	5 - 10	
GA5152	B-wings on Attack, 170 pcs.	5 - 10	
GA5153	Friends of Jabba, 70 pcs.	5 - 10	
GA5154	Jabba Throne Room, 70 pcs	5 - 10	
GA5155	Death Star Scene, 70 pcs.	5 - 10	
Wicket and Friends boxed puzzles			
GA5160	Fishing, 35 pcs.	3 - 5	
GA5161	Swimming hole, 35 pcs.	3 - 5	

GA5162	Nature lesson, 35 pcs.	3 - 5	
Craft Master *ROTJ* Tray Puzzles			
GA5180	Gamorrean Guard, photo	3 - 6	
GA5181	Leia and Wicket, photo	3 - 6	
GA5182	Darth Vader, photo	3 - 6	
GA5183	Wicket the Ewok, photo	2 - 5	
GA5184	Ewoks on Hang Gliders, cartoon	2 - 5	
GA5185	Wicket and R2-D2, cartoon	2 - 5	
GA5186	Ewok Village, cartoon	2 - 5	
GA5187	Kneesaa & Baga, cartoon	2 - 5	
Match Blocks tray puzzles			
GA5300	*ROTJ* pattern	3 - 6	
GA5301	Wicket the Ewok pattern	2 - 5	
Milton Bradley			
GA5321	*Star Wars: A New Hope*	10 - 15	
GA5322	*The Empire Strikes Back*	10 - 15	
GA5323	*Return of the Jedi*	10 - 15	
GA5325	3-D Millennium Falcon	20 - 30	
England (Waddingtons)			
SW boxed puzzles, 150 pcs.			
GA6110	Inside the Millennium Falcon	5 - 10	
GA6111	R2-D2 and C-3PO	5 - 10	
GA6112	Entering the city	5 - 10	
GA6113	Han Solo & Chewbacca	5 - 10	
SW boxed puzzles using scenes w/Kenner toys, 350 pcs.			
GA6134	Style A w/Death Star above	10 - 20	
GA6135	Style B, in mountains	10 - 20	
ROTJ boxed puzzles, 150 pcs.			
GA6190	Jabba the Hut	5 - 10	
GA6191	Luke	5 - 10	
GA6192	Chewie, Leia, Luke, Han, C-3PO	5 - 10	
GA6193	Darth Vader	5 - 10	

GA6110 GA6111 GA6112 GA6113

GA6135 GA6190 GA6191 GA6192 GA6193

GA6194 GA6195 GA6196 GA6197 GA6340

GA6420

GA6702 GA6704 GA6703 GA6813 (front) GA6813 (back) GA6923

GA7151 GA7154 GA7260

GA6194 *Ewoks: Sled ride*	3 - 5	
GA6195 *Ewoks: At home*	3 - 5	
GA6196 *Ewoks: Swimming hole*	3 - 5	
GA6197 *Ewoks: Nature lesson*	3 - 5	

France

GA6300 *Entrée dans la ville* (Capiepa/Waddingtons)	5 - 10
GA6301 *Yan Solo et Chiktabba* (Capiepa/Waddingtons)	5 - 10
GA6340 *Nature Lesson* (Ravensburger)	10 - 15

Germany (Parker Spiele)

GA6420 *Krieg der sterne* boxed mini-puzzles, 12 different, ea.	4 - 8

Greece (Thomas Theophanides)

GA6540 *ROTJ* boxed mini-puzzles, 8 different, ea.	3 - 6

Japan (Takara)

Boxed micro puzzles, 60 pcs

GA6701 Chewbacca & Han Solo	10 - 15
GA6702 Vader, full figure, w/spacecraft	10 - 15
GA6703 Vader head, Leia, Luke, droids	10 - 15
GA6704 Dogfight	10 - 15
GA6705 Luke, landspeeder, droids, escape pod	10 - 15
GA6706 C-3PO & R2-D2 in desert	10 - 15

Boxed mini-puzzles, 108 pcs

GA6810 Stormtroopers in corridor	12 - 20
GA6811 Victory celebration	12 - 20
GA6812 Preparing X-wngs. for combat	12 - 20
GA6813 Luke, landspeeder, droids, escape pod	12 - 20
GA6814 C-3PO & R2-D2 in desert	12 - 20

GA6815 R2-D2	12 - 20
GA6816 C-3PO, R2-D2 in control room	12 - 20
GA6817 Troopers stop landspeeder	12 - 20

Boxed puzzles, 500 pcs.

GA6920 Vader, full figure, w/spacecraft	15 - 30
GA6921 C-3PO & R2-D2 in desert	15 - 30
GA6922 Luke, landspeeder, droids, escape pod	15 - 30
GA6923 Stormtrooper mask, Luke, C-3PO, Han Solo	15 - 30

Boxed puzzles, 730 pieces

GA7030 Vader head, Leia, Luke, droids	20 - 45
GA7031 TIE ftrs. chasing X-wngs., Millennium Falcon	20 - 45

Large tray puzzles w/coloring scene on back

GA7040 Darth, full figure, & droids	15 - 25

GA7510　　　GA7511　　　GA7512　　　GA7513　　　GA7750　　GA7775

GA7775　　　　　　GA7790　　　　　　GA7840　　　GA7841

GA8200　　GA8203　　GA8204　　GA8205　　GA8208　　GA8210　　GA8215

GA8220　　GA8225　　GA8230　　GA8233　　GA8240　　GA8245　　GA8258

GA7041	R2-D2 & C-3PO	15 - 25
GA7042	R2-D2	15 - 25
GA7043	Luke, X-wing, droids	15 - 25

Plastic tray puzzles

GA7150	*SW* logo	15 - 25
GA7151	Victory celebration	15 - 25
GA7152	X-wing firing	15 - 25
GA7153	R2-D2	15 - 25
GA7154	R2-D2 & C-3PO in desert	15 - 25
GA7155	Darth, full figure, w/X-wng.	15 - 25

9-cube block puzzles w/6 different faces

| GA7260 | Black box, style A | 20 - 35 |
| GA7261 | Blue box, style B | 20 - 35 |

Netherlands **(MB International)**

GA7510	*ROTJ*: Gamorrean Guard	3 - 10
GA7511	*ROTJ*: Leia, Jabba, C-3PO, Bib Fortuna	3 - 10
GA7512	*ROTJ*: R2-D2 and Wicket	3 - 10
GA7513	*ROTJ*: Star Destroyer, Death Star, fighters	3 - 10

Spain

GA7750	*SW* Rompecabezas (Juguetes Borras)	25 - 45
GA7770	*SW* Classic plastic & cardboard puzzles (Del Mau), ea.	5 - 20
GA7775	*Droids/Ewoks* puzzles (Del Mau), ea.	
GA7780	*SW* Classic puzzles, box & frame (Didactecnica SA), ea	5 - 20
GA7790	*Droids* puzzles (Didactecnica SA), ea	

Sweden **(AB Prodessia)**

| GA7840 | *ROTJ*: Darth & Luke, 500 pcs. | 5 - 10 |
| GA7841 | *ROTJ*: Wicket, 500 pcs. | 3 - 6 |

ROLE-PLAYING

In 1987, West End Games began an extensive new line of *Star Wars* role-playing games. While it produced a few boxed board games, most of West End's prodigious output has appeared in hardcover and softcover books and booklets. It also has produced a variety of small metal gaming figures to accompany the games. They originally came in boxed sets—usually 10 to a box—but were then repackaged in smaller quantities and sold on rack cards. West End, with the agreement of Lucasfilm, has vastly expanded the *Star Wars* universe, providing new information, background material and histories that are of interest even to those who don't play the games. Some of these elements have also made their way into *Star Wars* novels. A live-action adaptation of the West End system was introduced in 1997.

Basic Rules

GA8200	*Star Wars* The Roleplaying Game	20 - 30
GA8203	*SW* The Roleplaying Game, 2nd ed.	20 - 30
GA8204	*SW* The Roleplaying Game, Expanded 2nd ed.	20 - 30
GA8205	*SW* Introductory Adventure Game, boxed set	10 - 20

Sourcebooks: first printings are hardcover

GA8208	The *Star Wars* Sourcebook	20 - 30
GA8209	hardcover, 2nd edition	15 - 25
GA8210	The Imperial Sourcebook	20 - 30
GA8211	softcover version	15 - 18
GA8212	hardcover, 2nd edition	15 - 25
GA8215	The Rebel Alliance Sourcebook	20 - 30
GA8216	softcover version	15 - 18
GA8217	The Rebel Alliance Sourcebook, 2nd ed.	20 - 30
GA8220	*Heir to the Empire* Sourcebook	20 - 30
GA8221	*Heir to the Empire*, softcover version	15 - 18
GA8225	*Dark Force Rising* Sourcebook	20 - 30
GA8226	*Dark Force Rising*, softcover version	15 - 18
GA8230	*The Last Command* Sourcebook	20 - 30
GA8233	*Thrawn Trilogy* Sourcebook (compiles and updates GA8220-30 to 2nd ed.), softcover	20 - 30
GA8235	*Dark Empire* Sourcebook	20 - 30
GA8240	The Movie Trilogy Sourcebook	20 - 30
GA8245	Han Solo and the Corporate Sector Sourcebook	18 - 24
GA8250	*The Truce at Bakura* Sourcebook	20 - 30
GA8255	*Shadows of the Empire* Sourcebook	20 - 30

GA8310	GA8312	GA8314	GA8316	GA8318	GA8320	GA8326
GA8328	GA8330	GA8410	GA8414	GA8422	GA8428	GA8430
GA8440	GA8446	GA8448	GA8450	GA8452	GA8454	GA8470
GA8610	GA8611	GA8612	GA8613	GA8614	GA8616	GA8618

GA8258	*Jedi Academy* Sourcebook	20 - 30	
GA8260	*Tales of the Jedi* Sourcebook	20 - 30	
GA8262	Movie Trilogy Special	20 - 30	
GA8264	X-wing Sourcebook	15 - 25	
Early Adventures (Adventure kits)			
GA8310	Tatooine Manhunt	8 - 12	
GA8312	Strike Force: Shantipole	8 - 12	
GA8314	Battle for the Golden Sun	8 - 12	
GA8316	Starfall	8 - 12	
GA8318	Otherspace	8 - 12	
GA8320	Scavenger Hunt	8 - 12	
GA8322	Riders of the Maelstrom	8 - 12	
GA8324	Otherspace II: Invasion	8 - 12	
GA8326	Crisis on Cloud City (with Sabaac deck)	8 - 12	
GA8328	Black Ice	8 - 12	
GA8330	The Game Chambers of Questal	8 - 12	
Later Adventures (softcover books)			
GA8410	Twin Stars of Kira	10 - 15	
GA8412	Supernova	10 - 15	
GA8414	The Politics of Contraband	10 - 15	
GA8416	Graveyard of Alderaan	10 - 15	
GA8418	Domain of Evil	10 - 15	
GA8420	Death in the Undercity	10 - 15	
GA8422	Planet of the Mists	10 - 15	
GA8424	The Isis Coordinates	10 - 15	
GA8426	The Abduction of Crying Dawn Singer	10 - 15	
GA8428	Mission to Lianna	12 - 20	
GA8430	Scoundrel's Luck	12 - 20	
GA8432	Jedi's Honor	10 - 15	
GA8440	Classic Adventures #1	12 - 18	
GA8442	Classic Adventures #2	12 - 18	
GA8444	Classic Adventures #3	12 - 18	

GA8446	Classic Adventures #4, Best of the Journal	12 - 20	
GA8448	Instant Adventures	10 - 15	
GA8450	No Disintigrations	10 - 15	
GA8452	Black Sands of Socorro	12 - 18	
GA8454	Imperial Double-Cross	8 - 12	
GA8456	Secrets of the Sisar Run	10 - 15	
GA8470	*SW* Adventure Journal, Vol. 1	15 - 25	
GA8471	*SW* Adventure Journal, Vol. 2 and up, ea.	10 - 15	
Books: Guide (softcover)			
GA8610	Galaxy Guide 1: *A New Hope*	10 - 15	
GA8611	Galaxy Guide 1: *A New Hope*, 2nd ed.	10 - 15	
GA8612	Galaxy Guide 2: Yavin and Bespin	10 - 15	
GA8613	Galaxy Guide 2: Yavin and Bespin, 2nd ed.	10 - 15	
GA8614	Galaxy Guide 3: *The Empire Strikes Back*	10 - 15	
GA8615	Galaxy Guide 3: *The Empire Strikes Back*, 2nd ed.	10 - 15	
GA8616	Galaxy Guide 4: Alien Races	10 - 15	
GA8617	Galaxy Guide 4: Alien Races, 2nd ed.	10 - 15	
GA8618	Galaxy Guide 5: *Return of the Jedi*	10 - 15	
GA8619	Galaxy Guide 5: *Return of the Jedi*, 2nd ed.	10 - 15	
GA8620	Galaxy Guide 6: Tramp Freighters	10 - 15	
GA8621	Galaxy Guide 6: Tramp Freighters, 2nd ed.	10 - 15	
GA8622	Galaxy Guide 7: Mos Eisley	10 - 15	
GA8624	Galaxy Guide 8: Scouts	10 - 15	
GA8626	Galaxy Guide 9: Fragments from the Rim	10 - 15	
GA8628	Galaxy Guide 10: Bounty Hunters	12 - 18	
GA8630	Galaxy Guide 11: Criminal Organizations	10 - 15	
GA8632	Galaxy Guide 12: Aliens—Enemies and Allies	10 - 15	
GA8650	Planets of the Galaxy, Vol. I	10 - 15	
GA8652	Planets of the Galaxy, Vol. II	10 - 15	
GA8654	Planets of the Galaxy, Vol. III	15 - 25	
GA8656	Planets Collection	15 - 25	
GA8658	*Shadows of the Empire* Planets Guide	10 - 15	

| GA8620 | GA8622 | GA8624 | GA8626 | GA8628 | GA8630 | GA8632 |

| GA8650 | GA8652 | GA8656 | GA8658 | GA8680 | GA8681 | GA8690 |

| GA8692 | GA8694 | GA8696 | GA8698 | GA8700 | GA8708 | GA8718 |

| GA8720 | GA8722 | GA8750 | GA8752 | GA8754 | GA8756 | GA8780 |

| GA8815 | GA8820 | GA8830 | GA8835 | GA8855 | GA8858 |

GA9010   GA9014   GA9016   GA9018   GA9020   GA9024   GA9026   GA9028   GA9032   GA9036

GA9045   GA9050   GA9092   GA9306   GA9308   GA9420

GA8835	Star Warriors	20 - 25	GA9095	Emperor	5 - 7

GA8835   Star Warriors   20 - 25
GA8850   Gamemaster's Handbook   10 - 18
GA8855   Gamemaster Screen, 2nd ed.   10 - 15
GA8858   Gamemaster Screen, 2nd ed., Revised   8 - 10

Miniatures

GA9010   Heroes of the Rebellion, boxed set   15 - 25
GA9012   Imperial Forces, boxed set   15 - 25
GA9014   Bounty Hunters, boxed set   15 - 25
GA9016   A New Hope, boxed set   15 - 25
GA9018   *The Empire Strikes Back*, boxed set   15 - 25
GA9020   *Return of the Jedi*, boxed set   15 - 25
GA9022   Stormtroopers, boxed set   15 - 25
GA9024   Rebel Characters , boxed set   15 - 25
GA9026   Mos Eisley Cantina, boxed set   15 - 25
GA9028   Jabba's Palace, boxed set   15 - 25
GA9030   The Rancor Pit, boxed set   20 - 30
GA9032   Rebel Troopers, boxed set   15 - 25
GA9034   Imperial Troopers, boxed set   15 - 25
GA9036   Zero-G Assault Troopers, boxed set   20 - 35
GA9042   *SW* Miniatures Battles (book)   15 - 25
GA9043   *SW* Miniatures Battles (book), 2nd ed.   10 - 15
GA9045   Miniatures Battles Starter Set (boxed)   30 - 40
GA9046   Miniatures Battles Companion (book)   10 - 15
GA9047   Miniatures Battles: Imperial Entanglements (book) 10 - 15
GA9048   Vehicles Starter Set (boxed)   30 - 40
GA9050   Mos Eisley Starter Set (boxed)   30 - 40

Miniatures - Blister Packs

GA9071   Heroes #1   5 - 7
GA9072   Heroes #2   5 - 7
GA9073   Stormtroopers #1   5 - 7
GA9074   Stormtroopers #2   5 - 7
GA9075   Rebel Troopers #1   5 - 7
GA9076   Rebel Troopers #2   5 - 7
GA9077   Users of the Force   5 - 7
GA9078   Pilots and Gunners   5 - 7
GA9079   Stormtroopers #3   5 - 7
GA9080   Imperial Crew with Heavy Blaster   5 - 7
GA9081   Imperial Army Troopers   5 - 7
GA9082   Imperial Navy Troopers   5 - 7
GA9083   Rebel Troopers #3   5 - 7
GA9084   Rebel Commandos #1   5 - 7
GA9085   Imperial Officers   5 - 7
GA9086   Stormtroopers #4   5 - 7
GA9087   Rebel Commandos #2   5 - 7
GA9088   Imperial Army Troopers #2   5 - 7
GA9089   Imperial Navy Troopers #2   5 - 7
GA9090   Bounty Hunters #1   5 - 7
GA9091   Rebel Troopers #4   5 - 7
GA9092   Bounty Hunters #2   5 - 7
GA9093   Droids #1   5 - 7
GA9094   Cloud City   5 - 7

GA9095   Emperor   5 - 7
GA9096   Bounty Hunters #3   5 - 7
GA9097   Denizens of Tatooine   5 - 7
GA9098   Sand Troopers   5 - 7
GA9099   Aliens of the Galaxy #1   5 - 7
GA9100   Jedi Knights   5 - 7
GA9101   Snowtroopers   5 - 7
GA9102   Hoth Rebels   5 - 7
GA9103   Scout Troopers   5 - 7
GA9104   Rebel Operatives   5 - 7
GA9105   Wookiees   5 - 7
GA9106   Mon Calamari   5 - 7
GA9107   Heir to the Empire Villians   5 - 7
GA9108   Ewoks   5 - 7
GA9109   Noghri   5 - 7
GA9110   Zero-G   5 - 7
GA9111   Skywalkers   5 - 7
GA9112   Encounter on Hoth   5 - 7
GA9113   Aliens of the Galaxy #2   5 - 7
GA9114   Jabba the Hutt   5 - 7
GA9115   Jabba's Servants   5 - 7
GA9116   DarkStryder #1   5 - 7
GA9117   DarkStryder #2   5 - 7
GA9118   Pirates   5 - 7
GA9119   Mos Eisley   5 - 7
GA9120   Gamorrean Guards   5 - 7
GA9121   Mos Eisley Cantina   5 - 7
GA9122   DarkStryder #3   5 - 7
GA9123   Aliens of the Galaxy #3   5 - 7
GA9124   Imperial Troop Pack   15 - 20
GA9125   Rebel Troop Pack   15 - 20
GA9126   Mos Eisley Cantina #2   5 - 7

Vehicle Miniatures - Blister Packs

GA9301   Landspeeder   8 - 12
GA9302   Imperial Speeder Bikes   8 - 12
GA9303   Rebel Speeder Bikes   8 - 12
GA9304   Storm Skimmer   8 - 12
GA9305   AT-PT   8 - 12
GA9306   Snowspeeder   12 - 18
GA9307   Bantha with Rider   8 - 12
GA9308   Rebel Tauntaun Patrol   8 - 12

Finland (Pro Games)

GA9410   Finnish, Danish, Norwegian and Swedish language
         versions of West End products   8 - 30

France (Jeux Descartes)

GA9420   French versions of West End products   8 - 30

Italy (Stratelibri S.R.L.)

GA9430   Italian versions of West End products   8 - 30

Spain (Joc International SA)

GA9460   Spanish versions of West End products   8 - 30

110

GA9510   GA9512   GA9620   GA9622   GA9730   GA9801

GA9810   GA9811   GA9812   GA9814   GA9915   GA9830

GA9820   GA9900   GA9901   GA9902   GA9910

GA0210   HH2015   HH2010   HH2013   HH2110 HH2112   HH2114   HH2116

VIDEO

Parker Brothers for Atari & Sears systems

GA9510	*SW*: Jedi Arena	5 - 15
GA9512	*ESB*	5 - 15
GA9514	*ROTJ*: Death Star Battle	5 - 15
GA9516	*SW*: The Arcade Game (also for Colecovision)	5 - 15

Empty advance displays boxes

GA9518	*SW: Revenge of the Jedi*, Game I	35 - 60
GA9520	*SW: Revenge of the Jedi*, Game II	35 - 60

Nintendo GA9610-42

GA9610	*Star Wars* (JVC)	25 - 35
GA9612	*The Empire Strikes Back* (JVC)	25 - 35
GA9620	Super *Star Wars* (JVC)	45 - 55
GA9622	Super *The Empire Strikes Back* (JVC)	45 - 60
GA9640	*Star Wars* for Gameboy (Capcom USA)	25 - 35
GA9642	*The Empire Strikes Back* for Gameboy (Capcom)	25 - 35
GA9644	Super *ROTJ*	45 - 60

Sega

GA9710	*Star Wars* for Game Gear (Sega/U.S. Gold)	25 - 35
GA9715	Rebel Assault (Sega CD-Rom) LucasArts	20 - 45
GA9730	*Star Wars* Arcade for Sega Genesis	20 - 45

Video Games for personal computers

GA9801	*Star Wars*, Broderbund	25 - 45
GA9805	Night Shift, Lucasfilm Games (*SW* character parody)	35 - 45
GA9810	X-wing, LucasArts Games	45 - 60
GA9811	Imperial Pursuit, LucasArts Games	35 - 45
GA9812	B-wing, LucasArts Games	35 - 45
GA9813	TIE fighter, LucasArts Games	45 - 60
GA9814	Rebel Assault, (CD-Rom) LucasArts Games	45 - 60

GA9820	*Star Wars* Chess (CD-Rom and PC), The Software Toolworks	35 - 50
GA9830	Dark Forces, (CD-Rom) LucasArts Games	35 - 50

England (Domark: conversions of Atari arcade games)

GA9900	*SW*	25 - 45
GA9901	*ESB*	25 - 45
GA9902	*ROTJ*	25 - 45

Japan

GA9910	*SW* for Japnese Nintendo (Victor Musical Industries)	35 - 45
GA9915	*SW: Attack on the Death Star* for Sharp X68000 and NEC9801 PCs (Namco Ltd.)	45 - 60

Spain (Walather Miller S.A.)

CR9975	*Droids*	35 - 45

HOUSEHOLD

DOOR SIGNS
Japan

HH0210	*SW/ROTJ* Stop/Welcome	5 - 15

HANGERS (Adam Joseph)

HH2010	Admiral Ackbar	3 - 9
HH2013	C-3PO	3 - 9
HH2015	Stormtrooper	3 - 9

HOOKS (Adam Joseph)

HH2110	Boba Fett	2 - 8
HH2112	C-3PO	2 - 7
HH2114	Darth Vader	2 - 8
HH2116	Emperor's Guard	2 - 7

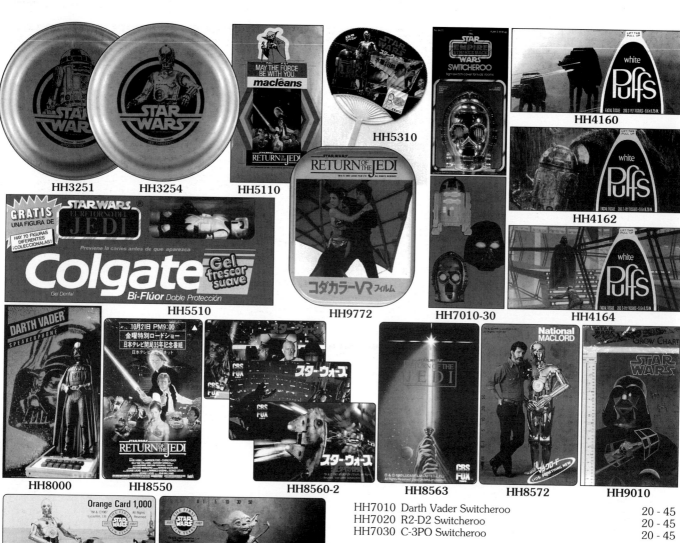

HH3251 HH3254 HH5110 HH5310 HH4160 HH4162 HH4164

HH5510 HH9772 HH7010-30

HH8000 HH8550 HH8560-2 HH8563 HH8572 HH9010

HH8570

HH8571

HOUSEHOLD PRODUCTS

HH3250	*SW* Pine-Sol bottle label	
HH3251	Artoo-Detoo flying disk (Pine-Sol)	15 - 25
HH3252	Stormtroopers flying disk (Pine-Sol)	15 - 30
HH3253	Chewbacca flying disk (Pine-Sol)	15 - 30
HH3254	See-Threepio flying disk (Pine-Sol)	15 - 30
HH3255	X-wing fighter flying disk (Pine-Sol)	15 - 30
HH3256	Darth Vader flying disk (Pine-Sol)	15 - 30
HH4160	Hoth tissue box (Puffs)	10 - 15
HH4162	Dagobah tissue box (Puffs)	10 - 15
HH4164	Bespin tissue box (Puffs)	10 - 15
Australia (Adrenalin Pty)		
HH5010	Johnson & Johnson Band-Aids	5 - 12
Canada		
HH5110	Macléans toothpaste promo sticker (Beecham)	8 - 12
Spain (Colgate/Palmolive SAE)		
HH5510	Colgate toothpaste w/Kenner *ROTJ* action figure	10 - 15

MIRRORS

Australia (Roy Lee Cin)		
HH6010	*ESB* decorated mirrors	15 - 45
England (Cosalt Exports Ltd.)		
HH6310	*SW* mirrors	15 - 40

SWITCH PLATE COVERS

Kenner made a line of Switcheroos, dimensional figures of *Star Wars* characters that completely covered a wall light switch plate. The switch itself fit into the back of the Switcheroo, and was controlled by a moving part of the figure.

HH7010	Darth Vader Switcheroo	20 - 45
HH7020	R2-D2 Switcheroo	20 - 45
HH7030	C-3PO Switcheroo	20 - 45

TELEPHONES/TELEPHONE CARDS

The Darth Vader speaker/telephone not only looks good, it works great. Still, so far there appear to be enough in the collectors market that the phones haven't risen in value much above the original price.

Telephone calling cards are a relatively new phenomenon in the U.S., but they have been used for years in Europe and Asia and have become a hot collectible, especially in Japan. The cards listed were available commercially or were special advertising promotions.

Telephones

HH8000	Darth Vader speaker phone (Comdial)	70 - 135
See also—**TOYS: Preschool**		

Telephone Cards

Japan		
HH8550	*ROTJ*: 1985 rerelease style 'B' poster art	15 - 25
CBS-Fox Video		
HH8560	*SW*: Falcon cockpit	15 - 25
HH8561	*ESB*: Lightsaber duel	15 - 25
HH8562	*ROTJ*: Falcon inside Death Star	15 - 25
HH8563	*ROTJ*: Style 'A' poster art	15 - 25
Panasonic/National/Maclord		
HH8570	C-3PO, R2-D2 in desert, 1st 10 years logo	35 - 45
HH8571	Yoda, 1st 10 years logo	45 - 65
HH8572	Lucas leaning on C-3PO	35 - 45
See also—**SHOW SOUVENIRS; STAR TOURS**		

OTHER

HH9010	*SW* "Grow" chart (Random House)	5 - 10
Australia (Crystal Craft)		
HH9450	*ROTJ* toothbrush holders,Darth, Royal Guard, Yoda, Wicket, R2-D2, C-3PO	5 - 12
Italy		
HH9560	Photo album (Fuji Audio Visual Systems)	5 - 15
Japan		
HH9770	Juice glass w/*SW* & Kodak logos (Kodak)	5 - 12

JE0010	JE0011	JE0012
JE1100	JE1215 JE3000	JE3001 JE3002
JE1210	JE1212	JE1213 JE1214

JE3112 JE4001 JE4002 JE4003 JE4004 JE4005 JE4006

JE3120 JE4050 JE4051 JE4052 JE4053 JE4056 JE4057 JE4700

JE4351 JE4355 JE4357 JE4359 JE4361 JE4363 JE4365 JE4371 JE4373

JE4710 JE5210-15

HH9771	Cylinder pencil sharpener w/droids & *SW* logo	5 - 12
HH9772	Metal tray w/*ROTJ* logo & Luke, Leia on sail barge	10 - 15

Paper photo cups w/*ROTJ* and Kodak logos

HH9773	Luke & Stormtroopers	2 - 5
HH9774	Leia & Jabba	2 - 5
HH9775	Leia, Luke on sail barge	2 - 5
HH9776	Star Destroyer	2 - 5
HH9777	R2-D2, C-3PO	2 - 5

JEWELRY

In the U.S., jewelry was marketed by Weingeroff Enterprises for *SW*, W. Berrie and Co. for *ESB*, Adam Joseph Industries for *ROTJ*, and Howard Eldon/A. Weiss and Creation Conventions for the *SW* 10th Anniversary. The lines were all distinctly different from each other. Individual pieces can still be found at reasonable prices, and occasionally full displays filled with jewelry go up for sale.

BARRETTES (Weingeroff Ent.)

JE0010	R2-D2	5 - 15
JE0011	C-3PO	5 - 15
JE0012	Darth Vader	5 - 15

BRACELETS (Weingeroff Ent.)

JE1100	Charms: C-3PO, R2-D2 and Darth Vader	15 - 25
JE1101	Charms: Stormtrooper, Chewbacca, X-wng.	15 - 25
JE1102	Charms: Chewbacca, R2-D2 and C-3PO	15 - 25
JE1210	Stormtrooper	10 - 20
JE1211	Darth Vader	10 - 20
JE1212	Chewbacca	10 - 20
JE1213	C-3PO	10 - 20
JE1214	X-wing	10 - 20
JE1215	R2-D2	10 - 20

DOG TAGS

***England* (Pastahurst Ltd.)**

JE2050	*SW* sterling silver	45 - 65

EARRINGS (Weingeroff Ent.)

Pierced

JE3000	R2-D2	5 - 10
JE3001	C-3PO	5 - 10
JE3002	Darth Vader	5 - 10
JE3003	Chewbacca	5 - 10

Dangling, clip-ons

JE3110	Darth Vader	5 - 15
JE3111	R2-D2	5 - 15
JE3112	C-3P0	5 - 15
JE3120	Full Earring Display	75 - 100

KEY CHAINS

Weingeroff Ent., metal

JE4001	*SW*: C-3PO	5 - 15
JE4002	*SW*: Darth Vader	5 - 15
JE4003	*SW*: X-wing	5 - 15
JE4004	*SW*: R2-D2	5 - 15
JE4005	*SW*: Stormtrooper	5 - 15
JE4006	*SW*: Chewbacca	5 - 15

Adam Joseph, brass

JE4050	*ROTJ*: Yoda	3 - 10
JE4051	*ROTJ*: Millennium Falcon	3 - 10
JE4052	*ROTJ*: Darth Vader	3 - 10
JE4053	*ROTJ*: R2-D2	3 - 10
JE4056	Wicket	3 - 10
JE4057	Kneesaa	3 - 10

Creation Conventions, plastic

JE4100	*SW*: Early McQuarrie Luke sticker art	3 - 5
JE4201	*ESB*: Darth in flames art	3 - 5
JE4202	*ROTJ*: Yoda sticker art	3 - 5

Third Dimension Arts Inc.

JE4300	Yoda hologram	25 - 35
JE4301	Darth Vader hologram	25 - 35
JE4302	X-wing hologram	25 - 35

Hollywood Pins

JE4351	New Republic	2 - 5
JE4353	Millennium Falcon	3 - 6
JE4355	Rebel Forces	3 - 6
JE4357	New Republic, antique finish	3 - 6
JE4359	Rebel Forces, antique finish	3 - 6
JE4361	Yoda Portrait	2 - 5
JE4363	Darth Vader Portrait	2 - 5
JE4365	Darth Vader Mask	4 - 7
JE4367	Darth Vader Mask, small	2 - 5

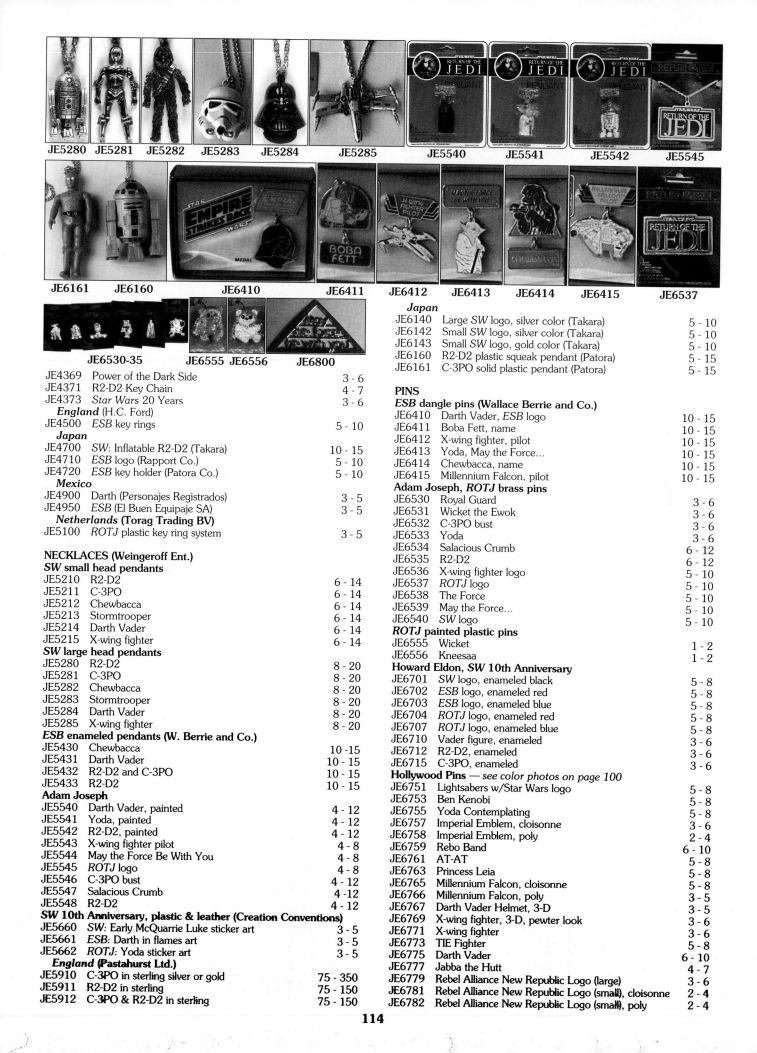

JE5280	JE5281	JE5282	JE5283	JE5284	JE5285	JE5540	JE5541	JE5542	JE5545

JE6161　　JE6160　　　　JE6410　　　JE6411　　JE6412　　JE6413　　JE6414　　JE6415　　JE6537

JE6530-35　　JE6555 JE6556　　JE6800

JE4369	Power of the Dark Side	3 - 6
JE4371	R2-D2 Key Chain	4 - 7
JE4373	*Star Wars* 20 Years	3 - 6
England (H.C. Ford)		
JE4500	*ESB* key rings	5 - 10
Japan		
JE4700	*SW*: Inflatable R2-D2 (Takara)	10 - 15
JE4710	*ESB* logo (Rapport Co.)	5 - 10
JE4720	*ESB* key holder (Patora Co.)	5 - 10
Mexico		
JE4900	Darth (Personajes Registrados)	3 - 5
JE4950	*ESB* (El Buen Equipaje SA)	3 - 5
Netherlands (Torag Trading BV)		
JE5100	*ROTJ* plastic key ring system	3 - 5

NECKLACES (Weingeroff Ent.)
***SW* small head pendants**

JE5210	R2-D2	6 - 14
JE5211	C-3PO	6 - 14
JE5212	Chewbacca	6 - 14
JE5213	Stormtrooper	6 - 14
JE5214	Darth Vader	6 - 14
JE5215	X-wing fighter	6 - 14

***SW* large head pendants**

JE5280	R2-D2	8 - 20
JE5281	C-3PO	8 - 20
JE5282	Chewbacca	8 - 20
JE5283	Stormtrooper	8 - 20
JE5284	Darth Vader	8 - 20
JE5285	X-wing fighter	8 - 20

***ESB* enameled pendants (W. Berrie and Co.)**

JE5430	Chewbacca	10 -15
JE5431	Darth Vader	10 - 15
JE5432	R2-D2 and C-3PO	10 - 15
JE5433	R2-D2	10 - 15

Adam Joseph

JE5540	Darth Vader, painted	4 - 12
JE5541	Yoda, painted	4 - 12
JE5542	R2-D2, painted	4 - 12
JE5543	X-wing fighter pilot	4 - 8
JE5544	May the Force Be With You	4 - 8
JE5545	*ROTJ* logo	4 - 8
JE5546	C-3PO bust	4 - 12
JE5547	Salacious Crumb	4 -12
JE5548	R2-D2	4 - 12

***SW* 10th Anniversary, plastic & leather (Creation Conventions)**

JE5660	*SW*: Early McQuarrie Luke sticker art	3 - 5
JE5661	*ESB*: Darth in flames art	3 - 5
JE5662	*ROTJ*: Yoda sticker art	3 - 5

England (Pastahurst Ltd.)

JE5910	C-3PO in sterling silver or gold	75 - 350
JE5911	R2-D2 in sterling	75 - 150
JE5912	C-3PO & R2-D2 in sterling	75 - 150

Japan

JE6140	Large *SW* logo, silver color (Takara)	5 - 10
JE6142	Small *SW* logo, silver color (Takara)	5 - 10
JE6143	Small *SW* logo, gold color (Takara)	5 - 10
JE6160	R2-D2 plastic squeak pendant (Patora)	5 - 15
JE6161	C-3PO solid plastic pendant (Patora)	5 - 15

PINS
***ESB* dangle pins (Wallace Berrie and Co.)**

JE6410	Darth Vader, *ESB* logo	10 - 15
JE6411	Boba Fett, name	10 - 15
JE6412	X-wing fighter, pilot	10 - 15
JE6413	Yoda, May the Force...	10 - 15
JE6414	Chewbacca, name	10 - 15
JE6415	Millennium Falcon, pilot	10 - 15

Adam Joseph, *ROTJ* brass pins

JE6530	Royal Guard	3 - 6
JE6531	Wicket the Ewok	3 - 6
JE6532	C-3PO bust	3 - 6
JE6533	Yoda	3 - 6
JE6534	Salacious Crumb	6 - 12
JE6535	R2-D2	6 - 12
JE6536	X-wing fighter logo	5 - 10
JE6537	*ROTJ* logo	5 - 10
JE6538	The Force	5 - 10
JE6539	May the Force...	5 - 10
JE6540	*SW* logo	5 - 10

***ROTJ* painted plastic pins**

JE6555	Wicket	1 - 2
JE6556	Kneesaa	1 - 2

Howard Eldon, *SW* 10th Anniversary

JE6701	*SW* logo, enameled black	5 - 8
JE6702	*ESB* logo, enameled red	5 - 8
JE6703	*ESB* logo, enameled blue	5 - 8
JE6704	*ROTJ* logo, enameled red	5 - 8
JE6707	*ROTJ* logo, enameled blue	5 - 8
JE6710	Vader figure, enameled	3 - 6
JE6712	R2-D2, enameled	3 - 6
JE6715	C-3PO, enameled	3 - 6

Hollywood Pins — *see color photos on page 100*

JE6751	Lightsabers w/Star Wars logo	5 - 8
JE6753	Ben Kenobi	5 - 8
JE6755	Yoda Contemplating	5 - 8
JE6757	Imperial Emblem, cloisonne	3 - 6
JE6758	Imperial Emblem, poly	2 - 4
JE6759	Rebo Band	6 - 10
JE6761	AT-AT	5 - 8
JE6763	Princess Leia	5 - 8
JE6765	Millennium Falcon, cloisonne	5 - 8
JE6766	Millennium Falcon, poly	3 - 5
JE6767	Darth Vader Helmet, 3-D	3 - 5
JE6769	X-wing fighter, 3-D, pewter look	3 - 6
JE6771	X-wing fighter	3 - 6
JE6773	TIE Fighter	5 - 8
JE6775	Darth Vader	6 - 10
JE6777	Jabba the Hutt	4 - 7
JE6779	Rebel Alliance New Republic Logo (large)	3 - 6
JE6781	Rebel Alliance New Republic Logo (small), cloisonne	2 - 4
JE6782	Rebel Alliance New Republic Logo (small), poly	2 - 4

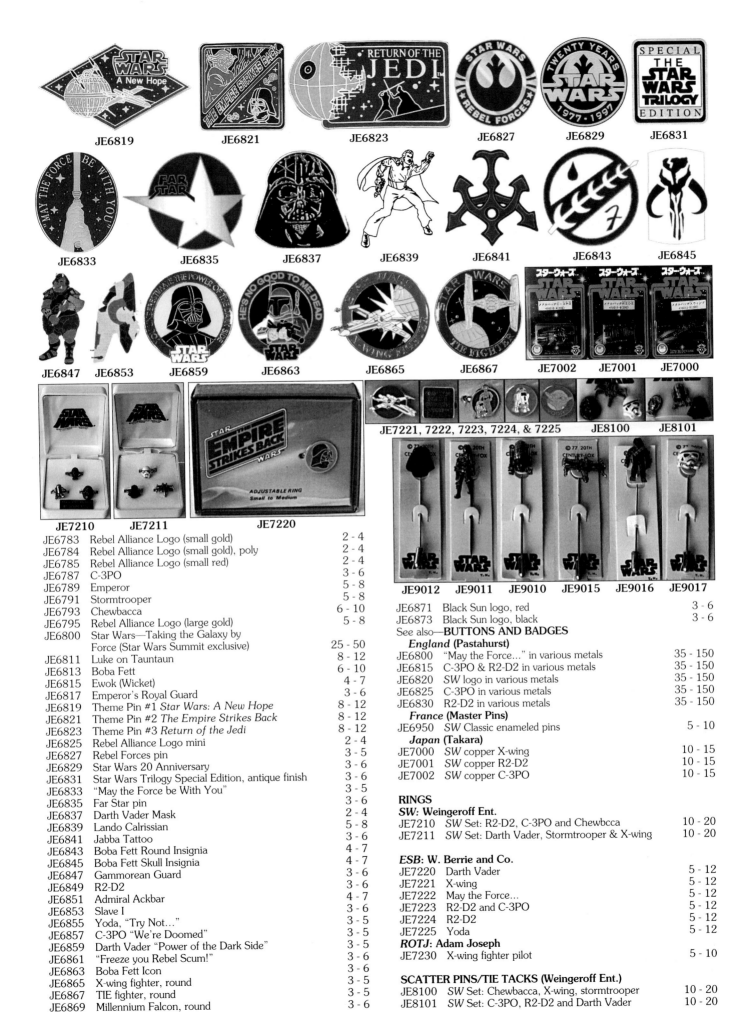

JE6819 JE6821 JE6823 JE6827 JE6829 JE6831

JE6833 JE6835 JE6837 JE6839 JE6841 JE6843 JE6845

JE6847 JE6853 JE6859 JE6863 JE6865 JE6867 JE7002 JE7001 JE7000

JE7210 JE7211 JE7220

JE7221, 7222, 7223, 7224, & 7225   JE8100   JE8101

JE9012 JE9011 JE9010 JE9015 JE9016 JE9017

JE6783	Rebel Alliance Logo (small gold)	2 - 4
JE6784	Rebel Alliance Logo (small gold), poly	2 - 4
JE6785	Rebel Alliance Logo (small red)	2 - 4
JE6787	C-3PO	3 - 6
JE6789	Emperor	5 - 8
JE6791	Stormtrooper	5 - 8
JE6793	Chewbacca	6 - 10
JE6795	Rebel Alliance Logo (large gold)	5 - 8
JE6800	Star Wars—Taking the Galaxy by Force (Star Wars Summit exclusive)	25 - 50
JE6811	Luke on Tauntaun	8 - 12
JE6813	Boba Fett	6 - 10
JE6815	Ewok (Wicket)	4 - 7
JE6817	Emperor's Royal Guard	3 - 6
JE6819	Theme Pin #1 *Star Wars: A New Hope*	8 - 12
JE6821	Theme Pin #2 *The Empire Strikes Back*	8 - 12
JE6823	Theme Pin #3 *Return of the Jedi*	8 - 12
JE6825	Rebel Alliance Logo mini	2 - 4
JE6827	Rebel Forces pin	3 - 5
JE6829	Star Wars 20 Anniversary	3 - 6
JE6831	Star Wars Trilogy Special Edition, antique finish	3 - 6
JE6833	"May the Force be With You"	3 - 5
JE6835	Far Star pin	3 - 6
JE6837	Darth Vader Mask	2 - 4
JE6839	Lando Calrissian	5 - 8
JE6841	Jabba Tattoo	3 - 6
JE6843	Boba Fett Round Insignia	4 - 7
JE6845	Boba Fett Skull Insignia	4 - 7
JE6847	Gammorean Guard	3 - 6
JE6849	R2-D2	3 - 6
JE6851	Admiral Ackbar	4 - 7
JE6853	Slave I	3 - 6
JE6855	Yoda, "Try Not…"	3 - 5
JE6857	C-3PO "We're Doomed"	3 - 5
JE6859	Darth Vader "Power of the Dark Side"	3 - 5
JE6861	"Freeze you Rebel Scum!"	3 - 6
JE6863	Boba Fett Icon	3 - 6
JE6865	X-wing fighter, round	3 - 5
JE6867	TIE fighter, round	3 - 5
JE6869	Millennium Falcon, round	3 - 6

JE6871	Black Sun logo, red	3 - 6
JE6873	Black Sun logo, black	3 - 6
See also—BUTTONS AND BADGES		

England (Pastahurst)

JE6800	"May the Force…" in various metals	35 - 150
JE6815	C-3PO & R2-D2 in various metals	35 - 150
JE6820	*SW* logo in various metals	35 - 150
JE6825	C-3PO in various metals	35 - 150
JE6830	R2-D2 in various metals	35 - 150

France (Master Pins)

JE6950	*SW* Classic enameled pins	5 - 10

Japan (Takara)

JE7000	*SW* copper X-wing	10 - 15
JE7001	*SW* copper R2-D2	10 - 15
JE7002	*SW* copper C-3PO	10 - 15

RINGS

SW: Weingeroff Ent.

JE7210	*SW* Set: R2-D2, C-3PO and Chewbcca	10 - 20
JE7211	*SW* Set: Darth Vader, Stormtrooper & X-wing	10 - 20

ESB: W. Berrie and Co.

JE7220	Darth Vader	5 - 12
JE7221	X-wing	5 - 12
JE7222	May the Force…	5 - 12
JE7223	R2-D2 and C-3PO	5 - 12
JE7224	R2-D2	5 - 12
JE7225	Yoda	5 - 12

ROTJ: Adam Joseph

JE7230	X-wing fighter pilot	5 - 10

SCATTER PINS/TIE TACKS (Weingeroff Ent.)

JE8100	*SW* Set: Chewbacca, X-wing, stormtrooper	10 - 20
JE8101	*SW* Set: C-3PO, R2-D2 and Darth Vader	10 - 20

KI0012

KI0171

KI0010

KI0270

KI0271

KI1215

KI1216

KI1217

KI1320

KI1322

KI1323

KI1210

KI1211

KI1425   KI1426   KI1427   KI2250

STICKPINS

JE9010	R2-D2	5 - 10
JE9011	C-3PO	5 - 10
JE9012	Darth Vader	5 - 10
JE9015	X-wing	5 - 10
JE9016	Chewbacca	5 - 10
JE9017	Stormtrooper	5 - 10

KITCHEN ITEMS

BOWLS (Deka Plastics)

KI0010	*SW* 14 oz. soup	6 - 15
KI0011	*SW* 16 oz. insulated	6 - 15
KI0012	*SW* 20 oz. cereal	6 - 15
KI0170	*ESB* 14 oz. soup	5 - 12
KI0171	*ESB* 20 oz. cereal	5 - 12
KI0270	*ROTJ* 14 oz. soup	5 - 12
KI0271	*ROTJ* 20 oz. cereal	5 - 12

CAKE PANS/KITS/ACCESSORIES (Wilton Enterprises)

KI1210	R2-D2 cake decorating kit	15 - 30
KI1211	Darth Vader cake decorating kit	15 - 30
KI1215	C-3PO cake pan	15 - 20
KI1216	Boba Fett cake pan	25 - 30
KI1217	Darth Vader cake pan	20 - 25
KI1218	R2-D2 cake pan	15 - 20
KI1320	*SW* C-3PO and R2-D2 cake tops	4 - 10
KI1322	*ESB* C-3PO and R2-D2 put ons	4 - 10
KI1323	Darth Vader and Stormtrooper plastic cake tops	4 - 10
KI1425	Chewbacca cake candle	3 - 6
KI1426	Darth Vader cake candle	3 - 6
KI1427	R2-D2 cake candle	3 - 6

CANDY MOLDS (Wilton Enterprises)

KI2250	*ESB* carded double set w/Darth, Chewie, C-3PO, Stormtrooper, R2-D2, Yoda	5 - 15

KI3510

KI4010   KI8010   KI6010

KI4120

KI4121

KI4122

KI4123

KI4131

KI4130

KI4500

KI4503

KI4505

KI5010	KI5011	KI5012	KI5013	KI5014	KI5015	KI5016	KI5017
KI5025	KI5026	KI5027	KI5028	KI5029	KI5030	KI5031	KI5032

KI5050	KI5051	KI5052	KI5053	KI5060	KI5061	KI5062

KI2252	*ROTJ/SW* I: Darth, Boba Fett, Stormtrooper	3 - 10
KI2255	*ROTJ/SW* II: Yoda, Chewie, droids	3 - 10
KI2260	*ROTJ/SW*: Large R2-D2	3 - 10

CHINA

KI3510	Plate, bowl and mug set (Sigma)	25 - 45

Spain (Deccoraciones Herrandiz)

KI3650	*Droids* cups and saucers	10 - 25

CUPS/MUGS (Deka Plastics)

KI4010	*SW* 10 oz.	5 - 10
KI4120	*ESB* Yoda 10 oz.	5 - 10
KI4121	*ESB* Vader, Boba Fett 10 oz.	5 - 10
KI4122	*ESB* Han, Leia, Luke 10 oz	5 - 10
KI4123	*ESB* Chewie, droids 10 oz.	5 - 10
KI4130	*ROTJ* Luke/Yoda, Darth/Guards	5 - 10
KI4131	*ROTJ* Droids/Wicket, Leia/Ewoks	5 - 10

See also—**CERAMICS**

DINNERWEAR SETS

KI4500	*ROTJ* Baby's first feeding set	4 - 8
KI4503	*ROTJ* Dinnerware Set	5 - 10
KI4505	Wicket 3 piece child's set	4 - 8

PAPER CUPS

American Can Co. and later James River-Dixie/Northern Inc. issued four different major series of disposable Dixie Cups for the *Star Wars* saga. The boxes themselves were colorful and each series had as many as 40 differently designed paper cups. There were mail-in premium offers as well as in-pack offers. The company also ran contests, offering everything from a limited-edition cloth patch to a personal appearance by Darth Vader.

***Star Wars* boxes**

KI5010	Droids	15 - 25
KI5011	Obi-Wan Kenobi	15 - 25
KI5012	Princess Leia	20 - 30
KI5013	Han and Chewbacca	15 - 25
KI5014	Luke Skywalker	15 - 25
KI5015	Stormtrooper	15 - 25
KI5016	TIE ftr./X-wing/Death Star	15 - 25
KI5017	Darth Vader	15 - 25

***The Empire Strikes Back* boxes**

KI5025	Yoda	12 - 20
KI5026	X-wing in swamp	12 - 20
KI5027	Luke on Tauntaun	12 - 20
KI5028	Twin-pod cloud car	12 - 20
KI5029	AT-ATs and snowspeeder	12 - 20
KI5030	Millennium Falcon	12 - 20

KI5068   KI5080   KI5500   KI5501   KI5502   KI6020

KI6510

KI8030 (3 sizes)

KI6030

KI6520

KI6530   KI8020 (11 oz.)   KI8020 (17 oz.)

LA7410   LA7410   LA7410

| KI5031 | Star Destroyer | 12 - 20 |
| KI5032 | Darth Vader | 12 - 20 |

Return of the Jedi boxes

KI5050	Luke/Yoda/B-wng.	10 - 15
KI5051	Jabba/Princess Leia	10 - 15
KI5052	Ewoks	10 - 15
KI5053	Emperor/Guard/Darth Vader	10 - 15

Star Wars Saga boxes

KI5060	Droids	10 - 15
KI5061	Leia/Han/Stormtroopers	10 - 15
KI5062	Darth Vader	10 - 15
KI5063	Luke and Yoda	10 - 15

Premiums/Promotions

KI5065	Collector's Kit: Rebel Alliance set. Poster of Luke and 4 5x7 action scene cards	10 - 25
KI5066	Collector's Kit: Empire set. Poster of Darth and 4 5x7 action scene cards	10 - 25
KI5067	SW logo T-shirt	10 - 25
KI5068	ESB story cards, 6 strips of 4, ea.	10 - 25
KI5070	Poster to hold story cards	15 - 20
KI5072	ESB logo on T-shirt and hat (Hawaiian Punch tie-in)	10 - 15
KI5075	ESB laminated placemats, 4 diff., ea.	15 - 30
KI5080	Darth Vader Appearance Sweepstakes:1,000 red, white and black Vader cloth patches for 4th prize.	45 - 65

Canada (Canada Cup Inc.)

KI5500	ROTJ Leia and Jabba	5 - 10
KI5501	ROTJ Emperor and Darth Vader	5 - 10
KI5502	ROTJ Luke, Yoda and X-wing	5 - 10

See also—**PARTY ITEMS**

PITCHERS/DECANTERS (Deka Plastics)

KI6010	SW 90 oz. w/top	15 - 25
KI6020	ESB 90 oz. w/top	15 - 25
KI6030	ROTJ 90 oz. w/top	15 - 25

PLATES (Deka Plastics)

KI6510	SW compartment plate	6 - 12
KI6520	ESB compartment plate	6 - 12
KI6530	ROTJ compartment plate	6 - 12

TABLEWARE

Australia (Roy Lee Cin)

| KI7050 | ESB plastic tableware | 5 - 10 |

TUMBLERS (Deka Plastics)

| KI8010 | SW 6 oz., 11 oz., or 17 oz. | 3 - 15 |

| KI8020 | ESB 6 oz., 11 oz., or 17 oz. | 3 - 12 |
| KI8030 | ROTJ 6 oz., 11 oz., or 17 oz. | 3 - 10 |

See also—**CUPS/GLASSES—COLLECTOR'S**

OTHER

Spain (Decoraciones Herrandiz)

| KI9200 | Droids porcelain jars | 10 - 25 |

LAMINATED CARDS

Japan

LC7010	SW assorted cards	10 - 25
LC7210	ESB assorted cards	8 - 20
LC7410	ROTJ assorted cards	8 - 20

Sweden (Ide and Resultat AB)

| LC8510 | ROTJ luminous hard plastic tags | 5 - 12 |

See also—**STATIONERY/SCHOOL SUPPLIES: Notepads**

LUGGAGE/CARRYALLS

BACKPACKS

Factors Inc.

LG0010	SW Han and Chewbacca	15 - 25
LG0012	SW Chewbacca	15 - 25
LG0015	SW May the Force Be With You	15 - 20
LG0130	ESB Darth and Stormtroopers, black	15 - 25
LG0132	ESB Darth and Stormtroopers, blue	15 - 25

Adam Joseph Industries

LG0560	ROTJ R2-D2 and C-3PO backpack (tear-shaped)	10 - 25
LG0561	ROTJ R2-D2 and C-3PO (school bag shaped)	10 - 20
LG0562	ROTJ R2-D2 and C-3PO (reversed design)	10 - 20
LG0565	ROTJ Yoda backpack (tear-shaped)	10 - 25
LG0566	ROTJ Yoda backpack (school bag shaped)	10 - 20
LG0567	ROTJ Yoda backpack (reversed design)	10 - 20
LG0570	ROTJ Darth Vader and guards	10 - 25
LG0577	ROTJ AT-AT	10 - 25
LG0580	ROTJ cast	10 - 25

LG0010   LG0012   LG0560   LG0561   LG0562   LG0565   LG0567

LG0570   LG0577   LG0590   LG0591   LG1050   LG1054   LG1220

LG1525   LG2010   LG2015   LG2020   LG2025   LG2030   LG2510   LG2520   LG2525   LG2530

LG3000   LG3020   LG4010   LG6010   LG6018   LG6130

LG6170   LG6171   LG6170   LG6172   LG6790   LG6791   LG6792   LG6793

LG0590	Wicket the Ewok backpack (tear-shaped)	10 - 20
LG0591	Wicket the Ewok backpack (school bag shaped)	8 - 15
LG0592	Wicket the Ewok backpack (reversed design)	8 - 15

Australia (Premier)

LG1010	*SW* R2-D2 and C-3PO, blue	15 - 25
LG1011	*SW* R2-D2 and C-3PO, yellow	15 - 25
LG1050	*ESB* Luke, Leia, Han, droids, blue	10 - 25
LG1052	Darth and Stormtroopers, black	8 - 20
LG1054	Darth and Stromtroopers, blue	8 - 20

England (Frankel & Roth)

LG1220	*ROTJ* Darth, Stormtrooper, C-3PO, Luke, Leia and R2-D2	10 - 25

Japan

LG1525	*SW* May the Force...	12 - 30

DUFFEL/BARREL BAGS (Adam Joseph)

LG2010	*ROTJ* Yoda	10 - 20
LG2015	*ROTJ* R2-D2 and C-3PO	10 - 20
LG2020	*ROTJ* Millennium Falcon	10 - 20
LG2025	*ROTJ* Darth Vader	10 - 20
LG2030	*ROTJ* Wicket	10 - 20

LAUNDRY BAGS (Adam Joseph)

LG2510	C-3PO and R2-D2	8 - 15
LG2520	Darth and Emperor's Guard	8 - 15
LG2525	Wicket the Ewok	5 - 10
LG2530	Wicket and Kneesaa	5 - 10

LUGGAGE (Adam Joseph)

LG3000	Darth Vader & Royal Guard suitcase, 3 sizes, ea.	15 - 55
LG3020	Wicket & Princess Kneesaa suitcase	15 - 25

SPORTS BAGS

Australia (Premier)

LG4010	*ESB* Vader, Stormtroopers, Luke, Han, droids, Leia	10 - 25

Japan (Maruyoshi Co.)

LG4220	*SW* sports bag	10 - 25

Spain (Industrias CYS)

LG4430	*SW* sports bag	10 - 25

TOILETRY (Adam Joseph)

LG5010	Princess Kneesaa Personal Care Bag	3 - 6

Japan (Maruyoshi Co.)

LG5510	*SW* mini-bag	5 - 10

TOTE

Factors

LG6010	*SW* C-3PO and R2-D2	5 - 15
LG6012	Darth "Vadar" Lives	5 - 15
LG6014	*SW* logo	5 - 15
LG6016	May the Force....	5 - 15
LG6018	*SW* Hilderbrandt	

Adam Joseph

LG6130	*ROTJ* C-3PO & R2-D2	5 - 12
LG6132	*ROTJ* Darth Vader school bag w/handle	5 - 15

LG7420   LG8010   LG8011   LG8012   LG8030   LU0010

LU0020   LU0021   LU0030   LU0110   LU0120

LU0121   LU0111   LU0140   LU0040   LU2000   LU2001

LU0041

LG6134	*ROTJ* Yoda	5 - 12
LG6136	*ROTJ* Wicket the Ewok	5 - 10
LG6170	*ROTJ* C-3PO & R2-D2 ditty bag	5 - 10
LG6171	*ROTJ* Sail Barge ditty bag	5 - 10
LG6172	*ROTJ* biker scout ditty bag	5 - 10

Australia (B and W Character Mdse)

LG6575	*ESB* tote	5 - 12

England (Frankel and Roth)

LG6780	*ESB* bag, Yoda	5 - 12
LG6781	*ESB* bag, Darth Vader	5 - 12
LG6782	*ESB* bag, Luke	5 - 12
LG6783	*ESB* bag, scenes	5 - 12
LG6790	*ROTJ* zippered or hand bag, Jabba	5 - 15
LG6791	*ROTJ* zippered or hand bag, 4 scenes	5 - 15
LG6792	*ROTJ* zippered or hand bag, Rebel hanger	5 - 15
LG6793	*ROTJ* zippered or hand bag, Luke w/blaster	5 - 15

Italy (Regis SpA)

LG6900	*ESB* school bags, ea.	5 - 15

Japan (Maruyoshi Co.)

LG7110	Luke and Leia canvas	5 - 15
LG7120	*SW* logo tote	5 - 15
LG7121	*SW* beach bag	5 - 15

Mexico (Peonajes Registrados)

LG7420	*ROTJ* Luke and Darth duel	5 - 12

New Zealand (Bing Harris Sargood Ltd.)

LG7550	*ROTJ* school bags, droids, Yoda, speeder bikes, ea.	5 - 15

Spain (Industrias CYS SA)

LG7650	*SW* schoolbags, ea.	5 - 15

OTHER

Adam Joseph

LG8010	*ROTJ* Wicket shaped shoulder bag	4 - 10
LG8011	*ROTJ* Kneesaa shaped shoulder bag	
LG8012	*ROTJ* Ewoks shoulder bag	4 - 10
LG8014	*ROTJ* Wicket & Kneesaa shoulder bag	4 - 10
LG8016	*ROTJ* Wicket shoulder bag	4 - 10
LG8020	Wicket and Baga lunch bag	4 - 10
LG8030	*ESB* Concorde Bag (American Can)	

Mexico (Personajes Registrados)

LG9290	Emperor, Luke, Darth plastic bags w/tie closings, ea.	3 - 6

LUNCH BOXES

There were at least a dozen varieties of metal and plastic *Star Wars* trilogy lunch boxes produced in the U.S. by King Seeley Thermos.

Collectors should look for them with their small plastic thermos jugs inside, and the prices reflect such a complete kit. We have listed bottles separately, because they were used in multiple boxes and are sometimes found for sale individually.

LU0010	*SW* metal w/black star field around sides	30 - 60
LU0020	*SW* metal w/character art on sides	30 - 45
LU0021	Blue thermos w/droids decal and yellow cup/cap	5 - 10
LU0030	*SW* light blue plastic dome: "Design Your Own," w/large sheet of stickers	25 - 40
LU0031	Same color light blue thermos, no design, w/white cup/cap	5 - 10
LU0040	*SW* red plastic w/art of Darth Vader and droids	20 - 35
LU0041	Same blue thermos as LU0021, but w/red cup/cap	5 - 10
LU0110	*ESB* metal w/photos of Luke/Yoda & snowtroopers	20 - 35
LU0111	Red thermos w/Yoda decal and yellow cap/cup	10 - 15
LU0120	*ESB* metal w/art of Luke/Yoda & Falcon cockpit	20 - 40
LU0121	Blue thermos w/Yoda decal and white cap/cup	10 - 15
LU0140	*ESB* red plastic w/photo of Chewie, Han, Leia, Luke in Hoth ice cave (came w/LU0111)	15 - 30
LU0150	*ESB* red plastic w/photo of X-wing and smaller photo montage (came w/LU0121)	15 - 30
LU0210	*ROTJ* metal w/art of Death Star/Vader and Luke in Jabba's palace	15 - 25
LU0211	Red thermos w/*ROTJ* logo and Wicket decal w/white cap/cup	5 - 10
LU0220	*ROTJ* red plastic w/cartoon art of Wicket and R2-D2	15 - 20
LU0310	*Ewoks* red plastic w/cartoon art of Wicket flying	15 - 20
LU0311	Red thermos w/*SW Ewoks* logo and cartoon art of Wicket and white cap/cup	5 - 10
LU0410	*Droids* light blue plastic w/cartoon art of C-3PO, R2-D2 & aliens	15 - 25
LU0411	Light blue thermos w/*SW Droids* logo & cartoon art of droids w/white cap/cup	5 - 10
LU0510	*Ewoks* lunch bag (Adam Joseph Industries)	

England (Thermos Ltd.)

LU2000	*ESB* red plastic w/*SW* logo & art of Vader, troopers on Hoth	15 - 30
LU2001	Red thermos w/Vader & troopers & white cap/cup	5 - 10
LU2040	*ROTJ* light blue plastic w/art of Wicket flying	15 - 20
LU2041	Light blue thermos w/decal of Wicket swinging & white cap/cup	5 - 10

| LU0210 | LU0211 | LU0220 | LU0310 | LU0410 | LU0411 | LU2040 |

| LU0510 | LU3010 | MA0010 | MA0025 | MB8010 | MO2009 |

Japan (Sakura Co. Ltd.)

LU3010	*SW* "Sports Pot and Seal Cooler" w/art of droids, yellow top; large thermos-like jug	25 - 35

New Zealand (Bing Harris Sargood Ltd.)

LU4050	*ROTJ* plastic lunch box	15 - 20

MAGNETS (Adam Joseph Industries)

MA0010	Chewbacca, Darth Vader, R2-D2 & Yoda multi-pack	3 - 12
MA0025	Wicket and Kneesaa	2 - 4

MAQUETTES

Maquettes are highly-detailed artists' proofs used as models for sculpture, animation, and other design applications. In recent years, limited-edition "maquettes" have been marketed as high-end collectibles.

Illusive Originals began producing Maquettes and similar character items for the *Star Wars* saga in 1995, debuting the line with a 1/1 scale Yoda replica. See page 100 for color photos.

MA5001 Yoda	400 - 750
MA5003 Admiral Ackbar	75 - 125
MA5005 Boba Fett	90 - 125
MA5011 Chewbacca head	150 - 175
MA5013 Jabba the Hutt	125 - 200
MA5015 Han Solo in Carbonite replica	900 - 1200

MOBILES

Spain (Ediciones Manantial)

MB8010	C-3PO card stock	45 - 65

See also—**FOOD: Cereal**

MODEL KITS/ROCKETS

The primary licensee for model kits was Kenner Products' affiliate MPC. The company's models were good enough to be used by Industrial Light & Magic in both *ESB* and *ROTJ* after some modifications. There were lots of innovations, including a Darth Vader action bust that made a raspy "breathing" sound; a lighted Millennium Falcon (first release only); "Structor" action models that actually walked after assembly; and "Mirr-a-kits," where only half a model was assembled and attached to a reflective surface to mimic a full model. A number of the kits were sold in boxes for several of the movies, and many were later reissued in the original box with a notable difference: the logo now read MPC/Ertl, reflecting the fact that the Ertl Co. had taken over the line. The company later became AMT/Ertl, and old kits were re-released in completely new packaging. A few kits were issued in a version that had to be glued as well as one that could be snapped together.

MPC's foreign affiliates, including Airfix in England, sometimes sold the models in different packaging, including one four-piece set. In Japan, there were some series of unusual models made of metal and wood. There were also a lot of unauthorized Japanese resin "garage kits," some issued as detailed likenesses, other as "deformed" or comic adaptations. More recently fully-licensed kits in resin and vinyl have come onto the market.

Star Wars MPC kits were sold with an *ESB* sticker attached to the shrink wrap shortly before the release of the second film. The sticker is easily removed (and comes off with the shrink wrap), and the kits are identical, so the effect of the sticker on value is negligible.

Values quoted for plastic kits assume *no construction or painting* has been started, and that the box is in good condition with little or no wear. High-end prices assume the original shrink wrap is intact. Plastic kits with construction or painting started, crushed boxes, or parts missing have little or no collectible value. For example, a Millennium Falcon kit with lights (MO2210) which has been started and partially painted would have a value of about $10 instead of $35 - 75, even if the box is in good condition.

This rule does not usually apply to resin kits, unless they are almost totally useless. This is because of the higer cost and lower availability of resin kits, as well as the ease of stripping the paint down to the original surface.

METAL

Japan (Tskuda Co.)

MO1010	AT-AT vs. Snowspeeder	90 - 110
MO1011	Snowspeeder vs. Scout Walker	90 - 110
MO1012	X-wing vs. TIE fighter	90 - 110
MO1013	Millennium Falcon vs. Slave I	90 - 110
MO1014	Star Destroyer	120 - 150
MO1015	Y-wing vs. TIE fighter (limited, paper bag only)	125 - 150

PLASTIC (MPC)

MO2009	*SW* Luke Skywalker's X-wing fighter (10" x 14" box)	35 - 45
MO2010	*SW* Luke Skywalker's X-wing fighter (8" x 14" box)	27 - 37
MO2011	*ROTJ* X-wing fighter	12 - 20
MO2012	*ROTJ* Snap X-wing fighter	12 - 20
MO2013	*ROTJ* MPC/Ertl X-wing	10 - 12
MO2014	*ROTJ* MPC/Ertl Snap X-wing	10 - 14
MO2015	*ROTJ* AMT/Ertl X-wing fighter	8 - 12
MO2016	*ROTJ* AMT/Ertl Snap X-wing	8 - 12
MO2017	AMT/Ertl X-wing fighter w/paint	10 - 15
MO2018	AMT/Ertl Limited Edition gold X-wing	18 - 32
MO2019	AMT/Ertl X-wing fighter flight display	15 - 20
MO2020	*SW* Darth Vader's TIE fighter (10" x 14" box)	30 - 35
MO2021	*SW* Darth Vader's TIE fighter (8" x 14" box)	22 - 28
MO2023	*SW* MPC/Ertl DV TIE fighter	10 - 12
MO2024	*SW* AMT/Ertl DV TIE fighter	8 - 11
MO2025	*SW* AMT/Ertl DV TIE fighter flight display	15 - 20
MO2026	*SW* AMT/Ertl DV TIE fighter w/paint	10 - 15
MO2030	*SW* Darth Vader figure w/Glo-Light saber	18 - 35
MO2033	*SW* MPC/Ertl DV figure	12 - 16
MO2035	*SW* AMT/Ertl DV figure	10 - 15
MO2040	*SW* Darth Vader action model	80 - 90
MO2050	*SW* R2-D2 original wide box	35 - 45
MO2051	*SW* R2-D2 second narrow box	25 - 35
MO2200	*ROTJ* R2-D2	10 - 20
MO2202	*SW* C-3PO original wide box	30 - 40
MO2204	*SW* C-3PO second narrow box	20 - 30
MO2206	*ROTJ* C-3PO	8 - 18
MO2207	*SW* Snap Darth Vader van	28 - 38
MO2208	*SW* Snap Luke Skywalker van	28 - 38
MO2209	*SW* Snap Artoo-Detoo van	28 - 38

MO2012 MO2020 MO2030 MO2040

MO2202 MO2204 MO2206 MO2051 MO2207

MO2208 MO2209 MO2210 MO2212

MO2400 MO2408 MO2410 MO2420

MO2430 MO2431 MO2440 MO2450

MO2210	*SW* Han Solo's Millennium Falcon w/lights	70 - 80
MO2212	*ROTJ* Millennium Falcon w/o lights	28 - 38
MO2214	*ROTJ* MPC/Ertl Millennium Falcon	17 - 22
MO2216	*ROTJ* AMT/Ertl Millennium Falcon	15 - 20
MO2218	AMT/Ertl Millennium Falcon cutaway	20 - 30
MO2400	*ESB* AT-AT	16 - 32
MO2404	*ROTJ* AT-AT	12 - 20
MO2406	*ROTJ* MPC/Ertl AT-AT	10 - 18
MO2407	*ROTJ* AMT/Ertl AT-AT	8 - 15
MO2408	*ESB* Slave I	45 - 55
MO2409	*ESB* AMT/Ertl Slave I	10 - 14
MO2410	*ESB* Star Destroyer	30 - 35
MO2412	*ESB* MPC/Ertl Star Destroyer	11 - 16
MO2413	*ESB* AMT/Ertl Star Destroyer	10 - 15
MO2414	AMT/Ertl Star Destroyer w/fiber optic lights	35 - 45
MO2420	*ESB* Luke Skywalker's Snowspeeder	15 - 35
MO2421	*ESB* MPC/Ertl Luke Skywalker's Snowspeeder	10 - 20
MO2422	*ESB* AMT/Ertl Luke Skywalker's Snowspeeder	8 - 18
MO2430	*ESB* Battle on Ice Planet Hoth	20 - 35

MO2431	*ESB* AMT/Ertl Battle on Ice Planet Hoth	10 - 14
MO2440	*ESB* Encounter w/Yoda on Dagobah	20 - 45
MO2441	*ESB* AMT/Ertl Encounter w/Yoda on Dagobah	10 - 14
MO2450	*ESB* Rebel Base	20 - 30
MO2451	*ESB* MPC/Ertl Rebel Base	12 - 18
MO2452	*ESB* AMT/Ertl Rebel Base	10 - 15
MO2600	*ROTJ* Speeder Bike	15 - 28
MO2601	*ROTJ* MPC/Ertl Speeder Bike	12 - 20
MO2602	*ROTJ* AMT/Ertl Speeder Bike	10 - 18
MO2610	*ROTJ* Snap TIE Interceptor	12 - 20
MO2612	*ROTJ* MPC/Ertl Snap TIE Interceptor	10 - 14
MO2613	*ROTJ* AMT/Ertl Snap TIE Interceptor	8 - 12
MO2614	AMT/Ertl Limited Edition gold TIE Interceptor	18 - 32
MO2615	*ROTJ* Snap A-wing fighter	12 - 20
MO2620	*ROTJ* MPC/Ertl Snap A-wing	10 - 15
MO2622	*ROTJ* Snap B-wing fighter	20 - 35
MO2623	AMT/Ertl Limited Edition gold B-wing	18 - 32
MO2624	*ROTJ* Shuttle Tyderium	20 - 30
MO2625	*ROTJ* MPC/Ertl Shuttle Tyderium	12 - 18

MO2600

MO2610

MO2614

MO2615

MO2622

MO2623

MO2624

MO2631

MO2633

MO2636

MO2626 *ROTJ* AMT/Ertl Shuttle Tyderium	10 - 15	
MO2630 *ROTJ* Jabba Throne Room	20 - 40	
MO2631 *ROTJ* AMT/Ertl Jabba Throne Room	10 - 14	
MO2633 *ROTJ* Y-wing fighter	35 - 45	
MO2635 *ROTJ* MPC/Ertl Y-wing	20 - 35	
MO2636 *ROTJ* AT-ST	8 - 12	
MO2639 *ROTJ* MPC/Ertl AT-ST	8 - 12	
MO2640 *ROTJ* MPC/Ertl 3-Piece Set: Snap X-wing, B-wing, TIE Interceptor	18 - 28	
MO2642 *ROTJ* AMT/Ertl 3-Piece Set: Snap X-wing, B-wing, TIE Interceptor	15 - 25	
MO2645 Imperial TIE fighter	15 - 20	
MO2650 *SOTE* AMT/Ertl Xizor's Virago	15 - 20	

Structors (wind-up motors)

MO2800 *ROTJ* C-3PO	20 - 25
MO2810 *ROTJ* AT-AT	20 - 25
MO2820 *ROTJ* AT-ST	20 - 25

Mirra-A-Kits

MO3010 *ROTJ* X-wing fighter	8 - 15
MO3020 *ROTJ* TIE Interceptor	8 - 15
MO3030 *ROTJ* Shuttle Tyderium	8 - 15
MO3040 *ROTJ* Y-wing fighter	8 - 15
MO3050 *ROTJ* AT-ST	8 - 15
MO3060 *ROTJ* Speeder Bike	8 - 15

England

Denys Fisher

MO4000 *SW* Darth Vader TIE fighter	35 - 45
MO4001 *SW* Luke Skywalker X-wing	30 - 40
MO4002 *SW* R2-D2	40 - 50
MO4003 *SW* C-3PO	40 - 50

Airfix

MO4010 *ESB* Luke Skywalker Snowspeeder	25 - 40
MO4011 *ESB* Battle on Ice Planet Hoth	30 - 45
MO4012 *ESB* Enocunter with Yoda on Degobah	30 - 50
MO4013 *ESB* AT-AT	20 - 35
MO4014 *ESB* Rebel Base	20 - 40
MO4015 *SW* Luke Skywalker X-wing fighter	20 - 30
MO4016 *ESB* Slave I	50 - 60
MO4017 *ROTJ* Jabba's Palace	20 - 45
MO4018 *ROTJ* Speeder Bike	15 - 30
MO4019 Imperial Star Destroyer	25 - 40
MO4020 *ROTJ* Imperial Shuttle Tyderium	25 - 35
MO4021 *SW* Millennium Falcon w/lights	80 - 100
MO4022 *ROTJ* Space Vehicle set w/X-wing, A-wing, B-wing and TIE Interceptor	35 - 45
MO4023 X-wing fighter (small)	15 - 20
MO4024 A-wing fighter	15 - 25
MO4025 TIE Interceptor	15 - 20
MO4026 *ROTJ* B-wing fighter	25 - 45
MO4027 AT-ST	15 - 20
MO4028 Y-wing fighter	40 - 45
MO2800 *ROTJ* C-3PO Structors	25 - 30
MO2810 *ROTJ* AT-AT Structors	25 - 30
MO2820 *ROTJ* AT-ST Structors	25 - 30

France (Meccano)

MO4200 *SW* Z-6PO	50 - 60
MO4210 *SW* D2-R2	50 - 60
MO4220 Darth Vader Bust	130 - 160
MO4230 Chasseur X (X-wing)	35 - 45
MO4240 Chasseur T.I.E. (DV TIE Fighter)	40 - 50
MO4250 Faucon Millénaire (Millennium Falcon)	80 - 110

Germany (Kenner Germany)

MO4550 *SW* C-3PO	40 - 55
MO4555 *SW* R2-D2	40 - 55
MO4560 *SW* TIE-Jäger	40 - 50
MO4565 *SW* X-Flügeljäger	40 - 50

Japan

Revell/Takara, all *SW*

MO5005 Motorized R2-D2 w/lights (motor not included)	100 - 120
MO5010 Motorized X-wing fighter w/lights (motor not incl.)	100 - 120
MO5020 R2-D2	75 - 100
MO5025 C-3PO	75 - 100

MO2810   MO3010   MO3020   MO3030   MO3040   MO3050   MO3060

MO4550	MO4555	MO4560	MO4565

MO5005	MO5010	MO6010	MO8000

MO8002	MO8004	MO8100	MO8102	MO8103	MO8105 MO8107

MO5030 Luke Skywalker X-wing fighter	75 - 100	
MO5035 Darth Vader TIE fighter	75 - 100	
Takara		
MO5250 X-wing fighter	100 - 120	
MO5255 R2-D2	100 - 120	
MO5260 C-3PO	100 - 120	
MO5265 TIE fighter	100 - 120	
Mexico (Lily-Ledy)		
MO5500 Nave Imperial de Darth Vader (DV TIE fighter)	40 - 55	
MO5510 Nave Supersonica de Luke Skywalker (X-wing)	40 - 55	
Netherlands (Clipper)		
MO5610 R2-D2	50 - 60	
RESIN		
Japan		
Tsukuda		
MO6010 Wicket W. Warrick	50 - 70	
Kaiyodo limited editions (white boxes, on 30 of each made)		
MO6200 Princess Leia 1/6	150 - 170	
MO6201 Han Solo 1/6	240 - 270	
MO6210 R2-D2 1/6	160 - 180	
MO6211 C-3PO 1/6	240 - 270	
MO6212 Stormtrooper w/Han head 1/6	240 - 270	
MO6213 Boba Fett 1/6	250 - 285	
MO6214 Darth Vader 1/6	255 - 300	
Argonauts/Aoshima Bunka Co. MO6430-33		
MO6430 TIE fighter 1/72	75 - 90	
MO6431 X-wing fighter 1/72	80 - 95	
MO6432 TIE Interceptor 1/72	75 - 90	
MO6433 Y-wing fighter 1/72	85 - 100	
MO6434 Millennium Falcon 1/144	90 - 110	
MO6435 Star Destroyer 1/6150	125 - 145	
VINYL		
Screamin' Products Inc.		
MO8000 Darth Vader 1/4	55 - 65	
MO8001 Darth Vader 1/6	40 - 50	
MO8002 C-3PO 1/4	55 - 65	
MO8003 C-3PO 1/6	40 - 50	
MO8004 Yoda 1/4	55 - 65	

MO8006 Han Solo 1/4	55 - 65
MO8007 Han Solo 1/6	35 - 45
MO8008 Stormtrooper 1/4	65 - 75
MO8009 Stormtrooper 1/6	35 - 45
MO8010 Chewbacca 1/4	65 - 75
MO8012 Boba Fett 1/4	65 - 75
MO8013 Boba Fett 1/6	40 - 50
MO8014 Tusken Raider 1/4	65 - 75
MO8016 Luke Skywalker 1/4	55 - 65
AMT/Ertl	
MO8200 Luke Skywalker	15 - 25
MO8202 Darth Vader	15 - 25
MO8204 Han Solo	15 - 25
MO8240 *SOTE* Xizor	15 - 25
MO8245 *SOTE* Emperor Palpatine	15 - 25
Canada (Polydata) 1/6 scale pre-painted, limited to 9,000	
MO8100 Luke Skywalker	25 - 35
MO8102 Ben "Obi-Wan" Kenobi	25 - 35
MO8103 Tusken Raider	25 - 35
MO8104 Princess Leia Organa	25 - 35
MO8105 Lando Calrissian	undetermined
MO8106 Chewbacca	undetermined
MO8107 Boba Fett	undetermined
MO8108 Grand Moff Tarkin	undetermined
MO8109 Han Solo	undetermined
MO8110 Gamorrean Guard	undetermined
Japan (Kaiyodo)	
MO8500 Han Solo 1/6	50 - 55
MO8502 Darth Vader 1/6	55 - 60
MO8504 Stormtrooper w/Han head 1/6	50 - 55
MO8506 Boba Fett 1/6	55 - 60
MO8507 R2-D2 1/6	40 - 45
MO8508 Princess Leia Organa 1/6	35 - 40
MO8510 C-3PO 1/6	40 - 45
Argonauts/Aoshima Bunka Co.	
MO8701 Darth Vader 1/8	75 - 90
MO8702 Stormtrooper 1/8	75 - 90
Reds	
MO8801 Darth Vader, 1/3, limited ed. of 500	450 - 600
MO8803 Resculpt of MO8801	400 - 500

| MO8104 | MO8500 | MO8502 |

| MO8850-53 | MO8910 | MO8920 | MO8930 | MO8935 |

| MO8801 | MO9000 | MO9010 | MO9020 | MO9021 | MO9030 | MO9041 |

| MO9045 | MO9046 | MO9047 | MO9051 | MO9052 |

WOOD

Estes Flying Model Kits (balsa)

MO8850	X-wing fighter	4 - 8
MO8851	Y-wing fighter	4 - 8
MO8852	A-wing fighter	4 - 8
MO8853	Star Destroyer	4 - 8

Japan **(Takara)**

MO8910	Landspeeder	125 - 150
MO8920	TIE fighter	125 - 150
MO8930	X-wing fighter	125 - 150
MO8935	R2-D2	125 - 150

MODEL ROCKETRY

These were made originally by Estes in 1978 and 1979. A separate rocket starter kit was required to launch most of the models available. Estes rereleased three of the kits as a *Star Wars* 15th Anniversary pro-motion. Several more were later produced in conjunction with the *Star Wars Special Edition* release in 1997.

MO9000	Proton Torpedo (boxed)	22 - 35
MO9010	TIE fighter kit (bagged)	16 - 27
MO9011	15th Anniversary TIE fighter kit (bagged)	14 - 22
MO9020	X-wing fighter outfit (boxed)	28 - 45
MO9021	X-wing fighter (bagged)	16 - 28
MO9022	15th Anniversary X-wing fighter (bagged)	14 - 22
MO9030	Maxi-Brute X-wing (boxed)	30 - 50
MO9040	Flying R2-D2 (boxed)	28 - 40
MO9041	Flying R2-D2 (bagged)	22 - 35
MO9042	15th Anniversary Flying R2-D2 (bagged)	14 - 22
MO9045	Flying R2-D2 (boxed)	15 - 30
MO9046	Darth Vader TIE Fighter	20 - 30
MO9047	Death Star	20 - 30

MU0010

MU0011

MU1200

MU1216

MU1220

MU1238　　　　MU1254

MU1264

MU1270

MU1273

MUSIC/SPOKEN WORD CODES

LP	LP Record Album	45	45 speed record	CDS	Compact Disc Single	RR	Reel to Reel tape
LP7	7-inch, 33 1/3 rpm	CD	Compact Disc	CAS	Cassette	8T	8-Track Tape

MO9051	X-wing Starter Set	20 - 30
MO9052	Death Star Starter Set	20 - 30
MO9053	Y-wing Starter Set	30 - 40
MO9054	A-wing Starter Set	30 - 40
MO9055	X-wing/Darth Vader's TIE Fighter	30 - 50
MO9056	Star Destroyer	undetermined
MO9057	Shuttle Tydirium	undetermined

MUSIC/SPOKEN WORD

The jewel in the *Star Wars* trilogy crown is, of course, the music of John Williams. His scores for the three films became instant classics, recorded not only by symphony orchestras but "translated" into disco, reggae, marches and other types of music played on everything from dual pianos to organs. In the days when vinyl was still king, record album jackets could be elaborate and collectible in their own right. But besides LPs and 45s, trilogy music has been available on tape (cassette, reel-to-reel and 8-track) and compact discs (full albums and singles).

The spoken word and *Star Wars* recordings were twinned from the start with the "Story of..." albums. In recent years, as audio books have become popular, most new *Star Wars* saga novels have appeared on tape. And the popular *SW* and *ESB* radio dramas were made available on tape and disc to an army of fans.

This category also includes a fairly large number of pieces of sheet music as well as carrying cases for recorded music.

CARRYING CASES (Buena Vista Records)

MU0010	*SW* record tote	10 - 20
MU0011	*ROTJ* cassette tote	10 - 15

MUSIC (SELECTED)

Star Wars

MU1200	*SW* LP: Original Soundtrack, John Williams/London Symphony 2 records, 2 sleeves, liner note insert, poster (20th Century Records)	15 - 25
MU1202	*SW* LP: Original Soundtrack, 2 records, 1 sleeve, no liner notes or poster (PolyGram Records)	10 - 20
MU1204	*SW* RR: Original Soundtrack, 4 track, 3¾ ips (20th Century)	15 - 30
MU1206	*SW* 8T: Original Soundtrack, twin pack (20th Century)	5 - 10
MU1208	*SW* CAS: same as MU1200	10 - 15
MU1210	*SW* CD: same as MU1200, 2 disc set (RSO)	15 - 25
MU1212	*SW* CAS: Original Soundtrack, 1979 pink label re-release (20th Century Records/RCA Music Service)	5 - 10
MU1214	*SW* CAS: Original Soundtrack, reduced price (Polygram)	5 - 10
MU1216	*SW* LP: The Story of *Star Wars* w/16-page color booklet (20th Century-Fox Records)	15 - 25
MU1218	*SW* LP: The Story of *Star Wars* w/slightly different 16 page booklet (Buena Vista Records)	10 - 15

MU1220	*SW* CAS: Same as MU1216 (in pouch or w/LP-sized cover, Buena Vista)	5 - 10
MU1222	*SW* CAS: Same as MU1216, but earlier Superscope Story Tapes version	15 - 25
MU1224	*SW* LP: The Story of *Star Wars* Picture Disc w/R2-D2 & C-3PO (20th Century-Fox Records) (also available in numbered edition)	10 - 35
MU1226	*SW* RR: Same as MU1216	15 - 30
MU1228	*SW* RR: Soundtrack & Story of...in black pebble-finish package embossed w/gold lettering (20th Century-Fox Records)	65 - 95
MU1230	*SW* 8T: Same as MU1216	5 - 10
MU1234	*SW* CAS: NPR production of *SW* (Highbridge Co.)	40 - 50
MU1236	*SW* CD: Same as MU1234	50 - 65
MU1238	*SW* LP: Christmas in the Stars (RSO Records)	15 - 35
MU1240	*SW* CAS: Same as MU1238, on header card, rare	45 - 55
MU1242	*SW* LP: Zubin Mehta Conducts Suites from *Star Wars* and *Close Encounters* (London)	10 - 15
MU1244	*SW* LP: Digital Space/Morton Gould. First digital recording of *SW* (Varese Sarabande)	10 - 15
MU1246	*SW* LP: *Star Wars*/Ferrante & Teicher (United Artists Records)	10 - 15
MU1248	*SW* 8T: Same as MU1246	5 - 10
MU1250	*SW* LP: Living in These *Star Wars*/The Rebel Force Band (Bonwhit Records)	15 - 20
MU1252	*SW* LP: Music From *Star Wars*/John Rose on organ of Cathedral of St. Joseph (Delos Records)	10 - 15
MU1254	*SW* LP: *Star Wars* and Other Galactic Funk/Meco (Millennium Records)	10 - 15
MU1256	*SW* 8T: Same as MU1254	5 - 10
MU1258	*SW* LP: *Star Wars* Dub, blue vinyl (Burning Sounds)	25 - 35
MU1260	*SW* LP: Music From *Star Wars*, Marty Gold Orchestra (Peter Pan Records)	5 - 10
MU1262	*SW* LP: Patrick Gleeson's *Star Wars*, synthesizer (Mercury)	10 - 15
MU1264	*SW* LP: Music From *Star Wars*/Electric Moog Orchestra (Musicor Records)	10 - 15
MU1268	*SW* 8T: Same as MU1264	5 - 10
MU1270	*SW* LP: *Star Wars* and A Stereo Space Odyssey/Colin Frechter (Damont Records	10 - 15
MU1272	*SW* CAS: Same as MU1270	10 - 15
MU1273	*SW* 8T: Same as MU1270	
MU1274	*SW* CAS: *Star Wars*, London Philharmonic & Cinema Sound Stage Orchestra (Stage & Screen Productions)	10 - 15
MU1276	*SW* LP: *Star Wars* by the Kid Stuff Repertory Company (Kid Stuff Records)	5 - 10
MU1278	*SW* LP: Tomita/Kosmos (RCA Red Seal)	10 - 15
MU1280	*SW* CD: Same as MU1278 (BMG Classics)	10 - 15

MU1298	MU1308	MU1504
	MU1520	
MU1522	MU1532	MU1536

MU1282 *SW* LP: Music From Other Galaxies & Planets/Don
Ellis and Survival (Atlantic Records) — 10 - 15

MU1284 *SW* LP: Spaced Out Disco/The Galactic
Force Band (Springboard Records) — 15 - 20

MU1286 John Williams' Symphonic Suites/Frank Barber (Angel) — 10 - 15

MU1288 *SW* LP: Music From John Williams' Close
Encounters *Star Wars*/Charles Gerhardt (RCA) — 10 - 15

MU1290 *SW* CD: Same as MU1288 (BMG Classics) — 10 - 15

MU1292 *SW* LP: *Star Wars*/Close Encounters
Richard "Groove" Holmes (Versatile Records) — 10 - 15

MU1294 *SW* LP: *Star Wars* and Other Space Themes,
Geoff Love (Moss Music Group) — 10 - 20

MU1296 *SW* 45: Main Title/Cantina Band, pink, blue on
white logo sleeve, early light blue label
(20th Century Records) — 10 - 15

MU1298 *SW* 45: Main Title/Cantina Band, picture sleeve
w/art from "D" sheet, updated label has Fox Film-like
logo in "stone" (20th Century-Fox Records) — 15 - 25

MU1300 *SW* 45: Fox Fanfare/Main Title (both sides),
promo copy (20th Century Records) — 10 - 15

MU1302 *SW* 45: Main Title b/w Funk, Meco, plain sleeve
(Millennium Records) — 10 - 15

MU1304 *SW* 45: Main Title/Cantina Band b/w Funk,
Millennium logo sleeve (Millennium Records) — 10 - 15

MU1306 *SW* 45: Title Theme b/w Close Encounters, plain
sleeve (Casablanca) — 10 - 15

MU1308 *SW* 45: What Can You Get A Wookiee For
Christmas b/w R2-D2 We Wish You a Merry
Christmas, picture sleeve (RSO Records) — 15 - 25

MU1310 *SW* 45: Light the Sky on Fire b/w Hyperdrive,
Jefferson Starship, black sleeve w/white letters: As
seen and heard on the CBS-TV *Star Wars*
Holiday Special (Grunt Records) — 15 - 20

MU1312 *SW* 45: Chewie The Rookie Wookiee b/w May
the Force Be With You, printed sleeve (Bonwhit) — 15 - 20

MU1314 *SW* 45: The *Star Wars* Stars b/w same,
The Force, promo (Lifesong Records) — 10 - 15

MU1316 *SW* 45: Space Holiday: Theme Music
From *Star Wars*, etc. (Pickwick Records) — 10 - 15

MU1318 *SW* LP7: *Star Wars*, 24-page Read-Along Book &
Record (Buena Vista Records) — 5 - 15

Canada

MU1400 *SW* 8T: Original Soundtrack, revised order
(20th Century Records/GRT of Canada Ltd.) — 5 - 10

MU1402 *SW* 8T: The Story of *SW* (20th Century/GRT of
Canada) — 5 - 10

England

MU1430 *SW* CAS: story of... (Rainbow) — 10 - 15

MU1432 *SW* CAS: Space Encounters, London
Philharmonic Orchestra (Artistry Quality/A&Q Ltd.) — 5 - 10

France

MU1450 *SW* LP: L'Histoire de La Guerre des Etoiles
(Story of *SW*) w/24-page booklet (Disques Ades) — 10 - 15

MU1452 *SW* LP7: La Guerre des Etoiles, 24-page Read-
Along Book & Record (Buena Vista Records) — 10 - 15

Germany

MU1470 *SW* LP: *Krieg der Sterne* w/8-page color booklet
(Fontana/Phonogram GmbH) — 15 - 20

MU1472 *SW* CAS: *Krieg der Sterne* (Remus Lessen &
Lauschen Filmbuch+Cassette) — 10 - 15

MU1474 *SW* CAS: *Krieg der Sterne*, sound-track
(20th Century Records) — 15 - 20

MU1476 *SW* CAS: *Krieg der Sterne*/Galactic
Music, Colin Frechter (Europa) — 10 - 15

MU1478 *SW* CAS: *Krieg der Sterne* (Story of *SW*) (Philips) — 15 - 20

Japan

MU1500 *SW* LP: Original Soundtrack, 2 records, 2 sleeves,
4-page liner note insert, poster, paper band (20th Cen.) — 25 - 35

MU1502 *SW* CD: Same as MU1500 (Polydor) — 10 - 15

MU1504 *SW* CDS: Christmas in the Stars, w/2 songs
from album (RSO Records) — 25 - 45

MU1506 *SW* CD: Also Sprach Zarathustra/*Star Wars*
Suite, Zubin Mehta (King Record Co.) — 10 - 20

MU1508 *SW* CD: *Star Wars*, Richard Hayman Symphonic
Orchestra (Sohbi Corp.) — 10 - 20

MU1510 *SW* CD: The Greatest "Musics" of John Williams,
including *Star Wars*, Film Studio Orchestra
(Victor Musical Industries Inc.) — 15 - 20

MU1512 *SW* LP: The Story of *Star Wars*, Japanese pressing/
English language w/paper band, booklet, 6-page
foldout, 2-page cut-out and assemble R2-D2
(King Records: FML-95) — 25 - 45

MU1514 *SW* LP: The Story of *Star Wars*, Japanese
language, otherwise same as MU1512 — 25 - 45

MU1516 *SW* LP: Zubin Mehta Conducts Suites from Star
Wars and Close Encounters. Silver metallic cover
w/insert (London) — 10 - 20

MU1518 *SW* LP: *Star Wars* Collector's Disk/Osamu Shoji
& the Polyphonic Ensemble Orchestra (Warner-
Pioneer Corp.) — 10 - 20

MU1520 *SW* 45: The Throne Room & End Title b/w
Princess Leia's Theme, picture sleeve of Japanese
version of style A (20th Century-Fox Records) — 15 - 30

MU1522 *SW* 45: Main Title b/w Oasis, Maynard Ferguson,
picture sleeve w/R2-D2 &C-3PO in desert
(CBS/Sony Inc.) — 15 - 30

MU1524 *SW* 45: Main Theme b/w Princess Leia's Theme,
David Matthews, picture sleeve w/tricked-out
SW logo (CTI Records) — 15 - 20

MU1526 *SW* 45: Main Title b/w Hotel California, Raymond
Lefevre, picture sleeve of sexy woman (Barclay) — 15 - 20

MU1528 *SW* 45: Main Title, promo copy in plain
cover; Don Ellis (Atlantic Recording) — 10 - 20

MU1530 *SW* 45: Main Title b/w Princess Leia's Theme,
Don Ellis, picture sleeve of silvery cosmos
(Atlantic Recording) — 10 - 20

MU1532 *SW* 45: Main Theme/Cantina Band b/w Funk,
Meco, picture sleeve similar to U.S. album cover
(RCA Records) — 15 - 25

MU1534 *SW* 45: Main Title b/w CE3K Main Title, Zubin
Mehta, picture sleeve of tricked-out *SW* logo
(London Records) — 10 - 20

MU1536 *SW* 45: Main Theme b/w long version, Graffiti
Orchestra, picture sleeve of X-wing & TIE
fighter battle (Prodigal) — 15 - 25

Mexico

MU1600 *SW* LP: *La Guerra de Las Galaxias*, (soundtrack)
2 records, 2 sleeves, no inserts (Gamma S.A.) — 10 - 15

MU1602 *SW* LP: *Star Wars* and Other Galactic
Funk/Meco (RCA Victor/Millennium) — 10 - 15

MU1604 *SW* 45: *La Guerra de las Galaxias*, from soundtrack, black sleeve w/white letters, (Gamma
S.A./20th Century Records) — 15 - 20

MU1606 *SW* 45: Main Theme/Cantina Band b/w Funk,
Meco, picture sleeve w/album art (RCA Victor/
Millennium Record Co.) — 15 - 20

MU1608 *SW* LP7: *La Guerra de las Galaxias*, 24-page
Read-Along Book & Record (Buena Vista Records) — 10 - 15

The Empire Strikes Back

MU2000 *ESB* LP: Original Soundtrack, John Williams/
London Symph., 2 records, 2 sleeves, 14- page
color booklet (RSO Records), rare — 35 - 50

MU2002 *ESB* CAS: Same as MU2000 — 15 - 25

MU2004 *ESB* LP: Original Soundtrack, abridged, 1 record,
1 sleeve (RSO Records) — 15 - 20

MU2006 *ESB* CAS: Same as MU2004 — 10 - 15

MU2008 *ESB* CD: Same as MU2004 (RSO) — 10 - 15

MU2010 *ESB* LP: Original Soundtrack, selected cuts for
programming use only; 1 record (RSO Records) — 20 - 30

MU2000

MU2012

MU2014

MU2016

MU2050

MU2408

MU3006

MU3048

MU4052   MU4054

MUSIC/SPOKEN WORD CODES							
LP	LP Record Album	45	45 speed record	CDS	Compact Disc Single	RR	Reel to Reel tape
LP7	7-inch, 33 1/3 rpm	CD	Compact Disc	CAS	Cassette	8T	8-Track Tape

MU2012 *ESB* LP: The Adventures of Luke Skywalker (RSO) 15 - 30

MU2014 *ESB* LP: The Story of *The Empire Strikes Back*; like MU2012, but repackaged (Buena Vista) 15 - 25

MU2016 *ESB* CAS: Same as MU2014, in pouch or w/LP-sized cover 10 - 15

MU2017 *ESB* LP: Special In-Store Play Disc featuring excerpts from soundtrack, Story of..., Meco, Empire Jazz, Boris Midney; plain white sleeve w/label (RSO Records) 15 - 20

MU2020 *ESB* LP: Special Radio Programming Material for *ESB*; style "A" poster on cover and timed scripts enclosed (Backstage Productions) 15 - 35

MU2022 *ESB* CAS: National Public Radio production of *ESB* (Highbridge Co.) 40 - 50

MU2024 *ESB* CD: same as MU2022 50 - 60

MU2026 SW/*ESB* CD: Limited edition boxed set of *SW* & *ESB* NPR productions (Highbridge) 150 - 200

MU2028 *ESB* LP: Empire Jazz, arranged by Ron Carter (RSO) 10 - 15

MU2030 *ESB* CAS: Same as MU2028 10 - 15

MU2032 *ESB* LP: Boris Midney/Music From *ESB* (RSO) 10 - 15

MU2034 *ESB* CAS: Same as MU2032 10 - 15

MU2036 *ESB* LP: Meco Plays Music From *ESB*, 10-inch (RSO) 10 - 20

MU2038 *ESB* LP: *ESB* Symphonic Suite, Charles Gerhardt/ National Philharmonic, (Varese Sarabande/Chalfont) 10 - 25

MU2040 *ESB* CAS: Same as MU2038 10 - 15

MU2042 *ESB* CD: Same as MU2038 10 - 15

MU2044 *ESB* 45: Imperial March b/w Battle in the Snow, logo sleeve (RSO Records) 10 - 15

MU2048 *ESB* CAS: Darth Vader/Yoda's Theme b/w The Force Theme, logo sleeve (RSO Records) 10 - 15

MU2050 *ESB* LP7: *The Empire Strikes Back*, 24-page Read-Along Book & Record (Buena Vista Records)

England

MU2150 *ESB* CAS: Story of... (Rainbow) 10 - 15

France

MU2200 *ESB* LP: L'Empire Contre-Attaque (Story of...) w/24-pagecolor booklet (Buena Vista/Disques Ades) 10 - 15

MU2202 *ESB* LP7: L'Empire Contre-Attaque, 24-page Read-Along Book & Record (Buena Vista Records) 10 - 15

Germany (R L & L Filmbuch + Cassette)

MU2300 *ESB* CAS: Das Imperium Schlagt Zuruck 10 - 15

Japan

MU2400 *ESB* LP: Original Soundtrack, 2 records, 2 sleeves, w/paper band, Japanese liner notes & 12-page color booklet (RSO Records/Polydor K.K.) 25 - 50

MU2402 *ESB* CD: Original Soundtrack, abridged, (Polydor) 15 - 25

MU2404 *ESB* LP: Boris Midney/Music From *ESB*, w/paper band (RSO/Polydor) 10 - 15

MU2406 *ESB* CD: *ESB* Symphonic Suite, Charles Gerhardt, (SLC Inc.) 10 - 20

MU2408 *ESB* 45: Imperial March (Darth Vader's Theme) b/w Yoda's Theme, from soundtrack (RSO Records) 10 - 15

MU2410 *ESB* 45: Main Theme b/w *SW* Main Title, Larry Nelson Orch./Double Power Brass Orch., picture sleeve w/both logos tricked out (Seven Seas) 10 - 15

Mexico

MU2500 *ESB* LP7: El Imperio Contraataca, 24-page Read-Along Book & Record (Buena Vista Records) 10 - 15

Return of the Jedi

MU3000 *ROTJ* LP: Original Soundtrack, John Williams/ London Symph., 1 record w/4-page color insert (RSO) 15 - 25

MU3002 *ROTJ* CAS: Same as MU3000 5 - 15

MU3004 *ROTJ* CD: Same as MU3000 10 - 15

MU3006 *ROTJ* LP: The Story of *ROTJ* w/16-page color booklet (Buena Vista Records) 10 - 15

MU3008 *ROTJ* CAS: Same as MU3006, in pouch or w/LP-sized cover 10 - 15

MU3010 *ROTJ* LP: The Story of *ROTJ*, Special Edition Picture Disc (Buena Vista Records) 15 - 20

MU3012 *ROTJ* LP: Meco's Ewok Celebration, cover is Ewok tracks on dirt (Arista Records) 10 - 15

MU3014 *ROTJ* LP: Meco Ewok Celebration, cover is Ewok hand lifting glass to a sun in a star field (Arista Records) 15 - 25

MU3016 *ROTJ* CAS: Same as MU3012 10 - 15

MU3018 *ROTJ* LP: Music From *ROTJ*, Charles Gerhardt/ National Philharmonic (RCA Red Seal) 10 - 15

MU3020 *ROTJ* CD: Same as MU3018 (BMG Classics) 10 - 15

MU3022 *ROTJ* CAS: The *Star Wars* Trilogy Varujan Kojian/The Utah Symphony (Varese Sarabande) 5 - 10

MU3024 *ROTJ* CD: Same as MU3022 10 - 15

MU3026 *ROTJ* LP: 1984 A Space Odyssey, John Williams/The Boston Pops (J&B Records) 10 - 15

MU3028 *ROTJ* LP: The *Star Wars* Trilogy, Varujan Kojian/ The Utah Symphony (Varese Sarabande) 10 - 15

MU3030 *ROTJ* LP: Pops in Space, John Williams/ Boston Pops (Philips) 10 - 15

MU3032 *ROTJ* LP: Out of This World, John Williams/ Boston Pops (Philips) 10 - 15

MU3034 *ROTJ* LP: By Request, John Williams/Boston Pops (Philips) 10 - 15

MU3036 *ROTJ* LP: Star Tracks, Erich Kunzel/ Cincinnati Pops (Telarc) 10 - 15

MU3038 *ROTJ* LP:Biola University Symphonic Band/In Concert, Symphonic Suite from *ROTJ* (Monarch) 15 - 20

MU3040 *ROTJ* 45: Ewok Celebration b/w logo sleeve, promo copy (Arista Records) 10 - 15

MU3042 *ROTJ* 45: Lapti Nek Overture, Urth, 12-inch 45 (Warner Bros.Records) 10 - 15

MU3044 *ROTJ* 45: Lapti Nek, Special Extended Dance Remix b&w cover, promo 12-inch 45 (RSO Records) 15 - 20

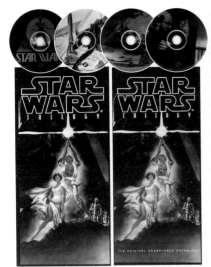

MU4068	**MU4086**	**MU4094**	**MU4098**

MU5008	**MU5010**	**MU5012**	**MU5014**	**MU5016**	**MU5020**	**MU5022**

MU3046 *ROTJ* 45: Lapti Nek Overture, logo sleeve, promo copy (Warner Bros. Records) ... 15 - 20

MU3048 *ROTJ* LP7 *Return of the Jedi*, 24-page Read-Along Book & Record (Buena Vista Records) ... 10 - 15

England

MU3150 *ROTJ* LP: The *Star Wars* Trilogy, Varujan Kojian/ The Utah Symphony (That's Entertainment Records) ... 10 - 15

France

MU3200 *ROTJ* LP: Le Retour du Jedi (Story of...) w/24-page color booklet (BV/Disques Ades) ... 10 - 15

MU3202 *ROTJ* 45 Les Petits Ewoks b/w Nos Amis les Ewoks, Dorothee, picture sleeve (Polygram) ... 10 - 15

MU3204 *ROTJ* LP7: Le Retour du Jedi, 24-page Read-Along Book & Record (Buena Vista Records) ... 10 - 15

Germany

MU3300 *ROTJ* LP:Die Ruckkehr der Jedi-Ritter (Story of...) w/16-page color booklet (Buena Vista Records/Metronome Musik) ... 10 - 15

MU3302 *ROTJ* CAS: Die Ruckkehr der Jedi Ritter (R L & L Filmbuch + Cassette) ... 10 - 15

Japan

MU3400 *ROTJ* LP: Original Soundtrack w/paper band, 4-page color insert (RSO Records/Polydor K.K.) ... 15 - 20

MU3402 *ROTJ* CD: Sames as MU3400 ... 15 - 20

MU3404 *ROTJ* LP: *Star Wars* Trilogy, Varujan Kojian/The Utah Symphony,w/paper band (Victor Musical Indus. 10 - 20

MU3406 *ROTJ* CD: Same as MU3404, (1986: JVC/Victor; 1991: Varese Sarabande) ... 10 - 20

New Zealand

MU3550 *ROTJ* LP: The Story of *ROTJ* w/16-page color booklet (His Masters Voice Records) ... 10 - 15

Star Wars Saga

MU4050 SWS LP: Ewoks Original Soundtrack, From *Caravan of Courage* and *The Battle for Endor* (Varese Sarabande) ... 10 - 15

MU4052 SWS LP: Rebel Mission to Ord Mantell, A Story from the *Star Wars* Saga (Buena Vista Records) ... 10 - 15

MU4054 SWS CAS: Same as MU4052 ... 5 - 10

MU4056 SWS CAS: *SW* Trilogy, 3 story of... tapes packed together in see-through pouch ... 15 - 20

MU4058 SWS LP: Big Daddy, includes *Star Wars* theme (Rhino Records) ... 10 - 15

MU4060 SWS CAS: Same as MU4058 ... 5 - 10

MU4062 SWS CAS: The *Star Wars* Trilogy, John Williams/ The Skywalker Symphony (Sony Classical) ... 5 - 10

MU4064 SWS CD: Same as MU4062 ... 10 - 15

MU4066 SWS CD: Kid Stuff: An Afternoon at the Movies, John Williams/The Boston Pops (Philips) ... 10 - 15

MU4068 SWS CD: *Star Wars* Trilogy: The Original Soundtrack Anthology (boxed set of 4 CDs w/ expanded scores of all 3 films, booklet) ... 45 - 65

MU4070 SWS CAS: Cinema Gala: *Star Wars*, etc., Zubin Mehta (London Records) ... 5 - 10

MU4072 SWS CD: Same as MU4070 ... 10 - 15

MU4074 SWS LP: Dare to be Stupid, "Weird Al" Yankovic, includes "Yoda" (CBS Records) ... 10 - 15

MU4078 SWS CD: Same as MU4074 (Scotti Bros.) ... 5 - 10

MU4080 SWS LP7: Droid World, 24-page Read-Along Book & Record (Buena Vista Records) ... 5 - 15

MU4082 SWS CAS: Same as MU4080 ... 5 - 15

MU4084 SWS LP7: Planet of the Hoojibs, 24-page Read-Along Book & Record (Buena Vista Records) ... 5 - 15

MU4086 SWS CAS: Same as MU4084 ... 5 - 15

MU4088 SWS LP7: The Ewoks Join the Fight, 24-page Read-Along Book & Record (Buena Vista Records) ... 5 - 15

MU4090 SWS CAS: Same as MU4088 ... 5 - 15

MU4092 SWS LP7: The Ewok Adventure, 24-page Read-Along Book & Record (Buena Vista Records) ... 5 - 15

MU4094 SWS CAS: Same as MU4092 ... 5 - 15

MU4096 SWS LP7: *Ewoks*: The Battle for Endor, 24-page Read-Along Book & Record (Buena Vista Records) ... 5 - 15

MU4098 SWS CAS: Same as MU4096 ... 5 - 15

MU5000 SWS LP7: *Star Wars* Adventures in Colors and Shapes, 24-page Read-Along Book & Record (Buena Vista) ... 5 - 15

MU5002 SWS CAS: Same as MU5000 ... 5 - 15

MU5004 SWS LP7: *Star Wars* Adventures in ABC, 24-page Read-Along Book & Record (Buena Vista Records) ... 5 - 15

MU5006 SWS CAS: Same as MU5004 ... 5 - 15

MU5008 SWS CAS: Heir to the Empire (Bantam Audio Cassette) ... 12 - 18

MU5010 SWS CAS: Dark Force Rising, (Bantam Audio Cassette) ... 12 - 18

MU5012 SWS CAS: The Last Command, (Bantam Doubleday Dell Audio Publishing) ... 12 - 18

MU8118   **PA0030**   **PA0032**   **PA0510**   **PA0520**   **PA0530**

PA0550   **PA0700**   **PA0720**   **PA0722**   **PA0840**   **PA0840**

MU5014	SWS CAS: The Truce at Bakura, (BDD Audio Publishing)	12 - 18
MU5016	SWS CAS: *Jedi Search* (BDD Audio Publishing)	12 - 18
MU5018	SWS CAS: *Dark Apprentice* (BDD Audio Publishing)	12 - 18
MU5020	SWS CAS: *The Courtship of Princess Leia* (BDD Audio Publishing)	12 - 18
MU5022	SWS CAS: *Dark Empire* (Time Warner AudioBooks)	12 - 18

England

MU5500	SWS CAS: Droid World (Rainbow)	5 - 15
MU5502	SWS CAS: Planet of the Hoojibs (Rainbow)	5 - 15
MU5504	SWS CAS: The Ewoks Join the Fight (Rainbow)	5 - 15

France

MU5550	SWS LP7: L'Aventure des Ewok, 24-page Read-Along Book & Record (Buena Vista Records)	5 - 15

Japan

MU5600	SWS CD: Pops in Space, John Williams/Boston Pops (Nippon Phonogram Co.)	15 - 20
MU5602	SWS CD: Out of This World, John Williams/Boston Pops (Nippon Phonogram Co.)	15 - 20
MU5606	SWS CD: The Greatest Music of John Williams, Film Studio Orchestra (JVC/Victor)	15 - 20
MU5608	SWS CD: Great Space Music Scores, Erich Kunzel/Cincinnati Pops (Nippon Phonogram Co.)	15 - 20
MU5610	SWS CD: The *Star Wars* Trilogy, John Williams/Skywalker Symphony (CBS/Sony Records)	15 - 25
MU5612	SWS CD: *Star Wars*/The Best of Space Music, John Williams/Boston Pops Orchestra (Philips)	15 - 20
MU5614	SWS CD: Movie Themes by 30,000 People's Requests (BMG Victor Inc.)	15 - 20
MU5616	SWS CD: Harrison Ford: Screen Star Music Library (King Record Co.)	15 - 20

SHEET MUSIC

MU8100	Main Theme/Original Piano Solo (Fox Fanfare & Bantha Music)	5 - 10
MU8102	Main Theme (Warner Bros.Publications)	5 - 10
MU8104	Main Theme/Dan Coates Piano Solo (Warner-Tamerlane & Bantha)	5 - 10
MU8106	Princess Leia's Theme (Fox Fanfare)	5 - 10
MU8108	Cantina Band (Fox Fanfare)	5 - 10
MU8110	*Star Wars* Deluxe Souvenir Folio of Music Selections (20th Century Fox)	10 - 25
MU8112	The *Star Wars* Picture Music Book (20th Century)	15 - 25
MU8114	*Star Wars* Medley Book (Fox Fanfare Music)	10 - 20
MU8116	Classic Film Scores: *Star Wars* Suite for Piano (Warner Bros.)	10 - 15
MU8118	Christmas in the Stars	15 - 20
MU8130	*ESB* Medley: Darth Vader/Yoda's Theme (Fox Fanfare & Bantha)	5 - 10
MU8132	Han Solo and the Princess (Fox Fanfare & Bantha Music)	5 - 10

MU8134	The Imperial March: Darth Vader's Theme (Fox & Bantha)	5 - 10
MU8136	Yoda's Theme (Fox & Bantha)	5 - 10
MU8138	*ESB* Deluxe Souvenir Folio of Music Selections and Photos	10 - 25
MU8139	*Return of the Jedi* music book	10 - 20
MU8140	The *Star Wars* Saga Souvenir Folio of Music Selections and Photos	10 - 25
MU8160	Ewok Celebration (Warner Bros.)	5 - 10
MU8162	Lapti Nek (Warner Bros.)	5 - 10
MU8164	Music from the *Star Wars* Saga book (Warner Bros.)	10 - 20
MU8180	*Christmas in the Stars*, Easy Piano	9 - 15

PAPERWEIGHTS

PA0110	*SW* plastic w/Darth Vader hologram (Third Dimension Arts)	20 - 35
PA0112	*SW* plastic w/Yoda hologram (Third Dimension Arts)	20 - 35

England (H.C. Ford and Sons)

PA1050	Stormtrooper/Darth Vader	10 - 20
PA1052	Luke/Leia	10 - 20
PA1054	R2-D2/C-3PO	10 - 20

See also—**CAST AND CREW**

PARTY ITEMS

With all the *Star Wars* napkins, plates, cups, table coverings, centerpieces, invitations, thank you notes and the like, it wasn't hard to throw a trilogy-themed party. Collectors, of course, seek these items without icing and spilled punch—mint in their original wrapping, actually. Enough of the party goods were produced that most of the items are still relatively plentiful and not overly expensive. Nearly all of the U.S. items were produced by Drawing Board Greeting Cards Inc., unless otherwise identified below.

BAGS: GIFT OR PARTY

PA0030	*ROTJ*: Luke/Vader duel 8-pack	5 - 10
PA0032	*Ewoks* party bag 8-pack	5 - 10

France (Compagnie Europeenne des Emballages)

PA0150	*ROTJ* paper bags 12 different designs, each	1 - 2
PA0165	*ROTJ* polyethylene bags 12 different designs, each	1 - 2

BALLOONS

PA0510	*ESB* 10-pack, assorted designs	5 - 8
PA0520	*ROTJ* 10-pack, assorted designs	5 - 8
PA0530	*ROTJ*: 4-pack of punch balloons, assorted designs	5 - 10
PA0540	*ROTJ*: Ewok 6-pack, assorted designs (K mart exclusive)	5 - 10
PA0550	*ROTJ*: Ewok 5-pack, assorted designs	5 - 8

Australia

PA0700	*ESB* giant balloons: R2-D2, Darth Vader, Stormtrooper, C-3PO, Millennium Falcon (Balloon Supply), each	1 - 2
PA0702	*ESB* Galaxy Balloons, pack of 8	2 - 4

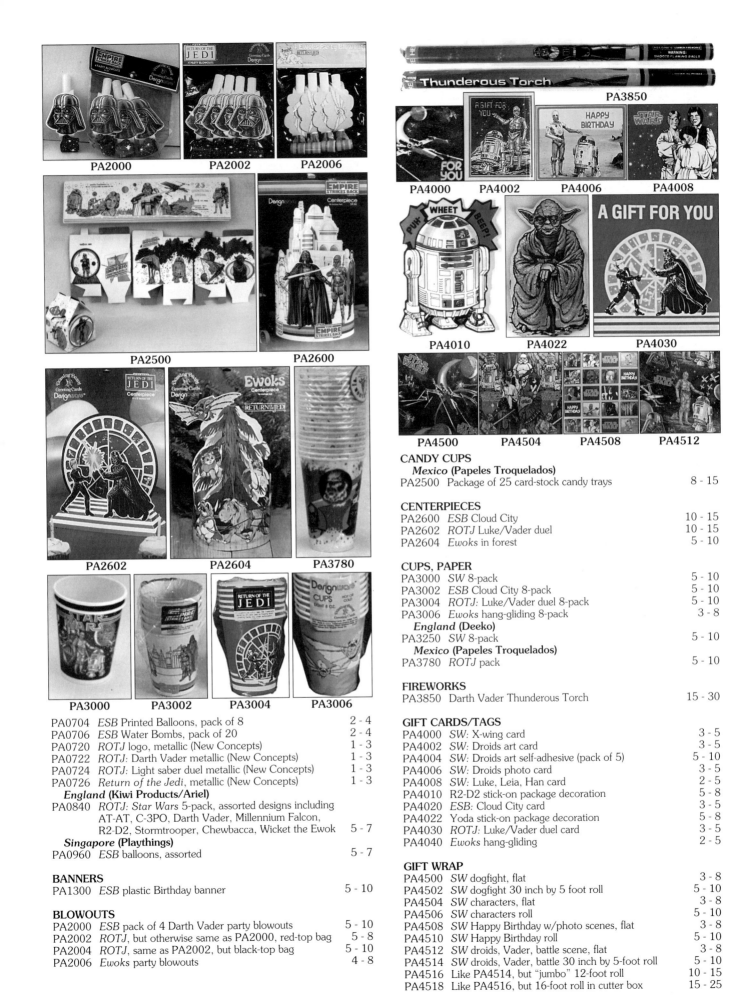

PA2000   PA2002   PA2006

PA2500   PA2600

PA2602   PA2604   PA3780

PA3000   PA3002   PA3004   PA3006

PA3850

PA4000   PA4002   PA4006   PA4008

PA4010   PA4022   PA4030

PA4500   PA4504   PA4508   PA4512

PA0704	*ESB* Printed Balloons, pack of 8	2 - 4
PA0706	*ESB* Water Bombs, pack of 20	2 - 4
PA0720	*ROTJ* logo, metallic (New Concepts)	1 - 3
PA0722	*ROTJ*: Darth Vader metallic (New Concepts)	1 - 3
PA0724	*ROTJ*: Light saber duel metallic (New Concepts)	1 - 3
PA0726	*Return of the Jedi*, metallic (New Concepts)	1 - 3

England (Kiwi Products/Ariel)

PA0840	*ROTJ*: Star Wars 5-pack, assorted designs including AT-AT, C-3PO, Darth Vader, Millennium Falcon, R2-D2, Stormtrooper, Chewbacca, Wicket the Ewok	5 - 7

Singapore (Playthings)

PA0960	*ESB* balloons, assorted	5 - 7

BANNERS
PA1300	*ESB* plastic Birthday banner	5 - 10

BLOWOUTS
PA2000	*ESB* pack of 4 Darth Vader party blowouts	5 - 10
PA2002	*ROTJ*, but otherwise same as PA2000, red-top bag	5 - 8
PA2004	*ROTJ*, same as PA2002, but black-top bag	5 - 10
PA2006	*Ewoks* party blowouts	4 - 8

CANDY CUPS
Mexico (Papeles Troquelados)
PA2500	Package of 25 card-stock candy trays	8 - 15

CENTERPIECES
PA2600	*ESB* Cloud City	10 - 15
PA2602	*ROTJ* Luke/Vader duel	10 - 15
PA2604	*Ewoks* in forest	5 - 10

CUPS, PAPER
PA3000	*SW* 8-pack	5 - 10
PA3002	*ESB* Cloud City 8-pack	5 - 10
PA3004	*ROTJ*: Luke/Vader duel 8-pack	5 - 10
PA3006	*Ewoks* hang-gliding 8-pack	3 - 8

England (Deeko)
PA3250	*SW* 8-pack	5 - 10

Mexico (Papeles Troquelados)
PA3780	*ROTJ* pack	5 - 10

FIREWORKS
PA3850	Darth Vader Thunderous Torch	15 - 30

GIFT CARDS/TAGS
PA4000	*SW*: X-wing card	3 - 5
PA4002	*SW*: Droids art card	3 - 5
PA4004	*SW*: Droids art self-adhesive (pack of 5)	5 - 10
PA4006	*SW*: Droids photo card	3 - 5
PA4008	*SW*: Luke, Leia, Han card	2 - 5
PA4010	R2-D2 stick-on package decoration	5 - 8
PA4020	*ESB*: Cloud City card	3 - 5
PA4022	Yoda stick-on package decoration	5 - 8
PA4030	*ROTJ*: Luke/Vader duel card	3 - 5
PA4040	*Ewoks* hang-gliding	2 - 5

GIFT WRAP
PA4500	*SW* dogfight, flat	3 - 8
PA4502	*SW* dogfight 30 inch by 5 foot roll	5 - 10
PA4504	*SW* characters, flat	3 - 8
PA4506	*SW* characters roll	5 - 10
PA4508	*SW* Happy Birthday w/photo scenes, flat	3 - 8
PA4510	*SW* Happy Birthday roll	5 - 10
PA4512	*SW* droids, Vader, battle scene, flat	3 - 8
PA4514	*SW* droids, Vader, battle 30 inch by 5-foot roll	5 - 10
PA4516	Like PA4514, but "jumbo" 12-foot roll	10 - 15
PA4518	Like PA4516, but 16-foot roll in cutter box	15 - 25

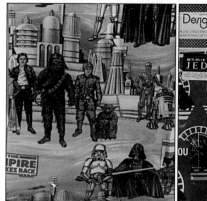

PA4520   PA4524

PA4528   PA4850   PA4970

PA5500

PA5502   PA5504   PA5506

PA4520	*ESB* Cloud City, flat	3 - 8
PA4522	*ESB* Cloud City roll	5 - 10
PA4524	*ROTJ* Luke/Vader duel, flat	3 - 5
PA4526	*ROTJ* duel roll	5 - 8
PA4528	*Ewoks* hang-gliding, flat	2 - 5
PA4530	*Ewoks* roll	5 - 8
***Australia* (Hallmark Australia)**		
PA4850	*ROTJ* design	3 - 8
***France* (Compagnie Europeenne des Emballages)**		
PA4970	*ROTJ* multi-character roll	5 - 10

HATS

PA5500	*SW* punch-out hats 8-pack	10 - 15
PA5502	*ESB* Cloud City cone hats 8-pack	5 - 10
PA5504	*ROTJ* Luke/Vader cone hats 8-pack	5 - 10
PA5506	*Ewoks* cone hats 8-pack	3 - 8
***Mexico* (Papeles Troquelados)**		
PA5750	*ESB* pack of 25 w/designs of Probot, Stormtrooper, Boba Fett, Darth Vader, C-3PO	10 - 20

PA5750

PA6000   PA6002   PA6004

PA6003   PA6006   PA6008

PA6020   PA6110   PA6112

PA6500   PA6502   PA7000

INVITATIONS

PA6000	*SW:* R2-D2 8-pack	10 - 15
PA6002	*SW:* C-3PO & R2-D2 8-pack	10 - 15
PA6003	*SW:* C-3PO & R2-D2 post cards	
PA6004	*ESB:* Cloud City 8-pack	10 - 15
PA6006	*ESB:* Heroes & villains 8-pack	10 - 15
PA6008	*ROTJ:* Luke/Vader duel 8-pack	10 - 15
PA6020	*Ewoks* 8 pack	5 - 10
***Australia* (Hallmark)**		
PA6110	*ROTJ:* Biker Scout	4 - 8
PA6112	*ROTJ:* Darth Invitations	5 - 9
***Denmark* (I. Chr. Olsen)**		
PA6250	*SW* children's invitations	8 - 12

NAME BADGES

| PA6500 | *SW* logo, adhesive 16-pack | 8 - 12 |
| PA6502 | *SW:* Vader head, adhesive 16-pack | 8 - 12 |

NAPKINS (All designs come in luncheon and beverage size packs)

PA7000	*SW:* C-3PO and R2-D2	10 - 15
PA7002	*ESB:* Cloud City	10 - 15
PA7004	*ROTJ* Luke/Vader duel	10 - 15
PA7006	*Ewoks*	6 - 12

PA7002   PA7004   PA7006

PA7250   PA7750

PA7505

PA8000   PA8050

Additional Placemats from PA8050

PA8250

PA8470   PA8472

PA8474   PA8476

PA8478   PA8480   PA8482

PA9000   PA9002   PA9010

Mexico (Papeles Troquelados)
PA7250 *ESB* napkins   5 - 15

PARTY PACKS (Table cover, plates, cups, napkins)
PA7505 *ESB*: Cloud City design   20 - 40

PLACE CARDS
PA7750 *SW*: C-3PO and R2-D2 8-pack   5 - 10

PLACEMATS
PA8000 *SW* maze paper placemats, 8-pack (Drawing Board)   10 - 20
PA8050 *ESB* box of 4, 4 different designs (Towle/Sigma)   5 - 10
Australia (Roy Lee Cin)
PA8250 *ESB* vinyl, 4 designs, set   20 - 35
England (Icarus Co)
SW or *ROTJ* logo laminated paper, 9" x11" or 12"x16", ea.
PA8470 Bounty hunters   10 - 20
PA8472 Vader and Stormtroopers   10 - 20
PA8474 C-3PO and R2-D2   10 - 20

PA8476 Lando, Chewbacca, Han   10 - 20
PA8478 Hoth: Luke on tauntaun   10 - 20
PA8480 Yoda on Dagobah   10 - 20
PA8482 Ewoks   10 - 20
See also—CERAMICS: Cups and Mugs; KITCHEN ITEMS: Premiums

PLATES, PAPER
PA9000 *SW* luncheon, 7" pack   10 - 15
PA9002 *SW* dinner, 9" pack   10 - 20
PA9010 *ESB* Cloud City, 7" pack   10 - 15
PA9012 *ESB* Cloud City, 9" pack   10 - 20
PA9020 *ROTJ* Luke/Vader duel, 7" pack   10 - 15
PA9022 *ROTJ* duel, 9" pack   10 - 20
PA9030 *Ewoks*, 7" pack   6 - 12
PA9032 *Ewoks*, 9" pack   6 - 15
England (Deeko)
PA9250 *SW*: Luke cake and dinner   10 - 20
Mexico (Papeles Troquelados)
PA9470 *ESB* design 25-pack   10 - 20

133

PA9012   PA9022   PA9250

PA9032   PA9030   PA9470

PA9600   PA9610

PA9620   PA9630   PA9750

TABLE COVERS

PA9600	*SW*: R2-D2 and C-3PO	10 - 20
PA9610	*ESB* Cloud City	10 - 20
PA9620	*ROTJ*: Luke/Vader duel	10 - 20
PA9630	*Ewoks* hang-gliding	8 - 15
England (Deeko)		
PA9750	*SW* design	10 - 20

See also—**KITCHEN ITEMS; STATIONERY**

PATCHES

Cloth patches to be sewn onto jackets and other clothing were first sold by Factors Inc. on rack cards inside plastic bubbles—including a version of the badge with Darth Vader's name misspelled as Vadar. Thereafter, the main source of patches became the *Star Wars/Lucasfilm* fan club. Some of them are fashioned after crew patches. Most of the patches remain fairly common, with the exception of the *Revenge of the Jedi* Yoda patch. When the third film was renamed, the patch was replaced by a similar one with the title *Return of the Jedi*. Below are the patches that were available commercially.

PC0010

PC0005

PC0030

PC5110

PC0035

PC0025   PC0001   PC0002

PC0020   PC5150   PC0015

PC5100   PC5160   PC5165

PC0001   PC3010   PC3020

PC5125   PC5140   PC5145

Factors

PC0001	*SW* pyramid logo, blue (w/stars) on yellow w/o ™	10 - 20
PC0002	*SW* pyramid logo, blue (w/stars) on yellow w/™	10 - 20
PC0005	*SW* outline logo, white on black, 3½" wide original	10 - 20
PC0010	*SW* outline logo, white on black, 4" wide	8 - 15
PC0015	May the Force be with You	8 - 15
PC0020	Brotherhood of Jedi Knights 3" wide original	10 - 20
PC0025	Brotherhood of Jedi Knights 3½" wide	8 - 15
PC0030	*SW* Rebel Forces, round yellow and blue on red	15 - 25
PC0035	Darth "Vadar" Lives, round w/Vader head	10 - 20

Kenner

| PC3010 | *SW/ESB* Sweepstakes Third Prize patch | 15 - 30 |
| PC3020 | *ROTJ* Patch (Kenner Internal) | 20 - 40 |

Fan Club

PC5100	Official *SW* Fan Club, yellow & red on black circle, 2 variations, ea.	5 - 15
PC5110	A New Hope triangular	5 - 15
PC5115	*ESB* logo w/*SW* outline in red	5 - 15
PC5120	*ESB* logo w/*SW* outline in white	5 - 15

PE0010

PL0005

PC5125	Vader in Flames (like crew patch)	5 - 15
PC5130	*Revenge* logo rectangular	15 - 25
PC5135	*ROTJ* logo rectangular	5 -15
PC5140	Yoda/*Revenge of the Jedi*	20 - 45
PC5145	Yoda/*Return of the Jedi*	5 - 15
PC5150	*Star Wars*: The First Ten Years	5 - 15
PC5155	*ESB* 10th anniversary	5 - 12
PC5160	*SW* Lucasfilm Fan Club, blue on maroon	5 - 10
PC5165	The Lucasfilm Fan Club, either gray or red on black	4 - 8

See also—**CAST AND CREW; KITCHEN ITEMS**

PEWTER

PE0010	*SW* Classic Millennium Falcon (Franklin Mint)	150 - 200
PE0100	*SW* Millennium Falcon (Rawcliffe Corp.)	95 - 145
PE0101	*SW* X-wing	95 - 145
PE0102	*SW* Vader's TIE fighter	95 - 145
PE0105	Luke/Leia (Kenner/F.A.O. Schwarz exclusive)	400 - 500

PINBALL—See **GAMES: Arcade**

PLAQUES AND SCULPTURE, LIMITED EDITIONS

The first "limited edition" item was a bronze sculpture of Yoda by artist Larry Noble, sold by Kilian Enterprises and the Lucasfilm Fan Club. Catch A Star, a division of The Scoreboard Inc., made other limited edition items—most of them signed—to sell on quarterly *Star Wars* collectible specials on the QVC home shopping channel. The number in brackets is the total number of the edition.

PL0005	Yoda bronze sculpture on wood base [50 made]	$650 - 850
PL0010	*SW*: R2-D2 and C-3PO photo plaque, unsigned [1000]	55 - 75
PL0012	*SW*: Marvel Special Edition comic #3, matted and framed, signed by Roy Thomas [975]	175 - 225
PL0014	*SW*: Death Star trench production art litho, matted and framed, signed by Ralph McQuarrie [1000]	95 - 150
PL0516	*ESB*: C-3PO photo plaque, signed by Anthony Daniels [1980 made]	65 - 95
PL0518	*ESB*: Luke carrying Yoda photo plaque, signed by Mark Hamill [1000]	65 - 95
PL1020	*ROTJ*: Luke in black photo plaque, signed by Mark Hamill [1000]	65 - 95
PL1022	*ROTJ*: cast in forest photo plaque, unsigned [2500]	40 - 55
PL1024	Gifted Images lithograph [500]	500 - 700

POSTERS, LOBBY CARDS, PRESS KITS, ETC.
See also—**CRAFTS**

POSTERS

There have been more posters produced for the *Star Wars* trilogy than any movie or movie series ever, making them an abundant and beautiful collectible. The *Star Wars* Special Edition added a new dimension, with posters in many more foreign languages than the original releases, although using the same art worldwide. Trilogy posters also are sought by non-*Star Wars* poster collectors because of the importance of the three films and the quality of the art used.

Most posters were produced in the thousands, are fairly widely available, and are therefore still affordable. Some, however, have taken on mythic proportions such as the *Star Wars* mylar (or shiny silver) advance; the *Star Wars* Happy Birthday poster, made for theaters still playing the film after a year; and, for non-theatrical, the *Star Wars* Concert poster, sold only at one performance at the Hollywood Bowl.

Poster collectors have mixed feelings about foreign posters and prices tend to be lower. Many of the original foreign posters have the same art as their American counterparts, but some—those from Poland, in particular—are knockouts. Prices of oversized posters—once shunned by many collectors—have jumped in recent years. Finally, there are promotional posters and posters used to advertise trilogy-related products. While usually not advertised in publications and not that easy to find, they remain mostly inexpensive. Looking at a large selection of them makes it clear how much *Star Wars* has influenced worldwide popular culture.

Collectors like to find posters rolled, in as pristine condition as possible. Many posters were distributed to theaters with a triple fold, but every trilogy one-sheet was available in rolled form at one time or another. Collectors need to be careful about condition—though posters can be restored—and bootlegs. Unfortunately, most of the *Star Wars* style A, B-advance and C one-sheets being sold widely today are bootlegs (the quality is a little less than perfect, with images a bit more hazy than they should be), as are many *Revenge of the Jedi* posters and the infamous U.S. Triple Bill poster. The artwork on fake style A posters is slightly smaller then the original, and the "©1977 Twentieth Century-Fox" line directly under the artwork on the left side is flush with the left border on the bootleg, rather than being indented about one-eighth inch like the real one. The color is also slightly different. Bootleg style B posters have some smearing around a few of the letters, and the oval union label to the left of center in the bottom border is missing. On style C bootlegs, the faces of the characters have a yellowish cast, rather than the original orange-brown flesh tone. Authentic triple-bill posters are large photo blow-ups—bootlegs are printed. Be ultra cautious in purchasing any of these. All posters in this book are known to exist.

Prices in this edition have been adjusted to more closely track recent sales and market trends. All top prices, except where noted, are for mint and rolled posters. Folded posters may be priced at well less than half mint rolled ones. Condition impacts price. Mint means no pin or staple holes, no tape, tears, stains or creases. For the handful of so-called "mylar" posters silk-screened in metallic colors onto plastic sheets and then backed by heavy paper or vinyl, it also means no de-lamination, or separation from the backing or bubbling of the surface. Poster values also depend on the quality of the image and how pleasing it is to a large number of people.

See pages 101-102 for color photos of major theatrical and other posters.

US POSTER SIZE GUIDE									
Insert	14x36	One sheet	27x41	Two-sheet	40x60	Three-sheet	41x81	Sm Billboard	82x84
Half sheet	22x28	Windowbox	30x40	Standee	40x60	Six-sheet	81x81	24-sheet	varies

THEATRICAL POSTERS

United States

Star Wars

PO0010	1976-27x41 Mylar Advance (heavy stock)		600 - 1,000
PO0011	1976-27x41 1st Advance: Silver-gray on black w/silver-gray border. No opening date		175 - 225
PO0012	1977-27x41 Teaser 'B'; white letters on blue field		175 - 250
PO0013	1977-6-sheet Teaser 'B' in 4 sheets: "STARTS MAY 25th"		750 - 1,000
PO0014	1977-27x41 'A' sheet		125 - 175
PO0015	1977-27x41 'A' sheet (heavy)		100 - 125
PO0016	1977-14x36 'A' sheet/Vert.		100 - 125
PO0017	1977-22x28 Horiz. Diff. art		200 - 350
PO0018	1977-30x40 'A' sheet		150 - 225
PO0019	1977-40x60 'A' sheet		225 - 275

PO0020	1977-3-sheet 'A' sheet	300 - 600
PO0021	1977-6-sheet 'A' sheet	300 - 750
PO0022	1977-Standee 'A' sheet	175 - 250
PO0023	1977-24-sheet 'A' sheet	750 - 1,000
PO0024	1977-27x41 Style 'A' Records w/black *SW*- & 20th Cnt-Fox Records logos	125 - 200
PO0030	1977-27x41 Style 'C'	225 - 300
PO0040	1978-27x41 Style 'D' ('Circus')	250 - 300
PO0041	1978-30x40 Style 'D'	125 - 150
PO0042	1978-40x60 Style 'D'	200 - 225
PO0043	1978-Standee Style 'D'	200 - 300
PO0044	1978-27x41 Style 'D' w/Fox Records oval in lower left corner	150 - 225
PO0045	1978-27x41 *SW*- Happy Birthday: "One year old today" w/cake and Kenner action figures	600 - 800

PO0050	1979-27x41 1979 Rerelease: 'It's Back' silver/blue w/red band	100 - 125
PO0055	1981-27x41 1981 Rerelease w/yellow stripe	60 - 75
PO0056	1981-14x36 1981 Rerelease/Vert.	45 - 60
PO0057	1981-22x28 1981 Rerelease/Horiz.	45 - 60
PO0060	1982-27x41 1982 Rerelease w/Revenge stripe	50 - 60
PO0061	1982-14x36 1982 Rerelease w/Revenge/Vert.	45 - 55
PO0062	1982-22x28 1982 Rerelease w/Revenge/Horiz.	45 - 55
PO0063	1982-30x40 1982 Rerelease w/Revenge stripe	50 - 60
PO0064	1982-40x60 1982 Rerelease w/Revenge stripe	55 - 75
PO0065	1982-Standee 1982 Rerelease w/Revenge stripe	75 - 100

PO0050	PO0060	PO0110	PO0310	PO0311

The Empire Strikes Back

PO0110	*ESB* Advance: "Coming to your Galaxy this Summer" 1980-27x41	150 - 225
PO0111	1980-45x58 NYC Subway	75 - 125
PO0112	1980-3-sheet	300 - 450
PO0113	1980-6-sheet	400 - 600
PO0114	1980-24-sheet, full billboard/ 6 pcs.	750 - 1,000
PO0120	1980-27x41 Style 'A'	175 - 225
PO0121	1980-14x36 Style 'A'/Vertical	100 - 150
PO0122	1980-22x28 Style 'A'/Horiz.	100 - 150
PO0123	1980-30x40 Style 'A'	250 - 300
PO0124	1980-40x60 Style 'A'	250 - 300
PO0125	1980-45x58 NYC Subway Style 'A' 'Opens Wed. May 21'	75 - 125
PO0126	1980-Standee Style 'A'	200 - 250
PO0127	1980-6-sheet	1,000-1,500
PO0130	1980-27x41 Style 'B'	75 - 100
PO0131	1980-14x36 Style 'B'/Vertical	60 - 75
PO0132	1980-22x28 Style 'B'/Horizontal	60 - 75
PO0133	1980-30x40 Style 'B'	85 - 115
PO0134	1980-40x60 Style 'B'	85 - 115
PO0140	1981-27x41 1981 Rerelease	40 - 60
PO0141	1981-14x36 1981 Rerelease/Vert.	35 - 45
PO0142	1981-22x28 1981 Rerelease/Horiz.	35 - 45
PO0143	1981-30x40 1981 Rerelease	45 - 60
PO0144	1981-40x60 1981 Rerelease	45 - 75
PO0150	1982-27x41 1982 Rerelease	40 - 60
PO0151	1982-14x36 1982 Rerelease/Vert.	35 - 45
PO0152	1982-22x28 1982 Rerelease/Horiz.	35 - 45
PO0153	1982-30x40 1982 Rerelease	45 - 65
PO0154	1982-40x60 1982 Rerelease	45 - 75
PO0155	1982-Standee 1982 Rerelease	100 - 125
PO0156	1982-24x38 Standee 1982 Rerelease mini-standee	50 - 75

Return of the Jedi

PO0210	1982-27x41 Revenge Advance w/opening date	250 - 350
PO0211	1982-27x41 Revenge Advance no date	350 - 450
PO0220	1983-27x41 Style 'A'	25 - 40
PO0221	1983-14x36 Style 'A'/Vert.	25 - 40
PO0222	1983-22x28 Style 'A'/Horiz.	25 - 40
PO0223	1983-30x40 Style 'A'	45 - 60
PO0224	1983-40x60 Style 'A'	50 - 75
PO0225	1983-Standee Style 'A'	175 - 200
PO0230	1983-27x41 Style 'B'	40 - 55
PO0231	1983-14x36 Style 'B'/Vert.	40 - 55
PO0232	1983-22x28 Style 'B'/Horiz.	40 - 55
PO0233	1983-30x40 Style 'B'	65 - 85
PO0234	1983-40x60 Style 'B'	75 - 100
PO0235	1983-3-sheet Style 'B'	300 - 350
PO0236	1983-27x41 Style 'B' International (No rating)	100 - 125
PO0237	1983-six-sheet Style 'B' small billboard in 4 sheets	300 - 450
PO0238	1983-24½x38½ Standee Style 'B' mini-standee	75 - 85
PO0239	1983-Standee Style 'B'	125 - 150
PO0245	1985-27x41 1985 Rerelease	35 - 40
PO0246	1985-14x36 1985 Rerelease/Vert.	35 - 40
PO0247	1985-22x28 1985 Rerelease/Horiz.	35 - 40

Ewok, Triple Bill

PO0310	1984-Ewok-27x41 Caravan of Courage 'A' sht Intl.	60 - 75
PO0311	1984-Ewok-27x41 Caravan of Courage' 'B' sht Intl.	60 - 75
PO0312	1984-Ewok-25x33 'Opens Nov. 25 on ABC'; like 'A' sht w/yellow border	125 - 150
PO0320	1985-Triple Bill-1985-27x41 photo enlargement from one of 9 theaters; *beware printed fakes*	3,000 - 4,500

Star Wars Trilogy Special Edition

The first price listed is for 1-sided posters; the second for 2-sided versions used in lightboxes. All posters are about 27x40 unless indicated. Various versions were also available in the following countries: Brazil, Bulgaria, Croatia, Czech Republic/Slovakia, Denmark, Egypt, England, Finland, France, Germany, Hungary, Italy, Lebanon, Norway, Poland, Romania, South Africa, Spain, Sweden, Switzerland, Turkey, Yugoslavia, Australia, India, Indonesia, Japan, Korea, Taiwan, Thailand. Prices should be about the same for similar-sized posters.

PO0410	1996-Ingot Advance	30 - 50
PO0415	1997-*SW* (style B)	25 - 45
PO0420	1997-*ESB* (style C)	30 - 45
PO0425	1997-*ROTJ* (style D, March 7)	30 - 45
PO0430	1997-*ROTJ* (style E, March 14)	30 - 45
PO0435	1997-Ingot (style D, March 14, 1-sided)	40 - 50
PO0440	1997-16x26-All 3 posters/Horiz. (1-sided)	20 - 40

FOREIGN POSTERS: A selection

Argentina

PO1201	*SW*-1978-27x41 like PO0030; stone litho look	20 - 35

Australia

PO1321	*SW*-1978-26x40 like PO0030 w/superscript: 'A long time ago…'	45 - 75
PO1322	*SW*-1978-13x27 Vert. like PO1321	20 - 30
PO1323	*ESB*-1980-26x40 Japanese art	35 - 45
PO1324	*ESB*-1980-13x27 Vert. like PO1323	20 - 30
PO1325	*SW*-1981-26x40 like US 1981 rerelease, no time period on banner	35 - 45
PO1326	*SW*-1981-13x27 Vert. like PO1325	15 - 25
PO1327	*ROTJ*-1983-26x40 like PO0230	25 - 35
PO1328	*ROTJ*-1983-13x27 Vert. like PO0231	15 - 20
PO1329	*SW*-1983-18x36 'Proudly presented by General Electric' (TV)	15 - 45
PO1330	*SW*-1983-24x9 GE/Kenner contest (TV)	10 - 25
PO1331	*SW* Saga-1983-40x59 Immunization poster w/R2 & C-3PO on Endor (heavy stock)	75 - 125
PO1332	*SW* Saga-1983-15x20 like PO1331, glossy stock	15 - 25
PO1333	*ROTJ*-1983-6x24 Logo mini-banner (white on black), Bing Harris Sargood	5 - 10
PO1334	Like PO0433, 6x48, two parts	10 - 15
PO1335	*ROTJ*-1983-16x24 Crystal Craft Gifts ad poster	10 - 15

PO0017

PO1350

PO1351

| PO2042 | | PO2046 | | PO2051 | | PO2846 | |

PO1336-42 ROTJ-1983-19x25 Shellacked Crystal Craft posters

PO1336	*ROTJ* Style B 1-sheet	5 - 15
PO1337	Luke & Leia	5 - 15
PO1338	Battle in front of Death Star	5 - 15
PO1339	Jabba the Hut	5 - 15
PO1340	Wicket	5 - 15
PO1341	Darth Vader	5 - 15
PO1342	R2-D2 and C-3PO	5 - 15
PO1343	Coupon for Crystal Craft Posters	
PO1345	*ROTJ*-1983-16x22 Peters w/Jedi Jelly (ice pops) w/Revenge and Style 'B' art and toys to win	15 - 25
PO1346	*ROTJ*-1983-9x14 PO1345 w/o toys	15 - 25
PO1347	*ROTJ*-1983-13x19 NSW Building Society Style 'B' art; (promo)	20 - 25
PO1350	Triple Bill-1985-27x41 Black, white, silver & red tri-logo & art from *SW* and *ESB* posters	45 - 75
PO1351	Triple Bill-1985-13x27 Vert.	25 - 45
PO1352	Ewok-1985-26x39½ 'Build an Ewok Adventure with Break' fruit drinks; needs 28 stickers	15 - 25

Belgium

PO1471	*SW*-1978-14x21 Miniature of US 'A' sht in French	15 - 25
PO1472	Like PO1471, but Flemish	15 - 25
PO1473	*SW*-1978-19x32 US 'C' sht in English, w/logo in lower right: "Maandblad Muziek Expres"	10 - 20
PO1474	*ESB*-1980-14x21 Miniature of US 'B' sht in Flemish	15 - 25
PO1475	*ESB*-1980-14x19 Miniature of US 'B' sht in French	15 - 25
PO1476	*ROTJ*-1983-14x21 like French, Jouin art with Clipper toys superscript in Flemish	10 - 20
PO1477	PO1476 w/handwritten ad in upper margin	5 - 15
PO1478	*ROTJ*-1983-14x21 Jouin art, Flemish title, all else in English	10 - 15
PO1479	Ewok-1985-14x21 Caravan of Courage-Struzan art, Flemish & French	10 - 20

Brazil

PO1591	*SW*-1978-25x36 like US 'C' sht	25 - 45
PO1592	*ESB*-1980-25x36 like Japanese art	25 - 45
PO1593	*ROTJ*-1983-25x36 like US 'B' sht	25 - 45

Canada

| PO1610 | *ROTJ*-1983-25x38 Slurpee (Coke) Collectors Cups | 15 - 35 |
| PO1612 | *ROTJ*-1983-13x18 As above, but cardboard with cutout for one cup | 20 - 35 |

PO1613-15 ROTJ-1983-24x36 General Mills (Canada) mail-in posters, logos in Eng. & Fr.:

PO1613	Revenge art w/25 small boxed cast photos at bottom (art)	10 - 20
PO1614	Darth Vader pointing (photo)	10 - 20
PO1615	Star Destroyer & TIE fighters en route to Death Star (photo)	10 - 20
PO1616	*SW* Kellogg-1984-20x30 C-3PO Cereal w/large letters at top & copyright below in Eng. and Fr.	10 - 15

Czechoslovakia

| PO1721 | *SW*-1990-23x33 Tom Jung 'A' sht art w/logo in Czech & English w/logo 'Lucernafilm Beta' | 45 - 75 |

Denmark

PO1825	*SW*-1977-24x33 Foreign 'A' sht	45 - 65
PO1826	*ESB*-1980-242x33 like US 'B' sht	35 - 50
PO1827	*ROTJ*-1983-24x33 like US 'B' sht	35 - 50

England

PO1941	*SW*-1977-30x40 Hildebrandt art	75 - 125
PO1942	*SW*-1978-30x40 Like US 'C' sht. Art by Cantrell	75 - 150
PO1943	PO1942 w/Oscar logo and '7 Academy Awards'	75 - 125
PO1944	*SW*-1978-20x30 For Sphere Books paperback version of novel-shows book cover	20 - 30
PO1945	*SW*-1978-11x19 Store window poster for Sphere soft w/ Hildebrandt art & photos	25 - 45
PO1946	*ESB*-1980-30x40 Like US 'B' sht w/B&W logo	65 - 95
PO1947	PO1946, logo in silver & black	65 - 125
PO1948	*SW/ESB*-1980-30x40 Double bill	75 - 125

PO1949-53 ESB-1980- Five poster set in red, white & blue w/B&W

PO1949	'Fun for everyone with...'-20x30	15 - 25
PO1950	'...space for a little romance'-20x30	15 - 25
PO1951	'The heroes return...'-20x30	15 - 25
PO1952	'...but so do the villains'-.20x30	15 - 25
PO1953	Thrills Excitement'-30x40	15 - 25
PO1955	*SW/ESB*-1980-20x30 Red, white & blue 'half crown' w/R2-D2 & C-3PO w/space for photo of Luke & Leia on Tatooine	45 - 60
PO1956	*ESB*-1980-Palitoy inside window *ESB* logo and stripes for border	35 - 50
PO1957	*ROTJ*-1982-30x40 *Jedi* advance in dayglo orange w/black and yellow	65 - 100
PO1958	PO1957 w/'Parker Video Games Available Here' snipe	55 - 75
PO1959	PO1957 w/'Toys Available Here'	55 - 75
PO1960	PO1957 w/'*Star Wars* Yogurts Available Here' snipe	55 - 75
PO1961	*ROTJ*-1983-31x40 Kirby art; designed by Feref Assoc. (No Ewoks) Glossy printers proof	45 - 85
PO1962	*ROTJ*-1983-27x40 Kirby art-same as above on flat paper (No Ewoks)	45 - 85
PO1963	*ROTJ*-1983-30x40 Similar to above, but w/Ewok and others	45 - 85
PO1964	*SW/ESB/ROTJ*-1983-27x39 '3 in one programme'	65 - 125

PO1965-68 ROTJ-1983-20x30 Double Crowns, vertical w/2 photos

PO1965	Robots in forest; Vader & troops	25 - 30
PO1966	Luke, Leia at Jabba's; Imp. cruiser	25 - 30
PO1967	Han/carbon; Han, Chewie caught	25 - 30
PO1968	Bibb Fortuna; Forest battle	25 - 30
PO1970	*ROTJ*-1983-16x23 Airfix logo on 2-sided photo poster: Han; Jabba throne room	5 - 10
PO1971	*ROTJ*-1983-16x23 *SW* Yogurts store poster w/5 cups and Darth in background	10 - 20

PO1972	*ROTJ*-1983-12x16 As above, but horizontal and w/o *ROTJ* logo	10 - 20
PO1973	*ROTJ*-1983-16x23 Eng/Fr. toy promo poster-pkg insert w/illus of B-wing ftr in center	5 - 10
PO1974	*ESB*-1984-15x22 Video promo Like US 'B' sht	10 - 20
PO1975	Ewok-1984-30x40 Like US 'B' sht	35 - 55

Finland

PO2036	*SW*-1978-16x24 Like US 'C' sht	35 - 50
PO2037	*ESB*-1980-16x24 Like US 'B' sht	35 - 50
PO2038	*ROTJ*-1983-16x24 Like US 'B' sht	35 - 50

France

PO2041	*SW*-1978-23x31 US 'A' sht in French	35 - 55
PO2042	*SW*-1978-47x62 US 'A' sht in French	75 - 100
PO2043	*SW*-1978/79-23x34 Near repro of #1, for commercial sale by F. Nugeron	15 - 25
PO2044	*ESB*-1980-15x20 Like US 'A' sht but in French and with Lando and Boba Fett at right (Used in Canada w/Quebec sticker)	25 - 35
PO2045	*ESB*-1980-47x62 US 'A' sht in French	75 - 100
PO2046	*ESB*-1980-47x6 US 'B' sht in French	50 - 75
PO2047	*ESB*-1980-39x59 Yoplait yogurt original art of heroes & villains w/cup of Yoplait floating & offer for poster collection/stickers	15 - 25
PO2048	*ESB*-1980-13x19 Yoplait as above	5 - 15
PO2049	*ESB*-1980-24x34 Four Yoplait posters on one sheet w/spaces for stickers; new art	15 - 30
PO2050	*ESB*-1981-21x29 US Style 'B' surrounded by spaces for stickers from Glacés Motta	20 - 30
PO2051	*ROTJ*-1983-47x62 Michel Jouin illus w/Ewoks, scenes. In French	45 - 75
PO2052	*ROTJ*-1983-23x63 US 'A' sht. Door poster: Le 19 Octobre	35 - 50
PO2053	*ROTJ*-1983-27x38 Like US Revenge advance, but 'Retour'; Editions du Weekend	15 - 30
PO2054	Ewok-1984-23x30 Like US 'B' sht	15 - 30
PO2055	Ewok-1984-45x62 Like US 'B' sht	25 - 35
PO2056	*ROTJ* TOYS-1984-12x25 In store promo poster w/cartoon-like art of space battle in front of Death Star from General Mills Fun Group	15 - 25
PO2057	*SW/ESB/ROTJ*-1985-23x62 Triple bill w/3 small posters	25 - 45
PO2058	*SW/ESB/ROTJ*-1985-23x62 Triple bill as above, but w/empty white blocks to write in times. 'La Saga de la Guerre des Etoiles'	25 - 45

Germany

PO2101-10 *SW*-1977-23x33 10-sheet Deko display, to be mounted as one panoramic scene, set	150 - 350
PO2101	TIE Ftr	
PO2102	C-3PO & R2-D2	
PO2103	Two X-wing ftrs.	

PO2104 Jawa & 'Tusken-Bandit'
PO2105 Large blue planet
PO2106 Luke & Leia
PO2107 Star Destroyer
PO2108 Obi Wan & Darth Vader
PO2109 X-wing & 'broken' red planet
PO2110 Chewbacca & Han Solo
PO2112 *SW*-1977-20x47 Krieg der Sterne logo in blue star field letters on silver w/*Star Wars* under, to be used as part of above display (2 in set, each 2-sheets glued together)
PO2113 *SW*-1977-16x27 Illus. battle scene, miniature of above: TIE ftrs, X-wings & Star Destroyer; red planet, Death Star. Horizontal   25 - 45
PO2114 *SW*-1977-25x35 Instruction sheet poster illustrating ways to hang *SW* Deko display: 10 - 15
PO2115 *SW*-1978-23x33 Like US 'A' sht w/silver background   45 - 60
PO2116 *SW*-1978-23x33 Like US 'C' sht (Cantrell art) w/silver background   45 - 60
PO2117 *SW*-1978-33x46 As above   55 - 75
PO2118 *SW*-1978-11x16 As above   20 - 30
PO2121 *SW*-1978-47x67 'Super-Poster im Panoramaformat' German Kenner wall poster in 2 sheets All major *SW* characters and vehicles Mint, rolled, w/sales flyer   25 - 40
PO2122-23 *ESB*-1980/2-23x33
PO2122 Film-1980 Illustrated. In center: Luke in flight outfit w/Yoda on shoulder   45 - 55
PO2123 Video-1982 As above, but w/snipe for CBS/Fox and mention of book & soundtrack   25 - 35
PO2124 *ESB*-1980-33x46 Art as above   45 - 55
PO2125 *ESB*-1980-11x16 Art as above   25 - 25
PO2126 *ESB*-1980-23x33 Like US 'B' sht   35 - 45
PO2127 *ESB*-1980-7x94 Banner: The Star Wars Continues (white on blue)   15 - 25
PO2128 *ESB*-1980-3x38 As above, w/ sticker backing   15 - 25

PO2131-38 *ESB*-1980-18x33 Character photo poster Deko display w/large blue caption bands
PO2131 Han Solo   15 - 22
PO2132 Darth Vader   15 - 22
PO2133 Yoda   15 - 22
PO2134 AT-AT   15 - 22
PO2135 Chewbacca   15 - 22
PO2136 Luke   15 - 22
PO2137 Leia   15 - 22
PO2138 C-3PO & R2-D2   15 - 22
PO2139 *ROTJ*-1983-23x33 *Jedi* Advance w/ all 3 logos and art from US 'A' sht   45 - 60
PO2140 *ROTJ*-1983-12x16 As above   15 - 25
PO2141 *ROTJ*-1983-11x19 Window card w/US 'A' sht art   10 - 20
PO2142 *ROTJ*-1983-33x46 US 'A' sht art: Opening Dec. 9   45 - 60
PO2143 *ROTJ*-1983-23x33 As above.   35 - 45
PO2144 *ROTJ*-1983-23x33 Like US 'B' sht   25 - 35
PO2145 *ROTJ*-1983-33x46 As above   25 - 45
PO2146 *ROTJ*-1983-12x16½ As above   15 - 20
PO2147 *ROTJ*-1983-23x33 Two-sided; *Jedi* toys (Genl Mills Gy.)   5 - 10

PO2151-56 *ROTJ*-1983 Deko display: Set of posters connected by hand holding lightsaber
PO2151 All 3 logos-16x34   20 - 25
PO2152 Darth Vader-16x34   20 - 25
PO2153 Luke & Leia-16x34   20 - 25
PO2154 Gamorrean Guard-16x34   20 - 25
PO2155 Yoda & heroes-16x34   20 - 25
PO2156 Vertical *ROTJ* logo banner-16x47   20 - 25

PO2160-62 *SW* SAGA-1985-23x33 Headlines on 'Star Wars' (SDI) over: "Star Wars Belongs Only in the Movies" w/film logos:
PO2160 *Star Wars*   25 - 50
PO2161 *Empire*   25 - 50
PO2162 *Jedi*   25 - 50
PO2163 Ewok-1985-23x33 'Caravan of Courage' (art by Struzan)   25 - 35
PO2164 Ewok-1985-33x46 As above   35 - 50
PO2165 Ewok-1985-11x16 As above   15 - 20
PO2166 Ewok-1985-47x66 Two sheets Different art-by Rob   45 - 50
PO2167 Ewok-1985-16x23 Painting of an Ewok w/'Caravan' logo, bright yellow background   15 - 30

PO2168 Ewok-1985-16x23 As above, w/different Ewok   15 - 30
PO2169 Ewok-1986-23x33 'Battle for Endor' (R. Casaro art)   20 - 30
PO2170 Ewok-1986-33x47 'Endor' Casaro art as above   30 - 40
PO2171 Ewok-1987-33x47 'Endor' video poster (Casaro)   15 - 25
PO2172 *SW* 10th-1987-11x16 *Star Wars* Fan Connection anniv. poster printed by color Xerox   5 - 15
PO2173 *SW* Saga-1987-12x17 Uni Film *Star Wars* Nacht Berlin screening of trilogy for 10th anniv.; miniposters of all 3 films   5 - 10
PO2174 Droids-1985-23x33 CBS/Fox for 4 Droids cartoon cassettes   5 - 15
PO2175 EWOKS-1985-16½x23 Scandecor #6988. Cartoon Wicket & Kneesaa swinging on vine   5 - 10

Hong Kong
PO2277 *SW*-1978-21x31 Like US 'C' sht   75 - 100
PO2278 *ESB*-1980-21x31 Like US 'A' sheet w/AT-ATs   75 - 100
PO2279 *ESB*-1980-21x31 Elements of US 'B' sht, but mostly Chinese   75 - 100

Israel
PO2380 *SW*-1977-25x37 Like US 'A' sht   45 - 75
PO2381 *ROTJ*-1983-25x37 Like US 'B' sht; matte   35 - 60

Italy
PO2482 *SW*-1978-39x55 Cartoon art by Papuzza   75 - 125
PO2483 *SW*-1978-53x78 Two-sheet like US 'A' sht   75 - 125

PO2484-87 *SW*-1978-18x26
PO2484 Photo: Troopers stop speeder   15 - 20
PO2485 Darth in Leia's ship   15 - 20
PO2486 Luke, Leia on Death Star bridge   15 - 20
PO2487 Luke and robots on Falcon   15 - 20
PO2488 *SW*-1978-26x37 Like half-sheets Stormtrooper on Bantha   35 - 50
PO2489 *SW*-1978-26x37 Like above. Main: Leia & Luke   35 - 50

PO2490-99 *SW*-1978-18x26
PO2490 Luke in Mil. Falcon cabin w/R2   7 - 10
PO2491 Luke, Leia on Death Star bridge   7 - 10
PO2492 Chewie, Luke, Obi, Han in Falcon   7 - 10
PO2493 Vader threatens Leia   7 - 10
PO2494 Han shoots Stormtroopers   7 - 10
PO2495 Stormtrooper; Obi, Luke & droids   7 - 10
PO2496 Leia & R2; Obi on Death Star   7 - 10
PO2497 Escape pod; Jawa   7 - 10
PO2498 TIE Ftrs in bay; Tusken Raider   7 - 10
PO2499 Jawas/Crawler; robots & spdr   7 - 10
PO2500 *SW*-1978-13x27 Vertical-like US 'A' sht   15 - 25
PO2501 *ESB*-1980-13x27 Vertical-like US 'B' sht   15 - 25
PO2502 *ESB*-1980-39x55 Like US 'B' sht   45 - 60

PO2503-14 *ESB*-1980-18x26 All silver backgrounds w/large photos
PO2503 C-3PO, Luke, Leia, Falcon/Hoth   7 - 10
PO2504 Luke emerges from Dagobah swamp   7 - 10
PO2505 C-3PO and R2 in ice cave   7 - 10
PO2506 Luke on Tauntaun   7 - 10
PO2507 Luke vs. Darth   7 - 10
PO2508 Darth, Lando, Boba Fett   7 - 10
PO2509 Chewie, C-3PO, Leia, Han on Falcon   7 - 10
PO2510 Lando, Leia, Han, Chewie   7 - 10
PO2511 Luke and R2 on Dagobah   7 - 10
PO2512 C-3PO looks through plotting chart   7 - 10
PO2513 Stormtroopers and Lobot   7 - 10
PO2514 Darth w/hand outstretched   7 - 10
PO2515 *ROTJ*-1983-39x55 Like US 'B' sht   35 - 50

PO2516-25 *ROTJ*-1983-18x26 Blue starfield backgrounds w/2 photos
PO2516 Skiff; Millennium Falcon   6 - 10
PO2517 Jabba; Lando fighting   6 - 10
PO2518 Surrounded by Ewoks; Yoda   6 - 10
PO2519 Star Destroyer; Heroes in forest   6 - 10
PO2520 Droids & Ewok; Luke, Leia on skiff   6 - 10
PO2521 Inside Death Star; Darth Vader   6 - 10
PO2522 Rebels' council; Gamorrean Guard   6 - 10
PO2523 Heroes captured; Han defrosting   6 - 10
PO2524 Heroes in Mil. Falcon; Biker Scout   6 - 10
PO2525 Forest battle; Han   6 - 10
PO0726 *ROTJ*-1983-13x27 US 'B' sht art   15 - 25
PO2527 Ewok-1985-13x27 'Caravan of Courage' daybill (US 'B')   10 - 15

PO2528 Ewok-1985-39x55 As above   25 - 45
PO2529 Ewok-1985-53x78 As above   30 - 50

Japan
PO2830 *SW*-1977-29x41 Advance. Mostly Japanese. '*SW*' in silver on blue/ star background   65 - 85
PO2831 *SW*-1977-20x29 As above   35 - 45
PO2832 *SW*-1977/78-29x40 'Drink Coca Cola *Star Wars*' (Battle scene illus by Shimaoka)   75 - 125
PO2833 *SW*-1978-29x41 'May the Force' but mostly in Japanese; Good guy photos in front of illus Darth; Illus of Academy Award   45- 65
PO2834 *SW*-1978-20x29 As above   35 - 45
PO2835 *SW*-1978-14x20 As above: Transit advertising (blank)   25 - 35
PO2836 *SW*-1978-20x29 Like US 'A' sht, but mostly Japanese, Oscar in lower left corner   35 - 45
PO2837 *SW*-1978-29x41 Seito version of US 'A' sht   45 - 75
PO2838 *SW*-1978-20x29 Seito version of US 'A' sht (gloss)   40 - 60
PO2839 *SW*-1978-20x29 All Eng. Small version of US 'A' sht   35 - 45
PO2840 *SW* Records-1978-20x29 King Records & Tapes; photo of R2 & C-3PO in ship corridor   15 - 25
PO2841 *SW* Factors badges-1978-14x20 For 10 Japanese Factors badge set   15 - 25

PO2842-43 *SW* 1978 Uncut printers proofs of die-cut figures
PO2842 R2-D2-50x62½   15 - 45
PO2843 C-3PO-38x75   15 - 45
PO2844 *SW*-1979-20x29 'It's Back!' blue & rerelease   25 - 35
PO2845 *ESB*-1979-29x41 Advance: Darth head photo; mostly in Japanese   45 - 75
PO2846 *ESB*-1980-29x41 '*SW* 2' but mostly in Japanese. All illus w/green Darth in background   45 - 60
PO2847 *ESB*-1980-23½x33 Similar to above, w/RSO records logo & English only '*SW TESB*'   25 - 40
PO2848 *ESB*-1980-20x29 '*SW* 2' mostly Japanese. Photo of cast in front of Bespin City and Darth head (Gloss and matte)   35 - 45
PO2849 *ESB*-1980-20x29 Duplicate of '*SW* 2' w/green Darth (Gloss and matte)   35 - 45
PO2850 *ESB*-1980-20x30 US International 'A' sheet w/Japanese in left border and dated Aug. 1980. Reverse has B&W of US Navy planes   5 - 10
PO2851 *ESB*-1980-21x29½ Like '*SW* 2' w/green Darth, backed w/photo of T. O'Neil & K. McNichol   5 - 10

PO2852-53 *ESB*-1980-21x30 Boy's Photo News (transit ads)
PO2852 No. 850: Star Destroyer   25 - 45
PO2853 No. 853: Falcon landing on Bespin   25 - 45
PO2854 *ESB*-1980-20½x30 Insert from May '80 'Screen' w/*ESB* advance backed w/B&W photo of Leia, Han, Luke & Chewie   5 - 15
PO2855 *SW*-1982-20x29 Illus, mainly Millennium Falcon; for Japanese-dubbed version   45 - 65
PO2856 *ROTJ*-1982-29x41 *Revenge* logo advance on star field   125 - 175
PO2857 *ROTJ*-1983-29x41 '*SW* 3' but mostly in Japanese. All photos Main: Imp. Destroyer & Death Star   35 - 55
PO2858 *ROTJ*-1983-29x40½ '*SW* 3' Horizontal. All photos, similar to above, but some different elements   35 - 45
PO2859 *ROTJ*-1983-21x34 US 'B' sheet. All Eng. except Japanese in top and bottom white borders   35 - 45
PO2860 *ROTJ*-1983-20x29 '*SW* 3' mostly in Japanese. Photos of good guys vs. Death Star, Vader   30 - 40
PO2861 *ROTJ*-1983-20x29 '*SW* 3' mostly in Japanese. like US 'A'   30 - 40
PO2862 *ROTJ*-1983-20x29 '*SW* 3' mostly in Japanese. like US 'B' (Gloss and matte)   25 - 35

PO2864 *ROTJ*-1983-39x62 *'SW 3'*
mostly in Japanese. like US 'B   35 - 50
PO2865 *ROTJ*-1983-14x20 *'SW 3'*
horizontal. Mostly in Japanese w/'A'
sht illus. on left and 3 photos on
top Blank white space beneath   15 - 25
PO2866 *ROTJ*-1983-14x20 Transit
poster (as above, but printing in
lower margin)   15 - 25
PO2867 *ROTJ*-1983-22x33 US 'A' sht
w/Japanese in lower and right
borders. Reverse is B&W of cast   5 - 10
PO2868 *ROTJ*-1983-21x34 US 'A' sht
backed by poster for 'Half a Loaf
of Kung Fu'   5 - 10
PO2869 *ROTJ*-1983-21x30 Yamakatsu
of R2 and C-3PO on orange-red
star field   75 - 125
PO2870 *ROTJ*-1983-21x34 US 'A' sht
w/Japanese in top and bottom
borders. Backed by Kung Fu poster 5 - 10
PO2871 *ROTJ*-1983-21x34 US 'B' sht
backed by of Japanese teenager   5 - 10
PO2872 *ROTJ*-1983-14x20 PNN News:
Cover cartoon w/*Jedi* and other
film characters   15 - 20
PO2873 *SW Misc.*-1983-20x28 'USA &
Japan: The Great Robot Exhibition'
R2-D2 and C-3PO w/others   25 - 35
PO2874 Ewok (Caravan)-1984-20x29
Like US 'B' sht   25 - 35
PO2875 Ewok (Caravan)-1984-20x29,
Photo illus   25 - 35
PO2876 Ewok (Caravan)-1984-20x29
Photo montage on red background
(sold in stores)   15 - 20
PO2877 *ROTJ*-1986-14x20 Cassette
promo poster using US 'A'   15 - 20
PO2878 *ROTJ*-1986-14x20 Cassette
promo; top one-third is *ROTJ*   15 - 20
PO2879 Ewok (Endor)-1987-20x29
Photo of girl at center w/Endor
in cut- out photo-filled letters at top
(gloss and matte)   20 - 30
PO2880 Ewok (Endor)-1987-20x29
Slightly different photo of girl, more
abstract sky in background   20 - 30
PO2881 Ewok (Endor)-1987-14x20
Magazine foldout poster w/elements
of first Endor poster, twinned w/
Japanese animation film by Bandai 5 - 10
PO2882 *SW-ROTJ*-1987-29x40 TOB
Magazine promo w/prominent
sketch of Lucas, R2-D2, Ewok, etc. 10 - 15
PO2883 *SW-ROTJ*-1987-14x20 As above,
but horizontal   10 - 15
PO2884 *SW-ROTJ*-1987-14x20 Promo
poster for Japanese-language
version: Industrial Light & Magic-
The Art of Special Effects   25 - 35
PO2885 *SW* 10PO-1987-20x28½
Panasonic Rally: R2, C-3PO, map of
Shibuya (neon yellow and pink)   25 - 35

PO2886-92 *SW* Panasonic-1987/8-41x57
PO2886 Lucas w/lightsaber   125 - 175
PO2887 Lucas w/camcorder, C-3PO
w/butterfly net   125 - 175
PO2888 Yoda w/earphones   125 - 175
PO2889 Two Ewoks   75 - 100
PO2890 Lucas balancing TIE Ftr on finger 125 - 175
PO2891 Chewbacca, Lucas w/pocket TV 125 - 175
PO2892 Darth Vader   125 - 175
PO2893-94 *SW* Panasonic-1987/8-29x40
PO2893 Lucas balancing TIE Ftr on finger 50 - 75
PO2894 Lucas w/camcorder, C-3PO w/net 50 - 75
PO2895-98 *SW* Panasonic-1987/8-14x40
PO2895 R2, C-3PO w/umbrella & computer 25 - 45
PO2896 Lucas, C-3PO w/net & 10 yr. logo 25 - 45
PO2897 Two Ewoks w/Japanese boy 15 - 25
PO2898 Jabba (PIA Intermedia Theater) 25 - 45
PO2899-00 *SW* Panasonic-1987/8-14x20
PO2899 Lucas balancing TIE Ftr on finger 25 - 45
PO2900 Yoda w/earphones   25 - 45
PO2901-03 *SW* Panasonic-1987/8-7x20
PO2901 Two Ewoks (vertical)   15 - 25
PO2902 Yoda (vertical)   25 - 40
PO2903 Millennium Falcon (vertical)   25 - 40
PO2904 Ewok (Endor)-1988-23x33
Video release w/new art   25 - 45

PO2905-06 *SW* Panasonic-1988
PO2905 28x40 Fair in Akihabara: Hot
pink background w/circular photo
of Lucas & *Jedi* figures in grass 125 - 175
PO2906 14x40 As above, horizontal 75 - 100
PO2907 *SW* Panasonic-1988-35x56
Plastic-coated outdoor banner w/
photo of Lucas & *Jedi* characters 225 - 350
PO2908-10 *SW* Panasonic-1988
PO2908 21x70 Silk-like cloth banner,
green top, photo of C-3PO
w/laptop and R2-D2   150 - 200
PO2909 21x70 Silk-like cloth banner,
pink top, photo of Lucas &
C-3PO w/butterfly net   150 - 200
PO2910 19½x35½ Silk-like cloth banner,
photo of C-3PO and red stripe
at bottom w/'Maclord'   150 - 200
PO2911-17 *SW* Panasonic-1988/9-41x57
PO2911 Lucas, Chewie & Wicket on metal
pole for satellite dish   125 - 175
PO2912 Sparky robot/flute, Lucas on
porch   85 - 125
PO2913 Sparky robot w/kite and small girl 50 - 65
PO2914 Sparky, Lucas & dog   85 - 125
PO2915 Wicket, Sparky skateboarding 50 - 65
PO2916 Lucas talks to illuminated Sparky 85 - 125
PO2917 Movie theater w/Lucas, Sparky
& many *SW* characters seated 125 - 175
PO2920-23 *SW* Panasonic-1988/9-14x20
PO2920 Lucas, Chewie & Wicket on metal
pole for satellite dish   25 - 45
PO2921 Sparky plays flute, Lucas on porch 20 - 30
PO2922 Wicket & Ewok w/large leaf 20 - 30
PO2923 R2-D2, C-3PO & laptop computer 25 - 45
PO2924-28 *SW* Panasonic-1988/9-14x42
PO2924 Sparky robot w/kite and small girl 25 - 45
PO2925 Lucas scratching beard, small
Sparky as rocket   35 - 55
PO2926 Profile of Lucas w/eyes closed 45 - 60
PO2927 3 kids w/Chewie, R2 & 2 Ewoks 35 - 55
PO2928 Sparky w/digital clock in stomach 25 - 30
PO2929-31 *SW* Panasonic-1988/9
PO2929 Lucas & Yoda floating 29x40 125 - 175
PO2930 14x40   65 - 85
PO2931 20x28½   35 - 50
PO2940-42 *SW* Panasonic-1988/9-21x70
PO2940 Cloth banner w/Yoda & Lucas 150 -200
PO2941 Cloth banner w/Sparky & Lucas 100 -135
PO2942 Cloth banner w/Sparky   65 - 75
PO2943 *SW* Panasonic-1989-41x114
Sparky robot on rocky desert for
Hi-Bit digital component show.
(Japan Railways two-sheet)   60 - 75
PO2944 *SW* Panasonic-1989-41x57 'Red
is the most difficult.' Black &
white of Lucas w/red flower 125- 175
PO2945 *SW* Panasonic-1989-14½x40½
B&W of Lucas w/red apple
suspended above his palm; for
audio/video VHS player   125 - 175
PO2946 *SW* Panasonic-1989-29x40
July Panasonic Fair/Sparky   35 - 45
PO2949-50 *SW* Panasonic-1989
PO2949 14x40½   75 - 100
PO2950 14x20 'Pure Red': B&W of Lucas
w/red flower; ad for Video FS90 50 - 65
PO2951 *SW* Panasonic-1989-14x20
Sparky: Super Festival in Dome 25 - 35
PO2952 *SW* Panasonic-1989-14x40
Lucas on high director's chair w/
characters from *SW*, Indy, Tucker,
Amer. Graffiti; for Maclord laptop 125 - 175
PO2953 *SW* Video-1989-20x29 *'SW* World'
photo montage from all 3 films and
cartoons for Japanese-dubbed release 45- 60
PO2954 Star Tours 1989-41x114
'Space Open!' Japan Railways 2-sht
for ST Tokyo Disneyland opening
July 12. One large Starspeeder, one
smaller flying over city w/lighted
Cinderella castle   75 - 125
PO2955 Star Tours-1989-29x40 'Space Open!'
JR Eastern Japan division, w/photo
of R2-D2 and C-3PO   45 - 60
PO2956 Star Tours-1989-29x40 As above,
no English except ST logo and
white border at bottom for writing 45 - 60

PO2957-59 Star Tours-1989-29x40
PO2957 Mickey's Space Fantasy: Mickey
in space suit floating between R2 &
C-3PO w/dancers in front of Star
Tours building on left, Castle on
right and two Starspeeders above 45 - 60
PO2958 As above, but w/yellow band at top
announcing special Day   45 - 60
PO2959 14x20 As above, horiz. transit ad 45 - 60
PO2960 Star Tours/Pana-1989-23x33
Photo of boy holding Star Tours/
Panasonic inflatable 'beach shuttle'
next to photo of castle and illus
of Starspeeder   60 - 75
PO2961-63 Star Tours/Pana-1989-14x40
PO2961 Invitation Sale Speeder, Castle,
Space Fantasy Mickey & Minnie 35 - 45
PO2962 Panasonic Fair Dec. 1-31, w/art
of Speeders, space mice & castle 35 - 45
PO2963 Panasonic Fair-29x40 Mostly
pink w/Speeder & space mice art
in lower right   45 - 55
PO2964 Star Tours-1989-14x20 Two
Starspeeders over city & Castle 25 - 35
PO2965 Star Tours-1989-33x47
Original silk-screened Tokyo
Disneyland entrance poster for ST,
w/printer's color blocks in
margin, 100 made   1500-2500
PO2966 Star Tours-1989-20x30
Silver mylar commercial poster:
Starspeeder pursued by TIE
fighters w/Tokyo Dland on
earth below, R2-D2 and C-3PO 15 -25
PO2967 Star Tours-1989-23x33
Similar to Space Fantasy, but
w/Mickey & Minnie in front of ST.
'National/Panasonic' at bottom 20 -35
PO2968 Star Tours-1990-232x33 Tokyo
Disneyland 1990 calendar w/small
photo of ST waiting area & speeder 15 - 25
PO2969 *SW*-1990-14x20 Silvery transit ad
for TV Week magazine w/R2-D2
and C-3PO as part of cover   15 - 25
PO2970-71 *SW* Panasonic-1990-14x40
PO2970 Lucas w/youngster dressed as
angel for Maclord video camera 125 - 150
PO2971 Lucas in field of floating red
roses for VCRFS700 EP Power 125 - 150
PO2972 CBS/FOX Video-1990-142x20
'Best Library' release of *SW* and
Sound of Music   15 - 25
PO2973 Star Tours-1990-29x40 Japan
Rail 'Disney Vacation' promo w/small
ST poster in lower right and star-
speeders flying above ST building 35 - 45
PO2974 Star Tours-1990-14x20 Transit ad
for Nikkei Trendy magazine 6/4/90
w/photo story on opening of Star
Tours Disney World (Michael Eisner
w/Lucas, Fisher, Hamill, etc.) 15 - 25
PO2975 Star Tours-1990-29x40 Mickey
Mouse Sports Festival w/small ST
logo lower right; for Saitama Pref 25- 40
PO2976 Star Tours-1990-29x40 Donald
Duck's American Oldies w/inset
of Starspeeder; Chiba Pref week 25 - 40
PO2977 Star Tours-1990-29x40 Travel
agency poster: The Kingdom of
Dreams and Magic; photo of
Japanese family, Mickey & Minnie,
C-3PO, lots of balloons   25 - 40
PO2978 Star Tours-1991-29x40 Disney
Vacation w/ST art included   25 - 40
PO2979 Star Tours-1991-29x40 Campus Day
w/small ST logo from Tokyu Travel 25 - 40
PO2980 Star Tours-1991-29x40
As above w/Tobu Travel logo   25 - 40
PO2981-82 Star Tours-1991-29x40
PO2981 Party Gras for Chiba citizens
w/inset of Starspeeder   25 - 40
PO2982 As above w/travel agency name 25 - 40
PO2983 CBS/FOX Video-1991-29x40
Photo collage for 'Best Library'
release of Trilogy in Japanese
dubbed and titled   25 - 45
PO2984 CBS/FOX Video-1991-20x29
'Best Library' release of *Jedi*
w/U.S. 'A' sht art   25 - 45

PO5020	**PO5026**	**PO5027**	**PO5028**	**PO5029**

PO2985 FOX Video-1991-20x29 Laser disc low price release of *SW*, other films w/photo of Han Solo — 15 - 30

PO2986 JVC/MNM Software-1991-14x20 'Attack on the Death Star' software — 35 - 40

PO2987 Lucasfilm Games-1992-7x20 'Attack on Death Star' game for PC-9801 — 20 - 30

PO2988 WOWOW-1992-14x40 Home Theater Channel *SW* Triple Bill for March '92 — 25 - 45

PO2989 GLSLA-1992-28x40 Announcing George Lucas's Super Live Adventure show. Black w/white & gold text. Lucas visage in red (1 of 28) — 250 - 400

PO2990-91 George Lucas Super Live Adventure-1992

PO2990 28x40 Full color Hiro montage art of Lucas films — 75 - 125

PO2991 20x29 As above — 50 - 75

PO2992 PIA-...1992-20x28 'Special Line-Up' w/one photo of Chewie & Han w/race cars and MC Hammer — 15 - 25

PO2993 GLSLA-1993-14x20 Transit car ad for GL Super Live show w/Hiro montage art (horizontal) — 25 - 30

PO2994-98 GLSLA-1993 Different Hiro montage art, predominantly *SW* but w/large Indy face and small Willow

PO2994 28x40 Running April 27-July 4 — 25 - 40

PO2995 28x40 As above, but w/bottom TFC band — 25 - 40

PO2996 28x40 Like A, but w/sticker for new venue, dates Sept. 15 - 26 — 25 - 40

PO2997 20x29 Smaller version of A — 25 - 35

PO2998 20 x29 Smaller version of C — 25 - 35

PO2999 GLSLA-1993-25x36 Figure w/large logo, GL signature & reddish photo of GL wearing sunglasses — 25 - 35

PO3100 Magazine-1993-14 x20 Cartoon of George Lucas' head springing out of C-3PO's body w/Luke on his shoulder fighting Darth; for GLSLA — 15 - 25

PO3101 Video-1993-20x28 Shinseido video chain w/lots of small video cases incl. *SW* — 15 - 25

PO3102 SF Music-1993-29x40 Cartoon of C-3PO leading orchestra w/ET, Yoda, Godzilla, Spock for 'Orchestra in Screen' CD and concert tour (Japan Railwayband at bottom) — 25 - 40

PO3103-04 Sezon Museum-1993-GEORGE LUCAS, scenes from; for Sezon Museum exhibit

PO3103 29x40 w/photo at bottom of special phone card — 75 - 100

PO3104 14 x20 — 45 - 60

PO3105 Sezon Museum-1993-29x40 Lucas name in gold w/R2, X-wing & TIE ftr & saber — 125 - 150

PO3106-08 Sezon Museum-1993-23x33 Suite of three posters on heavy stock w/copy of GL autograph

PO3106 *ROTJ* style 'B' art — 100 - 125

PO3107 1983 photo of Lucas and props — 100 - 125

PO3108 Battle photo montage w/Falcon, Death Star, X-wings & TIE ftrs — 100 - 125

Mexico

PO3850 *ESB* mini-posters, 6 different, ea.

New Zealand

PO4010-12 *ESB*-1980-23x35 commercial posters

PO4010 Luke as pilot — 15 - 25

PO4011 Photo montage w/large photo of Luke on Tauntaun & Han — 15 - 25

PO4012 Photo montage — 15 - 25

PO4013 *ESB*-1980-14x19 Tip-Top ad: Darth Vader/free masks — 25 - 35

PO4014 *ROTJ*-1983-12x19 Tip-Top ad: like US 'B' w/popsicle — 25 - 35

PO4015 *ROTJ*-1983-12x19 Tip-Top ad: Free Ewok stickers — 25 - 35

PO4016 *ROTJ*-1983-29x33 Macléans toothpaste offer to win tickets & posters; red, white & blue w/Style 'B' art and more stylized cartoon art — 25 - 35

PO4017 *ESB* video-1984-16 x32 'Coming Soon...' w/Bespin — 15 - 25

PO4018 Ewok-1985-27x41 Like US 'B' sht — 25 - 35

PO4019 Ewok-1985-13x27 As above — 15 - 25

Norway

PO4322 *SW*-1978-24 x33 Like US 'A' sht — 45 - 65

Poland

PO4523 *SW*-1979-26x38 Yellow C-3PO on black w/white spots — 75 - 125

PO4524 *ESB*-1982-26x38 Yellow, black & red on blue background w/indistinguishable face or mask — 65 - 85

PO4525 *ROTJ*-1984-26 x38 Illus of Darth Vader head exploding — 75 - 125

PO4526 *ROTJ*-1984-26 x38 Illus of Luke, Leia, Han & C-3PO — 65 - 85

South Africa

PO4630 *SW*-1978-28x40 B&W w/yellow overlay; US 'A' — 25 - 35

Spain

PO4740 *SW*-1978-27 x39 Like US 'C' sht (matte) — 35 - 60

PO4741 *SW*-1978-27x39 US 'C' sht art, glossy & no border; marked Grobes S.A.-Paris & Barcelona — 15 - 25

PO4742 *SW*-1978-27 x39 Like US 'D' sht (matte) — 35 - 60

PO4743 *SW*-1978-27 x39 Mostly white w/logo "cut out" from 'A' sht w/Time mag quote at top — 50 - 75

PO4744 *ESB*-1980-27 x39 Like Japanese art (matte) — 35 - 50

PO4745 *ESB*-1980-27 x39 Like US 'A' w/Lando & Boba Fett — 45 - 60

PO4746 *ESB*-1980-27 x39 Like US 'B' sht — 30 - 40

PO4747 *ROTJ*-1983-27 x39 Montage — 35 - 50

PO4748 Ewok-1985-27 x39 Like US 'B' sht — 20 - 30

PO4749 Ewoks/Droids-1986-9x13 Crecs chips promotion for 20 stickers — 20 - 30

PO4750 *SW* Saga-1987-27 x39 20th Fantasy Fox: B. de Pedro 4-color art w/montage of Fox SF films: Yoda, R2-D2, C-3PO, etc. for film festival — 35 - 50

Spanish Language (U.S. printing)

PO4751 *SW*-1978-27x41 Advance, white on blue — 75 - 125

PO4752 *SW*-1978-27x41 Hildebrandt art: 'SW/La Guerra de las Galaxias' — 75 - 125

PO4753 *SW*-1978-27x41 US 'C' sht Cantrell art — 75 - 125

PO4754 *ESB*-1980-27x41 US Darth Vader advance: Estara muy pronto en su galaxia. — 65 - 85

PO4755 *ESB*-1980-27x41 Japanese art; Mexico 'B' sht — 50 - 65

PO4756 *ROTJ*-1983-27x41 Advance Like US Revenge — 75 - 125

PO4757 *ROTJ*-1983-27x41 US 'A' sht in Spanish — 25 - 35

PO4758 *ROTJ*-1983-27x41 US 'B' sht in Spanish — 35 - 45

PO4759 Ewok-1985-27x41 Spanish Intl. 'A' sht — 25 - 35

PO4760 Ewok-1985-27x41 Spanish Intl. 'B' sht — 25 - 35

Sweden

PO4780 *SW*-1978-27 x39 Uses some of US 'A' sht art plus photo of Han & Chewie — 45 - 75

PO4781 *SW*-1978-13x27 As above — 30 - 40

PO4782 *SW*-1978-27x39 Luke, Leia, Chewie, Han (Scandecor) — 15 - 20

PO4793-94 *ESB*-1982-24x34

PO4793 Imperial Star Destroyer (Scanlite) — 15 - 20

PO4794 Millennium Falcon (Scanlite) — 15 - 20

PO4795 *ESB*-1980-27 x39 US 'B' sht art (no border) — 30 - 50

PO4796 *ESB*-1980-13x27 As above w/thin black border — 25 - 35

PO4797 *ROTJ*-1983-27 x39 US 'B' sht art (no border) — 25 - 35

PO4798 *ROTJ*-1983-13x27 As above, but vertical — 25 - 35

Yugoslavia

PO4890 *ROTJ*-1990-13x27 Neon magenta on navy w/tricked images of Falcon, Luke, Han & rear of C-3PO — 45 - 65

ADVERTISING & OTHER POSTERS
Star Wars: 1976-1979
Ballantine

PO5001 Photo blowup of McQuarrie art for 'Splinter of the Mind's Eye'-20x30 — 35 - 45

Burger Chef

PO5011 Fun Meal promo poster-23x35 — 35 - 45

PO5012 Fun Meal lightbox poster-29x29 — 50 - 75

PO5013 Collect all 7 action trays-13x56 — 45 - 50

Casablanca Records

PO5014 Meco album 'SW and Other Galactic Funk'-23x35 — 25 - 40

Chaykin Poster #1

PO5020 Star Wars Corp. Poster No. 1 20x29 — 250 - 450

Coke/Burger Chef

PO5026 Luke-18x24 — 5 - 10

PO5027 R2 & C3PO — 5 - 10

PO5028 Darth — 5 - 10

PO5029 Chewie — 5 - 10

Coke/Burger King

PO5030 Luke (w/white border)-18x24 — 5 - 10

PO5031 R2 & C3PO (Coke only)-18x24 — 5 - 10

PO5032 Darth (Coke only) — 5 - 10

PO5033 Chewie (Coke only) — 5 -10

Coke (7-11 Stores)

PO5034 Store poster: Collect set of 8 *SW* cups-14x22 — 25 - 40

Coke (Koolee Corp.)

PO5034a Star Wars Cups promo w/frozen Coke-24x36 — 45 - 50

Coke/Mr. Pibb

PO5035 Store poster w/photos of cups-18x30 — 20 - 40

PO5036 Store poster w/photo of X-wing fighter-22x35 — 20 - 40

Coca-Cola

PO5037 Collect set of 8 16-oz cups-18x30 — 25 - 40

| PO5070 | PO5085 | PO5086 | PO5087 | PO5110 |

| PO5235 | PO5236 | PO5237 | PO5290 |

Concert

PO5040	John Alvin art of R2-D2 and C-3PO w/instruments-24x37	800 - 1200
PO5075	With Close Encounters: Marin Laser Concert w/Obi Wan, Flash Gordon, French horn by McQuarrie-16x20	50 - 75
PO5077	Black & white: KMET presents Music from Outer Space-14x21	15 - 30

Don Post

| PO5045 | Don Post Studios poster for first 4 *SW* masks-18x25 | 30 - 40 |
| PO5046 | 'Men of a Thousand Faces' 16x25 | 25 - 40 |

Drawing Board

| PO5050 | 'The Force is With Us' (R2 & C-3PO)-17x24 | 15 - 25 |

Estes

| PO5051 | For flying model rockets-15x24 | 5 - 10 |

Factors

PO5052	Stormtroopers firing into 'tunnel of light'-20x28	25 - 40
PO5053	X-wing vs. TIE ftr with 3 circular photos-20x28	25 - 40
PO5054	Hildebrandt art-20x28	5 - 15
PO5055	R2 and C-3PO-20x28	5 - 15
PO5056	Darth Vader-20x28	5 - 15
PO5057	Luke-20x28	5 - 15
PO5058	Leia-20x28	5 - 15
PO5059	Cantina-20x28	15 - 25

Fan Club Poster #1

| PO5065 | Luke in Death Star trench (McQuarrie)-20x28 | 10 - 15 |

Health

| PO5070 | Immunization poster with R2 & C3PO-14x22 | 10 - 25 |

Lucasfilm

| PO5071 | Suite of 11 lithos of Boba Fett by Joe Johnston-14x18, each | 100 - 200 |

Pendulum Press

| PO5080 | Classroom poster for reading program-11x17 | 15 - 30 |

Procter & Gamble

PO5985	Darth vs. Obi Wan-18 x 23	5 - 10
PO5986	R2 & C3PO-18 x 23	5 - 10
PO5987	Luke, Han, Leia, Chewie-18 x 23	5 - 10

Supersnipe

| PO5088 | B&W window poster for show of original work of McQuarrie & Johnston at Supersnipe Gallery-11x17 | 15 - 25 |

| PO5089 | Numbered and hand-signed suite of 2 McQuarrie color lithos & 2 Johnston B&W sketches-18x24 | 400 - 750 |

Thermos

| PO5090 | Art from front of first metal lunchbox-20x28 | 15x25 |

Topps

| PO5095 | Premium poster of uncut sheet of blue border cards-22x29 | 25 - 50 |

20th Fox Film

| PO5100 | Color photo of Tie ftr/X-wing battle-17x22 | 10 - 20 |

20th Fox Film

| PO5101 | 2-part paper insert, blue on white with Hildebrandt art & touting Oscars-14x36 | 25 - 40 |

20th Fox Records

PO5103	Foil promo, black & silver, Vader head w/ 'Star Wars'-22x32	25 - 50
PO5104	Story of *SW* soundtrack-22x33	25 - 40
PO5105	Unfolded album insert-22x33	20 - 35

Vymura

| PO5106 | Store poster for wallpaper; like US 'C' sht-19x23 | 25 - 40 |

Weingeroff Ent.

| PO5107 | Red & black window poster for jewelry-23x35 | 25 - 40 |

Wonder Bread

PO5110	Wonder Bread cards promo-12x24	25 - 40
PO5111	Braun's Town Talk Bread promo-12x16	15 - 30
PO5012	Free 16 Trading cards promo-12x16	15 - 25

***The Empire Strikes Back*: 1980-1982**

Ballantine

| PO5200 | McQuarrie Bespin City-11x17 | 20 - 30 |

Burger King

| PO5205 | *ESB* glasses advance | 15 - 25 |
| PO5206 | *ESB* glasses | 25 - 35 |

Canada Packers

| PO5210 | Promo poster like *ESB* Advance-16x20 | 15 - 20 |

CBS/Fox Video

PO5215	Banner-11x47	25 - 40
PO5216	Mini-banner-6x23	5 - 15
PO5217	Promo w/Hildebrandt art-8x11	5 - 15
PO5218	Small *SW* 'A' sheet-20x28	10 - 20

Cincinnati Pops

| PO5220 | John Williams *Star Wars* Festival-18x28 | 65- 100 |

Coke by Boris

| PO5230 | Vader, crossed lightsabers-24x33 | 10 - 20 |

PO5235	Luke on Tauntaun-18x24	5 - 10
PO5236	Luke & Yoda-18x24	5 - 10
PO5237	Han in carbon freeze chamber-18x24	5 -10

Crisco, Duncan Hines, Pringles

PO5241	R2 & C-3PO photo-18x23	5 - 10
PO5242	Leia & Han photo-18x23	5 - 10
PO5243	Luke photo-18x23	5 - 10
PO5244	Darth photo-18x23	5 - 10

B Dalton Books

| PO5250 | Unusual B&W sketch of Darth and *ESB* logo-22x28 | 20 - 30 |

Dixie/Lipton

PO5255	Luke photo-22x28	5 - 10
PO5256	2.Darth Vader-22x28	5 - 10
PO5260	In-store w/Vader, droids, Leia & Luke, Dixie & *ESB* logos—15x42	30 - 45

Drawing Board

| PO5265 | Greeting Cards in-store promo like 'B' sht-17x24 | 15 - 25 |

Factors

PO5270	In-store promo poster: 'The Saga of *SW* Continues With' *ESB*-18x18	20 - 35
PO5275	Like 'A' sheet w/Lando, Boba Fett-20x28	5 - 10
PO5276	Darth and stormtroopers-20x28	5 - 10
PO5277	Boba Fett-20x28	5 - 10
PO5278	C-3PO and R2-20x28	5 - 10
PO5279	Yoda-20x28	5 - 10

Fan Club

| PO5285 | Like *ESB* 'A' sheet w/o words-20x27 | 10 - 15 |

Natl. Geo. WORLD 1980, 20x31

| PO5286 | Photo poster of Falcon vs. Star Destroyer-20x31 | 5 -10 |

MPC

| PO5290 | Model kit promo | 15 - 30 |

Natl. Public Radio

PO5295	*SW*; just art-17x29	100 - 150
PO5296	PO5295 w/station logo	45 - 60
PO5297	*ESB*; just art-17x28	100 - 125
PO5298	PO5297 w/station logo	35 - 50

Noble

| PO5300 | *ESB* concept art pencil signed by artist Larry Noble, later used for *ESB* 10th Anniv-17x22 | 50 - 85 |
| PO5301 | Reproduction of early graphite sketch for PO5300-11x16 | 25 - 40 |

Parker Bros.

| PO5305 | For first Atari video cart-24x36 | 10 - 25 |

RCA 1982

| PO5310 | RCA videodisk promo: Take home *SW* free-26x80 | 25 - 40 |

PO5590	Display for PO5601	PO5645	PO5646	PO5065

PO5311	Like PO5310-28x40	15 - 30

RSO Records

PO5315	*ESB* soundtrack: black background-24x36	15 - 40
PO5315a	Like PO5315-36x36	25 - 50
PO5316	*ESB* soundtrack: maroon background-24x36	25 - 50
PO5317	Printers proof of 4 *ESB* album covers for POP display-26x28	20 - 35
PO5318	Promoting 4 different *ESB* records-24x36	20 - 30

Topps 1980, 22x29

PO5325	Premium poster of uncut sheet of silver-border cards-22x29	25 - 50
PO5330	Topps mini movie posters: *SW* 'A'-12x20	5 - 10
PO5331	Topps mini movie posters: *ESB* 'A'-12x20	5 - 10

Valentine Greetings

PO5335	*ESB* photo montage: Vader, Luke-23x35	10 - 20
PO5336	Red border: 3 photos of Luke/Yoda-23x35	10 - 20
PO5337	Drk blue: 2 photos of R2, C-3PO-23x35	10 - 20

Weekly Reader 1980

PO5340	Book Club photo poster-14x21	5 - 10

Return of the Jedi/Classic Star Wars: 1983-86

Airborne Express

PO5510	'Express Wars 83' ad poster-17x22	15 - 30

Anabas Pdts

PO5515	Photo of Luke, Leia on sail barge-24x35	10 - 20
PO5516	Photo of Wicket w/*ROTJ* white logo-24x35	10 - 20

Atari

PO5520	*SW* arcade game-20x30	20 - 40

Ballantine

PO5525	'Art of *ROTJ*': photo of Imperial Shuttle-13x22	25 - 40

Break (Australia)

PO5527	Break juice drink promo for Ewok Adventure poster & stickers offer-10x11	15 - 25

Buena Vista Records

PO5530	For *SW* records-13x13	5 - 10
PO5531	Like PO5530-15x26	5 - 10

Burger King

PO5535	Movie advance ('Coming to a theater in your galaxy May 25th')-21x29	25 - 40
PO5536	Glasses promo banner-8x48	25 - 40
PO5540	Crew room poster for promo	20 - 30
PO5541	'They're Here! *ROTJ* Glasses'-8x48	25 - 40

CBS/Fox Video

PO5545	B&W w/Darth on pink background (Video CrossRoads Stores)-18x24	15 - 30

CBS/Fox Video

PO5550	'Don't be struck Empireless' 2-sided-14x24	5 - 15
PO5551	'Coming Soon' and *ESB* logo-23x24	5 - 15
PO5552	'Coming Soon' over *ESB* logo and 'B' sheet-23x58	5 -15
PO5554	*ESB* 'B' art with CBS/Fox logo-15x22	10 - 20
PO5555	'Coming soon....'; perforated top w/*ROTJ* logo-23x36	20 - 40
PO5556	Endor speeder bike-24x36	15 - 30

Coca-Cola

PO5560	For free 50-oz collector pitcher-22x28	20 - 40
PO5565	For in-theater promo w/cup stickers-18x24	15 - 30

Creation Con

PO5570	W/some *SW* art for 1983 cons-20x25	5 - 10

Del Rey

PO5575	For *ROTJ* paperback (like 'A')-14x22	10 - 20
PO5576	For Industrial Light & Magic book-20x30	25 - 40

Drawing Board

PO5580	'The excitement starts here'—20x30	15 - 25

Fan Club

PO5585	1983 member poster-20x27	10 - 20
PO5586	'*ROTJ* Poster Album'-22x33	10 - 15

Film Freak Shop

PO5590	Reprint of *ROTJ* 'B' w/o border-27x39	10 - 15

Hi-C

PO5595	Mail in offer; 2-sided w/Jabba & Ewoks blacked out-18x22	5 - 10
PO5596	Like PO5595, regular version-18x22	15 - 25

Kenner

PO5600	Sweepstakes: Darth, Nien Numb, Adm. Ackbar-16x20	25 - 30
PO5601	Two-sided: '*SW* is Forever' backed by photo of action figures-18x22	15 - 25

Melanie Taylor Kent

PO5605	'Hollywood Boulevard' poster-24x32	25 - 45

Kilian Ent

PO5610	L'Affiche *SW* Saga American Poster Checklist-27x41	15 - 30

Library Council

PO5615	Yoda: 'READ'-22x34	25 - 40

Marvel

PO5620	Cover of *ROTJ* special-24x32	15 - 25

Mall

PO5625	'Welcome to Jedi Adventure Center'-22x28	10 - 20

Noble

PO5630	Larry Noble poster for Space Fantasy/Northridge	5 - 10
PO5633	Student Union screening; B&W w/all 3 films-12x16	5 - 10

Olympics

PO5635	AFI Film Festival w/Vader-22x36	25 - 40

Omni Cosmetics

PO5640	'Introducing....'	15 - 25
PO5642	X-wing	15 - 25

Oral B

PO5645	Darth fighting Luke photo poster for dentists' offices-17x22	10 - 15
PO5646	Two-sided, with ad & coupons-17x22	5 - 10

Palomar College

PO5650	Exhibition of Phil Tippett models-12x18	15 - 25

Parker Bros.

PO5655	*SW Jedi* Arena video cart-23x36	10 - 25
PO5656	Death Star Battle video cart-23x34	10 - 25
PO5657	*SW* Arcade Game video cart-23x34	10 - 25
PO5658	*Jedi* Arena 'Honor Roll'-17x21	5 - 10

Pepperidge Farm

PO5660	*SW* cookies in-store poster-18x27	15 - 25

Procter & Gamble

PO5665	Lando fighting-17x22	5 - 10
PO5667	Luke at Jabba Palace-17x22	5 - 10
PO5668	R2 and Ewoks-17x22	5 - 10
PO5669	Leia and Jabba-17x22	5 - 10

RSO Records

PO5670	*ROTJ* soundtrack-22x33	15 - 30

Sales Corp. of America 1983, 22x34

PO5675	*ESB* advance sheet-22x34	5 - 10
PO5676	*ROTJ* Millennium Falcon-22x34	5 - 10
PO5677	Darth and Royal Guards-22x34	5 - 10
PO5678	*ROTJ* 'Revenge' art w/'Return'-22x34	5 - 10
PO5679	*ROTJ* 'A' sheet-22x34	5 - 10

PO5680	*ROTJ* 'B' sheet-22x34	5 - 10
PO5681	*ROTJ* forest scene w/cast-22x34	5 - 10
PO5682	*ROTJ* Ewok montage-22x34	5 - 10
PO5683	Like *SW* 'D' sheet -22x34	5 - 10
PO5684	Battle before Death Star-22x34	5 - 10
PO5690	Vader door poster (illustration)-26x70	10 - 20
PO5695	Ad poster for Darth door poster-11x23	5 - 10
PO5696	Ewoks: 'Friends come in all shapes and sizes'-17x22	25 - 35
PO5697	Promo for 12 mini posters-10x14	5 - 10

Scholastic Book Club

PO5700	Ewoks photo blue border-17x22	5 - 10
PO5701	Darth Vader-17x22	5 - 10

Stride Rite

PO5705	'Shoes...out of this world'; Vader, droids-22x28	15 - 25
PO5706	Glossy promo banner for *ROTJ* sneakers-16x44	25 - 40

Struzan

PO5715	Poster for Drew Struzan Illustration Inc. w/*SW* 'D' and 'Revenge' advance-16x39	25 - 40

Thermos

PO5720	Lunch kits-16x20	10 - 15

Topps

PO5725	Ad poster for stickers, album-9x13	5 - 10

Uniprints

PO5730	*ROTJ*	5 - 10

Underoos

PO5735	Proof sheet of 12 Leia heat transfers-25x38	20 - 30
PO5736	Proof sheet of 9 transfers: Han; Luke/Vader; Luke/Emperor/Royal Guards-25x38	20 - 30

Weekly Reader

PO5740	Book Club photo montage-16x20	5 - 10
PO5741	Wicket the Ewok-16x20	5 - 10
PO5742	Ewoks mother and child-17x22	5 - 10
PO5743	Animated Droids-17x20	5 - 10

Classic *Star Wars*: 1987-Present

Abrams Book

PO5800	'Films of Science Fiction and Fantasy' w/Vader-22x27	10 - 15

Bantam Books

PO5805	Tom Jung cover for 'Heir to the Empire'-17x22	15 - 25
PO5806	Drew Struzan cover for 'Glove of Darth Vader'-17x22	10 - 20
PO5807	Struzan cover for 'Truce at Bakura' giveaway-11x17	5 - 10

Bantam/Kilian Ent

PO5815	Tom Jung cover for 'Heir to the Empire' w/o words; signed-22x28	35 - 45
PO5816	Like PO5816, unsigned-22x28	10 - 15

Blockbuster Video

PO5817	Print of 3 1995 video package fronts-10x17	15 - 25

Broderbund

PO5820	*SW* video game for home PC; McQuarrie art-22x28	15 - 25

CBS-Fox Video

PO5825	Video poster for 1988 trilogy release-25x38	10 - 15
PO5826	Video poster for 1990 trilogy release; merges elements of posters of all 3 films-25x38	15 - 25

Center for the Arts

PO5828	'The Art of *SW*' show: photo/art montage w/Death Star, Yoda, droids-46x68	250 - 400
PO5828a	Like PO5828-14x24	10 - 20

PO5945	**PO5948**	**PO5980**

PO6491	**PO6495**

B Dalton
PO5830 'The Force is Back' 2-sided w/ covers of book and cassette for 'Dark Force Rising'-22x28 — 15 - 25

Children's Museum
PO5831 Children's Museum of Indianapolis: flight exhibit, includes Millennium Falcon-12x36 — 15 - 20

Dark Horse
PO5832 Dark Empire II, art by Dave Dorman-10x19 — 5 - 10

Decipher
PO5833 Large 'Expand the Empire' card on starfield-20x27 — 10 -20
PO5833a Gray/black w/photos of *SW* characters, vehicles-11x33 — 5 - 10
PO5833b Full color of Cantina backed w/card list-11x33 — 5 - 10

Draconis Studios (Canada)
PO5834 Vehicles of the Rebel Alliance-24x36 — 20 - 30
PO5834a Vehicles of the Empire-24x36 — 20 - 30
PO5834b Battle of Yavin litho, signed & numbered-23x32 — 45 - 65

ESB 10th Anniversary
PO5835 Larry Noble art in color, signed and numbered-27x41 — 40 - 55
PO5837 PO5835 Fan Club version folded-27x41 — 10 - 15
PO5837a PO5837 rolled-27x41 — 40 - 55
PO5839 Style A gold mylar with Vader mask, *ESB* and *ESB* 10th logos-27x41 — 150 - 200
PO5840 Style B silver mylar with large #10 & Luke on tauntaun-27x41 — 100 - 150
PO5841 Style B gold mylar marked 'test'-27x41 — 200 - 300

ESB 15th
PO5842 Kilian Ent. Boba Fett on gold mylar-27 x 41 — 100 - 150
PO5842a PO5842 marked Test Proof — 250 - 400

Fan
PO5842e Cover for Fan #5: Dark Horse 'Heir to the Empire'-16x22 — 5 - 10

Galoob
PO5842h 1996 Toy Fair Ralph McQuarrie art for Action Fleet: Death Star bay-18x21 — 150 - 200
PO5842i PO5842h, but Hoth Battle-18x21 — 150 - 200

Gifted Images
PO5843 Ken Steacy litho, art from Topps *SW* Galaxy I poster on heavy rag paper, signed & numbered-23x30 — 400 - 600

Hallmark
PO5844 Cardstock in-store for *SW* Shoebox card line-24x30 — 15 - 25

Highbridge Audio
PO5845 Larger version of original Celia Strain art for *SW* on NPR-22x32 — 50 - 75

Houston Film Festival
PO5846 Photo of C-3PO, Charlie Chaplin for 1995 fest-21x32 — 20 - 30

Industrial Light & Magic
PO5850 1975-1990 retrospective w/40 mini posters including *SW, ESB, Revenge,* Star Tours-27x39 — 50 - 75

IMAX
PO5851 For 'Special Effects' film-27x39 — 15 - 25.
PO5851a PO5851, for Cincinnati Museum Center-18x24 — 10 - 15

JVC
PO5855 For Super Nintendo *ESB*-23x37 — 20 - 30

Lucasfilm Fan Club
PO5860 Michael David Ward art of X-wings heading into battle-16x21 — 5 - 10

Lucasfilm Games
PO5865 Enhanced photo of destroyed AT-AT w/*ESB* logo-23x37 — 10 - 15

LucasArts Games
PO5866 Computer cover art for X-Wing PC game-16x23 — 10 - 15
PO5866a CG art of stormtroopers battle, Dark Forces CD-ROM-24x31 — 5 - 10
PO5866b Rebel Assault II w/movie-like credit block-27x36 — 5 - 10

Marin County Fair
PO5870 Red, white & black for '88 Fair featuring 'The Magic of Lucasfilm'-9x23 — 5 - 10

MGM/UA Home Video
PO5875 Ewoks: The Battle for Endor video-24x36 — 10 - 15
PO5876 The Ewok Adventure video-24x36 — 10 - 15

Mythical Realism Press/Glass Onion Graphics
PO5880 Yoda litho signed by Michael Whelan-19x22 — 135- 150

New Frontiers Pub
PO5881 Michael David Ward art of X-wings heading into battle at Death Star-25x37 — 100 - 150
PO5882 Michael David Ward art of C-3PO and R2-D2 gazing skyward-20 x 34 — 100 - 150

Nintendo/Lucas Games
PO5885 Premium poster, photo of Vader & *SW* logo in red-23x32 — 5 - 10
PO5886 Store display for PO5885, w/red band at top-23x33 — 10 - 15

Official *SW* Fan Club
PO5887 Tsuneo Sanda art: Falcon-25x36 — 10 - 20
PO5887a Tsuneo Sanda art: Slave I-25x36 — 10 - 20

Pitarelli
PO5888 Jeff Pitarelli print of his art for '95 Atlanta SF con program cover w/Vader-17x23 — 25 - 40

Portal Pubs
PO5890 *SW* 'C' sheet reprint-24x36 — 5 - 10
PO5891 *ESB* advance reprint-24x36 — 5 - 10
PO5892 Revenge art, but 'Return'-24x36 — 5 - 10
PO5893 *ROTJ* 'A' reprint-24x36 — 5 - 10
PO5895 Composite *ROTJ* battle scene-24x36 — 5 - 10
PO5896 Ewoks photo montage-12x36 — 5 - 10
PO5896b 1995 *SW* video key art-24x36 — 10 - 15
PO5896b 1995 *ESB* video key art-24x36 — 10 - 15
PO5896c 1995 *ROTJ* video key art-24x36 — 10 - 15
PO5896g 'All I need to know about life I learned from *Star Wars*'-24x36 — 10 - 15

Profondo Rosso
PO5897 Italian toy store showing shelves filled with sci-fi goodies, C-3PO and R2-D2 in doorway-18x27 — 20 - 30

Rarities Mint
PO5900 For silver, gold coins: *SW* 'A'-18x24 — 10 - 15

Rolling Thunder Graphics (Dave Dorman art)
PO5905 'Dark Empire' cover-19x24 — 45 - 55
PO5095a The Smuggler's Moon-19x24 — 45 - 55
PO5095b 'Dark Empire II'-19x24 — 45 - 55
PO5095c Boba Fett: Bounty Hunter-19x34 — 45 - 55
PO5095d Heroes of the Alliance-16x22 — 45 - 55
PO5095e Obi-Wan Kenobi: Jedi Knight-16x22 — 45 - 55

ROTJ 10th Anniversary (Kilian Ent.)
PO5910 Drew Struzan's 'Revenge' art, test proof/no logo-27x41 — 75 - 100
PO5911 'Return' logo in red foil-27x41 — 100 - 125
PO5912 'Return' logo in gold foil-27x41 — 75 - 100
PO5912a Like PO5912, hand signed 'drew'-27x41 — 100 - 150
PO5913 'Return' & LFL Fan Club logos in gold foil-27x41 — 65 - 80
PO5914 Kazo Sano unused *ROTJ* art w/gold credits-27x41 — 50 - 75

Star Tours
PO5915 Disneyland Cast Premiere Party (B & W)-17x24 — 40 - 65
PO5916 Imagineering Inaugural Flight-(Jan 5) 17x24 — 40 - 65
PO5920 'The Ultimate Adventure' travel poster title sheet-18x24 — 15 - 25
PO5921 Bespin-18x24 — 15 - 25
PO5922 Dagobah-18x24 — 15 - 25
PO5923 Endor (moon) -18x24 — 15 - 25
PO5924 Endor (Ewok village) -18x24 — 15 - 25
PO5925 Hoth-18x24 — 15 - 25
PO5926 Tatooine-18x24 — 15 - 25
PO5927 Yavin-18x24 — 15 - 25
PO5930 PSA/Walt Disney Travel Co. 'Magical Smiles' Tours includes X-wing and Starspeeders-20x30 — 25 - 40
PO5931 PO5930, but limited edition litho signed by Charles Boyer-18x24 — 80 - 100
PO5932 Oldsmobile promo: 1st anniversary of Star Tours by Kriegler-20x30 — 10 - 20
PO5933 Like PO5932 w/out Oldsmobile promo: 'Now the Experience is Real'-20x30 — 10 - 15
PO5934 Grand Opening at Disney-MGM Studios in Fla.; image is 2 M&M candies-24x36 — 5 -10
PO5935 Like PO5920, but no park name-18x24 — 10 - 15

Star Wars 10th
PO5940 John Alvin art: 'Mind's Eye,' signed-17x36 — 35 - 55
PO5941 PO5940, signed & numbered-17x36 — 40 - 60
PO5942 PO5940 unsigned-17x36 — 20 - 35
PO5945 Silver mylar teaser: The First 10 Years-27x41 — 75 -100
PO5946 Gold Mylar like PO5945-27x41 — 225 - 250
PO5947 British Gold Mylar with anniv. date of Nov. 28, 1977-27x41 — 100 - 150
PO5948 Style B, numbered and signed by Drew Struzan-27x41 — 100 - 125
PO5949 Bantha Tracks final issue centerfold as poster-22x25 — 10 - 15

Star Wars 15th (Kilian Ent.)
PO5950 Hildebrandt Bros. original art as a 'B' sheet, numbered-27x41 — 25 - 35
PO5951 PO5950 numbered and signed-27x41 — 50 - 65
PO5955 Reprint of *SW* 'D' sheet (Circus poster) by Struzan & White, numbered-27x41 — 15 - 25
PO5956 Like PO5950 but w/'A New Hope' logo, signed-27x41 — 50 - 60
PO5957 PO5956, unsigned-27x41 — 20 - 25

SW 15th: Kent
PO5960 Melanie Taylor Kent original remarqued serigraph w/artist's laser-cut mat-33x44 — 1800 - 2600
PO5966 Poster version of PO5960-24x36 — 20 - 35

PO6497   **PO6498**   **PO6499**   **PO6500**

PO6504   **PO6572**   **PO6573**   **PO6576**   **PO6571**

PO6577   **PO6578**   **PO6580**   **PO6581**   **PO6574**

T-Man

PO5970	Sci-Fi Café B&W poster by Howard Teman, includes Vader, Jabba, R2, C-3PO, Yoda, Falcon-22x47	10 - 15

Topps

PO5971	Ken Steacy art of Vader for *SW Galaxy I*-17x20	5 - 10
PO5971a	Boris art of droids for *SW Galaxy II*-17x20	5 - 10
PO5971b	McQuarrie bounty hunters for *SW Galaxy* mag-17x22	5 - 10

20th Cent Fox

PO5972	*SW* Special Edition, all 3 one-sheets by Drew, horizontal-16x26	20 - 35

20th Cent Fox Home Ent

PO5972a	Glossy Vader supergraphic for 1995 *SW* Trilogy video-27x41	15 - 25
PO5972b	PO5972 but horizontal with added line: Experience the Force in THX-36x48	25 - 30

Waldenbooks

PO5975	Cardboard 2-sided promo for newsletter w/Timothy Zahn on cover-17x22	10 - 15

West End Games 1987, 17x22

PO5980	'Fulfill Your Destiny'; departing X-wing ftr & first 3 games-17x22	10 - 15

Western Graphics

PO5982	'Collectors Edition': Boris *ESB* art-21x32	10 - 15
PO5982a	'Collectors Edition': *ROTJ* using *Revenge* art-21x32	10 - 15
PO5982b	1995 video art: *SW*/Vader-23x35	10 - 15
PO5982c	1995 video art: *ESB*/stormtrooper-23x35	10 -15
PO5982d	1995 video art: *ROTJ*/Yoda-23x35	10 - 15
PO5982e	3-D Wars: B-wings above 'Magic Eye' art-23x35	10 - 15
PO5982f	Original Selby Cantina art: 'You'll never find a more wretched hive of scum and villainy!'23x35	10 - 15

ZigZag Posters (Germany) 1993, 27x40

PO5985	*ESB* style 'A'-27x40	10 - 15
PO5985a	*ROTJ* style 'B'-27x40	10 - 15
PO5985b	*SW* style 'C'-27x40	10 - 15
PO5985c	*SW* style 'A'-27x40	10 - 15
PO5985d	British 3-in-1-27x39	10 - 15
PO5985e	*ESB* style 'B'-27x40	10 - 15
PO5985f	*Revenge* art with *Return* logo-27x40	10 - 15
PO5985g	*ESB* w/Japanese art but U.S. copy-27x40	10 - 15
PO5985h	Fan Club art: Luke X-wing in Death Star trench w/*SW* logo-27x40	10 - 15
PO5985i	Fan Club art: space battle w/*SW* logo-27x40	10 - 15

BANNER

One of the rarest theatrical items produced by National Screen Service for 20th Century Fox, this silk-screened banner could be ordered by theater owners for less than $30 in 1977. But today it is virtually impossible to find one, especially in mint condition.

PO6300	*SW* yellow-fringed silk-screened nylon banner, 105x24 inches, gold & white w/blue *SW* logo and images of Leia, Luke and the droids	1250 - 2000

LOBBY CARDS

Most lobby cards, whether paper, thin cardstock or actual photographic paper, are sold in sets. The exceptions are fairly esoteric cards from outside the U.S. Lobby cards were used to decorate theater lobbies and entrances with scenes that would entice would-be movie-goers. Most are in color but some—the Japanese and the main photo on the background-colored Mexican cards, for example—are in black and white. Some collectors call the U.S. 8x10 cards photo sets and reserve the name lobby cards for the larger 11x17 sets. The U.S. photobusta sets are oversized cards with photos of the main characters and major scenes from the films. The U.S. lobby card sets, once fairly common and available for $25 or so a set, have become much scarcer and pricier as a result. For the

Special Edition release in 1997, lobby cards printed in the U.S. were used only in other countries.

Star Wars

PO6400	8x10 w/border (8)	100 - 125
PO6410	8x10 borderless (8)	100 - 125
PO6420	11x14 w/border (8)	115 - 135
PO6430	11x14 borderless (8)	115 - 135
PO6440	Oversized photobusta card set	125 - 175

Photo portraits (12 x17):

PO6441	Luke	15 - 20
PO6442	Leia	15 - 20
PO6443	Han	15 - 20
PO6444	Chewbacca	15 - 20
PO6445	Grand Moff Tarkin	15 - 20
PO6446	Obi Wan Kenobi	15 - 20
PO6446a	All portraits on one sheet	50 - 75

Scenes (16x20)

PO6447	Tusken Raider attack	15 - 25
PO6448	Garbage pit	15 - 25
PO6449	The leap	15 - 25
PO6450	Final ceremony	15 - 25

Scenes (20x30)

PO6460	X-wing fighter	30 - 40
PO6461	Millennium Falcon/Death Star	30 - 40

The Empire Strikes Back

PO6470	8x10 w/border (8)	50 - 75
PO6471	8x10 borderless (8)	50 - 75
PO6480	11x14 w/border (8)	65 - 85
PO6481	11x14 borderless (8)	65 - 85
PO6490	Photobusta set	150 - 225

Photo portraits (12 x17)

PO6491	Luke	15 - 20
PO6492	Leia	15 - 20
PO6493	Han	15 - 20
PO6494	Chewbacca	15 - 20
PO6495	R2-D2 & C-3PO	15 - 20
PO6496	Lando	15 - 20
PO6496a	All portraits on one sheet	50 - 75

Scenes (16x20)

PO6497	Luke on tauntaun	15 - 25
PO6498	Hoth battle	15 - 25
PO6499	Darth on Hoth	15 - 25

| | PO6579 | | PO8020 | Mini-mylar from PO8020 | PO8055 | | PO8055 (Inside) | |

PO6500 Carbonite chamber 15 - 25
Scene (20x30)
PO6501 Vader in starfield 25 - 30
PO6502 Falcon Vs. Destroyer 25 - 30
PO6503 Luke Vs. Vader 25 - 30
PO6504 Han & Leia in carbon chamber 25 - 30
Return of the Jedi
PO6555 8x10 w/border (8) 45 - 65
PO6556 8x10 borderless (8) 45 - 65
PO6565 11x14 w/border (8) 55 - 75
PO6566 11x14 borderless (8) 55 - 75
PO6570 Photobusta set 175 - 250
Photo portraits (16x20)
PO6571 Luke & Vader 12 - 15
PO6572 Vader 12 - 15
PO6573 R2-D2 & C-3PO 12 - 15
PO6574 Cockpit of Shuttle 12 - 15
PO6575 Leia, Luke on barge 12 - 15
PO6576 Lando 12 - 15
PO6577 Luke 12 - 15
PO6578 Han 12 - 15
PO6579 Luke & lightsaber 12 - 15
PO6580 Leia, slave 12 - 15
PO6581 C-3PO, Chewie, Leia 12 - 15
Scene (17x30)
PO6585 Barge explodes (art) 20 - 30
Scenes (20x30)
PO6586 Forest battle 25 - 30
PO6587 Death Star approach 25 - 35
Caravan of Courage
PO6590 8x10 w/border (8) 20 - 30
PO6591 8x10 borderless (8) 20 - 30
PO6595 11x14 w/border (8) 20 - 30
PO6596 11x14 borderless (8) 20 - 30
Special Edition
Star Wars
PO6600 16x20 (6) 75 - 100
The Empire Strikes Back
PO6610 16x20 (6) 75 - 100
Return of the Jedi
PO6620 16x20 (6) 75 - 100
Czechoslovakia
PO6701 *Star Wars* 8x11 w/lower white
border; single card: photo of
Chewie & Han 25 - 30
France
PO6810 *Star Wars*: 8 x11 (24) 65 - 85
PO6840 *ESB:* 8 x11 (10, Series B) 65 - 85
PO6860 *Jedi:* 8x10 (11) 55 - 70
Germany
PO6900 *Star Wars* uncut sheet of 8 paper
lobby cards w/blue borders and
perforations-23x33 25 - 40
PO6901 As above w/8 different scenes 25 - 40
PO6910 *Star Wars:* 8 x11 (24) 65 - 75
PO6930 *Empire:* 8 x11 (20) 60 - 70
PO6950 *Jedi:* 8 x11 (22) 50 - 65
PO6975 Caravan of Courage: 8 x11 (18) 25 - 30
PO6990 *Endor:* 9 x12 (12) 25 - 30
PO7010 *ESB* paper lobby cards-23x33 25 - 40
PO7011 As above 25 - 40
PO7015 *ROTJ* paper lobby cards-23x33 25 - 35
PO7016 As above 25 - 35
Great Britain
PO7120 *Star Wars:* 8x10 (8) 60 - 80
PO7130 *Empire:* 8x10 (8) 55 - 75
PO7140 *Jedi:* 8x10 (8) 45 - 55
Japan
PO7150 *Star Wars:* 8x10 (4) 25 - 35
PO7155 *Empire:* 8x10 (4) 25 - 35
PO7160 *Jedi:* 8x10 (4) 25 - 35
PO7165 Caravan of Courage: 8x10 (4) 15 - 25
PO7170 Battle for Endor: 8x10 (4) 15 - 25
Mexico
PO7180 *SW:* 12x16 (8 w/ or w/o borders) 85 - 125
PO7190 *Empire:* 11x14 (8 w/borders) 85 - 125

Poland
PO7201 *SW* 9 x12: Single B&W card (Han
under Falcon) 15 - 25
Spain
PO7230 *Star Wars:* 11x14 (12) 75 - 95
PO7245 *Empire:* 11x14 (24) 65 - 85
PO7270 *Jedi:* 8x10 (12) 35 - 50
PO7285 Ewok Adventure (Caravan):
9 x13 (12) 20 - 25

PRESS KITS (SELECTED)

These folders packed with press releases, black and
white photos and sometimes color slides were sent
mainly to reviewers and reporters. They are prized by
collectors for their behind-the-scenes information and
great photos. Most have specially-designed covers.

PO8010 *Star Wars*-1977. Original w/
blue cover. *SW* in silver, "Press Kit"
at top in white w/silver Fox logo.
'Production Information Guide' first
page in goldenrod. Material stapled.
Brown bag w/17 photos. 150 - 200
PO8015 *Star Wars*-1978. Blue cover w/
silver *SW* and "Press Kit" at bottom
in silver w/Fox logo. White band:
New Material Summer '78. Brown
bag rubber-stamped "Star Wars"
w/8 photos. 125 - 150
PO8020 *Star Wars* Holiday Special
1978 Kit for Nov. 17 CBS-TV
Special. White cover, blue title,
w/six B&W photos, 4 pages of
info and 3 captioned photos w/
silver mylar promo mini-poster. 250 - 350
PO8025 NPR Presents...-1979. White
cover kit for National Public Radio
& BBC 'Star Wars' radio series. 45 - 55
PO8030 *The Empire Strikes Back*-1980
Original w/black cover and silver
logo. Stapled press material. White
bag w/18 photos and credit sheet 75 - 125
PO8035 Introducing Yoda (1980)
Follow-up kit w/color photo of Yoda
on purple cover. Two pages of info.
White bag w/3 photos & 1 slide. 35 - 50
PO8040 NPR Playhouse-1981 *Star Wars*
on radio; die-cut cover marquee
showing *SW* and 2 other titles.
w/press info, photo of Vader 25 - 35
PO8045 *The Empire Strikes Back*
NPR-1983 Many releases (including
recipe for Yoda's stew), 6 photos,
flyer, 'invitation' to listen; Cover is
B&W art by Strain. 35 - 50
PO8050 *Return of the Jedi*-1983
w/stapled 59-page production notes,
other press material. Brown bag set
of 16 stills stamped w/title. 50 - 75
PO8055 Introducing the Ewoks-1983
Follow-up kit w/color photo of Ewok
on black matte cover. Contains 2-page
release, 3 B&W photos in brown\
bag, color slide in cello bag and color
8x10 blowup of the slide. 35 - 50
PO8060 *The Empire Strikes Back* Video-
1984 CBS-Fox Video kit for
dealers w/1982 rerelease one-sht
cover; w/brochures, ad mats,
order forms, ad schedule. 20 - 30
PO8065 Year of the Jedi-1984 CTS
Promotions kit for Jedi Adventure
Centers in malls; release, 2 photos 15 - 25
PO8070 The Ewok Adventure-1984
ABC-TV kit (white cover w/brown

logo) w/press info, 5 captioned
photos 15 - 25
PO8075 Caravan of Courage-1984
Blue cover w/orange logo for Fox
Film intl. release of TV movie. w/set
of 8 8x10 color lobby cards 20 - 25
PO8080 *Star Wars:* The First Ten Years-
1987 Black pebbled cover w/red
embossed logo; press info on LFL
embossed letterheads. w/6 photos. 30 - 45
PO8085 Star Tours: Tokyo Disneyland-
1989 Advance press kit. Cover is
'Happy Five Years' TDL; w/2-page
release in Japanese and 3 5x7 B&W
photos with captions in Japanese
and English 35 - 45
PO8090 Star Tours: Tokyo Disneyland-1989
Cover is blue star field w/Star Tours/
TDL logo. w/4 releases, five 4x6
B&W stills and special ST edition of
TDL mag. 4
PO8095 Star Tours: Walt Disney World-
1990 Wrap-around full-color
cover w/letter, 12 press releases
(2 on Star Tours) and 10 photos
(3 on Star Tours). 20 - 25
PO8100 *Star Wars* Special Edition- Ingot
cover, information booklet,
technology breakthrough notes,
w/6 photos 30 - 45
PO8105 Special Edition Audio/Visual-generic
Fox cover, info booklet &
technology notes as above, video
tape and 2-page list 30 - 45
PO8110 *Return of the Jedi* Special Edition-
Struzan poster art cover w/new date
slash, info booklet & technology
notes,10 color slides each for
ESB and *ROTJ*, captions,
added crew bios 30 - 45

PRESSBOOKS

Pressbooks, or books of ad slicks, are sent to theater owners to use as clip art for newspaper ads. They
sometimes also contain suggestions on how to promote the film and other oddities. They should be purchased only in unclipped form. Most were printed by
Gore Graphics in Los Angeles, and have that company's logo and the date at the bottom of most pages.
Individual pressbook pages are worth $1 to $3 each.

PO8330 *SW* 1977 20 - 45
PO8335 *SW* 1978 15 - 35
PO8340 *SW* 1982 10 - 20
PO8345 *ESB* 1980 15 - 35
PO8350 *ESB* 1981 10 - 20
PO8355 *ESB* 1982 10 - 20
PO8360 *ROTJ* 1983 (May) 15 - 20
PO8361 *ROTJ* 1983 (July) 15 - 20
PO8365 *ROTJ* 1985 10 - 20
PO8370 *SWSE* 1997 10 - 15
PO8375 *ESBSE* 1997 10 - 15
PO8380 *ROTJSE* 1997 10 - 15

PROGRAMS

The program booklet for *Star Wars* was sold in
theater lobbies. For *ESB* and *ROTJ* there were "official collectors' edition" magazines that were sold
instead. Most foreign variations are almost exact
duplicates of the American ones, except for the colorful programs from Japan.

PO8810 *SW* program (George Fenmore) 15 - 30
PO8811 *SW* program, pebble stock cover 15 - 30
PO8815 *ESB* Official Collectors' Edition
(Paradise Press) 5 - 12

PO8810	**PO9450**	**PO9860**

PO8820	*ROTJ* Official Collectors' Edition (Paradise Press)	5 - 10
England		
PO8930	*SW* Souvenir Programme (Oscar Lerman)	8 - 15
Japan		
PO9040	*SW* program	45 - 55
PO9041	*ESB* program	40 - 50
PO9042	*ROTJ* program	35 - 40
PO9050	*SWSE* program	25 - 35

PRINTED MATERIAL

There are thousands of magazine covers that have been devoted to the *Star Wars* trilogy worldwide, and thousands more than have articles inside on the films. These generally sell anywhere from fifty cents or $1 to as much as $100 for a particularly rare issue of American Cinematographer with a cover and articles detailing the making of *Star Wars*. Here we list just a number of directly licensed poster magazines.

MAGAZINES: POSTER

PT3001	*SW* Official Poster Monthly (Paradise Press) #1	2 - 5
PT3002-4	*SW* Official Poster Monthly, Issues #2-4, ea.	2 - 5
PT3005-10	*SW* Official Poster Monthly, Issues #5-10, ea.	2 - 5
PT3011-18	*SW* Official Poster Monthly, Issues #11-18, ea	5 - 15
PT3031	*ESB* Official Poster Monthly, Issue #1	1 - 4
PT3032-5	*ESB* Official Poster Monthly, Issues #2-5, ea.	1 - 4
PT3050	*SW/ESB: The SW* Compendium #1 - #3	5 - 15
PT3071	*ROTJ* poster magazine, Issue #1	5 - 10
PT3072-4	*ROTJ* poster magazine, Issues #2 - #4	5 - 10
PT3081	*ROTJ* Compendium #1 (white cover)	5 - 15
PT3082	*ROTJ* Compendium #2 (red cover)	5 - 15
Denmark (A/s Interpresse)		
PT3120	Stjerne Krigen	5 - 10
England		
PT3240	*SW* Official Poster Monthly, (Galaxy Publications), ea.	5 - 10
PT3250	*ESB* Official Poster Monthly (Paradise Press), ea.	5 - 10
Finland (Oy Semic)		
PT3360	*Tähtien Sota*, ea.	5 - 10

CREDIT SHEETS

These cardstock sheets or folders are handed out to members of the press at early screening of films. They have the film's logo on one side and list all members of the cast and crew.

PO9450	*SW* credit sheet	5 - 10
PO9451	*ESB* credit sheet	5 - 8
PO9452	*ROTJ* credit sheet	3 - 5

TICKETS/STUBS

Tickets for special screenings hold some value. There are press preview tickets, tickets for charitable events and some for special promotional screenings, many of which were by invitation only. In Japan, colorful paper tickets for the premiere performances of many "event" movies are sold weeks or months in advance, often with poster art or some other key illustration from the marketing campaign for the film. When the perforated ticket part is torn off, the remaining stub is a collectible. Depending on their nature, tickets or stubs might be valued anywhere from $1 to $20 or more.

PO9810	*SW* press preview ticket	5 - 15
PO9820	*ESB* press preview ticket	5 - 10
PO9830	*ROTJ* press ticket	5 - 10
PO9840	*SWSE* premiere ticket	10 - 15
Australia		
PO9860	Paul's ice cream and radio station QLD premiere	5 - 8
Japan		
PO9100	Stub for *SW* opening	15 - 25
PO9110	Stub for *ESB*	10 - 20
PO9120	Stub for *ROTJ*	10 - 15
PO9125	Stub for *SWSE*	10 - 15
PO9126	Stub for *ESBSE*	10 - 15
PO9127	Stub for *ROTJSE*	10 - 15

France (Galaxy Publications)		
PT3480	*La Guerre des Étoiles*, ea.	5 - 10
Germany		
PT3500	*Krieg der Sterne*, ea. (Galaxy Publications)	5 - 10
PT3510	*Das Imperium Schlägt Zurück das poster journal* (Comics Film Merchandising), ea.	5 - 10
Italy (Galaxy Publications)		
PT3620	*Guerre Stellari*, ea.	5 - 10
Norway (Nordisk Forlag/Semic)		
PT3740	*Star Wars*, ea.	5 - 10
Sweden (AB Semic)		
PT3860	*Stjärnornas Krig Jättestor Poster Inuti*, ea.	5 - 10

MERCHANDISE CATALOGS

There are two kinds of catalogs that interest collectors. The first kind is printed by manufacturers to let retailers know what products will be available for the coming year. For *Star Wars* fans, the most interesting of these are the Kenner Products retailers catalogs prepared for Toy Fair in New York, for these show nearly every toy produced (and some that weren't, or variations) along with store displays that were available. Even less common are special "Pre-Pack" catalogs, which feature store displays; department store program catalogs, featuring special packaging combinations; Consumer Promotions catalogs; and repro art books, featuring line art of the toys.

PT3001	PT3002	PT3003	PT3004	PT3005	PT3006
PT3120	PT3240	PT3360	PT3480	PT3500	PT3620

PT3031   PT3081   PT5500   PT5506   PT5517   PT5527

PT5540   PT5546   PT5560   PT5700   PT5702   PT5703

PT5704   PT5706   PT5709

PT5707   PT5712   PT5714   PT5718   PT5720

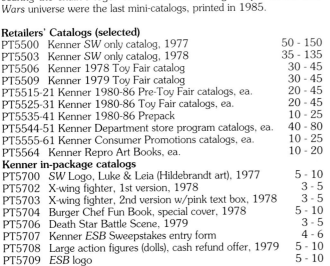

PT5724   PT5725   PT5726

PT7750   PT7751

The second type of catalog was more readily available to consumers. Almost all Kenner *Star Wars* toys were packed with a small pamphlet listing available *Star Wars* merchandise and previewing future items. Some mini-catalogs were also shipped with mail-in premiums or as part of special promotions, and were updated about once a year. The 1978 catalog was given out as a Burger Chef premium with an added cover bearing the chain's logo. Three different catalog "maps" of the *Star Wars* universe were the last mini-catalogs, printed in 1985.

Retailers' Catalogs (selected)

PT5500	Kenner *SW* only catalog, 1977	50 - 150
PT5503	Kenner *SW* only catalog, 1978	35 - 135
PT5506	Kenner 1978 Toy Fair catalog	30 - 45
PT5509	Kenner 1979 Toy Fair catalog	30 - 45
PT5515-21	Kenner 1980-86 Pre-Toy Fair catalogs, ea.	20 - 45
PT5525-31	Kenner 1980-86 Toy Fair catalogs, ea.	20 - 45
PT5535-41	Kenner 1980-86 Prepack	10 - 25
PT5544-51	Kenner Department store program catalogs, ea.	40 - 80
PT5555-61	Kenner Consumer Promotions catalogs, ea.	10 - 25
PT5564	Kenner Repro Art Books, ea.	10 - 20

Kenner in-package catalogs

PT5700	*SW* Logo, Luke & Leia (Hildebrandt art), 1977	5 - 10
PT5702	X-wing fighter, 1st version, 1978	3 - 5
PT5703	X-wing fighter, 2nd version w/pink text box, 1978	3 - 5
PT5704	Burger Chef Fun Book, special cover, 1978	5 - 10
PT5706	Death Star Battle Scene, 1979	3 - 5
PT5707	Kenner *ESB* Sweepstakes entry form	4 - 6
PT5708	Large action figures (dolls), cash refund offer, 1979	5 - 10
PT5709	*ESB* logo	5 - 10

PT5710	*ESB* logo (English & French flip book), 1980	5 - 10
PT5712	Luke and Yoda, 1981	3 - 5
PT5714	*Star Wars* Collections, Hoth photo w/silver border	3 - 5
PT5715	*Star Wars* Collections, Hoth photo w/gray border	5 - 10
PT5716	*ROTJ* logo, 1983	3 - 5
PT5718	Vader and Royal Guards, 1983	3 - 5
PT5720	Jabba the Hutt, 1984 w/77 figures listed	3 - 5
PT5722	Jabba the Hutt, 1984 w/79 figures listed	3 - 5

Kenner Planetary Maps (1985) PT5724-26

PT5724	Tatooine, the Planet	5 - 15
PT5725	The Death Stars	5 - 15
PT5726	Endor: The Sanctuary Moon	5 - 15
PT5730	*Revenge* product listing ad folder	30 - 75

West End Games

PT7750	Winter/Spring '88	1 - 4
PT7751	Spring '89	1 - 4

Japan

Takara in-package flyers

PT7901	Small flyer	3 - 5
PT7905	Large flyer w/rocket-firing R2, X-wing, Super-Control R2, die-cast toys	2 - 4
PT7910	Large flyer w/X-wing (2 sizes), 8" figures, other toys	2 - 4

| PT7901 | PT7905 | PT7910 | RA0010 | RA0020 |

| SH0055 | SH0050 | SH0055 | SH1140 | SH1150 | SH3200 | SH3812 | SH3814 | SH3816 |

| SO0010 | SO0014 | SO0040 | SO0554 | SO2070 |

NEWSPAPERS

A *Star Wars* newspaper was printed as a promotion in conjunction with the first film. The Yuma Daily Sun did a *Revenge of the Jedi* supplement.

PT8000	*Star Wars* newspaper	10 - 20
PT8010	Yuma Daily Sun *ROTJ* Revenge supplement	5 - 10

See also—COMICS: Comic Strips

PRESS KITS—See **POSTERS, LOBBY CARDS, PRESS KITS, ETC.**

RADIOS (Kenner Products)

RA0010	Luke Skywalker AM headset radio	250 - 1400
RA0020	R2-D2 radio	85 - 150

See also—FOOD: Beverages; WATCHES

SHOPPING BAGS/SHOW BAGS

Australia (Benson Trading Co.)

These printed plastic bags, purchased at fairs, contained a number of inexpensive toys and other goodies for youngsters.

SH0050	*ROTJ* show bag	3 - 5
SH0055	Ewoks show bag, 2 versions, ea.	3 - 5

Japan
Rapport Co.

SH1140	*ESB* logo and Darth Vader, plastic, silver or black	10 - 20
SH1150	*ROTJ* Luke & Leia on barge, 6 other photos, plastic	10 - 15
SH1152	*ROTJ* art collage, plastic	10 - 15
SH1154	*ROTJ* like SH3152, Kodak premium w/logo on back	10 - 15

Panasonic

SH2200	Ewok, George Lucas, Chewbacca "riding" on pole of satellite dish, coated paper	15 - 20

Yamakatsu Co.

SH3200	*ROTJ* Luke, Leia on barge on black bckgrnd, paper	15 - 20

Yukari Co.

SH3810	*SW* logo, white outline on black, paper	10 - 20
SH3812	*SW* Hildebrandt art, paper	10 - 20
SH3814	Photos of troopers, droids, Chewie, dewback, paper	10 - 20
SH3816	Descriptive graphics of R2-D2 and C-3PO, paper	10 - 20
SH3820	Descriptive graphics of R2-D2 and C-3PO, plastic	10 - 20
SH3822	*SW* logo w/Luke & Leia, plastic	10 - 20
SH3824	*SW* logo & X-wing fighter, plastic	10 - 20
SH3826	*SW* logo white outline on black, plastic	10 - 20

SHOW SOUVENIRS

The George Lucas Super Live Adventure was a live arena show staged in several cities in Japan in 1993 by Irving Feld and Kenneth

Feld Productions Inc. There were a number of *Star Wars* trilogy-related souvenir items, and others with at least partial *SW* art. Some items were later available in limited quantity through the fan club.

GEORGE LUCAS SUPER LIVE ADVENTURE
Apparel

SO0010	Baseball caps w/GLSLA logo on front, Lucasfilm on back in black, red or white, each	20 - 30
SO0014	Painters caps, one GLSLA all characters, one *SW* characters on white background, each	20 - 30
SO0016	Tyvek cap, blue w/LFL movie scenes	25 - 35
SO0018	Heavy denim jacket w/beige sleeves and GLSLA logo embroidered on back	150 - 200
SO0020	Black windbreaker w/gold GLSLA logo on front and across back	45 - 75
SO0022	Tyvek zippered jacket, blue w/movie scenes	55 - 95
SO0024	White polo shirt w/GLSLA logo embroidered in red, blue, yellow	30 - 45
SO0026	Black sweatshirt w/gold GLSLA logo on back	30 - 45
SO0028	Black T-shirt w/LFL characters in purple, blue	20 - 30
SO0030	Black T-shirt w/*SW* logo vertically and characters	20 - 30
SO0032	Green T-shirt w/LFL movie characters	20 - 30
SO0034	Black T-shirt w/*SW* space battle on front, *SW* opening crawl on back	20 - 30

Badges, metal

SO0040	GLSLA 6" w/LFL movie characters	5 - 15
SO0042	*SW* 2¼" w/heroes and villains against star field	5 - 15

Bags

SO0550	Paper shopping bag w/*SW* art on one side and GLSLA on other	5 - 15
SO0552	Plastic shopping bag like SO0050	5 - 15
SO0554	Small black fabric drawstring bag w/GLSLA logo, containing small white towel w/multi-colored LFL movie logos	10 - 20
SO0556	Blue Tyvek duffel bag w/LFL movie scenes	45 - 65
SO0558	Fabric handbags w/movie characters filling letters of GLSLA, black or cream, each	15 - 25

Cosmetics

SO1560	Ladies pocket compact mirror w/GLSLA logo	10 - 15

Cups, containers

SO2070	R2-D2 plastic figural mug and bank w/handle and slots for straw and coins	25 - 40
SO2072	Tall plastic cup w/lid and flexi-straw w/GLSLA logo	15 - 25
SO2074	Small plastic mug w/movie scenes and logo	10 - 15
SO2076	Plastic popcorn bucket w/lid and handle; one side is *SW* art and other is GLSLA art	15 - 25
SO2078	Ceramic black cup w/gold GLSLA logo and George Lucas picture	20 - 30

SO2074 SO2076 SO2580 SO2586 SO2590

SO2584 SO2588 SO2800 SO2802 SO2804

SO2592 SO2594

SO3230 SO3851 SO3852

SO3851 (loose) SO3852 (loose) SO3850

Electronics, electric

SO2580	Darth Vader Voice, shaped like Vader mouthpiece	40 - 65
SO2582	R2-D2 LCD target clock w/gun (shoot him and he beeps), premium	75 - 125
SO2584	Sonic Blaster, silver plastic w/lights, sound and vibration	20 - 35
SO2586	R2-D2 & C-3PO figural LCD alarm clock	55 - 80
SO2588	Spinning LED message machine, gold plastic w/lights that spell out "George Lucas Super Live" when twirled quickly	25 - 35
SO2590	Darth Vader swivel light w/blue light under Vader's spinning head	20 - 30
SO2592	Jedi Knight Lightsaber, gray plastic w/flashing light in blade	15 - 25
SO2594	Jedi Knight Lightsaber, gold plastic w/blade that lights up slowly to increasing humming sound	25 - 35
SO2596	Fantasma Darth Vader watch in black padded GLSLA case	50 - 75

Keychains

SO2800	Square plastic w/GLSLA logo scenes on other side	10 - 15
SO2802	Metal, shaped like R2-D2	10 - 15
SO2804	Painted vinyl w/metal ring and chain: R2-D2, C-3PO, Darth Vader, Yoda, each	10 - 20

Pennants

SO3020	Triangular w/movie characters	15 - 25
SO3022	Die-cut w/movie characters	15 - 25

Program

SO3230	GLSLA program book	25 - 35

Stationery

SO3540	Pen set, one of 3 w/*SW* art	10 - 20
SO3542	Paper and pen set w/GLSLA logo and movie scenes	10 - 20

Telephone cards

SO3850	GLSLA logo w/C-3PO & R2-D2	15 - 25
SO3851	GLSLA, explosion, Luke & Indy, with holder	15 - 25
SO3852	Luke holding lightsaber (mainly *SW* art) with holder	15 - 25

SO4060 SO4064

Toys

SO4060	Plush Ewoks w/capes, 8" and 15" versions	20 - 35
SO4064	Plush 12" Yoda w/vinyl head and fabric body	30 - 45
SO4066	Glitter stick w/small images of Yoda and other LFL characters amidst the glitter	15 - 25
SO4068	Illuminated glitter stick w/Mylar streamer	10 - 20
SO4070	Large inflatable Darth Vader bop (punching) bag	25 - 40

ICE CAPADES

Ewoks on Ice were one segment of the 1985 Ice Capades. A number of licensed Ewoks items were available at the souvenir counters.

SO5500	Program	10 - 15
SO5502	Fiber-optic flashlight	10 - 15
SO5504	Ice Capades & Ewoks triangular pennant	10 - 15
SO5505	Wicket & Kneesaa triangular pennant	
SO5506	Wicket die-cut felt pennant	10 - 15
SO5508	Kneesaa die-cut felt pennant	10 - 15
See also—**BUTTONS AND BADGES**		

TENTH ANNIVERSARY CONVENTION

Creation Conventions and Starlog magazine sponsored a three-day celebration in 1987 for the 10th anniversary of the release of *Star Wars*. Never before—and never since—had there been so many *Star Wars* trilogy collectibles in one place at one time. In addition to all the dealers' goodies, there were a number of special items for sale.

SO7610	*SW* 10th Program	5 - 10
SO7612	*SW* 10th pennant	10 - 20
SO7614	*SW* 10th black ceramic mug	5 - 15
SO7616	*SW* 10th magnetic pad/pencil holder, blue or lavender	8 - 12
SO7618	*SW* 10th cap	10 - 15
SO7620	*SW* 10th T-shirt	10 - 15
SO7622	*SW* 10th decorated notepads	5 - 10
SO7624	*SW* 10th color photos from films	5 - 7
SO7626	*SW* 10th Jacket (black w/patch on back)	100 - 125

See also—**BUTTONS AND BADGES; BUMPER STICKERS; PATCHES**

SPORTS/OUTDOOR ACTIVITY

BALLS
England (Vulli)

SP0120	*Star Wars* soccer ball, dark blue, white, black and red	20 - 35

Spain (Amaya SA)

SP0430	*SW* plastic balls	10 - 15

BICYCLES (Huffy)

SP1050	Kenner Speeder Bike pedal vehicle, won through sweepstakes (made for Kenner by Huffy)	600 - 950
SP1060	Ewoks Girls' First Bike, Kneesaa, Baby and Baga	75 - 125
SP1062	Ewoks Girls' Hi-Rise, Kneesaa	75 - 125
SP1064	*ROTJ:* R2-D2 and C-3PO Boys First Bike	100 - 225

Australia (Redline Engineering Pty. Ltd.)

SP1200	Bicycle Safety Flags	10 - 15

SP3708   SP3714   SP3710

SP1600   SP3700 SP3702 SP3704

SP3706

SP3712

SP4860   SP4862

SP6520   SP6522   SP6740   SP6742   SP6900

SP7550   SP7552

FRISBEES/FLYING DISCS See also—HOUSEHOLD; SHOW SOUVENIRS
Japan (Takara)

SP1450	Yellow w/paper *SW* logo & Luke and Leia	25 - 50
SP1452	Blue w/paper Darth Vader photo label	25 - 50

GO-ROUNDS (Kenner)

SP1600	Wicket Sit 'n Spin ride-on toy	35 - 70

GYM SETS (CBS/Gym Dandy)

SP2400	*ROTJ* Scout Walker Command Tower w/Speeder Bike Ride	350 - 700
SP2405	*ROTJ* Scout Walker Command Tower Swing Set w/Speeder Bike Ride	450 - 900
SP2410	SP2400 w/7 foot slide	350 - 500
SP2415	*ROTJ* Speeder Bike Swing add-on	100 - 200

KITES (Spectra Star)

SP3700	Darth Vader figure kite	10 - 15
SP3702	Luke Skywalker figure kite	10 - 15
SP3704	Wicket figure kite	10 - 15
SP3706	SW/*ROTJ* 8-panel box kite w/heroes, villains	10 - 15
SP3708	Ewoks on hang-gliders, 80" Mylar Octopus kite	10 - 15
SP3710	Speeder Bike scene, 50-foot Mylar Dragon kite	10 - 15
SP3712	*SW* montage, 42" Delta Wing kite	10 - 15
SP3714	Luke/Vader lightsaber duel, 64" Streamer kite	10 - 15
SP3716	*Droids* 80" Streamer kite	10 - 15

See also—**FOOD: Cereal**
Australia (G. and J. Barnes Nominees Pty. Ltd.)

SP4735	*ROTJ* box kite	10 - 15
SP4736	50 foot dragon kite	10 - 15
SP4737	Darth Vader	10 - 15
SP4738	Wicket the Ewok	10 - 15
SP4739	Luke Skywalker	10 - 15
SP4740	80 inch Ewoks Octopus kite	10 - 15

England (Worlds Apart Ltd.)

SP4860	*ROTJ* Darth Vader action stunt kite	15 - 25
SP4862	*ROTJ* Millennium Falcon stunt kite	15 - 25

PLAY HOUSES/TENTS
France (Le Panache Blanc)

SP5010	Space vehicle (child's tent)	25 - 55

Spain (Runesco)

SP5520	*SW* polyester tents	25 - 45

SKATES AND SKATEBOARDS (Brookfield Athletic)
Ice Skates

SP6520	Vader & Royal Guards, lace or Velcro	35 - 75
SP6522	Wicket, lace or Velcro	25 - 40

Roller Skates

SP6740	Vader & Royal Guards, lace or Velcro	35 - 60
SP6742	Wicket, lace or Velcro	25 - 40

Skateboards

SP6900	Luke/Vader duel	75 - 130

SWIMMING INFLATABLES
Australia (Stern's Playland Pty. Ltd.)

SP7550	*ROTJ* "speed boat"	10 - 20
SP7551	*ROTJ* "canoe"	10 - 20
SP7552	*ROTJ* R2-D2 Floaters	10 - 15
SP7553	*ROTJ* swim ring	10 - 15
SP7554	*ROTJ* Ewok bubble	10 -15
SP7555	*ROTJ* "Super Tuber"	10 - 15

Japan (Takara)

SP8000	*SW* swim ring	20 - 35
SP8012	*SW* beach ball	20 - 35

See also—**STAR TOURS: Miscellaneous**

SR0010	SR0011	SR0520	SR0520	SR1000

SR4000	SR5350	SR5860	SR5862	SR5863	SR6000	SR6200

STAMPS, STICKERS, AND DECALS

See also—CAST AND CREW; CRAFTS: Rubber Stamps; FOOD; HOUSEHOLD; STAR TOURS; STATIONERY: Labels; TRADING CARDS

DECALS

Two paintings by Ralph McQuarrie were printed on 4"x5" paper decal sheets. They were originally given away as renewal premiums through the *Star Wars* Fan Club, and were later sold through the club. Image Marketing issued several vinyl decals—one to a pack—in 1994.

SR0010	4"x5" decal: Bounty Hunters	5 - 10
SR0011	4"x5" decal: Yoda	3 - 9
SR0020	Darth Vader (Image Marketing)	4 - 8
SR0021	C-3PO and R2-D2 (Image Marketing)	4 - 8
SR0022	Yoda (Image Marketing)	4 - 8
SR0023	TIE fighter attacks Falcon (Image Marketing)	4 - 8
France		
SR0300	Die-cut C-3PO/R2-D2 decal	4 - 8
Japan (Tokyo Queen)		
SR0520	SW Decals, 2 diff., ea.	10 - 20
Mexico (Personajes Registrados S.A.)		
SR0700	*ROTJ* assorted decals	1 - 3

STAMPS

Stamp Kits (H. E. Harris and Co.)

A stamp collecting kit was produced in 1977 by H. E. Harris and Co. It included an album, 24 *Star Wars* seals, 35 space exploration postage stamps, a bag of 300 stamp hinges, and a plastic magnifying glass. The set was produced in at least three variation boxes, one polybag with a header and also was split apart and sold in six different polywrapped cardboard-backed packs with six *SW* seals and 10 regular space stamps each.

SR1000	*SW* boxed stamp kit	10 - 20
SR1005	*SW* bagged stamp kit	10 - 20
Stamp Envelopes		
SR2510	Death Star	3 - 6
SR2511	Heroes	3 - 6
SR2512	Tatooine residents	3 - 6
SR2513	Space ships	3 - 6
SR2514	Cantina scenes	3 - 6
SR2515	Escape from Death Star	3 - 6

STICKER ALBUMS

Edizioni Panini SpA of Italy, affiliated with Topps, did stamp albums and stamps for *Star Wars* and *Return of the Jedi*. Pacosa Dos Internacional of Spain did a different *Star Wars* album for Spanish-speaking countries and FKS Publishers Ltd. of England and affiliates did an album for *The Empire Strikes Back*. Yet another different *ROTJ* album was done by Editorial Ciarmar of Mexico. Most were published in many languages and sold mainly in European and Latin American countries. The albums and stickers were sold wherever non-sports trading cards could normally be found; the stickers were sold both in packs and in quantity through mail-in offers. Only the album and stickers for *ROTJ* were sold in the U.S.—by Topps. A completely different trilogy album and sticker set was sold in 1989 by Cedibra Editora Brasileira Ltda. of Brazil. Ideally for collectors, the albums should be mint and empty and come with a full set of stickers and at least one wrapper from a sticker package.

SR4000	*ROTJ* album/180 stickers (Topps/Panini)	20 - 40
Australia (Allen's Confectionery)		
SR5005	*ROTJ* album/180 stickers	15 - 35
Brazil		
SR5345	*SW* album/256 stickers (Panini)	
SR5350	*ROTJ* album/248 stickers (Shorebrook)	50 - 125
SR5352	Trilogy album/120 stickers (Cedibra Editora)	25 - 60
Costa Rica		
SR5600	*SW* album/187 stickers (Culturama de Centroamerica SA/Pacosa Dos Internacional)	50 - 125
England (FKS Publishers Ltd.)		
SR5700	*ESB* album/225 stickers	50 - 125
France		
SR5860	*ROTJ* album/180 stickers (France Images/Panini)	15 - 35
SR5862	*Ewoks* album/stickers (International Team)	
SR5863	Display box for SR8662	
Germany (Jolly Press/Panini)		
SR6000	*SW* album/256 stickers	50 - 125
SR6005	*ROTJ* album/180 stickers	15 - 35
Italy (Edizioni Panini)		
SR6200	*SW* album/256 stickers	50 - 125
SR6201	Display box for SR6200	25 - 45
SR6205	*ROTJ* album/180 stickers	20 - 40
Mexico		
SR6400	*SW* album/187 stickers (Pacosa Dos Internacional)	50 - 125
SR6405	*ROTJ* album/202 stickers (Editorial Ciarmar, S.A.)	45 - 60
SR6411	*ROTJ* album #1/40 stickers (Editorial Ciarmar)	
SR6412	*ROTJ* album #2/41 stickers (Editorial Ciarmar)	
SR6413	*ROTJ* album #3/41 stickers (Editorial Ciarmar)	
SR6414	*ROTJ* album #4/40 stickers (Editorial Ciarmar)	
SR6415	*ROTJ* album #5/40 stickers (Editorial Ciarmar)	
Netherlands (Vanderhout Internationale)		
SR6530	*ESB* album/225 stickers	50 - 125
Spain		
SR6600	*SW* album/187 stickers (Pacosa Dos Internacional)	50 - 125
SR6602	*ESB* album/225 stickers (Editorial FHER S.A.)	50 - 125
SR6603	*ROTJ* album (Pacosa Dos Internacional)	
SR6604	*ROTJ* sticker set/32 stickers (Chupa) w/poster	
SR6606	*Droids* album/225 stickers (Pacosa Dos Internacional)	35 - 60
SR6608	*Ewoks* album/225 stickers (Pacosa Dos Internacional)	30 - 50
Venezuela		
SR6870	*SW* album/stickers (Dive Press S.A.)	50 - 75

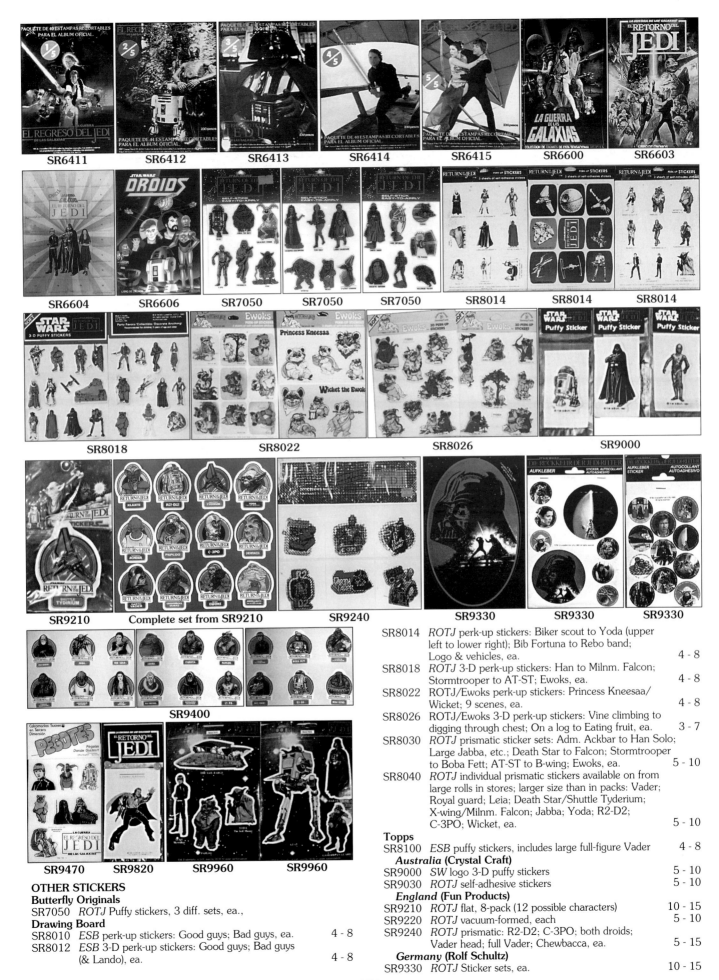

SR6411 SR6412 SR6413 SR6414 SR6415 SR6600 SR6603

SR6604 SR6606 SR7050 SR7050 SR7050 SR8014 SR8014 SR8014

SR8018 SR8022 SR8026 SR9000

SR9210 Complete set from SR9210 SR9240 SR9330 SR9330 SR9330

SR9400

SR9470 SR9820 SR9960 SR9960

OTHER STICKERS

Butterfly Originals

SR7050 *ROTJ* Puffy stickers, 3 diff. sets, ea.,

Drawing Board

SR8010 *ESB* perk-up stickers: Good guys; Bad guys, ea.   4 - 8

SR8012 *ESB* 3-D perk-up stickers: Good guys; Bad guys (& Lando), ea.   4 - 8

SR8014 *ROTJ* perk-up stickers: Biker scout to Yoda (upper left to lower right); Bib Fortuna to Rebo band; Logo & vehicles, ea.   4 - 8

SR8018 *ROTJ* 3-D perk-up stickers: Han to Milnm. Falcon; Stormtrooper to AT-ST; Ewoks, ea.   4 - 8

SR8022 ROTJ/Ewoks perk-up stickers: Princess Kneesaa/ Wicket; 9 scenes, ea.   4 - 8

SR8026 ROTJ/Ewoks 3-D perk-up stickers: Vine climbing to digging through chest; On a log to Eating fruit, ea.   3 - 7

SR8030 *ROTJ* prismatic sticker sets: Adm. Ackbar to Han Solo; Large Jabba, etc.; Death Star to Falcon; Stormtrooper to Boba Fett; AT-ST to B-wing; Ewoks, ea.   5 - 10

SR8040 *ROTJ* individual prismatic stickers available on from large rolls in stores; larger size than in packs: Vader; Royal guard; Leia; Death Star/Shuttle Tyderium; X-wing/Milnm. Falcon; Jabba; Yoda; R2-D2; C-3PO; Wicket, ea.   5 - 10

Topps

SR8100 *ESB* puffy stickers, includes large full-figure Vader   4 - 8

Australia **(Crystal Craft)**

SR9000 *SW* logo 3-D puffy stickers   5 - 10

SR9030 *ROTJ* self-adhesive stickers   5 - 10

England **(Fun Products)**

SR9210 *ROTJ* flat, 8-pack (12 possible characters)   10 - 15

SR9220 *ROTJ* vacuum-formed, each   5 - 10

SR9240 *ROTJ* prismatic: R2-D2; C-3PO; both droids; Vader head; full Vader; Chewbacca, ea.   5 - 15

Germany **(Rolf Schultz)**

SR9330 *ROTJ* Sticker sets, ea.   10 - 15

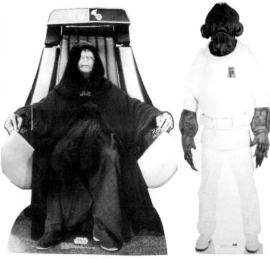

SS0010	SS0011	SS2289	SS2290	SS2291	SS2293

SS2285	Stormtrooper	20 - 30
SS2286	Darth Vader without lightsaber	20 - 30
SS2287	Chewbacca	20 - 30
SS2288	Yoda	20 - 30
SS2289	Boba Fett	20 - 30
SS2290	Han Solo in Carbonite	20 - 30
SS2291	Emperor Palpitine	20 - 30
SS2293	Admiral Ackbar	20 - 30
SS2295	Tusken Raider	20 - 30
SS2297	Princess Leia enslaved	20 - 30
SS2299	Ben Kenobi	20 - 30
SS2300	Jawa	20 - 30
SS2302	Darth Vader with lightsaber	20 - 30
SS2304	Royal Guard	20 - 30
SS2306	Han Solo as Stormtrooper	20 - 30

See also—**POSTERS, LOBBY CARDS, PRESS KITS, STORE DISPLAYS**

SS2295	SS2297	SS2299

Italy **(Sodecor)**
SR9400	Character stickers, 18 different, ea.	1 - 2

Mexico **(Personajes Registrados)**
SR9470	*ROTJ* Pegotes	3 - 8

Philippines **(Presswell Enterprises)**
SR9600	Ewok stickers	3 - 5

Spain **(Publi-Badge)**
SR9820	El Retorno del Jedi vinyl stickers	5 - 10

Switzerland **(Dufner and Cie.)**
SR9960	*ROTJ* sticker packs, 4 different	5 - 10

STANDEES

These photo-realistic die-cut cardboard pieces with cardboard easels are lifelike enough to scare your dog—or unsuspecting friends. They were offered for *Star Wars*, *Jedi*, and recently as a *SW* Classic line.

Factors Inc., near life size
SS0010	*SW*: C-3PO	25 - 40
SS0011	*SW*: R2-D2	25 - 40
SS0012	*SW*: Darth Vader	25 - 45
SS0013	*SW*: Chewbacca	25 - 45
SS0014	*ESB*: Boba Fett	35 - 55

Sales Corp. of America, 18" to 36" high
SS1150	*ROTJ*: Darth Vader & Royal Guards	15 - 25
SS1151	*ROTJ*: C-3PO & R2-D2	15 - 25
SS1152	*ROTJ*: Wicket W. Warrick	5 - 15

Advanced Graphics, near life size, 1993-1997
SS2280	Luke Skywalker	20 - 30
SS2281	C-3PO	20 - 30
SS2282	R2-D2	20 - 30
SS2283	Princess Leia	20 - 30
SS2284	Han Solo	20 - 30

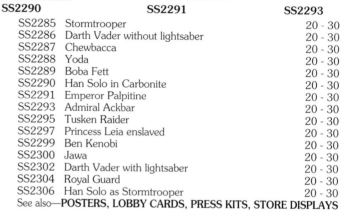

SS2280-88

ST0010   ST0210   ST0212   ST0611

STAR TOURS

Star Tours opened in Disneyland in Anaheim, California, in January, 1987. A project developed jointly by Disney Imagineering and Industrial Light & Magic, the ride has both excitement and humor as inexperienced pilot Rex takes his Starspeeder (a motion control simulator base) on an unexpected journey into the heart of a nasty battle. The stores connected to the Star Tours rides at all four Disney parks have carried an assortment of both Star Tours and *Star Wars* merchandise, most available nowhere else. And while the two U.S. parks sometimes have similar merchandise, there is little over-all duplication. These have effectively become the *Star Wars* boutiques that George Lucas envisioned when making the first film.

APPAREL

Hats

ST0010	D-White plastic visor w/logo	5 - 12
ST0011	D-White cloth , embroidered logo and orange/blue piping on bill	10 - 15
ST0012	D-Gray corduroy w/embroidered logo	10 - 15
ST0013	D-Black cloth w/white ST	10 - 15
ST0014	D-White painters' cap w/Rex, droids, Dland logo	10 - 15
ST0015	D-Black, "X-wing fighter Captain" silver embroidery	10 - 20
ST0210	W-White painters' cap w/Rex, droids & Dis/MGM logo	10 - 15
ST0211	W-Black Opening Day press cap w/ST logo & Walt Disney World	10 - 20
ST0212	W-Black cloth/mesh w/explosion behind ST logo	10 - 15
ST0213	W-Black w/*SW* embroidered in gold	10 - 20
ST0214	W-Black w/blue bill, blue embroidered *SW* logo, X-wng. in silver & blue, "May the Force…" on back	10 - 20
ST0215	W-Like ST0214 but silver embroidered Yoda on other side	10 - 20
ST0216	W-Like ST0215 but purple bill, embroidery	10 - 20
ST0217	W-Black, w/purple *SW* logo, Vader, "Master of the Dark Side"	10 - 20
ST0218	W-Black beanie, blue *SW* logo, silver X-wing, "May the Force…"	10 - 15
ST0410	T-Black nylon w/printed logo	10 - 20
ST0411	T-White cloth w/embroidered logo	10 - 20
ST0412	T-Black polished cotton , embr. logo	10 - 20
ST0610	E-Black cotton w/ST silver embr.	10 - 20
ST0611	E-Silver metallic polyester w/ST and logo in black	10 - 20

Jackets

ST1010	D-Gray satin w/ST logo in blue & orange	50 - 75
ST1012	D-Gray satin w/ST logo in hot pink, yellow & blue	50 - 75
ST1014	D-Gray "Launch Crew" for Imagineering and ILM workers	100 - 150
ST1016	D-Child's zippered windbreaker (light blue)	35 - 45
ST1018	D-Black satin w/silver glitter Dland logo on front & ST logo on back	50 - 75
ST1020	D-Black/aqua pull-over zippered poncho w/ST logo	35 - 50
ST1022	D-Black satin w/silver embroidered ST logo on front & ST on back	50 - 75
ST1210	W-Black satin w/silver glitter Dis/MGM logo on front and ST logo on back	50 - 75
ST1410	T-Silver satin w/blue piping, zippers, knit collar w/ST logo in blue and orange	60 - 95
ST1412	T-Like ST1410 but black w/orange	60 - 95
ST1414	T-Black zippered windbreaker w/ST blue & orange logo on front & back & TD on front (unlined)	45 - 55
ST1416	T-Like ST1414 but lined	55 - 65
ST1418	T-Orange lined windbreaker	55 - 65
ST1420	T-White lined windbreaker	55 - 65

ST5010

ST1610	E-Silver metallic polyester hooded windbreaker w/ED front & ST on back	55 - 70

Sweatshirts

ST2010	D-Black w/silver ST/Dland logo	20 - 35
ST2011	D-Blue w/silver ST/Dland logo	20 - 35
ST2012	D-White w/R2-D2, C-3PO, logo and "Now the Adventure…"	20 - 35
ST2013	D-Black w/vertical gray & black puffy logo	20 - 35
ST2014	D-White w/Speeder, Death Star, Rex, droids and ST Dland logo	20 - 35
ST2015	D-Red, black & white w/black elbow patches & logo	20 - 35
ST2016	D-White w/9 R2-D2s in neon colors w/ST logo	20 - 35
ST2017	D-Navy w/ST logo, TIE interceptor	20 - 35
ST2018	D-Black w/ST logo in reflective blue-green-purple	20 - 35
ST2310	W-Black w/silver sparkle logo	20 - 35
ST2311	W-White w/Rex in silver circle, Dis/MGM logo on back	20 - 35
ST2312	W-Light gray w/black, logo	20 - 35
ST2510	T-Black w/logo, T-Dland and "Now the Adventure…"	20 - 35
ST2511	T-Like ST2510 but gray	20 - 35
ST2512	T-White w/Speeder, Death Star, Rex, droids, and ST logo w/Tokyo Dland	20 - 35
ST2513	T-White w/blue star-field, "Been there…"	20 - 35
ST2514	T-White w/stylized metallic gold C-3PO, "Welcome to Tomorrowland Starport. Star Tours"	20 - 35
ST2515	T-White w/metallic silver R2-D2, "Welcome to…"	20 - 35
ST2710	E-Black w/flat silver ST and logo	20 - 35

T-shirts

ST3010	D-Black w/silver ST-Dland logo	10 - 25
ST3011	D-Blue w/silver ST-Dland logo	10 - 25
ST3012	D-White w/droids, logo: "Now the Adventure is Real"	10 - 25
ST3013	D-White w/small logo on front & sleeves, large logo on back	10 - 25
ST3014	D-White w/Death Star, Starspeeder, R2-D2, C-3PO, Rex and logos	10 - 25
ST3015	D-Like ST3014 but blue	10 - 25
ST3016	D-Black w/orange & blue logo and "Now the Adventure…"	10 - 25
ST3017	D-White w/pink, yellow, blue splatters w/robots, Speeder, X-Wings, ST logo	10 - 25
ST3018	D-Red "Jedi Master Yoda" shirt	10 - 25
ST3019	D-Blue w/ST logo and large X-wing	10 - 25
ST3020	D-White oversized w/large cartoon of robots, creatures, Starspeeder & logo	10 - 25
ST3021	D-Like ST3020 but black	10 - 25
ST3022	D-White w/R2-D2 and C-3PO, Speeder, ST and Dland logo	10 - 25
ST3033	D-White w/overall print (front & back) of Starspeeders, Cinderella's Castle w/red ST logo framed in yellow	10 - 25
ST3034	D-Black. Front is *SW* logo in yellow w/TIE ftr. pursuing X-Wing; rear is exploding Death Star , "splatter" star field	10 - 25
ST3035	D-Med. blue w/TIE interceptor, Death Star, *SW* logo in purple	10 - 25
ST3036	D-Black w/large A-wing, smaller B-wing & TIE ftr, green grid, "May the Force…" Back: blue "A long time ago…" in pyramid	10 - 25

STAR TOURS CODES			
D—Disneyland (Anaheim)	**W**—Walt Disney World/MGM (Orlando)	**T**—Tokyo Disneyland	**E**—Euro Disneyland

ST5014	**ST5017**	**ST5019**	**ST5023**	**ST5510**	**ST5511**

ST5512	**ST5513**	**ST5710**

ST5514

ST6812	**ST6814**	**ST6816**

ST3037 D-Black w/"Chewie" and illus of him on gray
       "splatter" star field .... 10 - 25

ST3038 D-Black w/aqua accents, 2 X-wings w/*SW* logo
       and type .... 10 - 25

ST3039 D-Black, child's w/Luke & Han, guns out, in
       front of large Darth head, X-Wings, Death Star .... 10 - 25

ST3040 D-White "Ewoks" logo in aqua w/glitter as is pond
       below, 2 Ewoks .... 10 - 25

ST3041 D-Black w/front & back Darth Vader supergraphic
       & *SW* triangular logo .... 10 - 25

ST3042 D-Black w/overall front & back C-3PO supergraphic
       & *SW* triangular logo .... 10 - 25

ST3043 D-Heather gray: Jedi Master Yoda, w/full figure illus. 10 - 25

ST3044 D-Heather gray w/black at neck, sleeves: *SW* logo
       embroidered in black outline w/silver fill-in .... 10 - 25

ST3045 D-Black w/battle in front of Death Star, *SW* logo
       in red .... 10 - 25

ST3046 D-Black. Front: Outlined *SW* logo in back of dogfight,
       SW crawl; back is TIE ftr. & exploding Death Star ... 10 - 25

ST3047 D-Black w/Chewbacca in silver letters and portrait
       in brown & gold w/glittery stars in back .... 10 - 25

ST3048 D-Black. Front: Aqua pyramid: "A long time
       ago…" w/*SW* logo Back: A-wing on green grid ...... 10 - 25

ST3049 D-Black w/C-3PO bust in metallic gold and R2-D2
       in silver w/metallic blue streaks .... 10 - 25

ST3050 D-Black w/heather gray: Two X-wngs over aqua
       grid, *SW* logo in yellow .... 10 - 25

ST3510 W-Blue w/ST logo and large TIE interceptor .... 10 - 25

ST3512 W-White w/Rex in silver circle, Dis/MGM logo
       and 'Rex' quote on back .... 10 - 25

ST3513 W-Navy w/large Rex on field of words "Star Tours" .. 10 - 25

ST3514 W-White w/ST logo over diamond-shaped Death
       Star trench .... 10 - 25

ST3515 W-White w/schematic of R2-D2 .... 10 - 25

ST3516 W-White w/schematic of C-3PO .... 10 - 25

ST3517 W-Hot pink w/silver ST logo and Dis/MGM on sleeve 10 - 25

ST3518 W-Black w/puffy ST logo and puffy explosive bursts
       w/white splatters .... 10 - 25

ST3519 W-Black long sleeve w/silver glitter Darth Vader
       on field of type .... 10 - 25

ST3520 W-Black shortsleeve Vader shirt like ST3519 .... 10 - 25

ST3521 W-White w/large Imperial Walker .... 10 - 25

ST3522 W-White w/R2-D2 and C-3PO, Speeder, ST and
       Dis/MGM logo .... 10 - 25

ST3523 W-Black Cutoff w/silver glitter logo .... 10 - 25

ST3524 W-Blue w/silver ST logo and Dis/MGM on sleeve ... 10 - 25

ST3525 W-Gray w/Starspeeder bursting through puffy ice field 10 - 25

ST3526 W-White w/9 squares of R2-D2 in different neon
       color combinations .... 10 - 25

ST3527 W-Black large Darth Vader w/lightsaber; below is
       outline of Luke/Darth duel .... 10 - 25

ST3528 W-Black w/large Darth head in blue, white, blue
       metallic & silver metallic .... 10 - 25

ST3529 W-Black w/*SW* logo & X-wings, Death Star
       w/deep reds and silver metallic .... 10 - 25

ST3810 T-White w/Speeder in front of Death Star, Rex,
       droids, and ST & TD logos .... 10 - 25

ST3811 T-Black Press Kit shirt w/logo & "Now the Adventure…" 10 - 25

ST3812 T-White kids w/blue star field: "Been there,
       Done that…Been to Endor too. Welcome, etc. .... 10 - 25

ST3813 T-White w/stylized yellow C-3PO on blue
       square and "Welcome to…" .... 10 - 25

ST3910 E-Black w/silver glitter ST and stars .... 10 - 25

ST3912 E-Black w/flat silver ST and logo .... 10 - 25

ST3913 E-White w/schematic of R2-D2 .... 10 - 25

ST3914 E-White w/schematic of C-3PO .... 10 - 25

Other shirts

ST4210 D-Aqua sleeveless, blue/orange logo .... 10 - 25

ST4211 D-White sleeveless, blue/orange logo .... 10 - 25

ST4212 D-Red polo w/small logo .... 10 - 25

ST4213 D-Gray polo w/small logo .... 10 - 25

ST4214 D-White crewneck, gray/black logo .... 10 - 25

ST4215 D-Red/white striped boatneck w/logo on pocket .... 10 - 25

ST4216 D-Like ST4215, but blue .... 10 - 25

ST4217 D-White lady's polo, red sleeves, red ST logo on top
       of multi-colors .... 10 - 25

ST4218 D-Black polo, small blue/orange logo .... 10 - 25

ST4219 D-White Ewok nightshirt, Kneesaa & Wicket .... 10 - 25

ST4220 D-Black tanktop w/ST logo in green/yellow
       metallic puffy type .... 10 - 25

ST4510 W-Black polo w/small pink/yellow logo .... 10 - 25

ST4511 W-Like ST4510 but white .... 10 - 25

ST4512 W-White shortsleeve cutoff w/artsy C-3PO in
       green, yellow, pink .... 10 - 25

ST4513 W-Like ST4512, but R2-D2 .... 10 - 25

ST4760 T-Black ribbed longsleeve polo w/pocket logo ...... 10 - 25

ST4761 T-Like ST4760 but white .... 10 - 25

ST4762 T-Black shortsleeve polo w/embroidered pocket logo 10 - 25

ST4763 T-like ST4762 but white .... 10 - 25

BADGES, STICKERS, PATCHES, KEYCHAINS

ST5010 D-Gray metallic bumper sticker .... 3 - 5

ST5011 D-Gray metallic glow-in-dark triangular sticker w/logo 2 - 5

ST5012 D-White/gold logo enameled pin .... 5 - 10

ST5013 D-White/gold logo enameled keychain .... 3 - 5

ST5014 D-Black rectangular "coming soon" badge for
       Imagineering, ILM .... 45 - 65

ST5015 D-Black logo badge .... 5 - 8

ST5016 D-Blue logo badge .... 5 - 8

ST5017 D-Badge w/droids, logo, space scene .... 5 - 10

ST5018 D-ST "wings" pin for press opening .... 25 - 45

ST5019 D-Round C-3PO ST pin: "Disneyland, 35 Years
       of Magic .... 10 -20

ST5020 D-Black logo pin, design in silver & blue) .... 5 - 10

ST5021 D-Black triangle logo keychain .... 5 - 10

D-Silvery "3-D Holographic buttons" on ST card

ST5022 ST logo .... 3 - 5

ST5023 Starspeeder w/logo .... 3 - 5

ST5024 R2-D2 and C-3PO .... 3 - 5

ST5025 D-"3-D Holographic Stickers" .... 5 - 10

D-Two-sided holographic keychains ST5026-29

ST5026 X-wing .... 3 - 5

ST5027 TIE interceptor .... 3 - 5

ST5028 Millennium Falcon .... 3 - 5

156

ST6824 ST6826 ST6910 ST7010 ST7014 ST7012

ST7016 ST7018 ST7410 ST7412 ST7712 ST7714 ST7720

ST7718 ST8614 ST8616 ST8210

ST8610

ST5029	Rex	3 - 5
ST5510	W-Glow-in-dark badge w/logo and Dis/MGM	5 - 10
ST5511	W-Badge w/droids, /ST logo and Dis/MGM	5 - 10
ST5512	W-Blue triangle cloth patch w/ST logo in pink & yellow	5 - 10
ST5513	W-Black rectangle cloth patch w/Star Tours in silver	5 - 10
ST5514	W-Silver metallic bumper sticker	5 - 10
ST5710	T-Triangle glow-in-dark sticker w/droids, logo and TDland	2 - 5
ST5711	T-Vinyl bumper sticker w/Rex. Speeder, droids	3 - 5
ST5712	T-Large silver badge w/space scene	5 - 10
ST5713	T-Like ST5712 but smaller and mirror-backed	5 - 12
ST5714	T-White enameled keychain w/logo	5 - 10
ST5715	T-Like ST5714 but black	5 - 10
ST5716	T-Square Lucite keychain w/black logo embedded	5 - 10
ST5717	T-ST Tokyo Dland "wings" pin for press opening	35 - 55
ST5718	T-Mini slide puzzle keychain w/C-3PO & speeder	15 - 30
ST5910	E-Clear plastic square keychain w/logo & EuroDland	10 - 12

CARRYALLS

ST6010	D-Black wet-look nylon bag w/straps; silver & blue Starspeeder going w/ST logo	15 - 25
ST6012	D-Backpack like ST6010	15 - 25
ST6014	D-Belly-bag like ST6010	10 - 20
ST6016	D-Wallet like ST6010	10 -15
ST6510	W-Black cloth bag w/silver sparkle logo	10 - 15
ST6512	W-Black nylon barrel bag w/ST logo in blue & silver	15 - 25
ST6514	W-Belly-bag like ST6512	10 - 20
ST6516	W-Shaving kit like ST6512	10 - 20
ST6518	W-Wallet like ST6512	10 - 15
ST6810	T-Black nylon zippered briefcase for Press Opening w/metal ST Tokyo Dland logo riveted on, "Star Tours Travel Agency" printed	60 - 125
ST6812	T-Black nylon shaving kit w/small metal ST logo	25 - 40
ST6814	T-Zippered wallet like ST6812	15 - 25
ST6816	T-Black nylon draw-string bookbag w/logo & TDland	15 - 20
ST6818	T-Like ST6816 but gray	15 - 20
ST6820	T-Black "sandwich" bag like ST6816	10 - 15
ST6822	T-Like ST6820 but gray	10 - 15
ST6824	T-Black nylon round zippered change purse w/ST, TD logos	10 - 15
ST6826	T-Black vinyl belly-bag w/orange satin patch & metal riveted ST logo	20 - 35
ST6910	E-Silver metallic polyester backpack w/logo in black	20 - 35
ST6912	E-Belly-bag like ST6910	15 - 25

CUPS, MUGS, GLASSES, PLATES, TRAYS

ST7010	D-Plastic mug, blue or white	4 - 8
ST7012	D-Tall silver ceramic mug	4 - 8
ST7014	D-Shorter silver ceramic mug	4 - 8

ST7016	D-Clear plastic double-walled tumblers w/pink liquid, glitter and TIE fighters floating inside	5 - 10
ST7018	D-Tumbler w/logo and droids	4 - 8
ST7410	W-White ceramic mug w/R2-D2	3 - 8
ST7412	W-White ceramic mug w/C-3PO	3 - 8
ST7710	T-White china tea cup w/logo	10 - 20
ST7712	T-Juice glass w/logo and droids	10 - 20
ST7714	T-Boxed china "Picture Plate" similar to Mylar poster	20 - 35
ST7716	T-Boxed ceramic ash tray w/logo, R2-D2, C-3PO	15 - 25
ST7718	T-Small rectangular tin tray w/Rex, Speeder, droids	15 - 25
ST7720	T-Round tin ash tray w/logo, droids	15 - 25
ST7910	E-Silver ceramic coffee mug w/logo, larger handle, different copyright	5 - 10

POSTERS, CARDS, PENNANTS

For posters, see—**POSTERS, LOBBY CARDS, PRESS KITS, ETC.**

ST8210	D-Cloth pennant	10 - 15

D-Postcards, 4 designs from ST posters ST8212-18

ST8212	ST theme poster	1 - 3
ST8214	Endor (Ewok forest home)	1 - 3
ST8216	Bespin (Cloud city)	1 - 3
ST8218	Tatooine (Jabba's palace)	1 - 3
ST8410	W-Cloth pennant	10 - 15
ST8610	T-Cloth pennant w/silver edge	15 - 25
ST8614	T-Foil postcard similar to Tokyo Dland Mylar poster	5 - 10
ST8616	T-Foil postcard similar to Dland "Ultimate Adventure" poster	5 - 10

E-3 Postcards w/EuroD on reverse

ST8810	*Star Wars* French poster	2 - 5
ST8812	*Empire* French poster	2 - 5
ST8814	*Jedi* French poster	2 - 5

STATIONERY ITEMS

ST9010	D-Ewok Color-Me cards	10 - 15
ST9012	D-Black rubberized mechanical pencil	3 - 5
ST9014	D-Black fat marker pen	3 - 5
ST9016	D-3-pen set: R2-D2, C-3PO, logo	5 - 8

D-Metallized pencils w/ST logo, speeder, droids, Rex ST9020-24

ST9020	Prism: silver or gold	1 - 2
ST9022	Stripes: silver or gold	1 - 2
ST9024	Stars: silver	1 - 2

ST9210

ST9310

ST9320

ST9316

ST9504

ST9510

ST9540

ST9712

ST9722

ST9723

ST9611

ST9524-29

ST9616

ST9618

ST9620

X-WING FIGHTER SQUADRON

HAN SOLO

BATTLE STATION

ST9724

ST9726

ST9728

ST9731

ST9730

ST9732

ST9505

ST9210	W-Rubber stamp set	5 - 10
ST9212	W-Notepad & pen set	5 - 10
ST9310	T-Tin pencil case w/Rex , front screen of Speeder	15 - 25
ST9312	T-Pen stand w/logo in Lucite	15 - 25
ST9314	T-Carded set of 3 black w/silver logo pencils	10 - 20
ST9316	T-Pencils w/dimensional Speeder: pink, green, blue	8 - 12
ST9320	T-Plastic pens w/"Star Tours," blue, orange, or black	5 - 12
ST9324	T-Clear plastic ruler	5 - 12

MISCELLANEOUS

ST9504	D-Boarding pass, January 8-9, 1987	15 - 25
ST9505	D-Admission bracelet, January 9-11, 1987	10 - 15
ST9510	D-Plush baby Ewok w/pink shawl	10 - 15
ST9511	D-Plush large Ewok w/green shawl	12 - 20
ST9512	D-Color-Me T-shirts (small pkg: Wicket, Kneesaa, Ewok group	10 - 15
ST9516	D-Color-Me T-shirts (large pkg: Wicket, Kneesaa, group, Latara ,Teebo	12 - 20
ST9520	D-Rubber figures from Spain: R2-D2, C-3PO, Ewok, ea.	2 - 5
ST9524-29	D-Rubber figures from China w/different paint job: R2-D2, C-3PO, Ewok, Yoda, trooper, Chewie, ea.	2 - 5
ST9540	D-ST Dland logo watch (opening weekend giveaway)	25 - 50
ST9541	D-Tomorrowland Slide Set #1	5 - 10
ST9544	D-Tomorrowland 3-reel Viewmaster set w/viewer	8 - 12
ST9546	D-Black water bottle, ST logo silver & blue Speeder	5- 12
ST9548	D-Videocassette: A Disneyland Day—Relive the Memories	12 - 20
ST9550	D-Clear plastic box w/M&Ms, silver R2-D2, gold C-3PO, ST logo	4 - 8
ST9551	D-Plastic "Robot Claw" w/SW sleeve and illus. of C-3PO	6 - 12
ST9552	D-Laser Space Pistol: silverized plastic, w/SW logo on Luke card	10 - 20
ST9610	W-Vader watch (black face w/gold outlined Vader)	30 - 45

ST9611	W-Water bottle w/black & silver logo	5 - 12
ST9613	W-Magnets: R2-D2; C-3PO, each	3 - 5
ST9615	W-Imperial Lord/Darth Vader "street sign"	5 - 12
ST9616	W-HQ/X-wing fighter Squadron "street sign"	5 - 12
ST9617	W-Moon of Endor/Ewok Village "street sign"	5 - 12
ST9618	W-Cpt. Millennium Falcon/Han Solo "street sign"	5 - 12
ST9619	W-Comdr. Rebel Alliance/Luke Skywalker "street sign"	5 - 12
ST9620	W-Millennium Falcon/Battle Station "street sign"	5 - 12
ST9710	T-Large rocketship-like inflatable raft w/ST Tokyo Dland logo & Panasonic insignia; premium	75 - 150
ST9712	T-Circular chair pad (black latch-hook rug w/logo)	35 - 50
ST9714	T-Hand towels w/embr. logo, blue or white, each	8 - 15
ST9716	T-Washcloths w/embr.logo, blue or white, each	5 - 15
ST9718	T-Silk scarf w/main poster scene	15 - 30
ST9720	T-Silk ad banner for opening	35 - 50
ST9722	T-Telephone card like litho entrance poster	20 - 30
ST9723	T-Telephone card, silver w/Speeder & C-3PO	20 - 30
ST9724	T-Press badge for opening, silver phone card in vinyl case	50 - 75
ST9726	T-300-piece jigsaw puzzle of litho entrance poster	15- 25
ST9728	T-Tin bank shaped like spacecraft	20 -35
ST9730	T-Black hand-held plastic mirror	10 - 20
ST9731	T-Brushed aluminum bottle opener	15 - 25
ST9732	T-Brushed aluminum spoon	15 - 25
ST9733	T-Commemorative holographic watch in plastic box w/wings pin for press	50 - 100
ST9736	T-Opening Day cardboard press kit "briefcase" w/press kit, 5 color slides, watch, t-shirt	50 - 75
ST9740	T-Pop-up invitation to ST party	20 - 35

ST9740

ST9743　　ST9820

ST9736

SY0010　　SY0320　　SY0450　　SY0560

SY0800　　SY0850　　SY1010　　SY1012　　SY1025　　SY1029

ST9742	T-Adult brown plush Ewok w/brown shawl	20 - 30
ST9743	T-Baby brown plush Ewok w/brown shawl	15 - 25
ST9744	T-Rubber figures from China as keychains: C-3PO, Yoda, Ewok, Trooper, Vader, Chewie. each	6 - 12
ST9810	E-Rubber figures from China: R2-D2, C-3PO, Yoda, Darth, Chewie, stormtrooper, Ewok, each	5 - 10
ST9820	E-Silver yo-yo w/black ST logo	12 - 25

STATIONERY/SCHOOL SUPPLIES

ADDRESS BOOKS (Antioch Publishing Co.)

SY0010	Drew Struzan cover art from "Glove of Darth Vader"	3 - 6
	England (H.C. Ford and Sons)	
SY0110	*ESB* address book	5 - 10

BINDERS, RING
Mead Corp.

SY0210	*SW*: Chewie & Han/Star Destroyer cover w/clip, notepad, file pockets	10 - 20
SY0211	*SW*: Photos of Leia, Luke, Obi Wan, Han	10 - 20
SY0212	*SW*: R2-D2 and C-3PO	10 - 20
SY0213	*SW*: Darth Vader photo	10 - 20
Stuart Hall		
SY0320	*ESB*: Darth and storm-troopers polybinder	5 - 12
SY0321	*ESB*: Luke on Dagobah	5 - 12
SY0322	*ESB*: Yoda seated	5 - 12
SY0323	*ESB*: C-3PO & R2-D2	5 - 12
SY0324	*ESB*: Aliens, 2-1B, bounty hunters, Ugnaught, Probot	5 - 12
	Australia (Reding Stationery)	
SY0450	*ESB*: C-3PO	5 - 15
	England (Letraset)	
SY0560	*SW*: X-wing fighter	10 - 25
	Japan (Tokyo Queen Co.)	
SY0670	R2-D2 & C-3PO	15 - 25
SY0671	Stormtroopers	15 - 25
SY0672	X-wing fighter	15 - 25
SY0673	Darth Vader	15 - 25

BOOK COVERS (Butterfly Originals)

SY0800	*ROTJ*: Speeder bikers backed w/Jabba	2 - 5
	Italy (Regis)	
SY0850	*ESB* plastic coated	2 - 5

CHALK OR MARKER BOARDS (Manton Cork Corp.)

SY0910	*ESB* chalkboard	15 - 25
SY0915	*ROTJ* Wicket & R2-D2	15 - 25
	Spain (Midena)	
SY0950	Droids board with felt-tip pen, bull's eye target	15 - 25

CORK BOARDS (Manton Cork Corp.)

SY1010	*SW* logo, explosion & spacecraft	15 - 25
SY1012	*SW* logo: Darth, Boba Fett, stormtroopers	15 - 25
SY1014	*SW* logo: Luke, Leia, Han, droids, Chewbacca	15 - 25
SY1021	*ESB* Yoda	15 - 25
SY1023	*ESB* Yoda, glow-in-dark	15 - 25
SY1025	*ESB* Darth Vader, full	15 - 25
SY1026	*ESB* Vader, head & torso	15 - 25
SY1029	*ESB* R2-D2 and C-3PO, figural (2 board set)	15 - 25
SY1031	*ESB* Luke on tauntaun, die-cut	15 - 25
ESB **Glo-Domes (glow-in-dark)**		
SY1112	AT-AT	10 - 20
SY1113	Chewbacca	10 - 20
SY1114	Darth Vader	10 - 20
SY1115	Luke on tauntaun	10 - 20
SY1116	C-3PO/R2-D2	10 - 20
SY1117	Yoda	10 - 20
ROTJ **non-glow**		
SY1231	*ROTJ* Ewoks home, 17x23	10 - 20
SY1232	*ROTJ* Jabba's palace, 17x23	10 - 20
SY1233	*ROTJ* Jabba, 11x17	10 - 20
SY1234	*ROTJ* Rebo band, 11x17	10 - 20
SY1235	*ROTJ* Darth/Luke duel 11x17	10 - 20
SY1236	*ROTJ* Ewoks/droids 11x17	10 - 20
SY1237	*ROTJ* Millennium Falcon, "May the Force…"	10 - 25

DESK CARDS

| | **Japan (Sankikogyo Co.)** | |
| SY1350 | *SW* assorted paper & plastic desk cards, each | 10 - 20 |

ENVELOPES

	England (Letraset)	
SY1450	*SW*: Droids/stormtrooper, 12-pack	10 - 15
	Japan	
SY1470	*SW*: Blue, Vader head & logo, 10-pack	10 - 20
SY1471	*SW*: White, X-wng. & Y-wngs.	10 - 20
SY1472	*SW*: White/lavender, droids	10 - 20

SY1031

SY1114

SY1116

SY1232

SY1234

SY1235

SY1236

SY1610

SY1611

SY1612

SY1614

SY1615

SY1616

SY1617

SY1618

SY1625

SY1450

SY1650

SY1656

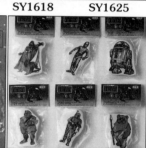
SY1670

SY1665

SY1680

SY1690

Box for SY1680

SY1664

SY1900

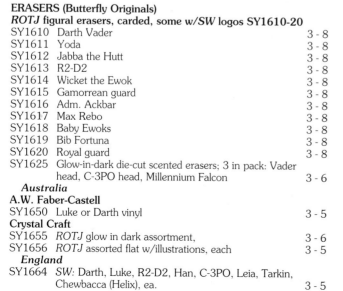

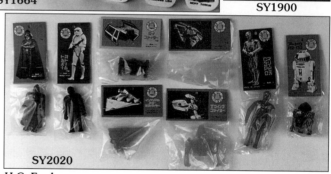
SY2020

ERASERS (Butterfly Originals)
ROTJ figural erasers, carded, some w/*SW* logos SY1610-20

SY1610	Darth Vader	3 - 8
SY1611	Yoda	3 - 8
SY1612	Jabba the Hutt	3 - 8
SY1613	R2-D2	3 - 8
SY1614	Wicket the Ewok	3 - 8
SY1615	Gamorrean guard	3 - 8
SY1616	Adm. Ackbar	3 - 8
SY1617	Max Rebo	3 - 8
SY1618	Baby Ewoks	3 - 8
SY1619	Bib Fortuna	3 - 8
SY1620	Royal guard	3 - 8
SY1625	Glow-in-dark die-cut scented erasers; 3 in pack: Vader head, C-3PO head, Millennium Falcon	3 - 6

Australia
A.W. Faber-Castell

SY1650	Luke or Darth vinyl	3 - 5

Crystal Craft

SY1655	*ROTJ* glow in dark assortment,	3 - 6
SY1656	*ROTJ* assorted flat w/illustrations, each	3 - 5

England

SY1664	*SW*: Darth, Luke, R2-D2, Han, C-3PO, Leia, Tarkin, Chewbacca (Helix), ea.	3 - 5

H.C. Ford

SY1665	*SW* purfumed erasers: Leia, Darth, Chewie, Luke, Han, or droids, ea.	3 - 5
SY1670	*ROTJ* flat, die-cut: R2-D2, Wicket, C-3PO, Gamorrean guard, Darth Vader, Bob Fett, ea.	3 - 5
SY1680	*ROTJ* perfumed erasers, in small plastic cases w/paper labels: Chewbacca, Wicket, droids, Han Solo, Darth Vader, Gamorrean guard, ea.	3 - 5
SY1690	*ROTJ* record erasers, shaped like LPs in album cover; colors are yellow, pink, gray w/2 covers: Luke/Vader duel, hands holding lightsaber upright, each	5 - 8

Finland (Playmix/Brio Scanditoy Oy)

SY1790	*ROTJ* erasers	3 - 5

Mexico (Personajes Registrados)

SY1900	*ROTJ* erasers	3 - 5

Box for SY2020	SY2040	SY2110	SY2120	SY2120	SY2120
SY2130	SY2130	SY2130	SY2130	SY2130	SY2130
SY2200		SY2280		SY2530	SY2531	SY2650
SY2350	SY2351	SY2352	SY2353	SY2354	SY2355

New Zealand **(Fortuna Industries Ltd.)**
SY1920 *ROTJ* erasers .... 3 - 5
Japan
Kosumosu Co.
SY1955 *ESB* mini-eraser .... 5 - 10
Maruka Toy Co.
SY2020 *SW* figural in various colors: Darth Vader, R2-D2,
stormtrooper, C-3PO, Y-wing, X-wing, Vader TIE ftr.,
sandcrawler, Star Destroyer, landspeeder, Milnm.
Falcon, in packs w/headers, each .... 8 - 15
Takara
SY2040 R2-D2 figural w/eraser as middle "leg" ... 15 - 25
Singapore **(A and T International Ltd.)**
SY2060 *ESB* erasers .... 2 - 5
Switzerland **(Uranium)**
SY2090 *ROTJ* radiergummi gomme .... 2 - 5

FOLDERS (PORTFOLIOS), FILE BOXES
SY2110 *SW*: Leia/Luke; Vader/Stormtroopers; Droids/
Droids; Obi-Wan/Troopers; Luke, Chewie, Han;
X-wing/TIE fighter, (Mead) ea. .... 8 - 12
Stuart Hall
SY2120 *ESB*: Darth and stormtroopers; Yoda; Luke on
Dagobah; C-3PO & R2-D2;5 photos, each ... 5 - 10
SY2130 *ROTJ*: Max Rebo Band; C-3PO, R2-D2 &
Wicket; Darth/Luke/Emperor; Jabba & Salacious
Crumb; Speeder bikers; B-wing & TIE ftr., each ... 5 - 10
Finland **(Playmix)**
SY2180 *ROTJ*: Death Star .... 8 - 12

Japan **(Tokyo Queen)**
SY2200 *SW* plastic file boxes: Stormtroopers; Darth Vader;
X-wing dogfight; Droids, ea. .... 25 - 35
SY2220 *ROTJ*: Lightsaber .... 8 - 12
Switzerland **(Uranium)**
SY2280 *ROTJ*: Droids; C-3PO; Vader, ea. .... 8 - 12

FRAMED ART
England
Silver-painted wood frames w/5" *ESB* art (Icarus) SY2350-55
SY2350 Darth Vader .... 20 - 30
SY2351 Luke Skywalker .... 20 - 30
SY2352 R2-D2 and C-3PO .... 20 - 30
SY2353 Yoda .... 20 - 30
SY2354 Chewbacca .... 20 - 30
SY2355 Boba Fett .... 20 - 30

GLUE/TAPE (Butterfly Originals)
SY2530 *ROTJ* color glue .... 3 - 6
SY2531 *ROTJ* tape dispenser/tape .... 4 - 8
Italy **(Beecham Italia S.p.A.)**
SY2650 *ROTJ*: UHU glue stick w/Kenner Ewok figure ... 30 - 60

GREETING CARDS (Drawing Board Greeting Cards Inc.)
See also—**CAST AND CREW**
SW juvenile birthday SY2800-05
SY2800 Chewbacca, 7 years .... 4 - 8
SY2801 Stormtrooper, 8 .... 4 - 8
SY2802 R2-D2, 9 .... 4 - 8

SY2803	Obi-Wan, 10	4 - 8
SY2804	Darth Vader, 11	4 - 8
SY2805	C-3PO, 12	4 - 8
SY2808	Mother's Day card	4 - 8
SY2809	Father's Day card	4 - 8

SW blue-border birthday, friendship, get well w/blue envelopes

SY2810	C-3PO, "Haven't written"	4 - 8
SY2811	Vader arm raised, "Write!"	4 - 8
SY2812	Chewie, "You're weird"	4 - 8
SY2813	Millennium Falcon, "Greetings"	4 - 8
SY2814	Droids in desert, "Lost"	4 - 8
SY2815	Obi-Wan, "May the Force"	4 - 8
SY2816	Dogfight, "Haven't had a minute"	4 - 8
SY2817	C-3PO, Luke, "Make 'em like you"	4 - 8
SY2818	Droids, "Happy Birthday"	4 - 8
SY2819	Luke firing, "HB"	4 - 8
SY2820	R2-D2, "HB"	4 - 8
SY2821	Vader full figure, "HB"	4 - 8
SY2822	Garbage pit, "HB"	4 - 8

SY2823	Droids, star-field, "HB"	4 - 8
SY2824	C-3PO, "Rusty? Get well"	4 - 8
SY2825	Chewie, "Not feeling well?"	4 - 8

SW Christmas

SY2830	Droids, star-field	5 - 8
SY2831	Obi-Wan	5 - 8
SY2832	SY2831 in 6-pack	15 - 20
SY2833	R2-D2 w/wreath	4 - 8
SY2834	X-wings	4 - 8
SY2835	SY2834 in 6-pack	15 - 20
SY2836	R2-D2 beaming Leia	4 - 8
SY2837	C-3PO w/Santa cap	4 - 8
SY2838	Droids in Santa caps	4 - 8
SY2839	SY2838 in 6-pack	15 - 20
SY2840	Chewbacca	4 - 8
SY2841	SY2840 in 6-pack	15 - 20
SY2842	Luke/Chewbacca/Han	4 - 8

SW Valentines

SY2845	Darth "Space Bulletin…"	4 - 8

SY2860   SY2864   SY2861   SY2865   SY2866   SY2863   SY2867   SY2862   SY2870   SY2868

SY2880   SY2881   SY2882   SY2883   SY2884   SY2885   SY2886   SY2887

SY2890   SY2892   SY2914   SY2915   SY2912   SY2910   SY2917   SY2916   SY2913   SY2911

SY2922   SY2930   SY2940   SY3030   SY3031   SY3034   SY3036   SY3039

SY2846	Droids "To Son…"	4 - 8
SY2847	R2-D2 "A Valentine Message…"	4 - 8
SY2848	C-3PO "Valentine Greetings"	4 - 8
SW Halloween, w/orange envelopes		
SY2850	Luke firing, "Deflector shields"	4 - 10
SY2851	Leia "For daughter"	4 - 10
SY2852	Dogfight, "Earthling boy"	4 - 10
SY2853	Millennium Falcon, "Earthling girl"	4 - 10
SY2854	Luke/Chewie/Han, "From The Alliance"	4 - 10
SY2855	Vader & bats, "Happy Halloween"	4 - 10
SY2856	C-3PO w/mask, "Trick or treat"	4 - 10
SY2857	Chewie & bats, "Do not fear"	4 - 10
SY2858	Obi-Wan & bats, "May the Force"	4 - 10
SW die-cut		
SY2860	Obi-Wan, "Happy Birthday"	5 - 12
SY2861	R2-D2, "Hello Earthling"	5 - 12
SY2862	Droids, "About your malfunction"	5 - 12
SY2863	Luke/Leia/Han, "HB"	5 - 12
SY2864	Stormtrooper, "HB"	5 - 12
SY2865	C-3PO, "HB"	5 - 12
SY2866	Darth Vader, "HB"	5 - 12
SY2867	Chewbacca, "HB"	5 - 12
ESB die-cut		
SY2868	Yoda, "Live to 800"	5 - 12
SY2869	Luke/Tauntaun, "HB"	5 - 12
SY2870	Boba Fett, "HB"	5 - 12
ESB fold-out birthday game cards		
SY2875	Leia/Chewie/Han on Cloud City, maze	4 - 10
SY2876	Vader in asteroid belt, maze	4 - 10
SY2877	Yoda on Dagobah, find hidden items in swamp	4 - 10
ROTJ birthday, friendship SY2880-87		
SY2880	Vader/Royal guards, "May the Force"	4 - 8
SY2881	Leia/Mogaar, "Special friend"	4 - 8
SY2882	Luke/Leia on speeder bike, "Thrilling birthday"	4 - 8
SY2883	C-3PO/Ewoks, "Royal birthday"	4 - 8
SY2884	Rebo band, "Birthday note"	4 - 8

SY2885	Ewoks, "Birthday surprises"	4 - 8
SY2886	Vader, Birthday command	4 - 8
SY2887	Wicket/R2-D2, "HB friend"	4 - 8
SY2890	*SW/ROTJ* classroom valentines, die cut or wrapped box	10 - 20
SY2892	Ewoks classroom valentines, die cut or wrapped box	8 - 15
SW/ROTJ embossed birthday		
SY2910	Droids, Gamorrean guard, aliens at party	5 - 8
SY2911	Female Ewok w/flowers	5 - 8
SY2912	Droids, R2-D2 carried aloft by balloons	5 - 8
SY2913	Droids in landspeeder	5 - 8
SY2914	Droids, C-3PO in chef's hat holding HB cake	5 - 8
SY2915	R2-D2 in forest w/Hoojibs	5 - 8
SY2916	R2-D2 one-droid band	5 - 8
SY2917	C-3PO a la Rodin's "Thinker"	5 - 8
Ewoks birthday, cartoon art by Pat Paris SY2920-27		
SY2920	Archery practice	4 - 8
SY2921	Swimming hole	4 - 8
SY2922	Baby Ewoks	4 - 8
SY2923	Fishing	4 - 8
SY2924	Hang-gliding	4 - 8
SY2925	Making music	4 - 8
SY2926	Learning about nature	4 - 8
SY2927	Kneesaa and Baga	4 - 8
SY2930	Kenner Preschool Birthday Club Card	5 - 10
Portal Publications		
SY2940	*SW* Classic: Main characters, die-cut fold-out "HB"	3 - 5
***Australia* (Hallmark Australia Ltd.)**		
SY3030	*ROTJ* Leia/Luke "HB"	4 - 8
SY3031	Stormtrooper "HB"	4 - 8
SY3032	Darth Vader birthday	4 - 8
SY3033	C-3PO and R2-D2 "HB"	4 - 8
SY3034	Wicket "You're my Favorite Human"	4 - 8
SY3035	C-3PO, "I like you"	4 - 8
SY3036	Jedi Cast	4 - 8
SY3037	Paploo "Keep Smiling"	4 - 8
SY3038	Sy Snoodles "I want the Truth"	4 - 8

SY3100

SY3410 SY3490 SY3556 SY3550 SY3552 SY3870 SY3880

SY3885 SY4000 SY4100 SY4150 SY4430

SY4410 SY4510 SY4520 SY4520 SY4530 SY4615

SY4620 SY4730 SY4821 SY4822 SY4840 SY4841 SY4842

SY3039	R2 and Wicket "Strange and Wonderful"	4 - 8
	Netherlands	
SY3100	Ewoks, 24 designs, ea.	3 - 6

LABELS
Australia **(Ancol)**

SY3410	*ESB* 6 school-book labels	5 - 10
	Netherlands	
SY3490	*ESB* 6 school lables	5 - 10

MARKERS **(Butterfly Originals)**

SY3550	*ROTJ* logo black, blue markers on C-3PO card	4 - 8
SY3552	*ROTJ* Darth Vader figural felt tip markers, individually bagged: black, red, blue, purple	5 - 10
SY3556	*ROTJ* thin markers w/Vader dimensional head on clip: black, blue, purple	3 - 6
	England	
SY3670	*SW* 10-color "fibre tip" set (Helix)	20 - 35

SY3680	*SW/ROTJ* markers w/*SW* logo and Luke, Vader, droids (H.C. Ford)	3 - 6

MEMO/MESSAGE BOARDS **(Junior Achievement of Cincinnati)**

SY3820	*SW* black plastic Message Center; 500 sold as project with Kenner & LFL permission	100 - 150
	Australia **(Reding)**	
SY3870	*ESB* clipboard	10 - 15
	England **(Icarus)**	
SY3880	*SW* logo memo boards w/wipe-off markers: Darth Vader; Leia, Han and Luke, ea.	15 - 20
SY3885	*ROTJ* logo memo boards w/wipe-off markers: AT-AT, R2-D2 & C-3PO, Chewbacca, ea.	15 - 20

MEMO PADS/BOOKS **(Stuart Hall)**

SY4000	*ESB* pocket memo pads: Boba Fett; Yoda; Luke; Aliens; C-3PO & R2-D2; Vader & stormtroopers, ea.	4 - 8

164

SY4825   **SY5500**

SY5150   **SY5504**

SY5508   **SY5520**   **SY5900**   **SY5902**

SY5935

SY5940   **SY5942**   **SY5944**

SY5946   **SY5970**   **SY6000**

England

SY4100	*SW: Stormtrooper Manual mini-notebook (Letraset)*	4 - 10
SY4150	*ROTJ pocket memo pads: Yoda/Luke/Vader; Droids/ Vader; Chewbacca/Han, ea. (H.C. Ford)*	2 - 4
SY4160	*ROTJ mini memo pads: Han; Droids; Leia; Vader; Luke X-wng. pilot; Yoda, ea. (H.C. Ford)*	1 - 3

NOTEBOOKS

SY4410	*SW spiral notebooks: Vader; Stormtroopers; Chewie & Han, R2-D2 & C-3PO; Leia, Luke, Obi-Wan, Han, (Mead) ea.*	6 - 12
SY4430	Mini-notebook w/Drew Struzan art cover (Antioch)	3 - 5

Stuart Hall

SY4510	*ESB 84-sheet spiral notebooks: C-3PO & R2-D2; Vader & troopers; Luke on Dagobah; Aliens, 2-1B, Ugnaught, Probot, bounty hunters; Bespin hallway, Hoth troopers, Luke, ea.*	5 - 10
SY4520	*ESB 50-sheet spiral notebooks: Vader silhouette; Chewbacca; Han/Leia/Luke on Hoth; Yoda; Boba Fett; Star Destroyer vs. Millennium Falcon; Vader in carbon freeze chamber; Han, Lando, Luke, Leia, Vader; Droids; ea.*	5 - 10
SY4530	*ROTJ 54-sheet spiral notebooks: Max Rebo Band; C-3PO, R2-D2 & Wicket; Darth/Luke/Emperor; Jabba & Salacious Crumb; Speeder bikers; B-wing & TIE fighter, ea.*	4 - 8

Australia (Reding Stationery)

SY4610	*ESB Project book*	5 - 10
SY4615	*ESB top-spiral steno notebook: Probot, 3 others, ea.*	5 - 10
SY4620	*ESB stapled 128-pg exercise book: Yoda, 3 others, ea.*	5 - 10

Columbia (Carvajal)

SY4730	*SW notebook*	4 - 8

England

H.C. Ford

SY4820	*ROTJ hard-cover small log books (diaries): Chewie/ Han/Falcon/Vader; Droids/Luke/X-wing/Vader, ea.*	5 - 10
SY4821	Notebook, Luke & Leia	5 - 10
SY4822	*ROTJ Exercise Book*	5 - 10
SY4825	*ROTJ mini-notebooks: Boba Fett; X-wing; Obi-Wan; Lando Calrissian, ea.*	3 - 5

Letraset

SY4840	*SW R2-D2's Memory Bank, 56-page lined notebook*	5 - 15
SY4841	*SW C-3PO's Exercise Book, 24-page lined & stapled*	5 - 15
SY4842	*SW Chewbacca's space notes*	5 - 15

Finland (Playmix)

SY4880	*ROTJ notebooks, each,*	4 - 8

Japan

SY5000	*SW lined spiral notebooks; main cover photos: Droids; Stormtroopers; C-3PO (Tokyo Queen), ea.*	10 - 20

SY5010	*SW lines stapled notebooks: Escape Pod; Hildebrandt art; Vader; Droids (Tokyo Queen), ea.*	10 - 20
SY5040	*ESB mini-notebooks, ea (Kosumosu Co.)*	10 - 15

Mexico (Kimberly Clark)

SY5150	*ROTJ notebooks, ea.*	5 - 10

NOTECARDS (Drawing Board)

SY5500	*SW: Droids art, blank, box of 10 w/envelopes*	10 - 20
SY5502	*SW Hildebrandt art, blank, box of 10 w/envelopes*	10 - 20
SY5504	*SW 3 assorted, blank, box of 12 w/envelopes: C-3PO; Vader; Chewbacca*	10 - 20
SY5508	*SW R2-D2 fold-overs, box of 12*	10 - 25
SY5510	*SW: R2-D2 Thank You cards, 8-pack w/envelopes*	10 - 15
SY5520	*Ewoks notecards, 4 designs, ea.*	3 - 5

England (Westbrook Publications)

SY5750	*ROTJ blank cards, logo plus assorted characters, ea.*	3 - 5

NOTEPADS/WRITING PADS

Drawing Board

SY5900	*SW: Wookiee Doodle Pad*	5 - 10
SY5902	*SW: Official Duty Roster (notepad w/Vader)*	5 - 10
SY5910	*ROTJ: Droppin' a line… (Ewoks on vine notepad)*	5 - 10
SY5912	*ROTJ: Notes (Ewok w/horn notepad)*	5 - 10

Stuart Hall

SY5930	*ESB tablets: Droids; Falcon & Star Dest.; 5 diff., ea.*	8 - 12
SY5935	*ESB Learn to Letter & Write tablets: Vader & troopers; Yoda; Boba Fett; Luke, ea.*	8 - 15
SY5940	*ROTJ Pencil Tablet: Wicket and R2-D2, 50 sheets*	5 - 12
SY5942	*ROTJ Doodle Pad: Rebo band*	4 - 10
SY5944	*ROTJ Scribble Pad: Droids outside Jabba's palace*	4 - 10
SY5946	*ROTJ Learn to Letter: Ewoks hang-gliding*	4 - 8

Australia (Reding)

SY5970	*ESB unlined jotter: Probot, 3 other designs*	8 - 15

Colombia (Carvajal)

SY5980	*ESB writing pads, multi-photo front with covers in red, green, orange, yellow, ea.*	5 - 12

England

SY6000	*SW: Princess Leia's Rebel Jotter, 50 sheets, (Letraset)*	10 - 15
SY6010	*ROTJ Sketch Pad (H.C. Ford)*	5 - 10

Finland (Playmix/Brio)

SY6020	*ROTJ pocket notebooks, ea.*	4 - 8
SY6030	*ROTJ mini-notebooks, ea.*	3 - 5

Greece (A Paullis)

SY6050	*ROTJ pencil tablets, ea.*	3 - 6

Japan

Rapport

SY6095	*ESB laminated desk sheet*	5 - 15

Box for SY6150   SY6150   SY6155

SY6100   *ROTJ* laminated desk sheet   5 - 15

Tokyo Queen
SY6150   *SW* Laminated cards, 4 diff., ea.   10 - 20
SY6155   *SW:* Lined bound notebooks: Vader/Rebel flight
       bay; Droids/Trooper in light tunnel; Dogfight/
       Droids; Escape Pod, ea.   10 - 20
SY6160   *SW:* Vinyl tri-fold cases w/mini-notepads, 8
       collectors' cards, class schedule card; fronts:
       Stormtroopers in desert; Vader; C-3PO & R2-D2;
       Han & Chewie, ea.   15 - 30

Yukari
SY6185   *SW* writing pad, Hildebrandt art w/plastic overlay   15 - 25
SY6186   *SW:* small dual-fold plastic cases w/pocket calendar,
       address card, class schedule: black, blue, green,
       white, ea.   12 - 25

PAPER (Stuart Hall)
SY6210   *ROTJ* Biker Scout colored construction paper pad   5 - 10
    Australia **(Reding Stationery)**
SY6240   *ESB:* Chewie looseleaf refill   3 - 5

PENCILS, PENCIL-TOPS
Butterfly Originals
SY6420   *ROTJ* character pencils: silver w/many characters;
       red w/Darth; gold w/C-3PO, packs of 4   5 - 10
SY6421   SY6420, retailer box   6 - 12
SY6430   *ROTJ* Pop-a-Point pencils, 2-pack, glittery red w/refills   4 - 8
SY6435   *ROTJ* Pop-a-Point color pencils, 6-pack   5 - 10
SY6440   *ROTJ* character-top pencils, B&W logo, art
       w/dimensional character tops: Vader; Royal
       guard; C-3PO; Wicket, ea.   4 - 8
Fantasma, Inc.
SY6465   *SW* Classic dichromate pencils: Darth Vader, 2 diff., ea.   2 - 5
SW/Lucasfilm Fan Club
SY6500   *SW* pencil, black on silver logo and character strip   3 - 5
SY6510   *ESB* pencils: red or blue logo and character strip   3 - 5

England
Helix
SY6560   *SW* regular pencils w/logo and "May the Force..."   2 - 4
SY6562   *SW* colored pencils like SY6560, box of 12 w/
       Stormtroopers on front   20 - 30
H.C. Ford
SY6575   *SW* logo pencil, 6-sided, mainly red white & blue
       w/Vader head   2 - 4
SY6580   *SW* logo perfumed square pencils: R2-D2 & C-3PO;
       Han & Chewie; Luke & Leia; Vader &
       Stormtrooper, ea.   2 - 4
SY6585   *SW* logo 4 colors in 1 pencils   2 - 4
SY6590   *SW* tag pencils w/puffy plastic starburst hanging
       from end: Vader; Luke & Leia; Droids, ea.   4 - 8
SY6500   *ROTJ* hand-painted molded vinyl pencil top figures:
       Adm. Ackbar; Gamorrean guard; Wicket; Royal guard;
       Vader; Bib Fortuna; Yoda; Luke X-wing pilot; Chewie;
       R2-D2; Han in Hoth parka, ea.   3 - 7
    Finland **(Playmix/Brio)**
SY6730   *ROTJ* square pencils   2 - 4
SY6734   *ROTJ* 4-in-1 pencils   2 - 4
SY6740   *ROTJ* tag pencils/markers   3 - 7
    Japan **(Rapport)**
SY6880   *ESB* "steel" mechanical pencil   15 - 25
    Singapore **(A and T International Ltd.)**
SY6900   *ESB* pencils   2 - 4
    Switzerland **(Uranium)**
SY7010   *ROTJ* pencils   2 - 4
SY7015   *ROTJ* starburst pencil tops   3 - 7

PENCIL CASES/BOXES
Butterfly Originals
SY7210   *ROTJ* zippered vinyl pouch: Luke/Vader duel   5 - 10

SY7015

SY6880 SY7010

SY7240

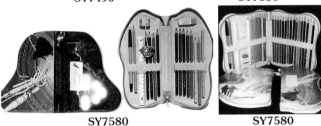

SY7490

SY7550

SY7610

SY8000

SY8010

SY7615

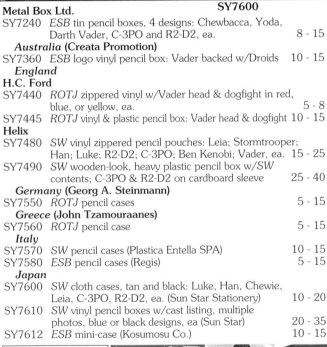

SY7580

SY7580

SY7670

SY7650

SY7800

SY7600

Metal Box Ltd.
SY7240 *ESB* tin pencil boxes, 4 designs: Chewbacca, Yoda,
Darth Vader, C-3PO and R2-D2, ea.   8 - 15
  Australia (Creata Promotion)
SY7360 *ESB* logo vinyl pencil box: Vader backed w/Droids   10 - 15
  England
H.C. Ford
SY7440 *ROTJ* zippered vinyl w/Vader head & dogfight in red,
blue, or yellow, ea.   5 - 8
SY7445 *ROTJ* vinyl & plastic pencil box: Vader head & dogfight 10 - 15
Helix
SY7480 *SW* vinyl zippered pencil pouches: Leia; Stormtrooper;
Han; Luke; R2-D2; C-3PO; Ben Kenobi; Vader, ea. 15 - 25
SY7490 *SW* wooden-look, heavy plastic pencil box w/*SW*
contents; C-3PO & R2-D2 on cardboard sleeve   25 - 40
  Germany (Georg A. Steinmann)
SY7550 *ROTJ* pencil cases   5 - 15
  Greece (John Tzamouraanes)
SY7560 *ROTJ* pencil case   5 - 15
  Italy
SY7570 *SW* pencil cases (Plastica Entella SPA)   10 - 15
SY7580 *ESB* pencil cases (Regis)   5 - 15
  Japan
SY7600 *SW* cloth cases, tan and black: Luke, Han, Chewie,
Leia, C-3PO, R2-D2, ea. (Sun Star Stationery)   10 - 20
SY7610 *SW* vinyl pencil boxes w/cast listing, multiple
photos, blue or black designs, ea (Sun Star)   20 - 35
SY7612 *ESB* mini-case (Kosumosu Co.)   10 - 15

SY7920

SY7615 *ROTJ* metal pencil boxes (Rapport)   15 - 25
  Mexico (Personajes Registrados)
SY7650 *ROTJ* vinyl case   3 - 8
  New Zealand (D.N. Russell and Co.)
SY7670 *ESB* silvery vinyl case   4 - 10

PENS (Butterfly Originals)
SY7800 *ROTJ* blue ink ball-point w/logo & characters, 2-pack 4 - 8
  New Zealand (Bic)
SY7850 *ESB* ball-point pens w/Vader, orange, lime green, ea. 3 - 7
See also—**CAST AND CREW, STATIONERY: Markers**

POSTCARDS
Classico
SY7920 *SW* Classic: More than 60 regular sized and oversized
postcards using photos and art from all 3 films, ea.   2 - 8

SY7440

SY7360

SY7445

SY7480

SY7921

SY8155

SY8420

SY8480

SY8600   SY8510   SY8700   SY8740   SY8741

SY8742   SY8760   SY8785   SY8792   SY8794   SY8790   SY8820

SY8838   SY8840   SY8930   SY8935   SY8940

SY7921 *SW* Special Edition: additional postcards
        featuring new CGI sequences   2 - 8

Drawing Board SY8000-10

SY8000 *SW* droids 20-pack: "Greetings, Earthling!"   10 - 15
SY8010 *ESB* set of 6: R2-D2 & C-3PO; Chewie, Han,
        Leia, Luke; Yoda; Han, Luke on tauntaun; AT-
        AT attack; Vader vs. Luke, each   3 - 6
SY8050 *SW* Classic multi-character dichromate (Fantasma) 3 - 6
  Finland (Playmix)
SY8100 Postcard book   10 - 20
  France (Images 'in)
SY8120 *ROTJ*: Trilogy posters, ea.   2 - 5
  Japan (Rapport Co.)
SY8150 *ESB* cards: 8 diff., ea.   4 - 7
SY8155 *ROTJ*, 8 diff., ea.
  Netherlands (Loeb)
SY8290 *ROTJ*: 12 cartoon-art scenes of Ewoks, ea.   2 - 4

RUBBER STAMPS See—CRAFTS: Rubber Stamps; STAR TOURS

RULERS (Butterfly Originals)

SY8400 *ROTJ* 6" lenticular w/logo & battle scenes   5 - 10
SY8410 *SW* logo 12" lenticular w/*ROTJ* vehicles & characters 10 - 15
SY8420 *ROTJ* 12" w/glossy paper label w/logo & characters   3 - 6
  England
  H.C. Ford
SY8480 *ROTJ* 6" ruler w/paper label: logo & characters   3 - 5
  Helix
SY8490 *SW* "May the Force" 6", isosceles & equilateral
        triangles, semi- circle in see-through plastic colors, ea. 5 - 10
SY8492 *SW* "May the Force" 12" solid blue ruler
        w/5 stormtroopers on back blasting away   7 - 15

  Japan (Rapport Co.)
SY8500 *ESB* plastic ruler   3 - 7
  Mexico (Personajes Registrados)
SY8510 *ROTJ* 12"   3 - 7
  New Zealand (Fortuna Industries Ltd.)
SY8520 *ROTJ* ruler   3 - 7

SCISSORS (Butterfly Originals)

SY8600 *ROTJ* safety scissors w/lenticular badge of
        Vader/Imperial shuttle   4 - 8

SCHOOL SETS (Butterfly Originals)

SY8700 *ROTJ* school kit   7 - 15
  England
  H.C. Ford
SY8740 *SW* logo stationery-pencil top gift set (Yoda memo) 10 - 25
SY8741 *SW* logo stationery-pencil top gift set (Leia memo) 10 - 25
SY8742 *ROTJ* logo boxed fancy stationery set   10 - 25
SY8760 *SW* "stationery set" w/mini-crayons,
        pencils, marker, pencil caps, sharpener, eraser,
        notepad: Vader & stormtrooper; Luke & Leia, ea. 10 - 20
SY8785 *ROTJ* assorted carded character stationery sets   5 - 12
  Helix
SY8790 *SW* Droids tin "Maths" set   20 - 45
SY8792 *SW* Chewie & Han vinyl snap School set   20 - 45
SY8794 *SW* Star Destroyer zippered vinyl School
        Drawing set   20 - 45
  Italy (Plastica Entella SPA)
SY8810 *SW* school sets   10 - 25
  Mexico (Personajes Registrados)
SY8820 *ROTJ* School set   10 - 20
  Spain (Estucheria Vipo SA)
SY8830 *SW* Classic plastic tote bag with school supplies 10 - 25
  Staedtler
SY8838 *ESB* school set   10 - 25
SY8840 *ROTJ* school sets: Luke/Vader; Luke & Ewoks, ea. 10 - 25
SY8842 *Caravan of Courage* school set   10 - 20

SCRAP BOOKS/PHOTO ALBUMS
  Australia (Reding)
SY8920 *ESB* C-3PO and Chewie   15 - 20

SY9014	SY9014	SY9014	SY9010

SY9015	SY9020	SY9021

SY9075	SY9070	SY9076

SY9190

SY9262	SY9264	SY9266	SY9310	SY9380	SY9550

England
SY8930 *SW* 32-page scrapbook: heroes & villains (Letraset) 15 - 20
SY8935 *ROTJ* Scrap Book (H.C. Ford)
Japan (Sun-Star)
SY8940 *SW* photo albums: R2-D2; C-3PO/X-wing, ea. 20 - 35

SHARPENERS/ACCESSORIES
Butterfly Originals
SY9010 *ROTJ* plastic w/baby Ewoks 3 - 6
SY9012 *ROTJ* round plastic: TIE ftr. 3 - 6
SY9014 *ROTJ* carded figural: R2-D2, Yoda, Vader, ea. 4 - 8
SY9015 *ROTJ* 48 loose-leaf foil reinforcements in pack 3 - 5
Craft Master/Kenner
SY9020 *ROTJ* Clip-A-Long Vader crayon holder & sharpener 5 - 10
SY9021 *ROTJ* Clip-A-Long R2-D2 compass w/crayon 5 - 10
SY9022 *ROTJ* Clip-A-Long Wicket magnifying glass 5 - 10
Australia (Crystal Craft)
SY9050 *ROTJ* round plastic: R2-D2 and other designs, ea. 3 - 5
England
SY9070 *SW* Death Star shaped tin litho sharpener (Helix) 35 - 65
SY9075 *ROTJ* oval w/label: Vader head/dogfight (H.C. Ford) 2 - 5
SY9076 *SW* logo domes plastic w/stormtrooper & Vader: red, blue or gray see-transparent plastic (H.C. Ford) 4 - 7
Finland (Playmix/Brio)
SY9100 *ROTJ* pencil sharpeners 3 - 5
Japan (Takara)
SY9115 *SW*: R2-D2 figural sharpener 15 - 25
Mexico (Creaciones Juanin, S.A.)
SY9190 *ROTJ* figural sharpeners: Gamorrean guard; Adm. Ackbar; Vader; Wicket; Yoda, R2-D2, ea. 4 - 8
New Zealand (Fortuna Industries Ltd.)
SY9195 *ROTJ* pencil sharpeners 3 - 5

STATIONERY (Drawing Board)
SY9260 *SW* boxed stationery w/X-wing on paper, battle inside envelope; box w/18 sheets, 12 envelopes 15 - 22
SY9262 *SW* lap pack folder (Hildebrandt art cover) w/10 printed sheets (droids), 10 plain, 10 envelopes 15 - 25
SY9264 *SW* boxed R2-D2 die-cut paper, 18 sheets, 12 envelopes 15 - 22
SY9266 *SW* Darth Vader head, 25 sheets in writing pad 10 - 20
England (Letraset)
SY9300 *SW*: Writing Pad for Intergalactic Messages: Droids & stormtrooper 10 - 15

SY9310 *SW* Space Writing Set in die-cut R2-D2 box: Pad, droid/trooper envelopes, mini-pad, 6 transfers 15 - 30
Finland (Playmix/Brio)
SY9360 *ROTJ* stationery set 10 - 20
SY9362 *ROTJ* writing set, space scene 10 - 20
Japan (Yukari)
SY9380 *SW* lap pack, clear plastic folders w/stationery pad w/6 envelopes: Vader; Droids, escape pod;Droids & red/yellow *SW* logo; Stormtrooper on dewback, droids, pyramid logo, ea. 20 - 40
SY9385 *SW* larger-size lap pack w/stationery pad (7x10 inches) and 6 envelopes: *SW* logo; X-wing; R2-D2; droids on pad & envelopes, ea. 25 - 45
New Zealand
SY9390 *ROTJ* writing set w/logo (Bing Harris Sargood Ltd.) 10 - 20
SY9410 *ROTJ* stationery pack (Fortuna Industries Ltd.) 10 - 20

STENCILS
Japan
SY9550 *SW* individually bagged stencils: R2-D2, C-3PO, Y-wing, X-wing, Landspeeder, MillenniumFalcon, Death Star, Star Destroyer, TIE, Darth TIE, ea. 3 - 7

STORE DISPLAYS

The displays retailers used to merchandise trilogy products are highly desirable. Kenner displays are great for showing off a toy collection and collecting them helps fans relive the excitement. Kenner displays range from cardboard or plastic shelf talkers to back-pieces of cardboard bins for action figures to large colorful end-cap displays.

Other displays are also interesting. One wallpaper display was in the shape of a three-dimensional TIE fighter. Some of the Burger King tie-in display pieces are huge and attractive. Foreign displays—ranging from a light-up Vader for a Japanese lightsaber from Takara to a card-stock dimensional R2-D2 to sell Panasonic audio and video products to a German standee for CBS/Fox Droids cartoons—are choice items. .

KENNER
Star Wars
SZ0010 Action figure shelf display bin & card: "12 Exciting Action Figures" 150 - 350
SZ0012 Action figure bin card w/photos of 12 100 - 150
SZ0014 Action figure long display card for 12 figures 125 - 250
SZ0016 Action figure bin card: Get a Free Boba Fett; 20 figs (photos) 100 - 250

SZ0012   SZ0020   SZ0020

SZ0024   SZ0028   SZ0030   SZ0070   SZ0110

SZ0050   SZ0050   SZ0148

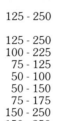

SZ0152   SZ1110   SZ1130

SZ0018	Action figure long display card: Collect all 21. Boba Fett offer	125 - 250
SZ0020	Action figure bin card: Collect all 21; Boba Fett offer w/sticker covering firing backpack	125 - 250
SZ0022	Action figure bin card w/photos: Collect all 21	100 - 225
SZ0024	Action figure hanger: 12	75 - 125
SZ0026	Action figure hanger: Collect all 21	50 - 100
SZ0028	Action figure display prepack w/header card	50 - 150
SZ0030	Action figure pole display w/header card	75 - 175
SZ0050	Boba Fett (action figure) long display card	150 - 250
SZ0060	Large *SW* Toy Center header/hanger card	150 - 350
SZ0065	Toy Center shelf talkers	10 - 20
SZ0070	Electronic Laser Battle Game display: plastic unit w/game, transformer, header card	225 - 350
SZ0100	Movie Cassettes counter display	50 - 75
SZ0110	Laser pistol/rifle display	125 - 250
SZ0120	Lightsaber header display	125 - 250
SZ0130	Two-sided, rect. folding sign, "*Star Wars* is Here"	45 - 65
SZ0144	*SW* Toy Galaxy hanger/header card	85 - 125
SZ0146	*SW* Toy Galaxy shelf talker	10 - 20
SZ0148	Die-cast vehicles shelf display bin & header card	125 - 225
SZ0150	Stuffed R2-D2 shelf display bin & header card	125 - 250
SZ0152	Counter standee for *SW* '81 rerelease: Save Your *SW* Movie Ticket Stubs (w/rebate coupons)	75 - 150
SZ0154	Shelf display for *ESB* Sweepstakes w/coupons	10 - 20

The Empire Strikes Back

SZ1110	Action figure hanger: Collect all 32	45 - 100

 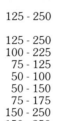

SZ2212   SZ2212

SZ1112	Action figure hanger: Collect all 41	45 - 85
SZ1114	Action figure 3-sided hanger: Collect all 48	45 - 85
SZ1116	Micro Collection 3-sided hanger	40 - 65
SZ1118	*ESB* shelf talker (flat plastic)	5 - 15
SZ1120	*ESB* shelf talker (embossed plastic)	8 - 16
SZ1122	*ESB* Micro Collection shelf talker (flat plastic)	5 - 15
SZ1124	Large hanging sign w/*ESB* logo in silver letters	125 - 300
SZ1126	Large hanging sign: Hoth battle scene/space battle	150 - 300
SZ1127	*ESB* logo: Heavy cardboard	60 - 120
SZ1128	*ESB* logo: Large metal sign	150 - 300
SZ1130	Yoda dimensional plastic hanger with *ESB* logo at bottom	75 - 150

Return of the Jedi

SZ2210	Action figure heavy cardboard sign: Collect All 65 (Imperial Guard, Bib Fortuna, etc.)	55 - 150
SZ2212	Action figure heavy cardboard sign: Collect All 79 (Imperial guard/Emperor)	55 - 150
SZ2214	Action figure bin (no illus.): Collect Them All	45 - 75
SZ2215	Large black floor bin for POTF figures w/header (Featuring Collector Coin sign)	45 - 75
SZ2216	Like 2215, w/*Droids/Ewoks* insert	
SZ2218	*ROTJ* Toy Center with heavy cardboard sign, raised silverized letters	100 - 250
SZ2220	Large tree display for Speeder Bike pedal-car sweepstakes	100 - 300
SZ2224	Speeder Bike pedal car display #2 w/heads of Ewok, Luke & C-3PO & die-cut *ROTJ* logo	100 - 250
SZ2226	Large heavy cardboard 2-sided sign: Battle scene	150 - 350

SZ2214

SZ2215

SZ2216

SZ2218

SZ2220

SZ2238

SZ2241

SZ2226

SZ4601

SZ4605

SZ4750

SZ4610

SZ5032

SZ5050

SZ5055

SZ6290

SZ2228

SZ2228	*ROTJ* shelf talker (plastic)	5 - 12
SZ2230	*ROTJ* shelf talker (cardboard): Free poster offer w/coupon pad	10 - 20
SZ2234	*ROTJ* shelf talker (cardboard): Free Anakin Skywalker w/pad	10 - 20
SZ2236	*ROTJ* shelf talker (cardboard): *ROTJ* Sweepstakes w/pad (VG)	10 - 20
SZ2238	Lightsaber floor display unit	75 - 125
SZ2240	Shelf box for plush Ewoks	30 - 60
SZ2241	Floor Display for plush Ewoks	40 - 85
SZ2242	Coloring books counter display	25 - 35

England/Germany (Kenner)

SZ4532	Kenner England/Germany: Plastic dimensional Vader head w/blinking red eyes	125 - 225

Germany

SZ4601	Action Figure Dump box: 12	150 - 200
SZ4605	Action Figure Dump box: 20	150 - 200
SZ4610	Action Figure Display w/Falcon Background	300 - 500

Japan (Takara)

SZ4750	Action Figure shelf box	95 - 190

OTHER STORE DISPLAYS (Selected)

Star Wars

SZ5010	Burger Chef 2-piece cardboard mobile: *SW* Posters & Death Star	35 - 50
SZ5012	Burger King 4-glass counter display	50 - 125
SZ5014	Burger King 2-part plastic hanger for glasses: Collect All 4	35 - 55

CBS/FOX Video SZ5030-32

SZ5030	*SW* 3-D silverized floor standee (Style A art)	75 - 250
SZ5032	*SW* 3-D silverized counter standee (A one-sheet)	50 - 100
SZ5050	Clark's Blinking-light triangular upright plastic display for shoes	200 - 350
SZ5055	Cheer, Dawn, Cascade posters display	10 - 25
SZ5060	Drawing Board Circular shelf hanger	25 - 40
SZ5062	Drawing Board 3-piece mobile: C-3PO, Stormtrooper, Darth Vader	25 - 35
SZ5080	General Mills in-store display for *Star Wars* kites	75 - 150
SZ6110	Random House C-3PO 3-D book bin floor dump	100 - 175
SZ6150	Texas Instruments Header card for digital watches	25 - 40

20th Century Fox Records SZ6290-94

SZ6290	Mobile: diecut R2-D2 backed by battle scene	35 - 50
SZ6292	R2-D2 3-D counter standee to hold 45s	35 - 55
SZ6294	*SW* & Story of *SW* large standee of droids	75 - 125

Weingeroff Enterprises SZ6350-52

SZ6350	Shelf standee for *SW* jewelry with Hildebrandt art	10 - 20
SZ6351	Shelf standee for *SW* earrings	15 - 25
SZ6352	Shelf tree (gray plastic) for *SW* necklaces	45 - 60

SZ6352   SZ7530   SZ7555   SZ7590   SZ8042

SZ6400

SZ6400	Wonder Bread Trading Cards shelf talker	10 - 15

The Empire Strikes Back

SZ7010	Burger King C-3PO & R2-D2 standee for glasses	100 - 200
SZ7012	Burger King Counter standee for Super Scene Collection w/laminated album	50 - 100
SZ7014	Burger King 4-glass counter display	45 - 85
SZ7016	Burger King Large 3-D standee with 'space kids'	65 - 125
SZ7017	Burger King contest translite	30 - 50
SZ7018	Burger King 2-piece cardboard mobile of Bespin City w/spacecraft	25 - 40
SZ7140	CBS/FOX Video *ESB* counter display	20 - 40
SZ7142	CBS/FOX Video Vader/Yoda plastic door sign	20 - 50
SZ7260	Dixie/Lipton Darth cardboard standee (waist up)	65 - 100
SZ7300	Deka *ESB*	75 - 110
SZ7410	Procter & Gamble Posters display (Crisco, Duncan Hines, Pringles)	50 - 125
SZ7530	Puffs tall dimensional in-store display	200 - 300
SZ7550	RSO/Polygram Records Hanging display with 2-sided Vader and 4-sided record-jackets	45 - 60

SZ8014

SZ7555	RSO/Polygram hanging display *ESB* style 'A' art	60 - 120
SZ7570	Sigma black plastic display shelf unit w/dimensional Vader head	75 - 150
SZ7590	Wallace-Berrie black plastic display unit for boxed jewelry w/dimensional Vader head	75 - 150
SZ7650	Wilton Enterprises display for cake pans, etc.	45 - 100

Return of the Jedi/Star Wars Classic

SZ8010	Adam Joseph Tall Royal Guard cardboard floor display with metal pegs	75 - 150
SZ8012	Adam Joseph plastic shelf rack w/hooks for jewelry: Vader & Royal guards	25 - 40
SZ8014	Adam Joseph dump displays, each	50 - 125

Bantam SZ8030-42

SZ8030	Large airbrushed R2-D2 floor dump for paperbacks	50 - 100

SZ8280

SZ2224   SZ5080

SZ8160

SZ8321

SZ8450

SZ8455

SZ8460

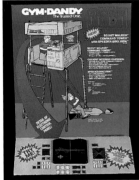
SZ8465

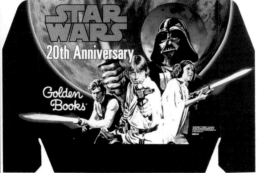
SZ8467

SZ8564

SZ8032	Large C-3PO back-of-bin standee for paperbacks	25 - 45
SZ8034	Top of dump card and front piece (back of Luke holding silvery lightsaber) for *Jedi Academy* series	20 - 35
SZ8036	Hanging mobile for 'Jedi Academy' (looks like box kite w/R2-D2 & C-3PO)	25 - 40
SZ8038	Plastic shelf talker: 'Official *SW* Book Center'	10 - 15
SZ8040	Die-cut Princess Leia w/pistols for *The Courtship of Princess Leia*	20 - 35
SZ8042	Die-cut Luke w/lightsaber for *Dark Apprentice*	30 - 60

SZ8160	Bradley Time display sign including C-3PO	20 - 30
SZ8165	Buena Vista *ROTJ* Records/tapes	15 - 20
SZ8280	Burger King Vader standee: Get Yours (glasses) Today	125 - 250
SZ8282	4-glass counter display	45 - 75
SZ8284	3-D hanger	35 - 75
SZ8320	Butterfly Originals die-cut Imperial Guard standee w/metal hooks	65 - 125
SZ8321	Butterfly Originals shuttle display w/hooks	45 - 85
SZ8440	CBS/FOX Video Mobile with 4 characters	25 - 40
SZ8442	CBS/FOX Video Lenticular speeder bike sign	45 - 75
SZ8444	CBS/FOX Video Sweepstakes box and pad	25 - 40
SZ8450	Coke/Pizza Hut tumbler display	35 - 60
SZ8455	Deka *ROTJ*	75 - 110
SZ8457	Drawing Board display, w/party zxsupplies	200 - 300
SZ8460	Hi-C Poster display	20 - 50
SZ8465	Gym Dandy *ROTJ* Tower w/Glider swing display	80 - 160
SZ8467	Golden Books display topper	10 - 25
SZ8480	Kellogg's C-3PO's Cereal standee	150 - 225
SZ8482	Kellogg's Folding sign: A New Force at Breakfast	20 - 30
SZ8484	Kellogg's Plastic shelf talker	15 - 30
SZ8520	Metallic Images counter standee (C.U.I. Inc.)	15 - 20
SZ8530	MPC Shelf Talker for models	10 - 20
SZ8540	Natural Balance large R2-D2 floor dump for *SW* multivitamins	65 - 150
SZ8560	Omni Cosmetics styrofoam figural R2-D2	125 - 250

SZ8560 / SZ8457 / SZ8480 / SZ8580 / SZ7012 / SZ7570

SZ8562

SZ8580

173

SZ9015

SZ8800   SZ8805   SZ9001   SZ9015

SZ9005

SZ9007   SZ9008   SZ9009   SZ9010   SZ9012

SZ9014

SZ8562	Omni cardboard Royal guard in-store display unit	100 - 200
SZ8564	Omni plastic display w/background	110 - 225
SZ8580	Oral-B toothbrush floor dump, 3 different header cards, each version	60 - 135
SZ8780	Pepperidge Farm large in-store cookies display	80 - 175
SZ8800	Random House bookmark counter box	20 - 50
SZ8810	RSO "All the *SW* Adventures..." shelf sign	30 - 60
SZ8820	Specialty Wallpaper TIE fighter 3-D in-store display bin unit	150 - 300
SZ8960	Stride Rite Ewok mobile	20 - 30

Star Wars Special Edition (Pepsico)

SZ9001	Display trim roll	10 - 20
SZ9003	Pole display w/C-3PO, Darth Vader, Yoda	15 - 30
SZ9005	Rotating Death Star	75 - 125
SZ9007	Darth Vader Standee	25 - 45
SZ9008	Chewbacca Standee	25 - 45
SZ9009	C-3PO Standee	25 - 45
SZ9010	R2-D2 Standee	25 - 45
SZ9012	Darth Vader dump display topper	30 - 75
SZ9014	Luke and Leia dimensional Standee	60 - 135
SZ9015	Flat hanging version of (similar to above)	15 - 35
SZ9017	R2-D2 Cooler	150 - 300

Taco Bell

| SZ9021 | Round hanging cup display | 60 - 120 |

Detail of SZ9025

SZ9017   SZ9023   SZ9025

SZ9027   SZ9028   SZ9029   SZ9030

SZ9050   SZ9200   SZ9400   SZ9430   SZ9435   SZ9444

TI0050   Lids from   TI0070   TI0071   TI0075   TI0510   TI0520
TI0050 & TI0060

SZ9023	Yoda/Cup standee	25 - 45
SZ9025	Yard signs, 4 different, each	15 - 30
SZ9027	Register topper	
SZ9028	2-sided window sticker w/prizes, Millennium Falcon	
SZ9029	Character window decals, each	10 - 25
SZ9030	Other window decals, each	5 - 10

Australia

SZ9050	Macléans "1000 Double Tickets…"	15 - 25

England (Palitoy)

SZ9100	Cardboard double-sided logo hanger (*SW/ESB*)	45- 65
SZ9102	Vinyl *ESB* window logo in red, black, silver	45- 65
SZ9104	Cardboard header card with battle scene backed by "Action Force"	20 - 40

Germany

SZ9200	*Droids* standee (large diecut cartoon R2-D2)	45 - 75

Japan

SZ9400	Large Darth Vader plastic standee w/lightbox for Lightsaber display (Takara)	250 - 350
SZ9420	Plastic filled hanging display for Japanese trading card packs (Topps)	65 - 125
SZ9430	Shelf box display for wind-up R2-D2s (Takara)	100 - 175
SZ9435	Shelf box display for central American Yo-yos	75 - 150

Panasonic

SZ9440	Large diecut Darth Vader photo standee (no advertising)	65 - 150
SZ9442	Large glossy C-3PO diecut standee w/ad in oval on stomach	65 - 150

SZ9444	Three-dimensional R2-D2 made of thin card-stock and foam-core w/plastic dome, about 26 in. high	100 - 250
SZ9446	Panasonic Star Tours standee	35 - 75
SZ9448	Plastic mini shelf standee: die-cut of Lucas & C-3PO	25 - 45
SZ9450	Heavy plastic die-cut card of Wicket, Lucas, Chewie	25 - 45
SZ9452	Mini-cardboard shelf standee: Yoda w/earphones	25 - 45
SZ9454	Plastic 3-D counter piece w/Yoda in earphones	35 - 55

TINWARE

See also—**BANKS; STATIONERY; STAR TOURS**

CONTAINERS

Chein Industries

TI0050	*ROTJ* 3½" high mini tins, 6 lid designs: Vader, Jabba, Ewoks, Rebo band, Droids, Leia/Luke/Han, ea.	4 - 10
TI0060	*ROTJ* 1" high trinket tins, same 6 lid designs as TI0050, ea.	3 - 6
TI0070	*ROTJ* rectangular carry-all tin w/handles & lid	10 - 20
TI0071	*ROTJ* round cookie tin w/lid	10 - 25
TI0075	*Ewoks* carry-all	10 - 20

Metal Box Ltd.

TI0510	*ESB* micro tins, 6 designs: Lando, Yoda, AT-ATs, Boba Fett, Luke/tauntaun, Luke/Vader duel, each	5 - 10
TI0520	*ESB* macro tins, 8 designs: Vader, Luke, Han, Leia, Probot, Yoda, Star Destroyer, Chewbacca, ea.	5 - 10
TI0530	*ESB* oval storage tin: Cloud City	10 - 20
TI0535	*ESB* square 1/4-pound tin: Probot, R2-D2, etc.	10 - 20

TI0540	TI0541	TI5210
TI5212	TI7000	TI7002

TL2280 · TL2000 · TL2030 · TL6730 · TL2270

| TL2270 | TL3051 | TL3060 | TL3061 | TL3062 | TL4050 | TL4200 | TL5070 |

TI0540	*ESB* space trunk: Luke, Leia, etc.			10 - 20
TI0541	*ESB* space trunk #2: Droids, Probot, etc.			10 - 20
	***Italy* (Vergani SpA)**			
TI1050	*ESB*: Metal locking candy container			10 - 20
	***Spain* (Mundi Paper SA)**			
TI1080	*SW* Classic metal pencil cube			10 - 20
TI1082	*SW* Classic money box			10 - 20

TRAYS (Chein Industries Inc.)
TI5210	*ROTJ* collage	10 - 20
TI5212	*ROTJ* Ewoks	10 - 20

WASTE BASKETS (Chein Industries)
TI7000	*ROTJ* collage	10 - 20
TI7002	*ROTJ* Ewoks	10 - 20
	***Japan* (Shibayama Sangyo Co.)**	
TI7250	*ESB* dust box	25 - 40
	***Spain* (Mundi Paper SA)**	
TI7480	*SW* Classic basket	10 - 20

TOILETRIES AND SUNDRIES

A small number of *Star Wars* fans felt cleanliness was next to, well, the Force. It took until *Jedi* for a company—Omni Cosmetics—to release such products in the U.S., although other countries had toiletries from the first film on. Many of the products are figural, including some sculpted soap. The figural liquid containers also are sought by "soakies" collectors. Omni, which shipped a wonderful Styrofoam R2-D2 unit with shelves to display its merchandise in stores, also issued some of its liquid products in non-character bottles to refill—or "refuel" as the company put it—the containers. These were also packaged as "Princess Leia's Beauty Bag" and "Luke Skywalker's Belt Kit."

BATH AND SHOWER GEL
***England* (Addis Ltd.)**
TL0250	*SW* Classic see-through tubes w/self-hangers & character decals: C-3PO; Chewbacca; Darth Vader; Gamorrean Guard; Han Solo; Luke Skywalker; Obi Wan; Princess Leia; R2-D2; Wicket the Ewok, ea.	5 - 10

BATH SPONGES
***England* (Addis Ltd.)**
TL1100	*SW* Classic figural sponge: Darth Vader	5 - 10

BUBBLE BATH (Omni Cosmetics)
TL2000	*SW* Classic figural plastic bottles: Leia; Darth Vader; Chewbacca; Jabba the Hutt , Wicket, Yoda, ea.	10 - 25
TL2030	*SW* Classic "refueling station" refill w/battle scene on front	5 - 15

***Australia* (B and W Character Merchandise)**
TL2250	*ESB* Darth Vader, R2-D2, ea.	10 - 20
	England	
TL2270	*SW* boxed figural plastic: Darth, R2-D2, ea. (Cliro)	15 - 25
TL2280	*SW* Classic bottles w/characters: C-3PO; Chewie; Darth Gamorrean Guard; Han Solo; Luke Skywalker; Obi Wan; Princess Leia; R2-D2; Wicket, ea. (Addis)	8 - 15

COMBS/BRUSHES (Adam Joseph Ind.)
TL3050	*SW* logo C-3PO & R2-D2 pop-up comb	5 - 15
TL3051	*ROTJ* logo Darth Vader pop-up comb	5 - 15
TL3052	*ROTJ* logo Leia as dancing girl pop-up comb	5 - 15
TL3060	Rebo band Comb-n-Keeper	5 - 15
TL3061	Landspeeder w/droids Comb-n-Keeper	5 - 15
TL3062	Kneesaa Comb-n-Keeper	5 - 10
TL3063	Wicket and Kneesaa Comb-n-Keeper	5 - 10

SHAMPOO (Omni Cosmetics)
TL4050	*SW* Classic shampoo in plastic figural bottles:Luke; Yoda; R2-D2, Darth Vader; Wicket; Jabba, ea.	10 - 25
TL4060	*SW* Classic "refueling station" refill w/battle scene on front	5 - 15

***Australia* (B and W Character Mdse.)**
TL4200	*ESB* Darth Vader, R2-D-2, ea.	10 - 20
	England	
TL4250	*SW* figural plastic bottles: Darth Vader, R2-D2 boxed, ea. (Cliro)	15 - 25

SOAP (Omni Cosmetics)
TL5050	*SW* Classic character soap, 4-ounce bars boxed w/ sculpted face of character Luke; Leia; Yoda; Darth Vader; Gamorrean Guard; Wicket; C-3PO	3 - 8
TL5070	*SW* Soap Collection No. 1, set of 4 1-ounce bars: Luke; Leia; Yoda: Chewbacca	7 - 15
TL5075	*SW* Soap Collection No. 2, set of 4 1-ounce bars: R2-D2; Lando Calrissian; C-3PO; Darth Vader	7 - 15
	England	
TL5200	*SW* boxed "soap models," figural boxed soaps: C-3PO; R2-D2; ea. (Cliro)	15 - 25
TL5230	*ESB* soaps (Consumer Products)	3 - 6
TL5250	*SW* Classic character soap, oval w/long-lasting label, sold in boxed sets: Luke and Darth Vader; R2-D2 & C-3PO; Wicket & Woklings, (Addis) ea. set	10 - 15

SOAP BOXES
***Japan* (Sakura)**
TL6200	*SW* plastic oval w/tray: R2-D2 and 3PO	20 - 30

TL6200   TL5250   TL5250   TL5250   TL6750   TL6751   TL6755

TL7070

TL5200   TL6900   TL7050   TL7065 TL8030   TL8050

TOILETRY SETS (England)

TL6730	*ESB* foam bath and shampoo (Consumer Products)	10 - 15
TL6750	Luke/Vader shower gel, sponge & soaps set (Addis)	15 - 25
TL6751	R2-D2 and C-3PO foam bath and soaps (Addis)	15 - 25
TL6755	Ewok foam bath and soaps (Addis)	10 - 15

TOOTHBRUSHES

Kenner Products

TL6900	*SW* battery-op w/*SW* graphics	60 - 125
TL6910	*ESB* battery-op	25 - 45
TL6920	*ROTJ* battery-op, J.C. Penney catalog only	50 - 100
TL6930	Wicket figural battery-op	25 - 40

Cooper Care/Oral-B

TL7050	*ROTJ* toothbrushes, Luke; Leia; Chewbacca and Han; C-3PO and R2-D2; Ewoks; Darth Vader; carded, ea.	4 - 8
TL7060	As TL7050, shrink wrapped w/o cards	2 - 6
TL7065	Toothbrush 3-packs w/Jedi Masters toothbrush, ea.	10 - 15
TL7070	*ROTJ* promotional material; for dentists: Dental Health Adventure coloring book, dental reminder postcards (Jabba and Bib Fortuna, Ewoks, Darth and Luke) membership cards, each item	3 - 12

See also—**POSTERS, LOBBY CARDS, PRESS KITS, ETC.**

TRAVEL KITS

TL8030	Princess Kneesaa Personal Care Bag (Adam Joseph)	10 - 15

Omni Cosmetics

TL8050	*SW* Classic Princess Leia Beauty Bag, clear vinyl w/straps and 2-ounce bottles of shampoo, cream rinse, cologne splash; 1-ounce bath soap; comb	15 - 25
TL8022	*SW* Classic Luke Skywalker Belt Kit, clear vinyl w/slots for belt and 2-ounce bottles of bubble bath and shampoo; 1-ounce soap; comb; toothbrush	15 - 25

TOYS See also—HOUSEHOLD; STORE DISPLAYS

ACTION FIGURES

Scaled action figures, vehicles, playsets, and other accessories are the heart of the *Star Wars* toy phenomenon. The figure count for the original classic series eventually hit 115, counting the cartoon *Droids* and *Ewoks*, the Max Rebo Band, and Yak Face, which was not retailed in the United states, but was sold in Canada and on Tri-Logo cards. Not included in this count are the much-promoted missile-firing Boba Fett and Vlix, a *Droids* figure exclusive to South America. The line was revived in 1995, and became more popular than ever.

There are numerous figure and card variations, plus special promotional combinations. The same figure can have a wide variety of values depending on condition, completeness, variation, and type of packaging. Packages are shown here in the order the figures were introduced, along with subsequent major packaging changes. It is estimated that there are nearly 2,500 different card and figure combinations in the classic series alone. Weapons and other accessories are shown slightly enlarged near each loose figure. Values are listed for each major variation known to our consulting panel of experts.

Most action figures sold throughout the world were the Kenner-designed figures. Takara produced the largest variety of non-Kenner *Star Wars* figures and toys, but Palitoy of England also made a number of unique items.

TO1104   TO1126   TO1130

Star Wars marked a major change in the action figure industry. Until 1977, most figures on the market were 8" or 12½". *Star Wars* figures were only 3¾" on the average so they would fit in space ships and other fantasy vehicles. Figures this size had been produced in the past, but none had ever enjoyed the phenomenal popularity of the *Star Wars* line. The response was so tremendous that smaller figures became the standard for the industry. *Star Wars* also produced high-quality, detailed playsets and accessories for the figures, which effectively signed the death warrant for the older, vinyl playsets.

The original figures were not available in time for Christmas in 1977. To fill the demand, Kenner produced "early bird" kits. The kits came in a large cardboard envelope which contained the following items: a cardboard display stand with detachable cards, a sheet of stickers, and the early bird certificate. This last item was mailed to Kenner. In return, the company promised to send four of the original figures (Luke Skywalker, Princess Leia, Chewbacca, and R2-D2) as soon as they were ready, and plastic pegs to complete the display stand. The sets were mailed between Feb 1 and June 1.

The first 12 figures are found packaged on cards in a variety of languages. More standardization was gradually introduced until Tri-logo cards in English, French, and Spanish replaced most packaging configurations outside the United States.

Figures were occasionally redesigned. Luke Skywalker, Darth Vader, and Ben Kenobi originally came with telescoping lightsabers. After a few shipments, the smaller of the two sections was glued in. Following the release of *The Empire Strikes Back*, R2-D2 figures came with a pop-up sensorscope. In conjunction with *Return of the Jedi*, the R2-D2 figure was redesigned again, this time with a pop-up lightsaber. C-3PO figures could be taken apart and carried around by other figures in a special pack. Boba Fett was originally advertised as a mail-in premium with a working rocket launcher. Two prototype mechanisms were designed in the hope of meeting legal standards, but the negative PR surrounding rocket-launching *Battlestar Galactica* vehicles killed the idea. Ads for the figure, already printed on other packages, were covered over with a sticker promoting the offer which did not mention the launcher. The figure itself arrived with a glued-in rocket and a note explaining the situation.

The *Star Wars* logo was regularly updated to that of the most recent film or figure series. Listings below include separate price estimates based on the card logo.

Most *Star Wars* fans know that George Lucas changed the name of the third film after millions had been spent on advertising and packaging for licensed products. Kenner had already printed 48 four-color *Revenge of the Jedi* figure cards, plus one two-color generic card. Cards for many more figures were designed as well, and exist on thinner card stock with squared-off bottom corners. No Kenner production figures mounted on these cards have ever been found, though many hobbyists have mounted figures with glue or heat pressure as conversation pieces. Boxes with the *Revenge* logo also exist for several vehicles and mini-rigs. The cards sell for $50-$125 each.

Following *Return of the Jedi*, characters from all three films were available on *Star Wars—The Power of the Force* packages. Some of these were *Jedi* characters exclusive to this packaging, while others were re-issues of figures from as far back as the original series. Each of these included a collector's coin with the figure. See **COINS: Action Figure Coins** for more details. Separate action figure lines with unique packaging were produced for the *Droids* and *Ewoks* animated television shows. A few characters from the main line were repeated, some re-cast with cartoon-like features, others merely re-packaged. Additional figures for *Droids/Ewoks* were planned, but never made it beyond the prototype stage.

Numerous mail-ins were offered, allowing kids to send proof of purchase seals to obtain new figures not yet available in stores. These offers included Boba Fett, Yoda, Nein Nunb, Admiral Ackbar, the Emperor and Anakin Skywalker.

Playsets and accessories changed too. The X-wing fighters released with the second film included "battle-damage" stickers. The original Tauntaun was molded in solid plastic, but was later released with a split rubber belly.

Toys were sometimes altered slightly and sold under different names. The Ice Planet Hoth playset was almost identical to the Land of the Jawas playset. The base was cast from the same mold, but in white plastic, and packaged with a new cardboard background. The Jabba the Hutt Dungeons were mostly plastic bases from the Droid Factory.

The Sonic Controlled Land Speeder and the Turret and Probot playset were J.C. Penny exclusives, while the Cantina Adventure Set and Jabba the Hutt Dungeon could only be found at Sears. The Cantina Adventure Set contained four figures, one of which was a taller, blue Snaggletooth which was not available individually. The other three figures were Greedo, Walrus Man and Hammerhead. The Jabba Dungeon came two ways: with EV-9D9, Amanaman, and Barada; or with Klaatu, Nikto, and 8D8.

Kenner marketed a larger set of figures in 1979, ranging in size from 7½" - 15" tall. Boba Fett and IG-88 were the only characters from *The Empire Strikes Back* produced in this size. The Princess Leia figure brings higher values if the original hairdo is intact. Listed prices assume the figure is in its original box.

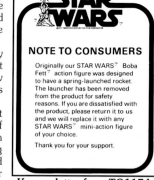

Kenner letter from TO1174

Separate action figure lines were produced for the Droids and Ewoks animated television shows. Collector's coins were included with each figure. A few characters from the main line were repeated in these lines, but were cast in a cartoon-like style as they appeared in the show. Additional figures for Droids/Ewoks were planned, but never made it past the prototype stage.

All figures were commercially available in the United States with the exception of the classic Yak Face. The figures were made available in Europe and the rest of the English-speaking world by Palitoy of London. Palitoy also produced four cardboard playsets which were not available in the United States. Two older figures on *Power of the Force* cards were only available in Australia. The original series of *Star Wars* figures was featured at retail from the spring of 1978 through the end of 1986. Toys continued to be available on a sell-through and closeout basis for several more years.

New *Star Wars* figures began to appear at retail in July, 1995, reviving the "Power of the Force" slogan. All figures were completely redesigned except for a limited-edition set of four reproduction figures. Old tooling for vehicles was altered slightly. The deco design is different, so new products are easily distinguished from the originals, but the production of virtually identical products has affected collectible values of loose vehicles. Card back coloration was switched from red/orange to green for 1997. A hologram sticker was also added to help commemorate the 20th anniversary. Virtually all figures can be found with or without the sticker.

The original Ben (Obi-Wan) Kenobi card had a typo on the back. When the change was made, the photo on the back was modified as well, making this the first variation in the new round. Boba Fett originally appeared with black "crescents" on the back side of his gloves instead of circles. This was really a paint mask problem on an irregular surface, but nonetheless resulted in a figure variation. Look for other variations as noted in the listings.

Han Solo in a Stormtrooper uniform was only available by mail for 2 proofs-of-purchase symbols from Kellogg's Fruit Loops. Another food premium was the "Spirit of Obi-Wan," a transparent blue version of Ben Kenobi which was available only through a Lay's snack promotion. The third mail-in offer was for a Bith (cantina band member), available as a Fan Club exclusive. B'omarr Monk was offered as an Internet exclusive, but could also be ordered with a special certificate from the Spirit of Obi-Wan offer.

Original lightsabers in 1995 were too long, but the problem wasn't corrected until 1996 when the size was shortened by approximately an inch. Some shorter sizes got packed at first, but all figures with lightsabers eventually came in a standard size.

Shadows of the Empire was the first subset of figures, including some new characters based on those in the book, special comic series, and video game of the same name.

The new *Star Wars* trilogy is scheduled for 1999. It is estimated that well over 100 new figures will be produced before toys from the new films are released. Announcements and photos of new additions, including any variations, are published monthly in *Tomart's Action Figure Digest* (see pages 6-7 for more information).

The values listed in this section apper in a more detailed format than elsewhere in this book. The three categories used are Complete No Package (abbreviated as CNP), Mint In Package (MIP), and Mint in Mint Package (MMP). A full explanation of these categories appears on page 8 of this guide.

The identity code numbers in this section are not consistent with Tomart's *Space Adventure Collectibles* or Tomart's *Encyclopedia and Price Guide to Action Figure Collectibles*.

See color photos starting on page 185.

TO1000

Display stand from TO1000

Stickers from TO1000

	Loose CNP	Star Wars MIP	Star Wars MMP	Empire MIP	Empire MMP	Jedi MIP	Jedi MMP	POTF MIP	POTF MMP	Tri-Logo MIP	Tri-Logo MMP
TO1000 Early Bird kit		300	550								
TO1005 Early Bird figures in mailing box w/12 pegs (includes Luke w/extending lightsaber)		1200	2000								
Original Star Wars figures (1978)											
TO1101 Chewbacca w/black bowcaster	10	80	180	45	100	25	60				
TO1102 Chewbacca w/green bowcaster	40	115	200								
TO1103 Chewbacca, card variation	10					25	60	75	130	50	100
TO1104 Luke Skywalker w/yellow hair and extending lightsaber	200	500	1350								
TO1105 TO1104 w/revised lightsaber	45	125	325	60	155	60	110			20	45
TO1106 Luke Skywalker w/brown hair	65			85	180	75	130			60	115
TO1108 Luke Skywalker, gunner card						70	125				
TO1111 Artoo-Detoo (R2-D2)	15	75	195	45	75						
TO1113 Princess Leia Organa	35	135	300	90	160	200	550			100	135
TO1115 Han Solo, original head (small)	26	200	550	500	850						
TO1116 Han Solo, second head (large)	21	150	500	100	180	40	80				
TO1119 Han Solo, photo variation/second head	21					85	150			75	95
TO1121 See-Threepio (C-3PO)	10	65	145	60	80						
TO1123 Stormtrooper	12	75	195	35	85	25	60	145	220		
TO1124 Stormtrooper, photo variation	12									30	40
TO1126 Darth Vader w/extending lightsaber	375	500	1600								
TO1127 Darth Vader w/revised lightsaber	15	65	225	35	90	18	40			15	30
TO1128 Darth Vader, photo variation	15					18	40	60	100		
TO1130 Ben (Obi-Wan) Kenobi, white hair and extending lightsaber	775	1000	1800								
TO1131 TO1130 w/revised lightsaber	18	90	200	45	90	20	60			20	30
TO1132 Ben (Obi-Wan) Kenobi, gray hair	18	90	200	45	90	20	55			20	30
TO1135 Ben (Obi-Wan) Kenobi, photo variation	18					30	60	65	100		
TO1137 Jawa (vinyl cape)	350	600	1600								
TO1139 Jawa (cloth cape)	18	75	150	50	80	20	40	65	90	40	60
TO1141 Sand People	15	85	200								
TO1142 Sandpeople	15			45	90						
TO1143 Tusken Raider (Sand People)	15					25	55			20	35
TO1145 Death Squad Commander	8	55	155								
TO1146 Star Destroyer Commander	8			45	70	20	40			50	75
Later Star Wars figures (1978-79)											
TO1151 Hammerhead	8	60	110	40	70	45	75			60	80
TO1153 Power Droid	9	60	120	40	90	40	90			60	80
TO1155 R5-D4	14	65	125	65	120	35	65			45	35
TO1157 Snaggletooth	10	60	120	40	70	45	90			15	35
TO1159 Blue Snaggletooth (Sears exclusive, came w/Cantina Adventure Set)	75-195										
TO1161 Greedo	10	65	95	65	95	25	65				
TO1163 Death Star Droid	12	65	95	60	90	40	65			40	65
TO1165 Walrus Man	10	65	95	60	90	40	65				
TO1167 Luke Skywalker X-wing Pilot	12	75	125	30	45	30	45	60	115	40	80
TO1169 Boba Fett (see also—TO1513)	22	400	900	120	300	65	125				
TO1171 Boba Fett, photo variation						65	125			40	75
TO1174 Boba Fett in mailer box w/letter	-	50	90								
Star Wars Three-figure sets											
TO1181 Hero Set (Han Solo, Leia, Ben)	-	300	900								
TO1183 Villain Set (Vader, Stormtrooper, Death Squad Commander)	-	300	800								
TO1185 Android Set (Chewbacca, R2-D2, C-3PO)	-	300	800								
Star Wars Three-figure sets w/backdrops											
TO1191 Hero Set (Han Solo, Luke X-wing Pilot, Ben)	-	500	800								
TO1193 Villain Set (Sand People, Boba Fett, Snaggletooth)	-	500	900								
TO1195 Android Set (Power Droid, R5-D4, Death Star Droid)	-	500	900								
TO1197 Creature Set (Greedo, Hammerhead, Walrus Man)	-	500	800								
The Empire Strikes Back (1980-82)											
TO1201 Luke Skywalker (Bespin Fatigues)	22			75	160						
TO1203 Luke Skywalker (Bespin Fatigues), revised card, yellow hair	22			75	145	50	77			20	40
TO1204 Luke Skywalker (Bespin Fatigues), revised card, brown hair	22			75	145	50	77			20	40
TO1207 Bespin Security Guard (white)	10			30	60	20	35			15	30
TO1209 Rebel Soldier (Hoth battle gear)	8			25	50	25	40			15	30
TO1211 FX-7 Medical Droid	8			40	70	40	60			12	20
TO1213 Han Solo (Hoth outfit)	10			40	70	25	40				
TO1217 Lando Calrissian	9			25	55						
TO1218 Lando Calrissian, white eyes and teeth	9			20	50	15	30			15	25
TO1221 Imperial Stormtrooper (Hoth battle gear)	18			50	95	25	50			15	25
TO1223 Leia Organa (Bespin gown) flesh collar	25			65	125						
TO1224 Leia Organa (Bespin gown) maroon collar	40			65	135						

	Loose CNP	Star Wars MIP	Star Wars MMP	Empire MIP	Empire MMP	Jedi MIP	Jedi MMP	POTF MIP	POTF MMP	Tri-Logo MIP	Tri-Logo MMP
TO1225 Leia (Bespin) photo variation, flesh	25			70	125	40	90			30	60
TO1226 Leia (Bespin) photo variation, maroon	40			70	110	50	90			30	60
TO1229 Bossk (Bounty Hunter)	10			40	90	35	70			30	60
TO1231 IG-88 (Bounty Hunter)	10			40	90	30	60			15	20
TO1233 2-1B	9			30	60	20	40			12	15
TO1235 Yoda w/orange snake	25			50	90						
TO1236 Yoda w/brown snake & darker cane	32			55	95	40	60				
TO1238 Yoda the Jedi Master card	25					30	55	200	475	25	35
TO1241 Ugnaught, blue smock	10			40	65	30	45			15	25
TO1242 Ugnaught, lavender smock	15			40	65	30	45			15	25
TO1245 AT-AT Driver	8			45	75	30	50	200	370	10	20
TO1247 Lobot	8			25	50	18	30			10	20
TO1249 Dengar	8			40	70	20	40			15	25
TO1251 Han Solo (Bespin outfit)	18			50	125	40	70			35	50
TO1255 Rebel Commander	8			30	45	10	25			12	18
TO1256 Rebel Commander, photo variation	8					15	30			15	30
TO1259 Imperial Commander	12			25	45	15	37			10	20
TO1261 Leia (Hoth outfit)	20			40	95	35	65				
TO1262 Leia (Hoth outfit) photo variation	20					35	65			25	55
TO1265 Artoo-Detoo (R2-D2) w/sensorscope	12			25	75	20	50			15	25
TO1267 See-Threepio (C-3PO) w/removable limbs	9			45	70	25	40	45	65	10	20
TO1269 4-LOM	10			45	95	25	55			15	25
TO1271 Zuckuss	13			40	80	25	60			15	25
TO1273 Imperial TIE Fighter Pilot	10			45	85	35	65				
TO1274 Imperial TIE Fighter Pilot, Tri-logo variation	10									35	50
TO1277 Bespin Security Guard (black)	9			35	50	15	30			20	30
TO1279 Cloud Car Pilot	22			35	45	20	40			20	30
TO1281 AT-AT Commander	8			25	40	15	25			15	25
TO1283 Luke Skywalker (Hoth battle gear)	12			45	75	35	60			20	40
TO1290 Action Figure Survival Kit (mail-in) w/Jedi training harness, 2 Hoth backpacks, 3 asteroid gas masks, grappling hook belt, and 5 laser weapons	12										

Empire Three-figure sets

	Loose CNP	Star Wars MIP	Star Wars MMP	Empire MIP	Empire MMP	Jedi MIP	Jedi MMP	POTF MIP	POTF MMP	Tri-Logo MIP	Tri-Logo MMP
TO1291 Hoth Rebel Set (Han Solo (Hoth outfit), Rebel Commander, FX-7) © 1980				600	1000						
TO1293 Bespin Alliance Set (Bespin Security Guard, Lando, Luke (Bespin fatigues) © 1980				600	1000						
TO1295 Imperial Forces Set (Bossk, Stormtrooper (Hoth), IG-88) © 1980				600	1300						
TO1297 Rebel Set (2-1B, Leia (Hoth outfit), Rebel Commander) © 1981				600	1200						
TO1299 Bespin Set (Han Solo (Bespin outfit), Ugnaught, Lobot) © 1981				600	1200						
TO1301 Imperial Set (Imperial Commander, Dengar, AT-AT Driver) © 1981				600	1000						
TO1303 Rebel Set (Leia (Hoth outfit), R2-D2 (Sensorscope), Luke (Hoth outfit) © 1982				600	1200						
TO1305 Bespin Set (C-3PO, Ugnaught, Cloud Car Pilot) © 1982				600	950						
TO1307 Imperial Set (Zuckuss, AT-AT Driver, TIE Fighter Pilot) © 1982				600	1250						

Empire Six-figure sets

	Loose CNP	Star Wars MIP	Star Wars MMP	Empire MIP	Empire MMP	Jedi MIP	Jedi MMP	POTF MIP	POTF MMP	Tri-Logo MIP	Tri-Logo MMP
TO1321 Box w/Rebel Soldier, C-3PO, R2-D2 (sensorscope), Han Solo (Hoth outfit), Darth Vader, and Stormtrooper (Hoth)				450	800						
TO1323 Box w/Darth Vader, Stromtrooper (Hoth), AT-AT Driver, Rebel Soldier (Hoth), IG-88, Yoda				450	800						

Return of the Jedi (1983)

	Loose CNP	Star Wars MIP	Star Wars MMP	Empire MIP	Empire MMP	Jedi MIP	Jedi MMP	POTF MIP	POTF MMP	Tri-Logo MIP	Tri-Logo MMP
TO1351 Bib Fortuna, brown cloak	10					18	40			8	15
TO1355 Ree-Yees	10					16	30			8	15
TO1357 Weequay	8					15	28			8	15
TO1359 Emperor's Royal Guard	10					15	40			10	20
TO1361 Chief Chirpa	8					15	30			8	15
TO1363 Lando Calrissian (Skiff guard disguise)	15					20	40			10	20
TO1365 Luke Skywalker (Jedi knight) blue saber	60					50	185				
TO1366 Luke Skywalker (Jedi knight) green saber	30					40	80	160	225	25	45
TO1369 Princess Leia Organa (Boushh disguise)	28					35	60			15	30
TO1371 Logray (Ewok medicine man)	8					15	30			10	20
TO1373 Squid Head	12					16	30			10	18
TO1375 Klaatu, tan arms	8					12	22			8	15
TO1376 Klaatu, gray arms	8					12	22			6	12
TO1379 Gamorrean Guard	10					18	35	100	200	10	15
TO1381 General Madine	8					16	30			10	15
TO1383 Nien Nunb	8					15	30			10	15
TO1385 Rebel Commando	14					20	33				

	Loose CNP	Star Wars MIP	Star Wars MMP	Empire MIP	Empire MMP	Jedi MIP	Jedi MMP	POTF MIP	POTF MMP	Tri-Logo MIP	Tri-Logo MMP
TO1386 Rebel Commando, photo variation	14									15	25
TO1389 Biker Scout	15					20	35	40	80	10	20
TO1391 Admiral Ackbar	8					15	26			10	20
TO1393 Nikto	18					20	30	100	200	10	15
TO1395 Klaatu (in Skiff Guard outfit)	18					20	30			10	20
TO1396 Klaatu (Skiff Guard outfit), photo variation	18									15	35
TO1399 B-Wing Pilot	8					15	20	20	30	8	20
TO1401 Han Solo (trench coat)	12					15	25	200	350	9	25
TO1405 Teebo	12					30	40	90	180	20	30
TO1407 AT-ST Driver	11					15	27	55	70	10	20
TO1409 Prune Face	10					15	27			8	20
TO1411 Wicket W. Warrick	18					20	38	115	145	10	25
TO1413 The Emperor	10					15	30	80	140	15	25
TO1415 Rancor Keeper	12					15	22			8	20
TO1417 Princess Leia Organa (in combat poncho)	28					30	45	60	100	20	35
TO1419 8D8	12					20	30			25	30
TO1421 Paploo	25					30	37	30	45	20	30
TO1423 Lumat	28					27	35	20	30	10	20
Jedi Three-figure sets											
TO1425 Rebel Set	-					450	850				
TO1427 Imperial Set	-					450	850				
Power of the Force (1985)											
TO1431 EV-9D9	80							110	165	85	125
TO1433 Artoo-Detoo (R2-D2) w/pop-up lightsaber	80							115	175	90	175
TO1435 Han Solo in Carbonite Chamber	125							150	250		
TO1436 TO1435, package variation w/figure on top	125									100	250
TO1439 Warok	32							40	60	30	50
TO1441 Imperial Dignitary	50							65	85	30	45
TO1443 Romba	28							30	55	20	30
TO1445 Barada	50							75	110	45	75
TO1447 Lando Calrissian (General Pilot)	60							90	145	40	90
TO1449 Anakin Skywalker	32							400	650	35	90
TO1451 Luke Skywalker (Imp. Stormtrooper outfit)	155							200	300	275	350
TO1453 Imperial Gunner	80							90	145	80	175
TO1455 Luke Skywalker (in battle poncho)	65							75	120	50	75
TO1457 A-Wing Pilot (see also TO1507)	60							85	125	50	75
TO1461 Amanaman	85							130	190	100	160
TO1465 Yak Face (weapon in Canada packs only)	150							350	1500	175	400
TO1470 Sy Snootles and the Rebo Band (boxed set)	80					100	175			100	175
TO1475 *Revenge of the Jedi* cards, ea	75-125										
TO1480 Action Figure two-packs, ea	-					15	40				
TO1485 Action Figure eight-packs, ea	-					45	175				
TO1490 Young Jedi Knight mail promotion w/figure	50										

Droids action figures	Loose CNP	Droids MIP	Droids MMP
TO1501 Kea Moll	7	12	25
TO1503 Thall Joben	7	12	20
TO1505 Jann Tosh	7	12	20
TO1507 A-Wing Pilot	60	80	125
TO1509 See-Threepio (C-3PO) w/gold POTF coin	15	30	80
TO1510 See-Threepio (C-3PO) w/gold Droids coin	15	25	80
TO1513 Boba Fett	22	250	425
TO1515 Tig Fromm	20	35	50
TO1517 Jord Dusat	8	12	20
TO1519 Kez-Iban	8	12	20
TO1521 Sise Fromm	22	40	80
TO1523 Artoo-Detoo (R2-D2) w/pop-up Lightsaber	35	30	55
TO1525 Uncle Gundy	8	15	25
TO1527 Vlix (foreign release only)	200	500	800

Ewoks action figures	Loose CNP	Ewoks MIP	Ewoks MMP
TO1531 Dulok Scout	8	12	18
TO1533 King Gorneesh	8	12	18
TO1535 Dulok Shaman	8	12	18
TO1537 Logray (Ewok medicine man)	8	14	20
TO1539 Wicket W. Warrick	8	14	20
TO1541 Urgah Lady Gorneesh	8	12	18

Large action figures, 12" scale

	Loose CNP	Star Wars MIP	Star Wars MMP	Empire MIP	Empire MMP	Jedi MIP	Jedi MMP	POTF MIP	POTF MMP	Tri-Logo MIP	Tri-Logo MMP
TO2001 C-3PO	66	80	175								
TO2003 Ben Kenobi	135	175	250								
TO2005 Jawa	90	160	235								
TO2007 R2-D2	60	85	135								
TO2009 Darth Vader	85	150	225								
TO2011 Princess Leia	85	150	250								
TO2013 Chewbacca	75	100	175								
TO2015 Luke Skywalker	110	175	300								
TO2017 Stormtrooper	105	150	225								
TO2019 Han Solo	185	375	550								
TO2021 Boba Fett	170	250	575	200	400						
TO2023 IG-88	235			600	850						

Vehicles

	Loose CNP	Star Wars MIP	Star Wars MMP	Empire MIP	Empire MMP	Jedi MIP	Jedi MMP	POTF MIP	POTF MMP	Tri-Logo MIP	Tri-Logo MMP
TO4500 X-wing Fighter	45	150	310	200	295						
TO4502 X-wing Fighter w/Luke and Han	-	400	850	-	-						
TO4503 X-wing Fighter w/"battle-damage" stickers	35			75	150			60	125		
TO4504 Imperial TIE Fighter	45	120	250	150	280						
TO4505 Imperial TIE Fighter w/Darth Vader & Stormtrooper	-	350	750								
TO4506 Imperial TIE Fighter w/"battle-damage"	40			100	185	75	125				
TO4507 Darth Vader TIE Fighter	65	85	125	125	200						
TO4508 TO4507, w/battle scene setting	200	500	750								
TO4509 TO4507, Collector's edition (1983)	35	60	80								
TO4511 Imperial Troop Transporter	35	75	150								
TO4513 Imperial Cruiser (Sears exclusive)	40			85	175						
TO4515 Millennium Falcon Spaceship	95	195	350	125	250	100	200				
TO4516 Millennium Falcon w/Han & Chewbacca	-	300	700								
TO4517 Land Speeder	25	45	75								
TO4519 Landspeeder with R2-D2 & C-3PO	-	90	200								
TO4520 Landspeeder, Collector's edition (1983)	25	35	50								
TO4521 Sonic Land Speeder (Penney's exclusive)	175	300	650								
TO4522 Radio-Controlled Jawa Sandcrawler	225	450	750								
TO4523 All-Terrain Armored Transport (AT-AT)	120			160	290	135	240				
TO4525 Scout Walker	35			55	95	50	75				
TO4527 Darth Vader's Star Destroyer	60			100	225						
TO4529 Rebel Armored Snowspeeder, pink or blue box	45			65	100						
TO4530 TO4529 w/Rebel Soldier (Hoth)	-			200	350						
TO4531 Rebel Transport	42			65	125						
TO4533 Twin-Pod Cloud Car	45			65	100						
TO4534 TO4533 w/Bespin Security Guard (white)	-			200	325						
TO4535 Slave I w/"frozen" Han Solo	45			95	180						
TO4536 TO4535 w/battle scene setting	225			250	400						
TO4537 Captivator (CAP-2)	8			15	30	10	20				
TO4538 TO4537 w/Bossk	-			75	150						
TO4539 Mobile Laser Cannon (MLC-3)	8			15	30	8	20				
TO4540 TO4539 w/Rebel Commander	-			75	150						
TO4541 Interceptor (INT-4)	8			10	30	8	20				
TO4542 TO4541 w/AT-AT Commander	-			75	150						
TO4543 Multi-Terrain Vehicle (MTV-7)	8			10	35	12	25				
TO4544 TO4543 w/AT-AT Driver	-			75	150						
TO4545 Personnel Deployment Transport (PDT-8)	8			10	30	8	20				
TO4546 TO4545 w/2-1B	-			75	150						
TO4547 Imperial Shuttle	175					250	350				
TO4549 Speeder Bike	20					27	40				
TO4551 Ewok Assault Catapult	20					15	35			15	35
TO4553 Ewok Combat Glider	20					20	40			20	40
TO4555 Ewok Battle Wagon	75							100	200		
TO4557 TIE Interceptor	80					95	150				

	Loose CNP	Star Wars MIP	Star Wars MMP	Empire MIP	Empire MMP	Jedi MIP	Jedi MMP	POTF/Droids MIP	POTF/Droids MMP	Tri-Logo MIP	Tri-Logo MMP
TO4559 A-wing Fighter, Droids box	200							450	650		
TO4561 B-wing Fighter	70					90	180			60	125
TO4563 Y-wing Fighter	70					90	180				
TO4565 Armored Sentinel Transport (AST-5)	8					15	25				
TO4567 Imperial Shuttle Pod (ISP-6)	8					15	25				
TO4569 Desert Sail Skiff	10					15	25				
TO4571 Endor Forest Ranger	12					15	25			15	25
TO4573 One-Man Sand Skimmer	50							35	75	40	65
TO4575 Imperial Sniper	70							50	80	40	65
TO4577 Security Scout	50							60	85	40	65
TO4579 Tatooine Skiff	275							450	650		
TO4583 Droids Side Gunner	35							35	80		
TO4585 Droids ATL Interceptor	35							45	100		

	Loose CNP	Star Wars MIP	MMP	Empire MIP	MMP	Jedi MIP	MMP	POTF MIP	MMP	Tri-Logo MIP	MMP
Creatures											
TO4601 Patrol Dewback	47	65	150	60	110						
TO4602 Patrol Dewback, Collector's edition (1983)	47	45	90								
TO4605 Wampa, box shows Rebel Commander	15			35	95						
TO4606 Wampa, box shows Luke in Hoth outfit	15			25	75	30	60				
TO4609 Tauntaun, solid belly (1980)	22			35	75						
TO4610 Tauntaun, open belly rescue feature (1982)	20			35	80						
TO4613 Jabba the Hutt playset	37					55	92				
TO4614 TO4613 in Sears line art box	20					50	65				
TO4615 Rancor Monster	35					35	75	40	80		
Playsets											
TO4631 Death Star Space Station	100	150	300								
TO4633 Droid Factory	65	85	150	80	170						
TO4635 Creature Cantina	42	85	150								
TO4637 Cantina Adventure Set (Sears exclusive)	215	300	650								
TO4639 Land of the Jawas Playset	45	85	170								
TO4641 Turret and Probot playset	45			75	135						
TO4643 Rebel Command Center (Sears exclusive)	50			100	275						
TO4645 Imperial Attack Base	25			35	90						
TO4647 Dagobah playset	30			45	75						
TO4649 Cloud City playset (Sears exclusive)	135			200	400						
TO4651 Hoth Ice Planet playset	55			85	165						
TO4652 TO4651 w/Imp. Stormtrooper (Hoth)	-			150	350						
TO4653 Jabba the Hutt Dungeon (Sears exclusive) w/EV-9D9, Amanaman, and Barada	215					250	375				
TO4655 Jabba the Hutt Dungeon (Sears exclusive) w/Klaatu, Nikto, and 8D8	50					70	125				
TO4657 Ewok Village	40					70	100				
Display Stands											
TO4670 Display stand (mail-in premium)	38	75	125								
TO4671 Display stand, store box version	38	350	600	400	800						
TO4675 Display arena (mail-in)	60			65	80						
Accessory Sets											
TO4701 Rescue on Hoth set w/figures	-									250	450
TO4703 Ewok Combat set w/figures	-									200	400
TO4705 Speeder Bike set w/figures	-									200	400
Other Accessories											
TO4751 Tri-Pod Laser Cannon	8			10	20	8	16				
TO4753 Vehicle Maintenance Energizer	8			10	20	8	16				
TO4755 Radar Laser Cannon	8			10	20	8	16				
Storage cases											
TO4800 Star Wars vinyl storage case	12	25	50								
TO4810 Empire vinyl storage case, 2 styles, ea	12			25	50						
TO4815 Darth Vader bust case (plastic)	8			18	40	15	40				
TO4816 TO4815 w/IG-88, Bossk & Boba Fett	-			125	175						
TO4817 TO4815 w/Luke Bespin, Vader, & Yoda											
TO4818 Jedi vinyl storage case	50					100	200				
TO4820 Chewbacca bandolier strap	8					5	15				
TO4825 C-3PO bust case, gold chrome	15					25	50				
TO4830 Laser rifle case	25					25	45				

1995 Power of the Force	CNP	MIP	MMP
TP5001 Luke Skywalker, long lightsaber	5	20	30
TP5003 Luke Skywalker, short lightsaber	3	6	10
TP5007 Han Solo	3	6	10
TP5009 Chewbacca	3	6	10
TP5011 Ben (Obi-Wan) Kenobi, original card back	15	40	55
TP5012 Ben (Obi-Wan) Kenobi, revised card back	15	50	70
TP5013 Ben (Obi-Wan) Kenobi, short lightsaber	3	6	9
TP5017 R2-D2	3	6	9
TP5019 Darth Vader, long lightsaber	5	20	30
TP5021 Darth Vader, short lightsaber	3	6	12
TP5023 Stormtrooper	4	9	12
TP5025 Princess Leia Organa	4	10	15
TP5027 C-3PO	3	6	9
TP5029 Han Solo in Stormtrooper armor (Froot Loops mail-in)	20	25	35
1996 Power of the Force figures			
TP5031 Boba Fett, crescent on hands	20	40	55
TP5032 Boba Fett, circle on hands	3	6	9
TP5035 Lando Calrissian	3	6	9
TP5037 Luke Skywalker in X-wing Fighter Pilot Gear, long lightsaber	5	25	35
TP5039 TP5037, short saber	3	6	9
TP5043 Classic Edition 4-pack	12	42	57
TP5045 Han Solo in Hoth Gear, open hand	6	12	18
TP5046 Han Solo in Hoth Gear, gripping hand	3	6	9
TP5049 Luke Skywalker in Dagobah Fatigues, long lightsaber	5	25	35
TP5051 Luke Skywalker in Dagobah Fatigues, short lightsaber	3	6	9
TP5053 TIE Fighter Pilot	3	6	9
TP5055 Yoda	4	9	12
TP5057 Luke Jedi Knight (brown vest)	20	60	70
TP5058 Luke Jedi Knight (black vest)	3	6	9
TP5059 Luke Jedi Knight (theater exclusive)	-	70	120
TP5061 Han Solo "In Carbonite with Carbon Freezing Chamber"	4	15	20
TP5062 Han Solo "In Carbonite Block"	4	6	12
TP5065 Tatooine Stormtrooper	4	25	35
TP5066 Sandtrooper	4	6	9
TP5069 Luke (Stormtrooper disguise), red card	4	35	40
green card	4	6	9

TP5071 Tusken Raider (closed hand)	10	20	30
TP5072 Tusken Raider (open hand) red card	3	15	25
green card	3	6	9
TP5075 Greedo, red card	3	15	25
green card	3	6	9
TP5077 Death Star Gunner, red	3	15	30
green card	3	6	9
TP5079 Jawas, red card	3	15	25
green card	3	6	9
TP5081 R5-D4, straight trigger	10	25	35
TP5082 R5-D4, L-shaped trigger	3	6	9
TP5084 Momaw Nadon "Hammerhead," red	3	15	25
green card	3	6	9

Star Wars deluxe figure assortment, 1996

TP5085 Crowd Control Stormtrooper	5	9	12
TP5087 Luke w/Desert Skiff	5	9	12
TP5089 Han w/Smuggler Flight Pack	5	9	12

Shadows of the Empire figures, 1996

TP5091 Dash Rendar	5	8	10
TP5093 Chewbacca (Snoova)	5	8	10
TP5095 Xizor	5	8	10
TP5099 Leia (Boushh disguise)	5	8	10
TP5101 Luke Skywalker (Coruscant Guard)	6	9	12
TP5105 Boba Fett/IG-88 2-pack	8	13	16
TP5107 Xizor/Vader 2-pack	8	13	16

1997 *Power of the Force* figures

TP5111 Spirit of Obi-Wan (mail-in)	12	18	22
TP5113 AT-ST Driver	3	6	9
TP5115 2-1B Medic Droid	3	6	9
TP5117 Luke Skywalker in Hoth Gear	3	6	9
TP5119 Bossk	3	6	9
TP5121 Hoth Rebel Soldier	3	6	9
TP5123 Cantina Band Member (Fan Club)	15	24	28
TP5125 Bib Fortuna	3	6	9
TP5127 Han Solo (Endor Gear)	3	6	9
TP5129 Lando Calrissian (Skiff Guard)	3	6	9
TP5131 Emperor Palpatine	3	6	9
TP5133 Rebel Fleet Trooper	3	6	9
TP5135 ASP-7 Droid	3	6	9
TP5137 Admiral Ackbar	3	6	9
TP5139 4-LOM	3	6	9
TP5141 Dengar	3	6	9
TP5143 Grand Moff Tarkin	3	6	9
TP5145 Ponda Baba	3	6	9
TP5147 Weequay, Skiff Guard	3	6	9
TP5149 Garindan (Long Snoot)	3	6	9
TP5151 Bespin Han Solo	3	6	9
TP5153 Princess Leia Organa (Jabba's Prisoner)	4	5	10
TP5155 Luke Skywalker (Ceremonial Outfit)	3	6	9
TP5157 Princess Leia (Ewok Ceremonial)	3	6	9
TP5159 Bespin Luke Skywalker	3	6	9
TP5161 B'omarr Monk (Internet Exclusive)	10	15	20
TP5163 Malakili (Rancor Keeper)	3	6	9
TP5165 Gamorrean Guard	3	6	9
TP5167 Nien Numb	3	6	9
TP5169 EV-9D9	3	6	9
TP5171 Saelt-Marae (Yak Face)	3	6	9
TP5173 Royal Guard	3	6	9
TP5175 Snowtrooper	3	6	9
TP5177 Endor Rebel Soldier	3	6	9
TP5179 General Lando Calrissian	3	6	9

Sam's Club 3-Packs

TP5181 R2-D2, Stormtrooper, C-3PO	-	15	30
TP5183 Luke, Ben, Vader	-	15	30
TP5185 Lando, Han, Chewbacca	-	15	30

Star Wars deluxe figure assortment, 1997

TP5191 Boba Fett	7	10	12
TP5193 Probe Droid	7	10	12
TP5195 Hoth Rebel Soldier	7	10	12
TP5197 Snowtrooper	7	10	12

Star Wars Power F/X assortment, 1997

TP5201 Ben Kenobi	8	12	14
TP5203 Darth Vader	8	12	14
TP5205 R2-D2	8	12	14
TP5207 Emperor Palpatine	8	12	14
TP5209 Luke Jedi Knight	8	12	14

Star Wars Cinema Scene 3-Packs, 1997

TP5211 Death Star Escape	15	25	35
TP5213 Cantina Showdown	15	25	35

Star Wars Beast assortment, 1997

TP5221 Dewback and Sandtrooper	10	15	20
TP5223 Ronto and Jawa	10	15	20
TP5225 Jabba the Hutt and Han Solo	10	15	20
TP5227 Tauntaun and Luke Skywalker	10	15	20

Vehicles and accessories, 1995

TP5501 Landspeeder	6	10	15
TP5503 TIE fighter	10	15	25
TP5505 X-wing fighter	12	18	30
TP5507 Millennium Falcon	25	40	55
TP5509 Imperial AT-ST (Scout Walker)	10	12	30

Vehicles and accessories, 1996

TP5511 Speeder Bike w/Biker Scout figure	5	9	14
TP5515 Rebel Snowspeeder	10	20	30

Shadows of the Empire vehicles, 1996

TP5521 Swoop vehicle w/figure	5	9	13
TP5523 Boba Fett's Slave I	10	20	30
TP5525 Dash Rendar's Outrider	10	20	30

Vehicles and accessories, 1997

TP5531 Slave I (1997 box)	10	20	30
TP5533 Luke's T-16 Skyhopper	10	20	30
TP5535 Speeder Bike w/Luke Endor, flesh hand on package	5	15	25
TP5536 TP5535, black hand on package	5	12	15
TP5539 Cruisemissile Trooper	5	12	15
TP5541 Darth Vader's TIE Fighter	10	15	22
TP5545 A-Wing Fighter	10	15	22
TP5547 Speeder Bike w/Leia Endor	5	9	15
TP5549 Imperial AT-AT w/ Driver & Commander	35	70	80

Star Wars Action Playsets, 1997

TP5551 Detention Block Rescue	8	10	15
TP5553 Death Star Escape	8	10	15
TP5555 Mos Eisley pop-up (mail-in)	20	30	40
TP5557 Hoth Ice Battle	10	15	20
TP5559 Endor Ambush	10	15	20

Storage Cases

TP5751 Collectors Case (1996)	8	10	12
TP5753 Talking C-3PO Carry Case (1997)	10	15	20
TP5755 Millennium Falcon Carry Case w/Wedge Antilles figure (1997), wrong deco on figure	25	30	40
TP5756 TP5755, corrected deco on figure	10	20	25

12" Collector Series figures, 1996

TP5801 Luke Skywalker	10	20	30
TP5803 Han Solo	10	20	30
TP5805 Obi-Wan Kenobi	10	30	50
TP5807 Darth Vader	10	20	30

12" Collector Series figures, 1997

TP5811 Lando Calrissian	9	18	25
TP5813 Luke Skywalker (Bespin)	10	20	30
TP5815 Tusken Raider w/ gaderffii stick	12	24	32
TP5817 TP5815 w/blaster and macrobinoculars	12	24	32
TP5819 Boba Fett	10	20	30
TP5821 Stormtrooper	10	22	32
TP5823 Princess Leia	10	22	32
TP5825 Luke Skywalker (X-wing Pilot)	10	20	30
TP5827 C-3PO	10	20	30
TP5829 Chewbacca	10	20	30
TP5831 Admiral Ackbar	10	20	30
TP5833 TIE Fighter Pilot	10	20	30

12" Collector Series Exclusives, 1997

TP5835 Han Solo & Luke Skywalker in Stormtrooper Gear (Kay-Bee)	50	135	175
TP5837 Grand Moff Tarkin & Imperial Gunner (FAO)	35	75	100
TP5839 Luke w/Wampa (Target)	50	150	190
TP5841 Han Solo w/Tauntaun (Toys "Я" Us)	50	150	190

Cantina Band (Wal-Mart) TP5843-53

TP5843 Figrin D'an	15	30	40
TP5845 Doikk N'ats	15	30	40
TP5847 Ickabel	15	30	40
TP5849 Nalan	15	30	40
TP5851 Tech	15	30	40
TP5853 Tedn	15	30	40
TP5855 Greedo (JC Penny)	25	70	100
TP5857 Electronic Obi-Wan vs. Darth Vader 2-Pack (JC Penny Catalogs)	35	75	110
TP5859 Sandtrooper (Diamond Comics and others)	15	30	40
TP5861 Bib Fortuna & Luke Jedi Knight (FAO)	35	75	100
TP5863 AT-AT Driver (Service Merchandise)	25	50	75

Promotional Catalog advertisement for TO1290

TO1101 TO1104 TO1106 TO1111 TO1113 TO1115 TO1116 TO1121

TO1101

TO1101

TO1101

TO1103

TO1103

TO1105

TO1105

TO1106

TO1108

TO1111

TO1113

TO1113

TO1115

TO1116

185

TO1123   TO1126   TO1127   TO1130   TO1132   TO1137   TO1139   TO1141

TO1116

TO1118

TO1121

TO1121

TO1123

TO1123

TO1123

TO1123

TO1124

TO1127

TO1127

TO1127

TO1128

TO1131

TO1131

TO1131   TO1132   TO1135   TO1137   TO1139

TO1139   TO1139   TO1139   TO1141   TO1142

TO1143   TO1145   TO1145   TO1146   TO1146

TO1151   TO1151   TO1151   TO1153   TO1153

All accessory combinations shown have been confirmed with sealed packaged samples. Other combinations may also exist, as substitutions were made for out-of-stock items.

TO1145   TO1151   TO1153   TO1155   TO1157   TO1159   TO1161   TO1163

TO1153   TO1155   TO1155   TO1155   TO1157

TO1157   TO1157   TO1161   TO1161   TO1161

TO1163   TO1163   TO1163   TO1165   TO1165

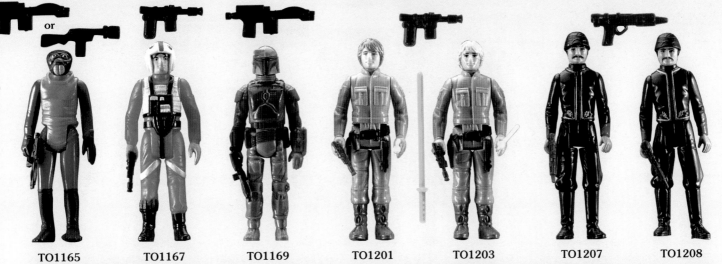

TO1165   TO1167   TO1169   TO1201   TO1203   TO1207   TO1208

TO1165   TO1167   TO1167   TO1167   TO1169

TO1169   TO1169   TO1171   TO1201   TO1203

TO1204   TO1204   TO1207   TO1207   TO1209

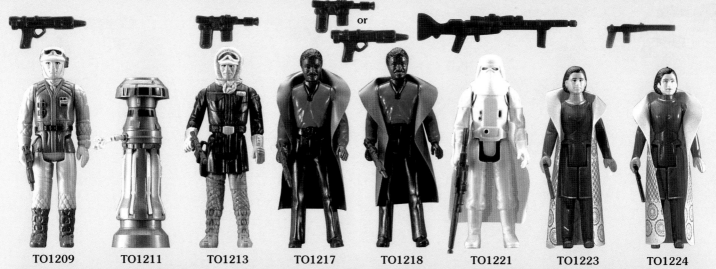

TO1209   TO1211   TO1213   TO1217   TO1218   TO1221   TO1223   TO1224

TO1209   TO1211   TO1211   TO1213   TO1213

TO1217   TO1218   TO1218   TO1221   TO1221

TO1223   TO1226   TO1226   TO1229   TO1229

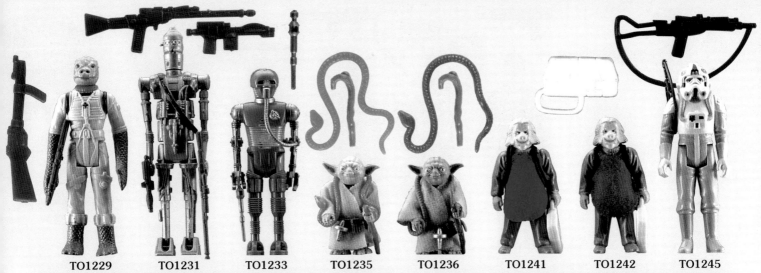

TO1229   TO1231   TO1233   TO1235   TO1236   TO1241   TO1242   TO1245

TO1231

TO1231

TO1233

TO1233

TO1235

TO1236

TO1237

TO1238

TO1238

TO1241

TO1241

TO1245

TO1245

TO1247

TO1247

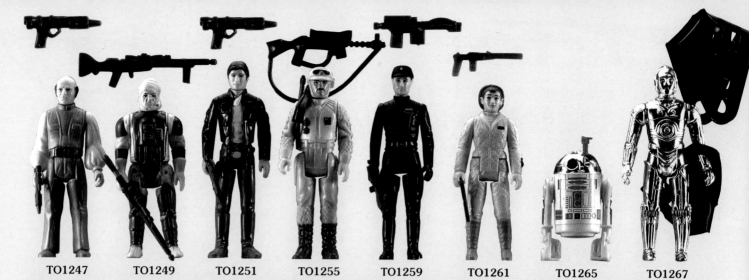

TO1247   TO1249   TO1251   TO1255   TO1259   TO1261   TO1265   TO1267

TO1249   TO1249   TO1251   TO1251   TO1255

TO1255   TO1256   TO1259   TO1261   TO1261

TO1265   TO1265   TO1267   TO1267   TO1267

TO1269   TO1271   TO1273   TO1277   TO1279   TO1281   TO1283

TO1269

TO1269

TO1271

TO1271

TO1273

TO1273

TO1277

TO1277

TO1279

TO1279

TO1281

TO1281

TO1283

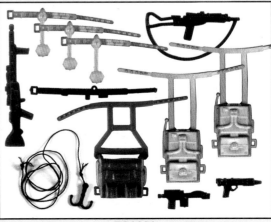
TO1290

TO1351

TO1355

TO1357

TO1359

TO1361

TO1363

TO1365
(shown w/o cape)

TO1366

TO1369

TO1371

TO1373

TO1375

TO1376

TO1351

TO1355

TO1357

TO1359

TO1361

TO1363

TO1365

TO1369

TO1369

TO1371

TO1379   TO1381   TO1383   TO1385   TO1389   TO1391   TO1393

TO1373   TO1373   TO1376   TO1379   TO1381

TO1383   TO1385   TO1386   TO1389   TO1389

TO1391   TO1393   TO1395   TO1399   TO1399

TO1395	TO1399	TO1401	TO1402	TO1405	TO1407	TO1409

TO1401	TO1401	TO1405	TO1405	TO1407

TO1407	TO1409	TO1411	TO1413	TO1413

TO1415	TO1417	TO1419	TO1421	TO1421

TO1411   TO1413   TO1415   TO1417   TO1419   TO1421   TO1423

TO1431   TO1433   TO1435   TO1439   TO1441   TO1443   TO1445

TO1423   TO1431   TO1433   TO1435   TO1436

TO1439   TO1441   TO1443   TO1445   TO1447

TO1447   TO1449   TO1451   TO1453   TO1455   TO1457   TO1461

Weapon included
in Kenner Canada
packages only

Staff for TO1461   TO1466   TO1470   TO1471   TO1472

TO1449   TO1449   TO1451   TO1453   TO1455

TO1457   TO1461   TO1465   TO1465   TO1470

198

TO1501 TO1503 TO1505 TO1507 TO1509

Coin from
TO1509

Coin from
TO1510

TO1513 TO1517 TO1519

TO1521 TO1523 TO1525 TO1527 TO1531

TO1533 TO1535 TO1537 TO1539 TO1541

TO1191

TO1193

TO1181

TO1183

TO1185

TO1191

TO1193

TO1297

TO1299

TO1301

TO1303

TO1305

TO1321

TO1323

TO1195

TO1197

TO1195

TO1197

TO1291

TO1293

TO1295

TO1307

TO1425

TO1427

TO1475

TO1480

TO2001

TO2003

TO2005

TO2007

TO2011 TO2015 TO2017 TO2019

TO2009 TO2013 TO2021 TO2023

TO4500 TO4501 TO4504 TO4505

TO4511

TO4513

TO4515

TO4507   TO4508   TO4508

TO4517   TO4518   TO4521

TO4522   TO4525   TO4527

TO4523   TO4529   TO4533

TO4531   203   TO4535

TO4537

TO4539

TO4539

TO4540

TO4541

TO4543

TO4543

TO4545

TO4547

TO4549

TO4555

TO4551

TO4553

TO4557

TO4559

TO4563

TO4565

TO4567

TO4569

TO4571

TO4561

TO4573

TO4575

TO4577

TO4579

TO4583

TO4585

TO4601

TO4602

TO4605

TO4606

TO4609

TO4610

TO4613

TO4615

TO4631

TO4633

TO4635

TO4637

TO4639

TO4643

TO4651

TO4641

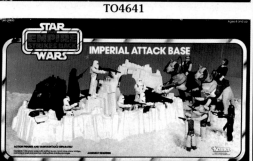

TO4645

TO4657

TO4647

TO4649

TO4653

TO4655

TO4651

TO4651

TO4653

TO4655

TO4671

TO4675

TO4701

TO4703

TO4705

TO4815

TO4815

TO4800

TO4810

TO4820

TO4830

TO4825

Lightsaber sizes for all figures were reduced in 1996. A standard size was eventually established, but a variety of different lengths appeared during the transition. Shorter lightsabers were initially packed in plastic inserts intended for the original size, then later appeared with a new insert made for the shorter size. Packages with the original insert and short lightsaber command a value equal to that of the long lightsabers. Shorter lightsabers in revised inserts are worth less in general. Oddball sizes not standard to either production version may become the most valuable in the long run, but market evidence is insufficient for pricing at this time.

TP5001 TP5007 TP5009 TP5011 TP5017 TP5019

TP5001 TP5007 TP5007 TP5009 TP5009

TP5011 TP5012 File Card TP5013 TP5017 TP5017

TP5011 File Card

TP5107   TP5023   TP5027   TP5025   TP5029   TP5031   TP5105

TP5019

TP5021

TP5023

TP5023

TP5023

TP5025

TP5025

TP5027

TP5027

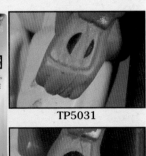

TP5031

TP5032

TP5031

TP5032

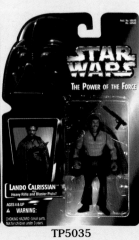

TP5035

TP5037

TP5039

209

TP5035　　TP5037　　TP5045　　TP5049　　TP5053　　TP5055

TP5058　　TP5061　　TP5065　　TP5069　　TP5072

CLASSIC EDITION 4-PACK

TP5043

Weapons from TP5043

TP5045 Detail

TP5045

TP5046 Detail

TP5049　　TP5053　　TP5053　　TP5055　　TP5055

TP5075   TP5077   TP5079   TP5079   TP5081   TP5084

TP5057   TP5058   TP5059   TP5061

TP5061 Detail

TP5062 Detail

    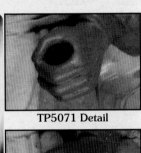 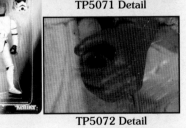

TP5065   TP5066   TP5069   TP5069

TP5071 Detail

TP5072 Detail

TP5071   TP5072   TP5075   TP5075   TP5077

TP5087

TP5089

TP5085

TP5091   TP5093   TP5095   TP5107   TP5099   TP5101

STAR WARS THE POWER OF THE FORCE

COLLECTION 1

DEATH STAR GUNNER
IMPERIAL BLASTER AND ASSAULT RIFLE

WARNING: CHOKING HAZARD—Small parts. Not for children under 3 years.

TP5077

STAR WARS THE POWER OF THE FORCE

COLLECTION 2

JAWAS
GLOWING EYES AND JONEATION BLASTERS

WARNING: CHOKING HAZARD—Small parts. Not for children under 3 years.

TP5079

STAR WARS THE POWER OF THE FORCE

COLLECTION 2

JAWAS
GLOWING EYES AND BLASTER PISTOLS

WARNING: CHOKING HAZARD—Small parts. Not for children under 3 years.

TP5079

STAR WARS THE POWER OF THE FORCE

COLLECTION 2
AGES 4 & UP

R5-D4
CONCEALED PHOTON MISSILE LAUNCHER

TP5081

STAR WARS THE POWER OF THE FORCE

COLLECTION 2
AGES 4 & UP

R5-D4
CONCEALED PHOTON MISSILE LAUNCHER

WARNING: CHOKING HAZARD—Small parts. Not for children under 3 years.

TP5082

TP5081 Detail

TP5082 Detail

STAR WARS

AGES 4 AND UP

WARNING: CHOKING HAZARD—Small parts. Not for children under 3 years.

DELUXE
CROWD CONTROL
STORMTROOPER
With FLIGHT-ACTION THRUSTER PACK AND CAPTURE CLAW

GALACTIC EMPIRE

TP5085

STAR WARS

AGES 4 & UP

DELUXE
LUKE SKYWALKER'S
DESERT SPORT SKIFF
With BLASTING ROCKET LAUNCHER AND RAPID-DEPLOY WINGS

REBEL ALLIANCE

TP5087

STAR WARS

AGES 4 & UP

DELUXE
HAN SOLO
with SMUGGLER FLIGHT PACK
Plus BATTLE-PIVOTING BLASTER CANNONS AND CARGO CLAW

REBEL ALLIANCE

TP5089

TP5105   TP5111   TP5113   TP5115   TP5117   TP5119   TP5121

STAR WARS®
SHADOWS OF THE EMPIRE

DASH RENDAR
with HEAVY WEAPONS PACK

TP5091

STAR WARS®
SHADOWS OF THE EMPIRE

CHEWBACCA
IN BOUNTY HUNTER DISGUISE
with VIBRO AXE AND HEAVY BLASTER RIFLE

TP5093

STAR WARS®
SHADOWS OF THE EMPIRE

PRINCE XIZOR
with ENERGY BLADE SHIELDS

TP5095

STAR WARS®
SHADOWS OF THE EMPIRE

LEIA
IN BOUSHH DISGUISE with
BLASTER RIFLE AND
BOUNTY HUNTER HELMET

TP5099

STAR WARS®
SHADOWS OF THE EMPIRE

LUKE SKYWALKER
IN IMPERIAL GUARD DISGUISE
with TASER STAFF WEAPON

TP5101

STAR WARS
SHADOWS OF THE EMPIRE

EXCLUSIVE DARK HORSE
COMIC BOOK INCLUDED!

ULTIMATE BATTLE OF BOUNTY HUNTERS!

BOBA FETT vs. IG-88

TP5105

STAR WARS
SHADOWS OF THE EMPIRE

EXCLUSIVE DARK HORSE COMICS
COMIC BOOK INCLUDED!

EPIC CLASH FOR GALACTIC CONTROL!

PRINCE XIZOR vs. DARTH VADER

TP5107

TP5123

STAR WARS®
THE POWER OF THE FORCE

COLLECTION 2

AT-ST DRIVER
with BLASTER RIFLE AND PISTOL

TP5113

STAR WARS®
THE POWER OF THE FORCE

COLLECTION 2

2-1B MEDIC DROID
MEDICAL DIAGNOSTIC COMPUTER

TP5115

STAR WARS®
THE POWER OF THE FORCE

COLLECTION 2

LUKE SKYWALKER IN HOTH GEAR
with BLASTER PISTOL AND LIGHTSABER

TP5117

STAR WARS®
THE POWER OF THE FORCE

COLLECTION 2

BOSSK
with BLASTER RIFLE AND PISTOL

TP5119

STAR WARS®
THE POWER OF THE FORCE

COLLECTION 2

HOTH REBEL SOLDIER
with SURVIVAL BACKPACK AND BLASTER RIFLE

TP5121

TP5125   TP5127   TP5129   TP5131   TP5133

TP5135   TP5137   TP5139   TP5141   TP5143

STAR WARS — THE POWER OF THE FORCE

BIB FORTUNA   HAN SOLO IN ENDOR GEAR   LANDO CALRISSIAN AS SKIFF GUARD   EMPEROR PALPATINE   REBEL FLEET TROOPER

TP5125   TP5127   TP5129   TP5131   TP5133

STAR WARS — THE POWER OF THE FORCE

ASP-7 DROID   ADMIRAL ACKBAR   4-LOM   DENGAR   GRAND MOFF TARKIN

TP5135   TP5137   TP5139   TP5141   TP5143

TP5145

TP5147

TP5149

TP5151

TP5153

TP5155

TP5157

TP5159

TP5161

TP5163

TP5165

TP5167

TP5169

TP5171

STAR WARS
THE POWER OF THE FORCE

COLLECTION 3
Asst. No. 69705
No. 69706

PONDA BABA
WITH
BLASTER PISTOL AND RIFLE

AGES 4 & UP

⚠ WARNING:
CHOKING HAZARD-Small parts.
Not for children under 3 years.

TP5145

STAR WARS
THE POWER OF THE FORCE

COLLECTION 3
Asst. No. 69705
No. 69707

WEEQUAY™ SKIFF GUARD
WITH
FORCE PIKE AND BLASTER RIFLE

AGES 4 & UP

⚠ WARNING:
CHOKING HAZARD-Small parts.
Not for children under 3 years.

TP5147

STAR WARS
THE POWER OF THE FORCE

COLLECTION 3
Asst. No. 69705
No. 69708

GARINDAN (LONG SNOOT)™
WITH
HOLD-OUT PISTOL

AGES 4 & UP

⚠ WARNING:
CHOKING HAZARD-Small parts.
Not for children under 3 years.

TP5149

STAR WARS
THE POWER OF THE FORCE

COLLECTION 1
Asst. No. 69570
No. 69710

BESPIN HAN SOLO™
WITH
HEAVY ASSAULT RIFLE AND BLASTER

AGES 4 & UP

⚠ WARNING:
CHOKING HAZARD-Small parts.
Not for children under 3 years.

TP5151

STAR WARS
THE POWER OF THE FORCE

COLLECTION 1
Asst. No. 69570
No. 69683

PRINCESS LEIA ORGANA™
JABBA'S PRISONER

AGES 4 & UP

⚠ WARNING:
CHOKING HAZARD-Small parts.
Not for children under 3 years.

TP5153

TP5173   TP5175

EMPEROR'S ROYAL GUARD   SNOWTROOPER

TP5173   TP5175   TP5179

COLLECTOR PACK

TP5181

TP5191

TP5193   TP5195   TP5197

MALAKILI (RANCOR KEEPER)   GAMORREAN GUARD   NIEN NUNB   EV-9D9   SAELT-MARAE (YAK FACE)

TP5163   TP5165   TP5167   TP5169   TP5171

DELUXE BOBA FETT   DELUXE PROBE DROID   DELUXE HOTH REBEL SOLDIER   DELUXE SNOWTROOPER

TP5191   TP5193   TP5195   TP5197

TP5203   TP5201   TP5205

TP5207   TP5209

TP5201   TP5203   TP5205   TP5207   TP5209

TP5211   TP5213

217

TP5211

TP5213

TP5221

TP5223

TP5225

TP5221

TP5223

TP5225

TP5511

TP5521

218

TP5501

TP5503

TP5507

TP5505

IMPERIAL AT-ST (SCOUT WALKER)

TP5509

TP5515

TP5511

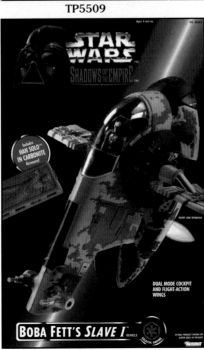

TP5521

TP5523

TP5531

Figure from TP5535-36   Figure from TP5545   Figure from TP5547   Figures from TP5549   TP5756   Figure from TP5755

TP5525

DASH RENDAR'S *OUTRIDER*
With Cockpit & Gun Turret You Fully Rotate in Battle!

TP5533

LUKE'S T-16 SKYHOPPER
2 VEHICLES IN 1 WITH DETACHABLE COCKPIT!

SPEEDER BIKE
WITH LUKE SKYWALKER IN ENDOR GEAR
BIKE EXPLODES APART AND EJECTS LUKE!

TP5535

TP5535 Detail   TP5536 Detail

TP5539

CRUISEMISSILE TROOPER
WITH TWIN PROTON TORPEDO LAUNCHERS

TP5541

DARTH VADER'S TIE FIGHTER
With LAUNCHING LASER CANNONS!

TP5545

A-WING FIGHTER
WITH PIVOTING LASER CANNONS AND RETRACTABLE TRIPOD LANDING GEAR

TP5751

OFFICIAL COLLECTOR CASE
For all your figures and accessories!

TALKING C-3PO CARRY CASE
Holds a Galaxy of Figures & Accessories!
TRY ME!

TP5753

MILLENNIUM FALCON CARRY CASE
AUTHENTICALLY STYLED REPLICA, HOLDS A GALAXY OF FIGURES & ACCESSORIES!

WEDGE ANTILLES
EXCLUSIVE WEDGE ANTILLES

TP5755

TP5547   TP5551   TP5553

TP5555, folded   TP5555, open

TP5801   TP5803   TP5805

TP5807   TP5811   TP5813

TP5815 Detail

TP5815-17   TP5815   TP5817 Detail   TP5819

TP5821   TP5823   TP5825

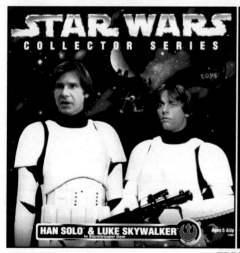

TP5835   TP5837

ACTION FIGURES, INTERNATIONAL				
Brazil (Glassite)			TO2214 Kez Iban	10 - 20
			TO2215 Thall Joben	10 - 20
POTF: O Poder da Força 1988-89			TO2216 Vlix	400 - 1200
TO2201 Chewbacca	40 - 125		**Canada**	
TO2202 R2-D2	40 - 125		TO2400 Canadian Kenner 3¾" figures	See Tri-Logo prices
TO2203 Guerreiro Imperial	40 - 125		TO2440 Hero Set	500 - 900
TO2204 Luke Skywalker	40 - 125		TO2441 Villain Set	500 - 900
TO2205 Princesa Leia	50 - 150		TO2442 Creature Set	500 - 900
TO2206 Han Solo	50 - 175		TO2443 Droids set	500 - 900
TO2207 C-3PO	40 - 125		TO2500 *ESB* 3-figure packs (Sears exclusives), ea.	250 - 450
Droids 1988-89			TO2505 *ESB* 4-figure packs (Sears exclusives), ea.	250 - 450
TO2210 R2-D2	50 - 75		TO2550 Canadian versions of *Droids* figures, ea.	8 - 18
TO2211 C-3PO	50 - 75		**England**	
TO2212 Jord Dusat	10 - 20		TO2750 U.K. versions of Kenner 3¾" figures (Palitoy)	U.S. + 30%
TO2213 Kea Moll	10 - 20		TO2760 U.K. large figures (Denys Fisher, Palitoy)	U.S. + 10%

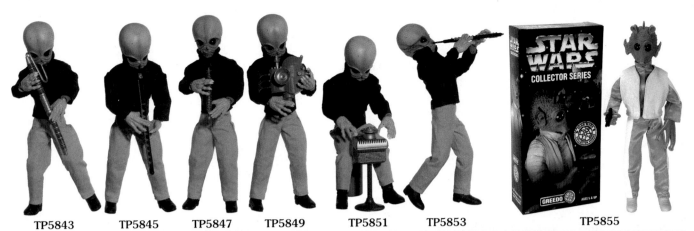

TP5843   TP5845   TP5847   TP5849   TP5851   TP5853   TP5855

TP5839   TP5841   TP5857

TO2201   TO2202   TO2203   TO2204   TO2205

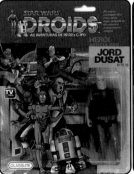

TO2206   TO2207   TO2211   TO2212   TO2213

France, La Guerre des Etoiles (Micro-Meccano)
French versions of Kenner 3¾" figures (square cards)

TO2801	Chiquetaba	40 - 60
TO2802	Luc	50 - 75
TO2803	D2 R2	40 - 60
TO2804	Leïa	40 - 60
TO2805	Yan Solo	55 - 80
TO2806	Z6 PO	40 - 60
TO2807	Soldat Impérial	35 - 55
TO2808	Dark Vador	50 - 75
TO2809	Ben Kenobi	40 - 60
TO2810	Jawa	25 - 35
TO2811	Homme de Sables	40 - 60
TO2812	Le Cdt de l'Etoile Noire	40 - 60
TO2813	Hammerhead	40 - 60
TO2814	Power Droïd	35 - 55
TO2815	D5 R4	35 - 55
TO2817	Snaggle Tooth (regular)	40 - 60

TO2214

TO2215

TO2216

TO2550

TO2550

TO2441

TO2442

TO2443

TO2500

TO2810

TO3050

TO3305

TO3400

TO3401   TO3402

TO2818	Greedo	40 - 60
TO2819	Death Star Droïd	35 - 55
TO2820	Walrus Mam	40 - 60
TO2821	Luc Pilote	50 - 75

French versions of Kenner Large Action Figures

TO2950	Princesse Leïa	100 - 175
TO2951	Luc	175 - 250
TO2952	Z6 PO	100 - 150
TO2953	Yan Solo	350 - 450
TO2954	Chiquetaba	75 - 100
TO2955	Dark Vador	65 - 150
TO2956	Soldat Impérial	65 - 150

Germany
Krieg der Sterne (GMI)

TO3001	Chewbacca	40 - 60
TO3002	Luke Skywalker	50 - 75
TO3003	Artoo-Detoo (R2-D2)	40 - 60
TO3004	Princess Leia Organa	40 - 60
TO3005	Han Solo	55 - 80
TO3006	See-Threepio (C-3PO)	40 - 60
TO3007	Stormtrooper	35 - 55
TO3008	Darth Vader	50 - 75

TO3009	Ben (Obi-Wan) Kenobi	40 - 60
TO3010	Jawa	25 - 35
TO3011	Sand People (Tusken Raider)	40 - 60
TO3012	Star Destroyer Comander	40 - 60
TO3013	Walrus Man	40 - 60
TO3014	Hammerhead	40 - 60
TO3015	Power Droid	35 - 55
TO3016	Luke Skywalker X-wing Pilot	50 - 75
TO3017	R5-D4	35 - 55
TO3018	Death Star Droid	35 - 55
TO3019	Greedo	40 - 60
TO3020	Snagletooth	40 - 60
TO3050	*YPS* Comic w/Snowtrooper premium	50 - 100

Italy **(Harbert)**

TO3300	Italian versions of Kenner 3¾" figures	40 - 100
TO3305	C1P8	20 - 50
TO3350	Uhu Stic glue sticks w/Ewoks, each	

Hong Kong **(1997 Commemoratives)**

TO3400	12" Commemorative Set	100 - 150
TO3401	3¾" Rebel Set	60 - 75
TO3401	3¾" Imperial Set	60 - 75

Japan
Star Wars 3¾"

TO3450	Japanese versions of 3¾" *SW* figures (Takara), ea.	35 - 175
TO3454	C-3PO w/variation head	75 - 150
TO3456	Stormtrooper w/variation head	50 - 100
TO3458	Darth Vader w/variation head	50 - 100

Star Wars 8" action figures

TO3500	Chewbacca	250 - 600
TO3501	Darth Vader	250 - 500
TO3502	"Stoom" Trooper	250 - 500
TO3503	C-3PO	250 - 500

TO3454	TO3500	TO3501	TO3501	TO3502

TO3551	TO3552	TO3553	TO3554	TO3555	TO3556	TO3557	TO3558	TO3559

TO3560	TO3561	TO3562	TO3563	TO3564	TO3565	TO3600	TO3650

TO3746	TO3747	TO3748	TO3749	TO3750

Star Wars **large action figures (Takara)**

TO3530	Luke	175 - 325
TO3531	Leia	175 - 350

Empire Strikes Back **3¾"(Popy)**

TO3551	#1 Boba Fett	150 - 325
TO3552	#2 Darth Vader	75 - 125
TO3553	#3 R2-D2	75 - 125
TO3554	#4 C-3PO	75 - 125
TO3555	#5 Luke Skywalker (Bespin fatigues)	75 - 125
TO3556	#6 Han Solo (Hoth gear)	75 - 125
TO3557	#7 Chewbacca	75 - 125
TO3558	#8 Luke Skywalker	75 - 125
TO3559	#9 Han Solo	100 - 250
TO3560	#10 Snowtrooper	75 - 125
TO3561	#11 Death Star Droid	75 - 125

TO3562	#12 Luke in Hoth gear	75 - 125
TO3563	#13 Luke in X-wing gear	75 - 125
TO3564	#14 R5-D4	75 - 125
TO3565	#15 Stormtrooper	75 - 125

Return of the Jedi **3¾" (Takara)**

TO3600	Japanese *Jedi* figures	U.S. + 20%

Power of the Force, 1995+

TO3650	Japanese 1995 *POTF* figures, w/trading card	U.S. + 20%
Mexico		

Large *SW* **action figure (Lili-Ledy)**

TO3746	Darth Vader	200 - 600
TO3747	Han Solo	200 - 575
TO3748	Hombre de las Dunas	600 - 1250
TO3749	Luke Skywalker	200 - 575
TO3750	Princesa Leia Organa	200 - 550

TO3751	Ar-tu-ri-to R2-D2	200 - 550
TO3752	Jawa	200 - 575

El Retorno de Jedi/El Regreso del Jedi (Kenner/Lili-Ledy SA)

Kenner *Jedi* figures were repackaged on Spanish packages for distribution in Mexico. The first assortment carried the logo *El Retorno de Jedi*. This was changed to *El Regreso del Jedi* for later assortments. Some figures were packaged with both logos.

First assortment: *El Retorno de Jedi/El Regreso del Jedi*

TO3901	Luke Skywalker (Bespin Fatigues), yellow hair	75 - 170
TO3903	Luke Skywalker (Bespin Fatigues), brown hair	60 - 150
TO3905	Han Solo (Bespin Outfit)	50 - 125
TO3907	Darth Vader	35 - 85
TO3909	C-3PO	60 - 80
TO3911	R2-D2	45 - 75
TO3913	Yoda (orange snake)	50 - 90
TO3914	Yoda (brown snake)	55 - 95
TO3917	Lando Calrissian (Skiff Guard disguise)	20 - 40
TO3919	Squid Head	16 - 30
TO3921	Klaatu	16 - 30
TO3923	Gammorrean Guard	18 - 35
TO3925	Ree-Yees	16 - 30

Later assortments: *El Regreso del Jedi*

TO3927	Nien Nunb	16 - 30
TO3929	Chief Chirpa	15 - 30
TO3931	Logray	15 - 30
TO3933	Leia (Bespin Gown), flesh collar	40 - 90
TO3934	Leia (Bespin Gown), maroon collar	50 - 95
TO3937	Chewbacca	45 - 100
TO3939	Obi-Wan Kenobi (white hair)	60 - 155
TO3940	Obi-Wan Kenobi (grey hair)	45 - 90
TO3943	Stormtrooper	35 - 85
TO3945	Boba Fett	120 - 190
TO3947	General Madine	15 - 30
TO3949	Guardia Emperator	15 - 40
TO3951	"Weeguay"	15 - 30
TO3953	Imperial TIE Fighter Pilot	35 - 65
TO3955	Bib Fortuna (brown vest)	18 - 40
TO3957	Princess Leia (Boussh Disguise)	35 - 60
TO3959	Biker Scout	12 - 28
TO3961	Star Destroyer Commander	20 - 40

TO3963	Imperial Commander	15 - 35
TO3965	Hombre Clamar	15 - 35
TO3967	Luke Skywalker (Jedi Knight Outfit)	40 - 80
TO3969	Chief Chirpa	15 - 30
TO3971	Paploo	30 - 45
TO3973	Wicket W. Warrick	20 - 38
TO3975	Lumat	20 - 30
TO3977	The Emperor	15 - 30
TO3979	AT-ST Driver	15 - 30
TO3981	Prune Face	15 - 30
TO3983	Lando Calrissian (with and without white teeth)	20 - 40
TO3987	Teebo	30 - 40
TO3989	Han Solo in trench coat	15 - 25
TO3991	Jawa (brown vest)	20 - 40
TO3993	Klaatu Skiff Guard Outfit	20 - 30
TO3995	Rebel Commander	15 - 30
TO3997	Princess Leia (in combat poncho)	30 - 45
TO3999	8D8	20 - 30
TO4011	B-Wing Pilot	15 - 30
TO4013	Cloud Car Pilot	20 - 40
TO4015	Rancor Keeper	30 - 45
TO4017	Zuccuss	25 - 60
TO4019	Nikto	20 - 30
TO4021	C-3PO w/removable limbs	25 - 40

Spain

TO4150	Spanish versions of Kenner 3¾" *ESB* figures	U.S. + 15%
TO4150	Spanish versions of Kenner 3¾" *ROTJ* figures	U.S. + 15%

ACTION FIGURE VEHICLES, PLAYSETS, AND ACCESSORIES, INTERNATIONAL

Australia (Toltoys)

TO4932	Death Star Playset	300 - 600

Brazil (Glasslite)

TO5070	Caça Estelar ASA-X	80 - 300
TO5072	Nave Interceptadora	90 - 325
TO5074	Nave Imperial	80 - 250
TO5085	Interceptador Tático ATL	30 - 90
TO5090	Nave de Combate	30 - 90

Canada (Kenner Canada)

TO5100	Death Star Playset	400 - 1000

England (Palitoy)

TO5117	Land Speeder	60 - 140
TO5135	Slave I	95 - 200
TO5232	Death Star Playset	300 - 600
TO5233	Droid Factory	200 - 500
TO5235	Cantina	175 - 425
TO5239	Land of the Jawas	175 - 425

France

TO5260	Chasseur X avec son et lumière	80 - 160
TO5261	Chasseur TIE standard	80 - 160
TO5262	Chasseur TIE de Dark Vador	90 - 180
TO5263	Aéroglisseur	60 - 100
TO5264	Transporteur de troupes	85 - 170
TO5270	L'Etoile Noire	150 - 400
TO5271	Le Marché des Jawas	125 - 250

TO3751   TO3752   TO3911

TO4150   TO4200   TO5070   TO5072   TO5074

TO5085   TO5090   TO5117   TO5135

TO5100   TO5232

TO5233   TO5235   TO5239   TO5300

TO5402   TO5450   TO5451

Germany

TO5300	Speeder Bike set, carded	200 - 500

Mexico (Lily Ledy)

TO5304	TIE Fighter	90 - 140
TO5306	Darth Vader's TIE Fighter	100 - 150
TO5325	*ROTJ* Scout Walker	60 - 100
TO5329	Rebel Armored Snowspeeder	65 - 125
TO5337	CAP-2 Capturador	10 - 20
TO5339	CLM-3 Cañón Laser Móuil	10 - 20
TO5341	NT-4 Interceptor	10 - 20
TO5349	Speeder Bike	15 - 45
TO5351	Millennium Falcon	125 - 250
TO5353	Y-wing	90 - 180
TO5355	Ewok assault catapult	15 - 35
TO5357	Ewok combat glider	20 - 40
TO5359	B-wing	90 - 180
TO5361	AST-5	15 - 25
TO5363	Tri-pod laser cannon	15 - 30
TO5365	Vehicle Maintenance Energizer	15 - 30
TO5367	Radar Laser Cannon	15 - 30
TO5369	Imperial Shuttle	225 - 300
TO5371	Rancor Monster	35 - 75
TO5373	Darth Vader Collector case	18 - 40
TO5375	Chewbacca Bandolier Strap	5 - 15
TO5393	Jabba the Hutt playset	40 - 90

BEND-EMS (Just Toys) 1992-94

TO5401	Luke	3 - 6
TO5402	Luke w/Topps trading card	5 - 8
TO5403	C-3PO	3 - 6
TO5404	C-3PO w/Topps trading card	5 - 8
TO5405	Darth Vader	4 - 6
TO5406	Darth Vader w/Topps trading card	4 - 6
TO5407	Stormtrooper	4 - 6
TO5408	Stormtrooper w/Topps trading card	4 - 6
TO5409	R2-D2	4 - 6
TO5410	R2-D2 w/Topps trading card	4 - 6
TO5411	Leia	4 - 6
TO5412	Leia w/Topps trading card	4 - 6
TO5413	Ewok	4 - 6
TO5414	Ewok w/Topps trading card	4 - 6
TO5415	Chewbacca	4 - 6
TO5416	Chewbacca w/Topps trading card	4 - 6
TO5417	Yoda	4 - 6
TO5418	Yoda w/Topps trading card	4 - 6
TO5419	Obi-Wan	4 - 6
TO5420	Obi-Wan w/Topps trading card	4 - 7
TO5421	Han Solo w/Topps trading card	4 - 7
TO5423	Bib Fortuna w/Topps trading card	4 - 7
TO5425	Wicket, the Ewok w/Topps trading card	4 - 7
TO5427	The Emperor w/Topps trading card	4 - 7
TO5450	8-piece gift set: Luke, C-3PO, Darth Vader, Stormtrooper, R2-D2, Leia, Ewok, Emperor	14 - 20
TO5451	4-piece gift set: Obi-Wan, Leia, Han, C-3PO w/cards	8 - 12
TO5453	4-piece gift set: Stormtrooper, Wicket, Yoda, Chewbacca, w/cards	8 - 12
TO5455	4-piece gift set: Stormtrooper, R2-D2, C-3PO, Vader, w/cards	8 - 12
TO5456	4-piece gift set: Stormtrooper, R2-D2, C-3PO, Vader, w/o cards	8 - 12
TO5458	4-piece gift set: Emperor, R2-D2, C-3PO, Vader w/cards	8 - 12
TO5480	Trading card 0 (mail-in premium)	1 - 3

DIE-CAST AND MICRO FIGURES, VEHICLES AND PLAYSETS

Numerous spaceships and other vehicles from the *Star Wars* saga were produced in die-cast metal and plastic. The micro-collection X-wing and TIE Fighter were designed to fall apart on impact, producing a "crash" effect.

The Kenner Micro Collection sets consisted of molded plastic settings and die-cast painted metal figures. Each could be purchased individually

TO6001	TO6003	TO6005	TO6007	TO6008

TO6009	TO6010	TO6011	TO6012

  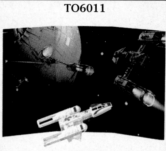 

TO6013	TO6017	TO6017	TO6017

TO6015	TO6019	TO6021	TO6052

or several could be bought at once in larger "world" sets. Additional Hoth Rebel and Snowtrooper figures were available through a "build your armies" mail-in offer.

Galoob introduced *Star Wars* to their *MicroMachines* line in 1994, and sales of the brand overall doubled within a year. In later years, new products were mixed in with old and packages were updated regularly to freshen the appearance of the line. Only the original packaging of each product is shown here.

In 1996, Galoob added larger-scale *Action Fleet* vehicles to the line, each with limited-articulation figures.

TO6001	Land Speeder	30 - 70
TO6003	X-wing Fighter	40 - 80
TO6005	TIE Fighter	30 - 75
TO6007	Darth Vader TIE Fighter, large wings	30 - 70
TO6008	TO6007, small wings	600 - 800
TO6009	Imperial Cruiser	45 - 200
TO6010	Imperial Cruiser w/background	425 - 550
TO6011	Millennium Falcon	35 - 195
TO6012	Millennium Falcon w/background	425 - 550
TO6013	Y-wing Fighter	30 - 175
TO6014	Y-wing Fighter w/background	425 - 550
TO6015	Snowspeeder	30 - 80
TO6017	TIE Bomber	400 - 925
TO6019	Slave I	30 - 90
TO6021	Twin-Pod Cloud Car	25 - 70

Micro Collection (Kenner) TO6050-6076

TO6050	Death Star Escape	20 - 50
TO6051	Death Star Trash Compactor	70 - 110
TO6052	Death Star World (includes TO6050-51)	75 - 160
TO6053	Hoth Ion Cannon	30 - 55
TO6054	Hoth Turret Defense	25 - 50
TO6055	Hoth Wampa Cave	20 - 45
TO6056	Hoth Generator Attack	20 - 50
TO6057	Hoth World (includes TO6053-55)	100 - 175
TO6058	Bespin Gantry	15 - 40
TO6059	Bespin Freeze Chamber	50 - 95
TO6060	Bespin Control Room	15 - 40

| TO6053 | TO6054 | TO6055 | TO6056 |

| TO6058 | TO6059 | TO6060 | TO6061 |

| TO6070 | TO6071 | TO6072 | TO6074 | TO6076 |

| TO6101 | TO6102 | TO6103 | TO6104 |

| TO6105 | TO6106 |

Micro Machines (Lewis Galoob Toys) 1994 Carded Vehicles

TO6101	#1: X-wing, Millennium Falcon, Star Destroyer	6 - 10
TO6102	#2: TIE Fighter, AT-AT, Snowspeeder	6 - 10
TO6103	#3: AT-ST, Jabba's Sail Barge, B-wing	6 - 10
TO6104	#4: Blockade Runner, Sandcrawler, Y-wing	6 - 10
TO6105	#5: Slave I, Twin-Pod Cloud Car, TIE Bomber	6 - 10
TO6106	#6: Speeder Bike w/Rebel, Shuttle Tyderium, A-wing	6 - 10

Micro Machines 1995-97 Carded Vehicles

TO6121	#I TIE Interceptor, Star Destroyer, Blockade Runner	6 - 10
TO6122	#II Landspeeder, Millennium Falcon, Sandcrawler	6 - 10
TO6123	#III Darth Vader's TIE Fighter, Y-wing, X-wing	6 - 10
TO6124	#IV Probot, AT-AT, Snowspeeder	6 - 10
TO6125	#V Rebel Transport, TIE Bomber, AT-ST	6 - 10
TO6126	#VI Escort Frigate, Slave I, Twin-Pod Cloud Car	6 - 10
TO6127	#VII Mon Calamari Star Cruiser, Jabba's Sail Barge, Speeder Bike w/Rebel	6 - 10
TO6128	#VIII Speeder Bike w/Imperial, Shuttle Tyderium, TIE Fighter	6 - 10
TO6129	#IX Executor, B-wing, A-wing	6 - 10
TO6130	#X T-16 Skyhopper, Lars Family Landspeeder, Death Star II	6 - 10
TO6131	#XI Cloud City, Mon Calamari Rebel Cruiser, Escape Pod	6 - 10
TO6132	#XIII Battle-damaged X-wings (red, blue, and green)	6 - 10

TO6061	Bespin World (includes TO6058-60)	100 - 160
TO6062	"Build Your Armies" mail-in figures, set of 6	15 - 30
TO6063	Individual Micro-Collection figures	3 - 10
TO6064	Individual Micro-Collection figures, unpainted	1 - 3
TO6070	X-wing	20 - 75
TO6071	X-wing w/background from TO4675	75 - 150
TO6072	TIE fighter	15 - 50
TO6073	TIE fighter w/background from TO4675	50 - 125
TO6074	Millennium Falcon (Sears exclusive)	200 - 450
TO6076	Snowspeeder (J.C. Penney exclusive)	125 - 275

TO6122

TO6132

TO6151

TO6171

TO6201

TO6205

TO6206

TO6209

TO6251

TO6252

TO6253

TO6255

TO6257

TO6259

TO6261

TO6263

TO6267

Micro Machines X-Ray Fleet (carded, 1996-97)

TO6151	#I: Darth Vader's TIE Fighter, A-wing	5 - 8
TO6152	#II: X-wing, AT-AT	5 - 8
TO6153	#III: Millennium Falcon, Sandcrawler	5 - 8
TO6154	#IV: Slave I, Y-wing	5 - 8
TO6155	#V: TIE Bomber, B-wing	5 - 8
TO6156	#VI: AT-ST, A-wing	5 - 8
TO6157	#VII: TIE Fighter, Landspeeder	5 - 8

Micro Machines *Shadows of the Empire* (carded, 1996)

TO6171	#I: IG-2000, Guri, Darth Vader, Asp, Stinger	6 - 10
TO6172	#II: Virago, Emperor, Prince Xizor, Swoop	6 - 10
TO6173	#III: Outrider, Dash Rendar, Luke Skywalker, LE-BO2D9 (Leebo), Hound's Tooth	6 - 10

Micro Machines Figure Collections

TO6201	Imperial Stormtroopers	6 - 10
TO6202	Ewoks	6 - 10
TO6203	Rebel Pilots	6 - 10
TO6204	Imperial Pilots	6 - 10
TO6205	Droids (boxed set)	6 - 10
TO6206	Jawas	6 - 10
TO6207	Imperial Officers	6 - 10

TO6281

TO6283

TO6301	TO6302	TO6303	TO6304

| TO6305 | TO6311 | TO6312 | TO6351 |

| TO6306 | TO6306 | TO6322 |

| TO6353 | TO6355 | TO6357 | TO6359 |

| TO6361 | TO6363 | TO6365 | TO6367 |

| TO6401 | TO6403 | TO6405 | TO6407 |

TO6208	Echo Base Troops	6 - 10
TO6209	Classic Characters	6 - 10
TO6210	Imperial Naval Troopers	6 - 10
TO6211	Rebel Fleet Troopers	6 - 10
TO6212	Tusken Raiders	6 - 10

Micro Machines Boxed Figure/Vehicle Assortments

TO6251	Rebel Forces Gift Set	10 - 15
TO6252	Imperial Forces Gift Set	10 - 15
TO6253	Rebel vs. Imperial Forces Gift Set	10 - 15
TO6255	Galaxy Battle Collector's Set (K mart)	10 - 20
TO6257	11 Piece Collector's Gift Set (Kay-Bee)	10 - 20
TO6259	Master Collector's Edition (Toys "Я" Us)	15 - 25
TO6261	Han/Millennium Falcon 2-pack (Fan Club)	30 - 40
TO6263	Collector's Edition: *Star Wars*	6 - 10
TO6264	Collector's Edition: *The Empire Strikes Back*	6 - 10
TO6265	Collector's Edition: *Return of the Jedi*	6 - 10

TO6409 TO6451 TO6453 TO6452 TO6471 TO6479

TO6501 TO6503 TO6505 TO6507

TO6509 TO6511 TO6515 TO6517

TO6519 TO6521 TO6523 TO6525

TO6527 TO6529 TO6531 TO6533

TO6513 TO6535

TO6267	Collector's Gift Set (bronze finish, Toys "Я" Us)	12 - 18
TO6269	Darth Vader w/Star Destroyer 2-pack (Fan Club)	15 - 25
TO6281	Micro 3-pack (film & Toy Fair 1997 Exclusive)	25 - 40
TO6283	Trilogy Gift Set	15 - 35

Micro Machines Playsets

TO6301	Death Star playset	10 - 15
TO6302	Hoth Base playset	10 - 15
TO6303	Endor Planetary Power Station playset	10 - 15
TO6304	Planet Dagobah	10 - 15

TO6551 TO6553

TO6555 TO6557

TO6561 TO6563

Micro Machines Die-Cast (2 packaging styles)		
TO6471	Jawa Sandcrawler	6 - 12
TO6473	Millennium Falcon	6 - 12
TO6475	X-wing Starfighter	6 - 12
TO6477	Y-wing Starfighter	6 - 12
TO6479	Imperial Star Destroyer	6 - 12
TO6481	TIE Fighter	6 - 12
Micro Machines Action Fleet (larger scale vehicles w/figures)		
TO6501	Luke's X-wing Starfighter	8 - 16
TO6503	Darth Vader's TIE Fighter	8 - 16
TO6505	Imperial AT-AT	8 - 16
TO6507	Imperial Shuttle *Tydirium*	8 - 16
TO6509	Rebel Snowspeeder	8 - 16
TO6511	A-wing Starfighter	8 - 16
TO6513	Luke's Landspeeder/Imperial AT-ST (Kay-Bee)	10 - 30
TO6515	Y-wing Starfighter	8 - 16
TO6517	TIE Interceptor	8 - 16
TO6519	Slave I	8 - 16
TO6521	Jawa Sandcrawler	8 - 16
TO6523	Rancor	8 - 16
TO6525	Bespin Cloud Car	8 - 16
TO6527	TIE Bomber	8 - 16
TO6529	TIE Fighter	8 - 16
TO6531	Virago	8 - 16
TO6533	B-wing Starfighter	8 - 16
TO6535	Remote Control AT-AT (Kay-Bee)	10 - 30
TO6537	X-wing repaint (2 stripes) w/Wedge	8 - 16
TO6539	X-wing repaint (6 stripes) w/Porkins	8 - 16
TO6541	Y-wing repaint (red stripes) w/gold pilot	8 - 16
TO6543	Y-wing repaint (blue stripes) w/blue leader	8 - 16
TO6545	A-wing repaint (green) w/Mon Mothma and pilot	8 - 16
TO6547	Snowspeeder repaint (black, grey, and yellow)	8 - 16
Action Fleet Series Alpha		
TO6551	Imperial AT-AT	12 - 20
TO6553	Imperial Shuttle	12 - 20
TO6555	Snowspeeder	12 - 20
TO6557	X-wing Starfighter	12 - 20
Action Fleet Flight Controllers		
TO6561	Rebel Flight Controller	15 - 22
TO6563	Imperial Flight Controller	15 - 22
Action Fleet Battle Packs		
TO6571	#1 Rebel Alliance	7 - 12
TO6572	#2 Galactic Empire	7 - 12
TO6573	#3 Aliens and Creatures	7 - 12
TO6574	#4 Galactic Hunters	7 - 12
TO6575	#5 Shadows of the Empire	7 - 12
TO6576	#6 Dune Sea	7 - 12
TO6577	#7 Droid Escape	7 - 12
TO6578	#8 Desert Palace	7 - 12
TO6579	#9 Endor Adventure	7 - 12
TO6580	#10 Mos Eisley Spaceport	7 - 12
TO6581	#11 Cantina Encounter	7 - 12
Action Fleet Playsets		
TO6601	Ice Planet Hoth	10 - 26
TO6602	Death Star	10 - 26
TO6603	Yavin Rebel Base	10 - 26
***Action Masters* (Kenner, 1994)**		
TO6621	Luke Skywalker	10 - 15
TO6622	R2-D2	10 - 15
TO6623	C-3PO	10 - 15
TO6624	Darth Vader	10 - 15
TO6626	Figure 6-pack (white background)	15 - 30

TO6305	Planet Tatooine	10 - 15
TO6306	Millennium Falcon	10 - 15
TO6311	Luke's Binoculars/Yavin Rebel Base	10 - 15
TO6312	Vader's Lightsaber/Death Star Trench	10 - 15
TO6322	Double Takes Death Star Playset	30 - 60
Micro Machines Transforming Head Playsets		
TO6351	Darth Vader/Bespin	12 - 18
TO6353	R2-D2/Jabba's Desert Palace	12 - 18
TO6355	C-3PO/Cantina	12 - 18
TO6357	Stormtrooper/Death Star	12 - 18
TO6359	Chewbacca/Endor	12 - 18
TO6361	Rebel Pilot/Hoth	12 - 18
TO6363	Boba Fett/Cloud City	12 - 18
TO6365	TIE Fighter Pilot/Academy	12 - 18
TO6367	Royal Guard/Death Star II	12 - 18
Mini Action Sets		
TO6401	I: Boba Fett, Admiral Ackbar, Gamorrean Guard	8 - 12
TO6403	II: Nien Numb, Greedo, Tusken Raider	6 - 10
TO6405	III: Jawa, Yoda, Princess Leia (Boushh)	6 - 10
TO6407	IV: Bib Fortuna, Figrin D'an, Scout Trooper	6 - 10
TO6409	Mini Action Boxed Set	6 - 10
TO6411	V: Bossk, Duros, Sandtrooper	6 - 10
TO6413	VI: 2-1B, Weequay, Emperor's Royal Guard	6 - 10
TO6415	VII: 4-LOM, Rebel Pilot, Snowtrooper	6 - 10
TO6417	VIII: Wampa, Wicket, TIE Fighter Pilot	6 - 10
TO6419	IX: Salacious Crumb, Jabba the Hutt , AT-AT Driver	6 - 10
Micro Machines Epic Collections		
TO6451	I: *Heir to the Empire*	6 - 10
TO6452	II: *Jedi Search*	6 - 10
TO6453	III: *The Truce at Bakura*	6 - 10

TO6571 TO6572 TO6573 TO6574 TO6575

TO6576	TO6577	TO6578	TO6579	TO6580	TO6581

TO6601	TO6602	TO6603

TO6621	TO6622	TO6623	TO6624	TO6626

TO6628	TO6629	TO6630	TO6631

TO6800	TO6801	TO6802	TO6803	TO6804	TO6860

TO6627	TO6626 with yellow background	15 - 30
TO6628	TO6626, *POTF*-style package	20 - 35
TO6629	Figure 4-pack	18 - 32
TO6630	Figure 4-pack, *POTF*-style package	20 - 35
TO6631	Gold C-3PO (mail-in)	20 - 25

England

TO6650	UK Death Star w/Argos truck (Argos exclusive)	15 - 20

Germany

TO6700	Landspeeder	10 - 55
TO6701	X-wing	15 - 65
TO6702	TIE fighter	15 - 65

234

TO6850　　　　TO6851　　　　TO6852　　　　TO6855　　　　TO7045

TO7061　TO7062　　TO7063　　TO7064　　TO7065　TO7066　TO7067　TO7068　TO7071　TO7073

TO7075　　　TO7076　　　　TO7077　　　TO7079　　　TO7081　　　TO7083

TO7085　　TO7087　　TO7089　　TO7091　　TO7093　　TO7095　　TO7092　　TO7097　　TO7099　　TO7101

Japan		
Space Alloy Toys		
TO6800	R2-D2	150 - 300
TO6801	C-3PO	150 - 300
TO6802	X-wing	150 - 300
TO6803	TIE fighter	150 - 300
TO6804	Landspeeder	150 - 300
Die-Cast Figures (Takara) TO6850-55		
TO6850	Darth Vader	75 - 175
TO6851	C-3PO	75 - 175
TO6852	R2-D2	75 - 175
TO6855	Smaller R2-D2 in hanging window box	75 - 150
TO6860	Takara versions of Kenner die-cast vehicles, ea.	45 - 90

FIGURES—NON-JOINTED

TO7045	Yoda the Jedi Master	20 - 60
Out of Character/Dakin Inc., 1993		
TO7061	Luke in X-wing pilot uniform	20 - 50
TO7062	Han Solo	10 - 15
TO7063	Chewbacca	10 - 15
TO7064	Darth Vader, two sizes, ea.	10 - 15
TO7065	Luke in Jedi outfit	10 - 15
TO7066	Leia	10 - 15
TO7067	R2-D2	10 - 15
TO7068	C-3PO	10 - 15

TO7200   TO7207   TO7208   TO7209   TO7210   TO7660

TO7700   TO7702   TO7704   TO7706

TO7708   TO7710   TO7901   TO8110

Applause 12" scale figures

TO7071	Luke and Yoda	12 - 17
TO7073	Han Solo in Stormtrooper disguise	12 - 17
TO7075	Leia w/R2-D2	12 - 17
TO7076	Leia in poncho w/removable helmet	12 - 17
TO7077	Chewbacca w/C-3PO	12 - 17
TO7079	Darth Vader, cloth cape	12 - 17
TO7081	Darth Vader, plastic cape	12 - 17
TO7083	Tusken Raider	12 - 17
TO7085	Emperor Palpatine	12 - 17
TO7087	Dash Rendar	12 - 17
TO7089	Prince Xizor	12 - 17
TO7091	Obi-Wan Kenobi	12 - 17
TO7092	Glow-in-the-dark Obi-Wan Kenobi (Puzzle Zoo)	17 - 22
TO7093	R2-D2	12 - 17
TO7095	Greedo	12 - 17
TO7097	Lando Calrissian in Skiff Guard disguise	12 - 17
TO7099	TIE Fighter Pilot	12 - 17
TO7101	Wedge Antillies	12 - 17

Applause PVC figurines w/round bases

TO7200	PVC 6-pack w/display base	6 - 22
TO7201	Chewbacca	3 - 5
TO7202	Han Solo	3 - 5
TO7203	Luke Skywalker	3 - 5
TO7204	C-3PO	3 - 5
TO7205	R2-D2	3 - 5
TO7206	Darth Vader	3 - 5
TO7207	Boba Fett	3 - 5
TO7208	Stormtrooper	3 - 5
TO7209	Emperor Palpatine	3 - 5
TO7210	Princess Leia (Bespin)	3 - 5
TO7211	Greedo	3 - 5
TO7212	Lando	3 - 5
TO7213	Spirit of Obi-Wan	3 - 5
TO7214	TIE Fighter Pilot	3 - 5
TO7215	Wedge Antillies	3 - 5
TO7216	Yoda	3 - 5

Cinemacast

TO7500	Logo Statue w/certificate	100 - 125

Spain

TO7660	*SW* PVC figurines (Comics Figuras), ea.	5 - 15

PLAY-DOH SETS

A typical set includes a plastic mat printed with a background from one of the films, three hinged molds, a plastic spaceship, three 6-oz cans of Play-Doh, and a plastic trimmer.

TO7700	*Star Wars* action set	20 - 50
TO7702	Attack the Death Star	25 - 55
TO7704	Ice Planet Hoth	25 - 55
TO7706	Dagobah	20 - 30
TO7708	Jabba the Hutt	20 - 30
TO7710	Wicket the Ewok	20 - 30
England		
TO7901	*SW* Adventure Modelling Set (Palitoy)	30 - 75

PLAYMATS

England (Recticel Sutcliffe Ltd.)

TO8110	*SW* Playmat	90 - 150
TO8111	*ESB* Playmat	75 - 125
TO8112	*ROTJ* Playmat	60 - 100

PLUSH FIGURES

Stuffed versions of R2-D2 and Chewbacca were made by Kenner in 1979. R2 has a built-in squeak mechanism. Plush toys were not seen again until the release of Return of the Jedi, when stuffed Ewoks and Woklings were released.

TO8500	R2-D2	30 - 55
TO8501	Chewbacca	35 - 55
TO8505	Wicket	15 - 30
TO8506	Princess Kneesaa	15 - 30
TO8507	Paploo	20 - 35
TO8508	Latara	20 - 35

Woklings

TO8515	Gwig	10 - 15
TO8516	Malani	10 - 15
TO8517	Wiley	10 - 15
TO8518	Mookiee	10 - 15
TO8519	Leeni	10 - 15
TO8520	Nippet (white)	10 - 15
TO8521	Nippet (brown)	10 - 15

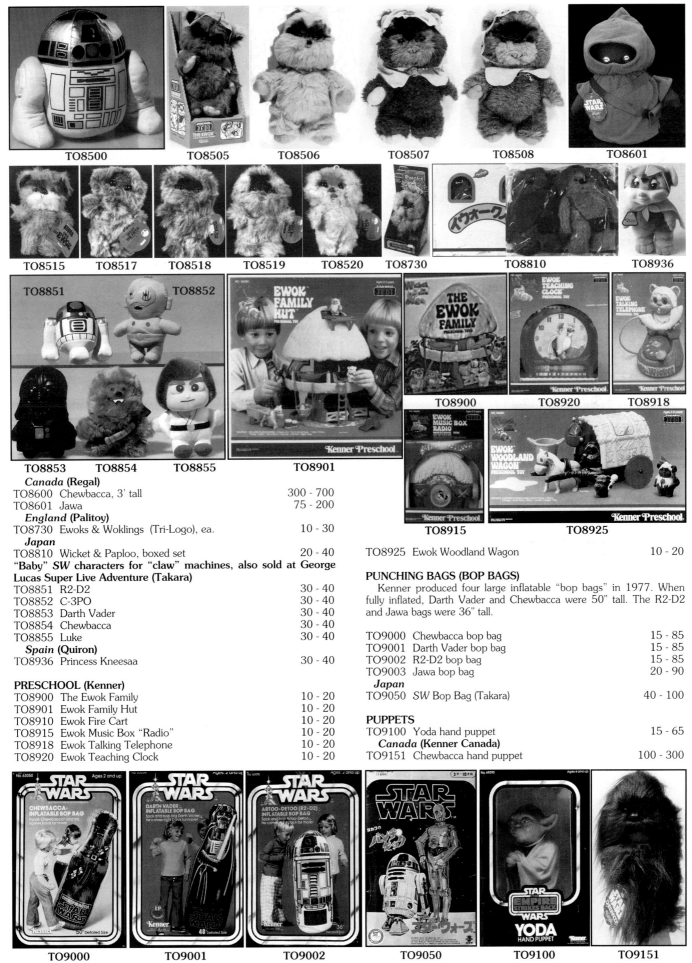

TO8500	TO8505	TO8506	TO8507	TO8508	TO8601
TO8515	TO8517	TO8518	TO8519	TO8520	TO8730	TO8810	TO8936
TO8851	TO8852	TO8901	TO8900	TO8920	TO8918
TO8853	TO8854	TO8855		TO8915	TO8925

Canada (Regal)
TO8600 Chewbacca, 3' tall   300 - 700
TO8601 Jawa   75 - 200
England (Palitoy)
TO8730 Ewoks & Woklings (Tri-Logo), ea.   10 - 30
Japan
TO8810 Wicket & Paploo, boxed set   20 - 40
"Baby" *SW* characters for "claw" machines, also sold at George
Lucas Super Live Adventure (Takara)
TO8851 R2-D2   30 - 40
TO8852 C-3PO   30 - 40
TO8853 Darth Vader   30 - 40
TO8854 Chewbacca   30 - 40
TO8855 Luke   30 - 40
Spain (Quiron)
TO8936 Princess Kneesaa   30 - 40

PRESCHOOL (Kenner)
TO8900 The Ewok Family   10 - 20
TO8901 Ewok Family Hut   10 - 20
TO8910 Ewok Fire Cart   10 - 20
TO8915 Ewok Music Box "Radio"   10 - 20
TO8918 Ewok Talking Telephone   10 - 20
TO8920 Ewok Teaching Clock   10 - 20

TO8925 Ewok Woodland Wagon   10 - 20

PUNCHING BAGS (BOP BAGS)
   Kenner produced four large inflatable "bop bags" in 1977. When
fully inflated, Darth Vader and Chewbacca were 50" tall. The R2-D2
and Jawa bags were 36" tall.

TO9000 Chewbacca bop bag   15 - 85
TO9001 Darth Vader bop bag   15 - 85
TO9002 R2-D2 bop bag   15 - 85
TO9003 Jawa bop bag   20 - 90
Japan
TO9050 *SW* Bop Bag (Takara)   40 - 100

PUPPETS
TO9100 Yoda hand puppet   15 - 65
   Canada (Kenner Canada)
TO9151 Chewbacca hand puppet   100 - 300

TO9000	TO9001	TO9002	TO9050	TO9100	TO9151

TO9200   TO9301   TO9301   TO9310

TO9400   TO9450   TO9540   TO9542   TO9760

TO9650   TO9651   TO9654

TO9671   TO9673

RACING SETS

| TO9200 | *Star Wars* Duel at Death Star (Fundimensions, 1978) | 50 - 125 |
| TO9201 | TO9200 in white box w/line art | 50 - 100 |

REMOTE CONTROLLED/BATTERY OPERATED

The Kenner radio-controlled R2-D2 and Sandcrawler were operated by a controller with an easily-broken wire. The Sandcrawler is more difficult to find. The "Cobot" was approved by Lucasfilm after it was made.

TO9300	Radio-controlled R2-D2	40 - 95
TO9301	Radio-controlled R2-D2 w/obstacle course	315 - 365
TO9310	Radio-controlled Jawa Sandcrawler	85 - 500
TO9315	"Cobot" R2-D2-like robot w/Coke can body	200 - 400
Canada		
TO9380	Sandcrawler	150 - 500
England		
TO9400	Talking R2-D2 (Palitoy)	300 - 500
Italy		
TO9450	C1P8 radiocomandato (Harbert)	15 - 75
Japan (Takara)		
TO9540	Battery-operated R2-D2 bump and go	75 - 150
TO9542	Super control R2-D2 (disk-firing)	200 - 450

See also—**TOYS: Action Figure vehicles, playsets, and accessories; TOYS: Die-Cast and Micro Figures, Vehicles and Playsets**

VEHICLES, OTHER

Perhaps the most incongruous items from this category were the Kenner SSP vans, designed to take advantage of the custom van craze of the '70s. The large Takara X-wing had interchangeable parts.

Plastic

TO9650	Darth Vader SSP Van (Kenner, 1978)	20 - 175
TO9651	Luke and heroes SSP Van (Kenner, 1978)	20 - 175
TO9654	SSP Van set w/both vans	50 - 300
TO9671	Rebel Blockade Runner (Kenner, 1997)	15 - 25
TO9673	Imperial Star Destroyer (Kenner, 1997)	15 - 25
TO9681	X-wing Flight Simulator (Kenner, 1997)	15 - 25
TO9683	Power Racing Speeder Bike (Kenner, 1997)	15 - 25
Japan (Takara)		
TO9755	X-wing, large	100 - 250
TO9756	X-wing, small	75 - 150
TO9760	Inflatable X-wing	80 - 175

See also—**FOOD CONTAINERS/PREMIUMS: Cereal; TOYS: Action Figures; TOYS: Die-Cast**

TO9781

TO9783

TO9756

TO9801

TO9802

TO9808

TO9803

TO9805

TO9811

TO9813

TO9815

TO9817

TO9818

TO9850

WEAPONS—GUNS

The laser pistol was a replica of the gun carried by Han Solo. It was identified as a *Star Wars* item by a sticker bearing the logo of the most recent film. Guns with the original logo are more valued. The 3-position laser rifle had a folding stock and front grip. The biker scout laser pistol was a replica of a gun used in Return of the Jedi. All three had a "secret" button in the handle grip that energized the motor for the noisemaker. There was also an "action figure" carrying case shaped like a laser rifle. Kenner re-used two of the gun molds in 1996, adding a new, brightly-colored deco job. New guns were added in 1997.

TO9800	Han Solo Laser Pistol, *Star Wars* sticker (1977)	20 - 150
TO9801	Same as TO9800, but w/*ESB* sticker	15 - 135
TO9802	Same as TO9800, but w/*ROTJ* sticker	15 - 90
TO9803	3-Position Laser Rifle	100 - 225
TO9805	*ESB* Electronic Laser Rifle	20 - 175
TO9806	*ROTJ* Electronic Laser Rifle	20 - 175
TO9808	Biker Scout Laser Pistol	40 - 125
TO9811	Heavy Blaster (1996)	10 - 20
TO9813	Blaster Rifle (1996)	15 - 25

TO9854

TO9861

TO9863

TO9857 **TO9900** **TO9955**

TO9815	Chewbacca's Bowcaster	15 - 25
TO9817	Water Blaster (silver)	10 - 20
TO9818	Water Blaster (black)	10 - 25
England **(Palitoy)**		
TO9830	*SW* 3-Position Laser Rifle	100 - 300
TO9831	*SW* Han Solo Laser Pistol	100 - 300
Japan **(Takara)**		
TO9840	*SW* 3-Position Laser Rifle	150 - 350
TO9841	*SW* Han Solo Laser Pistol	40 - 170
Mexico		
TO9845	Biker Scout Laser Pistol	

See also—**TOYS: ACTION FIGURE ACCESSORIES**

WEAPONS—LIGHTSABERS

The first toy adaptation of the lightsaber was essentially a flashlight connected to an inflatable vinyl "blade." A patch kit was included for repairs. "The Force" lightsaber was a hollow plastic tube molded in yellow or red which whistled when moved. New lightsabers were released in conjunction with the new action figures in the late '90s, featuring a teloscoping plastic blade and electronic sound effects. All were produced by Kenner.

TO9850	Inflatable lightsaber (1977)	35 - 175
TO9851	*Star Wars* lightsaber	30 - 90
TO9852	"The Force" lightsaber (1980), red or yellow, ea.	30 - 75
TO9853	*ROTJ* lightsaber, red or green, ea.	30 - 65
TO9854	*Droids* battery-operated lightsaber (1985)	60 - 200
TO9861	Luke Skywalker's Lightsaber (1996)	20 - 30
TO9863	Darth Vader's Lightsaber (1997)	20 - 30
Japan		
TO9870	*SW* lightsaber w/color change disks (Takara)	150 - 375

See also—**SHOW SOUVENIRS**

OTHER

TO9875	3D Character Yoyos, ea.	5 - 10
Canada **(Kenner Canada)**		
TO9880	Darth Vader utility belt	200 - 1000
TO9881	Luke Skywalker utility belt	200 - 1000
TO9882	Princess Leia utility belt	200 - 1000
TO9900	Walking Wind-up R2-D2 (Takara figure on card)	150 - 400
Italy		
TO9925	Bagatelle game	60 - 85
Japan **(Takara)**		
TO9950	Wind-up R2-D2	50 - 90
TO9955	Central American Yoyo	10 - 30

TRADING CARDS

Topps Co. issued five different trading card and sticker sets for the first film. Each included 66 cards and 11 stickers. There are two versions of card #207 from the fourth series. The first is the infamous "X-rated" or "excited" C-3PO. The way the set's compiler tells it, the color transparency he received from the Lucasfilm photo archives showed the golden droid with an extra appendage due to the angle of the shot. Neither he nor anyone else, he says, caught the rather obvious addition until the sets were printed. At the request of George Lucas, a diabetic, Topps introduced *Star Wars* sugar free bubble gum in 1978, mainly as a regional test. Each had one of 56 movie photos printed inside. Topps produced three sets for *The Empire Strikes Back* and two for *Return of the Jedi*. There were 33 stickers in the first *Jedi* set, but each sticker was printed with borders in different colors (either red, yellow, green or purple). Stickers from the first series were sometimes mistakenly packaged with second series cards. As a result, stickers intended for the second set (#34-55) are harder to find. Topps also included *SW* and *ESB* movie posters as part of an overall movie-poster set, and did an oversized series of 30 photo cards for *ESB*. There is also a rare test set and wrapper for the *ESB* oversized set. After a decade's pause, Topps reentered the *Star Wars* universe with three acclaimed sets of all-art cards, *Star Wars* Galaxy I through III, also sequentially numbered and with special chase and promotional cards. The first Galaxy set was offered in an altered factory version with foil-stamped cards and packed in a box capped by a vacuum-formed plastic Millennium Falcon. There was also a 16-card set offered inside Wonder Bread, and Burger King offered a set of 36 cards in 1981 that contained scenes from *Star Wars* and *The Empire Strikes Back*. They came in perforated strips of three (see **FOOD CONTAINERS/PREMIUMS**). A 20-card embossed tin set from Metallic Images, comes packed in a full-color tin box. The foreign sets were often reprints of the Topps series, but others were totally different.

TO9870

Topps		
Star Wars series 1, blue border (1977)		
TR0101-66	Individual cards, 1-66, ea.	.75 - 1.50
TR0167	Set of 66 cards	70 - 90
TR0171-81	Individual stickers, 1-11, ea.	2 - 4
TR0182	Set of 11 stickers	30 - 40
TR0185	Waxed wrapper (C-3PO)	2 - 5

TR0186	Unopened wax packs, ea.	10 - 12
TR0187	Box, full (36 wax packs)	350 - 400
TR0188	Box, empty	20 - 25
TR0189	Uncut sheet, cards or stickers	150 - 300
Star Wars series 2, red border (1977)		
TR0201-66	Individual cards, 67-132, ea.	.25 - .50
TR0267	Set of 66 cards	30 - 40
TR0271-81	Individual stickers, 12-22, ea.	1 - 2
TR0282	Set of 11 stickers	20 - 25
TR0285	Waxed wrapper (Vader)	1 - 3

TR0286	Unopened wax packs, ea.	8 - 10
TR0287	Box, full (36 wax packs)	250 - 300
TR0288	Box, empty	5 - 15
TR0289	Uncut sheet, cards or stickers	125 - 250
Star Wars series 3, yellow border (1977)		
TR0301-66	Individual cards, 133-198	.25 - .50
TR0367	Set of 66 cards	25 - 35
TR0371-81	Individual stickers, 23-33, ea.	4 - 5
TR0382	Set of 11 stickers	40 - 50
TR0385	Waxed wrapper (R2-D2)	1 - 3

TO9880 **TO9881** **TO9882**

TR0100 series cards

TR0170 series stickers

TR0186   TR0187

TR0200 series cards

TR0270 series stickers

TR0300 series cards

TR0370 series stickers

TR0386   TR0586

TR0386	Unopened wax packs, ea.	8 - 10
TR0387	Box, full (36 wax packs)	250 - 300
TR0388	Box, empty	5 - 15
TR0389	Uncut sheet, cards or stickers	125 - 200

Star Wars series 4, green border (1978)

TR0401-66	Individual cards, 199-264	.25 - .50
TR0467	Set of 66 cards	25 - 35
TR0468	Card #207, "X-rated" version	30 - 40
TR0469	Card #207, redone	1 - 3
TR0471-81	Individual stickers, 34-44, ea.	1 - 2
TR0482	Set of 11 stickers	20 - 25
TR0485	Waxed wrappers (Ben & Luke), ea.	1 - 3

TR0400 series cards

TR0468   TR0469

TR0470 series stickers

TR0500 series cards

TR0570 series stickers

TR0600 series wrappers

TR0665

TR0486	Unopened wax packs, ea.	5 - 7
TR0487	Box, full (36 wax packs)	150 - 200
TR0488	Box, empty	5 - 15
TR0489	Uncut sheet, cards or stickers	125 - 200

Star Wars series 5, orange border (1978)

TR0501-66	Individual cards, 265-330	.25 - .50
TR0567	Set of 66 cards	25 - 35
TR0571-81	Individual stickers, 45-55, ea.	1 - 2
TR0582	Set of 11 stickers	20 - 25
TR0584	Wrapper (X-wing), w/Kenner ad	1 - 3
TR0585	Wrapper (X-wing), w/Press sheet ad	1 - 3
TR0586	Unopened wax packs, ea.	4 - 5
TR0587	Box, full (36 wax packs)	100 - 150
TR0588	Box, empty	5 - 15
TR0589	Uncut sheet, cards or stickers	125 - 200

Star Wars Sugar Free Gum (1978)

TR0601-56	Individual wrappers, 1-56, ea.	3 - 5
TR0660	Set of 56 wrappers	150 - 250
TR0665	Unopened packs, ea.	4 - 6
TR0670	Box, empty	10 - 15

TR0675

TR1000 series cards

TR1192   TR1378

TR1200 series cards

TR0673	Flattened foil box wrapper	5 - 15
TR0675	Box, full w/foil wrap intact	100 - 200

ESB series 1, red and gray border (1980)

TR100-132	Individual cards, 1-132, ea.	.20 - .40
TR1135	Set of 132 cards	25 - 40
TR1141-73	Individual stickers, 1-33, ea.	2 - 3
TR1175	Set of 33 stickers	70 - 75
TR1176	Waxed wrapper (red), candy ad	1 - 2
TR1176a	TR1176, press sheet ad	1 - 2
TR1176b	TR1176, fan club ad	1 - 2
TR1177	Unopened wax packs, ea.	4 - 5
TR1178	Box, full (36 wax packs)	120 - 125
TR1179	Box, empty	5 - 10
TR1180	Uncut sheet, cards or stickers	100 - 200
TR1190	3 wax packs in poly wrapper	15 - 20
TR1191	Poly wrapper for TR1190	2 - 5
TR1192	80 cards on card w/collecting box	20 - 25
TR1193	51 unwrapped cards in clear rack pack: Vader header card	8 - 10
TR1194	Vader header card from TR1193	3 - 5
TR1195	Full rack pack display (24 packs)	50 - 75
TR1196	Empty rack pack display	5 - 10
TR1197	Collector box (mail-in or w/TR1192)	3 - 5

ESB series 2, blue and gray border (1980)

TR1201-332	Individual cards, 133-264	.20 - .30
TR1335	Set of 132 cards	20 - 25
TR1341-73	Individual stickers, 34-66, ea.	2 - 3
TR1375	Set of 33 stickers	60 - 70
TR1376	Waxed wrapper (blue), candy ad	1 - 2
TR1376a	TR1376, press sheet ad	1 - 2
TR1376b	TR1376, fan club ad	1 - 2
TR1376c	TR1376, collecting box ad	1 - 2
TR1377	Unopened wax packs, ea.	3 - 4
TR1378	Box, full (36 wax packs)	90 - 100
TR1379	Box, empty	5 - 10
TR1380	Uncut sheet, cards or stickers	100 - 200
TR1390	51 cards in clear rack pack w/header card	8 - 10
TR1391	Vader header card from TR1390	3 - 5
TR1392	Full rack pack display of TR1390	50 - 75
TR1393	51 cards in clear rack pack: Droids wrapper	8 - 10
TR1394	Droids wrapper from TR1393	3 - 5
TR1395	Full rack pack display of TR1393	50 - 75
TR1396	Empty display for TR1390/TR1393	3 - 5

ESB series 3, yellow and green border (1980)

TR1401-88	Individual cards, 265-352	.20 - .25
TR1535	Set of 88 cards	20 - 25
TR1541-68	Individual stickers, 67-88	1 - 1.25
TR1575	Set of 22 stickers	15 - 20

TR1400 series cards

TR1540 series stickers

TR1576	Waxed wrapper (yellow), candy ad	1 - 2
TR1576a	TR1576, press sheet ad	1 - 2
TR1576b	TR1576, fan club ad	1 - 2
TR1576c	TR1576, collecting box ad	1 - 2
TR1577	Unopened wax packs, ea.	2 - 3
TR1578	Box, full (36 wax packs)	80 - 90
TR1579	Box, empty	5 - 10
TR1580	Uncut sheet, cards or stickers	100 - 200

TR1600 series cards

ESB 5x7" large photo cards (1980)

TR1601-30	Individual photo cards, 1-30 (checklist on back)	1 - 2
TR1640	Set of 30 cards	30 - 35
TR1641	Unopened crimped paper pack	2 - 3
TR1644	Paper wrappers, ea.	1 - 2
TR1646	Empty display box	5 - 10
TR1648	Full display box (36 packs)	25 - 50

Back of TR1650

TR1650	Large photo cards, test series (back has art instead of photos), ea.	3 - 10
TR1685	Test card set	150 - 225
TR1687	Wrapper for test series, sealed w/tape, not crimped	15 - 25
TR1688	Empty test box (plain yellow)	50 - 75
TR1689	Full test box (36 packs)	350 - 500

TR2000 series cards

TR2140 series stickers

ROTJ series 1, red border (1983)

TR2001-132	Individual cards, 1-132	.10 - .20
TR2135	Set of 132 cards	15 - 20
TR2141-51	Individual stickers, 1-11 (yellow or purple borders), ea.	.40 - .50
TR2152-62	Individual stickers, 12-22 (blue or red borders), ea.	.40 - .50
TR2163-73	Individual stickers, 23-33 (orange or green borders), ea.	.40 - .50
TR2175	Set of 66 stickers (all variations)	25 - 30
TR2176	Wrapper (Luke, Vader, Wicket or Jabba)	1 - 2
TR2177	Unopened wax packs, ea.	1.50 - 2.50
TR2178	Box, full (36 wax packs)	45 - 50

TR2177   TR2277

TR2179	Box, empty	5 - 10
TR2180	Uncut sheet, cards or stickers	75 - 150
TR2190	45 unwrapped cards in clear rack pack: Wicket header card	5 - 10
TR2191	Wicket header card from TR2190	3 - 5
TR2193	Full rack pack display (24 packs)	30 - 45
TR2194	Empty rack pack display	8 - 12

ROTJ series 2, blue borders (1983)

TR2201-88	Individual cards, 133-220	.20 - .25
TR2295	Set of 88 cards	20 - 25
TR2301-22	Individual stickers, 34-55	.50 - .75
TR2325	Set of 22 stickers	10 - 15
TR2331	Wrapper (Leia, C-3PO, Wokling, or Lando)	1 - 2
TR2335	Unopened wax packs, ea.	1.50 - 2.50
TR2341	Box, full (36 wax packs)	45 - 50
TR2342	Box, empty	5 - 10
TR2343	Uncut sheet, cards or stickers	75 - 150

TR3000 series cards

TR3172

Star Wars Galaxy 1 (1993)

TR3001-140	Individual cards 1-140	.20 - .30
TR3145	Set of 140 cards	20 - 30
TR3151-6	Foil chase cards 1-6	12 - 15
TR3161	Redemption card for autographed series 1 card (blue, 1 per case)	50 - 75
TR3162	Autographed card	5 - 10
TR3170	Unopened foil pack	2 - 2.50
TR3171	Foil wrapper	.25 - .50
TR3172	Full display box (36 foil packs)	50-65
TR3173	Empty display box	1 - 2
TR3180	Set of 2 uncut sheets (contest giveaway)	50 - 100
TR3185	Uncut sheet of 6 foil cards (mail-in/contest giveaway)	95 - 100

TR3190

TR3190	Millennium Falcon factory set	80-100
TR3191	Set of 140 foil-stamped cards from TR3190	40-50
TR3192	Hologram card #1 (Vader) from TR3190	20-25
TR3201-6	Individual prism cards 1-6 from TR3190	5-8
TR3211	TR3190 w/publisher's proof sticker on box, limited to 500 sets	95 - 125
TR3215	Binder w/TR3781	35-50

Series 1 Promo Cards

TR3221	Leia (126), Non-sport Update vol.4, #2, con premium	6 - 10
TR3223	Stormtrooper (136), con premium	10 - 20
TR3225	Jabba (104), Non-sport Update vol.4, #2, Starlog #191	6 - 10

TR3243

TR3227	Boba Fett/Dengar (101), Dark Horse	10 - 15
TR3229	Leia/Stormtrooper double card (Adv. Comics)	20 - 30
TR3231	Alt. checklist "Look for series 2" (Just Toys)	5 - 20
TR3233	#0, Vader (box art)	10 - 20
TR3235	5.75" x 7.75" card (Previews)	25 - 35
TR3237	1994 San Diego Comicon 9-up sheets, 3 different, each	10 - 25
TR3241	1995 San Diego Comicon 9-up	10 - 25
TR3243	QVC *Art of SW Galaxy* 9-up	10 - 25

TR3300 series cards

TR3471

Star Wars Galaxy 2 (1994)

TR3301-435	Individual cards 141-275	.15 - .30
TR3440	Set of 135 cards	15 - 20
TR3441-6	Foil chase cards 7-12	8 - 10
TR3451	Redemption card for autographed series 2 card (pink, 1 per case)	50 - 60
TR3452	Autographed card	5 - 10
TR3461	Foil wrapper (album offer)	.25 - .50
TR3462	Foil wrapper (book offer)	.25 - .50
TR3463	Foil wrapper (sheet contest)	.25 - .50
TR3465	Unopened foil packs, ea.	1 - 1.50
TR3471	Full display box (36 foil packs)	35 - 40
TR3473	Empty display box	1 - 2
TR3475	Set of 2 uncut sheets (contest giveaway)	100 - 150
TR3477	Uncut sheet of 6 foil cards (mail-in/contest giveaway)	70 - 100
TR3480	Factory tin set	85 - 100
TR3481	set of 135 foil-stamped cards from TR3480	40 - 50
TR3482	Hologram card #2 (Droids) from TR3480	20 - 25
TR3491-6	individual prism cards 7-12 from TR3480	5 - 8

Series 2 promo cards

TR3500	#00, Vader by McQuarrie	10 - 15
TR3501	#P1, Rancor (243), Advance Comics 2/93, Cards Illustrated #2 & con promo	5 - 10
TR3502	#P2 Luke Jedi (265), Non-sport Update	10 - 15
TR3503	#P3 Yodas praying to statue (not released)	500+
TR3504	#P4 Jawas w/ C-3PO (228)	10 - 40

TR3170   TR3465

TR3511   TR3657   (detail)   TR3721

TR3625   TR3744

TR3745

TR3505	#P5 Han/Chewie (261), Cards Illus.	5 - 10
TR3506	#P6 Boba Fett (26), Hero #12	5 - 10
TR3507	Sandpeople (271), Just Toys/Dark Horse	10 - 15
TR3508	Ewoks vs. Biker Scout, Triton	
	Comic Cards and Collectibles #2	10 - 15
TR3509	5x7" card, Previews vol. 4, #2	10 - 15

Star Wars Galaxy 3 (1995)

TR3511-600	Individual cards 276-365	.10 - .20
TR3605	Set of 90 cards	8 - 12
TR3611-22	LucasArts cards L1-L12	.20 - .25
TR3625	Set of 12 LucasArts cards	2 - 3
TR3626-715	1st day cards 276-365	.50 - 1
TR3717	Set of 90 1st day cards	60 - 100
TR3721-6	Etched foil chase cards 13-18	5 - 6
TR3731-6	Clearzone chasecards 1-6	8 - 10
TR3741	Wrapper (magazine ad)	.25 - .50
TR3742	Wrapper (book offer)	.25 - .50
TR3743	Wrapper (contest ad)	.25 - .50
TR3744	Unopened foil packs, ea.	1 - 1.50
TR3745	Full display box (36 foil packs)	38 - 40
TR3746	Empty display box	1 - 2
TR3747	Magazine ad coupon	.10 - .20
TR3748	Uncut sheet (contest giveaway)	100 - 150
TR3749	Sheet of 6 foil cards (contest giveaway)	100 - 150

Series 3 promo cards

TR3750	#000 *Zorba the Hutt* art, *SW* Galaxy	5 - 10
TR3751	Boba Fett (258), from TR3480	10 - 30
TR3753	#P2 Snowtroopers (363), con promo	5 - 15
TR3755	#P3 Vader, Non-sport Update vol.6, #4	5 - 10
TR3757	#P4 Luke kneeling, Combo #7	5 - 10
TR3759	#P5 AT-AT (357), Advance Comics	5 - 10
TR3761	#P6 Luke/Yoda/Ben/Vader (310)	4 - 5
TR3763	Error card: P5 front, P6 back	50 - 60
TR3765	#P7 Leia with twins (336), Wizard	5 - 10
TR3767	#P8 Vader and Boba Fett (361), Cards Illus.	5 - 10
TR3769	5.5x7.5" card, Previews 11/95	5 - 15

Miscellaneous *Star Wars* Galaxy Cards

TR3771	*Truce at Bakura* art (Waldenbooks giveaway)	10 - 25
TR3781	#SWB1, Tarkin & Vader (*SW Galaxy* binder)	15 - 25
TR3791	#SWGM1 Cloud Car (*SW Galaxy*)	15 - 25
TR3792	#SWGM2 Shuttle/Coruscant (*SW Galaxy*)	15 - 25
TR3793	#SWGM3 Snowspeeder/AT-AT (*SW Galaxy*)	5 - 10
TR3794	#SWGM4 Dagobah (*SW Galaxy*)	5 - 10
TR3801	#DH1 Droid battle (Dark Horse)	5 - 10
TR3802	#DH2 Boba Fett (Dark Horse)	5 - 10
TR3803	#DH3 Falcon & Star Destroyer (Dark Horse)	5 - 10
TR3811	#C1 Emperor (*SW Galaxy*)	4 - 5
TR3812	#C2 Luke & Xizor (*SW Galaxy*)	4 - 5
TR3813	#C3 Han Solo (*SW Galaxy*)	4 - 5
TR3814	#C4 Vader (*SW Galaxy*)	4 - 5

Just Toys Bend-Ems cards, TR3821-48

TR3821	A Vader (4)	4 - 5
TR3822	B C-3PO (11)	4 - 5
TR3823	C R2-D2 (12)	4 - 5
TR3824	D Snowtroopers (137)	4 - 5
TR3825	E Yoda (10)	4 - 5
TR3826	F Chewie (8)	4 - 5
TR3827	G Luke (3)	4 - 5
TR3828	H Ben (6)	4 - 5
TR3829	I Han (7)	8 - 10
TR3830	J Leia (5)	4 - 5
TR3831	K The Emperor (14)	8 - 10
TR3832	L Wicket (129)	8 - 10
TR3833	M Boba Fett (13)	8 - 10
TR3834	N Trench battle (16)	8 - 10
TR3835	O Second Death Star (26)	8 - 10
TR3836	P Lando (9)	8 - 10
TR3837	Q Vader Boris art (71)	8 - 10

TR3771   TR4035

TR3838	R Luke X-wing pilot (87)	8 - 10
TR3839	S Young Mon Calamari (98)	8 - 10
TR3840	T Sand People (110)	8 - 10
TR3841	U Emperor's Royal Guard (112)	8 - 10
TR3842	V Gamorrean Guard (118)	8 - 10
TR3843	W Bib Fortuna (121)	8 - 10
TR3844	X Luke & Vader on Dagobah (241)	8 - 10
TR3845	Y Millennium Falcon crew (202)	8 - 10
TR3846	Z Luke & Leia (264)	8 - 10
TR3847	AA *ESB* art (195)	8 - 10
TR3848	BB *SW* art (167)	8 - 10
TR3851	SD-1 Darth Vader (5x6.5")	
	autograph card (limited to 7500)	10 - 20
TR3852	SD-2 Millennium Falcon (5x6.5")	
	autograph card (limited to 7500)	10 - 20
TR3853	Black & white Falcon art (5x7")	
	autograph card (limited to 5000)	5 - 15
TR3861	Quad card w/art from *SW Galaxy* #1-4	4 - 5

Star Wars Caps (1995)

TR3901-70	Individual caps 1-70	.30 - .40
TR3975	set of 70 caps	15 - 25
TR3981-90	Individual Galaxy Caps 1-10	1 - 2
TR3995	Set of 10 Galaxy Caps	10 - 15
TR4001-8	Black slammers 1-8, ea.	.75 - 1
TR4010	Set of 8 black slammers	5 - 8
TR4011-8	Silver slammers 1-8, ea.	.75 - 1
TR4020	Set of 8 silver slammers	5 - 8
TR4021-8	Gold slammers 1-8, ea.	.75 - 1
TR4030	Set of 8 gold slammers	5 - 8
TR4031	Unopened pack (4 caps, 1 slammer)	2 - 3
TR4032	Wrapper	.25 - .50
TR4033	Rulebook	.20 - .25
TR4035	Full box (48 packs)	30 - 35
TR4036	Empty box	1 - 2
TR4041	0-A promo cap (*SW Galaxy*)	4 - 5
TR4042	0-B promo cap (*SW Galaxy*)	4 - 5

TR4101   TR4220

TR4250

Star Wars Widevision (1993)

TR4101-220	Individual cards 1-120	.25 - .35
TR4225	Set of 120 cards	15 - 25
TR4231-40	Chase cards 1-10	20 - 25
TR4245	Wrapper (magazine ad)	.25 - .50
TR4246	Wrapper (album offer)	.25 - .50
TR4247	Wrapper (book offer)	.25-.50
TR4250	Unopened foil packs, ea.	3 - 4
TR4251	Full display box (24 foil packs)	100 - 125
TR4252	Empty display box	1 - 2
TR4255	Widevision Binder w/TR4280	25 - 30
TR4260	Steel card set (1-6, mail-in)	70 - 100

Star Wars Widevision promo cards

TR4270	#SWP0 Awards ceremony (w/TR3480)	20 - 30
TR4271	#SWP1 Mos Eisley checkpoint (37) Non-sport	
	Update vol. 5, #6, Up N Coming 12/94	
	(Canada), convention giveaway	5 - 10
TR4272	#SWP2 Millennium Falcon cockpit (60),	
	Advance Comics #72	10 - 20
TR4273	#SWP3 Vader's TIE and wingmen (105),	
	SW Galaxy #1	10 - 15
TR4274	#SWP4 Star Destroyer underside (2),	
	Wizard #42	5 - 10
TR4275	#SWP5 Vader choking rebel (8), Tuff Stuff	5 - 10
TR4276	#SWP6 Leia, C-3PO in war room (107),	
	Cards Illustrated #14	10 - 15
TR4280	00 Luke/X-wing in hanger bay	10 - 15

TR4251   TR4491

TR4285	5.5x7.5" Han in gun port (79), Previews	10 - 30

Kenner Classic 4-Pack cards, TR4291-4

TR4291	#K-01 Vader choking rebel (8)	5 - 15
TR4292	#K-02 Luke in gun port (80)	5 - 15
TR4293	#K-03 Falcon cockpit (60)	5 - 15
TR4294	#K-04 Han in Cantina (45)	5 - 15

TR4301

TR4500   TR4471

TR4481   TR4482

TR4483   TR4484

Empire Strikes Back Widevision (1994)

TR4301-444	Individual cards 1-144	.25 - .35
TR4450	Set of 144 cards	25 - 30
TR4451-60	Chase cards 1-10	10 - 15
TR4471-6	4x5.75" Mini poster cards 1-6	8 - 10
TR4481	Wrapper (AT-AT Walkers)	.25 - .50
TR4482	Wrapper (Luke and Yoda)	.25 - .50
TR4483	Wrapper (Falcon/Star Destroyer)	.25 - .50
TR4484	Wrapper (Vader in Freeze Chamber)	.25 - .50
TR4485	Unopened foil packs, ea.	1.50 - 2
TR4491	Full display box (24 foil packs)	45 - 50
TR4492	Empty display box	1 - 2
TR4495	Set of 2 uncut sheets (QVC)	100 - 150

Empire Strikes Back Widevision promo cards

TR4500	#0 Vader in meditation chamber (*SW Galaxy*)	5 - 10
TR4501	#P1 Vader tortures Han, Adv. Comics , cons	5 - 10
TR4502	#P2 AT-ATs (22) Non-sport Update #4	5 - 10
TR4503	#P3 Luke, Yoda and R2 (54), Tuff Stuff	10 - 15
TR4504	#P4 Luke hangs in shaft (118), Combo	10 - 20
TR4505	#P5 Slave I (111) con giveaway	25 - 50

TR4495

243

TR4506 #P6 Medical frigate (143), Wizard   5 - 10
TR4507 5.25x7.5" P1/P2/P3 triple card
        (direct comic distributors promo)   10 - 20

Return of the Jedi Widevision (1995)
TR4601-744 Individual cards 1-144   .25 - .35
TR4750 Set of 144 cards   20 - 25
TR4751-60 Chase cards 1-10   10 - 12
TR4765 3-D redemption card (Boba Fett)   40 - 50
TR4770 DIII 0 Admiral Ackbar 3-D chase card
        (mail-in/con promo)   25 - 30
TR4771 Retailer envelope for TR4770   5 - 10
TR4781-6 Mini poster cards 1-6   7 - 10
TR4791 Wrapper (Jabba)   .25 - .50
TR4792 Wrapper (Han)   .25 - .50
TR4793 Wrapper (B-wings)   .25 - .50
TR4794 Wrapper (Luke/Biker Scout)   .25 - .50
TR4795 Unopened foil packs, ea.   1.50 - 2
TR4801 Full display box (24 foil packs)   40 - 45
TR4802 Empty display box   1 - 2
TR4805 Set of 2 uncut sheets (QVC)   100 - 150

Return of the Jedi Widevision promo cards
TR4810 #0 Anakin/Yoda/Ben (*SW Galaxy*)   5 - 10
TR4811 #P1 Han, Luke, Lando Skiff (*SW Galaxy*)   5 - 10
TR4812 #P2 Luke & Scout on speeders (Adv. Comics) 10 - 15
TR4813 #P3 Han & Leia in bunker, Non-Sport Update 5 - 10
TR4814 #P4 Emperor (Cards Illustrated)   5 - 10
TR4815 #P5 Jabba & Bib Fortuna (Wizard)   5 - 10
TR4816 #P6 Han, Luke, & Chewie in
        Jabba's throne room (con promo)   20 - 40
TR4821 5.5x7.5" 0 card in stars (Previews)   5 - 15

Star Wars Mastervisions (6½ x10¼" - 1995)
TR4851-86 Individual cards 1-36   1 - 2
TR4890 Full display box (36 card set)   35 - 40
TR4891 Empty box   1 - 2
TR4895 7x10½" Bounty Hunters promo card by
        McQuarrie (*SW Galaxy*)   5 - 10
TR4896 #P2 6½x10¼" Tauntaun/AT-ATs promo
        card by McQuarrie (*SW Galaxy*)   5 - 10

Star Wars Finest (1996)
TR4901-90 Basic cards (silver backs) 1-90   .40 - .50
TR4995 Set of 90 cards   25 - 40
TR5001-90 Refractor cards (gold backs) 1-90   8 - 10
TR5095 Set of 90 refractor cards   650 - 750
TR5101-6 Embossed chase cards 1-6   5 - 8
TR5111-4 Matrix chase cards 1-4   5 - 10
TR5121 Redemption card for Jedi Legacy card   40 - 50
TR5122 Mastervisions 6.5x10" "A Jedi Legacy"   40 - 50
TR5123 Retailer envelope for TR5122   5 - 10
TR5131 Wrapper (book ad)   .25 - .50
TR5132 Wrapper (*SOTE* ad)   .25 - .50
TR5133 Wrapper (Magazine ad)   .25 - .50
TR5134 Wrapper (Binder offer)   .25 - .50
TR5135 Unopened foil packs, ea.   3 - 5
TR5140 Full display box (36 foil packs)   60 - 80
TR5141 Empty display box   1 - 2
TR5145 *SOTE* set reservation coupon   .10 - .20

TR5150 Uncut refractor sheet (QVC, ltd. to 250) 450 - 500
TR5152 *SW* Finest binder w/TR5171   20 - 25
Star Wars Finest promo cards
TR5161 #SWF1 Boba Fett (34), *SW Galaxy*   5 - 10
TR5162 #SWF2 Vader in TIE (20), *SW Galaxy*   5 - 10
TR5163 #SWF3 Luke on Tauntaun, Non-Sport Update   5 - 10
TR5165 7x10¾" Dealer promo (Bib Fortuna,
        Han and Chewie)   20 - 25
TR5166 TR5165, refractor coated   50 - 100
TR5171 Binder 1, Han & Chewie   5 - 10

Shadows of the Empire (1996)
TR5201-72 Individual cards 1-72   .20 - .30
TR5273-78 Gold-edged character cards 73-78   6 - 8
TR5279-82 Foil character cards 79-82   8 - 10
TR5283-300 Individual cards 83-100   .20 - .30
TR5301 Set of 90 basic cards (w/o TR5273-82)   15 - 18
TR5305 Redemption card for TR5306   40 - 50
TR5306 Autographed Mastervisions Hildebrandt card 40 - 50
TR5307 Non-auto. Hildebrandt case topper card   40 - 50
TR5308 Retailer envelope for TR5307   5 - 10
TR5311 Wrapper (Boba Fett)   .25 - .50
TR5312 Wrapper (Luke)   .25 - .50
TR5313 Wrapper (Vader)   .25 - .50
TR5314 Wrapper (Xizor)   .25 - .50
TR5320 Unopened foil packs, ea.   2 - 3
TR5321 Full display box (36 foil packs)   40 - 45
TR5322 Empty display box   1 - 2
TR5325 Uncut sheet cards (QVC)   50 - 75

Shadows of the Empire promo cards
TR5331 #SOTE1 Xizor (78), *SW Galaxy*   5 - 10
TR5332 #SOTE2 Vader (80), Adv. Comics   5 - 10
TR5333 #SOTE3 Luke (73), *SW* Finest   5 - 10
TR5334 #SOTE4 Dash Rendar (32), *SW Galaxy*   5 - 10
TR5335 #SOTE5 Boba Fett (82), QVC   5 - 10
TR5336 #SOTE6 Guri (79), Overstreet's Fan   5 - 10
TR5337 #SOTE7 Droids (76), Combo   5 - 10
TR5340 5½ x7½" card (Previews)   10 - 15

Star Wars 3D (1997)
TR5401-63 Individual cards 1-63   1 - 2
TR5470 Set of 63 cards   100 - 125
TR5475 #M1 Death Star Multi-Motion card   25 - 35
TR5481 Wrapper   .25 - .50
TR5482 Unopened foil pack   3 - 5
TR5485 Full display box (63 different), each   60 - 75
TR5486 Empty display box (63 different), each   3 - 5
TR5491 #3Di 1 Vader on Death Star, *SW Galaxy*   5 - 10
TR5492 #3Di 2 Luke/Vader (McQuarrie) dealer promo 20 - 30
TR5495 #M2 Ronto & Jawas MM card,
        SW 20th Anniversary Magazine   5 - 7
TR5498 #P1 *ESB* AT-ATs, *SW* 20th Ann.   5 - 7

The Star Wars Trilogy: SE Widevision (1997)
TR5501-72 Individual cards 1-72   .25 - .35
TR5575 Set of 72 cards   15 - 20
TR5581-6 Laser cut chase cards 1-6   6 - 8
TR5588-9 Hologram chase cards 1-2   4 - 6
TR5591 #1-3D rebel fleet launch 3D card   25 - 30
TR5601 Wrapper (20th ann. magazine ad)   .25 - .50
TR5602 Wrapper (*SW Galaxy* magazine ad)   .25 - .50
TR5605 Unopened foil packs, ea.   1 - 2

TR5611 Full display box (24 foil packs)   40 - 50
TR5612 Empty display box   1 - 2
Special Edition Hobby set promo cards
TR5621 #P1 Stormtroopers & dewback,
        San Diego Comicon 1996   5 - 7
TR5622 #P2 Jabba (26), *SW Galaxy*   5 - 7
TR5623 #P3 Rebel Fleet (40), Wizard   5 - 7
TR5624 #P4 Sandcrawler (4) *SW* 3D   8 - 10
TR5625 #P5 Jawa (17) *SW* 3D   8 - 10
TR5626 #P6 Falcon/Mos Eisley (32) *SW* 3D   8 - 10
TR5627 #P7 Landspeeder/Mos Eisley, Wizard   5 - 7
TR5628 #P8 Jabba palace dancers (67), Combo   5 - 7
TR5629 #0 Lasercut *SW* 20th Ann. Mag.   4 - 6
Kenner action figure accessory cards TR5631-34
TR5631 #H1 Millennium Falcon Escaping
        Mos Eisley (33)   5 - 10
TR5632 #H2 Massassi ruins/Yavin IV (38)   5 - 10
TR5633 #H3 Han Solo and Jabba the Hutt   5 - 10
TR5634 #H4 ASP Droids   5 - 10
Galoob boxed set cards TR5636-40
TR5636 #G1 R2-D2 on the X-Wing (41)   5 - 10
TR5637 #G2 TIE Fighter chasing X-Wing   5 - 10
TR5638 #G3 Luke in Landspeeder   5 - 10
TR5639 #G4 Mos Eisley   5 - 10
TR5640 #G5 Jawa riding Ronto   5 - 10
TR5651 Pack of 9 Widevision cards w/o holo stamp
        (Pepsi) 4, 27, 55, 68, 69, 79, 89, 95, 135 20 - 25

The *SW* Trilogy: The Complete Story (1997)
TR5701-72 Individual cards 1-72   .25 - .35
TR5775 Set of 72 cards   10 - 15
TR5781-6 Laser cut chase cards 1-6   6 - 8
TR5791 Wrapper (Yoda & Vader)   .25 - .50
TR5795 Unopened foil pack   1 - 2
TR5796 Full display box (36 foil packs)   45 - 55
TR5797 Empty display box   1 - 2

Star Wars Vehicles (1997)
TR5801-72 Individual cards 1-72   .20 - .30
TR5875 Set of 72 cards   20 - 25
TR5881-4 Cut-Away chase cards   8 - 10
TR5885-6 3D cards   12 - 15
TR5887 Redemption Card for 5888   40 - 50
TR5888 Uncut Luke/Leia 3D card   40 - 50
TR5889 Retailer envelope for TR5888   5 - 10
TR5891 Wrapper (Imperial Shuttle)   .25 - .50
TR5895 Unopened foil pack   1 - 3

TR9025

TR9001-20

TR9031-50

YODA	BOBA FETT	DARTH VADER	R2-D2
TR9036	TR9040	TR9043	TR9047

TR5896	Full display box (36 foil packs)		40 - 50
TR5897	Empty display box		1 - 2

Star Wars **Vehicles dealer promo cards**

TR5901	#P1 Speeder Bikes	15 - 20
TR5902	#P2 Imperial Shuttle	15 - 20
TR5903	#P1 refractor version of TR5801	40 - 50
TR5904	#P2 refractor version of TR5802	80 - 100

Metallic Images/C.U.I. Inc. (tin card sets in tin boxes)

TR9001-20	*SW* set (20), w/tin	35 - 60
TR9025	Promo card (*SW* Style 'A' one-sheet art)	5 - 10
TR9031-50	*ESB* set (20), w/tin	35 - 60
TR9055	*ESB* Promo card	5 - 10
TR9061-80	*ROTJ* set (20), w/tin	35 - 60
TR9101-20	*SW*: The Art of Ralph McQuarrie set (20)	35 - 60
TR9131-6	*Dark Empire* set (6), w/tin	10 - 20
TR9141-6	*Dark Empire II* set (6), w/tin	10 - 20

Australia **(Scanlens/Allen's Confectionery)**

TZ6000	*SW* cards, same as U.S., ea	.15 - .50
TZ6100	*ESB* cards, same as U.S., ea	.15 - .50
TZ6200	*ROTJ* cards, same as U.S., ea	.15 - .50

Canada **(O-Pee-Chee Ltd.)**

TZ6500	*SW* cards, same as U.S., ea	.15 - .50
TZ6600	*ESB* cards, same as U.S., ea	.15 - .50
TZ6700	*ROTJ* cards, same as U.S., ea	.15 - .50

TR9061-80

TR9063	TR9065	TR9076	TR9078

TR9101-20

TR9101	TR9102	TR9104

TR9141-6

TR9131-6

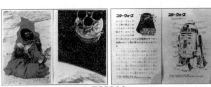

TZ8000

TZ8501	TZ8502	TZ8504	TZ8530

TZ8554

TZ8553

Japan **(Yamakatsu/Topps)**

TZ8000	*SW* 3½x5-inch , unnumbered, 36 in set, ea.	1 - 3
TZ8040	Set	55 - 85
TZ8042	Clear 4-pack w/header card	6 - 12
TZ8046	"Gamble book" w/33 cards in paper pockets, string tied w/cover	55 - 75

Mexico
Laboratorios y Agencias Unidas S.A.

TZ8400	*SW* classic cards, same as U.S., ea	.15 - .40

Sonric's

TZ8501-30	*SW: TSE* cards, ea.	1 - 2
TZ8531	Set of 30 cards	45 - 55
TZ8551	Unopened packs, (1 card per pack) ea.	2 - 3
TZ8552	Wrappers, ea.	.25 - .50
TZ8553	Darth Vader Helmet gum (1 in each pack)	1 - 2
TZ8554	Full display box (12 packs)	20 - 30
TZ8555	Empty display box	2 - 4

Netherlands **(Monty Fabrieken)**

TZ9000	*ROTJ* small cards, 1-100, ea.	.15 - .50
TZ9010	Set	20 - 45
TZ9011	Paper envelope wrapper	1 - 3
TZ9012	Box, full	35 - 50
TZ9013	Box, empty	3 - 5
TZ9015	Uncut sheet of 100	60 - 95

Philippines **(Presswell Enterprises)**

TZ9200	Ewok trading cards	

Spain **(Editorial Fher S.A.)**

TZ9300	*ESB*: El Imperio Contraataca small cards, 1-225, ea.	.25 - 1
TZ9350	Set	85 - 150
TZ9352	Wrapper	1 - 2

Sweden **(Nellba AB)**

TZ9500	*ROTJ*: Stjärnornas Krig cards	1 - 2
TZ9600	Uranium Trading Cards, set	15 - 30

See also—GAMES: Card Games; **FOOD CONTAINERS/ PREMIUMS; STAMPS, STICKERS AND DECALS**

WD0010	WD6200	WP1040	WP5020

WALL DECORATIONS (Fantasma Inc.)

WD0010	*SW* Laser Light Wall Decor: Falcon hologram	30 - 45

England **(Icarus)**

WD5100	*ROTJ* laminated wall posters, ea.	10 - 20

Germany **(Kennerspeil-Germany)**

WD6200	*SW* 2-piece wall poster: 6x8 feet	30 - 45

WALLPAPER

Wallpapers to Go

WP1030	*ROTJ* overall pattern, pre-pasted vinyl double roll	35 - 45
WP1032	*ROTJ* matching border w/portraits of characters	20 - 30
WP1040	*ROTJ* spacecraft blueprints, dark blue, pre-pasted vinyl double roll	35 - 45
WP1042	*ROTJ* spacecraft blueprints, dark brown, pre-pasted vinyl double roll	35 - 45
WP1050	*ROTJ/Ewoks* green, pre-pasted vinyl double roll	20 - 35
WP1052	*ROTJ/Ewoks* yellow, pre-pasted vinyl double roll	20 - 35
WP1054	*Ewoks* border	15 - 20

England **(Imperial Chemicals Limited)**

WP5010	*SW* overall pattern, pre-pasted vinyl double roll	35 - 65
WP5020	*ESB* overall pattern, pre-pasted vinyl double roll	35 - 65

Germany **(Bammental)**

WP6060	*ROTJ/Ewoks* pebbled surface, pre-pasted vinyl double roll	20 - 35
WP6062	Border for WP6060	10 - 20
WP6064	Combined rolls of WP6060 and WP6062	20 - 40

WATCHES AND CLOCKS

CLOCKS

Most clocks were made by Bradley Time Inc., which also used the trade names Elgin and Welby.

Bradley Time

WT0010	*SW/ESB* wind-up Talking Alarm Clock w/dimensional C-3PO & R2-D2	25 - 55

| WT0020 | WT0030 | WT0032 | WT0040 | WT1060 |

  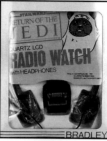     

| WT5414 | WT5000 | WT5002 | WT5003 | WT5110 |

| WT3110 | WT3113 | WT3140 | WT5111 | WT5114 | WT5116 | WT5226 |

| WT5118 | WT5119 | WT5122 | WT5124 | WT5126 | WT5128 | WT5210 | WT5212 | WT5214 | WT5228 |

WT0012 *SW* logo like WT0010, but later quartz battery-op clock version 35 - 65

WT0020 *SW* 3-D Electronic Quartz Clock w/droids and clock as center of TIE fighter 25 - 50

WT0030 *ESB* R2-D2 and C-3PO quartz battery-op wall clock 25 - 45

WT0032 *ESB* logo Vader and troopers quartz battery-op wall clock 25 - 45

WT0040 *ROTJ* quartz Portable Clock Radio, AM/FM 20 - 40

Clock-Wise division of Avant-Glass

WT1060 *SW* Classic beveled glass wall clock w/Death Star battle scene 25 - 40

NOVELTY ITEMS

WT3110 *SW* logo Radio Watch w/headphones 30 - 55

WT3113 *ROTJ Ewoks* Radio Watch w/headphones 30 - 55

WT3120 *ROTJ* LCD Clock and Calculator Ruler 25 - 45

WT3130 *SW* logo 3-Way "Anywhere" Clock: Droids clock as pendant, clip-on or stick-on 15 - 30

WT3135 *ROTJ* Wicket the Ewok Whistle Time (watch/whistle) 10 - 20

WT3140 *ROTJ* Biker Scout stopwatch 45 - 60

WATCHES

The first *Star Wars* watches were digital, made by Texas Instruments. The largest number, however, were made and sold by Bradley Time, which produced both digital and analog watches. Although collector interest is high, watches must be in working condition. If you're collecting to keep, not wear, the watches, make sure you remove the battery, which can leak and ruin the watch. Watch bands are often replaced or missing, and damage to the face (scratches, dirt, etc.) lessens the value considerably. Some collectors only collect watches in their original packaging, and that's how we've priced them below. Many watches were available only through Sears, J.C. Penney's or Montgomery Ward catalogs, and come in inexpensive vinyl pouches. Because of their relative scarcity, these watches are highly collectible.

In later years 3-D Arts produced three true hologram watches. About 50 samples of a fourth watch with the face of C-3PO were produced, but the watch was never generally available. Fantasma has also produced imaginative trilogy watches.

Texas Instruments

WT5000 Digital w/*SW* logo in black on silver face plate, black vinyl band, R2-D2 & Vader on opposite sides 50 - 100

WT5001 Digital, blue face plate w/droids above, Vader below 50 - 100

WT5002 Digital, blue face plate w/droids, gray plastic band & sheet w/10 decals for watch face 50 - 100

WT5003 Digital, black & silver face plate w/Vader & X-wings w/decal sheet 50 - 100

Bradley Time

WT5110 *SW* logo, C-3PO & R2-D2 in desert against blue sky, adult size w/gold metal case, dark blue vinyl strap, black plastic box 65 - 125

WT5111 Like WT5110, but child's size w/silver casing & light blue vinyl strap in blue & clear plastic case w/Vader & "Official *Star Wars* Watch" 50 - 100

WT5112 Later version of WT5111 w/more pronounced copyright & trademark lines, in plastic box 50 - 100

WT5114 R2-D2, C-3PO against black face, white *SW* logo, black vinyl band 50 - 100

WT5116 R2-D2, C-3PO like WT5114, but numbers on silver inner bezel ring, black Cycolac case & strap w/brushed silver inserts 55 - 125

WT5117 Digital Blue face w/silver *SW* logo below window 45 - 65

WT5118 Digital musical R2/3PO, w/red *SW* logo on round black star-field face, time window cuts into C-3PO at left, black vinyl strap 55 - 125

WT5119 Same as WT5118, w/oval face 60 - 150

WT5120 Same face as WT5118, but blue *SW* logo & non-musical, on blister pack 45 - 75

WT5121 Digital R2/3PO, w/blue *SW* logo above time window on black face, R2-D2 & C-3PO below, black vinyl strap, *SW* logo window box 45 - 75

WT5122 WT5121 in clear case 50 - 80

WT5123 WT5121 on blister card 60 - 90

WT5124 Digital 3PO/R2, X-wings on wide oval face, black plastic band w/slots 45 - 85

WT5126 Digital C-3PO Musical Alarm & animated read-out display, w/small R2-D2, X-wing, TIE ftr., SW logo in red/yellow on square blue face, black plastic band w/slots 60 - 125

WT5128 Digital *Droids* TV series logo, w/cartoon R2-D2 and C-3PO, black vinyl strap, blister-pack 35 - 60

WT5210 Vader w/lightsaber, red *SW* logo on white face, black vinyl band 50 - 100

WT5212 Vader w/saber, white *SW* logo on gray face, black vinyl band 50 - 100

WT5214 WT5212 w/black inner bezel ring w/Saturn & stars, black Cycolac case & strap w/silver inserts 65 - 125

WT5226 Digital Vader changing-image dial (Vader head/*SW* logo), blue face w/time window under "DV," black vinyl band 50 - 100

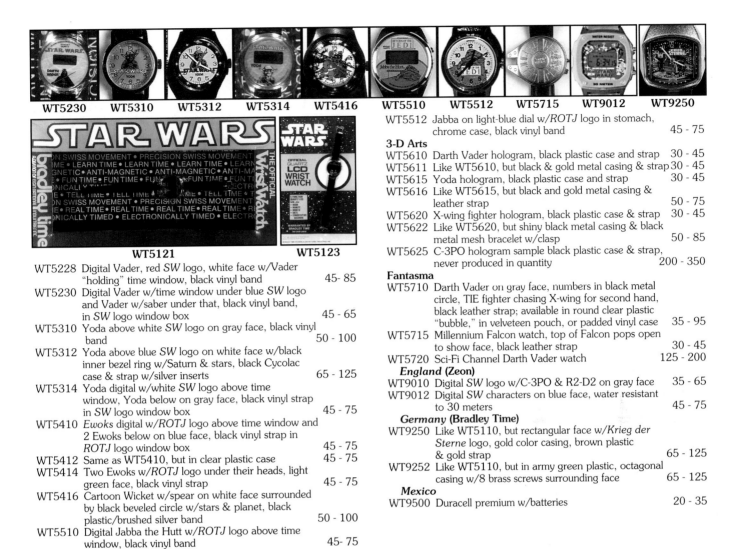

WT5230　WT5310　WT5312　WT5314　WT5416　　WT5510　WT5512　WT5715　WT9012　WT9250

WT5121　　　　　　　WT5123

WT5228 Digital Vader, red *SW* logo, white face w/Vader "holding" time window, black vinyl band　45- 85

WT5230 Digital Vader w/time window under blue *SW* logo and Vader w/saber under that, black vinyl band, in *SW* logo window box　45 - 65

WT5310 Yoda above white *SW* logo on gray face, black vinyl band　50 - 100

WT5312 Yoda above blue *SW* logo on white face w/black inner bezel ring w/Saturn & stars, black Cycolac case & strap w/silver inserts　65 - 125

WT5314 Yoda digital w/white *SW* logo above time window, Yoda below on gray face, black vinyl strap in *SW* logo window box　45 - 75

WT5410 *Ewoks* digital w/*ROTJ* logo above time window and 2 Ewoks below on blue face, black vinyl strap in *ROTJ* logo window box　45 - 75

WT5412 Same as WT5410, but in clear plastic case　45 - 75

WT5414 Two Ewoks w/*ROTJ* logo under their heads, light green face, black vinyl strap　45 - 75

WT5416 Cartoon Wicket w/spear on white face surrounded by black beveled circle w/stars & planet, black plastic/brushed silver band　50 - 100

WT5510 Digital Jabba the Hutt w/*ROTJ* logo above time window, black vinyl band　45- 75

WT5512 Jabba on light-blue dial w/*ROTJ* logo in stomach, chrome case, black vinyl band　45 - 75

3-D Arts

WT5610 Darth Vader hologram, black plastic case and strap　30 - 45

WT5611 Like WT5610, but black & gold metal casing & strap　30 - 45

WT5615 Yoda hologram, black plastic case and strap　30 - 45

WT5616 Like WT5615, but black and gold metal casing & leather strap　50 - 75

WT5620 X-wing fighter hologram, black plastic case & strap　30 - 45

WT5622 Like WT5620, but shiny black metal casing & black metal mesh bracelet w/clasp　50 - 85

WT5625 C-3PO hologram sample black plastic case & strap, never produced in quantity　200 - 350

Fantasma

WT5710 Darth Vader on gray face, numbers in black metal circle, TIE fighter chasing X-wing for second hand, black leather strap; available in round clear plastic "bubble," in velveteen pouch, or padded vinyl case　35 - 95

WT5715 Millennium Falcon watch, top of Falcon pops open to show face, black leather strap　30 - 45

WT5720 Sci-Fi Channel Darth Vader watch　125 - 200

England (Zeon)

WT9010 Digital *SW* logo w/C-3PO & R2-D2 on gray face　35 - 65

WT9012 Digital *SW* characters on blue face, water resistant to 30 meters　45 - 75

Germany (Bradley Time)

WT9250 Like WT5110, but rectangular face w/*Krieg der Sterne* logo, gold color casing, brown plastic & gold strap　65 - 125

WT9252 Like WT5110, but in army green plastic, octagonal casing w/8 brass screws surrounding face　65 - 125

Mexico

WT9500 Duracell premium w/batteries　20 - 35

LIST OF WORLDWIDE LICENSEES

This list has been carefully compiled and edited using the resources of Lucasfilm Ltd. It may, however, include some licensees which never actually went into production, or list categories which a licensee never made. We have tried to eliminate such listings and would appreciate feedback for future editions.

The headquarters cities and contract periods were accurate at the time the licenses were issued. The list is mainly of prime licensees, although sub-licensees are listed whenever possible. If no termination date is listed, the contract was still in effect as of late 1997.

A & T International Ltd. (Singapore) 1981-82
Empire: Pencils & erasers in Singapore, Malaysia
A. H. Prismatic (Brighton, England) 1994-96
Embossed holograms, film/photo polymer holograms, holographic foil products in U.K.
A. H. Prismatic (San Francisco, CA) 1994-96
Photopolymer holograms, laser gram postcards, embossed hologram products, holographic foil products in U.S. & Hungary
A. Hankin & Co. Pty. Ltd. (Newcastle, Australia) 1980-84
Empire: Pinball machines in Australia
A. Pallis S.A. (Athens, Greece) 1983-84
Jedi: Stationery in Greece
A. W. Faber-Castell (Filford, Australia) 1980-81
Empire: Erasers, pens, pencils, rulers in Australia, New Zealand, Fiji, Papua New Guinea
AB Prodessia (Djursholm, Sweden) 1983-84
Jedi: Cardboard jigsaw puzzles in Sweden
Abbott Mead Vickers BBDO (London, England) 1996
Themed television advertising campaign for Tunes medicated hard candy in U.K.
Abril Controjornal (Portugal) 1996-97
Comics in Portugal
Acamas Toys (Nottinghamshire, England) 1982-85
Empire & Jedi: Costumes & masks in UK, Ireland
Acme Merchandising (Rockdale, NSW, Australia) 1994-97
Adult & child t-shirts, caps, polo toms, sweatshirts, crop tops in Australia; t-shirts & caps in New Zealand

Acme Merchandising (Rockvale, NSW, Australia) 1994-97
T-shirts & caps in New Zealand
Action One Communication (Brussels, Belgium) 1993-
Star Wars Classic: Pins in Belgium
Adam Joseph Industries (San Francisco, CA) 1982-85
Empire, Jedi & Ewoks: Laundry bags, luggage, tote bags, backpacks, photo buttons, wallets, luggage tags, jewelry, key chains, night lights, plastic coin banks, bike accessories, rubber stamps, rainwear (coats, ponchos, umbrellas, hats,) magnets, brush and mirror sets, throw pillows in U.S., Canada, Scandinavia, Finland, Germany, Austria, Switzerland, France, Italy, Belux, U.K.
Addis Ltd. (Hertford, England) 1984-85
Star Wars, Empire, Jedi & Ewoks: Bath preparations and sets, shampoo, soap, talcum powder in U.K., Channel Islands, Ireland
Adrenalin Pty. Ltd. (St. Leonards, Australia) 1983
Jedi: Near pack promotion for **Johnson & Johnson Band-Aids**. Premium items: Darth Vader Posters, **Parker Bros.** *Empire* and *Jedi Arena* video games in Australia
Advance Bank Australia Ltd. [NSW Building Society] (Sydney, Australia) 1983-85
Jedi & Ewoks: Bank accounts w/special bankbook, poster and sticker premium in Australia
Advanced Graphics (Pittsburg, CA) 1993- , 1996-97
Star Wars Classic: Life-like cardboard standees of trilogy characters in U.S.

Agence Mandarine (Paris, France) 1988
Star Wars: Advertising campaign on billboards for video cassette using Yoda in France
A.H. Prismatic Photopolymer holograms, lasergram postcards, embossed hologram products and holograph foil products
Aladin (France) 1994
Use of name & characters for night club event in France
Allen's Confectionery Ltd. (Alexandria, Australia) 1983-84
Jedi: **Topps** cards w/bubble gum and character containers w/candy, **Panini** stamp albums and stamps in Australia, New Zealand
Amate Textile (Mexico) 1983-84
Jedi: T-shirts and sweatshirts in Mexico
Amaya S.A. (Pamplona, Spain) 1986-87
Star Wars & Droids: PVC non-inflatable balls in Spain
Amber Publishing Ltd. (Poland) 1995-2001
Bantam, Ballantine, Berkley books in Poland
American Can Co. (Greenwich, CT) 1980-82
Empire: **Dixie** cups; promotions with ice tea and lemonade mixes including T-shirt decorated w/*Star Wars* renderings, story card posters w/cards, hats, placemats; sweepstakes entry on back of Dixie package w/grand prize a screening of *ROTJ* w/a personal appearance by Darth Vader and bonus prize of a *Star Wars Saga* patches, in U.S. and Canada
American Marketing Enterprises (New York, NY) 1993-
Star Wars Classic: Screen-printed T-shirts using Topps *Star Wars* Galaxy art for distribution in comics and specialty shops in U.S.

American Publishing Corp. (Watertown, MA) 1980-85
Empire, Jedi & Ewoks: **Presto Magix** rubdown dry transfers in U.S., Canada
American Telecommunications (El Monte, CA) 1981-85
Empire & Jedi: Darth Vader speaker telephone in U.S., Canada, Europe, Australia and New Zealand
American Toy & Furniture Co. (Chicago, IL) 1982-85
Jedi & Ewoks: Juvenile furniture including toy chests, desks, night stands, book/showcases, table and chair sets, clothes racks, activity peg desks and chests, easels, rocking chairs in U.S. and Canada
American Supply/ASC (Talence, France) 1977-79 *Star Wars:* Belts, socks in Germany, The Netherlands, Belgium, Luxembourg, France, Denmark, Ireland, U.K.
Amora (Dijon, France) 1983-84
Jedi: Mustard glass container (4 different) in France
Amro Bank N.V. (Amstelveen, Netherlands) 1982
Empire: R2-D2 illustration on mobile and inserted in political journal "**Elsevier and HP**" and in company magazine **AMROFACET** in Netherlands
Anabas Products Ltd. (Essex, England) 1983-84
Jedi: Posters in U.K., Ireland, Italy, Germany
Ancol (Punchbowl, Australia) 1981
Empire: Self-adhesive school book labels in Australia
Andrews & McMeel (Kansas City, MO) 1994-95
Magic Eye 1995 3-D wall calendar in U.S.

Antioch Australia Pty Ltd. (Leichhardt, NSW, Australia) 1995-97
Journals, bookmarks, Book of Days, pocket address books & notebooks, collector albums, wallet cards, book plates in Australia

Antioch Limited (Berkshire, U.K.) 1994-95
Bookmarks, book plates, notebooks, address books, Book of Days, collectors albums, journals, doorknob hangers, wallet cards, memo boards in U.K.

Antioch Publishing Co. (Yellow Springs, OH) 1992- , 1995-98
Star Wars Classic: Bookmarks and bookplates, pocket note and address books, blank books, book of days in U.S. and Canada. Wallet cards, doorknob hangers, memo boards, bookmarks, bookplates, blank journals in U.S. and Canada

Aoshima Bunka Co. (Shizuoka, Japan) 1992-
Star Wars Classic: Soft vinyl model kits under **Argonauts** brand of *Star Wars* characters and vehicles in Japan

Applause, Inc. (Woodland Hills, CA) 1994-97
Vinyl dolls, resin figures, non-articulated figurine & vehicles, shadow-box diarama with non-articulated resin or PVC figurine, mugs, PVC key chains, bas relief plates, ceramic wall masks, chess sets, limited-edition framed art, lithographic prints, ceramic figural housewares, PVC mouse cover, ceramic bookends, Puzzle Cube in U.S.; entire line in Belgium, Netherlands, Luxembourg

Apple & Egg Productions (Purmerend, Netherlands) 1982-84
Empire & Jedi: Pin-back buttons in Belgium, Netherlands, Luxembourg

Arnot's Biscuits Pty. Ltd. (Homebush, N.S.W., Australia) 1985-87
Star Wars & Droids: Biscuits (cookies) in Australia

Arnott Harper Pty. Ltd. (Campsie, Australia) 1983-84
Jedi: Premium stickers w/pet food in Australia

Artemur, S.A. (Madrid, Spain) 1986-87
Star Wars & Droids: Bed sheets, padded quilts, padded sleeping bags, padded bedspreads, cushions, cotton/polyester cloth fabric pieces in Spain

Artfolio Limited (Edinburgh, Scotland) 1996-97
2-D plastic refrigerator magnets in U.K.

Asatsu, Inc. (Tokyo, Japan) 1995-96
TV & radio commercials, print campaign in Japan

Ata-Boy, Inc. (Hollywood, CA) 1994-96
Photographic refrigerator magnets in U.S.

Atari Games Inc. (Milpitas, CA) 1987-90
Star Wars Classic: Video game software for home/personal computers and game machines—a conversion of the coin-operated *Star Wars, ESB* and *ROTJ* arcade games, Europe, Australia, New Zealand

Atari, Inc. (Sunnyvale, CA) 1982-85
Star Wars, Empire & Jedi: Coin-operated video games worldwide

Australia United Foods (Queensland, Australia) 1983-86
Star Wars & Jedi: On-pack promotions w/**Paul's** and/or **Peters** ice cream and iced confectionery in Australia

Axcel Books do Brasil, Editora (Rio de Janeiro, Brazil) 1995-97
"Official Strategy Guides" in Brazil

Azbooka Publishers (St. Petersburg, Russia) 1996-97
Bantam books in Russia

Azrak-Hamway International, Inc. (New York, USA) 1994-97
Steel Tec construction sets in U.S.

B & W Character Merchandise (North Sydney, Australia) 1980-82
Empire: Umbrellas, rainwear, PVC painting smock, headgear, tote bags, soap, bubble bath, talcum powder, bath gel in Australia, Singapore, Malaysia

Bakers Promotions (New York, NY) 1977
Star Wars: Bread promotion w/trading cards in U.S.

Ballantine Books [see also **Random House**] (New York, NY) 1977- , 1994-2044
Star Wars, Empire, Jedi, Droids, Ewoks & Star Wars Classic: Story books, sketch books, album, iron-on transfer book, blueprints, portfolio, illustrated editions, art books, notebooks, quiz books, "guidebook". Reprints with new covers in U.S. and Canada; *Star Wars Technical Journal, Essential Guide to Vehicles & Vessels, Essential Guide to Characters*, NPR dramatization in U.S., terrorities & possessions.
Sub-Licensees and affiliates include:
Australia: **Horwitz Grahame Books**
Brazil: **Distribuidora Record, Livraria Francisco Alves Editora S.A.**
Bulgaria: **Lettera Publishers**
Canada: **Editions France-Amerique Ltee**
Czechoslovakia: **Premiera, Slovensky Spisovatel Publishers**
Finland: **Werner Soderstrom**
France: **Presse de la Cite, Hachette, Flammarion, Editions Hemma, Editions Des Deux Coqs D'or**
Germany: **Goldmann-Verlag, Uniparts Verlag, Xenos Verlagsgesellschaft**
Greece: **Pocketbooks, Multieditions Ltd.**
Netherlands: **A.W. Bruna & Zoons, Heron House**
Hungary: **Pendragon Konyvkiado, Mora Ferenc Ifjusagi**
Iceland: **Orn Org Orlygur**
Israel: **Ramdo, Shalgi Publishing Co.**
Italy: **Edizione Mondadori, Sperling & Kufer**
Japan: **Kladakawa Shoten, Sanrio, Bandai Co., Asahi Shimbunsha Ltd., Dynamic Sellers Ltd.**
Norway: **Freidhos Forlag, H.K. Koch**
Portugal: **Portugalia Editora Lda., Editora Abril, Livraria Francisco**
Poland: **Interart Publishers**
Spain: **Argos, Yanez, Ediciones Zeta, Carvajal y Cia., Editorial Roma, Plaza Joven, Editorial Planeta S.A.**
Sweden: **Bokforlags AB Tilden**
U.K.: **Sphere Books, Futura Books, Collins Publishers**
Yugoslavia: **Mladost, Forum Oour Marketprint, Politka Publishing House**

Balloon Supply Australia Pty. Ltd. (Terrey Hills, Australia) 1980-82
Empire: Party balloons in Australia, New Zealand, Fiji, Papua, New Guinea, New Caledonia, Singapore, Malaysia

Baltro Italiana (Rome, Italy) 1977-79
Star Wars: Corduroy pants and skirts, denim pants and skirts, wool and waterproof jackets in Netherlands, Belgium, Austria, Italy, Luxembourg, Germany, Switzerland, Greece, France, Corsica, Liechtenstein, Monaco, Spain, Portugal

Bantam Audio Publishing (New York, NY) 1990-, 1994-2042
Star Wars Classic: Audio version of *Star Wars* spin-off novels worldwide. Audio boxed set, versions, adaptations worldwide

Bantam Books (New York, NY) 1990- , 1994-2070
Star Wars Classic: Story books, novels, juvenile novels, short stories, illustrated books worldwide. Adult novels, Smithsonian Exhibit companion book, hardcover novels worldwide
Sub-Licensees and affiliates include:
Australia: **Transworld Publishers Pty**
Brazil: **Editora Noval Cultural**
Czech and Slovak Republic: **Bonus Press S.A., Nakladatelstvi Olympia**
France: **Les Presses de la Cite, Pocket Junior**
Germany: **Wilhelm Goldmann Verlag, Wilhelm Heyne Verlag**
Hungary: **S-King**
Italy: **Sperling & Kupfer Editori**
Japan: **Kaiseisha, Take Shobo**
Korea: **Koreaone Media Ltd.**
Poland: **Amber Publishing Ltd.**
Portugal: **Publicacoes Europa-Americ**
Spain: **Ediciones Martinez Roca**

Barrett Sportswear (Bloomington, MN) 1993-
Star Wars Classic: Adult T-shirts for Musicland, Suncoast Video, Sci-Fi Channel in U.S.

Basstoy International Corp. (Don Mills, Ontario, Canada) 1997-98
Starbles in Canada

Bastei-Verlag (Germany) 1994-2000
Magic Eye calendar, wall calendar in Germany, Austria, Switzerland; *The Art of...* in Germany

Beecham Cosmetics [Formerly **Jovan Inc.**] (Chicago, IL) 1983-84
Jedi: Natural and artificial soap products, toiletry products including bubble bath and cosmetic products for children and adults under the **Omni Cosmetics** line in U.S., Canada and Mexico

Ben Cooper Inc. (New York, NY) 1977-85
Star Wars, Empire, Jedi & Ewoks: Costumes, masks under $20, masquerade play suits, masquerade ponchos in U.S., Canada, and Australia

Benson Trading Company (Victoria, Australia) 1983-84
Jedi: Show bags, stickers, stationery items in Australia

Berkeley Fashions Pty Ltd (South Yarra, Victoria, Australia) 1996-98
Children's fashion tops, cotton shorts/pants, fleece & towelling tops/shorts & pants, cardigans, caps sourced from **Changes** in Australia

Berkley Publishing Group (New York, NY) 1994-07
Young adult novels, young Jedi Knights books, junior Jedi Knights books in U.S. and Phillipines

Best Buy Toys A.S. (Denmark) 1996-98
Watches in Denmark, Norway, and Finland

Bibb Company (New York, NY) 1977-85
Star Wars, Empire, Jedi & Ewoks: Towels, beach towels, sheets, pillowcases, comforters, drapes, bedspreads, slumber bags, blankets, window shades, beach throws, pillow shams, fabric, worldwide. Throw pillows, chambray shirts and jeans, corduroy jeans, toddler suits, shirts and slacks, boys swimwear and gym shorts in U.S. and Canada. Also under **"Barth & Dreyfuss"** brand
Sub-Licensees and affiliates include:
Australia: **Nouveau International Pty.**
Canada: **Dominion Textile Ltd. [Esmond division]**
U.K.: **Horrockes Ltd.**

Bienengraeber Marketing & Vert (Hamberg, Germany) 1994-95
Galoob Micro Machines in Germany

Big Balloon (Heemstede, The Netherlands) 1996-97
Three issues of *Shadows of the Empire* in Belgium, The Netherlands, Luxembourg

Bing Harris Sargood Ltd. (Auckland, New Zealand) 1983-84
Jedi: Towels, sheets, quilt covers, bedspreads, pillowcases (all **Bibb Co.** design), masks, children's T-shirts, sweat shirts, pajamas, tank tops, shorts, rainwear, stationery including pens, pencils, posters, hats, plastic lunch boxes in New Zealand

Black Horse Oy (Parola, Finland) 1996-98
Men's & boy's underwear, pajamas, sweatshirts & pants, t-shirts, swimwear, socks in Sweden, Finland, Norway, Russia

Boeder Deutschland GmbH (Florsheim/Main, Germany) 1996-97
Computer accessories in Germany, Austria, Switzerland, Belgium

Bonnier Carlsen (Stockholm, Sweden) 1995-98
Hardcover & trade paperback editions, **Berkley** books in Sweden

Books on Tape, Inc. (Costa Mesa, CA) 1994-98
Books in Tape in U.S.

Boxtree (London, U.K.) 1992- , 1994-99
Star Wars Classic: Gamebooks in U.K. Technical manual from **Star Log**, graphic novels, books, trade paperbacks from **Ballantine**, strategy guides in U.K.; **Dark Horse** graphic novels & comics, graphic novels, comics, trade paperbacks in U.K.

The Bradford Exchange (Niles, IL) 1995-99
3-D cold-cast porcelain and/or resin collector plates in U.S.

Bradley Time Inc. [Elgin] (New York, NY) 1977-85
Star Wars, Empire, Jedi & Ewoks: Mechanical wrist watches, digital watches, wall clocks, talking clocks, novelty items such as ruler with clock, virtually worldwide. (Most clocks under **"Welby Clock"** brand)

Brady Publishing (Indianapolis, IN) 1994-97
TIE Fighter Strategy Guides in U.S.

Brasoft Productos de Informatic (Sao Paulo, Brazil) 1994
Floppy-disk versions of computer games in Brazil

Brava Soft Furnishings Pty. Ltd. (St. Peters, Australia) 1980-84
Empire & Jedi: Bean bag chairs in Australia

Bridge Farm Dairies Ltd. (Suffolk, England) 1983-86
Jedi, Star Wars Classic & Droids: Yogurt containers in U.K.

British Shoe Corp. (Leicester, England) 1982-86
Empire, Jedi & Ewoks: Infants' bedroom slippers in U.K.

Broderbund Software, Inc. (San Rafael, CA) 1988-93
Star Wars Classic: Computer software game based on *Star Wars* in U.S.

Brookfield Athletic Shoe Co. (East Brookfield, MA) 1982-85
Jedi & Ewoks: Roller skates, ice skates and skate boards in U.S.

Brown Shoe Co. of Canada, Ltd. (Perth, Ontario, Canada) 1996-97
Children's & young men's athletic & skateboard shoes, beachwear & canvas shoes, sport sandals, hikers, weather boots in Canada

Bucci Imports Ltd. (Honesdale, PA) 1986- , 1996
Star Wars Classic: **West End Games** (see also for sub-licensees and affiliates): role playing, adventure board, book, miniature metallic figures distributed worldwide

Budget Books Pty Ltd. 1994-96
Glow in the Dark Colouring Books for Kids-Four in Australia and New Zealand

Buena Vista Home Video (Burbank, CA) 1990-
Star Wars Classic: 25 seconds of **Star Tours** footage in **Disneyland** sing-along videocassettes distributed worldwide

Burgschmiet Verlag GmbH (Nurnbert, Germany) 1996-99
Bantam: *The Illustrated SW Universe* in Germany, Austria, & Switzerland

Burton's Gold Medal Biscuits (Slough, England) 1983-84; (Bracknell, Berkshire, England) 1996-98
Jedi: Biscuits (cookies) in U.K., Ireland. Tins with sweet biscuits in U.K.

C.P.E.E.A. Ltd. (North Parmatta, Australia) 1983-84
Jedi: Promotion for **IBM** personal computers using Darth Vader posters and shelf cards in Australia

Calzados Nimer S.A. (Alicante, Spain) 1986-87
Star Wars & Droids: Children's footwear in vulcanized rubber w/top synthetic weave in Spain

Campina Ijsfavrieken B,V. (Roermond, Netherlands) 1983
Jedi: Ice cream packaged in character wrappers (& sticker promotion) in Netherlands, Benelux

Canada Cup Inc. (Brampton, Ontario, Canada) 1982-85
Jedi: 5 oz. & 9 oz. decorated disposable cups in Canada

Canada Game Limited (Concord, Ontario, Canada) 1995-96
POGs and slammers in Canada

Carlsen Forlag A.S. (Denmark) 1994-2000
Trade paperbacks and **Bantam** books in Denmark

Carlsen Verlag GmbH (Germany) 1994-2000
Dark Horse comic books and trade paperback editions in Germany, Austria, Switzerland; **Berkley** books in Denmark

Carvajal, S.A. (Bogota, Columbia) 1982-83
Empire & Jedi: Children's activity notebooks of 50-100 pages w/printed covers, school portfolios in Columbia

Catch A Star Collectibles (Cherry Hills, NJ) 1992-
Star Wars Classic: Specially made plaques and other collectibles distributed through **QVC** channel specials and retail in U.S.

CBS Toys (New York, NY) 1983-86
Jedi: **Gym-Dandy** in-ground or ground anchored outdoor activity equipment for children including swing sets.

Cedco Publishing Co. (San Rafael, CA) 1989-90, 1994-97
Star Wars Classic: 1990/1991 calendar in U.S., Australia, New Zealand. 1996 wall calendar & datebook using **Topps** trading-card images, 1997 calendars in U.S.

Center for the Arts (San Francisco, CA) 1994-95
"The Art of Star Wars" exhibit in U.S.

Central Mills, Inc. DBA Freeze (New York, NY) 1996-2000
Short- & long-sleeved t-shirts, tank tops, muscle t-shirts, long-sleeved fleece, fashion tops in U.S.

Ceraliment Lu Brun (Athis Mons, France) 1980-81
Empire: Small plastic vacuum-molded squares of characters affixed to cookie packages in France

Cereal Partners Espana (Barcelona, Spain) 1995-96
Promotional premiums (video, t-shirts, caps, pins) for Chocapic & Golden Grahams cereals in Spain

Cesar, S.A. (Saumur, France) 1978-83
Star Wars & Empire: Children's and adult's masks in Germany, Netherlands, Belgium, Luxembourg, France, Italy, U.K. Denmark, Ireland

Changes (Glendale, NY) 1994-97
Stipple images, heat transfers & other designs on t-shirts & sweatshirts in U.S.; adult t-shirts with stipple & portrait art in Canada

Charleston Hosiery Mills (Cincinnati, OH) 1977-85
Star Wars, Empire, Jedi & Ewoks: Children's knit hosiery in U.S.

Chaulnes Textile Industrielle (Chaulnes, France) 1996-98
Bedding in France and Belgium

Chein Industries, Inc. (Burlington, NJ) 1983-86
Jedi & Ewoks: Tin products including decorated containers, wastebaskets, and trays distributed in U.S.

Cherry Cindy's Creation (Manila, Philippines) 1991-93
Ewoks character clothing in the Philippines

Cheryl Playthings, Ltd. (London, England) 1977-79
Star Wars: Children's C-3PO playsuit in U.K., Ireland, Denmark, Finland, Iceland, Australia, Netherlands, Belgium, Austria, Italy, Luxembourg

Chiat/Day, Inc. Advertising (Venice, CA) 1994-96
Energizer Darth Vader commercial in U.S.

Chocolates La Cibeles Mieres-Siero (Oviedo, Spain) 1983-84
Jedi: Cardboard adhesive badges inside lids of chocolate spread and cocoa powder in Spain

Chronicle Books (San Francisco, CA) 1991- , 1995-2000
Star Wars Classic: "*Star Wars:* From Concept to Film to Collectible" worldwide. *Star Wars:* postcard books, 1997 vehicles calendar in U.S.
Sub-Licensees and affiliates include:
Japan: **Bandai Co.**

Chupa Chups Diversification (Barcelona, Spain) 1983-84
Jedi: Chewing gum and candies with stickers included as in-pack premium in Spain

Chupa Chups S.A. (Barcelona, Spain) 1996-98
Lollipops and lollipop holders in Europe; Fantasy Ball, Port-A-Chups and Pop-Machine in Argentina, Uruguay, Paraguay, Bolivia, New Zealand

Cie Sun City Sarl (Aubervilliers, France) 1996-97
T-shirts, sweatshirts, tracksuits, shorts-suits, polos for juniors and teens in France

Circculo Do Livro (Sao Paulo, Brazil) 1995-98
T. Zahn and **Bantam** books in Brazil

Clarks of England (Norwalk, CT) 1978-79
Star Wars & Empire: Shoes in U.S., Canada

Classico (San Rafael, CA) 1989-
Star Wars Classic: Large and small postcards in U.S.

Classico San Francisco (Corte Madera, CA) 1994-97
Postcards in U.S. and U.K.

Cleveley's Shoe & Slipper Co. Ltd. (Lancashire, England) 1978-79
Star Wars: Children's slippers in U.K., Ireland

Cliro Perfumeries, Ltd. (London, England) 1977-78
Star Wars: Character soaps, children's bubble bath and shampoo in U.K., West Germany, Austria, Belgium, Australia, Hong Kong, Denmark, Egypt, Spain, Finland, France, Greece, Iran, Israel, Italy, Norway, Portugal, Netherlands, Sweden, Switzerland

Clock I Sverige A.B. (Stockholm, Sweden) 1995
33 Restaurant promotion in Sweden

CMI Marketing Services (Singapore) 1996-97
Distribute products from **A.H. Prismatic, Third Dimension Arts, Fisher Space Pen, Zanart (OSP), Advanced Graphics, Hollywood Pins, Antioch Publishing, Ata-Boy, Portal, Western Graphics, Crystal Craft, Tin Signs** in Singapore

Coca-Cola Co. (Atlanta, GA) 1977-85
Star Wars: Drinking glasses, plastic cups, posters, paper trays or meal boxes, book covers, perforated stamps, small cards, soft-drink bottle crowns in U.S., Argentina, Australia, Brazil, Canada, Denmark, France, Ireland, Italy, Japan, Mexico, Spain, Sweden, U.K, Germany
Empire & Jedi: Drinking glasses, plastic cups w/lids, posters, perforated stamps, small cards, paper trays or meal boxes, book covers, small robots incorporating Lucasfilm design patent for R2-D2, calendars, pin-back buttons, bookmarks, T-shirts, pen and pencil sets, posters, plastic pitchers and cups w/lids distributed in various territories worldwide
Promotions w/various chains worldwide including **Burger Chef, Burger King, Kentucky Fried Chicken, 7-11 Stores, Hungry Jack's, Pizza Hut, Jollibee**

Coca-Cola Export Corp. (Silverwater, Australia & Auckland, New Zealand) 1983-84
Jedi: Plastic cup and glassware premium, mobile display, counter cards in Australia and New Zealand

Colgate/Palmolive, SAE (Madrid, Spain) 1986-87
Star Wars & Droids: In-pack premium of 415,000 *Star Wars* action figures with **Colgate** dental cream distributed in Spain

Collectors Guide Publishing (Burlington, Ontario, Canada) 1994-97
Crystal casting porcelain statues in U.K.

Colombine B.V. (Belgium) 1996-97
Products imported from **Hamilton, Fisher Space Pen Co., Rawcliffe, Willets, Crystal Craft Aus, Hollywood Pins, Ata-Boy, Ralph Marlin, Thinkway Toys, Fox Productions, Star Jars, Antioch, Peter Kolb** in Belgium, the Netherlands, Luxembourg

Colorvision International, Inc. (Orlando, FL) 1994-96
Customized computer portraits in U.S.

Comdial Consumer Communications (New York, NY) 1981-85
Empire & Jedi: Darth Vader speaker telephone in U.S., Canada, Europe, Australia, New Zealand

Comics Figuras (Barcelona, Spain) 1986-87
Star Wars & Droids: PVC figurines, maximum height 10 cm., hand-painted, not articulated in Spain

Commonwealth Savings Bank (Sydney, Australia) 1980-82
Empire: Darth Vader and R2-D2 plastic banks given away w/new account in Australia

Compagnie Europeenne Des Emballages (Thouars, France) 1983-84
Jedi: Gift paper, paper bags, polyethylene bags in France

Concesiones de Bebidas Carbonicas (Zaragoza, Spain) 1984
Jedi: Sales promotion for **Konga** brand lemon, orange and cola carbonated beverages in Spain (action figure giveaway)

Consumer Products (Storrington, Sussex, England) 1980-81
Empire: Toiletries: shampoo, bubble bath, talcum powder, soap in U.K.

Cosalt Exports, Ltd. (South Humberside, England) 1977-79
Star Wars: Decorated mirrors in U.K. Ireland, European Common Market

Courleciel (Courvevoie, France) 1995-96
Star Wars: SW Fan Magazine in France & French-speaking countries

CPC Espana S.A. (Barcelona, Spain) 1987
Droids: Promotion of CPC ready-mixed custards w/Ewoks on package in Spain

CPG Products (Cincinnati, OH) 1984-85
Jedi: Collectors coins (promotional tie-in w/**Kenner** mini-action figures) and 7,500 Speeder Bike ride-on toys used as premium in U.S.

Craft House Corporation (Toledo, OH) 1995, 97
Paint-By-Number, Collector's medallion, Wall Plaque in U.S.

Creaciones Juanin S.A. (Tola, Mexico), 1980-81, 83-84
Empire: Children's rigid masks in Mexico
Jedi: Decorated vinyl figurines w/pencil sharpeners in the base, rigid plastic masks, in Mexico

Creata Promotion (Castle Hill, Australia) 1980-81
Empire: Pencil cases, purses, disco bags in Australia

Creation Conventions Inc. (Mineola, NY) 1987
Star Wars Classic: Star Wars 10th Anniversary Conventions and products including buttons (3 designs), bumper stickers, note pad, T-shirts, photographs from the movies in U.S.

Crecspan S.A. (Barcelona, Spain) 1986-87
Droids: In-pack stickers w/snack line in Spain

Croner-Tyco Toys Pty Ltd. (Tullamarine, Victoria, Australia) 1995-97
Rubie's character costumes/masks; **Applause** PVC colllector assortment, PVC danglers, assorted vinyl dolls, assorted figural mugs, statutettes, collector art, puzzle can in Australia

Croner Trading (Victoria, Australia) 1983-84
Jedi: Masks and costume sets (using designs from **Acamas Toys**), distributed in Australia

Crown & Andrews (Granville, NSW, Australia) 1995-96
POGs, art & film from **Canada Games** in Australia

Crown Wallcovering Ltd. (Lancaster, England) 1985-87
Star Wars & Droids: Wall coverings in U.K., Ireland

Crystal Craft (Queensland, Australia) 1983-84, 1995-97
Jedi & Ewoks: Posters, stationery items, personal goods (much sub-licensed from **Adam Joseph**) in Australia. **Rawcliffe** pewter products; **Willitts** collector film cels, tumblers, wall clocks, key rings, magnets, pins, badges; **Advanced Graphics** life-size cardboard standees in Australia; mugs, plates, pens, pewter, **Willitts** film cells, classware clocks, key rings, magnets, pins/badges in New Zealand

CUI Inc. (Wilmington, NC) 1993- , 1994-97
Star Wars Classic: Tin trading cards in a metal collectors' box in U.S. Collector steins in U.S.

D.N. Russell & Co. (Christchurch, New Zealand) 1980-81
Empire: Pencil cases in New Zealand

Dakin Inc. (Woodland Hills, CA) 1983-85, 1992-93
Jedi: Photo buttons, wallets, luggage tags, hair accessories, combs, jewelry, brush and mirror sets, paper weights, key chains, night lights, luggage, magnets, tote bags, hooks, throw and autograph pillows, backpacks, plastic coin banks, rulers, markers, glue dispensers, pens, tape, safety scissors, foil reinforcements, pencil boxes, rubber stamps, self-inking stamps, ceramic mugs, puffy and other stickers in Australia (**Adam Joseph** line)
Star Wars Classic: Ceramic mugs, rotocast dolls (Darth Vader, Luke Skywalker [2 versions], Han Solo, Princess Leia, Chewbacca, C-3PO) in U.S. for exclusive sale at **Suncoast Motion Picture Co.**

Dal Mau Carles Pla, S.A. (Gerona, Spain) 1986-87
Star Wars & Droids: Plastic and cardboard puzzles in Spain

Danbury Mint (Norwalk, CT) 1992-
Star Wars Classic: Direct-order pewter chess set in U.S., Canada

Danon Markeging International (Scoresby, Victoria, Australia) 1996-97
Quilt covers, pillow cases, sheet sets, comforters, cushions, curtains and curtain fabric, bath and beach towels, face washes in Australia

Dark Horse Comics (Milwaukie, OR) 1990- , 1995-97
Star Wars Classic: Comic books, newspaper comics reprints, compilations worldwide. Comic books, collections, graphic novels, limited-edition bronze sculptures in U.S.
Sub-Licensees and affiliates include:
Germany: **Carlsen Verlag GmbH**
Italy: **News Market SRL**
Spain: **Norma Editorial S.A.**

Dark Horse France (Paris, France) 1995-97
Hardcover novels and comics in France and French-speaking countries

Data East Pinball (Melrose Park, IL) 1991-
Star Wars Classic: Pinball games w/effects by ILM from *Star Wars* trilogy distributed worldwide

Davenport (Abbotsford, Victoria, Australia) 1994-98
Boxer shorts, socks, ties, vests, sleepwear, kimonos, pajamas in Australia and New Zealand

Decipher, Inc. (Norfolk, VA) 1995-98
Collectible card games in U.S., Canada, Mexico

Decoraciones Herrandiz (Barcelona, Spain) 1986-88
Droids: Crystal glasses, porcelain jars, large cups, cups and saucers in Spain

Deeko Ltd. (London, England) 1977-79
Star Wars: Children's party paper goods: paper napkins, paper table covers and paper party cases in U.K., Ireland, Europe, Scandinavia, Australia, New Zealand, Africa, Middle East

Deerfield Pty Ltd. (Ringwood, Victoria, Australia) 1996-97
Character costumes in Australia

Deka Plastics (Elizabeth, NJ) 1978-85
Star Wars, Empire, Jedi & Ewoks: Plastic tableware: mugs, tumblers, salad bowls, soup bowls, decanters, divided plates in U.S., Canada, Korea, Saudi Arabia, South Africa, Taiwan, England, Ireland, France, Venezuela, Australia

Dekkertoys Limited (Hertfordshire, U.K.) 1995-96
Children's dress-up outfits in U.K.

Deluxe Corporation (Shoreview, MN) 1995-98
Personal checks and checkbook covers in U.S.

Dentsu, Inc. (Osaka, Japan) 1987-
Star Wars Classic: **Star Tours** inflatable raft as a premium through **Panasonic** dealers in Japan; postcards and telephone cards in Japan; print, billboard, transit and television advertising using *Star Wars* characters in Japan

Didactecnica S.A. (Barcelona, Spain) 1986-87
Star Wars & Droids: Table games w/board in box, cardboard jigsaw puzzles in box or frame, plastic and cardboard dominos in Spain

Distribution Network (London, U.K.) 1993-1995-97
Star Wars Classic: Shirts and caps in U.K. Adult caps & T-shirts, sweatshirts, fashion tops, limited-edition jackets, limited-edition fine-art prints, ceramic mugs in U.K.

Dive Press S.A. (Caracas, Venezuela) 1978-79
Star Wars: Stamp story album in Venezuela

Don Ling's (Butterfield, MN) 1993-
Star Wars Classic: Removable tattoos in U.S.

Don Post Studios, Inc. (North Hollywood, CA) 1977-90
Star Wars, Empire, Jedi, Star Wars Classic: Rubber, vinyl or plastic pull-over masks to retail at a minimum of $20.00 worldwide

Donau-Plastic Stefan Stern GMB (Wien, Austria) 1996-97
Address book, telephone index, blotting pad, book box, binder, pencil box & pouch, mini organizer, clipboard, ring binder, level arch file, pencil pot, mutipurpose case, poetry & photo albums, diary, pencil case, rucksack, fountain & fiber pens, exercise books, college block, identity card etui, school bag, colour pens in Germany, Austria, Switzerland, Hungary, Czech Republic

Dorfman-Pacific Co. Inc. (Oakland, CA) 1987-88
Star Wars Classic: Caps in U.S.

Double R Apparel Ltd. (MMI) (Montreal, Quebec, Canada) 1996-98
Boys' sleepwear, pajamas in Canada

Doubleday Book Club (Garden City, NY) 1994-00
Book club rights in U.S.

Doubleday Book & Music Club (New York, NY) 1995-2000
Book club & direct market rights to **Bantam's** *Children of the Jedi* and *Star Wars Technical Journal* in U.S.

Doubleday Direct, Inc. (Garden City, NY) 1996-01
Star Wars: Shadows of the Empire as Science Fiction Book Club selection in U.S.

Downpace (London, U.K.) 1995-97
Mugs, key rings, magnets, pewter vehicles, figurines, hanging ship figurines, **Willitts** collector film frames, **Crystal Craft** special-edition lithographs, frosted glasses in U.K.

Drawing Board Greeting Cards Inc. (Dallas, TX) 1978-85
Star Wars, Empire, Jedi & Ewoks: Gift wrap and tags, correspondence notes, greeting cards, paper party goods (plates, napkins, table covers, cups, placemats, invitations, place cards, hats, centerpieces, party puzzles), postcards, padded stationery w/matching envelopes, package decorations, stationery stickers, party banners, blow-outs, balloons, party cups, stickers, in U.S., Canada, Venezuela, Columbia, Hong Kong, Singapore
Sub-Licensees and affiliates include:
Australia: **Valentine Publishing Co.** (also New Zealand)
Canada: **RFI Industries**
Ecuador: **Technigraphics**
Panama: **Lewis Services**
Venezuela: **Profood, Carka**

Drew Pearson Marketing, Inc. (Hopkins, MN) 1995-97
Baseball & novelty caps, fashion hats, winter headwear in U.S.

Drew Struzan (Westlake Village, CA) 1996-97
Limited-edition prints of original artwork for "The Crystal Star" in Japan

Dufner & Cie. (Renens/Lausanne, Switzerland) 1983-84
Jedi: Stickers of 16 characters in Switzerland

Ed. Haas Nahrmittel GmbH. (Truan, Austria) 1996-98
PEZ candy dispenser in Hong Kong, Indonesia, Korea, Malaysia, Philippines

Ediciones Este (Barcelona, Spain) 1984-85
Jedi: 240 stamps and stamp album in Spain

Ediciones Manantial S.A. (Madrid, Spain) 1977-78
Star Wars: Rotating calendar and paper mobile in Spain, Canary Islands

Ediciones Martinez Roca (Barcelona Spain) 1994-01
Trade paperbacks, **Bantam** and **Berkley** books, novels in Spain

Ediciones du Weekend (Aulnay sous Bois Cedex, France) 1983-84, 1991-92
Jedi & Star Wars Classic: Posters, mini-posters, postcards in France

Editorial Ciamar S.A. (Mexico) 1983-85
Jedi: Posters, stamps and stamp albums in Mexico

Editorial Magro Ltda. (Sao Paulo, Brazil) 1996-98
Mos Eisley *Cantina Pop-Up Book* from **Little Brown** & White Heat in Brazil

Editorial Magro S.A. (Piso, Mexico) 1981-82
Empire: Rub-down transfers to be applied to illustrations, in Mexico, Peru, Ecuador, Dominican Republic

Edizioni Panini (Modena, Italy) 1977-79, 1983-84
Star Wars: Stamp story albums and stamps in Netherlands, Belgium, Austria, Italy, Luxembourg, Germany, Switzerland, Greece, France, Corsica, Liechtenstein, Monaco, Finland, Sweden, Iceland, Denmark, Norway
Jedi: Collectors stamps and stamp albums in U.K., Italy, Benelux, Germany, Switzerland, Greece, France, Yugoslavia, Austria

E. Gluck Corp. (Long Island City, NY) 1994-95
Wrist watches in U.S.

Egmont (Denmark) 1996-98
Books with audio tapes in Sweden, Norway, Denmark, Finland, Iceland

Ehapa Verlag GmbH (Germany) 1995-2000
Dark Horse comics in Germany, Switzerland, Austria

El Buen Equipaje S.A. (Xochimanca, Mexico) 1981-84
Empire & Jedi: Vinyl belts, metal buckles, key rings, costume jewelry in Mexico

Elliott Wave International (Gainsville, GA) 1995-2070
Text from *The Empire Strikes Back Notebook* to be used in book *Aerodynamic Trading* worldwide

Erregiochi (Lucca, Italy) 1981-83
Empire: Costumes for carnival in Italy

Ertl Company (Dyersville, IA) 1989- , 1994-96
Star Wars Classic: Model kits: re-release of plastic model kits in replica boxes worldwide except South America. Model kits worldwide

Estes (Penrose, CO) 1996-98
Model rocket kits, flying model space vehicle kits, static balsa wood model kits in U.S.

Estes Industries (Penrose, CO) 1977-81, 1993-
Star Wars & Empire: Flying model rocket kits in U.S., Canada, West Germany, Netherlands, Belgium, Luxembourg, France, Italy, U.K., Ireland, Denmark
Star Wars Classic: Re-release of original kits in U.S.

Estucheria Vipo S.A. (Barcelona, Spain) 1986-87
Star Wars & Droids: Pencil case (filled), plastic tote bag with school items in Spain

Euro Disney (France) 1994-
Film footage for souvenir video in France

Euro-Fashions (Amsterdam, Netherlands) 1983
Jedi: Posters and *Star Wars* products as prizes in quiz contest for purchasers of **McGregor** products, in Benelux (Dutch language only)

F.X. Schmid (Munich, Germany) 1978-79
Star Wars: Card games for children in Germany, Switzerland, France, Austria, Netherlands

Faciem (Paris, France) 1995-96
Cardboard stand-ups in France

Factors, Etc./The Image Factory (Bear, DE) 1977-81
Star Wars: Posters, T-shirt heat transfers, pin-back photo buttons, patches, silk-screened T-shirts, tote bags, caps, jewelry (through sub license to **Weingeroff Ent.**, Providence, RI), first year of *Star Wars* Fan Club, in U.S., Canada and nearly all other countries
Empire: Posters (including Yoda promotional poster for **Xerox**), silk-screened T-shirts and sweat shirts, heat transfers, badges, buttons, patches in U.S., Canada, Australia, New Zealand, U.K., Ireland, Germany, Netherlands, Luxembourg, Singapore, Malaysia, Philippines, Hong Kong, South Africa, Mexico, Central and South America

Fairland Investments (Sydney, Australia) 1981-82
Empire: PVC thongs in Australia

Famosa S.A. (Onil, Spain) 1994-97
Galoob Micro Machines in Spain

Fantasma Inc. (Woburn, MA) 1992-
Star Wars Classic: Watches, 3-D bookmarks, laser pens, 3-D postcards, streamer and other pencils, laser bumper stickers, 3-D magnets and key chains, laser spinner, mug, wall decor in U.S.

Irvin Feld & Kenneth Feld Productions Inc. (Vienna, VA) 1993-
Star Wars Classic: **George Lucas Super Live Adventure:** Live-action arena show in Japan, with merchandise including key chains, clocks, vinyl bop bags, pens, laser rifles, plush toys, mugs, banks, Darth Vader voice-changers, dome lights, T-shirts, painters' caps, sword, pin-back buttons, popcorn bucket, jackets, duffel bag in Japan

Festcolor Industria (Taboao da Serra San Paulo, Brazil) 1989-90
Star Wars Classic: Masks in Brazil

Film Freakshop (Ar den Haag, Netherlands) 1983-84
Jedi: Original *ROTJ* film poster in Benelux

Filmwelt Berlin (Berlin, Germany) 1995-97
Postcards, notepaper, giftwrap, tags, ribbon, bookwrap, writing pads, exercise, address & file books, file labels, deskmats, placemats, erasers, pencil sharpeners, bookmarks, pinwalls & figurines, buttons, mouse pads, cups, posters, pins, stickers, blueprints, greeting cards, planners, table calendars, keyrings in Germany, Austria, Switzerland

Fisher Space Pen Co. (Boulder City, NV) 1994-96
Bullet & collector pens and refills in U.S.

Flaggen Und Fahnenhandel Pehl (Mittenwald, Germany) 1997-98
Display flags in Germany, Austria, Switzerland

Fleer GmbH (Walldorf, Germany) 1983-85
Jedi: **Fleer** bubble gum promotion w/a series of *Star Wars* pictures on wrappers in Germany, Austria, Switzerland

Flex-print (Albury, Australia) 1980-81
Empire: Heat transfers in Australia

Flomo Plastics Industrial Co. (Taipei, Taiwan) 1996-98
Pencil cases, stationery, pencils, pens, erasers, ruler/stencil, clip, sharpener, scissors, tape dispenser, stamp set, glue, memo pad, stationery gift sets, paper products, bags, housewares, coin banks, key chain/ring in Taiwan

Flotilla Shoes Ltd. (Somerset, England) 1983-85
Jedi: Footwear in U.K.

Fonsash Pty. Ltd. (Glenhaven, Australia) 1985-86
Star Wars & Droids: Costumes in Australia

Fortuna Industries Ltd. (Mt. Wellington, New Zealand) 1984-85
Jedi: Erasers, pencil sharpeners, rulers, pin-back badges, school bags, stationery pack, masks in New Zealand

Fossil Partners, L.P. (Richardson, TX) 1996-97
Collectible analog watches in U.S.

Fox Fanfare Music, Inc. (Los Angeles, CA) 1977-81
Star Wars & Empire: Sheet music worldwide

Fox Productions B.V. (Amsterdam, The Netherlands) 1996-97
T-shirts, sweaters, caps in Belgium, the Netherlands, Luxembourg

France Quick (Bagnolet, France) 1995
Fast-food promotions in France & Belgium

Frankel & Roth International (Crawley, England) 1982-84, 1986-88
Empire & Jedi: Children's schoolbags, rayon pencil cases, backpacks in U.K., Ireland
Droids: Schoolbags in U.K., Ireland

Franklin Mint (Franklin Center, PA) 1992-
Star Wars Classic: Pewter replica models w/precious metals distributed worldwide

Friedlander Publishing Group (Pittsburgh, PA) 1996-2000
Dave Dorman's Art of Star Wars paperback and hardcover in U.S.

Friedrich W. Heye Verlag GmbH (Unterhaching, Germany) 1996-97
1997 & 1998 wall calendars and "agendas" in Germany, Austria, Switzerland

Frito-Lay of Puerto Rico (San Juan, Puerto Rico) 1982
Empire: Plastic stick-ons inserted into packages of **Doritos, Tostitos, Fritos, Munchos, Cheetos, Fantastix, Funyuns** in Puerto Rico, the Virgin Islands

Fromagerie Bel (Paris, France) 1984-85
Jedi: 18 stickers used as a premium for **La Vache qui Rit** in France

Fuji Audio Visual System Co. (Tokyo, Japan) 1978-79
Star Wars: Photo album in Japan and **Ken Films** sub-licensee

Fuji Film (Tokyo, Japan) 1982-83
Empire: Paper cut-outs inserted into packages of blank cassettes in Germany

Fun Products Ltd. (Whingate, Leeds, England) 1982-84
Empire & Jedi: Flat and 3-D stickers, pin-back badges in U.K.; key rings in Israel

Funtastic Pty Ltd. (South Oakleigh, Victoria, Australia) 1996-97
Diary school kits, letter sets, spiral note pad, ring binders, stationery bum bag, pencil pack, stationery set, #-D molded eraser, pencil case photo albums in Australia

Funworks (Disney Publishing) (Burbank, CA) 1996-98
Shimmer, Super Pop-Up, flip, Swing into Action, Toy in Spine & Punch-Out books in U.S. and Canada

G & J Barnes Nominees Pty. Ltd. (Victoria, Australia) 1984
Jedi & Ewoks: Kites (**Spectra Star**) in Australia

Gemma Designs Limited (Hampshire, England) 1996-98
Greeting, gift & roll wrap, gift tags, party invitations & favors, thank you pads, height charts in U.K.

General Biscuits Italia (Mortara, Italy) 1980-81
Empire: Promotion for packaged sweet biscuits in Italy

General de Confiteria (Barcelona, Spain) 1986-87
Star Wars & Droids: Promotion using Droids name and images for chewing gum, lollipops, jellies, gummys in Spain

General Electric Co. (Portsmouth, VA) 1984
Empire & Jedi: Poster given away upon visiting a store selling **GE** VCRs in U.S.

General Foods Corp. (Auckland, New Zealand) 1980-84
Empire: Badge and sticker premium w/**Twinkies** in New Zealand, New South Wales; paper cut-out mask premium for **Tip Top Ice Cream** in New Zealand
Jedi: Ice Cream and iced confectionery packages in New Zealand

General Mills (Minneapolis, MN) 1978-83
Star Wars, Empire & Jedi: In and on-package promotions using trading card sets, punch-out cardboard vehicles, kites, place mats, plastic tumblers in U.S. and Canada; 8-page 4-color in-pack booklets, posters in Canada Kenner Products

General Mills Fun Group [See also **Kenner**] (Minneapolis, MN) 1981, 1985
Empire: Costumes, play suits, ponchos, masks in Australia, New Zealand
Star Wars & Droids: Board games, paint by number kits, vehicles, articulated figures in Spain

Georg A. Steinmann Lederwarenfabrik GmbH (Nuremberg, Germany) 1983-85
Jedi: Pencil cases and bags, school kits in Germany, Austria, Switzerland

George Fenmore Associates (New York, NY) 1977-78
Star Wars: Souvenir program book for theater sale worldwide except Japan

Giftcraft Limited (Brampton, Ontario, Canada) 1995-97
Vinyl dolls, resin figures, vehicles, diorama, mugs, key chains, bas-relief plates, wall masks, chess sets, framed art, lithographic prints, ceramic figural housewares, cookie jars, salt & pepper shakers, PVC mouse cover, ceramic bookends in Canada

Gifted Images Publishing Ltd. (Baldwin, NY) 1994-96
Original art images reproduced as series of limited-edition lithographs in U.S.

Glasslite S.A. (Sao Paulo, Brazil) 1987-90
Star Wars Classic: Action figures, vehicles, weapons in Brazil

Glow Zone Products Pty Ltd. (Fairfield, Victoria, Australia) 1994-95
Glow in the Dark stickers, posters, wall plaques in Australia

Golden Turtle Press (Richmond, CA) 1995-97
1997 wall calendars in U.S.

Goldmann Verlag (Munich, Germany) 1994-2003
Bantam novels & **Ballantine** pocket books in Germany; books in Germany, Austria, Switzerland; short-story anthologies worldwide

Grand Concepts (Montreal, Quebec, Canada) 1996-98
Pyramid, book, tote & duffel bags, backpacks, fanny packs, luggage, collectible umbrellas in Canada

Grand Toys Ltd. (Dorval, Quebec, Canada) 1995-97
Kites, action packs in Canada

Great Scott, Inc. (Brampton, Ontario, Canada) 1996-97
Nylon flags in Canada

Great Scott, Inc. (Katonah, NY) 1995-97
Nylon flags in U.S.

Gringoire Brossard (Pithiviers, France) 1983-84
Jedi: Sales promotion for pastries in France (action figure giveaway)

Grosvenor of London Limited (London, England) 1994-97
3-D bubble bath, 3-D topper, 3-D soap, soap dish, toothbrush holder in U.K.

GTI Telecom, Inc. (Winter Park, FL) 1996-97
Pre-paid plastic telephone cards in U.S.

H.C. Ford & Sons (NCF) Ltd. (London, England) 1981-84
Empire & Jedi: Address books, scrap pads, memo pads, notepads, postcards, pencils, erasers, rulers, pencil tops, pencil sharpeners, pencil cases, key rings in U.K., France

H.J. Heinz & Co. (Middlesex, England) 1978
Star Wars: On-label premium of **Helix International** school sets w/**Heinz** "Baked Beans with Sausage" in U.K.

Hallmark Australia Ltd. (Victoria, Australia) 1983-84
Jedi: Greeting cards, gift cards, invitations, thank you cards and gift wraps in Australia, New Zealand

Hallmark Cards Australia (North Clayton, Victoria, Australia) 1995-97
Greeting cards, stationery, gift wrap, wrapping papers, invitation pads, sticket sheets in Australia

Hallmark Cards, Inc. (Kansas City, MO) 1994-97
Greeting cards, stationery, gift wrap, ornaments, party goods, calendars, puzzles, stickers, t-shirts, mugs in U.S.

Hallmark New Zealand (New Zealand) 1995-97
Cards, wrap, invitations, sheet stickers in New Zealand, Rarotonga, Fiji

Halva AB (Helsinki, Finland) 1983-84
Jedi & Ewoks: Licorice, fruit candies in Finland

The Hamilton Collection, Inc. (Jacksonville, FL) 1994-98
Commemorative 15th Anniversary collector plates in Canada; porcelain trading cards & decal collector plates, decal photo ceramic plates in U.S.; Collector Plates Ships Collection & **Willitts** film frames via mail order only in U.K.

The Hamilton Collection U.K. (Worchester, U.K.) 1994-95
Test plate & three porcelain collector plates via direct response & mail order only in U.K.

Hamilton Group (Jacksonville, FL) 1986-
Star Wars Classic: Collector's plates, mugs, framed canvas prints in U.S., U.K.

Harley Inc. (Montreal, Quebec, Canada) 1988-90
Star Wars Classic: T-shirts, sweatshirts, jogging suits, pants, shorts, tank tops, polo shirts, pajamas in Canada

Harmony Foods Pty Ltd. (Parkville, Victoria, Australia) 1996-98
Confectionery & containers, including **Galoob** Micro Machine or **Canada Games** milk caps in Australia

Harry N. Abrams Inc. (New York, NY) 1992-
Star Wars Classic: Lucasfilm-related books that include *Star Wars* in U.S.

Hasbro Australia Ltd. (Eastwood, New South Wales, Australia) 1996-97
Seven puzzles in Australia

Hasbro Games Group (Beverly, MA) 1994-97
Card games, board games, jigsaw puzzles, still photo license for Picture Pursuit game, collectibles card games in U.S.; board, card, & travel games in Canada

Hasbro International, Inc. (Uxbridge, Middlesex, U.K.) 1995-97
Board & collectible card game in Germany, Austria, Switzerland, France, Italy, Spain, Portugal, U.K.; puzzles in U.K., Germany, France, Italy, Spain, Sweden

Hasson Productions Inc. (Newport Beach, CA) 1993-
Star Wars Classic: Limited edition prints and posters created by Michael David Ward in U.S.

Hayjax Manufacturing (Manchester, England) 1983-86
Empire, Jedi, Star Wars Classic & Droids: Sheets, pillowcases, duvet covers, bedspreads, quilted bedspreads, sleeping bags, curtains, towels, sheets in U.K., Ireland

Hebron Marketing (Metro Manila, The Phillipines) 1996-97
Erasers, pencils, pencil cases, sharpeners, key chains, backpacks, wallets, school bags, **Thinkway** coin banks in the Philippines

Heel Verlag GmbH (Konigswinter, Germany) 1995-98
Chronicle books in Germany, Austria, Switzerland

Heliotex (Bernex-GE, Switzerland) 1983-84
Jedi: Sweatshirts and T-shirts in Switzerland

Helix International (West Midlands, England) 1977-79
Star Wars: Children's and school stationery supplies in U.K., British Commonwealth (except Canada), Middle East, Caribbean and West Indies

Hemglass AB (Strangnas, Sweden) 1984-85
Jedi: "**Star Mint**" and "**Big Star**" ice cream in Sweden

Hengstenberg Mustard (Esslingen, Germany) 1982-84
Empire & Jedi: Collectible mustard jars/glasses (6 per set) in Germany

Hennes & Mauritz (Stockholm, Sweden) 1995
Princess Leia t-shirts in Sweden

Heraclio Fournier S.A. (Vitoria, Spain) 1986-87
Droids: Playing cards in Spain

Hershey Chocolate Co. (Hershey, PA) 1980
Empire: On-pack promotion: scenes printed on the back of 6-pack cartons of **Hershey's Milk Chocolate, Milk Chocolate w/Almonds, Reece's Peanut Butter Cups, Mr. Goodbar, Krackle, Watchamacallit, Kit Kat** in U.S.

Highbridge Co. (St. Paul, MN) 1992-
Star Wars Classic: CD and cassette versions of **National Public Radio** *Star Wars* and *Empire* radio dramas worldwide

Hitari Ltd. (Leeds, England) 1996-97
Radio-controlled Darth Vader figure in U.K.

Hogar Y Moda (Barcelona, Spain) 1983-84
Jedi: 4 posters inserted in "Lecturos" publication

Holeproof (Pacific Dunlop Div) (Australia) 1996-98
Socks, children's underwear in Australia

Hollywood Pins Co. (Los Angeles, CA) 1993- , 1995-97
Star Wars Classic: cloisonne, enamel and metal collectors pins in U.S. Collector lapel pins & key chains in U.S.

Home Entertainment Magazine (London, England) 1995

Hope Industries (Farmingdale, NY) 1996-97
Character watches in U.S.

Hot Shots (Australia) Pty Ltd. (Thomastown, Victoria, Australia) 1996-97
Rolling Thunder lithographs, **New Frontier** prints, **Zanart** lobby cards in Australia

Howard Eldon & A. Weiss (Van Nuys, CA) 1987-88
Star Wars Classic: Star Wars 10th Anniversary pin and jewelry in U.S., Canada

Huffy Corp. (Miamisburg, OH) 1983-85
Jedi & Ewoks: Metal frame bicycles in U.S.

Humet Textile S.A. (Barcelona, Spain) 1986-87
Droids: Towels in Spain

I. Chr. Olsen Kunstforlag Spielkarlenfabrik (Hellerup, Denmark) 1977-78
Star Wars: Children's invitation cards in Denmark

Icarus Co. [Formerly **Wessex Giftware**] (Dorset, England) 1981-83
Empire & Jedi: Laminated placemats, memo boards, mini-framed prints in U.K.

Ice Capades (Hollywood, CA) 1985-86
Ewoks: Ewoks on Ice show and related merchandise incl. programs, badges, pennants, penlights

Ide & Resultat AB (Stockholm, Sweden) 1984-85
Jedi: Luminous hard plastic tags, light-up badges, 1984 Advent calendar in Sweden

Ideal Loisirs (France) 1994-95
Galoob Micro Machines in France

Ilmage Marketing (Harwood Heights, IL) 1992-
Star Wars Classic: Vinyl decals in U.S.

Illusive Concepts (Danbury, CT) 1994-96
Collector series of maquettes & busts in U.S.

Images 'in (Paris, France) 1983-84
Jedi: Postcards in France

Impact Posters (Five Dock, NSW, Australia) 1995-97
Posters of all sizes in Australia

Impala-Soc. Editorial S.A. (Lisbon, Portugal) 1996-98
Dark Horse & **White Heat** pop-up books in Portugal

Imperial Chemical Industries Ltd. (Cheshire, England) 1977-81
Star Wars & Empire: Wallpaper worldwide

Imperial Feather Corp. (Toronto, Ontario, Canada) 1994-95
Slumber mates & bags, comforters, pillow cases in Canada

Impressions Plus (Selangor, Malaysia) 1996-98
Star Wars: Comics in Malaysia, Singapore, Brunei

Industrias CYS S.A. (La Eliana, Valencia, Spain) 1986-87
Star Wars & Droids: Schoolbags, school wallets, sports bags in Spain

Infotainment World, Inc. (San Mateo, CA) 1994-97
Strategy guides worldwide

The Ink Group (Waterloo, NSW, Australia) 1996-97
1997 calendars in Australia, U.K.

The Ink Group New Zealand (Auckland, New Zealand) 1995-97
1997 commemorative calendar in New Zealand

Int'l Distrib. Electronique (France) 1996-97
Character ID cards in card wallet in France

Introduct Holland (Ijsselstein, Netherlands) 1983-84
Jedi: Paper and vinyl stickers in Belgium, Netherlands, Luxembourg

Irwin Publishing (Concord, Ontario, Canada) 1995-2070
Text excerpts from *The Courtship of Princess Leia* to be used in Irwin Publishing book in U.S.

Iwamoto Co. Ltd. (Tokyo, Japan) 1980-81
Empire: Cloth handkerchiefs in Japan

J.& L. Randall Ltd. (Herts., England) 1983-85
Jedi: Coin sorters in U.K.

J. Inglis Wright Ltd. (Auckland, New Zealand) 1983
Jedi: Posters and stickers for near-pack promotion for **Beecham Ltd.'s Macleans** toothpaste in New Zealand

J. P. Belgium (Brussels, Belgium) 1983-84
Jedi: Carnival masks and costumes in Benelux

James River-Dixie/Northern Inc. (Greenwich, CT) 1983-85
Jedi: Disposable cups (5 oz. & 9 oz.) in U.S.

Jigyungsa Publishing Company (Seoul, Korea) 1996-98
Look Look books & junior novelizations in Korea

JNH Toys (Chelteham, Victoria, Australia) 1994-95
CUI, Inc. metal trading cards, **Thinkway** banks, **Placo** key chains in Australia

John Steinberg Inc. (Los Angeles, CA) 1987
Star Wars: 10th Anniversary special edition poster by John Alvin distributed worldwide

John Tzamouranes (Athens, Greece) 1984
Jedi: Bags, schools bags, pencil cases, plastic rulers and stickers in Greece

Jollibee Food Corp. (Quezon City, Philippines) 1983
Jedi: Promotion giving away tumblers w/purchase of 20 oz. drinks, T-shirts at discount price w/purchase in the Philippines

Josman S.A. (Denia, Alicante, Spain) 1980-81, 86-87
Empire & Droids: Masquerade costumes and masks for children in Spain

Jovan, Inc. (Chicago, IL) 1981-83
Empire & Jedi: **Omni Cosmetics** brand shampoo and bubble bath in figural containers, soap w/embossed characters, travel kits in U.S., Canada, Mexico

JPM Automatic Machines Ltd. (Solihull, U.K.) 1995-97
Amusement machines in U.K., Belgium, the Netherlands, Luxembourg, Germany, Austria, Switzerland

Just Toys (New York, NY) 1992-
Star Wars Classic: PVC **Bend-em's** figures and collectors carrying cases in U.S.

Just Toys Products Inc. (East Kowloon, Hong Kong) 1994-95
PVC **Bend-Ems** & injected-molded figures, carry cases, **Talk-Ems** in Belgium, The Netherlands, Luxembourg, Germany, France, Spain

Kaiyodo Co. (Osaka, Japan) 1992-
Star Wars Classic: Soft vinyl model kits of *Star Wars* characters and vehicles in Japan

Kash N' Gold Limited (Ronkonkoma, NY) 1996-98
Two novelty telephones, universal remote control in U.S.

Keehn Scenes, Inc. (Santa Rosa, CA) 1994-95
Unisex t-shirts sold only to **Suncoast Motion Picture Co.** and **Musicland** in U.S.

Kellogg (Aust.) Pty. Ltd. (Botany, Australia) 1980-84
Empire, Jedi & Ewoks: Series of 8 cutouts printed on **Kellogg's Corn Flakes; Kellogg's Corn Flakes** and **Rice Bubbles** in-pack and back-pack promotions: 16 collectible picture disk game cards and sweepstakes in Australia, New Zealand

Kellogg Canada, Inc. (Etobicoke, Ontario, Canada) 1996
Instant-win promotion on Honey Nut Corn Flakes, Bran Flakes, and Corn Flakes in Canada

Kellogg Co. (Battle Creek, MI) 1982-84
Jedi: **C-3POs** breakfast cereal and related promotional on-/in-pack items including masks, trading cards and stickers, plastic rockets in U.S., Canada

Ken Films, Inc. (Fort Lee, NJ) 1977-82
Star Wars & Empire: 8mm film for the home movie market distributed worldwide
Sub-Licensees and affiliates include:
- Australia: **Home Talkie Co.** (also New Zealand)
- France: **Super 8 Filmiport**
- Germany: **U.F.A.**
- Greece: **Kinofot**
- Italy: **I.E. International**
- Japan: **Toei Video Co.**
- Scandinavia: **Novio**
- South America: **Latincolor**
- Spain: **Cine Para Aficionados** (also Portugal)
- U.K.: **Mountain Films**

Kenner Products (Cincinnati, OH) 1977-91, 1994-97
Star Wars, Empire, Jedi, Droids & Ewoks: Master worldwide toy license, including following major subsidiaries or affiliates:
- Argentina: **Top Toys**
- Australia: **Toltoys Pty. Ltd.** (also New Zealand)
- Benelux: **Clipper/Deska**
- Canada: **Regal Toys, Parker Brothers, Kenner Products Canada**
- France: **Micro-Meccano, GMI Jeux et Jouets**
- Germany: **General Mills Inc. Germany**
- Hong Kong/Far East: **General Mills Hong Kong**
- Italy: **Harbert/Editrice Giochi, GM Products Corp.**
- Japan: **Takara Co., Tsukuda Co., General Mills Asia**
- Mexico: **Lili-Ledy S.A.**
- Scandinavia: **A.B. Alga**
- Spain: **P.B.P. S.A., General Mills Juguetes S.A.**
- U.K.: **Palitoy, Denys Fisher, Chad Valley Associates**
- U.S.: **Fundimensions**
- Venezuela: **Ziade S.A.**

Items include action figures, dolls, play environments, vehicles and other accessories, die-cast vehicles, toy weapons, modeling compounds, board games, crafts, puzzles, inflatables. Other brands in the group include **Fundimensions, MPC, CPG/Creative Products Group, Airfix** (in Europe), **Craftmaster, Parker Brothers**
Licensed products in Europe, Japan, U.S., Canada

Kennerspeil-Germany (General Mills Fun Group) (Nieder-Roden, Germany) 1979
Star Wars: Wallpaper posters (approximately 6x8 feet) in Germany

Kent Gida (Istanbul, Turkey) 1996-97
Bubble gum with special anniversary edition high-gloss collectible stickers in Turkey

Kiddy Fun AG (Switzerland) 1994-95
Galoob Micro Machines and Micro Scale portable playsets in Switzerland

Kidnap Furniture Ltd. (County Claire, Ireland) 1984-86
Star Wars, Jedi & Droids: Headboards, foot boards, bedside footlockers, children's desks in U.K., Ireland

Kidnation, Inc. (St. Louis, MO) 1996-98
Children's & young men's footwear: athletic, sport sandals, hikers, weather boots, skateboard shoes, beach wear & canvas shoes

Kilian Enterprises (Wichita, KS) 1987- 96
Star Wars Classic: Star Wars Trilogy one-sheet poster checklist; *Star Wars* 10th Anniversary mylar posters; *Empire* 10th Anniversary regular and mylar posters; *Jedi* 10th Anniversary foil-printed posters; Yoda cast bronze sculpture; various other Trilogy posters using art of the Hildebrandt brothers, Tom Jung, Drew Struzan, Larry Noble and others, in U.S.

Kimberly Clark de Mexico (Piso, Mexico) 1981, 83-84
Empire & Jedi: Lined notebooks w/printed covers in Mexico

King International Limited (Surrey, England) 1994-95
1000-piece limited-edition jigsaw puzzle in U.K.

King-Seeley Thermos Co. (Norwich, CT) 1977-85
Star Wars, Empire, Jedi, Droids & Ewoks: Lunch kits and insulated bottles together and separately in U.S., and for *Star Wars* also in Canada, U.K., Australia, Norway, France, Germany, Sweden, Belgium, Saudi Arabia, Kuwait, Netherlands

Kinnerton Confectionery Ltd. (London, England) 1996-98
Commemorative ceramics, 3-D embossed tins, polystone figure tins all to be filled with chocolate or jelly beans, classic Easter eggs, chocolate advent calendars, mini-chocolate figures, lollipops (only to be sold to **Marks & Spencer**) in U.K.

Kiwi Products UK Ltd. (Kent, England) 1983-84
Jedi: Balloons in U.K.

Kodak Japan (Tokyo, Japan) 1983
Jedi: Premiums including paper cups printed with color photos, small metal tray, printed small glass, plastic banner in Japan

Kodak, S.A. (Madrid, Spain) 1983
Jedi: 1983 Calendars for customers in Spain

Kortex Pty. Ltd. (Victoria, Australia) 1983-84
Jedi: T-shirts, sweat suits in Australia

Kosumosu Co. (Tokyo, Japan) 1978-80
Star Wars: Small stationery items

Kraft Foods Ltd. (Gloucestershire, England) 1980
Empire: Mail-in offer for one of four different sets of rubdown transfers in U.K.

Krisalis Software, Ltd. (Rotherham, U.K.) 1994
Star Wars, Empire, Return: Laser Squad game in U.K.

Landmark General Corp. (Novato, CA) 1993-
Star Wars Classic: Calendars using art from Topps' *Star Wars* Galaxy trading card set in U.S.

Lansay (Argenteuil, France) 1996-97
Money boxes and electronic boxes in France

Lap ICS Ltd. Debrecen (Debrecen, Hungary) 1996-98
6 **Berkley** Young Jedi Knights books in Hungary

Le Panache Blanc (Issoudin, France) 1978-79
Star Wars: Children's costumes in France

Leathershop Inc. (San Francisco, CA) 1977-78
Star Wars: Belts/brass buckles in U.S., Canada

Lee Company (New York, NY) 1979, 1983-85
Star Wars, Empire, Jedi, Droids & Ewoks: Belts, belt buckles and suspenders in U.S. and Canada

Lee Wards Creative Crafts Inc. (Elgin, IL) 1980-82
Empire: Latch hook rug and pillow-cover kits; metal and plastic window hanging kits (cooking crystals) in U.S.

Legends in 3 Dimensions (Los Angeles, CA) 1996-98
Limited-edition cold-cast resin busts in U.S.

Lego Direct Marketing, Inc. (Enfield, CT) 1995
Still photo license agreement in U.S.

Leisure Dynamics (South Oakleigh, Victoria, Australia) 1996-98
Playballs from **Unice, S.A.** in Australia

Letraset Consumer Products Ltd. (Kent, England) 1977-78
Star Wars: Action transfers, children's and school stationery supplies in U.K., Ireland, Australia, South Africa, Scandinavia, Netherlands, Benelux, Austria, Italy, Germany, Switzerland, Greece, France, Liechtenstein, Monaco

Lewis Galoob Toys (San Francisco, CA) 1992- , 1994-97
Star Wars Classic: Miniatures of Star Wars Trilogy vehicles made of die-cast metal and plastic, and portable playsets and micro figures marketed under **Micro Machines** brand in U.S., Canada. Micro Machines and playsets in Japan, Denmark, Finland, Singapore, U.S. Italy, Canada, Belgium, The Netherlands, Luxembourg, U.K., Norway, Iceland, Israel, Germany, Austria, Switzerland, Greece, Cyprus, Hong Kong, Columbia, Costa Rica, Chile, Equador, Argentina
Sub-Licensees and affiliates include:
- France: **Ideal Loisirs**
- Switzerland: **Kiddy Fun AG**
- United Kingdom: **Toy Options Ltd.**

LFL Fan Club (Aurora, CO) 1987-
Star Wars Classic: Lucasfilm Fan Club magazine, special merchandise distributed worldwide

Liberte A/S (Vamdrup, Denamrk) 1996-98
Children's printed nightwear, underwear, swimwear, and bathrobes in Sweden, Denmark, Norway, Finland, Iceland

LIF-SUD SpA (Vomano, Teramo, Italy) 1977-79
Star Wars: Licorice twists in Netherlands, Benelux, Austria, Italy, Germany, Switzerland, Greece, France, Liechtenstein, Monaco, Spain, Portugal

Lifesavers (Australia) Ltd. (Victoria, Australia) 1985
Ewoks: Build-a-poster promotion w/**Break Fruit Drinks**

Lincoln Industries Ltd. (Auckland, New Zealand) 1983-84
Jedi: Masks and costume sets (using **Acamas Toys** designs) in New Zealand

Lincoln Playcorp Ltd. (Auckland, New Zealand) 1995-96
AH Prismatic: photopolymer holograms, lazergram postcards, embossed hologram products and hologram foil products; **CUI**: tin trading cards in New Zealand

Lintas: Campbell-Ewald (Warren, MI) 1994
Use of words in Chevrolet Impala SS ad in magazines in U.S.

Little Brown & Co. (Boston, MA) 1996-98
Ballantine book *Splinter of the Mind's Eye* in U.K.

Loeb, Uitgevers, VB (Amsterdam, Netherlands) 1984-85
Ewoks: Postcards, greeting cards in Benelux

Longman Publishers (Essex, England) 1983
Star Wars: Star Wars easy reading edition distributed worldwide except U.S., Canada

Lookout Management (Los Angeles, CA) 1979-81
Star Wars: Use of Jawa character in advertising and promotion of film and record album "Rust Never Sleeps" worldwide

Los Angeles Times Syndicate (Los Angeles, CA) 1979-84
Star Wars: Newspaper comic strip distributed in U.S., Canada

LSM Promotions (Coral Springs, FL) 1990
Star Wars Classic: Ewok premium items from **Blockbuster Video** in U.S.

J.C. Lucas (Manila, The Philippines) 1996-98
Coloring books; coin banks; party goods; posters/wall decor; handsized jigsaw puzzles; paper stationery; folders; diaries; memo, note & writing pads; address books in the Philippines

LucasArts Games (San Rafael, CA) 1990-
Star Wars Classic: Computer and game-mode video games distributed worldwide
Sub-Licensees and affiliates include:
- Taiwan: **Unalis Corp.**
- South Korea: **Dong Seo International Inc.**
- Singapore: **Telahin Enterprises** (also Philippines, Thailand, Malaysia, Indonesia)

Lyons Maid Ltd. (London, England) 1978-80
Star Wars & Empire: Iced lollies and ice cream with decorated wrappers in the U.K., Ireland

M.S.D. International (Paris, France) 1982-83
Empire & Jedi: T-shirts and sweatshirts in France

Magic Press SRL (Pavone, Italy) 1996-97
Dark Horse books and comics in Italy

Main Event Toys Inc. (Mississauga, Ontario, Canada) 1996-98
Poster Clings Inc. wall activity mat, **World Wide Licenses** watches in Canada

Manhattan Entertainment (Auckland, New Zealand) 1995-96
Glow-Zone Universe Packs in New Zealand

Manton Cork Corp. (Brentwood, NJ) 1979-85
Star Wars, Empire & Jedi: Decorative cork boards and chalkboards in U.S.

Manufacturas Quiron (Barcelona, Spain) 1986-87
Droids: Rubber dolls of C-3PO and R2-D2 in Spain

Marks and Spencer Ltd. (London, England) 1977-78
Star Wars: Children's pajamas, PVC aprons, slippers, socks, bed linens in the U.K., Ireland, France Belgium, Scandinavia in its own retail stores

Marubeni Co. (Tokyo, Japan) 1983
Jedi: Handkerchiefs in Japan

Maruyoshi Co. (Tokyo, Japan) 1978-79
Star Wars: Beach, sports and tote bags in Japan

Marvel Comics (New York, NY) 1977-
Star Wars, Empire, Jedi, Droids & Ewoks: Comic books, paperbacks of comics distributed in U.S., Canada
Sub-Licensees and affiliates include:
- Argentina: **Editorial Columbia, Editoria Abril**
- Australia/New Zealand: **Federal Publishing Co.**
- Brazil: **Bloch Editores, Editoria Abril**
- Canada: **Les Editions Heritage**
- Chile: **Aracuaria Ltda.** (also Peru, Argentina)
- Columbia: **Greco Ltda.** (also most of rest of South America)
- Denmark: **A.S. Interpresse** (also Sweden, Norway)
- Finland: **Kustannus Oy Seimic**
- France: **Edition Lug** (also Africa, Benelux, Switzerland)
- Germany: **Williams-Verlag** (also Austria), **Zellschriften-Und Buch Verlag Interpath, Gutenburghus**
- Hungary: **Isjusagi Lapkiado Vallalnt**
- Israel: **Audiovision**
- Italy: **Arnoldo Mondadori Editore, Edizioni L'Isola Trovata SRL, Editoriale del Corriere della Sera**
- Mexico: **Organizacion Editorial Novaro S.A.** (also Central America)
- Netherlands: **Oberon, Junior Press**
- Portugal: **Agency Portugesa de Revistas, Dsitri Sociedade Editora Lda.**
- Scandinavia: **Semic International**
- South Africa: **Super Comix Pty. Ltd.**
- Spain: **Editorial Bruguera S.A., Ediciones Forum, Ediciones Vertice**
- U.K.: **Marvel U.K., Brown Watson**
- Yugoslavia: **Politka Publishing House**

Maryborough Knitting Mills Ltd. (Victoria, Australia) 1977-78
Star Wars: T-shirts and sweatshirts in Australia

Masport (France) 1994-96
Costumes, playhouses, masks, POGs & slammers in France

Master Footwear (Manila, Philippines) 1992-93
Star Wars Classic: Ewoks character shoes, slippers and socks in the Philippines

Master Pins (Paris, France) 1990-92
Star Wars Classic: Enamel pins in France

Maynards (London, England) 1984-86
Jedi: Sugar and chocolate confectionery in U.K.

MBI Inc. (Norwalk, CT) 1993-
Star Wars Classic: Motion picture celluloid art prints in U.S.

MB International BV (Zeist, Netherlands) 1983-84
Jedi: Cardboard jigsaw puzzles in Benelux

McCall Pattern Co. (New York, NY) 1981-85
Empire, Jedi & Ewoks: Patterns for costumes; paper patterns for appliqués for quilts, pillows, wall hangings distributed worldwide except Japan and Europe

McDonald's Family Restaurant (North Sydney, Australia) 1980
Empire: Fast food premiums in conjunction w/**Coca-Cola** (drinking glasses, cups, posters, perforated stamps, paper trays, book covers, soft drink bottle crowns in Australia

Mead (Dayton, OH) 1977-78, 1996-98
Star Wars: School binders; wire and zip out theme books, portfolios in U.S., Canada, Saudi Arabia. Binders, pencil pouch, theme books, portfolios or folders, memo pads, stationery, writing instruments, paper tablets, note cards & envelopes, CD-ROM & diskette holders, mouse pads, wrist rests, **Peg Board Products** in U.S.

Media Works (Tokyo, Japan) 1996-2001
Bantam novels, Manga-style books in Japan

Meija Seika Co. Ltd. (Tokyo, Japan) 1978-79
Star Wars: **Choco-bowl** candy w/mini toy premium in Japan

Melanie Taylor Kent Ltd. (Encino, CA) 1989-
Star Wars Classic: T-shirt w/reproduction of Hollywood Boulevard artwork in U.S.; 15th Anniversary *Star Wars* serigraph and poster in U.S., Japan

Metal Box Ltd. (Berkshire, England) 1980-82
Empire: Metal coin banks and small metal containers in U.S., Canada, U.K., Sweden, France, Denmark, Belgium, Netherlands, Norway, Germany

Metric Media, Inc. (Toronto, Canada) 1980
Empire: Collector's circular picture trading cards for **York Peanut Butter** in 6 designs

and premium posters in Canada
J.M. Meulenhoff B.V. (Amsterdam, The Netherlands) 1995-99
Micro Games America (Los Angeles, CA) 1991- ; (North Hills, CA) 1994-97
Star Wars Classic: Hand-held games for *Star Wars, Empire* and *Jedi* distributed worldwide. LCD hand-held games, molded youth or personal electronics in U.S.; LCD hand-held games in U.K.; LCD hand-held games; walkie-talkies; Millennium Falcon cassette player, CD player & AM-FM radio; clock radio; power talker; bike radio, R2-D2 robot record/playback device in Canada
Midena (Barcelona, Spain) 1986-87
Droids: Blackboard w/felt-tip pen, bull's eye target in Spain
Mind Circus (Santa Monica, CA) 1978-79
Star Wars: Jim Rumpf-sculpted mugs of Chewbacca, Obi Wan Kenobi and Darth Vader marketed under **California Originals** brand in U.S.
Miracle Images Verlags GmbH (Augsburg, Germany) 1995-96
Memberships, name rentals, sale of licensed products through newsletter & conventions in germany, Austria, Switzerland
Mister Badges (Da Harmelen, Netherlands) 1983-84
Jedi: Pin-back badges in France
Modern Graphics (Restatt, Germany) 1995-98
Starlog Technical Journals in Germany; **Rawcliffe** pewter vehicles, ships figurines, **Willitts Design** collector film frames & gift products, cardboard stand-ups, **Ballantine** books in Germany, Austria, Switzerland
Mondragon Textilvertries GmbH (Munich, Germany) 1983-84
Jedi: T-shirts and sweatshirts in Germany, Austria
Monty Fabrieken B.V. (Je Leiderdorp, Netherlands) 1983-84
Jedi: Trading cards in Benelux (Dutch language only)
Morinaga & Co. Ltd. (Tokyo, Japan) 1978-79
Star Wars: Candy and snacks in decorated boxes w/mini toy premiums including caramels, stick crackers and rice snacks in Japan
Motta Ice Cream (Nanterre, France) 1980-82
Empire: Ice cream wrappers; posters and 30 different stickers inserted into ice cream boxes in France, Monaco
Mousetrak Canada Computer Access (Canada) ?, 1994-96
Mousepads
Moustrak Inc. (Carson City, NV) 1993-
Star Wars Classic: Computer mouse pads in U.S.
Mr. Australia Garments Pty. Ltd. (Newtown, Australia) 1981-84
Empire: Shavecoats and bath robes w/matching pants in Australia, New Zealand
Jedi: Terry-towel bath robes in Australia
Mundi Paper S.A. (Barcelona, Spain) 1986-87
Star Wars & Droids: Metal wastepaper basket, metal pencil cube, metal money box, file w/mini-pads, money purse, telephone book, distributed in Spain
Mythical Realism Press (Kenilworth, IL) 1991-
Star Wars Classic: Limited edition reproductions of Yoda cover from **Ballantine Books** *My Jedi Journal* painted by Michael Whelan in U.S.
Nabisco Ltd. (Victoria, Australia & Herts., England) 1978-79
Star Wars: Star Wars posters in Weeties cereal in Australia; Letraset transfer sheet as in-pack premium w/Shreddies cereal in U.K.
Namco Ltd. (Tokyo, Japan) 1987-89
Star Wars Classic: Star Wars video game cartridge for **Nintendo Game System** in Japan only; 1988 promotional Trilogy calendars—one for corporate giveaway, one for sale to public—in Japan
National Library for the Blind (Cheshire, England) 1995
Produce three titles in Braille worldwide
National Public Radio (Washington, DC) 1994-96
Empire: Broadcast of 10-part radio series in U.S.
Natural Balance (Castle Rock, CO.) 1991-93
Star Wars Classic: Vitamin tablets in character shapes in U.S., Canada, Mexico
Nellba AB (Falsterbo, Sweden) 1983-84
Jedi: Trading cards in Sweden
Nestlé Co., Inc. (White Plains, NY) 1979-80
Star Wars: **Weingeroff** pendant jewelry as premium promoted on **Nestlé's** chocolate bars and **Nestlé's Quik** in U.S.
Nestlé Co. (France) 1989-90
Star Wars Classic: Promotion for **Nestlé's Crunch** bars in France
Nestlé Co. (Santiago, Chile) 1982
Empire: Promotion for **Savory Ice Cream** w/collectible stamps and **Kenner** lightsabers in Chile
Network Distributors Ltd. (Alexandria, NSW, Australia) 1994-96
Topps trading cards and albums in New Zealand
New Concept Import Services Pty. Ltd. (Victoria, Australia) 1980-81, 1983-84
Empire: Iron-on transfers in Australia
Jedi: Balloons in Australia
New Dimension Holographics (Concord West, NSW, Australia) 1995-97
A.H. Prismatic stickers, key rings, badges, bookmarks, gift boxes, postcards, pencil tins in Australia
New Frontiers Publishing (Malibu, CA) 1994-95
Limited-edition prints & poster prints created by Michael David Ward in U.S.
Newsagents Direct Distribution (Alexandria, NSW, Australia) 1994-95
Topps trading cards and albums in Australia
Nintendo of America (Redmond, WA) 1995-2001
Ultra 64 Home System for "Shadows of the Empire" worldwide
Nippon Gohu Co. Ltd. (Tokyo, Japan) 1978-79
Star Wars: Sneakers and boots in Japan
Nishimura Seni Kogyo Co. Ltd. (Osaka, Japan) 1978-79
Star Wars: Rubber belts for children, cloth belts for juniors in Japan
Nonpareil Communications Inc. (Rochester Hills, MI) 1993-
Star Wars Classic: Cut-away view posters of *Star Wars* vehicles in U.S.
Norben Products (Montreal, Canada) 1977-79, 1994-96
Star Wars: Masquerade costumes & playsuits, vinyl and rubber masks in Canada, Bermuda, Bahamas. Halloween masks, costumes, make-up kits, dress-up accessories in Canada
Norma Editorial, S.A. (Barcelona, Spain) 1995-99
Star Wars Classic: Comics, **Marvel** reprints, **Dark Horse** comics in Spain
Northlight Productions Ltd. (West Yorkshire, England) 1977
Star Wars: Night light in U.K., Ireland, Australia, New Zealand, Africa, Europe
Nouveau International (East Botany, Australia) 1982-84
Empire & Jedi: Sets of sheets and pillowcases, tablecloths, washcloths, towels (using **Bibb Co.** designs) in Australia
Nupa S.A. (Barcelona, Spain) 1978-79
Star Wars: Likeness of characters printed on paper and distributed in cakes (cosquitos) in Spain and the Balearic and Canary Islands
O.S.P. Publishing, Inc. (Bell, CA) 1994-96
Reprints of trilogy motion picture scripts including one-sheet image, movie stills, studio & film logos in U.S.
Ogawa-Gomu Co. (Tokyo, Japan) 1978-84
Star Wars, Empire & Jedi: Rubber pull-over masks
Oral B Laboratories [formerly **CooperCare Inc.**] (Palo Alto, CA) 1983-85
Jedi: Promotional kit offered to dentists including patient motivation pamphlets, appointment reminder postcards, club membership cards, posters w/oral hygiene statement in U.S., Canada, Japan; toothbrushes in U.S., Canada, Mexico, Austria, Belgium, Ireland, Denmark, France, U.K., Germany, Italy, Spain, South Africa, Australia, Hong Kong, Indonesia, Japan, Malaysia, Philippines, Singapore, Taiwan, Thailand, Switzerland, Netherlands, South Korea; with 2-sided poster premium in U.S.
Oriental Trading Company (Hong Kong) 1994-95
Galoob Micro Machines and playset in Hong Kong and Macau
Oscar Lerman (London, England) 1978-79
Star Wars: Souvenir program sub-licensee in U.K.
Oy Halva AB (Helsinki, Finland) 1985-86
Star Wars & Droids: Licorice box illustrations for jelly babies in Finland
Oz Druck Und (Rheinfelden, Germany) 1995-96
5 issues of *Star Wars Fan Magazine* in Germany, Switzerland, Austria
P & J Promotions (West Sussex, U.K.) 1995-96
Phone cards in U.K.
Pace-Minerva (Edinburgh, Scotland) 1983-84
Empire & Jedi: Posters in U.K., Ireland
Pacosa Dos Internacional (Barcelona, Spain) 1977-78, 1983-84, 1986-87
Star Wars, Jedi & Droids: Non-adhesive stamps and albums in Spain, the Balearic and Canary Islands
Panini Espana S.A. (Girona, Spain) 1996-97
1997 20th Anniversary sticker album and stickers in Spain and Portugal
Panini SPA (Modena, Italy) 1996-97
1997 collector's sticker album & stickers in Sweden, Norway, Denmark, Finland, France, Germany, Austria, Switzerland
Panini UK Limited (Turnbridge Wells, U.K.) !996-97
1997 20th Anniversary Sticker Album & stickers in UK
Panrico S.A. (Barcelona, Spain) 1983-84, 86-87, 92
Jedi: Promotion for chocolate-covered pastry w/in-pack premium in Spain
Droids: Children's pastry using Droids in sales promotion w/in-pack premium, advertising materials: posters, display boxes, packaging in Spain
Star Wars Classic: Snack cakes and premiums (polyethylene figurines) in Portugal
Papeles Troquelados S.A. & Industrias Fiesta de Morelos (Iztapalapa, Mexico) 1980-83
Jedi: Paper plates, wax paper cups, paper napkins, light board face masks, cone-shaped hats, light board paper trays in Mexico
Paradise Press (Ridgefield, CT) 1977-79
Star Wars, Empire & Jedi: Poster magazines, tabloids in U.S., Canada
Sub-Licensees and affiliates include:
Australia:/New Zealand: **Horwitz Grahame Books**
Brazil: **Editora Safira**
Denmark: **A.S. Interpresse**
Finland: **Kustannua Oy Semic**
Germany: **Marcus Verstl**
United Kingdom: **Galaxy Publications**
Paramount Pictures (Hollywood, CA) 1994
Use of Darth Vader in motion picture *Indian in the Cupboard* worldwide
Parker Bros. Games (Beverly, MA) 1977-90
Star Wars, Empire, Jedi & Ewoks: Games and home video games distributed worldwide
Party Professionals (Rancho Cucamonga, CA) 1991-95
Star Wars Classic: Full overhead masks originally sold by Don Post Studios in U.S.; rubber, full overhead masks to sell at minimum retail price of $25 in U.S.
Pastahurst Ltd. (London, England) 1977-79
Star Wars: Gold and silver jewelry; pendants, brooches, lapel pins, charms in U.K., Ireland, Australia, Europe, Middle East
Patora Co. Ltd. (Tokyo, Japan) 1980-81
Empire: Key holders, pendants, brooches in Japan
Patty Marsh Productions (San Anselmo, CA) 1991-
Star Wars Classic: "Color Me" T-shirts and cards (Ewoks only) in U.S.
PCA Apparel Industries (New York, NY) 1996-97
Boy's pajamas in sizes 2-20 in U.S., its territories & possessions.
Pegasus Sport Limited (Albany, New Zealand) 1996-97
Spectra Star kites, Frisbees & yo-yo's in New Zealand
Pendulum Press Inc. (West Haven, CT) 1978-79
Star Wars: Remedial reading multi-media kit in U.S.
Penshiel Ltd. (Manchester, England) 1982-85
Empire & Jedi: pajamas and dressing gowns in U.K.
Pepperidge Farms Inc. (Norwalk, CT) 1982-85
Empire & Jedi: Star Wars cookies; 10 oz. tumblers for near-pack and mail-in promotions; distributed in U.S., Bermuda, Japan
Pepsico, Inc. (Purchase, NY) 1996-
Advertising, promotions & premiums for licensee's beverages, restaurants & snack foods (**Pepsi-Cola North America**; **Pepsi-Cola International**; **PepsiCo Foods International**; **PepsiCo Restaurants International**; **Frito-Lay, Inc.**; **Pizza Hut, Inc.**; **Taco Bell Corp.**; **KFC Corp.**) in world (excluding Russia, China & India)
Pepsi Cola France (Paris, France) 1995
In-store promotion for Pepsi-Cola in supermarkets in France
Perfect Fit Clothing Co. Pty. Ltd. (Bendigo, Australia) 1980-81
Empire: T-shirts, sweatshirts, hooded sweatshirts, tops in Australia
Personajes Registrados S.A. (Nuevo Leon, Mexico) 1983-84
Jedi & Ewoks: Stickers, puffy stickers, decals, key rings, small note books, school kits, plastic wallets, round plastic bags w/drawstring in Mexico
PEZ Candy, Inc. (Orange, CT) 1996-1998
Vertical candy/gum dispensers with 3-D character heads in U.S.
Phase Verlag (Germany) 1994-95
Non-exclusive use of R2-D2 image on book *Der Woolminator* in Germany
Photon Productions (Matraville, Australia) 1996-97
Star Wars Galaxy Magazine issues 1-12, 1996 in Australia
Pinder Lane Productions (HBO) (New York, NY) 1996
Permission for Jane Goodall/HBO commercial in U.S. and Canada
Pizza Hut (Pymble, Australia) !995-96
Star Wars Fun Cup, a premium, Kids Works promotion in Australia, New Zealand
Placo Products, Co. (Commerce, CA) 1996-98
Character die-cast key chains in Canada, France, Spain, U.K., Channel Islands, Eire, Hong Kong, Indonesia, Korea, Malaysia, Canada
Plastica Entella SPA (Chiavari, Italy) 1977-79
Star Wars: Pencil and school cases in Italy, France, Belgium, U.K.
Playcorp Pty., Ltd. (North Melbourne, Australia) 1994-98
JusToys Bend-ems, Talk-ems, carry cases; Micro Machines miniature vehicles in Australia, New Zealand; **Galoob** Droids Micro Machines, backpacks, bags & belts, products & 3-D blow molded bubble bath/shampoo bottles, **Thinkway Toys** 3-D PVC banks, **Spectra Star** Kite, Kite Fliders & Kite Accessories, Yoyos & Flying Discs, Pyramid apparel accessory bags & school bags, belts bags, backpacks, roll bags, wallet sport bags, mini packs, library bags, wet packs, three-in-one set, back-to-school bags, roll-on luggage in Australia
Playmix/Brio Scanditoy Oy (Helsinki, Finland) 1983-84
Jedi: Pencils, pencil sets and cases, sharpeners, erasers, notebooks, exercise books, writing paper and envelopes, invitation cards, wrapping paper, postcards in Finland, Norway, Sweden, Denmark
Playthings (Singapore) 1982-85
Empire: Lollipops, balloons, sun visors distributed in Singapore, Malaysia. *Jedi:* Silk-screened T-shirts in Singapore
Playthings Private Limited (Singapore) 1996-97
Star Wars, Empire, Jedi: **Micro Games** handheld electronic toys, Darth Vader medallion, Virtual Sharkin pinball, Intimidator, Three in One, Two in One, Darth & Stormtrooper Mix N Match Walkie Talkies, Darth Vader Poser Talker, sculptured cassette player, Darth Vader AM/FM clock radio & bike clock, Talking R2-D2 in Singapore, Malaysia, Hong Kong, Indonesia. Children's & adults t- & polo shirts, caps, vinyl dolls, resin figurines, non-articulated figurines, shadow box diorama, mugs, PVC key chains & mouse cover, ceramic wall masks, chess set, ceramic figural housewares, ceramic bookends, puzzle cube, costumes, Screamin' model kits, **Thinkway** coin banks, Rawcliffe pewter products, **CUI** metallic cards, mousepads, **Grosvenor** toiletries, Great Scott banners, **Don Post** & **Steve Altmann** masks, **Illusive Concepts** maquettes in Singapore, Malaysia, Hong Kong, Indonesia, Philippines, Taiwan, Thailand.
Playtoy Industries (Toronto, Canada) 1994-97
Steel Tec construction sets in Canada
Playworks International (Brooklyn, Australia) 1996-98
Watches in Australia
Pocket Junior (Paris, France) 1995-99
Bantam books in France, French-speaking Switzerland & Belgium
Polaroid Corporation (Cambridge, MA) 1994-97
Still photo license for brochure in U.S.
Polydata Resources Corp. (Thornhill, Canada) 1994-97
Character PVC model kits in Canada. Vinyl figure model kits in U.S.
Polydor Records Ltd. (London, England) 1980
Empire: **RSO** record albums w/premium gift of posters carried on **Express Dairies Ltd.** milk floats and bottle collars in U.K., Ireland
Polygram Records Inc. (New York, NY) 1979-93
Star Wars, Empire, Jedi, Ewoks: Soundtracks and other records distributed worldwide, some under **RSO Records Inc.** label
Portal Publications (Corte Madera, CA) 1987-88, 90-97
Star Wars Classic: Reproductions of 4 Trilogy one-sheets, 12 mini-posters, Darth Vader door poster, other posters in U.S. Posters in U.K., Channel Islands and Eire.
Premiere Luggage Co. Pty. Ltd. (Broadway, Australia) 1980-81
Empire: Schoolbags (back-pack and carry) in Australia, Fiji, New Guinea
Present Needs Ltd. (Kent, England) 1983-84
Jedi: Badges and key rings in U.K.
Preservenbedrijj BV (Breda, Netherlands) 1981
Empire: **U.F.O. Potato Chips** premium of stickers to be affixed to posters in Netherlands
Presses de la Cite (Paris, France) 1995-2002
Bantam books in France, French-speaking Belgium & Switzerland; novelizations in France, French-speaking Belgium.
Presswell Enterprises (Quezon City, Philippines) 1991-93
Star Wars Classic: Ewok stickers, trading cards, coloring books, board games, party favors in the Philippines
Prima Publishing (Rocklin, CA) 1993-2000
Star Wars Classic: Computer and video game hint books in U.S., Canada, U.K., Ireland, Australia, New Zealand. Strategy guides and hint books in U.S. & Canada; strategy guides in Germany, Austria & Switzerland.
Procter and Gamble Co. (Cincinnati, OH) 1978, 1980-81, 1983-84
Star Wars: Near-pack premium posters w/purchase of **Cheer, Cascade, Dawn, Ivory Snow** in U.S.
Empire: **Puffs** brand facial tissue in U.S.; poster free w/purchase of **Crisco, Pringles, Duncan Hines Cake Mix** in U.S.
Jedi: Posters used as near-pack and on-pack promotion offers w/**Crisco Oil, Crisco Shortening, Jiff Peanut Butter, Pringles Potato Chips** in U.S., Canada
P & G (Geneva, Switzerland) 1983-84
Jedi: Self-liquidating poster offer to promote detergent in Switzerland
P & G (Osaka, Japan) 1980
Empire: Promotion for detergent in Japan
P & G (Mexico City, Mexico) 1981

Empire: Self liquidating premium of a set of 6 different mini posters in Mexico
Productas Yupi (Cali, Columbia) 1985-87
Star Wars: Yupi snack foods promotion using tiny *Star Wars* plastic figures as premiums in Columbia, Venezuela, Ecuador, Panama, Peru
Promode Company Ltd. (Taipei, Taiwan) 1995-96
Star Wars Dark Empire: comic books in Taiwan; posters, post cards & trading cards using artwork from **Dark Horse** comics in Taiwan.
Promostaff S.A. (Barcelona, Spain) 1986-87
Droids: Premium promotion w/**Pilas Secas Tudor S.A.** blister-packed batteries and in-pack stickers in Spain
PT Mitra Indotra Abadi (Jakarta, Indonesia) 1996-97
Sticker activity and exercise books in Indonesia
Publi-Badge S.A. (Madrid, Spain) 1983-84
Jedi: Cardboard puzzles, metal badges, vinyl stickers, posters in Spain
Publicacoes Europa-Americ (Portugal) 1994-2001
Bantam books in Portugal
Publications International, LTD (Lincolnwood, IL) 1996-99
"Play-A-Sound Book" in U.S. and Canada
Putnam Berkley/Dark Horse (New York, NY) 1996-2072
3 *Dark Forces* graphic story albums in U.S.
Pye Records Ltd. (London, England) 1977-78
Star Wars: Record sub-licensee
Pyramid Handbags 1996-97
Children's back-to-school & apparel accessory bags in U.S.
Queen Co. Ltd. (Tokyo, Japan) 1978-79
Star Wars: Notebooks, memo pads, scribble pads. paper pads, binder, communications folder, book file, handy case, eraser in Japan
Radio Musyka Fakty (Krakow, Poland) 1996
Star Wars: products for traveling show in Poland
Rainbow Book Distribution Lt. (Vancouver, B.C., Canada) 1995-96
1997 calendar in Canada
Rainbow Productions Limited (Surrey, England) 1994-96
Meet-&-greet costume characters for U.K.
Ralph Marlin & Co. Inc. (Waukesha, WI) 1992- , (Hartland, WI) 1995-97
Star Wars Classic: Neckties, boxer shorts, caps, T-shirts in U.S. & Canada. Neckties, scarves, boxer shorts, pocketed jam shorts, caps, T-shirts in U.S.
Random House [Ballantine Books] (New York, NY) 1977, 1994-2002
Star Wars, Empire, Jedi, Droids & Ewoks: Story books, pop-up books, activity books, grow chart, educational books, teachers' guides, calendars, cut-out books, bookmarks and bookplates, puzzle books
Sub-Licensees and affiliates include:
Belgium: **Zuidnerderlandse Uitgeverij NV**
Brazil: **Editoria Acti-Vita, Livraria Francisco Alves Editora S.A., Editora Abril**
Canada: **Editions France-Amerique Ltee, Les Editions Heritage Inc.**
Chile/Colombia/Ecuador/Peru/ Venezuela: **Edinorma Internazional**
France: **Librairie Hachette, Flammarion**
Germany: **Bastei Verlag**
Greece: **Turtle Publications**
Netherlands: **A.W. Bruna**
Hungary: **MOKEB/Hungarofilm**
Israel: **Sabzerou Bros. Ltd.**
Italy: **Edizioni Paoline, Sperling e Kupfer**
Japan: **Futami Shobo, CBS/Sony Publishing Co., Kodansha Ltd.**
Portugal: **Pulicacoes Europa America**
Spain: **Ediciones**
Sweden: **Inernordic Marketing**
United Kingdom: **Futura Books, Octopus Books**
Rapport Co. Ltd. (Tokyo, Japan) 1980-84
Empire & Jedi: Shopping bags, mechanical pencils, key holders, paper pads, picture post-cards, rulers, badges, stickers in Japan
Rarities Mint Inc. (Anaheim, CA) 1987-89
Star Wars Classic: Gold and silver coins in 6 different designs and four styles in U.S., Canada; tenth-ounce gold coin in necklace in Japan
Ratcliffe Bros. Ltd. (London, England) 1978-79
Star Wars: **Bibb Co.** sub-licensee
Rawcliffe Corp. (Providence, RI) 1992, 1995-97
Star Wars Classic: Pewter vehicles in U.S. and Canada; pewter vehicles & figurines in U.S.
Rayman/Ridless Products Group (New York, NY) 1983-85
Jedi: Earmuffs in U.S.
RCA Sales Corporation (Indianapolis, IN) 1982
Star Wars: Material to accompany promotion of one videodisk copy of the movie *Star Wars* to be given away w/each purchase of an **RCA** Videodisk Player in U.S.
Recticel Sutcliffe Ltd. (West Yorkshire, England) 1982-84
Empire & Jedi: Floor playmats in U.K., Ireland
Reding Stationery (Victoria, Australia) 1980-81
Empire: School supplies including notebooks, binders, pencil tablets, theme books, pocket notebooks, portfolios in Australia
Redline Engineering Pty. Ltd. (Victoria, Australia) 1983-84
Jedi: Bicycle safety flags in Australia
Red Tulip Chocolates Pty. Ltd. (Prahran, Australia) 1980-82
Empire: Lollipops, jellies in Australia, Singapore, Malaysia
Reds Inc. (Tokyo, Japan) 1992-93, 1994
Star Wars Classic: A one-third scale Darth Vader vinyl doll in limited edition of 500 in Japan; 80-cm non-articulated Darth Vader vinyl dolls in Japan.
Reed International Books (Dingley, Victoria, Australia) 1996-98
Berkley books & **Random House** adventure books in Australia; **Random House** junior novelisations in U.K.
Regis SpA (Bologna, Italy) 1980-81
Empire: Pen and pencil cases, school bags in Italy
Reknown Inc. (Tokyo, Japan) 1978-79
Star Wars: Shorts, sport shirts, sweaters, windbreakers, pajamas, high socks in Japan
Renault (France) 1994-95
Premiums & promotional products in France
Rhino Records, Inc. (Los Angeles, CA) 1996-99
Music recordings in U.S. & Canada
Riddell, Inc. (Chicago, IL) 1996-98
Character helmet reproductions in U.S.
Rivertown Trading Company Inc. (Saint Paul, MN) 1992-
Star Wars Classic: Thermochromatic ceramic mugs (w/"disappearing" ink) in U.S.
Rolf A. Schultz (Mitterskirchen, Germany) 1983-85
Jedi: Stickers in Germany, Austria
Rolling Thunder Graphics (Shalimar, FL) 1994-96
Limited-edition lithographs using image from **Dark Horse** comics in U.S.
Roman Ceramics Corp. (Mayfield, KY) 1977-79
Star Wars: C-3PO and R2-D2 ceramic cookie jars and banks (including Darth Vader) in U.S. and Canada
Rose Art Industries, Inc. (Livingston, NJ) 1994-97
Plastic desks & accessories, 3-D cork puzzle figures, puzzles, vinyl rub offs & rub ons, sand-art kits, temporary tattoos, Lite Art backlit pegboards, Colorbloom, lap desks, stamper sets, light catchers, peelable paint, activity cases, & poster art in U.S.
Rowntree-Mackintosh (Paris, France) 1981
Empire: **Smarties** chocolate candy promotion using figures and vehicles made by **Kenner** affiliate **Micro-Meccano** in France
Roy Lee Cin Agencies Pty. Ltd. (Sydney, Australia) 1981
Empire: Ceramic money boxes and coffee mugs, placemats, plastic tableware, decorated mirrors, jewelry in Australia, New Zealand, Fiji
Royal Animated Art Inc. (Los Angeles, CA) 1989-, (Beverly Hills, CA) 1994-97
Star Wars Classic: Ewoks & Droids TV animation cells distributed worldwide. Serigraphs and Ewoks & Droids TV animation cells & background paintings distributed worldwide.
Royal National Institute for the Blind (Peterborough, England) 1995-2066
Talking books for the blind worldwide
Royal Scandinavian Bathrooms (Denmark) 1994
Permission to use EWAC on products in Denmark
Rubie's Costume Co., Inc. (Richmond Hill, NY) 1994-96
Costumes & masks in U.S.
Runesco (Madrid, Spain) 1986-87
Star Wars & Droids: Polyester tents in Spain
Rusich/Kluch (Smolensk, Russia) 1995-99
Russian-language hardcover books in Russia
Russitch (Smolensk, Russia) 1995-99
Russian-language hardcover books in Russia; **Berkley** books in Russia
Saatchi and Saatchi, (New York, NY) 1994-96
Use of phrase in corporate commercial in U.S.
Sage Co., Inc. (Taipei, Taiwan) 1996-98
Adult & children's t-shirts/bottoms, vests, jackets, jogging suits, socks, caps, towels in Taiwan
Sakura Co. Ltd. (Tokyo, Japan) 1978-79
Star Wars: Lunch box, thermos, soapbox in Japan
Sales Corporation of America (San Francisco, CA) 1982-85
Empire, Jedi, Droids & Ewoks: Posters, mounted die-cut standees, gloves, mittens, leg warmers, scarves, shorts, jackets, jeans, headgear, sweatshirts, other shirts, pants, skirts in U.S., Canada
Salvesa S.A. (Barcelona, Spain) 1986
Star Wars Classic: Lollipops in Central America
San Carlo SPA (Milano, Italy) 1995
Promotion of salted snacks with premiums in Italy
Sankikogyo Co. Ltd. (Tokyo, Japan) 1978-79
Star Wars: Desk cards (paper and plastic) in Japan
Sans Interdit Sarl (Paris, France) 1996-97
T-shirts, sweatshirst, windbreakers, caps, canvas record bags in France
Sao Paulo Alpagatas S.A. (Sao Paulo, Brazil) 1989-91
Star Wars Classic: Sneakers in Brazil
Scandecor International (Uppsala, Sweden) 1977-81
Star Wars & Empire: Posters, poster magazines in U.K., Germany, Austria, Benelux, Denmark, Greece, Egypt, Spain, Finland, Iran, Israel, Italy, Norway, Portugal, Netherlands, Sweden, Switzerland
Schmidt Spiel & Greizeit GmbH (Eching, Germany) 1995-97
POGs in Germany, Switzerland, & Austria
Schneidinger Freres (Zurich, Switzerland) 1983-84
Jedi: Bed linens, curtains in Switzerland
Schweppes, S.A. (Madrid, Spain) 1996
Use of Darth Vader in TV commercial in Spain
Sci Fi World (Concord, Ontario, Canada) 1994-97
Fine-art poster prints in Canada
Sci Pub Tech (Grosse Pointe Park, MI) 1996-98
Interior cutaway posters of space vehicles in U.S.
The Score Board, Inc. (Cherry Hill, NJ) 1994-1996
Autographed & unautographed products in U.S.
Screamin' Products Inc. (Albany, NY) 1991, 1994-96
Star Wars Classic: Molded 1/4 scale PVC model kits; 1/4 scale vinyl model kits in U.S.
Screenbrook Limited (Cambridge, England) 1980-82
Empire: Posters, lampshade kits in U.K., Ireland
Seaco S.A. (Barcelona, Spain) 1996-97
Rubber masks from **Party Professionals** in Spain
Sega Enterprises (Tokyo, Japan) 1992-
Star Wars Classic: Video game for **Sega Genesis** 16 bit console distributed worldwide except Europe, South America; high-end arcade games worldwide
Seio Insatsu Co. (Tokyo, Japan) 1983-84
Jedi: T-shirts, bags, handkerchief
Selene Industria Textil Ltda. (Cerquiho, SP, Brazil) 1996-97
Socks & stockings in Brazil
Semic International (Sundbyberg, Sweden) 1995-97
Comic albums from **Dark Horse** in Sweden, Norway, Denmark, & Finland
Semic Press AB (Stockholm, Sweden) 1996-97
Dark Horse *SW Classic Vol. 1* in trade paperback in Sweden
Shibayama Sangyo Co. Ltd. (Nagoya, Japan) 1980-81
Empire: Small and large steel dust bins in Japan
Shogakukan Production Co. Ltd (Tokyo, Japan) 1995-98
Dark Horse comics in Japan
Shorebrook S.A. (Ypiranga, Brazil) 1983-85
Jedi: Stamp albums and stamps in Brazil
Sifriat Ma' Ariv Publishing (Tel Aviv, Israel) 1994-96
Books in Israel
S-King Kiado (Hungary) 1994-97
Hungarian-language paperback books in Hungary
Smith & Masons Ltd. (London, England) 1978-79
Star Wars: **Ann Street Brewery** advertisement in the Channel Islands
Smithsonian (Washington, DC) 1995-98
National Air & Space Museum exhibition in U.S.
Sociedade Representatcoes (Portugal) 1994-95
Galoob Micro Machines in Portugal
Society Anselme (Langeais, France) 1977-79
Star Wars: Children's costumes in France, Belgium, Switzerland
Sodecor (Ogliate Comasco, Italy) 1983-84
Jedi: Stickers in Italy
Software Toolworks (Novato, CA) 1992-
Star Wars Classic: Interactive computer chess game for various formats worldwide
Sound Source Interactive (Westlake Village, CA) 1994-97
Visual & audio "clips" on disk for **Apple**, **IBM**, & compatible personal computers in U.S., Canada, U.K., & Australia
Sound Source Unlimited (Westlake Village, CA) 1992-
Star Wars Classic: Trilogy-related audio and video "clips" on disk for **Apple** and **IBM**-compatible computers in U.S.
Spearmark International (Cambridgeshire, England) (1994-96)
Melamine mugs, bowls, plates; acrylic tumblers; lunch boxes; wobble bottles; alarm clocks; poster clocks; watches in U.K., Channel Islands, Eire, & the Isle of Man
Spectra Star (Santa Monica, CA) 1994-96
Kites & accessories, kite gliders, yo-yo's, flying discs in U.S.
Spectra Star Kites (Pacoima, CA) 1983-87
Star Wars Classic, Droids & Ewoks: Kites in U.S., Canada
Spencer Gifts (Egg Harbor Township, NJ) 1996-97
LED-enhanced wall decor in U.S. & Canada
Spendrups Bryggerier (Bandhagen, Sweden) 1984-86
Jedi: Carbonated soft drink in Sweden
Sperling & Kupfer Editori 1994-2001
Bantam titles in Italy
Spirit Art (Edina, MN) 1993-
Star Wars Classic: Greeting cards in U.S.
Sports Stamps Collectors Ass'n. (Hicksville, NY) 1995-96
International postage stamps as souvenirs in U.S.
S.R.M. Company, Inc. (Jenkintown, PA) 1994
Staedtler (Barcelona, Spain) 1984-86
Jedi & Ewoks: Pencil cases in Spain
Staffordshire Potteries Ltd. (Staffordshire, England) 1983-84
Jedi: Ceramic mugs in U.K.
Star Jars, Inc. (N. Palm Beach, FL) 1995-97
Collector cookie jars in U.S.
Starfire U.K. Ltd. (Edinburgh, Scotland) 1982-83
Empire & Jedi: Flashing electronic badges in U.K.
Starlog Communications (New York, NY) 1993-, 1996-97
Star Wars Classic: Star Wars technical journal magazines worldwide in English except Australia, New Zealand, Ireland and U.K. Repackage of magazines with three new 8-page gatefold inserts in English, worldwide excluding U.K. & Ireland
Stern's Playland Pty. Ltd. (Lurnes, Australia) 1983-84
Jedi: Plastic inflatable swim ring, arm bands, tubes, inflatable rigid wall pools, surf riders, air mattress under **Aqua Fun Australia** Pty. Ltd. brand name distributed in Australia, New Guinea, Solomon Islands, Noumea, Tahiti, Fiji
Stormin' Norman Products (New York, NY) 1980-81
Empire: Character jackets, shirts, shorts, pants, sweat suits, T-shirts in U.S.
Streets Ice Cream Pty. Ltd. (Turrella, Australia) 1980-81
Empire: Ice cream bars and ice popsicles in Australia
Stride Rite Footwear Inc. (Cambridge, MA) 1982-84
Empire, Jedi & Ewoks: Sneakers; canvas leather, or fabric shoes; boots, sandals, slippers, shoelaces in U.S., Canada
Stuart Hall Co. (Los Angeles, CA) 1980-85
Empire, Jedi & Ewoks: School supplies: wire bound theme books, portfolios, ring binders, pocket notebooks, pencil tablets, erasers, pencil sharpeners, rulers, plastic memo boards, safety scissors, tape dispensers, glitter glue, reinforcements, book covers in U.S., Canada
Sun Press Oy (Tampere, Finland) 1985-86
Star Wars & Droids: 3-D poster magazines in Finland
Sun Star Stationery Co. Ltd. (Tokyo, Japan) 1978-81
Star Wars & Empire: Pen and pencil cases (cloth, vinyl), paper pads, pass cases in Japan
Sun Ya Publications (HK) Ltd. (Hong Kong) 1996-97
Star Wars Classic: reprints of **Dark Horse** comic books in Hong Kong
Sunrise Company (Los Angeles, CA) 1994-95
Still photo to be used in publication in Japan
Suzuki Shoten & Co. Ltd. (Osaka, Japan) 1980-81
Empire: Baseball caps, sun visors in Japan
Takara Co. Ltd. (Tokyo, Japan) 1978-79, 1991-92
Star Wars, Star Wars Classic: Original toys for *Star Wars*; plush dolls of "baby" *Star Wars* characters for "crane" arcade machines in Japan
Takashimaya Singapore, Ltd. (Singapore) 1996
Live show & photo session in Singapore
Take Shobo 1996-2001
Star Wars, Empire, Return: novels and **Bantam** books in Japan
Tavener Rutledge Ltd. (Liverpool, England) 1978-79
Star Wars: Marshmallow candy molded in the shape of Star Wars characters in U.K., Ireland, Denmark, Norway, Sweden, Finland, Germany, Netherlands, Benelux, France, Italy
Televoz (Lisbon, Portugal) 1994
Audiotext phone line for game in Portugal
Texas Instruments Inc. (El Segundo, CA) 1977
Star Wars: Digital watches distributed worldwide
Textile Artesa S.A. (Barcelona, Spain) 1986-87
Star Wars & Droids: Suspenders and belts in Spain
Thermos Ltd. (Brentwood, Essex, England) 1977-84
Star Wars, Empire, Droids & Ewoks: Insulated flasks, plastic lunch boxes in U.K., Ireland, Norway, Sweden, France, Belgium, Denmark, Australia
Thinking Cap Co. (Los Angeles, CA) 1980-82
Empire: Flannel, cotton/polyester caps, including Yoda w/ears in U.S., Canada
Thinkway Toys (Markham, Ontario, Canada) 1994-97
PC molded coin banks in the U.S.; PVC coin banks with & without sound in Canada
Third Dimension Arts Inc. (San Rafael, CA) 1991-, 1994-97
Star Wars Classic: Watches, key rings, pen-

dants, clear paperweights, all w/dichromate holograms in U.S. Watches, key rings, pendants, all w/dichromate holograms in U.S.

Thomas Forman & Sons Ltd. (Nottingham, England) 1981-82
Empire: Calendars in U.K.

Thomas Salter Ltd. (Fife, Scotland) 1983-85
Jedi, Star Wars, Droids & Ewoks: Rub-down paper transfers in U.K., Ireland, Benelux, France, Germany, Italy

Thomas Theophanides (Athens, Greece) 1983-84
Jedi: Jigsaw puzzles in Greece

Thought Factory (Sherman Oaks, CA) 1977-78
Star Wars: Posters in U.S.

Thyrring Agency (Klampenborg, Denmark) 1984-85
Jedi: T-shirts, sweatshirts in Denmark

Tidsskriften Foretagsekon-Mi (Gothenburg, Sweden) 1984
Jedi: Picture of R2-D2 and C-3PO on the front page of business magazine (**Foretags Ekonomi** Nov./Dec.) distributed in Sweden

Tiger Electronics, Inc. (Vernon Hills, IL) 1996-98
Electronic games, personal products, feature-based novelty items, & organizers in the U.S.

Tin Signs International (New York, NY) 1994-96
Metal signs in the U.S.

Titan Books, Ltd. (London, U.K.) 1994-99
The Art of... books, trade paperback editions, script books, **Ballantine** books, fan magazine in the U.K.

TM Semic (Warszawa, Poland) 1997-98
Six-part comic series in Poland

Toho Co. (Tokyo, Japan) 1980-81
Empire, Jedi & Ewoks: Souvenir programs, posters, pads, badges in Japan

Tomart Publications (Dayton, OH) 1993-, 1995-97
Star Wars Classic: Guide to worldwide *Star Wars* collectibles, worldwide. *Star Wars:* catalog & price guide 2nd edition & limited special edition in U.S.

Tomokuni Tebukuro Co. Ltd. (Ohkawagun, Japan) 1978-79
Star Wars: Children's gloves in Japan

Top Toys (Buenos Aires, Argentina) 1979-82
Empire: Toys, games, crafts in Argentina

Topps Canada, Inc. (Mississauga, Ontario, Canada) 1995-96
Trading cards, stickers & sticker albums, limited-edition lithographs in Canada

Topps Chewing Gum Inc. (Brooklyn, NY) 1977-85, 1991-
Star Wars, Empire, Jedi, Star Wars Classic: Picture trading cards, pressure sensitive stickers sold w/or w/o gum; small plastic figural candy containers, distributed worldwide or through affiliates, or in limited territories depending on product; for *Empire*, two paper poster premiums depicting uncut card sheets, puffy stickers, trading card file box; illustrated book based on *Star Wars Galaxy*, in U.S.
Sub-Licensees and affiliates include:
Australia: **Scanlens Sweets** (also New Zealand)
Canada: **O-Pee-Chee Ltd.**
Italy: **Edizioni Panini SpA**
U.K.: **Trebor Ltd.**

The Topps Company, Inc. (New York, NY) 1994-97
Trade paperback of trading cards, *Star Wars Galaxy Magazine*, picture trading cards, binders, stickers, 20th Anniversary souvenir & poster magazines in the U.S.

Torag Trading BV (Roermond, Netherlands) 1983-84
Jedi: Plastic key ring system in Benelux

Touchline Promotions Ltd. (London, England) 1983-84
Jedi: Pocket-size coin holders in U.K.

Towle/Sigma Giftware Corp. (New York, NY) 1980-85
Empire, Jedi & Ewoks: Ceramic items including mugs, figurines, coin banks, cookie jars, canisters, bookends, picture frames, children's dishes, music boxes, etc.; silver-plated coin banks; placemats, in U.S. and Canada

Toy Options, Ltd. (Lees, Oldham, England) 1994-95
Micro Machines from **Galoob** & PVC moulded money boxes in the U.K.

Toys N Things (Singapore) 1996-97
Waist/belt, tote, school, sling, shopping, duffle, hand, shoe, beach, lunch & drawstring bags; backpacks; briefcases; wallets; coin & keychain pouches in Singapore and Brunei

Tradescene Pty Ltd. (North Melbourne, Victoria, Australia) 1995-96
Steel Tec metal & plastic construction sets sourced from **Remco**; LCD hand-held & cartridge games from **Micro Games**; hand-held & headset walkie-talkies; cassette and CD players; AM-FM & clock radio in Australia

Transworld Publishers Limited (London, U.K.) 1994-05
Novels in the U.K.; **Bantam/Dell/Doubleday** Junior Novelisation in Australia

Transworld Publishers Pty Ltd (Australia) 1996-00
Paperback books in Australia

Trebor Sharps Ltd. (Essex, England) 1977-78, 1980-81
Star Wars, Empire: Children's confectionery chews in U.K., Ireland, Germany, Austria, Belgium, Denmark, Egypt, Spain, Finland, France, Greece, Iran, Israel, Italy, Norway, Portugal, Netherlands, Sweden, Switzerland

Trends International (Toronto, Canada) 1993- ; (Mississauga, Ontario, Canada) 1996-97
Star Wars Classic: Posters, doodle kits, locker cards, buttons in Canada; posters in Canada

Trielle Corporation (Sydney, Australia) 1994-97
Star Wars: 1997 color diary; *Star Wars Classic:* Series 1-2, Dark Empire 1-2, Dark Lords of the Sith 1-12, Heir to the Empire, River of Chaos, Splinter of the Mind's Eye, Tales of the Jedi, NADD Collection in Australia

Tsukuda Co. (Tokyo, Japan) 1980-85
Empire & Jedi: Plastic model kits, toys under license from **Fundimensions** & **Kenner**

Tsurumoto Room Co. Ltd. (Tokyo, Japan) 1978-79
Star Wars: Silk-screened of transfer T-shirts in Japan

20th Century Fox Japan (Tokyo, Japan) 1983-84
Jedi: Brochures to promote advance ticket sales in Japan

Twentieth Century-Fox Records (Los Angeles, CA) 1977-78
Star Wars: Soundtrack and "Story of..." albums and cassettes

Twentieth Television (Beverly Hills, CA) 1994-96
Eight seconds of *Star Wars* theme in "The Simpsons" promotion in U.S.

Ubisoft S.A. (Montreuil-sous-Bois, France) 1991-
Star Wars Classic: Interactive CD-ROM disks compatible w/**Nintendo** systems distributed worldwide

Union Sales Ltd. (London, England) 1982-84
Jedi: T-shirts and sweatshirts in U.K.

Union Underwear Co. Inc. (Bowling Green, KY) 1980-85
Empire, Jedi & Ewoks: Coordinated underwear sets in U.S., Canada, Central and South America (except Mexico), U.K., Ireland, Germany, Austria, Switzerland, Denmark

Uniprints Co. (Bowling Green, KY) 1982-85
Empire, Jedi & Ewoks: Imprinted knit shirts, sweatshirts, jerseys in U.S., Canada

United Biscuits Ltd. (Twickenham, England) 1977-78
Star Wars: Snack food promotion w/**Outer Spacers** in U.K., Ireland

Uranium (Baar, Switzerland) 1983-84
Jedi: Pencil tops, pencil erasers, sharpeners in Germany, Austria, Switzerland

Urweider (Lausanne, Switzerland) 1983-84
Jedi: Costumes and masks (**Acamas** design) distributed in Switzerland

U.S. Gold Limited (Birmingham, England) 1992-
Star Wars Classic: Video games for **Sega Genesis** in Europe, South Africa and for other **Sega** systems worldwide

Valentine N.Z. Ltd. (Auckland, New Zealand) 1980-81
Empire: Scrapbooks, jotter pads, notebooks, greeting cards, posters in New Zealand

Valhalla (Rakoczi, Hungary) 1994-99
Books & **Bantam** books in Hungary; roleplaying games, miniatures rules & games, adventure board games, flipbook games & supplements in Hungarian language worldwide

Varese Sarabande (North Hollywood, CA) 1985-86
Ewoks: Soundtrack album in U.S.

Vasilios Dagiacos (Athens, Greece) 1983-84
Jedi: Collectors cards inserted in chocolate wafer packages in Greece

Vergani SpA (Cremona, Italy) 1980-81
Empire: Wrapped boiled sweets in Italy, distributed in locked metal box

Verlagsgesellschaft MBH & Co. (Koln, Germany) 1996-2001
Star Wars Chronicles, **Berkley** books in Germany, Austria, Switzerland, and worldwide

Victor Musical Industries Inc. (Tokyo, Japan) 1991-
Star Wars Classic: Interactive video game for the **Sharp X6800** and **NEC9801** personal computers in Japan; possible CD-ROM games for other game platforms worldwide

Vinilos Romay S.A. (Grutas, Mexico) 1980-81
Empire: Decorated plastic coin banks in Mexico

Virgin Publishing, Ltd. (London, U.K.) 1996-98
Star Wars Chronicles by **Chronicle** Books in U.K.

Vivid Imaginations Limited (England) 1994-95
Bend-Ems, "Talk Ems" with carry cases sourced from **JusToys** in U.K.

Vulli (Berkshire, England) 1983-84
Jedi: Soccer balls in U.K., Ireland

Waddingtons Games (Leeds, England) 1995-96
Plaster moulding sets; coloring by numbers; designer fashion box with plain t-shirt, paints, image; POGs in U.K.

Waddingtons House of Games (Leeds, England) 1981-84
Empire, Jedi & Ewoks: Jigsaw puzzles (including poster of puzzle) in U.K., Ireland, Germany, Finland

Wallace Berrie Co. (Van Nuys, CA) 1980-81
Empire: Jewelry including pins, rings, pendants, key chains in U.S., Canada

Wallpapers to Go Inc. (Hayward, CA) 1983-86
Jedi & Ewoks: Flexible wallpaper coverings in U.S., Canada, Australia, Hong Kong, U.K., Ireland

Walls Ice Cream (Singapore & Kuala Lumpur, Malaysia) 1978-82
Star Wars & Jedi: Packaging for ice cream bars and ice popsicles in Singapore, Malaysia

Walls Sausage (London, England) 1978
Star Wars: Promotion using **Letraset** transfers in U.K., Ireland

Walt Disney Co. (Burbank, CA) 1986-
Star Wars Classic: **Star Tours** attractions and merchandise at theme parks worldwide. Items include pennants, postcards, posters, decals, buttons, bumper stickers, stickers, mugs, shopping bags, key chains, memo pads, pen set, mechanical and other pencils, pen and pad sets, sports bottles, magnets, patches, signs, PVC figurines, plushes, souvenir books, guide books, fanny packs, back packs, tote bags, purses, wallets, shirts, hats, jackets, pins

Walt Disney Records (Burbank, CA) 1980-92, 1996-98
Star Wars, Empire, Jedi, Ewoks: Records and cassettes w/books and carrying cases in U.S., Canada, Australia, New Zealand, South Pacific Islands, U.K., Ireland, South Africa. Read-Along paperback books & audio cassettes in U.S. and Canada

Walther Miller S.A. (Barcelona, Spain) 1986-88
Droids: Computer software game in Spain

Warner Audio Video Entertainment (Los Angeles, CA) 1994-99
Audio adaptations in the U.S.

Warner Bros. Music (Burbank, CA) 1979- ; (Los Angeles, CA) 1996-97
Star Wars, Empire, Jedi: Sheet music, anthologies. Music publishing worldwide

Warner Kids (Los Angeles, CA) 1994-2001
Audio tapes & softcover juvenile books previously published by **Buena Vista Records**, cassettes or CDs & related books, novelty format books in U.S.

Werner Soderstrom Osakeyhtio (Helsinki, Finland) 1996-99
Bantam books in Finland

West End Games Inc. (Honesdale, PA) 1986-
Star Wars Classic: Role playing games, adventure board games, rule and source books, miniature metallic figures distributed worldwide (see **Bucci Imports Ltd.**)
Sub-Licensees and affiliates include:
Finland: **Pro Games LTC**
France: **Jeux Descartes**
Germany: **Welt der Spiele GmbH**
Italy: **Stratelibri S.R.L.**
Spain: **Joc Internacional S.A.**

Westbrook Publications (Bedford, England) 1983-85
Jedi: Blank cards in U.K.

Western Graphics Corp. (Eugene, OR) 1993- , 1995-97
Star Wars Classic: Posters from Bantam book covers, **Dark Horse** comics and Topps *Star Wars* Galaxy in U.S. Wall, 3-D, & locker posters in U.S.

Wilhelm Heyne Verlag (Munchen, Germany) 1997-2004
Bantam books in Germany, Austria, & Switzerland

Wilker Bros. (New York, NY) 1977-85
Star Wars, Empire, Jedi & Ewoks: Knit or woven silk-screened pajamas, children's nightgowns in U.S.

William E. Coutts Co. (Willowdale, Ontario, Canada) 1994-98
Greeting cards, stationery, party items, calendars, puzzles, stickers in Canada

Willitts Designs 1994-97
Limited-edition film cell, Star Globe Halodome, & bookends in U.S.

Wilton Enterprises (Woodbridge, IL) 1980-83
Empire: Molded cake pans, cake decorating kits, cake decorations, cake candles, candy molds in U.S., Canada

Wimpy International Ltd. (London, England) 1978
Star Wars: Specially produced Letraset packs as premium w/purchase in U.K.

Wolper Manufacturing Corp. (Metro Manila, Philippines) 1996-98
Adult, teen, boys crewneck & fashion t-shirts/bottoms, woven & denim long- & short-sleeved shirts/bottoms in the Philippines

The Wonder Projects Co., Ltd. (Bangkok, Thailand) 1996-97
Crewneck & fashion t-shirts/bottoms, ls/ss shirts/bottoms, jackets, undergarments in woven & denim fabrics, pajamas, Big Trees, beachcovers, ceramic mugs in Thailand

World International (Cheshire, England) 1997
64-page hardcover 1998 Annual in U.K.

World Wide Licenses Ltd. (Kowloon, Hong Kong) 1996-98
LCD watches, quartz analog watches in U.K.

Worlds Apart Ltd. (London, England) 1983-84, 1996-98
Jedi: Kites in U.K. Kites, yo-yos, boomerangs, flying discs & gliders in U.K.

Wrebbit, Inc. (Montreal, Quebec, Canada) 1995-97
3-D foam/cardboard-based puzzle in Canada

Wright and Company (Gothenburg, Sweden) 1983-84
Jedi: T-shirts and sweatshirts in Sweden

Xerox Education Publications (Middletown, CT) 1983-84
Jedi: Posters to promote **Weekly Children's Book Club** in U.S.

Yagi Shoten Co. Ltd. (Osaka, Japan) 1980-81
Empire: T-shirts in Japan

Yamakatsu Shoten Co. Ltd. (Tokyo, Japan) 1978-79
Star Wars & Jedi: Trading cards in Japan (sub-licensee of **Topps**); posters, paper shopping bags, laminated cards, door plates in Japan

Yap Company Ltd. (Tokyo, Japan) 1984-85
Jedi: Souvenir program booklets distributed at "U.S.-Japan Robot Exhibition" in Japan

Yoplait S.A. (Madrid, Spain) 1980-81
Empire: Use of characters on stickers/posters w/yogurt purchase in Spain

Yurkari Co. Ltd. (Tokyo, Japan) 1978-79
Star Wars: Letter paper, envelopes in Japan

Zanart Publishing Inc. (Van Nuys, CA) 1993- , 1996-97
Star Wars Classic: Lobby cards/print portfolios with embossed, etched or foiled prints in U.S. Prints/blueprints & limited-edition framed lithographs in U.S.

Zap Limited (Lancashire, England) 1996-97
Bed linens, duvet, valence, fitted sheet & pillowcases, curtains in U.K.

Zeon Ltd. (London, England) 1985-87
Star Wars Classic: Watches in U.K., Ireland

Zig Zag Poster Productions (Stuttgart, Germany) 1993- ; (Ostfildern, Germany) 1995-98
Star Wars Classic: Posters in Germany, Austria, Switzerland

INDEX

ABOUT THE AUTHORS

Stephen J. Sansweet, a writer, public speaker, and collector, has transformed his love for the *Star Wars* saga into a busy career. He is the author or co-author of six books, with three more in the works, writes columns and feature articles for magazines, and has traveled the world as a Lucasfilm liaison to *Star Wars* fans everywhere.

Sansweet was born in Philadelphia and got his bachelor's degree from Temple University, where he was named outstanding graduate in journalism. He was a feature writer for the Philadelphia Inquirer before joining The Wall Street Journal as a staff reporter. Transferred to Los Angeles, he wrote on a wide range of topics from multinational corporate bribery to the civil rights of mental patients, and for three years covered Hollywood. He was named deputy bureau chief in 1983 and served as the Journal's Los Angeles bureau chief for nine years starting in March 1987.

In 1996, Sansweet joined Lucasfilm Ltd. as Director of Specialty Marketing to help promote *Star Wars* to fans both old and new. He started collecting robots and space toys in the mid-1970s, and over the years that has been transformed into the largest private collection of *Star Wars* memorabilia in the world.

Among Sansweet's books are: *The Punishment Cure*, (1976); *Science Fiction Toys And Models*, (1980); *Star Wars: From Concept To Screen To Collectible*, (1992); *Tomart's Price Guide To Worldwide Star Wars Collectibles*, (1994, revised 1997); and *Quotable Star Wars: I'd Just as Soon Kiss A Wookiee* (1996). Books in 1998 include the long-awaited *Star Wars Encyclopedia* (Del Rey); *Star Wars Scrapbook: The Essential Collection* (Chronicle Books); and the miniature *Star Wars Collectibles* (Running Press).

The California resident also writes collectibles columns for the *Star Wars Insider* and Topps' *Star Wars Galaxy* magazine, has been an editor and writer of five sets of *Star Wars* trading cards for Topps Inc. and has been a co-host on QVC *Star Wars* Collection broadcasts. Above all else, he is a fan who just can't wait until that day in May 1999 when, in a darkened theater, the screen lights up with those magic words: *Star Wars: Episode I.*

T.N.Tumbusch is the editor of *Action Figure Digest* magazine. The toys and related items of his childhood formed the foundation of the Tomart *Star Wars* collection.

Tumbusch discovered the value of nostalgia items at an early age, when he was caught playing with "toys" from his father's radio premium collection. He wrote his first book, *Space Adventure Collectibles* (1990), while still in college. After graduation he became editor of *Action Figure Digest* magazine in 1991. He is a co-author of *Tomart's Encyclopedia and Price Guide to Action Figure Collectibles* (1996), and has managed the production of numerous other price guides on contemporary collectibles. He lives in Dayton, Ohio with his wife Susan.